D1590829

Indigenous and Black Confraternities in Colonial Latin America: Negotiating Status through Religious Practices

Edited by
Javiera Jaque Hidalgo
and Miguel A. Valerio

Amsterdam University Press

The publication of this book is made possible by funding support from the editors' academic departments.

Cover image by: Camilo Blas, *Boceto para 'Procesión del Señor de los Milagros'*, 1947. (c) Museo de Arte de Lima
Cover design: Coördesign
Lay-out: Crius Group, Hulshout

ISBN 978 94 6372 154 7
E-ISBN 978 90 4855 235 1
NUR 685

Every effort has been made to obtain permission to use all copyrighted illustrations reproduced in this book. Nonetheless, whosoever believes to have rights to this material is advised to contact the publisher.

Printed and bound by CPI Group (UK) Ltd, Croydon, CR0 4YY

Table of Contents

Introduction

Negotiating Status through Confraternal Practices

Javiera Jaque Hidalgo
Miguel A. Valerio

Confraternities (lay Catholic brotherhoods or sodalities) emerged in medieval Europe's urban centers, especially among migrant groups, as sites of popular devotion, kinship, and mutual aid.[1] Modeled on the Roman collegium, burying the dead was one of their main functions.[2] They first appeared in Rome around 1267 under the pontificate of Clement IV; there is record of the first institution of pious people whose function was to free captive Christians from the Saracens.[3] Depending on their geographical location, and the social and ethno-racial origins of their members, brotherhoods were dedicated to different devotions, namely Christ, the Virgin, or a patron saint, which could be venerated in different locations – such as convent and parish churches. One of the primary functions of indigenous and black confraternities was to provide burial for members and individuals who would otherwise not receive proper funeral rites nor have places to be buried because of their ethno-racial backgrounds. Confraternities organized devotional processions celebrating their patron saints, a festive aspect that defined them. The penitent character of many of the ceremonies that linked them to mendicant orders may be both related to the pious example

---

1   See Catherine Vincent, *Les confréries médiévales dans le royaume de France: XIIIᵉ-XVᵉ siècle* (Paris: Albin Michel, 1994). In the scholarship about sodalities in Spanish America the term confraternity is more common, while brotherhood is more common in the literature about Brazil, but these terms are used here and elsewhere interchangeably.
2   Roman collegia were either civic or religious societies. Burial collegia were very prevalent: see Jonathan S. Perry, *The Roman Collegia: The Modern Evolution of an Ancient Concept* (Leiden: Brill, 2006).
3   See Marcial Sánchez Gaete, "Desde el Mundo Hispano al Cono Sur americano: una mirada a las Cofradías desde la historiografía en los últimos 50 años," *Revista de Historia y Geografía* no. 28 (2013): 59-80.

Javiera Jaque Hidalgo and Miguel A. Valerio. *Indigenous and Black Confraternities in Colonial Latin America: Negotiating Status through Religious Practices.* Amsterdam: Amsterdam University Press, 2022
DOI: 10.5117/ 9789463721547_INTRO

of the Passion of Christ as well as a validation of practices employed by marginalized subjects looking for a way of becoming visibly legitimized by the dominant culture, as Nicole von Germeten analyzes in her book on Afro-Mexican confraternities.[4] The mendicant orders often supported the efforts of confraternities, seeing in them the opportunity to teach Catholic doctrine to the poor and promote their particular devotions.[5] So, upon arrival in the Americas, the mendicant orders promoted confraternities among the indigenous and black populations. The Jesuits, a new order founded in 1540, joined these efforts. Religious orders saw confraternities as useful sites for evangelizing what they considered reluctant neophytes. But indigenous and black *cofrades* and *irmãos* (or confraternity members) had active roles in their confraternities from the beginning, using them to mitigate some of the worst indignities of life under colonialism through mutual aid and redefine their status in colonial society. The chapters in this volume explore the varied strategies indigenous and black *cofradías* and *irmandades* (or brotherhoods) employed to achieve these ends.

Employing a transregional and interdisciplinary approach, this volume explores indigenous and black confraternities founded in colonial Spanish America and Brazil between the sixteenth and eighteenth centuries. It presents varied cases of religious confraternities founded by subaltern subjects in rural and urban spaces to understand the dynamics and relations between the peripheral and central areas of colonial society, underlying the ways in which colonial subjects navigated the colonial domain with forms of social organization and cultural and religious practices. The volume analyzes indigenous and black confraternal cultural practices as forms of negotiation and resistance shaped by local devotional identities that also transgressed imperial, religious and ethno-racial hierarchies.[6] The analysis of these practices probes the intersections of ethno-racial identity and ritual devotion, as well as how the establishment of black and indigenous religious confraternities carried the potential to subvert colonial discourse.

Many of the confraternities discussed in this volume were multiethnic, or better, panethnic, that is, encompassing men and women from different

---

4   See Nicole von Germeten, *Black Blood Brothers: Confraternities and Social Mobility for Afro-Mexicans* (Gainesville: University Press of Florida, 2006), 17.

5   See Elizabeth W. Kiddy, "*Congados, Calunga, Cadombe*: Our Lady of the Rosary in Minas Gerais, Brazil," *Luso-Brazilian Review* 37, no. 1 (2000): 47-61.

6   Our understanding of race is aligned with María Elena Martínez, *Genealogical Fictions: Limpieza De Sangre, Religion, and Gender in Colonial Mexico* (Stanford: Stanford University Press, 2013), Rachel Sarah O'Toole, *Bound Lives: Africans, Indians and the Making of Race in Peru* (Pittsburgh: University of Pittsburgh Press, 2012), and others from this camp.

geocultural backgrounds. This underscores the group dynamics that characterized the formation of these corporate bodies where the desire to achieve
common aims overcame geocultural differences among indigenous and
African groups that found themselves colonialized in new or even their
own ancestral spaces. Few however were multiracial. Farman Sweda's case
study here focuses on one exception.

We hope that the united efforts of drawing a representative map of the
social and religious practices, as well as the diversity of identities linked
to religious confraternities in the region that were constituted or founded
by Afrodescendants and Indigenous people, can contribute to previous
academic efforts, which though they provide crucial insights on local and
ethnic-specific dynamics, have not drawn yet a regional overview. Our
desire is to shed light on a broader panorama that incorporates representative cases of cultural and religious practices associated with religious
confraternities.

The aim in compiling this volume is to present a long-overdue regional
map of the religious and cultural practices associated with indigenous
confraternities, as well as those of African or Afrodescendants, from early
to late colonial times featuring the work of scholars from varied fields and
regions. The chapters in this volume display a variety of cases studied from
rural, semi-urban, as well as urban spaces of colonial Latin America. The
main goal of this collected volume is to generate a compendium that we hope
will contribute to better understanding of the ways in which colonialized
subjects navigated the colonial domain by appropriating – in an empowering
fashion – European practices and institutions, transforming and creating
their own identities. By adopting and adapting European religious and
cultural practices, indigenous and African-descent people were able to
challenge imposed devotional identities by contesting oppressive imperial,
religious and racial norms, creating room for their own devotional, ritual,
and cultural expression.

It is our hope that this volume will move the study of black and indigenous brotherhoods forward, bringing to the fore of several fields of studies
(history, sociology, literature, art history, etc.) how subaltern subjects in
colonial Latin America used these institutions to define and constantly
redefine their position in local communities. At the same time, we wish
to highlight how both black and indigenous actors responded in similar
ways to the new world Europeans brought Africans to and brought to
Indigenous people, but also how each drew on their own cultural repertoires
to creolize these institutions as they developed new cultural phenomena
and contributed to the broader cultural becoming taking place at the

regional level. The chapters that make up this volume give priority to black and indigenous *cofrades'* and *irmãos'* vocality and offer new ways to account for the formation of black and indigenous Catholic subjectivities in colonial Latin America. We hope that new research will add greater depth and breadth to this undertaking.

General Structure of Confraternities

While not identical throughout the Iberian Atlantic, confraternities had a generally uniform governing structure. Members normally elected twelve (and in some places twenty-four) brothers and sisters annually to a governing board led by a *mayordomo* (steward), or sometimes two *mayordomos*, who were also elected, by either all the members or the board. In Brazil the members of the board were called *juizes* (judges) while in Spanish America they were called *los doce* (twelve) or *los veinticuatro* (twenty-four). Among the members of the board there was a secretary, who communicated information to the board and the members, a treasurer who managed the brotherhood's finances, and a scribe, who kept record of the confraternity's activities. Members of host religious orders or parishes would act as spiritual directors. Due to high levels of illiteracy among Afrodescendants and Amerindians, for most of the sixteenth century and part of the seventeenth the scribe was a lettered white member or spiritual director. The board, especially the *mayordomo/s*, was responsible for seeing to it that the brotherhood's statutes (which were set down in writing for easy reference) were observed (Figure I.1).

The statutes, called by various names in Spanish, such as *reglas* (rules), *constituciones* (constitutions), *fundación* (charter), or *ordenanzas* (ordinances), and *compromisso* (promise) in Portuguese, were the guiding principles of every confraternity. It is thus remarkable that a largely illiterate people became so reliant on the written word many from its fold could not read. Statutes ranged from ten to twenty stipulations, which can be divided into three sets. The first set of rules normally governed membership. The next set of rules concerned devotion. As we discuss above, many confraternities were dedicated to the Virgin and/or a saint. Membership required engaging in certain devotional practices, such as praying the Rosary, on a regular basis, maintaining the patron's altar or shrine, and celebrating their feast day with solemn mass, procession, and other displays of religious piety. The final set of rules set out the confraternities' care for infirm and deceased members. These normally involved caring for sick members, attending the

COMPROMISSO
da Irmandade de
S. BENEDITO
cita na Matriz da Praya
defta Cidade da Bahia que
seus devotos Irmãos haõ de
guardar feito no
ANNO
de
1684.

Figure I.1. Anonymous, Fontispiece of *Compromisso da irmandade de S. Benedito*, Salvador, Brazil, 1684. Archivo Estadual da Bahia. Photograph by Miguel A. Valerio, June 2016.

funerals of deceased members, attending the annual masses for their souls, and remembering them when praying the Rosary, for example. Members were normally buried in the brotherhood's church, whether its own or a host parish or monastery.

Brotherhoods financed their activities with membership fees, alms members collected in the streets – sometimes for a particular purpose, such as a sick member, a funeral, or their feast – and, especially in the case of Brazil, revenue from loans and real estate.[7] Besides the activities listed above, brotherhoods also built or maintained altars or shrines for their patrons, and in Brazil, constructed their own ornate baroque churches.[8] Afro-Brazilian *irmãos*, many of whom were architects, artists, and artisans, gave these sanctuaries Afro-centric iconographies, especially in the black saints with which they filled them.[9] Like their feast day celebrations, these temples constituted powerful public statements through which the brotherhoods expressed their corporate and ethnic identities, devotion, and, more poignantly, asserted their humanity in an anti-BIPOC[10] world. These activities underscore the kind of power brotherhoods wielded in colonial Latin America. In order to recognize the differences between indigenous and black sodalities writ large, in what follows we focus on each set individually, before summarizing the chapters that make up this volume.

Indigenous Confraternities

Confraternities and brotherhoods in colonial Latin America generated a space for association for marginalized groups within the colonial structure allowing, in a new community of subjects uprooted from their origin, new forms of association, validation, mutual aid, and cultural agency. Indigenous confraternities fulfilled a central social role that went beyond religious aspects: members were able to navigate the segregated urban fabric, be part of a community on which to count in instances of need, as well as to access spaces and social statuses reserved for hegemonic subjects in the colonial society, as many of the chapters in this volume contend. Maria Candela de Luca argues in Chapter 9 that in the context of disaggregated societies, such as Andean communities, Marian devotion created a sense of community between groups previously under conflict, functioning then as a socially cohesive instrument.

---

7   For a case study of Afro-Brazilian brotherhoods' finances, see Patricia Ann Mulvey, "Slave Confraternities in Brazil: Their Role in Colonial Society," *The Americas* 39, no. 1 (1982): 39-68.
8   See Miguel A. Valerio, "Architects of Their Own Humanity: Race, Devotion, and Artistic Agency in Afro-Brazilian Confraternal Churches in Eighteenth-Century Salvador and Ouro Preto," *Colonial Latin American Review* 30, no. 2 (2021): 238-271.
9   See José Roberto Teixeira Leite, "Negros, pardos e mulatos na pintura e na escultura brasileira do século XVIII," in *A mão afro-brasileira: significado da contribuição artística e histórica*, ed. Emanoel Araújo (Sao Paulo: Técnica Nacional de Engenharia, 1988), 13-54.
10   Acronym for black, indigenous, and people of color.

In the context of Spanish America, indigenous confraternities were first founded by mendicant friars in the sixteenth century, right after the fall of Tenochtitlan. As indicated by Laura Dierksmeier, Franciscan friars played a key role in the evangelization process in Mexico and were responsible for the foundation of the earliest and largest number of confraternities.[11] Archival records indicate that the Franciscans established the first indigenous confraternity as early as 1527, before the diocese of Mexico City was founded in 1529. In this manner, as studied in the latest book on indigenous confraternities in the context of New Spain by Dierksmeier, indigenous confraternities "fulfilled a wide range of charitable functions, including the administration of hospitals, giving food to the needy, providing small banking services, raising funds to release debt prisoners, and burying the dead."[12] Due to the great decline in the indigenous populations during these years, indigenous sodalities assumed the responsibility not only of taking care of the sick, but also burying the bodies of indigenous people that otherwise would have been abandoned on the outskirts of the new colonial city. This Mexican model was followed as the Spanish empire expanded to South America.

In urban and semi-urban colonial contexts, indigenous people negotiated their place in society through various tactics, such as learning trades that would allow them to integrate into the urban economy: they worked as cobblers, tailors, metalsmiths, or carpenters. Groups of indigenous people of different ethnic groups settled in specific neighborhoods, in the case of Santiago de Chile, for example, la Chimba neighborhood, on the northwest side of the Mapocho River (*mapocho*, "on the other side," in Quechua). From there they built social and commercial networks and became owners of *solares* (city lots), livestock, and various goods, listed in detail in their testaments.[13] Migrant indigenous people formed "confraternities of a mixed and plural nature, where members of different origins and condition coexisted and practiced their religiosity, thus responding to the complex multiethnic realities that were articulated in Spanish American cities and, at the same

11   See Laura Dierksmeier, *Charity for and by the Poor: Franciscan-Indigenous Confraternities in Mexico, 1527-1700* (Norman: University of Oklahoma Press, 2020), 1. As stated in the Introduction, "According to the Third Mexican Council, more than 300 indigenous confraternities operated in Mexico City a few decades after the conquest [...] Indigenous confraternities operated in nearly every village in colonial Mexico, with up to hundreds of members in each city": 11-12.
12   Ibid., 1.
13   See Julio Retamal, *Testamentos de "Indios" en Chile colonial: 1564-1801* (Santiago: RIL Editores, 2000). In this volume Retamal compiles more than a hundred wills and associated legal documents of indigenous people of diverse origins dictated in the city of Santiago.

time, to the demographically smaller dimensions of cities such as Santiago."[14] Notarial documentation is a prime source to analyze social mobility and the ways in which both indigenous and black people inhabited the social map, in material and symbolic terms, as well as how they participated in corporate religious forms such as confraternities. From them we can learn about the various ritual aspects associated with the festivals and festive practices in which confraternities occupied a pivotal role, as well as the production of testaments, and the funeral rituals, in which many times confraternities were in charge by request of the indigenous man or woman who dictated the will.

Testaments are a record of the ways in which indigenous migrants from different regions and ethnic groups navigated the colonial city. Their production resignified the European legal discourse in which they were framed and transformed. They also underscore indigenous identity formation in the processes of adaptation and survival to the challenges of forced or free displacement from their places of origin to the colonial city, with confraternities being a central player in the relocation processes.[15] However, the notarial archive to which the wills belong is, as Valenzuela reminds us elsewhere, fragmentary in nature, since it allows us to know the testimony of those indigenous people who achieved a certain material autonomy by serving as artisans and, in some cases, owning land on the margins of the city. Thus, "it is a group that represents the indigenous people most integrated into colonial society and its administrative practices, to the point that they resort to the western mechanism of the will to leave written testimony – with legal validity – of their wishes and inheritances, material and immaterial."[16]

Indigenous people who migrated to the colonial urban centers – such as the Mapuche people, who migrated from different regions of Chile and Argentina, as well as the so-called "Cuzco Indians" studied by Valenzuela in this volume – learned very early as we see it exemplified in documentation from the second half of the sixteenth century, mechanisms of adaptation to

14 Jaime Valenzuela Márquez, "Devociones de inmigrantes. Indígenas andinos y plurietnicidad urbana en la conformación de cofradías coloniales (Santiago de Chile, siglo XVII)," *Historia* 1, no. 43 (2010): 204. Unless otherwise noted, all translations are ours.

15 Hugo Contreras analyzes the forced and free migrations that took place at the end of the 16th century and the beginning of the seventeenth century in south central Chile due to the founding of the city of Concepción in 1550 by Pedro de Valdivia: "Indios de Tierra adentro en Chile central. Las modalidades de la migración forzosa y el desarraigo (fines del siglo XVI y comienzo del siglo XVII)," in *América en diásporas: esclavitudes y migraciones forzadas en Chile y otras regiones americanas (siglos XVI-XIX)*, ed. Jaime Valenzuela (Santiago: RIL editores, 2017), 161-196.

16 Valenzuela Márquez, "Devociones de inmigrantes," 216-217.

the colonial system either through the use of legal discourses such as wills, or by association with secular religious groups, such as confraternities. In their contribution Enrique Cruz and Grit Kirstin Koeltzsch point out that the rural indigenous population that migrated to the cities of Charcas and Santiago de Chile in the seventeenth century formed urban indigenous confraternities to maintain community ties and family relationships.[17] In both forms of appropriation, we find the result of a syncretic cultural practice and religious production.

We can also find in indigenous testaments a record of the permanence of pre-Hispanic modes of social organization within the limits defined by both the European legal discourse and institutions that, in turn, were adapted to colonial contingencies. Notarial documents produced by Indigenous people in the seventeenth century reveal the importance that religious confraternities had in the lives of the testators. Indigenous religious affiliations are also clearly reflected through the places where they indicate they want to be buried. In this way, we can see a large number of examples in notarial documents in which testators expressly declare their desire to make donations in favor of specific confraternities to which they belonged and that were, as well, associated with those religious orders.[18] Through the study of these legal documents, it is possible to know the dynamics of social organization. Works such as that of Joanne Rappaport, Tom Cummins, Mathew Restall, Karen Vieira-Powers, and Susan Kellogg, among others, argue that the texts produced by indigenous people are key to understanding their participation in the social formation of colonial Latin America.[19] In the study of indigenous confraternities, the use of notarial records becomes necessary because there are so few archives that present thematic catalogs dedicated to confraternities.[20] The researcher's work then becomes focused on collecting fragments, documenting objects and practices with the aim of

17   See Enrique Cruz, "'Esclavos españoles, indios y negros': notas para el estudio de las relaciones interétnicas en las cofradías religiosas del norte del Virreinato del Río de la Plata," *Boletim do Museu Paraense Emílio Goeldi. Ciências* Humanas 8, no. 2 (2013): 454.

18   See Julio Retamal, *Testamentos de "Indios" en Chile colonial: 1564-1801* (Santiago: RIL Editores, 2000), 49.

19   See Joanne Rappaport and Tom Cummins, *Beyond the Lettered City: Indigenous Literacies in the Andes* (Durham: Duke University Press, 2012); Susan Kellogg and Matthew Restall, eds., *Dead Giveaways: Indigenous Testaments of Colonial Mesoamerica and the Andes* (Salt Lake City: The University of Utah Press, 1998), 1-11; Karen Vieira-Powers, *Andean Journeys: Migration, Ethnogenesis, and the State in Colonial Quito* (Albuquerque: University of New Mexico Press, 1995).

20   A notable exeception is F. Javier Campos y Fernández de Sevilla, *Catálogo de cofradías del Archivo del Arzobispado de Lima* (Lima: IEIH, 2014).

giving a full image as possible that is representative of the dynamics associated with indigenous confraternities. Through the analysis of confraternal constitutions, testaments dictated or written by their members, registries of donations, and expenses for the ceremonies and festivities we can learn from the circumstances that enabled the creation of these organizations, as well as from daily practices, which can be read from the perspective of material culture studies. Legal complaints presented by indigenous people to defend their right, for example, to the use of spaces designated for devout practices and rituals associated with religious confraternities to which they belonged also provide us with representative examples on how indigenous people navigated legal procedures as a strategy of resistance against colonial rule.[21]

Confraternities' ways of grouping, on the other hand, responded to social, ethnic and professional factors. However, while belonging to a confraternity often represented a form of social validation, membership did not always embrace belonging to a certain group. Confraternities, frequently, were multiethnic, formed by people from different social strata and *calidades*, such as Spaniards, mestizos, Indians, and blacks, as well as their membership in certain artisans' guilds:

> Being a member of a confraternity, especially for people from discriminated, undervalued, and uprooted groups – in the case of geographically displaced individuals or groups – not only implies closer proximity to the possibility of *post mortem* salvation, but also a specific form of integration, community regeneration, social mobility and recognition [...] acting as an additional source of socio-religious positioning.[22]

In many cases these confraternities were founded by indigenous people themselves and represented an instance of community and solidarity among the most marginalized members of colonial society. On the other hand, the instances of corporate organization around confraternities allowed greater agency for indigenous women – as well as for Afro-Mexican women, as von Germeten indicates in her study of black brotherhoods in Mexico, and Gómez and Walker show in their contributions to this volume – who

21 For a case study of indigenous complaints presented before ecclesiastical justice, see Macarena Cordero Fernández, "La cofradía de Nuestra Señora de Guadalupe. Querellas y defensas indígenas ante la justicia eclesiástica. Colina, Chile, siglo XVII-XVIII. Un estudio de caso," *Revista de Humanidades*, no. 33 (2016): 79-104.
22 Valenzuela made a comprehensive literature review regarding the brotherhoods as spaces for social and ethnic integration: Valenzuela, "Devociones de inmigrantes," 209.

not only participated actively as members and benefactors, but were also founders of confraternities.[23] A similar case of agency that challenged the patriarchal structure of Hispanic culture can be seen in the confraternity of Our Lady of Copacabana at the Church of San Francisco in Santiago de Chile founded by Ana Vebún, a Mapuche woman from the island of Chiloé.[24] Similarly, in Cruz and Koeltzsch's contribution to this volume we see another example of indigenous empowerment in the viceroyalty of Peru. The authors argue that the festive culture connected to religious confraternities helped legitimize the indigenous governors' authority as well as popularize indulgence in drinking and feasting.

The practices as well as the objects associated with indigenous confraternities presented above are analyzed in the chapters compiled in four parts in which this volume is organized. Through them we can learn about the different nature of varied indigenous confraternities in urban and rural contexts across colonial Spanish America. Despite traditional monoethnic depictions of indigenous communities, confraternities were pluri-ethnic spaces where migrant and displaced subjects were able to seek aid and to form communities. Being part of these lay religious corporations, as well as participating in the festive culture linked to them, was a conducive way to display their cultural practices as well as their syncretic religious beliefs and identities. Confraternal cultural and religious practices, from the proliferation of devotional images to religious festivals, helped consolidate a space for indigenous people trying to navigate, resist, and survive colonial rule.

Black Confraternities

The first black *cofradía* was founded in Seville toward the end of the fourteenth century by that city's archbishop, Gonzalo Mena Roelas (r. 1393-1401), for infirm blacks.[25] As Karen B. Graubart has suggested, these Afrodescendants may have been West Africans enslaved into the Iberian Peninsula through the Trans-Saharan slave trade (eighth-fifteenth centuries).[26]

---

23   See von Germeten, *Black Blood Brothers*, 11.
24   To see an annotated transcription of her testament, see Retamal, *Testamentos de "Indios,"* 55.
25   Carmen Fracchia, *"Black but Human": Slavery and the Visual Arts in Hapsburg Spain, 1480-1700* (Oxford: Oxford University Press, 2019), 48-55; Isidro Moreno, *La antigua hermandad de los negros de Sevilla: etnicidad, poder y sociedad en 600 años de historia* (Seville: University of Seville, 1997), 23-56.
26   Karen B. Graubart, *"So color de una cofradía'*: Catholic Confraternities and the Development of Afro-Peruvian Ethnicities in Early Colonial Peru," *Slavery and Abolition* 33, no. 1 (2012): 43-64.

However, Afro-Sevillanos – the Iberian-born descendants of these West Africans – would eventually take control of the confraternity and make it their own. In fifteenth-century Barcelona and Valencia, Afro-Iberians would establish confraternities of their own accord.[27] The Dominicans also founded two black *cofradías* in Seville. In Lisbon, blacks were admitted to Portuguese Rosary brotherhoods starting in the mid-fifteenth century.[28]

The Afro-Iberians that accompanied the first Spanish-American colonizers may have been *cofrades* in Europe or the Caribbean who brought the practice to the Americas, for black brotherhoods already appear in the colonial archive in 1549.[29] That year, Lima's *cabildo* (city council) complained that the blacks were having drunken *fiestas* and engaging in robberies "so color de una cofradía" [under the guise of a confraternity].[30] A similar complain was made in Mexico City in 1598.[31] These complaints demonstrated that while religious orders relied on confraternities to minister to indigenous and black populations, secular officials were suspicious of their motives. Diocesan officials also believed that blacks used confraternities to perform non-Catholic rituals.[32]

As documented by von Germeten, New Spain (or colonial Mexico, 1521-1821) had the second largest number of black *cofradías*: fifty-nine.[33] In a recent article, Valerio reperiodized Afro-Mexican confraternities to show that they were active earlier than had been claimed.[34] There he posits that like the first blacks in Lima, "black conquistadors" in Mexico City may have joined the city's first confraternities in the 1530s. He also demonstrates that Afro-Mexican brotherhoods began to appear in the archive in the 1560s,

27 Iván Armenteros Martínez, "De hermandades y procesiones: la cofradía de esclavos y libertos negros de *Sant Jaume* de Barcelona y la asimilación de la negritud en la Europa premoderna (siglos XV-XVI)," *Clio: Revista de Pesquisa Histórica* 29, no. 2 (2011): http://www.revista.ufpe.br/revistaclio/index.php/revista/article/viewFile/234/130; Debra Blumenthal, "'La Casa dels Negres': Black African Solidarity in Late Medieval Valencia," in *Black Africans in Renaissance Europe*, edited by Thomas F. Earle and Kate J. P. Lowe (Cambridge: Cambridge University Press, 2010), 225-246.
28 Jorge Fonseca, *Religião e liberdade: os negros nas irmandades e confrarias portuguesas (séculos XV à XIX)* (Lisbon: Humus, 2016), 23-37.
29 Matthew Restall, "Black Conquistadors: Armed Africans in Early Spanish America," *The Americas* 57, no. 2 (2000): 171-205; Graubart, "*So color de una cofradía*,"; Miguel A. Valerio, "'That there be no black brotherhood': The Failed Suppression of Afro-Mexican Confraternities, 1568-1612," *Slavery and Abolition* 42, no. 2 (2021): 293-314.
30 Graubart, "*So color de una cofradía*."
31 See Valerio, "'That there be no black brotherhood'."
32 Ibid.
33 von Germeten, *Black Blood Brothers*, Appendix.
34 Valerio, "'That there be no black brotherhood'."

when it had been previously claimed that they were founded in the late 1590s or early 1600s. Most Afro-Mexican confraternities were attached to monasteries or parishes run by the orders that protected them. Colonial Peru, by contrast, had fifteen black *cofradías*.[35] Brazil, one of the few places where black *irmandades* are still active and remain a central part of some Afro-Brazilian communities, had 165 confraternities in the eighteenth century.[36] Three have been documented in the Viceroyalty of the Rio de la Plata. Work remains to be done on Colombia, Chile, Central America, and the Caribbean.

Afrodescendants' main aim in founding or joining confraternities was to form community in the diaspora, pool their meager resources to care for each other in times of need, and express their Afro-Catholic identity through devotional and festive practices.[37] Indeed, caring for ill members and poor blacks was a major tenet of black sodalities. This principle can be seen in the oldest surviving constitution of a black *cofradía*, that of Barcelona (1455): "It shall be a statute of this confraternity that if any member falls into poverty through illness or loss of goods or any other manner, the board shall provide for their sustenance, medicine, or any other need."[38] To this end, black brotherhoods founded, sought to establish, or worked at health care institutions. For example, in 1568, a mulatto brotherhood in Mexico City petitioned Philip II of Spain (r. 1556-1598) for land to build a "hospital," because "the ones in the city only care for Spaniards and Indians."[39] Although the king initially granted the mulatto *cofradía*'s petition, they were ultimately unsuccessful because the viceroy, Enríquez de Almanza (r. 1568-1680), asked the monarch to reverse his decision because he didn't want to allow "black gatherings for this or any other purpose."[40] Notwithstanding, Afro-Mexican confraternities were able to care for their infirm *cofrades* and poor blacks in at least two of the city's hospitals: Our Lady of the Conception founded

---

35   Frederick P. Bowser, *The African Slave in Colonial Peru, 1524-1650* (Stanford: Stanford University Press, 1974), 247-249.

36   Mulvey, "The Black Lay Brotherhoods of Colonial Brazil: A History," (Ph.D. diss., City University of New York, 1976), 304.

37   See von Germeten, *Black Blood Brothers*, 1-10; Elizabeth W. Kiddy, *Blacks of the Rosary: Memory and History in Minas Gerais, Brazil* (University Park: Pennsylvania State University Press, 2007), 15-38; Mulvey, "The Black Lay Brotherhoods of Colonial Brazil," 1-37.

38   Archivo General de la Corona de Aragón, 3298, Ordenanzas de la cofradía de los cristianos negros de Barcelona, (March 20, 1455).

39   Archivo General de Indias (hereafter AGI), México 98, Ynformaçion recibida en la Audiencia Real de la Nueva España a pedimiento de çiertos mulatos para ocurrir con ella ante su magestad (1568).

40   AGI, México 19:82, Carta del virrey Martín Enríquez, f. 1v. (April 28, 1572).

by Harnán Cortés for the native population; and Our Lady of the Helpless (Nuestra Señora de los Desamparados), established in 1582 by the Spaniard Pedro López, who was the doctor of the Dominicans, for "three groups [géneros de gente] that no hospital wanted to cure, which are mestizos, mulattos, and blacks, free or slave."[41]

While Afro-Mexican confraternities were not allowed to establish their own health care institutions, Afro-Peruvians, by comparison, were in fact forced to do so. And whereas in Mexico City blacks were allowed to minister to infirm blacks in the city's hospital for the indigenous population – which was run by a religious order – and later in the hospital for blacks, mulattos, and mestizos – which was administered by the Dominicans – in Lima, blacks were excluded from the city's health care institutions for Spaniards and the indigenous population.[42] In Lima, two "hospitals" located outside the city walls were dedicated to the care of infirm blacks: San Lázaro, for enslaved Africans, and San Bartolomé, initially established for free Afro-Limeños but eventually available to all Afro-Limeños.[43] These hospitals were founded and staffed by members of the city's black confraternities, especially their female members.[44] As von Germeten has noted, in Afro-Mexican confraternities, women too were principally responsible for Afro-Mexicans' "medical" care.[45]

Another pivotal activity of black confraternities was the burial of members and poor blacks. In a world that disposed of deceased slaves' bodies in "dung heaps or open fields" – as Dom Manuel I of Portugal (r. 1469-1521) put it 1515 – this confraternal function was so important to Afrodescendants, for whom proper burial was crucial, that in the 1970s Patricia A. Mulvey argued that black brotherhoods emerged as a "form of death insurance."[46]

41   Agustín Dávila y Padilla, Historia de la fundación y discurso de la provincia de Santiago de México de los Predicadores (Brussels: Ivan de Meerbeque, 1625), 446; Ignacio Bejarano, editor, Actas del cabildo de la Ciudad de México, vol. 14 (Mexico City: Aguilar e Hijos, 1889-1911), 7:548, 7:572; Archivo General de la Nación (Mexico), Tierras, 3556: 4, Testamento del fundador Dr. Pedro López, f. 38r. See Luis Martínez Ferrer, "Pedro López y los negros y mulatos de la ciudad de México (1582-1597)," in Socialización y religiosidad del médico Pedro López (1527-1597): de Dueñas (Castilla) a la ciudad de México, edited by Martínez Ferrer and María Luisa Rodríguez-Sala (Mexico City: UNAM, 2013), 179-216; Lourdes Mondragón Barrios, Esclavos africanos en la Ciudad de México: el servicio doméstico durante el siglo XVI (Mexico City: Euram, 1999), 57.

42   Jouve Martín, The Black Doctors of Colonial Lima: Science, Race, and Writing in Colonial and Early Republican Peru (Montreal: McGill-Queen's University Press, 2014), 10-11.

43   Ibid., 13-14; Nancy E. van Deusen, "The 'Alienated' Body: Slaves and Castas in the Hospital de San Bartolomé in Lima, 1680 to 1700," The Americas 56, no. 1 (1999): 1-30.

44   Ibid.

45   von Germeten, Black Blood Brothers, 41-70.

46   Mulvey, "The Black Lay Brotherhoods of Colonial Brazil," 15. On the importance of proper burial to Afrodescendants, see Kiddy, Blacks of the Rosary; José João Reis, Death is a Festival:

This claim is borne out by the fact that from the medieval period to the early nineteenth century, confraternities were the sole providers of burial services for Afrodescendants.[47] Thus, membership in confraternities was a way for Afrodescendants to finance dignified burial through installments in advance. Members were normally buried in the habit and church of the religious order that hosted the brotherhood.[48] Black confraternities also buried poor blacks who were not members.

As stated above and as explored by Lucilene Reginaldo, Célia Borges, and Marina de Mello e Souza in their chapters, black brotherhoods also expressed their devotion through festive practices. One specific performance, festive kings and queens, which have been traced back to Africa, became particularly associated with black brotherhoods.[49] Black confraternities' festive practices were also the most problematic aspect for colonial officials and their white neighbors alike. In fact, black *cofradías* entered the colonial archive for the first time through an accusation: in 1549, Lima's *cabildo*

Funeral Rites and Rebellion in Nineteenth-Century Brazil, trans. H. Sabrina Glehill (Chapel Hill: University of North Carolina Press, 2003). For another example of Europeans' neglect of deceased slaves' bodies, see Alonso de Sandoval, *Treatise on Slavery*, trans. Nicole von Germeten (1627; Indianapolis: Hacket, 2008); 70-71.

47   See Reis, *Death is a Festival*.

48   See Archivo Arzobispal de Lima, Tribunal de Bienes de Difuntos, vol. 31, exp. 39, Testamento de Juana Barba, morena libre, (Lima, 1651), translated by Jouve Martín in "Death, Gender, and Writing: Testaments of Women of African Origin in Seventeenth-Century Lima, 1651-1666," in *Afro-Latino Voices: Narratives from the Early Modern Ibero-Atlantic World, 1550-1812*, ed. Kathryn Joy McKnight and Leo J. Garofolo (Indianapolis: Hackett, 2009), 105-125; Archivo General de la Nación (Mexico, hereadter AGN), Bienes Nacionales, 1175: 11 Testamento de Juan Roque, negro libre (1623), translated by von Germeten in "Juan Roque's Donation of a House to the *Zape* Confraternity, Mexico City, 1623," in *Afro-Latino Voices*, 83-103.

49   Kiddy, *Blacks of the Rosary*; Marina de Mello e Souza, *Reis negros no Brasil escravista: História da festa de coroação de Rei Congo* (Belo Horizont: Editora da Universidade Federal de Minas Gerais, 2002); Tamara J. Walker, "The Queen of *los Congos*: Slavery, Gender, and Confraternity Life in Late-Colonial Lima, Peru," *Journal of Family History* 40, no. 3 (2015): 305-322; Jeroen Dewulf, *From the Kingdom of Kongo to Congo Square: Kongo Dances and the Origins of the Mardi Gras Indians* (Lafayette: University of Louisiana at Lafayette Press, 2017); Patricia Fogelman and Marta Goldberg, "*El rey de los congos*: The Clandestine Coronation of Pedro Duarte in Buenos Aires, 1787," in *Afro-Latino Voices*, 155-173; Cécile Fromont, "Dancing for the King of Congo from Early Modern Central Africa to Slavery-Era Brazil," *Colonial Latin American Review* 22, no. 2 (2013): 184-208; Miguel Valerio, "Black Confraternity Members Performing Afro-Christian Identity in a Renaissance Festival in Mexico City in 1539," *Confraternitas* 29, no. 1 (2018): 31-54; "A Mexican *Sangamento*?: The First Afro-Christian Performance in the Americas," in *Afro-Catholic Festivals in the Americas: Performance, Representation, and the Making of Black Atlantic Tradition*, edited by Cécile Fromont (University Park: Pennsylvania State University Press, 2019), 59-74; "The Queen of Sheba's Manifold Body: Creole Black Women Performing Sexuality, Cultural Identity, and Power in Seventeenth-Century Mexico City," *Afro-Hispanic Review* 35, no. 2 (2016): 79-98.

complained that the blacks of the city met "so color de una cofradía" [under the guise of a confraternity] to engage in drunkenness and non-Catholic rituals.[50] A similar complaint was made in Mexico City, in 1598, by the city's chief prosecutor, Guillén Brondat:

> The black residents of this city meet under the guise of confraternities [*so color de cofradía*] in the monasteries of Santo Domingo and San Agustin, and hospitals of Our Lady of Conception, and the Helpless. And for this they have a box, which they call the treasury, with three keys, and their treasurer, majordomo, secretary, and prior. In this box they gather great sums of gold pesos stolen from their masters and other residents of this city.[51]

Brondat's complaint exemplifies the anxiety felt by some colonial authorities, who expressed doubt that these black brotherhoods were earnest expressions of Catholic belief and functioned instead as fronts for more pernicious activities. Brondat's inclusion of the stolen gold pesos also gives testimony to the common association between blackness and criminality in colonial Latin America – a stain not even confraternity membership could remove – and suggests that such groups could only sustain themselves through illicit means. In his 1609 report, Viceroy Luis Velasco the Younger made the same claim: that any money Afro-Mexicans had "de fuerça seria hurtado" [was necessarily stolen].[52] In the end though, as the main hosts of Afro-Latin American festive practices, confraternities were the birthplace of modern Latin American music and dance.[53]

In Mexico and other parts of the Americas, black *cofrades* were charged, arrested, tortured, and sometimes hanged and quartered for the confraternal custom of electing and crowning a royal court. Less than a year before Holy Christ of the Expiration appeared with their king in Mexico City's celebration of the beatification of Ignatius of Loyola, Afro-Mexicans were accused of electing and crowning a king, queen, "y otros muchos oficios [que hay] en la casa real" [and many other titles of a royal court] on Christmas Eve 1608, as part of a plot to overthrow Spanish rule and replace it with an African

50   *Libros de cabildo de Lima*, ed. Bertram T. Lee and Juan Bromley, vol. 4 (1534-1637, first printed edition: Lima: Impresores San Martin, 1935-1948), 55-56. See Graubart, "'*So color de una cofradía*'."
51   *Actas del cabildo*, 115.
52   AGI, México R. 17, N. 63, Carta del virrey Luis de Velasco, el joven, f. 3r (February 13, 1609).
53   See John Charles Chasteen, *National Rhythms, African Roots: The Deep History of Latin American Popular Dance* (Albuquerque: University of New Mexico Press, 2004), 165-188.

kingdom.[54] This accusation had been made the first time in 1537 and would be made again in 1612.[55] In Buenos Aires, in 1787, Pedro Duarte, the *mayordomo* of the city's black confraternity of St. Balthazar, was tried for the same reason.[56] Like Mexico's 1608 coronation, St. Balthazar's coronation of Duarte had also taken place on Christmas Eve, the beginning of the Catholic holiday that would culminate on the Epiphany, the brotherhood's feast day. Yet black confraternities managed to survive these dangerous misunderstandings of their festive practices, no doubt with the help of the religious orders, as a 1702 Mexican Inquisition case shows.[57] In that case, the city's oldest black confraternity, St. Nicholas of Mount Calvary (or Tolentino), was accused by a white neighbor of processing through the streets without ecclesiastical permission. This brotherhood had been accused of the same offense in 1600.[58] In 1600, the diocesan prosecutor recommended excommunication and corporal punishment to the penitents. In 1702, however, the inquisitor found that their practices "no resulta cosa de heregia, ni sabor de ella, y que solo pareze haver sido una devoçion yndiscreta" [it is not nor does it look heretical, but only seems to have been an indiscreet devotion], and they constituted "cosa mui corriente y husada en esta ciudad" [a very common and habitual thing in this city].[59] The fact that the inquisitor was a member of the Dominican order may have made the difference here.

As outlined above, Africans and their descendants availed themselves of confraternities to form community through brotherhood, support each other through mutual aid, express their Afro-Catholic and creole

---

54   AGI, Mexico 73, R.1, N.4, Carta de López de Azoca, alcalde del crimen de la Audiencia de México, ff. 1r, 2r. (February 8, 1609).

55   AGI, Patronato 184, R. 27, Informe del virrey Antonio de Mendoza, s.f. (December 10, 1537); Biblioteca Nacional de España, MS 2010, Relacion del alçamiento que negros y mulatos libres y cautivos de la Ciudad de Mexico de la Nueva España pretendieron hazer contras los españoles por Quaresma del año de 1612, y del castigo que se hizo de los caveças y culpados, in Papeles varios de Perú y México, ff. 158-164 (1612).

56   Escribanía Mayor de Gobierno, Buenos Aires, Sala IX, 36:4:3, leg. 75, exp. 10, Información hecha para esclarecer lo que expone Farías en su memorial contra Pablo Agüero, ambos negros (January 23, 1787). See Fogelman and Goldberg, "*El rey de los congos*'."

57   Huntington Library (hereafter HL), Mexican Inquisition Papers, Series II, Box 6, HM35169, Autos contra diferentes personas que formavan nueba religion de san Agustin (1702). See Farman Sweda, "Black Catholicism"; Joan Cameron Bristol, "Afro-Mexican Saintly Devotion in a Mexico City Alley," in *Africans to Spanish America: Expanding the Diaspora*, ed. Sherwin K. Bryant, Rachel S. O'Toole, and Ben Vinson III (Urbana: University of Illinois Press, 2014), 114-135.

58   AGN, BN, vol. 810, exp. 28, Contra algunos mulatos que han fundado cofradia y salido en procesion sin licencia, f. 1r (1600).

59   HL, Mexican Inquisition Papers, Series II, Box 6, HM35168, Autos contra diferentes personas que formavan nueba religion de san Agustin, sf (1702).

identities, and redress their colonial status through festive performances. The chapters in Part II of this volume explore the varied strategies from art collecting to festive performances that black *cofrades* and *irmãos* used to (re)negotiate their colonial condition through confraternal life. They show that confraternities were (and in some cases remain) a central part of Afrodescendant social life. While these chapters elucidate a great deal about black brotherhoods, they are also an invitation for further research, especially in the areas that have received less attention, such as Chile, Argentina, and Panama.

Chapter Summaries

The volume is organized geographically, with sections corresponding to Mexico, the Andean region, Chile, and Brazil. In Chapter 1, "Religious Autonomy and Local Religion among Indigenous Confraternities in Colonial Mexico, Sixteenth-Seventeenth Centuries," Laura Dierksmeier analyzes why confraternities were indispensable charitable institutions for Amer-indians in colonial Mexico. Not only did missionaries see the potential of confraternities as a vehicle for evangelization, but also indigenous people themselves used Christianity as a tool for their protection and survival. Whether it be in their hospital work or in economic transactions, indigenous people ultimately became advocates of their own Christianity to advance their social status and power, and to negotiate their community positions. Indigenous customs were by no means eradicated within the new colonial society, and evidence of hybrid practices and local religion can be seen in the activities of confraternity members. By drawing on indigenous symbols and styles and fusing Christian saints with ancestral deities, indigenous people formed a Christianity of their own that was neither fully "orthodox" nor wholly "unorthodox." Between these two extremes, confraternal life fluctuated dynamically. What emerges from confraternity records, often written in Nahuatl with finances recorded in Aztec currencies, can aptly be called "Nahua Christianity," a combination of pre- and post-conquest religiosity.

In Chapter 2, "Confraternities of People of African Descent in Seventeenth-Century Mexico City," Cristina Verónica Masferrer León discusses black confraternities in colonial Mexico City, their form of organization, their beliefs and practices, as well as their connection to specific instances of resistance. This analysis shows that confraternities were communal spaces that allowed Afro-Mexicans to develop social relations that in turn allowed them to recreate and preserve certain elements of their identity, while also allowing them to interact with members of other ethnic groups. This chapter also underscores that while confraternities allowed Afro-Mexicans to integrate into colonial society, they were nevertheless seen as a threat to the established order, precisely due to the cohesiveness of their social relations.

Krystle Farman Sweda's contribution, Chapter 3, "'Of All Type of *Calidad* or Color': Black Confraternities in a Multiethnic Mexican Parish, 1640-1750," moves beyond the traditional depiction of black confraternities as sites of distinct cultural community formation separate from Spanish, indigenous, or mixed sacred organizations to argue that the complex social relationships forged by persons of African descent within a multiethnic colonial parish formed the foundation of their religious communities. In the daily social interactions that occurred in the sacred and secular spaces of the parish, black parishioners discussed their conceptions of communal behavior with individuals of "all types of color or *calidad*" – as the document studied in this chapter put it – fostering a sense of Christian unity that emerged in the formation of confraternal orders. Based on a shared spirituality framed by black expertise in Christian practices, sacred communities functioned within the dynamic cultural and social milieu of the colony, not as a distinct social organization, a recognition that ultimately places black Catholics as the center of local expressions of the Catholic faith.

Sweda's case study is unique as many of the sodalities discussed in the other chapters are multiethnic, but not multiracial, as we noted above. Chapter 4 also crosses the racial line to compare the artistic practices of black and indigenous confraternities. Taking advantage of Lima's rich documentary record, Ximena Gómez's chapter, "Confraternal 'Collections': Black and Indigenous *Cofradías* and the Curation of Religious Life in Colonial Lima," begins the process of recovering the images, material culture, and devotional interactions of black and indigenous confraternities that have been erased by colonialism. Gómez proposes that if we consider each confraternity as a "collection," we can situate their documented sacred images and possession as "inventory items" that were actively collected and thoughtfully displayed, rather than objects that were passively owned. She argues that black and indigenous confraternities curated their religious and social experiences and, thereby, came to visually define the artistic religious landscape of Lima in the sixteenth and seventeenth centuries.

Karen Graubart's Chapter 5, "Of Greater Dignity than the *Negros*": Language and In-Group Distinctions within Early Afro-Peruvian *Cofradías*," looks at how enslaved and free men and women of African origins in Lima joined Catholic *cofradías* in order to form community. She examines earliest records of Lima's African-descent *cofradías*, which reveal some of the ways that members found community, as well as dealt with growing schisms and fissures due to the Atlantic slave trade and local racialized hierarchies. Graubart highlights how Peruvians of African descent drew upon their contemporary experiences, adapting the European rhetoric of "difference" deployed against them, to identify and police their own divisions during the first century of the institutionalization of African slavery in Spanish America. The documents she analyzes also provide us with an early history of how African *naciones*, often misdiagnosed as ethnicities, came to be central to diasporic identities.

African-descent women played essential roles in confraternity life in colonial Latin America. From New Spain to Peru, Brazil, and other parts of the region, in contexts both rural and urban, they collected alms, cared for sick members, and were front and center in ceremonies, festivals, and public performances (as well as behind the scenes preparing for and cleaning up after them). These roles provided enslaved and free women alike opportunities to preserve ties to their communities and ancestors, wield autonomy and social influence, and to shape narratives about their histories and cultural identities. At the same time, however, confraternities often imposed strictures on African-descent women by tying their place within organizational hierarchies to their legal condition, marital status, and ancestral makeup. In Chapter 6, "African-Descent Women and the Limits of Confraternal Devotion in Colonial Lima, Peru," Tamara J. Walker examines a selection of eighteenth-century records from Lima's national archive that feature inventories of material possessions belonging to free women of African descent, especially religious paraphernalia, including rosaries, statuary, plaques of the Virgin Mary, and depictions of Marian apparitions. Taken together, within and across each inventory, these diverse devotional items provide an opportunity to think about African-descent women's extra-confraternal devotional practices in colonial Lima, that is, how Afro-Peruvian *cofradas* overcame the limits imposed upon by colonial society and their own male *cofrades*. Like Gómez's chapter, Walker shows how Afro-Peruvian *cofradas* redefined their colonial condition through the collection of sacred objects.

In Chapter 7, "Glaciers, the Colonial Archive and the Brotherhood of the Lord of Quyllur Rit'i," Angélica Serna analyzes the role of dance performances representing Amazonian identities in the annual Andean pilgrimage of Quyllur Rit'i, the most important annual religious pilgrimage in the southern Andes that involves devotional activities including dancing, singing, and dramatized life cycle events centered around both glaciers and a Catholic shrine to a miraculous image. Serna argues that these performances allow for the interaction of territorial and ritual practices. Her analysis of the history and context of these dances during the pilgrimage brings into discussion how ethnic identities emerge in relation to places such as glaciers and changes in climate across both time and space.

In "Immigrants' Devotions: The Incorporation of Andean Amerindians in Santiago de Chile's Confraternities in the Seventeenth Century," Chapter 8, Jaime Valenzuela Márquez discusses the main confraternities founded in colonial Santiago de Chile by indigenous immigrants from the Andes. These individuals formed social networks and relations, settled in the periphery of the city, and performed artisan labor. This chapter seeks to connect religious practices, social networks, and labor spaces through an analysis of the religious corporations that linked these loci of agency to one another. The ninth chapter of this volume, Maria Candela de Luca's "The Marian Cult as Resistance Strategy: The Territorialized Construction of Devotion in the Province of Potosí, Charcas in the Eighteenth Century," studies indigenous confraternities' Marian devotion in eighteenth-century Potosí, Bolivia. This period saw an explosion in Marian devotion, manifested through a prolif-eration of images, particularly paintings and statues, articulated through numerous confraternities. This chapter proposes to draw a devotional map, highlighting the mechanism of devotion around these images and their relation to various churches in Potosí and indigenous confraternities. This analysis underscores the tensions among the different social groups in this space and their competition for sacred space, as well as points out how these transformations were projected onto the political and religious belief system. De Luca argues that, in the context of disaggregated societies such as the Andean, Marian devotion creates a sense of community affecting groups previously under conflict, functioning then as a socially cohesive instrument.

Chapter 10, Enrique Normando Cruz and Grit Kirstin Koeltzsch's contribu-tion, "Between Excess and Pleasure: The Religious Festivals of the Indigenous People of Jujuy, Seventeenth-Nineteenth Centuries," explores the religious festivals staged by the indigenous confraternities of colonial Jujuy, in the viceroyalty of Peru. They argue that these festivals helped consolidate Spanish rule over these individuals, sustaining that festival culture helped legitimize the indigenous governors' authority and popularized a penchant for the excess of food and drink.

Célia Borges's chapter, "Black Brotherhoods in Colonial Brazil: Devotion and Solidarity," Chapter 11, explores solidarity among Afro-Brazilian *irmandades.* There were innumerable black brotherhoods in colonial Brazil. With the objective of promoting devotional practices, brother-hoods had a central role in fostering solidarity among the members. Afro-Brazilians and enslaved Africans made up the black Rosary brotherhoods of colonial Brazil. Endorsed by the Church and Crown, these institutions constituted Afro-Brazilians' sole means of social association. This chapter studies the meaning of membership in Afro-Brazilian brotherhoods and emphasizes the centrality of rituals in the formation of new social identities. Chapter 12, Marina de Mello e Souza's "Cultural Resistance and Afro-Catholicism in Colonial Brazil," adds to Borges' argument. Lay brotherhoods were a major form of social organization in colonial Brazil. These brotherhoods were dedicated to mutual aid and devotion to the Virgin Mary and certain saints. There were white, mestizo, black, rich, mid-income and poor brotherhoods. Black brotherhoods elected a king among their charges. His authority was recognized by the community he represented, and he was a respected mediator with slave-owners, priests, and colonial authorities. Brotherhoods offered Afro-Brazilians possibilities for affirming their identity and a social space. Afro-Brazilian brotherhoods show that Afro-Brazilians did not only achieve their own space through revolt and resistance, but also through negotiation and the adoption of European institutions.

Lucilene Reginaldo's Chapter 13, "'Much to See and Admire': Festival, Parade, and Royal Pageantry among Afro-Bahian Brotherhoods in the Eighteenth Century," studies Afro-Brazilian irmandades' festive prac-tices in Brazil's colonial capital until 1763. Brotherhoods' patron feasts were their main devotional and social activity. Celebrated annually, the feast was the moment of the greatest public visibility for members. The celebration could bring a great deal of prestige to the governing board and the whole brotherhood, attracting new members. Beyond this, the feast was an opportunity for the brotherhood to show its capacity to organize funerals, along with burial at a holy place, which constituted a key source of income and a major attraction for potential members. This was also another aspect of the celebrations: they functioned as a space for dancing, music, and the consumption of food and alcoholic beverages. The election and coronation of kings and queens was a unique part of this aspect of the celebration. This chapter analyzes the festivities organized by black brotherhoods in eighteenth-century Salvador, Brazil, underscoring various aspects of their confraternal life and the economic and political activity (within and without the brotherhood) undertaken to stage these festivities.

About the authors

Miguel A. Valerio

Miguel A. Valerio is assistant professor of Spanish at Washington University in St. Louis. His research focuses on the African diaspora in the literatures and cultures of the early modern Iberian world, particularly Afro-confraternities' festive practices. His work has appeared in *Afro-Hispanic Review*, *Confraternitas*, *Slavery and Abolotion*, *Colonial Latin American Review* and the *Journal of Festive Studies*. His book, Sovereign Joy: *Afro-Mexican Kings and Queens, 1539-1640*, which studies Afro-Mexican confraternities' festive practices, will be published with Cambridge University Press in 2022.

Javiera Jaque Hidalgo

Javiera Jaque Hidalgo is an assistant professor of Spanish in the Department of Modern and Classical Languages and Literatures in Virginia Tech. Her topic of research is the literature and culture of Colonial Latin America with a focus on Jesuit missions in Chile. More recently her research focus is on indigenous migration to urban spaces. She has published her research in *A Contracorriente, Una revista de estudios latinoamericanos, Rocky Mountain Review, Revista Chilena de Literatura, and Revista Provinciana. Revista de literatura y pensamiento*. She is currently working in her first monograph entitled *Misiones Jesuitas en la Frontera de Arauco: Resistencia Mapuche, Negociación y Movilidad Cultural en la Periferia Colonial (1593-1641)*, in which she analyzes the frontier dynamics among Mapuche people and Jesuit missionaries in the seventeenth century.

Bibliography

Armenteros Martínez, Iván. "De hermandades y procesiones: la cofradía de esclavos y libertos negros de *Sant Jaume* de Barcelona y la asimilación de la negritud en la Europa premoderna (siglos XV-XVI)." *Clio: Revista de Pesquisa Histórica* 29, no. 2 (2011): s/p.

Bejarano, Ignacio, ed. *Actas del cabildo de la Ciudad de México*, 52 vols. Mexico City: Aguilar e Hijos, 1889-1911.

Blumenthal, Debra. "'La Casa dels Negres': Black African Solidarity in Late Medieval Valencia." In *Black Africans in Renaissance Europe*, edited by Thomas F. Earle and Kate J. P. Lowe, 225-246. Cambridge: Cambridge University Press, 2010.

Bowser, Frederick P. *The African Slave in Colonial Peru, 1524-1650*. Stanford: Stanford University Press, 1974.

Bristol, Joan Cameron. "Afro-Mexican Saintly Devotion in a Mexico City Alley." In *Africans to Spanish America: Expanding the Diaspora*, edited by Sherwin K. Bryant, Rachel S. O'Toole, and Ben Vinson III, 114-135. Urbana: University of Illinois Press, 2014.

Campos y Fernández de Sevilla, F. Javier. *Catálogo de cofradías del Archivo del Arzobispado de Lima*. Lima: IEIH, 2014.

Chasteen, John Charles. *National Rhythms, African Roots: The Deep History of Latin American Popular Dance*. Albuquerque: University of New Mexico Press, 2004.

Contreras, Hugo. "Indios de Tierra adentro en Chile central. Las modalidades de la migración forzosa y el desarraigo (fines del siglo XVI y comienzo del siglo XVII)." In *América en Diásporas: esclavitudes y migraciones forzadas en Chile y otras regiones americanas (siglos XVI-XIX)*, edited by Jaime Valenzuela, 161-196. Santiago: RIL Editores, 2017.

Cordero Fernández, Macarena. "La cofradía de Nuestra Señora de Guadalupe. Querellas y defensas indígenas ante la justicia eclesiástica: Colina, Chile, siglo XVII-XVIII. Un estudio de caso." *Revista de Humanidades*, no. 33 (2016): 79-104.

Cruz, Enrique. "'Esclavos españoles, indios y negros': notas para el estudio de las relaciones interétnicas en las cofradías religiosas del norte del Virreinato del Río de la Plata." *Boletim do Museu Paraense Emílio Goeldi. Ciências Humanas* 8, no. 2 (2013), 449-458.

Dávila y Padilla, Agustín. *Historia de la fundación y discurso de la provincia de Santiago de México de los Predicadores*. Brussels: Ivan de Meerbeque, 1625.

van Deusen, Nancy E. "The 'Alienated' Body: Slaves and Castas in the Hospital de San Bartolomé in Lima, 1680 to 1700," *The Americas* 56, no. 1 (1999): 1-30.

Dewulf, Jeroen. *From the Kingdom of Kongo to Congo Square: Kongo Dances and the Origins of the Mardi Gras Indians*. Lafayette: University of Louisiana at Lafayette Press, 2017.

Dierksmeier, Laura. *Charity for and by the Poor: Franciscan-Indigenous Confraternities in Mexico, 1527-1700*. Norman: University of Oklahoma Press, 2020.

Farman Sweda, Krystle. "Black Catholicism: The Formation of Local Religion in Colonial Mexico." Ph.D. diss., City University of New York, 2020.

Fogelman, Patricia, and Marta Goldberg. "*El rey de los congos*: The Clandestine Coronation of Pedro Duarte in Buenos Aires, 1787." In *Afro-Latino Voices: Narratives from the Early Modern Ibero-Atlantic World, 1550-1812*, edited by Kathryn Joy McKnight and Leo J. Garofolo, 155-173. Indianapolis: Hacket, 2009.

Fonseca, Jorge. *Religião e liberdade: os negros nas irmandades e confrarias portuguesas (séculos XV à XIX)*. Lisbon: Humus, 2016.

Fracchia, Carmen. *"Black but Human": Slavery and the Visual Arts in Hapsburg Spain, 1480- 1700*. Oxford: Oxford University Press, 2019.

Fromont, Cécile. "Dancing for the King of Congo from Early Modern Central Africa to Slavery Era Brazil." *Colonial Latin American Review* 22, no. 2 (2013); 184-208.

von Germeten, Nicole. *Black Blood Brothers: Confraternities and Social Mobility for Afro- Mexicans.* Gainesville: University Press of Florida, 2006.

——. "Juan Roque's Donation of a House to the *Zape* Confraternity, Mexico City, 1623." In *Afro-Latino Voices*, 83-103.

Graubart, Karen B. "'*So color de una cofradía*': Catholic Confraternities and the Development of Afro-Peruvian Ethnicities in Early Colonial Peru," *Slavery and Abolition* 33, no. 1 (2012): 43-64.

Jouve Martín, José Ramón. *The Black Doctors of Colonial Lima: Science, Race, and Writing in Colonial and Early Republican Peru.* Montreal: McGill-Queen's University Press, 2014.

——. "Death, Gender, and Writing: Testaments of Women of African Origin in Seventeenth-Century Lima, 1651-1666." In *Afro-Latino Voices*, 105-125.

Kellogg, Susan, and Matthew Restall, eds. *Dead Giveaways. Indigenous Testaments of Colonial Mesoamerica and the Andes.* Salt Lake City: University of Utah Press, 1998.

Kiddy, Elizabeth W. "*Congados, Calunga, Cadombe*: Our Lady of the Rosary in Minas Gerais, Brazil." *Luso-Brazilian Review* 37, no. 1 (2000): 47-61.

——. *Blacks of the Rosary: Memory and History in Minas Gerais, Brazil.* University Park: Pennsylvania State University Press, 2007.

Lee, Bertram T., and Juan Bromley. *Libros de cabildo de Lima.* Lima: Impresores San Martín, 1935-1948.

Martínez Ferrer, Luis. "Pedro López y los negros y mulatos de la ciudad de México (1582- 1597." In *Socialización y religiosidad del médico Pedro López (1527-1597): de Dueñas (Castilla) a la ciudad de México*, edited by Martínez Ferrer and María Luisa Rodríguez Sala, 179-216. Mexico City: UNAM, 2013.

Mello e Souza, Marina de. *Reis negros no Brasil escravista: História da festa de coroação de Rei Congo.* Belo Horizont: Editora da Universidade Federal de Minas Gerais, 2002.

Mondragón Barrios, Lourdes. *Esclavos africanos en la Ciudad de México: el servicio doméstico durante el siglo XVI.* Mexico City: Euram, 1999.

Moreno, Isidro. *La antigua hermandad de los negros de Sevilla: etnicidad, poder y sociedad en 600 años de historia.* Seville: University of Seville, 1997.

Mulvey, Patricia Ann. "The Black Lay Brotherhoods of Colonial Brazil: A History." Ph.D. diss., City University of New York, 1976.

——. "Slave Confraternities in Brazil: Their Role in Colonial Society." *The Americas* 39, no. 1 (1982): 39-68.

Perry, Jonathan S. *The Roman Collegia: The Modern Evolution of an Ancient Concept.* Leiden: Brill, 2006.

Rappaport, Joanne, and Tom Cummins. *Beyond the Lettered City: Indigenous Literacies in the Andes.* Durham: Duke University Press, 2012.

Reis, José João. *Death is a Festival: Funeral Rites and Rebellion in Nineteenth-Century Brazil*. Translated by H. Sabrina Glehill. Chapel Hill: University of North Carolina Press, 2003.

Restall, Matthew. "Black Conquistadors: Armed Africans in Early Spanish America." *The Americas* 57, no. 2 (2000): 171-205.

Retamal, Julio. *Testamentos de "Indios" en Chile colonial: 1564-1801*. Santiago: RIL Editores, 2000.

Sánchez Gaete, Marcial. "Desde el Mundo Hispano al Cono Sur americano: una mirada a las Cofradías desde la historiografía en los últimos 50 años." *Revista de Historia y Geografía* no. 28 (2013): 59-80.

Sandoval, Alonso de. *Treatise on Slavery*. Translated by Nicole von Germeten. Indianapolis: Hacket, [1627] 2008.

Teixeira Leite, José Roberto "Negros, pardos e mulatos na pintura e na escultura brasileira do século XVIII." In *A mão afro-brasileira: significado da contribuição artística e histórica*, edited by Emanoel Araújo, 13-54. Sao Paulo: Técnica Nacional de Engenharia, 1988.

Valenzuela Márquez, Jaime. "Devociones de inmigrantes. Indígenas andinos y plurietnicidad urbana en la conformación de cofradías coloniales (Santiago de Chile, siglo XVII)." *Historia* 1, no. 43 (2010).

Valerio, Miguel A. "'That There Be No Black Brotherhood': The Failed Suppression of Afro Mexican Confraternities, 1568-1612." *Slavery and Abolition* 42, no. 2 (2021): 293-314.

——. "Black Confraternity Members Performing Afro-Christian Identity in a Renaissance Festival in Mexico City in 1539." *Confraternitas* 29, no. 1 (2018): 31-54.

——. "A Mexican *Sangamento*?: The First Afro-Christian Performance in the Americas." In *Afro-Catholic Festivals in the Americas: Performance, Representation, and the Making of Black Atlantic Tradition*, edited by Cécile Fromont, 59-74. University Park: Pennsylvania State University Press, 2019.

——. "The Queen of Sheba's Manifold Body: Creole Black Women Performing Sexuality, Cultural Identity, and Power in Seventeenth-Century Mexico City." *Afro-Hispanic Review* 35, no. 2 (2016): 79-98.

——. Architects of Their Own Humanity: Race, Devotion, and Artistic Agency in Afro-Brazilian Confraternal Churches in Eighteenth-Century Salvador and Ouro Preto." *Colonial Latin American Review* 30: 2 (2021): 238-271.

Vieira-Powers, Karen. *Andean Journeys: Migration, Ethnogenesis, and the State in Colonial Quito*. Albuquerque: University of New Mexico Press, 1995.

Vincent, Catherine. *Les confréries médiévales dans le royaume de France: XIIIᵉ-XVᵉ siècle*. Paris: Albin Michel, 1994.

Walker, Tamara J. "The Queen of *los Congos*: Slavery, Gender, and Confraternity Life in Late Colonial Lima, Peru." *Journal of Family History* 40, no. 3 (2015): 305-322.

Part I

Indigenous and Black Confraternities

in New Spain

1   Religious Autonomy and Local
     Religion among Indigenous
     Confraternities in Colonial Mexico,
     Sixteenth-Seventeenth Centuries[1]

Laura Dierksmeier
Universität Tübingen

Abstract
Confraternities were indispensable charitable institutions in colonial
Mexico. Not only did missionaries see the potential of confraternities as
a vehicle for evangelization, but also indigenous people themselves used
Christianity as a tool for their own protection and survival. Whether it be
in their hospital work or economic transactions, indigenous people ultimately became advocates of their own Christianity to advance their social
status and power, and to negotiate their community positions. Indigenous
customs were by no means eradicated within the new colonial society, and
evidence of hybrid practices and local religion can be seen in the activities
of confraternity members. By drawing on indigenous symbols and styles
and fusing Christian saints with ancestral deities, indigenous people formed
a Christianity of their own that was neither fully "orthodox" nor wholly
"unorthodox." Between these two extremes, confraternity life fluctuated
dynamically. What emerges from confraternity records, often written in
Nahuatl with finances recorded in Aztec currencies, can aptly be called
"Nahua Christianity," a combination of pre- and post-conquest religiosity.

1   This chapter is a reworked version of Chapter 4 from Laura Dierksmeier, *Charity for and by
the Poor: Franciscan and Indigenous Confraternities in Mexico, 1527-1700* (Norman: University of
Oklahoma Press, 2020). I have received assistance from several Nahuatl scholars, both in terms
of translations of archive sources and from the meticulous groundwork their scholarship has
provided. I thank especially Louise Burkhart, Annette Richie, Barry Sell, Rosa Yañéz Rosales,
and John F. Schwaller. I am indebted also to Renate Dürr and Jeffrey Burns for feedback on
earlier drafts of this chapter.

Javiera Jaque Hidalgo and Miguel A. Valerio. *Indigenous and Black Confraternities in Colonial
Latin America: Negotiating Status through Religious Practices.* Amsterdam: Amsterdam University
Press, 2022
DOI: 10.5117/ 9789463721547_CH01

Keywords: Indigenous confraternities, Nahua Christianity, Mexico, Franciscan, sixteenth century

Confraternities were indispensable charitable institutions in colonial Mexico. Not only did missionaries see the potential of confraternities as a vehicle for evangelization, but also indigenous people themselves used Christianity as a tool for their own protection and survival. Whether it be in their hospital work or economic transactions, indigenous people ultimately became advocates of their own Christianity to advance their social status and power, and to negotiate their community positions. Indigenous customs were by no means eradicated within the new colonial society, and evidence of hybrid practices and local religion can be seen in the activities of confraternity members. By drawing on indigenous symbols and styles and fusing Christian saints with ancestral deities, indigenous people formed a Christianity of their own that was neither fully "orthodox" nor wholly "unorthodox." Between these two extremes, confraternity life fluctuated dynamically. What emerges from confraternity records, often written in Nahuatl with finances recorded in Aztec currencies, can aptly be called "Nahua Christianity," a combination of pre- and post-conquest religiosity.[2] This chapter focuses on the area of central Mexico to augment examples of hybrid indigenous-Catholic practices meticulously traced for other regions of Mexico, including Michoacán, Oaxaca, Jalisco, and the Yucatán.[3]

Nahua Christianity

By the end of the sixteenth century, missionaries boasted that only a few remnants of indigenous beliefs were to be found. As with Islam in Spain,

[2] Nahua Christianity is also referred to as Nahua Catholicism. On the topic see, for example, Charles Dibble, "The Nahuatilization of Christianity," in *Sixteenth-Century Mexico: The Work of Sahagún*, ed. Munro Emerson (Albuquerque: University of New Mexico Press, 1974), 225-233; Louise M. Burkhart, *The Slippery Earth: Nahua-Christian Moral Dialogue in Sixteenth-Century Mexico* (Tucson: University of Arizona Press, 1989); Albert Meyers and Diane Elizabeth Hopkins, ed., *Manipulating the Saints: Religious Brotherhoods and Social Integration in Postconquest Latin America* (Hamburg: Wayasbah, 1988); Martin Austin Nesvig, ed., *Local Religion in Colonial Mexico* (Albuquerque: University of New Mexico, 2006).
[3] See Mark Z. Christensen, *Nahua and Maya Catholicisms: Texts and Religion in Colonial Central Mexico and Yucatan* (Stanford: Stanford University Press, 2013); Louise M. Burkhart, Barry D. Sell, and Gregory Spira, *Nahua Christianity in Performance* (Norman: University of Oklahoma Press, 2009).

missionaries in Mexico used the largest and most important religious structures as foundations for churches, transforming ancient holy locations for Nahuas into Christian sacred sites. The Nuestra Señora de los Remedios Church in Cholula, built on top of the Great Pyramid (*Tlachihualtepetl*), demonstrates this legacy.[4] The conversion of indigenous architecture into cross-bearing parishes could not, though, be conflated with the much more complicated conversion of individuals.

Christian saints, European hymns, the Aztec calendar, and omen reading were all part of indigenous spirituality at the same time. The interrelatedness of Catholic and indigenous beliefs was especially enduring for those born after the conquest: oral histories of the past combined with the only visible reality those people had witnessed of Spanish Catholicism and its tolling church bells, trumpeted confraternity processions, and Inquisition *autos da fé*.

Christian and Nahua elements of daily life in colonial Mexico can seldom be separated neatly into two separate groups. Rather, local religion in Mexico can often be referred to as Nahua Christianity, which presumes two belief systems coexisted and influenced one another, where there was neither a comprehensive replacement of past beliefs, nor did indigenous traditions continue unaltered by Catholic influences. Indigenous people were simultaneously Christians and Nahuas, of differing and changing degrees.[5] In a passage from Domingo de San Antón Muñón Chimalpahin Quauhtlehuanitzin's writings, we find a paradigmatic example[6]:

4   Catholic rituals had also been carried out with indigenous people, where one can only speculate as to the reception of such traditions. In an account by Friar Mendieta, Franciscan priests washed the feet of disabled indigenous people (who were deaf, blind, or had restricted mobility) to commemorate the washing of the feet of the disciples by Jesus. Indigenous nobles were also required to care for the poor in a fashion atypical of their stratified social hierarchy. After the washing of the feet, the indigenous people received a meal in imitation of the Last Supper: *Holy Wednesday: A Nahua Drama from Early Colonial Mexico* (Philadelphia: University of Pennsylvania Press, 1996), 81-82.

5   See David R. Galindo, *To Sin No More: Franciscans and Conversions in the Hispanic World, 1683-1830* (Stanford: Stanford University Press, 2018); David Tavárez, ed., *Words and Worlds Turned Around: Indigenous Christianities in Colonial Latin America* (Boulder: University of Colorado Press, 2017); Jonathan Truitt, *Sustaining the Divine in Mexico-Tenochtitlán: Nahuas and Catholicism, 1523-1700* (Norman: University of Oklahoma Press, 2018).

6   See Susan Schroeder, *Chimalpahin and the Kingdoms of Chalco* (Tucson: University of Arizona Press, 1991); Domingo Chimalpahin, *Annals of His Time: Don Domingo de San Antón Muñón Chimalpahin Quauhtlehuanitzin*, ed. James Lockhart, Susan Schroeder, and Doris Namala (Stanford: Stanford University Press, 2006), 5. Chimalpahin records information about political officers, earthquakes, plagues, and abnormal events in Mexico City beginning two years before Chimalpahin's birth (from oral histories) and ending with his own first-hand accounts.

7 House year, 1577. In this year mother Teresa de Jesús [...] wrote her book named *De las moradas*. In this year, in the month of January 31, there was sickness; during the 28 of February there was sickness; in the 31 of March the sickness abated. And during this time there were deaths all over New Spain; we commoners died, and the blacks, but only a few Spaniards died. And in this year there clearly appeared a comet with a very distinct tail; radiance arose from it, beginning while there was a bit of daylight. And at this time striping [for gladiatorial sacrifice] was performed as it was in ancient times; with it they honored the rulers.[7]

The "seventh year of the house" is the way of keeping the date in the Aztec calendar, a glyph (e.g., a house, rabbit, reed, or flint) represented each year. The calendar read as a circle with inner concentric circles. After 52 years, the cycle would begin again. In addition, comet sightings were significant omens of impending events.[8] Chimalpahin's account, with its Aztec elements, included Saint Teresa of Ávila and her 1577 work *De las moradas*.

The process of combining indigenous and Spanish belief systems can be observed through confraternity records. One source unearthed and translated by Nahuatl Scholar Annette Richie instructed confraternity members to take the crucifix seriously:

All that is set in order in relation to what belongs to the Holy confraternity, it is not a plaything, a joke. You will not consider it as such. All of the brethren, when there is mass, the brethren who are in the confraternity, they will not look upon the cross as if it is dead. Truly, every day it is Him, the child Jesus, whom we summon at our supper and our breakfast (night and day).[9]

The fact that the regulations state that the confraternity was not a plaything, or a joke implies that it might have seemed so at first. Making sense of Catholic symbols and adapting them to a Nahua understanding of the world, was a central part of confraternity life in colonial Mexico.

But if confraternities and their associated tenets of faith did not make sense, why would indigenous people voluntarily join confraternities in

---

7   Ibid., 27.

8   Alexus McLeod, *Astronomy in the Ancient World: Early and Modern Views on Celestial Events* (Cham: Springer, 2016), 71.

9   Annette D. Richie, "Confraternity and Community: Negotiating Ethnicity, Gender, and Place in Colonial Tecamachalco, Mexico" (Ph.D. diss., New York State University, Albany, 2011), 132.

colonial Mexico? First, the potential political and social advantages of affiliating oneself with the new dominant religion should not be underrated.[10] Also, aside from seeking benefits within the new social order, new converts can be a faith's most fervent defenders, as violent clashes between indigenous Catholics and their nonbelieving counterparts attests.[11] Yet, the most likely reason indigenous people, or Spaniards for that matter, joined confraternities was for the extensive benefits they offered. A small entry fee (which could be waved when one could not afford it) provided insurance and assurance during times of hardship, poor health, and death, providing members access to small loans, health care and medicines, and a burial with a guaranteed attendance by fellow members. Confraternities were a sort of early modern social security system. They also provided fraternal benefits of feast celebrations and local advantages for community dialogue, community policing, and locally elected leaders for a limited term of office. Moreover, various "Catholic" rituals that intended to gain protection from natural disasters had elements that could have fit into non-Catholic worldviews and sufficed as reasons for joining.

For example, the Parish of Saint Josef located in Puebla and its associated confraternity demonstrate the spiritual convictions of an ethnically mixed confraternity. According to their records, members needed to take actions to appease God, so that he would not punish them with storms, floods, droughts, or high winds. From 1634 to 1889, the Confraternity of Saint Joseph (Cofradía de San José) operated out of this parish.[12] On July 15, 1634, written on parchment "for future memory," is the receipt of a papal license given to the sodality to bless items on the day of their patron saint, Saint Joseph (March 19). These blessed items could help them ward off natural disasters, they claimed.[13] The Confraternity of Saint Joseph had requested permission by the leader of the sodality to bless "palms, olive branches, small pieces of bread, and other honest things" to give to the confraternity members "and to the rest of the loyal Christians" to invoke the intervention of Saint Joseph to help them "become free of so much punishment."[14] The sodality,

---

10   See, for example, the records of a request for indigenous tribute to be used to build a church in 1578: Library of Congress (hereafter LOC), Stephen Harkness Collection, doc. XXXVI; or the request by indigenous people for money to help them repair their church: ibid., doc. XXXVII.

11   Ryan Dominic Crewe, *The Mexican Mission: Indigenous Reconstruction and Mendicant Enterprise in New Spain, 1521-1600* (Cambridge: Cambridge University Press, 2019), 63-77.

12   Although this confraternity ended in the late nineteenth century, confraternities still exist today at this church. In fact, confraternity members were gathered in black and purple uniforms preparing for upcoming processions while I was working in the parish archive.

13   Parroquia de San José, Puebla, Mexico, box 142, unbound pages without page numbers.

14   Ibid.

the document adds, is dedicated to the glorious Saint Joseph, "to whose dedication they founded a notable confraternity of brothers, who exercise many pious works, with much confidence that the said Saint will liberate them from formidable punishment."[15] The petition was approved by the papacy on September 19, 1634 in Rome under the Piscatory Ring.[16]

Whereas in the Puebla Confraternity of Saint Joseph sodality members united to carry out charitable works to ward off punishment from God, other confraternities in Mexico were founded to maintain and protect a shrine, such as in San Marcos Parish, founded in 1538. Mayor Hernando de Elgueta erected a shrine in honor of Saint Blaise, the doctor, bishop, and Christian martyr widely revered in Spain for his alleged miraculous healings. The shrine was built on the major throughway between Mexico City and Cholula. Several confraternities operated out of this parish.[17]

At first glance, one may think that indigenous groups carried out "Christian" ritual sacrifices to appease Aztec gods. After all, according to popular knowledge, that was one of the main characteristics of Aztec society.[18] But superstitious motivations were no more Aztec than they were Christian. The waving of blessed olive branches was believed to invoke Saint Joseph to protect followers from God's temper. In Spain, confraternity members even submerged statutes of the Virgin Mary into nearby rivers in attempts to ward off flooding.[19] While Spaniards emphasized the superstitious rituals of indigenous people, they were less critical of various Catholic practices occurring simultaneously on the Spanish homeland.

Further evidence of such "Nahua Catholicism" can be found within confraternity documents written in Nahuatl. In one indigenous sodality constitution written by Alonso de Molina, members were to celebrate the Virgin Mary's vigil

---

15   Ibid.

16   Ibid.

17   The parish of San Marcos was eventually purchased by the Carmelitas Descalzas and most of the extant confraternity records derive from the eighteenth century, including the Confraternity of the Blessed Sacrament (Cofradía del Santísimo Sacramento, 1722-1884), Confraternity of Our Lady of the Good Event (Cofradía de Nuestra Señora del Buen Suceso, 1745-1827), Confraternity of Our Lady of Sorrows (Cofradía de Nuestra Señora de los Dolores, 1775-1788), and the Confraternity of the Sacred School of Christ (Cofradía de la Santa Escuela de Cristo, 1789-1800). PSM, box 85.

18   Susan Toby Evans, *Mexico and Central America: Archaeology and Culture History* (New York: Thames & Hudson, 2013); Matthew A. Boxt and Brian D. Dillon, *Fanning the Sacred Flame: Mesoamerican Studies in Honor of H. B. Nicholson* (Boulder: University Press of Colorado, 2012); Catherine R. DiCesare, *Sweeping the Way: Divine Transformation in the Aztec Festival of Ochpaniztli* (Boulder: University Press of Colorado, 2009); E.C. Wells and Karla L. Davis-Salazar, *Mesoamerican Ritual Economy: Archaeological and Ethnological Perspectives* (Boulder: University Press of Colorado, 2007).

19   See Maureen Flynn, *Sacred Charity: Confraternities and Social Welfare in Spain, 1400-1700*, ed. Flynn (Ithaca: Cornell University Press, 1989), 31.

with forms of reverence typical of pre-Hispanic traditions: "They will adorn things with flowers, they will shake reeds, grasses and other good flowers here in the home of our beloved mother Saint Mary."[20] Confraternity members were to fear the punishment of God if not all of the people in the hospital were cured, a situation that ultimately would require them to be in a constant state of fear. This fear mirrors Aztec sacrifices to appease their ever-angry gods. A passage in the confraternity regulations demonstrates religious sacrifice that overlapped between indigenous and Christian traditions:

> Our Lord God the Giver of Life knows and is truly angry if many persons here are terminally ill in the hospital and dying who cannot restore themselves to health. Because of that you need to fast right away, beat yourselves with whips and go around in procession saying [the seven] penitential psalms and the litany [of the saints] three times in one week (on Monday and Wednesday and Friday).[21]

God was also to be feared if the members did not make sufficient offerings. Sodality members were to fear God's punishment for failing to "make offerings in church." When they failed to offer enough, God would "take their property and their goods from them and a great famine will happen to them, [and] God gives them a great sickness."[22] Since a bilingual person oversaw the writing of this confraternity constitution, we do not know if the text aimed to manipulate Aztecs to fear the Christian God, or if this writing style was simply a Nahua way to contend with the new Christian religion.

The confraternity members were also to revere Jesus and venerate Mary and Saint Francis. Members were to kiss the feet of Jesus on the crucifix to help with the healing of the sick:

> Behold the cross of our Lord Jesus Christ on which He died and saved people everywhere in the world! Let all of us kiss it, cry before it because of our sins. Let all of us kiss His feet because of the loving of our beloved Savior Jesus Christ. And right away because of that they will give it to the sick person; he will kiss its feet first, afterwards all the members of the cofradía [will do the same].[23]

---

20   Alonso de Molina, Barry D. Sell, Larissa Taylor, and Asunción Lavrin, *Nahua Confraternities in Early Colonial Mexico: The 1552 Nahuatl Ordinances of Fray Alonso de Molina, OFM* (Berkeley: Academy of American Franciscan History, 2002), 101.

21   Ibid., 111.

22   Ibid., 99.

23   Ibid., 115.

Jesus, the regulations reported would "have pity on the poor and sick."[24] Prayers to the "noblewoman Saint Mary" were also said to "give you what your hearts want, what you desired."[25] The Virgin Mary could be asked for anything that could be granted either on earth or in heaven, "because she is very much the compassionate one."[26] One could place their hopes in Mary, because "the noblewoman Saint Mary is not a despiser of people."[27] The sodality regulations also mention that Mary "had mercy on a person who was an idolater."[28]

Franciscan Friar Mendieta also wrote about the processions of native confraternities carried out by thousands of indigenous members. In 1595, Mendieta claimed: "On Holy Thursday, the procession of the True Cross went out with more than 20,000 Indians, and more than 3,000 penitents, with 219 insignias of Christ and insignias of his Passion." Many *cofrades* dressed in white, carried white candles, and processed in the early hours of the morning before it turned to dawn. Mendieta exclaimed, "It is one of the loveliest and most solemn processions in Christendom. And so said Viceroy Don Martín Enríquez, that it was one of the things most worth seeing that he had ever seen in his life."[29] The reality of that moment was likely still different than Mendieta's biased report of "innumerable" participants in the processions. But numerous indigenous people chose unquestionably to partake voluntarily in confraternity processions.

Indigenous Saints

In an attempt to avoid "superstitious" motivations, the Council of Trent condemned the cult of the saints. In 1564, the Council concluded: "Frequent visits to shrines dedicated to the saints with the goal of achieving their help is useless."[30] Shrine visits could be interpreted as an idolization of saints as gods. In practice, however, both indigenous and Spanish confraternity members showed an unyielding dedication to the cult of saints. Since a

---

24 Ibid., 95.
25 Ibid., 135.
26 Ibid.
27 Ibid., 137.
28 Ibid., 139.
29 Mendieta as translated by Burkhart in *Holy Wednesday*, 84.
30 Translation by author from Council of Trent, *El sacrosanto y ecuménico Concilio de Trento traducido al idioma castellano: agrégase el texto latino corregido según la edición auténtica de Roma, publicada en 1564* (Madrid: Ramón Ruiz, 1798).

particular saint could take on different meanings for different people, the saints had the potential to reconcile two spiritual worldviews within one material world. Elizabeth Penry has likewise argued that indigenous people were attracted to the Christian cult of saints because of its familiarity and compatibility with indigenous deities.[31] Indigenous variations of Christianity observed by Penry include offering coca leaves and corn beer instead of sacramental bread and wine during mass and the Virgin Mary appearing to believers through shamanistic performances.[32]

Christianity among indigenous Mexicans was taken up with strong fervor after the appearance of the Virgin of Guadalupe to the indigenous man Juan Diego Cuauhtlatoatzin on the hill of Tepeyac in 1531.[33] Cuauhtlatoatzin deserves our attention because his account of a miraculous appearance is the reason for the spread of the cult of the indigenous Virgin Mary, which would become the largest Marianist devotion worldwide, and the focus of many indigenous confraternities. Bishop Juan de Zumárraga reportedly did not believe Juan Diego's account until he came to him with an image of the Virgin Mary and roses that bloomed out of season as proof of the miracle of her appearance to him.[34] Although scholars disagree as to the number of devotees to the Virgin in the sixteenth century, a strong cult to Guadalupe had formed by the seventeenth century, bolstered by written accounts of Juan Diego's visions.[35] For his visions and the authentication of

31   This information comes from a lecture titled "Cofradías in Colonial Latin America" given at the annual meeting of the Latin American Studies Association in Puerto Rico in May 2015. For details, see Elizaeth Penry, "Canons of the Council of Trent in Arguments of Priests and Indians over Images, Chapels and Cofradías," in *The Council of Trent: Reform and Controversy in Europe and Beyond (1545-1700)*, ed. Wim François and Violeta Soen, vol. 3, (Göttingen: Vandenhoeck and Ruprecht, 2018), 277-299.

32   See previous note.

33   Luis Lasso de la Vega, *The Story of Guadalupe: Luis Laso de a Vega's Huei Tlamahuiçoltica of 1649*, ed. Lisa Sousa, Stafford Poole, James Lockhart, and Miguel Sánchez López, (Stanford: Stanford University Press, 1998).

34   D.A. Brading, *Mexican Phoenix: Our Lady of Guadalupe: Image and Tradition across Five Centuries* (Cambridge: Cambridge University Press, 2003), 86.

35   The shrine of Guadalupe currently receives more visitors today than any other Marian shrine in the world. Located within the large boundaries of what constitutes "Mexico City," the shrine of the Virgin of Guadalupe is so crowded that visitors can only pass by momentarily on a people-moving conveyor belt. For the Virgin of Guadalupe and her legacy, see Paul Badde, *María of Guadalupe: Shaper of History, Shaper of Hearts* (San Francisco: Ignatius Press, 2008); Ernesto de la Torre Villar and Ramiro Navarro de Anda, *Nuevos Testimonios Históricos Guadalupanos* (Mexico City: FCE, 2007); Brading, *Mexican Phoenix*; Stafford Poole, *Our Lady of Guadalupe: The Origins and Sources of a Mexican National Symbol, 1531-1797* (Arizona: University of Arizona Press, 1995); Ernesto de la Torre Villar and Ramiro Navarro de Anda, *Testimonios Históricos Guadalupanos* (Mexico City: FCE, 1982).

reported miracles, Juan Diego himself eventually became Latin America's first indigenous saint, beatified in 1986. Followers of Juan Diego's Guadalupe included sodality members, who honored the Virgin as their patron saint, such as sodalities in both Puebla and Mexico City.

Confraternity-run shrines for devotions to the Virgin Mary (also called Marian devotions) were common throughout Latin America. One such confraternity dedicated to the Virgin of Guadalupe was said in a letter by Viceroy Enríquez to have hundreds of sodality members: "They say there are 400 cofrades."[36] After detailing the extensive property owned by this confraternity, the viceroy's mention of so many *cofrades* appears to demarcate a potential threat instead of to express his happiness with the success of the indigenous-Christian shrine.[37] Emma Sordo published a study on various confraternities dedicated to Our Lady of Copacabana in Peru, which was committed to praying to the Virgin for the manifestation of miracles.[38] Sordo argues that 112 native confraternities (*cofradías de naturales*) existed in fourteen native parishes in Potosí. There, it was largely believed by the local population that the Virgin could accomplish miracles.[39] Augustinian chroniclers between 1583 and 1653 had logged more than 200 miracles associated with the Virgin of Copacabana.[40] Sordo argues that for Andean people who had previously worshiped the mountains, it was not a coincidence that there were even special confraternities who claimed opposite sides of the mountain to worship. The sun-facing side was revered by a confraternity from Copacabana Parish and the shaded side was worshiped by a sodality from San Pedro Parish.[41]

A reason for the interest of indigenous people in the cult of saints may have been due to their familiarity with human-god figures acting as "sacred intermediaries, who granted favors in exchange for the cult rendered by their devotees, and with the complex systems of ritual and organization that upheld these cults."[42] An account from Peru by mestizo Inca Garcilasco

---

36   A letter from Viceroy Don Martin Enriquez notes the confraternity dedicated to the Our Lady of Guadalupe shrine: Archivo General de Indias (hereafter AGI) Mexico 19, N.159, Carta del virrey Martín Enríquez, f. 6 (September 23, 1575).

37   Ibid.

38   Emma Sordo, "Our Lady of Copacabana and her Legacy in Colonial Potosí," in *Early Modern Confraternities in Europe and the Americas: International and Interdisciplinary Perspectives*, ed. Christopher F. Black and Pamela Gravestock (Aldershot: Ashgate Publishing, 2006), 187-203.

39   Ibid., 190.

40   Ibid., 191.

41   Ibid., 192.

42   Mario Rodríguez León, "Invasion and Evangelization in the Sixteenth Century," in *The Church in Latin America, 1492-1992*, ed. Enrique Dussel (Tunbridge Wells: Burns & Oates, 1992), 78.

de Vega starkly incorporates indigenous confraternity practices into the Christian feast of Corpus Christi in Cuzco:

> The floats looked like those carried by the confraternities on such feast days in Spain [...] The Indians carried all the decorations, ornaments and instruments which they used to celebrate their principal feasts in the time of their Inca kings [...] Some wore lion skins, others carried the wings of a very large bird which they call *cuntur* [...] and others came with painted emblems, such as fountains, rivers, lakes, mountains, and caves, because they said that their first fathers came from such things [...] With these things those Indians solemnized the feasts of their kings, with the same things (adding to them as much as they were able) [...]. [T] hey celebrated in my times the feasts of the Most Holy Sacrament [...] as people now disabused of their gentile past.[43]

Indigenous people dressed in lion skins, carrying bird wings and painted symbols of sacred mountains brought their former religious symbols into their new religious sphere. This incorporation of religious objects with sacred significance suggests that indigenous people understood well the intention of the Catholic confraternity processions to worship collectively something held to be collectively holy (even if indigenous reactions to the symbols of Christ were unsentimental and ambiguous). In short, indigenous and Catholic traditions were combined and often fused in sodality processions.[44]

Amy Remensnyder has compared the reception of the Virgin Mary by Jews and Muslims in Spain with that of indigenous people in Latin America.[45] She concludes that converted Jews rejected the Virgin far more than did Muslims. Remensnyder accounts for this difference due to an aversion for any praise of a woman's womb. Muslims, on the other hand, accepted Mary, Remensnyder holds, because she was already the most important female figure in the Qur'an. Similarly, indigenous people, she claims, acknowledged Mary in large

43   Ibid. For the original text in Spanish, see Garcilaso de la Vega and Augusto Cortina, *Comentarios reales* (Buenos Aires: Espasa Calpe Argentina, 1950).

44   For indigenous saints in Latin America, see Jeanette Favrot Peterson, *Visualizing Guadalupe: From Black Madonna to Queen of the Americas* (Austin: University of Texas Press, 2014); Allan Greer and Jodi Bilinkoff, *Colonial Saints: Discovering the Holy in the Americas, 1500-1800* (New York: Routledge, 2003); Ronald J. Morgan, *Spanish American Saints and the Rhetoric of Identity, 1600-1810* (Tucson: University of Arizona Press, 2002); Stephanie Wood, "Adopted Saints: Christian Images in Nahua Testaments of Late Colonial Toluca," *The Americas* 47, no. 3 (1991): 259.

45   Amy G. Remensnyder, *La Conquistadora: The Virgin Mary at War and Peace in the Old and the New Worlds* (New York: Oxford University Press, 2014).

numbers because they were already familiar with female goddesses having
a comparable function. Spaniards therefore used indigenous devotion to
the Virgin as a means for furthering conversion. This instrumentalization
of the Virgin Mary has led to much literature on her role as "the female
conqueror" (*la conquistadora*) of Mexico.[46]

Nahua Scribes, Currencies, and Local Leaders

Archival manuscripts make it clear that indigenous confraternities kept
their records in indigenous languages.[47] Even confraternities with Spanish
members wrote their records in Nahuatl when indigenous members outnum-
bered Spaniards. Nonetheless, certain Spanish words were not translated.
Nahuatl sodality documents from 1610 to 1620 show these examples: days
of the week (e.g., *lunes, domingo*), months (e.g., *marzo, octubre*), religious
holidays (e.g., Semana Santa, Jueves Santo), confraternity-specific words
(e.g., *cofradía*), measurements (e.g., *medio*, referring to half a bushel of
peanuts), and items used in celebrating mass, such as candles (*candella*)
and wine (*vino*).[48]

Nahuatl had different stylistic norms and usages than did Spanish.
The writing by Nahuatl scribes involved self-reflective questions that
are not seen in Spanish confraternity documents.[49] For example, in the
Confraternity of Our Lady of Solitude of San Miguel Coyotlan, a con-
templative passage appears: "Did you just uselessly make a vow? Or did
you come to give delight to your flesh? What do you think of yourself?
What do you think you are? What counsel have you given yourself?"[50]

46 Ibid.
47 Professor Louise Burkhart and Dr. Annette Richie were very kind in helping me translate
and decipher these Nahuatl documents from the Archivo Histórico del Museo Nacional de
Antropología e Historia (hereafter AHMNA): Fondo Franciscano (hereafter FF), microfilm roll
29, vol. 91, and roll 43, vol. 129. Dr. Richie helped me at length with several pages of Nahuatl text,
and I am indebted to her for her generosity, expertise, and kindness.
48 AHMNA, FF, roll 29, vol. 91, Gastos de una cofradía en Nahuatl, 1610; FF, roll 43, vol. 129, 1615.
49 See Mónica Díaz, *Indigenous Writings from the Convent: Negotiating Ethnic Autonomy in
Colonial Mexico* (Tucson: University of Arizona Press, 2010); Yanna Yannakakis, *The Art of Being
in-between: Native Intermediaries, Indian Identity, and Local Rule in Colonial Oaxaca* (Durham:
Duke University Press, 2008). For an annotated bibliography of 3,000 texts from colonial Mexico
that have been transcribed from the original Nahuatl manuscripts, see Ascensión H. de León-
Portilla, *Tepuztlahcuilolli: Impresos en náhuatl (historia y bibliografía)* (Mexico City: UNAM,
1988).
50 Confraternity of Our Lady of Solitude, *Our Lady of Solitude of San Miguel Coyotlan, 1619: A
Rare Set of Cofradía Rules in Nahuatl*, ed. Barry D. Sell (Mexico City: UNAM, 2000), 135.

Such questions seen in Nahuatl sodality documents show reflection over spiritual questions and were most likely written by children of indigenous nobles who were trained in Franciscan schools and held minor positions in the Church.

In one remarkable example, an ethnically mixed confraternity kept its recorded finances in two languages, depending on who gave the donation. Spanish donations were recorded in Spanish, while mestizo and indigenous donations were logged in Nahuatl. Being able to use written Nahuatl (albeit in an alphabetized form) as an official language allowed for a realm of linguistic autonomy. Finances were also recorded in Nahuatl, and sometimes Nahuatl and Spanish appeared side by side in the same list of donations, depending on the language preference of the scribe.[51] A fusion of languages was indicative of a synthesis of two coexisting cultures in need of practical solutions for cooperation.

Even though Nahuatl was used as a standard language for recordkeeping, there were at times mandates to translate certain legal documents, such as testaments of wealthy indigenous nobles, from Nahuatl into Spanish. Translations sometimes resulted in mistranslations—and we do not know whether the changes were intentional.[52] After all, at the same time in Spain, authors were censored by the Inquisition for writing in the foreign languages of French, German, and Italian.

Confraternity records also reveal that indigenous autonomy was visible in the realm of finances. Currencies other than coins in use before the conquest were still permitted decades later as standard units of value. Under the Aztec Empire, tribute was collected in "gemstones, multicolored feathers, aromatics, tiger skins, amber, and live eagles."[53] Woven cloth, red seashells, gold dust, and sandstone beads also held great value. But cacao beans, the fruit of the cocoa tree, was the main form of Aztec currency.[54] The cacao beans could be handled and counted easily, and they also had a food value. But, as with coins, there could be manipulation in that "some would debase the beans—removing the nutritious content of the hull and replacing it with

51   Ibid.
52   For examples of mistranslations of indigenous last wills and testaments, see Teresa Rojas Rabiela and Elsa Leticia López Rea, *Vidas y bienes olvidados: testamentos indígenas novohispanos* (Mexico City: Centro de Investigaciones y Estudios Superiores en Antropología Social, 2002).
53   Pedro Carrasco Pizana and Johanna Broda, *Economía política e ideología en el México prehispánico* (Mexico City: Editorial Nueva Imagen, 1978), 15.
54   Cacao beans as currency are still in use today in some remote regions of Mexico and Guatemala: ibid.

dirt to restore normal weight."[55] Despite the risk of manipulation, indigenous people were permitted to continue to use cacao beans as currency, even after the issue of minted coins.[56]

Nahuatl sodality records from 1615 show that peanuts (*cacahuatl*) were also still in use as a valid currency. The fact that peanuts were recorded in the confraternity disbursement list with a numerical amount shows that they had a monetary value. Peanut donations ranged from one to four *tomines* (Spanish coins).[57] Nahua protagonists in Christian social institutions could use confraternities to fulfill their needs using pre-Hispanic currencies that were accessible and convenient.

Indigenous confraternities were also allowed to elect their own leaders without Spanish intervention or oversight. Even though missionaries often instituted confraternities, priests were not in full control of them. Because of the relatively small number of friars, missionaries often complained that all their time was dedicated to celebrating mass and administering the sacraments. Entire parishes were left in the hands of indigenous assistants. Rural and remote mission parishes, in particular, were often left unattended with no local priest to provide the sacraments for which the residents once had been instructed to observe.[58] This general sentiment is well-captured in a 1567 letter from a Mexican bishop to the king. Fray Francisco de Toral, bishop of Yucatán wrote:

> Evangelical ministers are needed here to teach the natives the law of God, for there is no one to instruct them. There are about fourteen friars for 150 leagues of inhabited land, and of these there are only three who can preach, two others are beginners; there is need for fifty friars.[59]

---

55   Ibid.

56   All coins minted in the New World were made of silver. Gold was reserved for coins made in Spain. One *tomín* was equivalent to 140 cacao beans: ibid. For descriptions of use of Aztec currencies to pay tribute (blankets, feathers, etc.), see René Acuña, *Relaciones geográficas del siglo XVI* (Mexico City: UNAM, 1982), 398.

57   AHMNA, FF, roll 43, vol. 139. The donor's ethnicity was listed in Spanish when the person was not indigenous.

58   Charles Gibson, *The Aztecs Under Spanish Rule: A History of the Indians of the Valley of Mexico, 1519-1810* (Stanford: Stanford University Press, 1964), 103.

59   Letter written by Fray Francisco de Toral, bishop of Yucatán, to the king, 1567. A distance of 150 leagues was approximately equal to 800 km or 500 miles. Although fourteen friars are referenced in this quotation, the bishop notes that only three had finished their vows and were authorized to preach; two others were still in training: James Lockhart and Enrique Otte, *Letters and People of the Spanish Indies, Sixteenth Century* (Cambridge: Cambridge University Press, 1976), 204-207.

Friars generally did not have substantial influence over the mundane, day-to-day operations and finances of confraternities. The elected leaders of the confraternities handled daily tasks independently. Oversight came instead in the form of several yearly inspections by Church *visitadores*, who would scrutinize confraternity finances for orthodoxy.

Confraternity leadership may have been one of few situations where local residents could directly elect the people who would make decisions affecting their lives. Whether this autonomy was used to recreate preconquest nobility hierarchies or to express true commitment to an individual leader, is a matter of academic debate among scholars of colonial Mexico.[60] Amos Megged uses the term an "unholy marriage" to refer to indigenous relationships in confraternities that at times exacerbated pre-Hispanic conflicts between nobles and commoners.[61] From Nahuatl records in 1563, we know of at least one conflict over whether the confraternity leaders were real nobles.[62] This suggests that certain indigenous people tried to enforce previous hierarchies within the new Christian institutions. But the ability to enforce previous nobility titles was made difficult as such titles were often unrecognized by the Spanish and known only through oral histories.

Inclusivity and Ethnic Boundaries

Most confraternities in colonial Mexico appear to have included both men and women, and women sometimes held leadership roles.[63] Archival sources suggest that black and indigenous confraternities elected women into higher offices than did Spaniards in Mexico. Female indigenous officers were called *cihuateopisquis*, which Annette Richie explains as "officials in charge of women."[64] Richie has also found the existence of a female scribe

---

60   David Cahill, "The Long Conquest: Collaboration by Native Andean Elites in the Colonial System, 1532-1825," in *Technology, Disease, and Colonial Conquests, Sixteenth to Eighteenth Centuries: Essays Reappraising the Guns and Germs Theories*, ed. George Raudzens (Boston: Brill, 2003), 87.

61   Amos Megged, "The Religious Context of an 'Unholy Marriage': Elite Alienation and Popular Unrest in the Indigenous Communities of Chiapa, 1570-1680," *Ethnohistory* 46, no. 1 (1999): 149-172.

62   Richie, "Confraternity and Community," 83.

63   This is different from Portugal, where larger numbers of highly discriminatory confraternities excluded women: Isabel dos Guimarães Sá, "Assistance to the Poor on a Royal Model: The Example of the Misericórdias in the Portuguese Empire from the Sixteenth to the Eighteenth Century," *Confraternitas* 13, no. 1 (2002): 13.

64   Richie, "Confraternity and Community," 54.

in an indigenous confraternity from 1612, by the name of Maria Xuarez.[65] In Andahuaylilllas, Peru, the Confraternity of Our Lady of Monserate "was open only to unmarried Indian women."[66]

The existence of confraternities based exclusively on a single ethnicity were less common than one might expect.[67] As marriage licenses in sixteenth-century Mexico display, intermarriage among ethnically diverse populations was commonplace.[68] Spaniards married mestizos, indigenous people married black slaves, and as the years passed, the combinations became sizable.[69] Racial mixing through marriage made exclusive confraternities unattractive to couples who belonged to different ethnic groups. The well-known *castas* paintings from eighteenth-century Mexico display the extent to which racial mixing could result in a long list of hybrid identities.[70] The Confraternity of the Blessed Sacrament, established in most parish churches, often accepted any parishioner who wanted to join.

Social interactions through labor and trade made it likely that Spaniards would share a sodality with members of various ethnicities. This was true for the Confraternity of the Blessed Sacrament in Tula Hidalgo, Mexico.[71] From the membership book, we know this was an inclusive confraternity that had Spanish, creole, and indigenous members. In rural contexts, letters from Spanish settlers show us that they were not always better situated than

---

65 Ibid., 143.

66 Susan Migden Socolow, *The Women of Colonial Latin America* (Cambridge: Cambridge University Press, 2000).

67 Some confraternities in Spain explicitly banned black people, or those of mixed black-Spanish blood (e.g., Cofradía de los Nazarenos, 1532, Priego de Córdoba; Cofradía de Ánimas del Purgatorio de la Iglesia de Santa María, 1587 in Manzanilla, Huelva; and Hermandad y Cofradía de la Santa Vera Cruz, 1575, Palomares del Río). Other confraternities had no specific ethnic regulations and decided on a case-by-case basis. La Hermandad de los Negritos (Brotherhood of the Blacks), established between 1394 and 1400 and one of the earliest confraternities in Seville, Spain, was founded exclusively for black members, both free and enslaved. The regulations required enslaved members to bring a signed letter of permission from their masters stating that they could join. Also, in Seville, a sodality of mulatos was formed in 1572, La Hermandad del Calvario de San Ildefonso (Saint Ildephonsus Calvary Brotherhood). This confraternity only allowed members of mixed blood: José Sánchez Herrero and Silvia María Pérez González, ed., *CXIX reglas de hermandades y cofradías andaluzas: siglos XIV, XV y XVI* (Huelva: Universidad de Huelva, 2002).

68 LOC, Stephen Harkness Collection, doc. XXXVIII.

69 See Leon Yacher, *Marriage, Migration and Racial Mixing in Colonial Tlazazalca, Michoacán, Mexico, 1750-1800* (Syracuse: Syracuse University, Department of Geography, 1977).

70 See Ilona Katzew, *Casta Painting: Images of Race in Eighteenth-Century Mexico* (New Haven: Yale University Press, 2004).

71 Bernardo Mendel Latin American Collection, Cofradía del Santísimo Sacrament, mss.

their indigenous counterparts.[72] Moreover, the sodality accepted not only men but also women and children. With the guidance of a Franciscan friar, two Spanish men and two local men (creole or indigenous) led this *cofradía*.

Association also occurred for indigenous people of different social strata. In one Nahuatl confraternity constitution, such integration was made explicit: "This is called a Decree and really in it [...] were set forth all of the cofrades who belong to the said Holy confraternity, and also all the caciques [*tlatoque*] and nobles [*pipiltin*] and all of the little commoners [*macehualtzitzintin*] who willingly were counted within the said Holy Confraternity."[73] As will also be seen with indigenous confraternity-run hospitals, much emphasis was put on the equality of indigenous sodality members, suggesting that their relations under the Aztec Empire were no less stratified than those of the Spanish in Spain. The breakdown of a strict indigenous social hierarchy with the onset of a new Spanish colonial order made social and ethnic mixing in indigenous confraternities more commonplace than would have likely occurred in the former Aztec order.

The Cofradía de la Santissima Trinidad in Atlixco, Mexico, established in 1626, included a wide range of ethnicities, predominantly Spanish, *moreno* and *mulato* members. This very interesting document, which covers the 1626-1681 time period, records the various members of the Confraternity of the Blessed Sacrament.[74] To organize its members by name, the sodality made an alphabetical index (*abecedario)*, where small cut-outs at the top of each page made it possible to thumb through the member list quickly, much like a modern address book. The members were not listed into categories by ethnicity but by alphabetical order, where it was also listed if the person had Spanish, indigenous, *mestizo*, *moreno*, or *mulato* heritage. Likewise, in a predominantly indigenous confraternity with records kept in Nahuatl, members listed as Spanish, *pardo*, and black were members of equal standing.[75]

Even with significant proof of cross-ethnic admittance to confraternities throughout Mexico, confraternities did not always stay clear of ethnic hierarchies. In the Confraternity of Charity in Mexico City, which ran an orphanage of girls, the inventory list from 1574 shows that the orphan house relied on the slave labor of five people.[76] One of the slaves, Catalina, was

72 See Lockhart and Otte, *Letters and People of the Spanish Indies.*
73 Richie, "Confraternity and Community," 129.
74 Parroquia Santa María de la Natividad, box 103, Cofradia de la Santissima Trinidad.
75 AHMNA, FF, roll 43, vol. 139.
76 Benson Latin American Collection, Genaro Garcia Collection, *Libro de cabildos*, 1538-1584.

only eight years old; she had been donated by the Viceroy Martín Enríquez to live and work in the house. Catalina was of African descent, but the description "*negra criolla*" implies she was born in Mexico like the other girls in the house. In essence, we have the paradox of her location and her role as a vulnerable orphan in need of protection, forced to serve orphans with lighter skin and "purer" blood.[77]

Archival records also at times demonstrate reliance by Spanish confraternities on forced indigenous labor. For example, Gaspar de Aldaña, the *mayordomo* of the Confraternity of the True Cross (Cofradía de la Veracruz) in Mexico City filed a legal petition for two indigenous people from an *encomienda* to be sent to the sodality for assistance in cleaning the church.[78] While indigenous confraternities often shared cleaning tasks among members, Spanish confraternities could avail themselves of the compulsory labor of those on lower rungs of the social ladder.

Some confraternities also decided to restrict admittance by ethnicity or profession. The ethnic composition of a sodality in Mexico usually had to do with its geographic location, and areas with large Spanish, mestizo, indigenous, mulatto, and black populations were more likely to have single-ethnicity confraternities. Cities such as Mexico City and Puebla had large enough Spanish populations to contain multiple confraternities made up of only Spanish members.[79] Confraternities acting also as guilds were at times strictly Spanish, as non-Spanish people were prohibited in some trades. In fact, most professions with guilds had associated confraternities.[80] Even though certain trades excluded non-Spanish groups, a few exceptions were made. The regulations for a sodality of dressmakers in 1565 stipulated that: "Because there are few dressmakers, one is permitted to examine Spaniards, blacks, and Indians."[81] In 1574, a confraternity of candlestick

---

77 It was then customary for black children to be sold separately from their slave parents. Hence, we rarely read about black orphans in the early colonial period because a black orphan was instead "just a slave" devoid of entitlements to a childhood.

78 Archivo General de la Nación (hereafter AGN), Indiferente Virreinal, box 5556, file 35 (1596).

79 This is confirmed by Aurea Zafra Oropeza: *Las cofradías de Cocula, Guadalajara, Jalisco* (Guadalajara: H. Ayuntamiento Constitucional de Guadalajara, 1996), 26.

80 Spaniards created a monopoly over work that they preferred to carry out. Few Spaniards, for example, were willing to work as agricultural laborers or miners. Typically, trades of choice pertained to well-paid skilled labor, such as painters, embroiderers, schoolteachers, silk workers, or specialized tailors of military or clothing worn by nobles. These professions all required proper licensing and passing of trade-specific examinations, controlled by the guilds: Manuel Carrera Stampa, *Los gremios mexicanos: la organización gremial en Nueva España, 1521-1861* (Mexico City: Iberoamericana, 1954), 79-127. Table was created by author from information in ibid., 299-319.

81 Ibid.

makers prohibited other ethnicities, but exceptions could be made: "No black, mulatto, nor mestizo can have a store, nor be examined, unless they are of full confidence, and complete these ordinances."[82] Exceptions were few and far between, but they did exist.

Even inquisitors had their own confraternity in Mexico, like in Spain. The Confraternity of Saint Peter Martyr in Mexico was made up of officials from the Holy Office of the Inquisition.[83] The Saint Peter Martyr Confraternity warrants a brief overview in this study because it reveals how similar institutions could function differently when their membership changed. The Inquisition confraternity had donation requirements, financial assets, fines, expenditures, behavior expectations, practices, and procedures dissimilar from indigenous confraternities. Even the ways of joining differed. The groups were all "confraternities," but many elements were adapted to their members.

After Philip II established the court of the Inquisition in Mexico in 1571, all staff members were *required* to join the Cofradía de San Pedro Mártir.[84] While one may assume indigenous people were forced to join confraternities, there is in fact only one known colonial Mexican confraternity made up explicitly of non-voluntary members, and all members were Spanish. Meetings were held in the Convent of Saint Dominic, as confraternities of inquisitors in Spain and Mexico were required to meet in Dominican convents.[85] The confraternity required 25 pesos for its entrance fee and 50 pesos for annual dues.[86] This was considerably more expensive than any indigenous sodality, although the salaries of Inquisition staff were much higher than typical indigenous wages. Inquisitors came only from Spain, but the courts and prisons could not operate without indigenous staff. Local indigenous people were even hired to carry out secret executions. Thus, a poor indigenous man could be put in charge of the death of a Spaniard. Despite being necessary to the operation of the Inquisition, indigenous assistants were not invited into the Inquisition confraternity. The Inquisition confraternity provided assistance to orphans, with dowry

82   Ibid., 241.
83   Richard Greenleaf has published a vivid history of this confraternity, which prompted me to pursue additional information from the original sources in the Library of Congress. Greenleaf's publication is, however, very complete, and I cannot add significant new details, aside from a few images from the microfilm. I recommend Greenleaf's article for this topic: Richard E. Greenleaf, "The Inquisition Brotherhood: Cofradía de San Pedro Martir of Colonial Mexico," *The Americas* 40, no. 2 (1983): 171-207.
84   Ibid., 172.
85   Ibid.
86   Ibid., 174. For donations to the confraternity from 1656-1712, see AGN, Cofradías y Archicofradías, vol. 17, file 1-4.

payments being covered by the sodality. Sick and disabled people were supported alongside other pious works. This charity, though, had its limits. Confraternity members also used their institution to organize searches for heretics who were to be arrested by the Inquisition.[87]

Each ethnic group at times excluded members of other ethnicities.[88] One set of 1595 indigenous regulations in Nahuatl read: "May there be no Spaniards [yspanoles], no blacks [tliltic], no mulattoes [mulato], no mulatas [molata]."[89] Members of one ethnicity may have been better able to relate to one another in terms of appearance, customs, self-expression, language, social status, personality traits, piety, or humor. Garcilasco de la Vega noticed the same phenomenon for mestizos in Cuzco: "And the natural mestizos of Cuzco [had] a sodality that was made up of only them. They did not want Spaniards to enter."[90] Indigenous groups could prevent Spanish people from entering their confraternities, and the same was true for mestizos, mulattos, and blacks. The ability to form a group with exclusive entry requirements allowed confraternity members to increase their social status by excluding people "unworthy" of entry.

Confraternities have been credited with allowing for continued ancestral worship and rebuilding ethnic identities. Nicholas Terpstra argues: "In some cases, these groups became shelters for indigenous cultural identity in a context that suppressed all other non-Catholic or non-Hispanic cultural institutions."[91] Association in confraternities has also been associated with levels of social prestige that would be less accessible otherwise in colonial society, as fraternization between indigenous nobles and commoners would not have taken place in the same social groups before the conquest. In

---

87 Ibid., 175. In some instances, the Inquisition confraternity sequestered property of alleged Jews before putting them on trial. These procedural improprieties eventually leaked to Spain and the Inquisitor of Seville reprimanded them: ibid. Illegal actions may have been prompted by the sodality's bankruptcy and even forced members to purchase a copy of their confraternity constitution. The financial position of the sodality only improved when the Senior Inquisitor Francisco Garzarón decided to name the king of Spain as the *visitador general* of New Spain. Suddenly in the early 1700s, contributions of silk and vestments with gold embroidery began arriving from the Philippines as endowments for the confraternity: ibid., 182.

88 For changing perspectives on ethnicity and social status at the end of the colonial period, see Jaime E. Rodríguez, *'We Are Now the True Spaniards': Sovereignty, Revolution, Independence, and the Emergence of the Federal Republic of Mexico, 1808-1824* (Stanford: Stanford University Press, 2012).

89 Richie, "Confraternity and Community," 129.

90 Garcilaso de la Vega, *Historia general del Perú, ó, Commentarios reales de los Incas* (Madrid: Villalpando, 1800), 165.

91 Nicholas Terpstra, "De-institutionalizing Confraternity Studies: Fraternalism and Social Capital in Cross-Culture Contexts," in Black and Gravestock, *Early Modern Confraternities*, 267.

addition, focus on the works of mercy to be carried out by confraternities provided a sanctioned justification for indigenous people to help one another while acting in the name of the Catholic faith. There is a convenient overlap between a Catholic mandate to feed the hungry and local efforts to prevent starvation, as confraternity records often show funds spent to feed the hungry. Confraternities were, in short, important institutions by which forms of community relations, which had been dismantled by Spanish invasion battles and *encomiendas,* could be in part reestablished, albeit in a different form.[92]

Conclusion

Nahuatl sodality sources represent a general tendency for Spanish authorities to allow confraternities to keep their records in Nahuatl, to use pre-Hispanic currencies, and to elect their own indigenous leaders within Catholic institutions. These examples of autonomy were likely factors for continued voluntary participation of indigenous people in colonial Mexican confraternities. Sodalities also mixed indigenous people of different social ranks. Caciques (*tlatoque*), nobles (*pipiltin*), and commoners (*macehualtzitzintin*) may have cooperated for the first time in administering to the needs of their communities. Confraternities also brought indigenous people into closer contact with Spaniards and prompted them to see one another in a fraternal context. Spaniards may have for the first time substituted the word "*indio*" for the specific indigenous names of their fellow *cofrades*. In turn, Spaniards could also be seen by indigenous people as migrants with the vulnerabilities associated with living in a new homeland. Franciscan confraternities thus fostered fraternity not only among Spaniards and indigenous people but also among Spaniards from different geographical and linguistic backgrounds, and among indigenous people who previously belonged to stratified social groups. The results were often hybrid forms of local religion, specific to each city, town, parish, or confraternity.

About the author

Laura Dierksmeier is a postdoctoral researcher in the German Research Foundation (DFG) research group "Resource Cultures" at the University of Tübingen in Germany. Previously, she worked as a researcher in the

---

92   Rodríguez León, "Invasion and Evangelization," 76.

research group "Religious Knowledge in Pre-Modern Europe, 800 – 1800."
Her dissertation, completed in 2016 at the University of Tübingen, focused
on indigenous confraternities in colonial Mexico. Dierksmeier received the
Bartolomé de las Casas Dissertation Award from the University of Fribourg
in Switzerland in 2017. She recently finished an edited book together with
Fabian Fechner and Kazuhisa Takeda entitled: *Indigenous Knowledge as a
Resource: Transmission, Reception, and Interaction of Knowledge between
the Americas and Europe, 1492-1800.*

Bibliography

Archives

Mexico
Archivo General de la Nación (Mexico City)
    Cofradías y Archicofradías, Vol. 17, File 1-4
    Indiferente Virreinal, box 4619, file 37, 1596; box 5556, file 35, 1596
Archivo Histórico del Museo Nacional de Antropología e Historia (Mexico City)
    Fondo Franciscano, Roll 29, Vol. 91; Roll 43, Vol. 139; Roll 43, Vol. 129
Parroquia de Santo Ángel (Puebla)
    Box 72, 1671. Cofradía de Nuestra Señora de Guadalupe
PParroquia de San José (Puebla)
    Box 142. Cofradía de San José
Parroquia Evangelista San Marcos (Puebla)
    Box 85. Cofradía del Santísimo Sacramento
        Cofradía de Nuestra Señora del Buen Suceso
        Cofradía de Nuestra Señora de los Dolores
        Cofradía de la Santa Escuela de Cristo
Parroquia Santa María de la Natividad (Atlixco)
    Box 103. Cofradía de la Santissima Trinidad

Spain
Archivo General de Indias (Seville)
    Audiencia de México, Cartas y expedientes de personas eclesiásticas, México, 19, 159

United States
Benson Latin American Collection (University of Texas, Austin)
    Genaro Garcia Collection
        Libro de cabildos de cofradia denominada del Sanctisimo Sacramento de
        la charidad y colexio de las monjas rrecoxidas. 1538-1584. 146 L. 32 Cm. G22

Lilly Library (Indiana University Bloomington)
     Bernardo Mendel Latin American Collection
     Confraternity del Santisimo Sacrament, L.A. mss.
Library of Congress

Internet Source

http://www.thecounciloftrent.com/ch22.htm

Primary Sources

Acuña, René. *Relaciones geográficas del siglo XVI*. Mexico City: UNAM, 1982.
Chimalpahin, Domingo. *Annals of His Time: Don Domingo de San Antón Muñón Chimalpahin Quauhtlehuanitzin*, edited by James Lockhart, Susan Schroeder, and Doris Namala. Stanford: Stanford University Press, 2006.
Confraternity of Our Lady of Solitude. *Our Lady of Solitude of San Miguel Coyotlan, 1619: A Rare Set of Cofradía Rules in Nahuatl*. Edited by Barry D. Sell. Mexico City: UNAM, 2000.
Council of Trent. *El sacrosanto y ecuménico Concilio de Trento traducido al idioma castellano. Agrégase el texto latino corregido según la edición auténtica de Roma, publicada en 1564*. Madrid: Ramón Ruiz, 1798.
Lockhart, James, and Enrique Otte, eds. *Letters and People of the Spanish Indies, Sixteenth Century*. Cambridge: Cambridge University Press, 1976.
Molina, Alonso de. *Nahua Confraternities in Early Colonial Mexico: The 1552 Nahuatl Ordinances of Fray Alonso de Molina, OFM*. Edited by Barry D. Sell, Larissa Taylor, and Asunción Lavrin. Berkeley: Academy of American Franciscan History, 2002.
Rojas Rabiela, Teresa, Elsa Leticia Rea López, and Constantino Medina Lima. *Vidas y bienes olvidados: testamentos indígenas novohispanos*. Mexico City: Centro de Investigaciones y Estudios Superiores en Antropología Social, 2002.
Sánchez Herrero, José, and Silvia María Pérez González. *CXIX reglas de hermandades y cofradías andaluzas: siglos XIV, XV y XVI*. Huelva, Spain: Universidad de Huelva, 2002.
Vega, Garcilaso de la. *Historia general del Perú, ó, Commentarios reales de los Incas*. Madrid: Impr. de Villalpando, 1800.

Secondary Sources

Badde, Paul. *María of Guadalupe: Shaper of History, Shaper of Hearts*. San Francisco: Ignatius Press, 2008.
Boxt, Matthew A., and Brian D. Dillon. *Fanning the Sacred Flame: Mesoamerican Studies in Honor of H. B. Nicholson*. Boulder: University Press of Colorado, 2012.

Brading, D.A. Mexican Phoenix: *Our Lady of Guadalupe: Image and Tradition across Five Centuries*. Cambridge: Cambridge University Press, 2001.

Burkhart, Louise M. *The Slippery Earth: Nahua-Christian Moral Dialogue in Sixteenth-Century Mexico*. Tucson: University of Arizona Press, 1989.

Burkhart, Louise M. *Holy Wednesday: A Nahua Drama from Early Colonial Mexico*. Philadelphia: University of Pennsylvania Press, 1996.

Burkhart, Louise M., Barry D. Sell, and Gregory Spira. *Nahua Christianity in Performance*. Norman: University of Oklahoma Press, 2009.

Cahill, David. "The Long Conquest: Collaboration by Native Andean Elites in the Colonial System, 1532-1825." In *Technology, Disease, and Colonial Conquests, Sixteenth to Eighteenth Centuries: Essays Reappraising the Guns and Germs Theories*, edited by George Raudzens, 85-126. Boston: Brill, 2003.

Carrasco Pizana, Pedro. *The Tenochca Empire of Ancient Mexico: The Triple Alliance of Tenochtitlan, Tetzcoco, and Tlacopan*. Norman: University of Oklahoma Press, 1999.

Carrera Stampa, Manuel. *Los gremios mexicanos: la organización gremial en Nueva España, 1521-1861*. Mexico City: Edición y Distribución Ibero Americana de Publicaciones, 1954.

Christensen, Mark Z. *Nahua and Maya Catholicisms: Texts and Religion in Colonial Central Mexico and Yucatan*. Stanford: Stanford University Press, 2013.

Díaz, Mónica. *Indigenous Writings from the Convent: Negotiating Ethnic Autonomy in Colonial Mexico*. Tucson: University of Arizona Press, 2010.

Dibble, Charles. "The Nahuatilization of Christianity." In *Sixteenth-Century Mexico: The Work of Sahagún*, edited by Munro Emerson, 225-233. Albuquerque: University of New Mexico Press, 1974.

DiCesare, Catherine R. *Sweeping the Way: Divine Transformation in the Aztec Festival of Ochpaniztli*. Boulder: University Press of Colorado, 2009.

Dierksmeier, Laura. *Charity for and by the Poor: Franciscan and Indigenous Confraternities in Mexico, 1527-1700*. Norman: University of Oklahoma Press, 2020.

Evans, Susan Toby. *Ancient Mexico and Central America: Archaeology and Culture History*. New York: Thames & Hudson, 2013.

Flynn, Maureen. *Sacred Charity: Confraternities and Social Welfare in Spain, 1400-1700*. Ithaca, NY: Cornell University Press, 1989.

Galindo, David R. *To Sin No More: Franciscans and Conversions in the Hispanic World, 1683- 1830*. Stanford: Stanford University Press, 2018.

Gibson, Charles. *The Aztecs Under Spanish Rule: A History of the Indians of the Valley of Mexico, 1519-1810*. Stanford: Stanford University Press, 1964.

Greenleaf, Richard E. "The Inquisition Brotherhood: Cofradía de San Pedro Martir of Colonial Mexico." *The Americas* 40, no. 2 (1983): 171-207.

Greer, Allan, and Jodi Bilinkoff. *Colonial Saints: Discovering the Holy in the Americas, 1500 1800*. New York: Routledge, 2003.

Hanke, Lewis. *Aristotle and the American Indians: A Study in Race Prejudice in the Modern World*. Chicago: H. Regnery, 1959.

Henderson, John. *Piety and Charity in Late Medieval Florence*. Oxford: Clarendon Press, 1994.

Katzew, Ilona. *Casta Painting: Images of Race in Eighteenth-Century Mexico*. New Haven: Yale University Press, 2004.

Lasso de la Vega, Luis. *The Story of Guadalupe: Luis Laso de la Vega's Huei Tlama-huiçoltica of 1649*, edited by Lisa Sousa, Stafford Poole, James Lockhart, and Miguel Sánchez López. Stanford: Stanford University Press, 1998.

León-Portilla, Ascensión H. de. *Tepuztlahcuilolli: Impresos en náhuatl (historia y bibliografía)*. Mexico City: UNAM, 1988.

Maffie, James. *Aztec Philosophy: Understanding a World in Motion*. Boulder: University Press of Colorado, 2014.

McLeod, Alexus. *Astronomy in the Ancient World: Early and Modern Views on Celestial Events*. Cham: Springer, 2016.

Megged, Amos. "The Religious Context of an 'Unholy Marriage': Elite Alienation and Popular Unrest in the Indigenous Communities of Chiapa, 1570-1680." *Ethnohistory* 46, no. 1 (1999): 149-172.

Meyers, Albert, and Diane Elizabeth Hopkins, eds. *Manipulating the Saints: Religious Brotherhoods and Social Integration in Postconquest Latin America*. Hamburg: Wayasbah, 1988.

Morgan, Ronald J. *Spanish American Saints and the Rhetoric of Identity, 1600-1810*. Tucson: University of Arizona Press, 2002.

Nesvig, Martin Austin, ed. *Local Religion in Colonial Mexico*. Albuquerque: University of New Mexico, 2006.

O'Brien, Terry J. *Fair Gods and Feathered Serpents: A Search for Ancient America's Bearded White God*. Bountiful: Horizon Publishers, 1997.

Pagden, Anthony. *The Fall of Natural Man: The American Indian and the Origins of Comparative Ethnology*. Cambridge: Cambridge University Press, 1982.

Penry, Elizabeth. "Canons of the Council of Trent in Arguments of Priests and Indians over Images, Chapels and Cofradías." In *The Council of Trent: Reform and Controversy in Europe and Beyond (1545-1700)*, edited by Wim François and Violeta Soen, 3: 277-299. Göttingen: Vandenhoeck and Ruprecht, 2018.

Peterson, Jeanette Favrot. *Visualizing Guadalupe: From Black Madonna to Queen of the Americas*. Austin: University of Texas Press, 2014.

Plate, S. Brent. *Key Terms in Material Religion*. New York: Bloomsbury Academic, 2015.

Poole, Stafford. *Our Lady of Guadalupe: The Origins and Sources of a Mexican National Symbol, 1531-1797*. Arizona: University of Arizona Press, 1995.

Remensnyder, Amy G. *La Conquistadora: The Virgin Mary at War and Peace in the Old and the New Worlds*. New York: Oxford University Press, 2014.

Richie, Annette D. "Confraternity and Community: Negotiating Ethnicity, Gender, and Place in Colonial Tecamachalco, Mexico." Ph.D. diss., New York State University at Albany, 2011.

Rodríguez, Jaime E. *"We Are Now the True Spaniards": Sovereignty, Revolution, Independence, and the Emergence of the Federal Republic of Mexico, 1808-1824.* Stanford: Stanford University Press, 2012.

Rodriguez, Junius P. *Encyclopedia of Slave Resistance and Rebellion.* Westport, CT: Greenwood Press, 2007.

Rodríguez León, Mario. "Invasion and Evangelization in the Sixteenth Century." In *The Church in Latin America, 1492-1992*, edited by Enrique Dussel, 43-54. Tunbridge Wells: Burns & Oates, 1992.

Schroeder, Susan. *Chimalpahin and the Kingdoms of Chalco.* Tucson: University of Arizona Press, 1991.

Socolow, Susan Migden. *The Women of Colonial Latin America.* Cambridge: Cambridge University Press, 2000.

Sordo, Emma. "Our Lady of Copacabana and her Legacy in Colonial Potosí." In *Early Modern Confraternities in Europe and the Americas: International and Interdisciplinary Perspectives*, edited by Christopher F. Black and Pamela Gravestock, 187-203. Aldershot: Ashgate Publishing, 2006.

Sweet, James H. *Recreating Africa: Culture, Kinship, and Religion in the African-Portuguese World, 1441-1770.* Chapel Hill: University of North Carolina Press, 2003.

Terpstra, Nicholas. "De-institutionalizing Confraternity Studies: Fraternalism and Social Capital in Cross-Cultural Contexts." In *Early Modern Confraternities*, 264-284.

Torre Villar, Ernesto de la, and Ramiro Navarro de Anda. *Testimonios históricos guadalupanos.* Mexico City: FCE, 1982.

Torre Villar, Ernesto de la, and Ramiro Navarro de Anda. *Nuevos testimonios históricos guadalupanos.* Mexico City: FCE, 2007.

Truitt, Jonathan. *Sustaining the Divine in Mexico Tenochtitlan: Nahuas and Catholicism, 1523 1700.* Norman: University of Oklahoma Press, 2018.

Wells, E.C., and Karla L. Davis-Salazar. *Mesoamerican Ritual Economy: Archaeological and Ethnological Perspectives.* Boulder: University Press of Colorado, 2007.

Wood, Stephanie. "Adopted Saints: Christian Images in Nahua Testaments of Late Colonial Toluca." *The Americas* 47, no. 3 (1991): 259-293.

Yacher, Leon. *Marriage, Migration and Racial Mixing in Colonial Tlazazalca, (Michoacán, Mexico), 1750-1800.* Syracuse: Syracuse University Press, 1977.

Yannakakis, Yanna. *The Art of Being In-between: Native Intermediaries, Indian Identity, and Local Rule in Colonial Oaxaca.* Durham: Duke University Press, 2008.

Zafra Oropeza, Aurea. *Las cofradías de Cocula, Guadalajara, Jalisco.* Mexico City: H. Ayuntamiento Constitucional de Guadalajara, 1996.

2 Confraternities of People of African Descent in Seventeenth-Century Mexico City[1]

Cristina Verónica Masferrer León
DEAS-INAH

Translated by Javiera Jaque Hidalgo

Abstract
This chapter discusses black confraternities in colonial Mexico City, their form of organization, their beliefs and practices, as well as their connection to specific instances of resistance. This analysis shows that confraternities were communal spaces that allowed Afro-Mexicans to develop social relations that in turn allowed them to recreate and preserve certain elements of their identity, while also allowing them to interact with members of other ethnic groups. This chapter also underscores that while confraternities allowed Afro-Mexicans to integrate into colonial society, they were also seen as a threat to the established order, precisely due to the cohesiveness of their social relations.

Keywords: Black confraternities, Mexico, resistance, African diaspora, Black Catholicism

In the capital of New Spain, the population of African origin was numerous and its participation in economic, social, political, and religious activities undoubted. In both America and Europe, Africans and Afro-descendants

[1] This text is a revised and updated translation of the article: "*Por las ánimas de los negros bozales*: Las cofradías de personas de origen africano en la ciudad de México (siglo XVII)," *Cuicuilco* 18, no. 51 (2011): 83-104.

Javiera Jaque Hidalgo and Miguel A. Valerio. *Indigenous and Black Confraternities in Colonial Latin America: Negotiating Status through Religious Practices.* Amsterdam: Amsterdam University Press, 2022
DOI: 10.5117/ 9789463721547_CH02

founded various confraternities: religious organizations formed mainly by
lay people that functioned as spaces for meeting and expression for their
members.[2] This chapter presents novel information that broadens our
knowledge about the black, *moreno*, and mulatto confraternities of Mexico
City, their forms of organization, their beliefs, and practices, as well as the
relationship between these corporate groups and uprisings that took place
in 1612. I intend to show that the confraternities of people of African origin
in the capital of New Spain were spaces of coexistence from which this
population developed social relationships that allowed members to recover
and recreate certain elements of their identities.

While these confraternities facilitated the integration of their members
into Novohispanic society, they were considered a threat to the order established precisely by these social relations. This was reflected in ordinances
that sought to control or eliminate them by associating them with the
early seventeenth-century uprisings of Africans and Afro-descendants.
This chapter reveals relevant aspects such as the forms of coexistence
and interaction that developed from the confraternities, the conflicts that
were generated within them and beyond, as well as the processes of resistance, cultural recreation, identity construction, and integration that these
institutions made possible.

Confraternities were formed not only by Spaniards, but also by indigenous
people of African and Asian origins, which shows that these corporations
were accepted and promoted both by the Church and by Novohispanic
society in general.[3] In fact, they were part of the efforts to evangelize Africans
and Afro-descendants in Europe and America.[4] The Novohispanic authorities sought to integrate them into the Church, modifying their previous

2   Isidro Moreno, *Cofradías y hermandades andaluzas: estructura, simbolismo e identidad*
(Seville: Government of Andalucía, 1985); Isidoro Moreno, Teresa Eleazar, and Ricardo Jarillo,
eds., *Cofradías de indios y negros: Origen, evolución y continuidades* (Mexico City: INAH, México,
2018); Ildefonso Gutiérrez, "Las cofradías de negros en la América Hispana, siglos XVI-XVIII,"
http://www.africafundacion.org/spip.php?auteur54
3   Alicia Bazarte, *Las cofradías de españoles en la Ciudad de México (1526-1869)* (México: UAM,
1989); Héctor Martínez Domínguez, "Las cofradías indígenas en la Nueva España," in *Primer
Anuario del Centro de Estudios Históricos* (Xalapa: Universidad Veracruzana, 1977), 54-71.
4   Solange Alberro, "Las representaciones y realidades familiares de los negros bozales en la
predicación de Alonso de Sandoval (Cartagena de Indias, 1627) y Nicolás Duque de Estrada (La
Habana, 1796)," in *La familia en el mundo iberoamericano*, ed. Pilar Gonzalbo and Cecilia Rabell
(Mexico City: IIS,1994), 73-89; Ildefonso Gutiérrez, "Los negros y la iglesia en la España de los
siglos XV y XVI," http://www.africafundacion.org/spip.php?auteur54; Sandra Negro y Manuel
Marzal, ed., *Esclavitud, economía y evangelización. Las haciendas jesuitas en la América Virreinal*
(Lima: Pontificia Universidad Católica del Perú, 2005).

religious practices and beliefs. This is observed in the Mexican Provincial Councils where the Spaniards were ordered bring their slaves to mass.[5] The importance of receiving religious instruction was also stressed, and Afro-descendants' participation as musicians in ecclesiastical ceremonies was sought out.[6]

Based on travelers' accounts, we know about the participation of people of African origin in processions, which undoubtedly formed part of their daily lives and religious lives. Gemelli Careri noted that during his stay in Mexico City at the end of the seventeenth century, there were processions of black and indigenous people during Holy Week. They were members of the confraternity of Santo Domingo, who went with "personas que se disciplinaban, y hacían otras penitencias," [people who whipped and flagellated themselves] accompanied by armed men, images, and "el sepulcro de Nuestro Señor" [the tomb of Our Lord].[7] The imposition of a new religion was not simple. This can be seen in the inquisitorial documents where they were accused, mainly, of *reniego* (apostasy) blasphemy, sorcery, bigamy, intimidation, and heresy.[8] It is important to remember that sometimes slaves denounced themselves or other people, which shows their understanding of New Spain's institutions. Furthermore, their masters or other acquaintances could also accuse them.[9]

Africans and Afro-descendants not only carried out practices condemned by the Holy Office, but also participated in religious activities accepted by the Church, as described above. In this sense, it is possible to consider that the religiosity of people of African origin was characterized by both obedience to and transgression of norms. Belonging to confraternities implied compliance, but at the same time gave members the opportunity

5   Francisco Antonio Lorenzana, *Concilios Provinciales, Primero y Segundo, celebrados en la muy noble, y muy leal Ciudad de México, Presidiendo el ILLmo y Rmo. Señor D.F Alonso de Montúfar, en los años 1555, y 1565* (1555 and 1565; reprint: Mexico City, 1769), 72; Mariano Galván Rivera, ed., *Concilio III Provincial Mexicano, celebrado en México el año 1585, confirmado en Roma por el Papa Sixto V, mandado observar por el gobierno español, en diversas* órdenes (1585; first edition: Mexico City), 140.

6   Antonio Zedillo, "Presencia de África en América Latina. El caso de México," in *Memoria del III Encuentro de Afromexicanistas*, ed. Luz María Martínez Montiel y Juan reyes (Mexico City: CONACULTA, 1993), 208-210.

7   Giovanni F. Gemelli Careri, *Viaje a Nueva España* (1700; reprint: Mexico City: UNAM, 1976), 73.

8   Solange Alberro, *Inquisición y Sociedad en México, 1571-1700* (México: FCE., 2004), 456; María Elisa Velázquez, *Mujeres de origen africano en la capital novohispana, siglos XVII y XVIII* (México: INAH, 2006), 241-247.

9   Alberro, *Inquisición y Sociedad*, 455-485.

to organize and develop their own practices and expressions, as shown in this study.

Confraternities of African and Afro-descendants in Mexico City

There were numerous confraternities of people of African origin in New Spain, for example, in Veracruz, Valladolid, Parral, and Mexico City.[10] In addition to being a religious space and an opportunity to gather, confraternities also offered support to the brothers, who received from it "botica, y Doctor, y diez pesos para ayuda de su entierro" [apothecary, and a doctor, and ten pesos to pay for their funeral].[11] Several authors agree that confraternities of Africans and Afro-descendants not only boosted Catholic religious fervor, but also fostered a sense of community and belonging to a group, the conservation and reproduction of cultural elements, and the building of alliances based on spiritual kinship.[12]

Based mainly on wills, Nicole von Germeten considered that the confraternities of Mexico City promoted ties between Africans and their descendants before 1650, but eventually were a means of integration into colonial society. For this researcher, the information on confraternities found in the wills showed the desire Afro-descendants had to hispanize themselves and to be more integrated into Novohispanic society. As stated previously, in this

10   Estela Roselló Soberón, "La cofradía de los negros: una ventana a la tercera raíz: El caso de San Benito de Palermo" (BA thesis, FFyL-UNAM, 1998); María Guadalupe Chávez Carbajal, "La negritud en Michoacán, época colonial," in *Presencia Africana en México*, ed. Lax Maria Matinez Montiel (Mexico City: Conaculta, 1994), 119-124; Nicole von Germeten, *Black Blood Brothers: Confraternities and Social Mobility for Afro-Mexicans* (Gainesville: University Press of Florida, 2006), and "Colonial Middle Men: Mulatto Identity in New Spain's Confraternities," in *Black Mexico: Race and Society from Colonial to Modern Times*, ed. Ben Vinson III and Matthew Restall (Aburqueque: University of New Mexico Press, 2009), 136-154.

11   Agustín de Vetancourt, *Chronica de la Provincia del Santo Evangelio de México* (1697; reprint: México: Porrúa, 1982), 36; Rafael Castañeda, "Piedad y participación femenina en la cofradía de negros y mulatos de San Benito de Palermo en el Bajío novohispano, siglo XVIII," *Nuevo Mundo/Mundos Nuevos* (2012), https://journals.openedition.org/nuevomundo/64478

12   See Estela Roselló Soberón, "La Cofradía de San Benito de Palermo y la integración de los negros y los mulatos en la ciudad de la Nueva Veracruz en el siglo XVII," in *Formaciones religiosas en la América colonial*, ed. María Alba Pastor and Alicia Mayer (México: UNAM, 2000), 229-242; Gutiérrez, "Las cofradías"; Luz María Martínez Montiel, *Negros en América* (México: Colecciones Mapfre, 1992), 112-113; Colin Palmer, *Slaves of the White God. Blacks in Mexico, 1570-1650* (Cambridge: Harvard University Press, 1976), 54-55; Nicolás Ngou-Mvé, "Mesianismo, cofradías y resistencia en el África Bantú y América Colonial" (2008), http://bibliotecavirtual.clacso.org.ar/ar/libros/aladaa/nico.rtf

chapter I analyze other types of documents in order to show the importance that the confraternities of seventeenth-century Mexico City had in the development of social relations between people of African origin, as well as some identity elements that they recovered and recreated within them.

Africans and Afro-descendants formed various confraternities in Mexico City beginning in the sixteenth century. For example, the Cofradía de San Nicolás de Tolentino was founded in the church of Santa Veracruz in 1560.[13] The Cofradía de Nuestra Señora de la Concepción was established at the Hospital de la Inmaculada Concepción in the sixteenth century.[14] Another confraternity, that of the Morenos de San Benito, has been of great importance since at least 1599.[15] It was initially founded in the church of Santa María la Redonda under the name of the Coronación de Cristo Nuestro Señor y San Benito and later moved to the Convent of San Francisco, as we will see later.[16] The Hermandad de Nuestra Señora de las Lágrimas was added to this confraternity. Another very important confraternity was that of Nuestra Señora de la Merced, which will be discussed in depth. In 1628 another confraternity was erected in the parish of Santa Veracruz, which requested the title of Cofradía de la Exaltación de la Cruz de los Negros.[17] The Cofradía de la Preciosa Sangre de Cristo was founded in the church of Santa Catalina in 1665.[18] Although the exact date of its constitution is unknown, the Cofradía de Nuestra Señora de las Angustias was originally instituted in the convent of San Francisco and in 1665 it was requested that it be passed to the Colegio de San Juan de Letrán.[19] In 1668, on the Monte del Calvario, a confraternity devoted to San Nicolás Tolentino was founded by mulattos; although it had the same name as the Confraternity of 1560, it was most likely a different one.[20] Other confraternities founded by blacks and mulattos in Mexico City between 1599 and 1706 were those

---

13 Alicia Bazarte, *Las cofradías*, 42.
14 Archivo General de la Nación (hereafter AGN), Indiferente Virreinal, caja 6486, exp. 040, f. 1 (1604).
15 Vetancourt, *Chronica*, 36.
16 Although von Germeten points out that its foundation was in 1600, Agustín de Vetancurt mentions that in 1599 this confraternity already existed: see von Germeten, *Black Blood Brothers*, 83; Vetancourt, *Chronica*, 36; Miguel A. Valerio, "'That There be No Black Brotherhood': The Failed Suppression of Afro-Mexican Confraternities, 1568-1612," *Slavery and Abolition* 42, no. 2 (2021): 293-314.
17 Alicia Bazarte, *Las cofradías*, 43, 64.
18 AGN, Indiferente Virreinal, caja 0906, exp. 028 (1690); von Germeten, *Black Blood Brothers*, 83.
19 AGN, Indiferente Virreinal, caja 4120, exp. 2 (1665).
20 von Germeten, *Black Blood Brothers*, 91.

of Santo Cristo de la Expiración, Nuestra Señora de la Concepción de Santa Efigenia, Nuestra Señora de la Concepción y Esclavos del Santísimo, San Roque, Nuestra Señora de los Dolores, San José, and the Derramamiento de la Sangre de Cristo.[21] According to von Germeten, one of the confraternities mentioned was founded by Africans from Zape nation, the Castilian denomination of the African ethnic group Kpwesi or Kpelle.[22] Its foundation was held at the Hospital de la Inmaculada Concepción and although von Germeten acknowledged that Biafara and Wolof Africans belonged to it, she considered it a mono-ethnic confraternity since several confraternities defended the ethnic exclusivity of their organization.[23] Von Germeten indicated that it was founded by Zapes and controlled by them in the first half of the seventeenth century, although by 1674 they were no longer mentioned. I have found information about this confraternity in the Ramo de Indiferente Virreinal del Archivo General de la Nación.[24] In the documents that I have reviewed, from 1604, 1622, and one after 1666, the Zapes are not referred to, but the confraternity of "blacks and free mulattos" is mentioned, although some slaves also belonged to it.[25] In addition, these documents mention that Bañol Africans, as well as other free people and slaves, were part of the confraternity, so although it is likely that it was founded by Zape people as von Germeten pointed out, it was not monoethnic as she proposed, but multiethnic, as Africans Biafara, Wolof and Bañol were part of the confraternity.

This means that Africans from various backgrounds related to one another through these organizations, within which they coexisted. Thus, it is possible to assert that this confraternity, like others, implied the association of people from Africa of various origins and Afro-descendants born in New Spain so that, despite their heterogeneity, these corporations encouraged the development of social relations between people of African origins. It is also important to note that in this period the denominations referring to origin seem to have had some relevance because people could recognize or

---

21 Sandra Nancy Luna García, "Espacios de convivencia y conflicto. Las cofradías de la población de origen africano en Ciudad de México, siglo XVII," *Trashumante*, no. 10 (2017): 38.

22 von Germeten, *Black Blood Brothers*, 86-88. On the Kpwesi or Kpelle, see Gonzalo Aguirre Beltrán, *La población negra de México* (México: FCE., 1972), 99-152.

23 von Germeten, *Black Blood Brothers*, 88.

24 It is a confraternity with the same name: "Cofradía de Nuestra Señora de la Conce[p]ción": AGN, Indiferente Virreinal, caja 6486, exp. 040, f. 1. It cannot be assured that it is the same, but it seems that it was because they correspond to the same time period.

25 AGN, Indiferente Virreinal, caja 6486, exp. 040, f. 1, 1604; caja 5695, exp. 37, 1622; caja 2831, exp. 017 (after 1666).

name them, although this does not seem to have limited the social relations between Africans and Afro-descendants, or with people of other origins.

Coexistence and Conflict in the Confraternities

The social relations within this confraternity were not peaceful, even among people of the same origin, confirming the complexity of these links. In 1604, Diego, a free black Bañol, expelled Pablo, who was also a black Bañol slave, from the confraternity of the Immaculate Conception, for no apparent reason.[26] It was said that Pablo had been a brother for twenty years, which allows us to assume that the confraternity already existed in 1584, although the exact date of its foundation is unknown. Belonging to the Cofradía de la Inmaculada Concepción for more than twenty years shows that these organizations fostered a sense of belonging to a group. We know that slaves could change their master and residence, so without a doubt having been part of this confraternity for so many years gave them some stability, as well as the possibility of knowing and relating to other confraternities of African origin. Being expelled from the congregation after twenty years must have significantly impacted Pablo's life. It is also important to add that Diego, the free black man referred to in the document, was "capitán de los negros de tierra bañol" [captain of the Blacks of Bañol],[27] which suggests that there was a group of Africans recognized as such that built social relationships with people of the same ethnic origin, as well as with Africans from other backgrounds and with Afro-descendants.

Information regarding this Immaculist confraternity appears later than the others. On February 26, 1622, Luis de Torres, a free *moreno*, responded to an accusation that had been made days earlier in which it was said that he had "usurped the alms" that had been collected.[28] He specified that, indeed, he had been "mayordomo de la cofradía de Nuestra Señora de la Concepcionsita [sic], en el Hospital del Marques del Valle, tiempo de tres meses, poco más o menos" [the leader of the Cofradía de la Nuestra Señora de la Concepcionsita [sic], at the Hospital del Marques del Valle, time of three months, more or less], and that he had received and spent "los pesos contenidos en esta memoria que presento" [the *pesos* contained

26 AGN, Indiferente Virreinal, caja 6486, exp. 040, f. 1 (1604).
27 AGN, Indiferente Virreinal, caja 6486, exp. 040, f. 1 (1604).
28 AGN, Indiferente Virreinal, caja 5695, exp. 37, f. 2v. (1622).

Table 1   Income from the Cofradía de Nuestra Señora de la Concepción

Brief Explanation	Detailed Explanation	Amount
	Incomes	
Alms	The document specifies that this amount was received, on January 1, 1622, from Juan Benites Camacho, who asked for alms with a new plate that was in dispute.	4 p. 4 t.
Alms	Alms received by Diego de la Cruz.	2 p. 1 t.
Alms	This amount was received from the servants of Don Juan de Samano, who collected it as alms.	2 p. 6 t.
Alms	It was received as alms, requested by Sebastian.	15 p.
Alms	On January 20, this amount was received from Pascuala, who collected it as alms.	3 p.
Alms	It is indicated that this amount was charged by "the mulatto next to the theater," who asked for it as alms.	1 p.
Alms	Alms requested by "the mulatto who lives next to the collection."	2 p. 4 t.
Alms	They were collected on January 22 as alms "for the burial of a sister."	6 t.
Alms	This amount of alms came the day Domingo de Hermosillo, slave of Don Juan Cortes, died in prison.	6 p.
Total income (according to the document)		24 p. 4 t.

Source: AGN, Indiferente Virreinal, box 5695, exp. 37, 7av-8av, 1622. The amounts are presented in gold *pesos*, of eight *tomines* each. p: *pesos*, t: *tomines*.

in this report that I present].[29] In response to this accusation, Torres asked and begged that a notary of the audiencia be appointed to receive the account books of the confraternity. Luis Núñez, the notary of the hearing, was appointed to receive these accounts from the confraternity that was founded, according to him, by "negros y mulatos libres" [blacks and free mulattos].[30]

It was ultimately decided that Luis de Torres should receive 24 *pesos* and a *tomín*, and in return he should forfeit a silver plate, four money boxes and a book, as well as "cinco cirios y una candela de libra y media que parece haber entrado en su poder" [five candles and candle weighing one and a half pounds that seems to have entered into his power].[31] To reach this decision, in the first days of March of the same year, an account of expenses and

29   Ibid., f. 3v.
30   Ibid., ff. 6v and 7v.
31   Ibid., f. 8 rv. A *tomín* was a one-eighth of a peso.

Table 2   Expenses of the Cofradía de Nuestra Señora de la Concepción

Brief Explanation	Detailed Explanation	Amount
	Expenses (*descargos*)	
Collection box painting	Matheo García, painter, was paid this amount "for the painting of three collection boxes for the confraternity."	15 p.
Collection box cost	A collection box for the confraternity was bought, on orders from Juan Benites Camacho.	4 p.
Ax rental	Expense for rent and reduction of axes for the confraternity and for burials. By axes, they referred to candles.	20 p. 4 t.
Book purchase	A book for the confraternity was bought by command of the chaplain.	1 p.
Silver plate purchase	On February 22, 1622, Cristobal third silversmith was paid, "for the silver and making of a plate for the confraternity."	35 p. 6 t.
Payment for a sung mass	This amount was paid to Pedro de Oceta "for the alms of a mass sung for Domingo de Hermosillo, black slave of Don Juan Cortes, who died in said hospital and was buried in it."	5 p. 2 t.
Total expenses (according to the document)		48 p. 5 t.

Source: AGN, *Indiferente Virreinal*, box 5695, exp. 37, 7av-8av, 1622. The amounts are presented in gold pesos, of eight *tomines* each. p: pesos, t: tomines.

alms was made. The information in the document has been summarized in the following tables.

Interesting information can be obtained from confraternal income and expenses. For example, in a few months La Concepción had a continuous movement of money, and expenses exceeded income, which could eventually have led to financial problems or disputes within the confraternity; in fact, the document has its origin in the lawsuit for the theft of alms. In addition, significant expenses were made to purchase the dish for alms, as well as for the purchase and painting of money boxes and for the candles that would be used by the confraternity and, specifically, for burials.

Both men and women were part of the confraternity. Some asked for alms and in other cases they were requested for women's burials. Although the amount collected for the burial of one of the sisters was low (6 *tomines*) compared to what was collected for the death of a male *cofrade* Domingo de Hermosillo (6 *pesos*), the amount that Pascuala collected (3 *pesos*) was greater than that collected by black or mulatto males, although the largest alms managed to be delivered to the confraternity were donated by a man (15 *pesos*).

Since the confraternity had been founded by free blacks and mulattos, according to the notary of the audience, the importance given to the burial of the slave Domingo de Hermosillo is interesting. A considerable amount (5 *pesos*, two *tomines*) was spent for a sung mass and for his burial at the Hospital de la Inmaculada Concepción. Although it was first indicated that he died in prison, it was subsequently noted that he died in the hospital where he was buried. In this way it is possible to observe the coexistence between enslaved and free people of African origin, which also shows the development of social relationships that favored a sense of belonging to a group formed by people of similar social and ethnic backgrounds. In addition, knowledge of confraternities shown by Africans and Afro-descendants reveals that *cofrades* used them to carry out activities accepted and promoted by Novohispanic society and its authorities, while allowing them to raise money for their own social purposes, thus building relationships and social networks.

The problems that arose from the collection of money were not exclusive to these confraternities. Something similar happened in 1666 with the Cofradía de Nuestra Señora de las Angustias, founded by "morenos."[32] On that occasion, the *mayordomo* (leader) of the confraternity, Andrés de la Cruz, who described himself as black, said that the confraternity's president, Joseph Limón, used to collect the money "del jornalillo que dan los hermanos para su curación" [from the *jornalillo* (salary) that the brothers give for their healing],[33] and distributed it at his will without documenting it. That is why the *cofrades* refused to distribute or pay anyone with money collected for specific purposes. Finally, it was requested that the accounts the other *cofrades* required be revealed, but this most likely did not happen, as later, in 1672, the same complaint was filed against Joseph Limón.[34]

The conflicts they had were not only internal, nor exclusively economic; confraternities also had problems with Novohispanic religious authorities. A year earlier, in 1665, Andrés de la Cruz had requested that Las Angustias move from the Convent of San Francisco to the Colegio de San Juan de Letrán because of problems with the Vicar of the Convent of San Francisco. They had decided to hold the feast of Nuestra Señora de las Angustias in accordance with their responsibilities and had paid for the mass alms, the sermon, and other necessary expenses. Despite this, problems arose since "el padre vicario de dicho convento [of San Francisco] salió, impidiéndonos el hacer dicha fiesta sin haber habido ningún pretexto por donde se nos prohíbe el celebrar nuestra fiesta" [The Vicar of the convent [of San Francisco]

---

32   AGN, Indiferente Virreinal, Caja 2475, exp. 34, f. 1 (1666).
33   Ibid.
34   AGN, Indiferente Virreinal, Caja 5424, exp. 072 (1672).

came out, preventing us from having this party, with no reason forbidding us from celebrating our feast].[35] It was added that they would leave behind "el retablo e imagen que se hizo a nuestra costa" [the altarpiece and image that was made at our expense] at San Francisco.[36] Thus, it is possible to know the importance that the members of this confraternity gave to their festivals, but it also allows us to know the purchasing power they had, with which they managed to commission the altarpiece they left in the Convent of San Francisco.

Despite his importance in the confraternity, Andrés de la Cruz did not enjoy freedom at that time. However, slavery did not prevent him from carrying out activities related to the confraternity. Thus, de la Cruz, who said he was a black slave of Dr. Don Simon Esteban de Alzate, played an active and very important role within the confraternity. Not only was he a founder member, but he also requested, in the name of the *cofrades*, the move from the Convent of San Francisco to the Colegio de San Juan, in addition to presenting two complaints against the president of the confraternity, Joseph Limón, for embezzling confraternity's funds. In the document from 1672 that repeats the same complaint from 1666, Andrés de la Cruz appears as a free black man, which shows the possibility of social and economic mobility of people of African origin.

The transition between slavery and freedom also forces us to think of this type of subjugation as a moment in the life of these people and in no way as an essential part of them. On the other hand, it highlights the fact that in the documents from 1665 and 1666 that refer to Las Angustias, Nicolás del Puerto appears as the canon of the Cathedral of Mexico City. Del Puerto was a man of African origin who had access to the University and important positions, eventually becoming Bishop of Antequera of Oaxaca.[37] These facts confirm the heterogeneity of the population of African origin in New Spain and the possibilities they had of transcending slavery and having significant social and economic mobility.

Although the *cofrades* did not always seek to use the confraternities as a means of social ascent, being part of them could influence their social status and the question remains whether they played any role in their liberation processes. Confraternities constituted real economic spaces that allowed

35 AGN, Indiferente Virreinal, Caja 4120, exp. 2 (1665).

36 Ibid., f. 8.

37 Precisely on those same dates Nicolás del Puerto had disputes with Simon Estevan Beltrán de Alzate, master of Andrés de la Cruz: see Leticia Pérez Puente, "La sangre afrentada y el círculo letrado. El obispo Nicolás del Puerto, 1619-1681," in *Promoción universitaria en el mundo hispánico. Siglos XVI al XX*, ed. Armando Pavón Romero (México: UNAM, 2012), 271-293.

for funds to be collected, which enabled Africans and Afro-descendants to carry out activities that involved an expense, such as the ceremonies for the death of a member, as well as the confraternity's celebrations. It is also very relevant to mention that the activities associated with a confraternity ensured the spatial mobility of its members.

Another confraternity was that of San Benito y la Coronación de Cristo, which was previously mentioned. In 1651, Juan Congo, who said he was of "mengala" caste,[38] made provisions for a funeral attended by his brothers from the confraternity upon his death. He was an African who owned a modest house, cattle, and other goods, which suggests that he enjoyed good economic conditions. In addition, his request indicates that burials had a special role in the experiences of the confraternities. Some years prior, in 1647, a complaint was filed against a member of the confraternity of San Benito de Palermo, probably in reference to the same member mentioned before, since it was also made in the Convento del Señor San Francisco.

Alonso de la Torre, black, and Pedro Camarena, rector and *mayordomo* of San Benito, asked that Francisco, a black slave of Mrs. Mariana, the widow of Melchor Cuellar, be expelled from the confraternity. The reason for such a drastic request was that it had upset the *cabildo* [town council or local government] that they had to host the procession: "dio voces y gritos por decir que no había de llevar yo el estandarte con cuya ocasión no se acaeció el dicho cabildo" [he cried and shouted to say that I was not to carry the banner on whose occasion the said council did not occur].[39] It was insisted that the slave should in no way be "admitido a ningún cabildo por ser tal alborotador" [admitted to any town council for being such a troublemaker].[40] This fact shows us that relations between members were not always peaceful, but rather sometimes generated conflicts.

However, without a doubt, relations developed between Africans and Afro-descendants who were part of these organizations, and they were sometimes close, as in the case of the rector and the *mayordomo* who jointly complained about the "troublemaker," Francisco. The document makes it

---

38   Could refer to "Benguela," a port in Angola: see Mariana P. Candido, "Tracing Benguela Identity to the Homeland," in *Crossing Memories: Slavery and African Diaspora,* ed. Ana Lucia Araujo, Mariana P. Candido, Paul Lovejoy (Trenton: World Press, 2011), 183-208. The name also has similarity to "bengala" [bengal], however the name "Juan Congo" does not seem to indicate a relationship with India, where the name probably comes from "bengala": Aguirre Beltrán, *La población negra,* 50-147.

39   AGN, Indiferente Virreinal, Caja 5593, exp. 46, f. 1 (1647).

40   Ibid.

clear that the rector is black, although nothing is said about the *mayordomo* with whom the complaint is filed. However, he was most likely black, *moreno*, or mulatto since the confraternity only admitted people of these qualities, and it was not until 1672 that Spaniards were admitted, which could have generated new conflicts among their members, as explored below.

Spaniards not Admitted to Black and Mulatto Confraternities

In 1700, Ambrocio Aniceto Galindo, a black slave and founder of the Cofradía de San Benito de Palermo filed a complaint against the admission of Spaniards, arguing that the confraternity was for "negros y mulatos por quienes se ha gobernado siempre y solamente este año pasado su mayordomo y diputados han admitido españoles que han votado y para que sin novedad se conserve en lo que debe" [blacks and mulattos who have always governed and only this past year their leader and deputies have admitted Spaniards who have voted and so that without incident it is conserved as it should be]. He requested that Spaniards be excluded so that the confraternity was preserved "solo en los negros y mulatos sin que se admitan ni a votar ni a los cargos" [only for blacks and mulattos without being admitted to vote or hold posts] people from another "calidad" [quality] or "piel" [skin].[41] In May of that year an *auto* [order] was issued to prohibit Spaniards' participation in the confraternity, but shortly afterward the reverse was ordered; Nicolás Flores (rector of the confraternity), Tomás de Esquivel (senior deputy), Manuel de la Crus (*mayordomo*) and Augustin Francisco de Herrera (*veedor*) assured that the confraternity was only for *morenos* and *pardos*, and demonstrated that since 1672 the treasurer had been ordered to be Spanish and to receive Spaniards, from whom they obtained "crecidas limosnas" [large amounts in alms]. The four also argued that the slave's claim was "maliciosa" [malicious] and it was of this nature because he was a slave.[42]

Thus, Africans and Afro-descendants constituted groups in which the coexistence between members could produce internal conflicts, which they sometimes attempted to resolve by resorting to Spanish methods in this manner; one observes involvement with the dominating system, while at the same time one can see the development of relations between people of this origin in the Novo-Hispanic capital. On the other hand, the early-eighteenth-century conflict between the members that has been described,

41   AGN, Indiferente Virreinal, Caja 0665, exp. 009 (1700).
42   Ibid.

regarding the growing participation of Spaniards in their confraternity,[43] shows the changes these groups underwent throughout the viceregal period, an aspect that von Germeten analyzes extensively.[44]

For the Souls of *Negros Bozales*: Cultural Recreation and Identity Construction Processes

The Cofradía de Nuestra Señora de la Merced deserves special mention because it is one of the confraternities that appears in the stories regarding the uprisings of the city in 1612, as will be discussed in the following section. There is news of this thanks to a document from 1664 which states that the congregation of La Santa Cruz had a dispute, without detailing the matter. This congregation had been founded in the church of Santa Teresa de Jesús, while the Cofradía de Nuestra Señora de la Merced was erected "en el convento de religiosos de dicha advocación por los negros de Guinea" [in the religious convent of this invocation by the blacks of Guinea].[45] The document requested to receive information regarding the accounts and councils (all documented in books), so that La Merced was not harmed by the problem indicated since, apparently, both of them had the same *mayordomo*.

The information we have comes from Jacinto de Baldés, "negro de nación Congo, mayordomo de la Cofradía de Nuestra Señora de las Mercedes" [black man from the Congo nation, *mayordomo* of the Cofradía de Nuestra Señora de las Mercedes].[46] The confraternity's books and alms accounts were requested from him, which he delivered, specifying the following: "Juro a Dios y a la Cruz [las cuentas] son ciertas y verdaderas y sin ningún fraude ni malicia" [I swear to God and the Cross [that the accounts] are true and correct and without any fraud or malice].[47] The books were sent to the court accountants to account for the alms and assets that these confraternities had in their possession, as well as for their expenses; with this information they could make the decision "que convenga" [that is suitable].[48] The concern that the authorities showed regarding the alms accounts suggests that the

---

43 In 1697 a similar conflict arose, due to the participation of a Spaniard, in the Confraternity of Nuestra Señora de la Concepción y Esclavos del Santisimo, which was considered a mulatto confratermity: Luna, "Espacios," 42.

44 von Germeten, *Black Blood Brothers*.

45 AGN, Indiferente Virreinal, caja 2299, exp. 008, f. 1v (1664).

46 Ibid.

47 Ibid.

48 Ibid.

congregation received a significant sum of money, and this allowed them to carry out actions that unsettled the ecclesiastics. Finally, it was ruled that the *mayordomo* should present all licenses to request alms and these would be revoked and canceled. We do not know if the licenses were actually repealed, if there was a possibility they would not be revoked, or if others were granted later. Controlling alms licenses, which undoubtedly represented a significant income, implied an act of intimidation and repression that threatened the continuity of the confraternity.

The *mayordomo* Jacinto de Baldés indicated that alms were settled "por mano de el Padre Fray Domingo Ximenes" [by Father Fray Domingo Ximenes], probably with the intention of giving more credibility to his accounts, but which could also suggest that Baldés could not write. The confraternity had several books: one of them settled the charity masses for the "ánimas de los hermanos difuntos" [souls of the deceased brothers]; in another, the private *cabildos* of the confraternity were inscribed; and in three others the alms that were requested "por las ánimas de los negros bozales [emphasis is mine]" (for the souls of the black *bozales*).[49] It is notable that for black *bozales* three books were required, while for the other purposes only one. This suggests that for the Africans and Afro-descendants of this confraternity, the black *bozales* had a special symbolic importance. It is not known exactly what was understood by "negros bozales." Traditionally, the word *bozales* has been used to refer to those who had just arrived in the Americas,[50] but the term *bozal* could also designate Africans who had not yet learned the Spanish or European language and cultural traits, and who had not left Africa.[51] According to the *Diccionario de Autoridades*, *bozal* meant "uncultured," and although it was ordinarily used in reference to blacks who had just arrived from the African continent, it also meant "rustic," that is, those who had remained in their own lands.[52] Therefore, I consider it more likely that they referred to the black *bozales* that had remained on the other side of the ocean, implying a link with their own ancestors or living relatives in Africa. Thus, the confreres who asked for alms "por las ánimas de los negros bozales," [for the souls of black *bozales*] maintained a symbolic bond with their ancestors through these spiritual acts, which could have represented the idea of a common origin.

49 Ibid.
50 Aguirre Beltrán, *La población negra*, 44.
51 Alonso de Sandoval, *Un tratado sobre la esclavitud,* ed. Enriqueta Vila Vilar (1627; reprint: Madrid: Alianza, 1987), 383, 380-381, 139.
52 Real Academia Española, *Diccionario de Autoridades*, vols. A-C (1732; reprint: Barcelona: Herder, 1987), 666.

This common past is fundamental to study ethnic and social identity and consciousness, because according to Richard Adams, "los grupos étnicos se definen en términos de un modelo de ascendencia, que especifica ciertas relaciones con los antepasados y que ratifica una continuidad de formas culturales seleccionadas, que significan o simbolizan la continuidad biológica y cultural con el pasado" [ethnic groups are defined in terms of an ancestry model, which specifies certain relationships with ancestors and ratifies a continuity of selected cultural forms, which mean or symbolize biological and cultural continuity with the past].[53] Besides, the "noción de pertenencia o membresía por adscripción a un pasado común" [notion of belonging or membership by ascription to a common past] is a constitutive element of ethnic or historical consciousness that is generated from "la valorización de aquellas formas tradicionales o de relativamente reciente adquisición que el grupo haya asumido como propias, en un momento dado de su proceso histórico" [the valuation of those traditional or relatively recently acquired forms that the group has assumed as its own, at a given moment in its historical process].[54] It should also be considered that holding masses or begging alms for the souls of Africans and Afro-descendants implied the adoption of Christian religious practices, which is reaffirmed by belonging to a confraternity and participating in their activities. We do not know what the practices were when praying, nor the way in which they understood the term *anima*, but it is possible that they still preserved some African traits. Thus, the confraternities were spaces for interaction, reproduction, and recreation of their own social and cultural elements that, at the same time, encouraged the integration of their members to the rest of Novohispanic society.[55]

As we have seen, in the confraternities of people of African origin of the seventeenth century, the strengthening of social relations allowed them to organize and defend themselves from external elements, although sometimes internal conflicts resulted. These problems should not be generalized, as

---

53 Richard Adams, *Etnias en evolución social: estudios de Guatemala y Centroamérica* (Mexico City: UAM, 1995), 38.

54 Miguel Bartolomé, "Conciencia étnica y autogestión indígena," in *Indignidad y descolonización en América Latina* (México: Nueva Imagen, 1979), 316.

55 As Barth points out, with its concept of ethnic boundaries, the interaction or acceptance of new norms does not imply the disappearance of a social group but is defined by the ethnic boundaries that are built between the groups that live together: Frederik Barth, Introduction to *Ethnic Groups and Boundaries: The Social Organization of Culture Difference*, ed. Barth (Long Grove: Waveland Press, 1998), 9-38. Regarding the processes of cultural recreation: see Sidney Mintz and Richard Price, *The Birth of Africa-American Culture: An Anthropological Perspective* (Boston: Beacon Press, 1992).

these, rather than peaceful activities or relationships, were more likely to be registered. Even in the documents that describe conflicts it is possible to observe other types of relationships and coexistence, as well as some of the daily activities carried out by the members of these organizations. For example, it should be noted that, beginning with confraternities, people of African origin could organize and resist religious pressures, which shows that these associations were also important spaces of power, in addition to significant economic spaces.

The links between slaves and free people, as well as between Africans and Afro-descendants, implied social relations between people with different economic resources and social positions. These confraternities preserved and reproduced their own elements, which encouraged the organization of a group with common goals and, perhaps, the definition of a common past that allowed them to share an identity. The social organization that these people achieved from the confraternities was important not only for the social, cultural, religious, and economic purposes indicated above, but also in relation to the fear the authorities showed in response, as well as for their possible relationship with the uprisings of the time. Were confraternities of Africans and Afro-descendants of the seventeenth century strong enough to break the Novohispanic order?

Uprisings and the Prohibition of Confraternities of People of African Origin in the Early Seventeenth Century

At the beginning of the seventeenth century, Novohispanic authorities believed there was an intrinsic relationship between confraternities and the uprisings of people of African origin from the capital of New Spain. This suspicion was undoubtedly strengthened by the uprisings and rebellions of Africans and Afro-descendants that occurred in various places in New Spain.[56] However, this was not the only reason; the authorities must have seen in these confraternities an organizational force that frightened them.[57]

56 María Guevara Sanginés, "El proceso de liberación de los esclavos en la América Virreinal," in *Pautas de convivencia étnica en la América latina colonial (indios, negros, mulatos, pardos y esclavos)*, ed. Juan Manuel de la Serna (Guanajuato: CCyDEL-UNAM, Gobierno de Guanajuato, 2005), 111-162; Adriana Naveda, "De San Lorenzo de los negros a los morenos de Amapa: cimarrones veracruzanos, 1609-1735," in *Rutas de la esclavitud en África y América Latina*, ed. Rina Cáceres (San José de Costa Rica: Editorial de la Universidad de Costa Rica, 2001), 157-174.

57 According to Pilar Gonzalbo "ignorance worsens situations of fear, provoques insecurity, bewilders reason and engender violence": "Reflexiones sobre el miedo en la historia," in *Una*

In fact, it is said that these confraternities "brought together the entire black and mulatto population of Mexico City," or at least an important sector of it.[58]

Although the attempts to suppress them had no effect, the fact that authorities insisted on doing so meant that Africans took advantage of the organizations that Europeans had imposed on them to – at least – interact with one another. We have seen that the confraternities had religious objectives that were not necessarily associated with violence, but which brought together Africans and organized Afro-descendants. That was how 1,500 blacks belonging to the "Cofradía de Nuestra Señora [de la Merced]"[59] protested in Mexico City at the end of 1611, when a black slave died from the beatings that her master, Luis Moreno de Monroy, had given her.[60] From there, a riot repressed by the Spanish authorities began, but they chose a King and Queen[61] from Angola and planned to revolt in the Holy Week of 1612.[62] Although Jonathan Israel doubts the existence of the plan, Colin Palmer stressed that it was a demonstration of solidarity, anger and indignation of blacks, which soon caused panic among the Spaniards. Rumor or not,[63] at the time there was talk of "motín y rebelión que intentaron hacer en esta ciudad los negros y mulatos" [a riot and rebellion that blacks and mulattos tried to hold in this city].[64]

In 1612, a pair of Portuguese slave traders who claimed to know the language of Angola, discovered a movement by listening to "unos negros que estaban discutiendo en el mercado de la Ciudad de México acerca de la supuesta conspiración" [blacks who were arguing in a Mexico City market

historia de los usos del miedo, ed. Pilar Gonzalgo, Anne Staples, and Valentina Torres Septién (Mexico City: COLMEX, 2009), 33.

58   Alicia Bazarte, Las cofradías, 43.

59   Although the invocation of the confraternity is not indicated, it seems that it was a confraternity devoted to "Nuestra señora de la Merced," or at least it was in the Convent of Mercy: see Junius Rodriguez, Encyclopedia of Slave Resistance and Rebellion (Westport: Greenwood Publishing Group, 2007), 321-322.

60   Palmer, Slaves of the White God, 138.

61   The importance of the coronation as an activity that refers us to the peoples of Bantu languages and their relationship with the confraternities in various parts of America is analyzed by Natalia Silva Prada: "El año de los seises (1666) y los rumores conspirativos de los mulatos en la ciudad de México: coronaciones, pasquines, sermones y profecías, 1608-1665," Nuevo Mundo/Mundos Nuevos (2012), http://journals.openedition.org/nuevomundo/64277

62   Jonathan Israel, Razas, clases sociales y vida política en el México colonial, 1610-1670 (México: FCE., 2005), 77.

63   Gonzalbo Aizpuru: "Among fears it is hard to distinguish between natural and cultural fears, for cultural fears have their origins in real fears": "Reflexiones," 32.

64   AGN, Ordenanzas, vol. 1, exp. 178, fs. 152r-153 (1612).

about the alleged conspiracy].[65] Domingo Chimalpáhin relayed that fear invaded the Spaniards since they said their slaves had assured them they would kill them; thus "estaban muy asustados, y andaban averiguando muchas cosas acerca de sus esclavos negros; estaban temerosos de ellos, y los trataban con mucho tiento cuando tenían que ordenarles algún trabajo" [they were very scared, and they were finding out many things about their black slaves; they were fearful of them, and treated them very carefully when they had to order them some work].[66] It was expected that on Holy Thursday the black population would rise up, so special elements were arranged to protect the city. During those days many processions went through the streets, although they were later banned (April 16, 1612).[67]

Beginning April 17, "soldados españoles con sus armas para vigilar," [Spanish soldiers with their weapons to guard] were posted not only on the roads but on the main canal.[68] Although the rebellion was alleged to have taken place in the capital of New Spain and the slave masters were frightened, apparently the rebels came from Acapulco and Veracruz; they were black *cimarrones* who lived on these coasts but who had previously fled from the Spaniards of Mexico City.[69] They undoubtedly believed that the blacks and mulattos of the capital would join the *cimarrones* that would supposedly arrive. The rebels' punishment was the gallows and dismemberment. According to Chimalpáhin, on Wednesday, May 2, body parts of six dismembered blacks hung on the main roads, while others were buried, as experts feared that their bodies would rot and "el hedor se convertiría en pestilencia, y luego con los vientos entraría a la ciudad de México y hallándose sobre nosotros nos causaría enfermedades" [the stench would become pestilence, and then the winds would carry it to Mexico City and would cause diseases upon reaching us].[70] On May 14, 1612 the "capitán de los negros ahorcados previamente" [captain of the previously hung blacks] was hung.[71]

In addition to the murders described above, another consequence for the African and Afrodescendant population, whether free or enslaved, was a variety of ordinances imposed in Mexico City. On April 3, an ordinance written the previous day was issued, stating that both free and enslaved

65   Israel, *Razas*, 77.
66   Domingo Chimalpáhin, *Diario,* ed. Rafael Tena (1624; first edition: Mexico City: Conaculta, 2001), 283.
67   AGN, Ordenanzas, vol. 1, exp.173, ff. 150-150r, (1612); Chimalpáhin, *Diario*, 283-285, 289.
68   Chimalpáhin, *Diario*, 285.
69   Ibid., 287.
70   Ibid., 299.
71   Ibid.

blacks and mulattos could not carry swords, daggers or any other type of weapons, even if they had licenses to carry them or used them in their service.[72] This ordinance was repeated on the 17th of the same month.[73] Chimalpáhin also mentioned these restrictions, which referred not only to weapons, but also requested "que las mujeres negras no podrían usar mantos negros, y la misma prohibición se impuso a las mulatas bajo penas" [that black women could not wear black cloaks, and the same ban was imposed on mulatto women under penalty].[74]

It was also forbidden for more than three blacks or mulattos, whether they were free or slaves, to assemble – in public or secretly, night or day – which prevented them from meeting under the pretext of "cofradías, bailes, plaças, tianguis[75], calles y otras partes," [confraternities, dances, squares, *tianguis*, streets, and other locations] because these resulted in "mucha inquietud a los vecinos, daños e inconvenientes de consideración a que conviene poner remedio" [much unease for the neighbors, damages, and considerable inconveniences that should be remedied].[76] In the event that they did not obey the ordinance, two hundred lashes would be given to each. Since they were forbidden to meet, even for the purposes of their confraternities, Spanish authorities decided to request "los priores y vicarios de los conventos y partes donde tienen las dichas cofradías no les admitan ni consientan tenerlas más de aquí adelante," [the priors and vicars of the convents and places where they have these confraternities not admit or consent to having them further from here on] or else they would receive the same punishment.[77]

The ordinances that were written as of April 1612 were multiple, but their duration should be taken into account. For example, the ordinance against the bearing of arms was repealed on September 29 of the same year, for the feast of San Miguel, so that Spanish masters could count on an accompaniment of armed blacks and mulattos.[78] It is likely that this was brought about solely for the masters' convenience, but tensions had no doubt eased. Regarding black and mulatto women being forbidden

72   AGN, Ordenanzas, vol. 1, exp. 164, f. 146 (1612).
73   AGN, Ordenanzas, vol. 1, exp. 172, ff. 149r (1612).
74   Chimalpáhin, *Diario*, 281.
75   *Tianguis* is the Castilianization of the Nahuatl word *tianquiztli* which means market, fair, or square: *Gran diccionario náhuatl de la Universidad Nacional Autónoma de México*, http://www.gdn.unam.mx/, accessed June 8, 2021
76   AGN, Ordenanzas, vol. 1, exp. 164, f. 146 (1612).
77   Ibid.
78   AGN, Ordenanzas, vol. 1, exp. 178, ff. 152-153 (1612).

to dress elegantly, some travelers, such as Thomas Gage and Giovanni Gemelli, who visited the city in 1625 and 1697, respectively, described that these women wore distinguished jewels and clothes.[79] With respect to the request that they not live alone and that they not meet in groups larger than three by either day or night, we can assume that these were equally unsuccessful, as some of the Marquis de Gelves's ordinances, in 1622 and 1623, requested that this be avoided, suggesting that it was still happening.

Although not considered an uprising of Africans or Afro-descendants, it is known that blacks and mulattos participated in important ways in the movement against the Marquis de Gelves in 1624.[80] One of the causes of this conflict was the imposition of strong restrictions that the Marquis had imposed on the Novohispanic population in general. Among the repressive ordinances issued under the government of the Marquis de Gelves was that of April 22, 1622, according to which the meetings of more than three blacks or mulattos, free or slaves, were prohibited under penalty of 200 lashes and to cut an ear off the apprehended slaves; if they were free they would be sentenced to serve three years of work in a mill.[81] The loss of one ear is included as a penalty, a radical measure that had not been presented even after the uprising of 1612. This ordinance affected both people of African origin, as well as slave masters, since it was specified that regulations should be enforced regardless of whether slaves belonged to the Spanish authorities or not.[82] Almost a year later, on May 22, 1623, authorities requested to prohibit black and mulatto confraternities from engaging in processions, assembling for meetings, or assembling for other reasons. Failure to comply with the ordinance would be punished with 200 lashes and three years of service in a mill.[83] Despite his religious aims and accordance with the social norms of the time, the Marquis de Gelves considered it necessary to control the actions and meetings of the confraternities.

Even after Gelves was overthrown, confraternities continued to cause distrust among the authorities. In 1665, it was requested that "se suprimieran las juntas y cofradías (de negros) porque había muchas en la Ciudad de México," [that the meetings and confraternities (of blacks) be suppressed

79   Thomas Gage, *Nuevo reconocimiento de las Indias occidentales* (1648; reprint: Mexico City: Conaculta, 1994); Gemelli Careri, *Viaje*.
80   Israel, *Razas*, 163.
81   AGN, Ordenanzas, vol. 4, exp. 40, ff. 41 av-41r (1622).
82   Ibid.
83   AGN, Ordenanzas, vol. 4, exp. 61, f. 60 (1623).

because there were too many in Mexico City] but, in addition, because they believed that their purpose was for "los negros se emborracharan y gastaran, robando lo que podían de las casas de sus amos para este efecto" [blacks to get drunk and spend money, stealing what they could from their masters' houses for this purpose].[84] On top of this was the authorities' fear of a possible mulatto conspiracy, as analyzed by Silva Prada.[85]

Conclusion

Through studying confraternities of people of African origins, it is possible to observe the way in which they made use of the spaces the Spaniards allotted them to form organized groups. These are, in this sense, manifestations of resistance, that is to say, "una forma de rebeldía compatible con la aparente sumisión" [a form of rebellion compatible with apparent submission].[86] Therefore, Africans and Afro-descendants cannot simply be considered transgressors of the Novohispanic order. We must consider that this was a heterogeneous population because, although some in fact rebelled openly against Spanish power, on other occasions they participated in colonial militias.[87] The same took place on a religious level; although they sometimes carried out practices for which they were blamed before the Inquisition, Afro-descendants also participated in Catholic religious activities such as processions and confraternities.

Confraternities were important forms of social organization that gave blacks, *morenos*, and mulattos the opportunity to meet and share an identity and a sense of community, where solidarity was especially valued. Thus, being part of these confraternities undoubtedly allowed them not only to form relations with other Africans and Afro-descendants, but also to comply with the Christian religious practices demanded by the Novohispanic

---

84   Lilia Serrano, "Población de color en la ciudad de México. Siglos XVI y XVII," in *Memoria del III Encuentro de Afromexicanistas*, 85.

85   Prada, "El año de los seises."

86   Pilar Gonzalbo Aizpuru, *Historia de la familia* (México: UAM, 1993), 28.

87   Juan Manuel de la Serna, "Integración e identidad, pardos morenos en las milicias y cuerpo de lanceros de Veracruz en el siglo XVIII," in *Fuerzas militares en Iberoamérica siglos XVIII y XIX*, ed. Juan Ortiz Escamilla (México: El Colegio de México, El Colegio de Michoacán, Universidad Veracruzana, 2005), 61-74. Ben Vinson III, "Los milicianos pardos y la relación estatal durante el siglo XVIII en México," in *Fuerzas militares en Iberoamérica siglos XVIII y XIX*, Juan Ortiz Escamilla (México: El Colegio de México, El Colegio de Michoacán, Universidad Veracruzana, 2005), 47-59.

authorities. The confraternities were also used as a form of cultural resistance where diverse elements blended.

In the confraternities of the seventeenth century were people of different ethnic groups or geographic origin, for example, Congo, Biáfara, Wolof, Bañol, Zape, Menguela, among others. Therefore we can say that the confraternities were multiethnic. In addition, they brought together both free and enslaved people, as well as people of different origins (blacks, *morenos*, mulattos, and sometimes mestizos), thus it can be considered that they sought to group Africans and Afro-descendants together, regardless of their ethnicity.

Although it was the Novohispanic authorities who began to impose this separation, people of African origins took advantage of this differentiation to develop their own religious and social organization based on European institutions. This is observed in some practices, such as burials and prayers for black *bozales*, which can only be understood as part of a confraternity that shared a fundamental fact: coming from Africa or – at least – descending from Africans. Despite this, it was by no means a homogeneous group. On the contrary, the ethnic diversity entailed by coming from Africa, as well as diverse personal characteristics, undoubtedly marked social relations.

The formation of a group that shared a social identity is an extremely complex phenomenon. Only in this way can we understand the existence of conflicts within groups of blacks and mulattos who, on the other hand, shared a sense of community and solidarity. Without these kinds of feelings, it would have been difficult for uprisings, riots, and rebellions to occur. This explains why Africans and Afro-descendants protested when a black female slave was beaten to death by her master, why they chose kings and queens, why their confraternities were banned in times of tension, why the authorities prohibited meetings of more than three parties, why they were accused of gambling and betting on their master's assets, why those who were free were accused of hiding and helping escaped slaves, and why they chose to have children, couples, godparents and *compadres* with people of the same origin and social position.[88]

The ordinances and stories about the uprisings show that these confraternities were so well-organized and were such strong forces of cultural reproduction that both the authorities and society in general feared they would bring about rebellions. This fear reflects the social relationships generated from them, the opportunity they offered to integrate their own

88   Cristina Masferrer León, *Muleke, negritas y mulatillos. Niñez, familia y redes sociales de los esclavos de origen africano de la Ciudad de México* (México: INAH, 2013).

elements into the religious activities allowed by the Church, as well as the way they represented social, cultural, economic, and social spaces of empowerment for people of African origin in the capital of New Spain. While they prayed for the souls of black *bozales*, confraternities allowed them to maintain a link with the land from which they came, as well as establish social relations between people of the same socio-ethnic group while connecting to greater Novohispanic society.

About the author

Cristina Masferrer is professor and researcher at the Ethnology and Social Anthropology Direction of the National Institute of Anthropology and History of Mexico (DEAS-INAH). Author of *Muleke, negritas y mulatillos. Niñez, familia y redes sociales de los esclavos de origen africano de la Ciudad de México* (INAH, 2013), as well as several publications on Afromexican population, childhood, education and racism. She studied Ethnohistory and Psychology, with a master's degree in Social Anthropology and a Ph.D. in History and Ethnohistory. She was awarded the National Prize "Francisco Javier Clavijero 2010." She coordinates the Seminar Anthropology and History of the Racisms, Discriminations and Inequalities (DEAS-INAH/SURXE-UNAM) with Olivia Gall.

Archivo General de la Nación (Mexico City)
    Indiferente Virreinal, caja 6486, exp. 040, 1604
    Indiferente Virreinal, caja 0906, exp. 028, 1690
    Indiferente Virreinal, caja 4120, exp. 2, 1665
    Indiferente Virreinal, caja 5695, exp. 37, 1622
    Indiferente Virreinal, caja 2831, exp. 017, after 1666
    Indiferente Virreinal, caja 2475, exp. 34, 1666
    Indiferente Virreinal, caja 5424, exp. 072, 1672
    Indiferente Virreinal, caja 5593, exp. 46, 1647
    Indiferente Virreinal, Caja 0665, exp. 009, 1700
    Indiferente Virreinal, Caja 2299, exp. 008, 1664
    Ordenanzas, vol. 1, exp. 178, 1612
    Ordenanzas, vol. 1, exp.173, 1612
    Ordenanzas, vol. 1, exp. 164, f. 146, 1612
    Ordenanzas, vol. 1, exp. 172, 1612
    Ordenanzas, vol. 4, exp. 40, 1622
    Ordenanzas, vol. 4, exp. 61, 1623

Bibliography

Adams, Richard. *Etnias en evolución social: estudios de Guatemala y Centroamérica*. Mexico City: UAM, 1995.

Aguirre Beltrán, Gonzalo. *La población negra de México*. Mexico City: FCE, 1972.

Alberro, Solange. *Inquisición y Sociedad en México, 1571-1700*. Mexico City: FCE, 2004.

—. "Las representaciones y realidades familiares de los negros bozales en la predicación de Alonso de Sandoval (Cartagena de Indias, 1627) y Nicolás Duque de Estrada (La Habana, 1796)." In *La familia en el mundo iberoamericano*, edited by Pilar Gonzalbo and Cecilia Rabell, 73-89. Mexico City: IIS, 1994.

Barth, Frederik. Introduction to *Ethnic Groups and Boundaries: The Social Organization of Culture Difference*, edited by Barth, 9-38. Long Grove: Waveland Press, 1998.

Bartolomé, Miguel. "Conciencia étnica y autogestión indígena." In *Indignidad y descolonización en América Latina,* 309-324. Mexico City: Nueva Imagen, 1979.

Bazarte, Alicia. *Las cofradías de españoles en la Ciudad de México (1526-1869)*. Mexico City: UAM, 1989.

Candido, Mariana P. "Tracing Benguela Identity to the Homeland." In *Crossing Memories: Slavery and African Diaspora,* edited by Ana Lucia Araujo, Mariana P. Candido, and Paul Lovejoy, 183-208. Trenton: World Press, 2011.

Castañeda, Rafael. "Piedad y participación femenina en la cofradía de negros y mulatos de San Benito de Palermo en el Bajío novohispano, siglo XVIII." *Nuevo Mundo/Mundos Nuevos* (2012). https://journals.openedition.org/nuevomundo/64478

Chávez Carbajal, María Guadalupe. "La negritud en Michoacán, época colonial." In *Presencia Africana en México*, edited by Lax Maria Matinez Montiel, 119-124. Mexico City: Conaculta, 1994.

Chimalpáhin, Domingo. *Diario*. Translated by Rafael Tena. Mexico City: Conaculta, [1624] 2001.

Gage, Thomas. *Nuevo reconocimiento de las Indias occidentales*. Mexico City: Conaculta, 1994.

Galván Rivera, Mariano, ed.. *Concilio III Provincial Mexicano, celebrado en México el año 1585, confirmado en Roma por el Papa Sixto V, mandado observar por el gobierno español, en diversas órdenes*. Mexico City, [1585] 1859.

Gemelli Careri, Giovanni F. *Viaje a Nueva* España. Mexico City: UNAM, 1976 [1700].

Germeten, Nicole von. *Black Blood Brothers: Confraternities and Social Mobility for Afro- Mexicans*. Gainesville: University Press of Florida, 2006.

—. "Colonial Middle Men: Mulatto Identity in New Spain's Confraternities." In *Black Mexico: Race and Society from Colonial to Modern Times*, edited by Ben Vinson III and Matthew Restall. Albuquerque: University of New Mexico Press, 2009, 136-154.

Gonzalbo Aizpuru, Pilar. *Historia de la familia*. Mexico City: UAM-Instituto Mora, 1993.

Gonzalbo Aizpuru, Pilar. "Reflexiones sobre el miedo en la historia." In *Una historia de los usos del miedo*, edited by Pilar Gonzalbo, Anne Staples, Valentina Torres Septién, 21-36. Mexico City: Colmex, 2009.

Gran Diccionario Náhuatl de la Universidad Nacional Autónoma de México, http://www.gdn.unam.mx/, accessed June 8, 2021.

Guevara Sanginés, María. "El proceso de liberación de los esclavos en la América Virreinal." In *Pautas de convivencia étnica en la América latina colonial. Indios, negros, mulatos, pardos y esclavos,* coordinated by Juan Manuel de la Serna, 111-162, Guanajuato: CCyDEL-UNAM, Gobierno de Guanajuato, 2005.

Gutiérrez, Ildefonso. "Las cofradías de negros en la América Hispana. Siglos XVI-XVIII" www.africafundacion.org/spip.php?auteur54, accessed June 7, 2021.

—. "Los negros y la iglesia en la España de los siglos XV y XVI," http://www.africafundacion.org/spip.php?auteur54, accessed June 7, 2021.

Israel, Jonathan. *Razas, clases sociales y vida política en el México colonial, 1610-1670*. Mexico City: FCE, 2005.

Lorenzana, Francisco Antonio. *Concilios Provinciales, Primero y Segundo, celebrados en la muy noble, y muy leal Ciudad de México, Presidiendo el ILLmo y Rmo. Señor D.F Alonso de Montúfar, en los años 1555, y 1565*. Mexico City, [1555 and 1565] 1769.

Luna García, Sandra Nancy. "Espacios de convivencia y conflicto. Las cofradías de la población de origen africano en Ciudad de México, siglo XVII," *Trashumante. Revista Americana de Historia Social* 10 (2017): 32-52.

Martínez Domínguez, Héctor. "Las cofradías indígenas en la Nueva España." *Primer Anuario del Centro de Estudios Históricos*, Centro de Estudios Históricos Prof. Carlos S. A. Segreti, 54-71. Xalapa: Universidad Veracruzana, 1977.

Martínez Montiel, Luz María. *Negros en América*. Mexico City: Colecciones Mapfre, 1992.

Masferrer León, Cristina. *Muleke, negritas y mulatillos. Niñez, familia y redes sociales de los esclavos de origen africano de la Ciudad de México*. Mexico City: INAH, 2013.

—. *"Por las ánimas de los negros bozales*: Las cofradías de personas de origen africano en la ciudad de México (siglo XVII)." *Cuicuilco*, 18, no. 51 (2011): 83-104.

Mintz, Sidney and Richard Price. *The Birth of Africa-American Culture: An Anthropological Perspective*. Boston: Beacon Press, 1992.

Moreno, Isidro. *Cofradías y hermandades andaluzas: estructura, simbolismo e identidad*. Seville: Governemt of Andalucía, 1985.

Moreno, Isidoro, Teresa Eleazar, and Ricardo Jarillo, eds. *Cofradías de indios y negros: Origen, evolución y continuidades*. Mexico City: INAH, 2018.

Naveda, Adriana. "De San Lorenzo de los negros a los morenos de Amapa: cimarrones veracruzanos, 1609-1735." In *Rutas de la esclavitud en África y América Latina*, compiled by Rina Cáceres, 157-174. San José: Universidad de Costa Rica, 2001.

Negro, Sandra and Manuel Marzal, comp. *Esclavitud, economía y evangelización. Las haciendas jesuitas en la América Virreinal.* Lima: Pontificia Universidad Católica del Perú, 2005.

Ngou-Mvé, Nicolás. "Mesianismo, cofradías y resistencia en el África Bantú y América Colonial," http://bibliotecavirtual.clacso.org.ar/ar/libros/aladaa/nico. rtf, accessed June 7, 2021.

Palmer, Colin. *Slaves of the White God: Blacks in Mexico, 1570-1650.* Cambridge: Harvard University Press, 1976.

Pérez Puente, Leticia. "La sangre afrentada y el círculo letrado. El obispo Nicolás del Puerto, 1619-1681." In *Promoción universitaria en el mundo hispánico. Siglos XVI al XX*, coordinated by Armando Pavón Romero, 271-293. Mexico City: UNAM, 2012.

Real Academia Española. *Diccionario de Autoridades*, vol. A-C. Barcelona: Herder, [1732] 1987.

Rodriguez, Junius. *Encyclopedia of Slave Resistance and Rebellion*. Westport: Greenwood Publishing Group, 2007.

Roselló Soberón, Estela. "La cofradía de los negros: una ventana a la tercera raíz: El caso de San Benito de Palermo." BA thesis. Mexico City: UNAM, 1998.

——. "La Cofradía de San Benito de Palermo y la integración de los negros y los mulatos en la ciudad de la Nueva Veracruz en el siglo XVII." In *Formaciones religiosas en la América colonial*, edited by María Alba Pastor and Alicia Mayer, 229-242. Mexico City: UNAM, 2000.

Sandoval, Alonso de. *Un tratado sobre la esclavitud.* Edited by Enriqueta Vila Vilar. Madrid: Alianza, [1627] 1987.

Serna, Juan Manuel de la. "Integración e identidad, pardos morenos en las milicias y cuerpo de lanceros de Veracruz en el siglo XVIII." In *Fuerzas militares en Iberoamérica siglos XVIII y XIX*, edited by Juan Ortiz Escamilla, 61-74. Mexico City: Colmex, 2005.

Serrano, Lilia. "Población de color en la ciudad de México. Siglos XVI y XVII." In *Memoria del III Encuentro de Afromexicanistas*, edited by Luz María Martínez Montiel and Juan Carlos Reyes, 72-88. Mexico City: CNCA, 1993.

Silva Prada, Natalia. "El año de los seises (1666) y los rumores conspirativos de los mulatos en la ciudad de México: coronaciones, pasquines, sermones y profecías, 1608-1665," *Nuevo Mundo/Mundos Nuevos* (2012). http://journals.openedition. org/nuevomundo/64277

Valerio, Miguel A. "'That There Be No Black Brotherhood': The Failed Suppression of Afro- Mexican Confraternities, 1568-1612." *Slavery and Abolition* 42, no. 2 (2021): 293-314.

Velázquez, María Elisa. *Mujeres de origen africano en la capital novohispana, siglos XVII y XVIII*. Mexico City: INAH, 2006.

Vetancourt, Agustín de. *Chronica de la Provincia del Santo Evangelio de México*. Mexico City: Porrúa, [1697] 1982.

Vinson III, Ben. "Los milicianos pardos y la relación estatal durante el siglo XVIII en México." In *Fuerzas militares en Iberoamérica siglos XVIII y XIX*, edited by Juan Ortiz Escamilla, 47-59. Mexico City: Colmex, 2005.

Zedillo, Antonio. "Presencia de África en América Latina. El caso de México." In *Memoria del III Encuentro de Afromexicanistas*, edited by Luz María Martínez Montiel y Juan Reyes, 208-210. Mexico City: Conaculta, 1993.

3 "Of All Type of *Calidad* or Color"

Black Confraternities in a Multiethnic Mexican Parish, 1640-1750

Krystle Farman Sweda
Independent Scholar

Abstract
This chapter moves beyond the traditional depiction of black confraternities as sites of distinct cultural community formation separate from Spanish, indigenous, or mixed sacred organizations to argue that the complex social relationships forged by persons of African descent within the multiethnic colonial parish formed the foundation of their religious communities. In the daily social interactions that occurred in the sacred and secular spaces of the parish, black parishioners discussed their conceptions of communal behavior with individuals of "all type of color or calidad" – as the document studied in this chapter put it – fostering a sense of Christian unity that emerged in the formation of confraternal orders. Based on a shared spirituality framed by black expertise in Christian practices, sacred communities functioned within the dynamic cultural and social milieu of the colony, not as a distinct social organization, a recognition that ultimately places black Catholics as the center of local expressions of the Catholic faith.

Keywords: Black confraternities, Mexico, African diaspora, Black Catholicism, interethnic solidarity

In August 1698, José de Santa María, a Spanish tobacco trader in Mexico City, received an invitation to accompany Isidro de Peralta to a confraternal organization in the nearby neighborhood of San Juan de la Penitencia. Isidro, a mulatto street vender, had founded the religious brotherhood for

Javiera Jaque Hidalgo and Miguel A. Valerio. *Indigenous and Black Confraternities in Colonial Latin America: Negotiating Status through Religious Practices.* Amsterdam: Amsterdam University Press, 2022
DOI: 10.5117/ 9789463721547_CH03

the communal devotions in honor of Saint Augustine. He indicated to José that he would learn to "practice devotions and matters of the spirit" from a local instructor at the gathering. Intrigued by the devotions, José decided to attend. "On one Sunday or feast day in the afternoon," he would later testify, he arrived at a house "where different men of all *calidades*" sat before an altar with "an image of Saint Augustine and some burning candles."[1] He remained at the gathering for "about a quarter of an hour," listening to "a chat or sermon" given by one of the attendees before everyone departed "for their own homes."[2] During the following year, he continued to assist in the festivities in San Juan de la Penitencia for most feast days until for "no reason good or bad" he left the confraternity. Later he would state that he enjoyed the devotionals because he did not believe "these gatherings could be bad since they pray to the Rosary of Our Lady."[3]

Around the same time, Gabriel de Sanabria, another tobacco trader in the central plaza, received a similar invitation from an acquaintance, a young Spanish man named Lucas de Mercado. Lucas, Gabriel declared, had informed him about a confraternity of "different men who, in the said gathering, address matters of devotion" to Saint Augustine. Lucas himself had visited a previous gathering organized by the same person, Isidro de Peralta, "who put together" the various devotions.[4] Deciding that "it was better than wandering around the city," Gabriel accompanied Lucas to the meeting. At the house, the two men joined a gathering of "multiple men of various status and *calidad*" who all sat before a post "like a pulpit," listening to a sermon for about a quarter of an hour.[5] After the homily, a member of the confraternity "read from a book of devotions for more than a half an hour" before they all "prayed the rosary of the crowns."[6] Pleased with the devotions, Gabriel accompanied Lucas to the meetings for three months, during which time he learned about two similar brotherhoods founded by Isidro, one also in honor of Saint Augustine and another held at the house of a clergyman in devotion to Saint Francis. For the next year, Gabriel attended

1   The Huntington Library (hereafter HL), Mexican Inquisition Papers, Series II, Box 6, HM35168, El Señor Fiscal de este Sancto Oficio contra Isidro de Peralta, mulato, por fundar a su modo una religión de San Agustín, f. 16r (1699). Another analysis of this case can be found in Joan Bristol, "Afro-Mexican Saintly Devotion in a Mexico City Alley," *Africans to Spanish America: Expanding the Diaspora*, ed. Sherwin K. Bryant, Rachel Sarah O'Toole, and Ben Vinson, III (Champaign: University of Illinois Press, 2012), 114-135.
2   HL, HM35168, f. 16r.
3   Ibid., f. 18v.
4   Ibid., f. 12v.
5   Ibid., ff. 14r, 12v.
6   Ibid., f. 12v.

the two confraternities until he stopped for "the precise reason of needing to attend to his occupation in the store."[7]

At the center of the multiple religious brotherhoods composed of men of "various status and *calidad*" rested the spiritual direction of one man: Isidro de Peralta, the mulatto street vender. In founding the confraternities, Isidro organized a variety of spiritual exercises for the men and women who attended the devotions. He invited local clergymen to give sermons, encouraged students at the university to recite devotional materials, guided prayers to the rosary, and, for special feast days, organized processions from a local church to the house of devotion.[8] All of his exercises spoke to the communal religious practices observed by the diverse individuals he invited to participate. Gabriel de Sanabria attended the confraternities in honor of Saint Augustine and Saint Francis precisely because "they had prayed the rosary and read for a book of devotions and made chats or sermons on virtuous matters."[9] José de Santa María participated in the confraternity dedicated to Saint Augustine for similar reasons. José explained to the inquisitor that the confraternities celebrated "most of the feast days together" with sermons and devotional prayers, which he considered "exercises of virtue."[10] Through the communal worship of the confraternities, Isidro de Peralta brought together individuals of "all *calidades*" around a shared set of religious practices. He organized the confraternities' devotions around his personal spiritual beliefs, inviting the people he interacted with on a daily basis to attend his celebrations.

Drawing from Isidro de Peralta's case and other examples of black confraternities, this chapter examines how sacred organizations provided an institutionalized social space for creoles of African descent to publicly enact their conceptions of communal Christianity alongside a diverse congregation. As a form of communal worship encouraged by ecclesiastical officials, approved by church authorities, and overseen by parish priests and local clergy, confraternities provided black Catholics with a social space to act upon their conceptions of community-driven Christianity without transgressing the boundaries of Catholic orthodoxy. Through the formal ties established between confraternities and the parochial system, specifically the location of the order's meetings and the presence of a member of the church hierarchy, ecclesiastical authorities acted to regulate and improve

7   Ibid., f. 14v.
8   Ibid., f. 6.
9   Ibid., f. 13r.
10   Ibid., f. 17r, 18v.

the beliefs, worship, and basic education of the Hispanic laity.[11] Despite the church's mandates for clerical supervision, confraternities generally functioned as self-governing institutions with limited ecclesiastical control, allowing the confraternity's officers and brothers a degree of freedom in how they enacted their devotions.[12] As *mayordomos*, deputies, rectors, and founders, black brothers of New Spain's various confraternities determined the religious activities required of the members by establishing constitutions with specific spiritual obligations, managing the brotherhood's finances, and organizing the various public processions and devotions for the congregation. Since these everyday decisions occurred with minimal oversight from ecclesiastical authorities, creole Christians were able to implement their well-informed conceptions of confraternal piety in a manner that placed their personal religious choices at the front of the congregation's devotional practices.

This black confraternal piety functioned almost entirely within the social environment of a diverse colonial parish where black creoles maintained spiritual connections with men and women of "various status and *calidad*." In the local churches, altars, and chapels, parish residents from disparate social backgrounds assembled in lay brotherhoods to discuss appropriate exercises for collective devotions based on their conceptions of a shared Catholic spirituality. Parish-centered processions and feast-day celebrations brought together separate social classes and various confraternities to express the spiritual sentiments that drove the religious life of their neighborhood. Within a single confraternity, the brotherhood's membership often mirrored the demographic diversity found within the boundaries of a colonial parish. Even in confraternities that restricted positions of authority – *mayordomos*, rectors, deputies, or treasurers – to a certain racial or social classifications, membership remained open to residents of an entire parish or individuals "of all type of *calidad* or color."[13] To be sure,

---

11   Christopher Black, "Confraternities and the Parish in the Context of Italian Catholic Reform," in *Confraternities and Catholic Reform in Italy, France, and Spain*, ed. John Patrick Donnelly and Michael W. Maher (Kirksville: Thomas Jefferson University Press, 1998), 1-26; Brian Larkin, *The Very Nature of God: Baroque Catholicism and Religious Reform in Bourbon Mexico City* (Albuquerque: University of New Mexico, 2010), and "Confraternities and Community: The Decline of the Communal Quest for Salvation in Eighteenth Century Mexico," in *Local Religion in Colonial Mexico*, ed. Martin Nesvig (Albuquerque: University of New Mexico Press, 2006), 189-213.

12   Larkin, "Confraternities and Community," 194.

13   Archivo General de Nación (hereafter AGN), Bienes Nacionales, caja 444, exp. 3, Constituciones de la nueva cofradía, f. 3v (1713); AGN, Bienes Nacionales, caja 444, exp. 4, Constitución de la Preciosa Sangre de Cristo, (1713); AGN, Bienes Nacionales, caja 863, exp. 4, Cofradía y

select congregations placed social restrictions on membership, requiring participants to be of a particular class, race, or occupational status, or at times demanding such a high entrance fee as to bar specific individuals.[14] But in confraternities founded by persons of African descent membership tended to reflect the very social interactions that sustained the parochial elements of black collective worship. The routine interactions that occurred in the colonial parish where black parishioners addressed their conceptions of appropriate religious behavior with their friends, family, neighbors, and casual acquaintances fostered the sacred social bonds that formed the foundation of their confraternal membership.

Images of black parishioners promoting communal devotions for the spiritual edification of "different men of all *calidades*" appears in stark contrast to traditional characterizations of black confraternities in the New World. As sacred organizations founded by persons of African descent, confraternities have traditionally appeared in historical studies as pivotal places for enslaved Africans to cultivate communal ties around a shared sense of corporate identity often associated with either an African ethnicity or a New World racial identity.[15] In the early era of the sixteenth and seventeenth centuries, as church authorities encouraged the foundation of confraternities

Congregación de Nuestra Señora del Rosario y San Antonio (1682); AGN, Bienes Nacionales, caja 1028, exp. 6, Constituciones de la Cofradía del Tránsito (1686); AGN, Bienes Nacionales, caja 1028, exp. 26, Cofradía de Nicólas de Penitencia de Acapulco (1691).

14   Multiple confraternities founded by elite Spaniards restricted membership to the town's wealthy elites or maintained an open membership policy with a high membership fee, thereby restricting members of a lower social class. In other confraternities, acceptance into the brotherhood required membership in an artisan guild, such as cobblers, tanners, or blacksmiths. For more, see Maureen Flynn, *Sacred Charity: Confraternities and Social Welfare in Spain, 1400-1700* (London: Macmillan Press, 1989); Clara García-Ayluardo, "Confraternity, Cult, and Crown in Colonial Mexico" (Ph.D. diss., University of Cambridge, 1989); Larkin, "Confraternities and Community" and *The Very Nature of God.*

15   Bristol, *Christians, Blasphemers, and Witches: Afro-Mexican Ritual Practice in the Seventeenth Century* (Albuquerque: University of New Mexico Press, 2007); Bryant, *Rivers of Gold, Lives of Bondage: Governing through Slavery in Colonial Quito* (Chapel Hill: University of North Carolina Press, 2014); Patricia A. Mulvey, "Black Brothers and Sisters: Membership in the Black Lay Brotherhoods of Colonial Brazil," *Luso-Brazilian Review* 17, no. 2 (1980): 253-279; Mariza de Carvalho Soares, *People of Faith: Slavery and African Catholics in Eighteenth-Century Rio de Janeiro* (Durham: Duke University Press, 2011); James Sweet, *Recreating Africa: Culture, Kinship, and Religion in the African-Portuguese World, 1441-1770* (Chapel Hill: University of North Carolina Press, 2003); Ben Vinson, III, *Bearing Arms for His Majesty: The Free-Colored Militia in Colonial Mexico* (Stanford: Stanford University Press, 2003), and *Before Mestizaje: The Frontiers of Race and Caste in Colonial Mexico* (Cambridge: Cambridge University Press, 2017); Nicole von Germeten, *Black Blood Brothers: Confraternities and Social Mobility for Afro-Mexicans* (Gainesville: University of Florida Press, 2006).

by individuals of African descent, enslaved Africans utilized their cultural awareness of the rituals and institutions of the Catholic Church to organize meaningful community associations within the dominant Christian system. Such associations mitigated the effects of social death by creating fictive kinship networks and corporate webs of relationships that would form the foundation for black social life in the Americas.[16] Since confraternities served as an institutionally recognized space where persons of African descent had the opportunity to gather without the watchful eye of their masters, enslaved Africans established corporate entities with individuals who expressed similar social, cultural, or ethnic ties. In recognizing the importance of this social space for community formation, scholars argued that for African-born individuals, the confraternity's connection to specific ethnicities in the New World transformed the Catholic institution into "veiled ethnic societies" where members perpetuated the social and cultural practices they brought with them from Africa.[17] Even in confraternities founded by first generations of black creoles and mulattos, they argued, the ethnic-based relationships established in former generations initially guided the development of their sodalities. Only as black creoles gradually formed a larger part of the overall population did black *cofrades* start to deemphasize their connections to African ethnicities or geographical locations, instead electing to designate their confraternities around a shared sense of racial corporate identity – as confraternities of blacks, mulattos, or morenos.[18]

Considered by historians a result of the demographic and cultural transformation that occurred in the seventeenth century, this gradual transition away from the African-influenced religious and social expressions and toward an identity founded entirely in the New World experience corresponded to black creoles' integration into Catholic society on terms

16   Herman Bennett, *Colonial Blackness: A History of Afro-Mexico* (Bloomington: Indiana University Press, 2009); Bryant, *Rivers of Gold*; Orlando Patterson, *Slavery and Social Death: A Comparative Study* (Cambridge: Harvard University Press, 1982); Sweet, *Recreating Africa*; Vinson, *Bearing Arms for His Majesty*; von Germeten, *Black Blood Brothers*.

17   Mulvey, "Black Brothers and Sisters," 258-257; Proctor, *Damned Notions of Liberty*, 46-56; Matthew Restall, *The Black Middle: Africans, Mayas, and Spaniards in Colonial Yucatan* (Stanford: Stanford University Press, 2013), 232-233; A.J.R. Russell-Wood, *Slavery and Freedom in Colonial Brazil* (Oxford: Oneworld, 2002), and "Black and Mulatto Brotherhoods in Colonial Brazil," *Hispanic American Historical Review* 54, no. 4 (1974): 567-602; Sweet, *Recreating Africa*, 207; von Germeten, *Black Blood Brothers*, 11-70.

18   Bristol, *Christians, Blasphemers, and Witches*; Vinson, *Bearing Arms for His Majesty*; Von Germeten, *Black Blood Brothers* and "Black Brotherhoods in Mexico City," in *The Black Urban Atlantic in the Age of the Slave Trade*, ed. Jorge Cañizares-Esguerra, Matt D. Childs, and James Sidburyn (Philadelphia: University of Pennsylvania Press, 2016), 248-268.

relevant to their socioracial status.[19] Under the New World social and economic conditions, identification with a particular racial category – whether
black, mulatto, pardo or moreno – associated individuals with a specific
social and personal identity recognized by both colonial authorities and
the people who composed their social networks. Since racial identification
functioned entirely within the fluid, at times ambiguous *sistema de castas*,
an association with a specific racial designation remained contextual,
relating to the local manifestations of social divisions that emphasized
how individuals of a certain racial classification figured into colonial
structures.[20] Premised on a person's *calidad*, the racial terms of this flexible
social hierarchy could be adapted by individuals or groups depending on
its usefulness in a particular setting. Within the religious institution of
the confraternity, an association with a racial corporate identity offered
Afro-descendants the possibility to forge a group solidarity that provided
protection in the repressive society of a racialized social order.[21] This
scholarly focus on the *sistema de castas* and the resulting formation of a
racial corporate identity directed historiographical discussions toward
an analytical framework that underscores how confraternities offered
opportunities for members to improve their local status and negotiate their
position in colonial society.[22] In these historical studies, the participation in
the Catholic rituals of the confraternity formalized the social relationships
necessary for black *cofrades* to address practical matters or advance their
immediate interests and material conditions – essentially to climb the
social ladder.[23] Since a group identity afforded a collective advantage in
a race-based social order, individual members could draw from the public
reputation and local renown of their confraternity to contest their social
status and secure positions of social prestige.

Scholars have presented a remarkable specificity to the position of
confraternities in the creation of black social networks, cultural formation,

19   Proctor, *Damned Notions of Liberty*; Vinson, *Bearing Arms for His Majesty*; Von Germeten,
Black Blood Brothers.

20   Vinson, *Bearing Arms for His Majesty*, 2-6; Von Germeten, *Black Blood Brothers*, 189.

21   Von Germeten, *Black Blood Brothers*; Sweet, *Recreating Africa*; Soares, *People of Faith*; Mulvey,
"Black Brothers and Sisters"; Vinson, *Bearing Arms for His Majesty*; Proctor, *Damned Notions*;
Bryant, *Rivers of Gold*; Nicholas Terpstra, "Ignatius, Confratello: Confraternities as Modes of
Spiritual Community in Early Modern Society," in *Early Modern Catholicism: Essays in Honour
of John W. O'Malley, S.J.*, ed. Kathleen M. Comerford and Hilmar M. Pabel (Toronto: Toronto
University Press, 2003), 175.

22   Von Germeten, *Black Blood Brothers*, 189; Vinson, *Bearing Arms*, 4-5.

23   Von Germeten, *Black Blood Brothers*; David Wheat, *Atlantic Africa and the Spanish Caribbean,
1570-1640* (Chapel Hill: University of North Carolina Press, 2016).

and racial solidarity. Such a characterization has rightfully privileged how persons of African descent utilized the Spanish Catholic institution to function under colonial Christian dominance, emphasizing social integration, access to material resources, social mobility, patterns of discrimination, and subversive actions against a hegemonic colonial power. But their focus on race relations precludes a serious examination into the intergenerational and interracial dynamics at play in the formation of black confraternal piety and their effects on communal worship in New Spain. For men and women, like Isidro de Peralta, their everyday religious practices occurred within a complex social formation where they maintained multigenerational ties to slaves, free blacks, Indians, Spaniards, and *castas*. As creoles born into a specific parish, where, in many cases, they were baptized, confirmed, and later married, black parishioners spent their entire adult life participating in an intensely localized communal worship. They regularly attended mass, participated in parochial feast celebrations, conducted pilgrimages to popular shrines, and partook in group devotionals known as *novenas*. In the everyday interactions of colonial life, black parishioners navigated their extensive social networks to participate in a common spirituality for Christian veneration. These personal, multiethnic interactions ultimately shaped the decisions on who entered the brotherhood and who could hold positions of authority. Black *cofrades*, who occupied positions of leadership over a diverse congregation, organized public devotions and communal worship that held significance to the ritual life of the individuals who composed this complex social formation.

Within a single confraternity, the brotherhood's membership often mirrored the social connections of their daily interactions. In the everyday contours of colonial life, black parishioners encountered the shifting social dynamics of an urban landscape where the marketplace, work spaces, and plazas enabled a remarkably varied group to interact with increasing familiarity. This familiarity, a result of the spatial proximity of marketplace stalls, artisan workshops, and routine interaction in the streets, afforded black Catholics a social environment to converse on spiritual matters with individuals who shared in their religious practices, individuals of "all *calidades*." Returning to Isidro de Peralta's various congregations as an example, the marketplace figured prominently in the transmission of his plans to form the communal devotions. While none of the witnesses explicitly stated that Isidro spoke to them about religious matters while in the central plaza, the fact that each of them mentioned their proximity to the Isidro at the marketplace and their neglect to mention a more intimate relationship suggests their social connections remained tied to their shared work space.

In his testimony, José de Santa María, the Spanish tobacco merchant in the plaza, highlighted the various patterns of interaction engaged by multiple men who worked at stands in the marketplace. He informed the inquisitor that he had first heard about the gathering from Isidro de Peralta, "who sells foodstuffs in the plaza," specifically noting that he knew no other information about Isidro besides his place of employment and his role in founding the multiple religious brotherhoods.[24] After the first house of devotion dispersed for an unspecified reason, José received an invitation from Isidro to another gathering dedicated to "the same order of Saint Augustine." As he attended the devotions, José explained to the inquisitor, he started to recognize the other participants who also maintained an occupation in the central plaza. He stated on one occasion that he recognized Gabriel de Sanabria, a Spaniard from a village in Michoacán, as "the man who sells tobacco near the gates of the central plaza," a store front not too distant from the stand occupied by Isidro.[25] He would later accompany Gabriel, and his friend Lucas de Mercado, to another one of the confraternities also dedicated to Saint Augustine. On another occasion, he recalled the regular presence of Antonio de Alarcon, "who usually assists his father in a stand in the plaza that sells wool," and Lazaro, a master swordsmith, at the services.[26] Throughout his interrogation, José continually referenced the importance of the market located "at the gates to the plaza" in the social connections Isidro maintained with his fellow participants.

Similarly, Gabriel de Sanabria noted the routine interaction of the multiple participants in the marketplace. His friend, Lucas de Mercado, a Spanish man who "had a small shop of merchandise near the gates of the plaza," had first introduced him to the gatherings after he had been invited by Isidro de Peralta, who maintained a stand near Lucas in the plaza.[27] Gabriel informed the inquisitor that he had no prior knowledge of Isidro, only that he "ha[d] noticed that he sells goods in the plaza,"[28] suggesting that their contact occurred solely in the context of brief interactions of the marketplace. He maintained a similar relationship to the other individuals he recognized at the various congregations that he attended over the course of the year. He recognized José Bravo, a man who was employed in his father's wool

---

24 HL, HM35168, f. 19r. José's exact words were "the solicitor of the expressed Religions is the said mulatto Isidro de Peralta, that he does not know on what he street he lives, only that he sells foodstuff in the plaza."

25 Ibid., f. 16v.

26 Ibid., f. 17v.

27 Ibid., f. 6r, 12v.

28 Ibid., f. 14v.

shop, when the people in attendance at the gathering referred to him as "the commissioner," implying that he held an important position within the congregation.[29] Apart from José Bravo, Gabriel informed the inquisitor that he "only remembered some Spanish man named de Santa María [José de Santa María]," who worked in front of the "new gates" of the plaza, and two brothers "named Juan and Gabriel Rodrigues," who held occupations as a chairmaker and a goldsmith, respectively.[30] He remembered little more about all four of the individuals apart from their place of employment and proximity to Isidro's stand near the gates to the central plaza, again suggesting that their familiarity remained tied to the marketplace.

Word had quickly spread through their various social networks, as individuals from outside the immediate neighborhood or marketplace started to attend the services, signifying a sense of a shared Catholic spirituality and conceptions of communal worship. José de Santa María indicated that men including José Zapata, a mulatto man who lives on the Calle de Corchero, and Francisco de Ugalde, a mulatto musician at the convent of Regina, attended the devotions to Saint Augustine without maintaining any apparent connection to Isidro de Peralta or the marketplace. Lucas de Mercado similarly noted that a musician at the convent of Jesus of Nazarene named Marco (no last name given), and a student at the university, Antonio Romiento, remained involved in the congregations during the year that he had attended. But the initial invitations for the various congregations occurred within the context of Mexico City's central plaza, where the participants of "various status and *calidad*" worked, socialized, and discussed their preferences for communal devotions. Within the context of their familiarity, however limited it may have been, Isidro had discussed his plans to form the congregations, inviting individuals he conversed with on a daily basis. Those individuals then extended an invitation to the people they presumed would be interested in the devotions. Through a transmission of information about the gatherings – when they would meet, what they would discuss, and which saint they worshiped – implies that Isidro's choices for a communal devotion spoke to the spirituality of the various parishioners he had invited.

Since Isidro de Peralta's congregations fell under inquisitorial scrutiny for their failure to obtain a license from the archbishop, a requirement for all confraternities in the colony regardless of racial classification, they offer a unique perspective on the racial composition of confraternities organized by individuals of African descent. Most extant sources on New Spain's

29   Ibid., f. 14r.
30   Ibid., f. 13v.

confraternities consist of membership records that typically only contain names without racial designations. In accounts maintained by the colony's confraternities, officials listed all members but simply specified the names and location of each individual, leaving it difficult to identify their racial background. At times, the list of names indicated individuals of a specific socioeconomic class through the use of *don* or *doña* and their dependents, which potentially included slaves or servants of a separate race.[31] But often more specific documentation appears in court cases, like Isidro's, than the confraternity's governing texts. When the *promotor fiscal* raided Isidro de Peralta's celebrations, he arrested a total of sixteen persons for their illicit devotions. Among those detained in the inquisitorial prisons, seven individuals were identified as mulatto or black, six were categorized as Spanish, and another three were described as mestizo.[32] Taking into consideration the racial classification of the witnesses brought before the inquisitor, primarily Spanish and mulatto, merely amplifies the remarkably varied group who attended the celebrations. In a complex social environment, the interactions forged as creole members of a particular neighborhood, parish, or marketplace guided the composition of their confraternities, with black *cofrades* inviting diverse individuals who shared in their Catholic spirituality and conceptions of communal worship.

In the everyday contours of colonial life, these intergenerational and interracial interactions that occurred between black creoles and their fellow parishioners affected how black *cofrades* determined who could join and who could lead their brotherhoods. In the majority of confraternities examined for this chapter, the constitutions written by black founders indicated how membership could draw from residents "of all type of *calidad* or color." Only one black brotherhood, the Confraternity of the Immaculate Conception in the Hospital of the Immaculate Conception, chose to explicitly limit membership to a single classification of people, stipulating that brothers should be "blacks from the Zape nation," an ethnic label in the early modern Iberian world that referred to Africans from coastal Sierra Leone.[33] Even though extant documentation remains limited to a legal dispute over the

---

31 AGN, Indiferente Virreinal, caja 2043, exp. 17, Cofradía de la Preciosa Sangre de Cristo (1732-1733); AGN, Indiferente Virreinal, caja 3492, exp. 10, Cofradía de la Preciosa Sangre de Cristo (1730); AGN, Indiferente Virreinal, caja 4989, exp. 051, Cofradía de la Preciosa Sangre de Cristo (1716-1731).
32 HL, Mexican Inquisition Papers, Series II, Box 6, HM 35169, Auto contra diferentes personas que formavan nueva religion de San Augustin, el principal, Isidro de Peralta, ff. 4r-6r (1702).
33 AGN, Bienes Nacionales, caja 1175, exp. 11, Mayordomo y los Diputados de la Cofradía de la Concepción (1634).

income from a house donated by Juan Roque, a free black *cofrade*, rather than a constitution, details indicate that the brotherhood remained in the hands of individuals identified as Zape for a significant amount of time. By the time the conflict over Juan Roque's donation escalated in 1644, the brotherhood had started to accept Africans of various ethnicities, including black creoles and mulattos, which remained a point of contestation for the officials of the organization. Despite this broader acceptance of a diverse Afro-Mexican population, the officers appeared to have limited the brotherhood's membership explicitly to Afro-descendants, prohibiting the presence of any person of Spanish or indigenous descent.[34]

Unlike the Confraternity of Immaculate Conception, most brotherhoods founded and led by black creoles accepted members regardless of their racial classification with membership eventually representing the changes of racial composition of their city, town, or neighborhood. In the city of Valladolid, the colonial capital of Michoacán, the Confraternity of Our Lady of the Rosary shifted its membership qualifications and leadership in response to the population changes of the seventeenth century. Originally founded under Spanish direction in 1586 for residents of all racial classifications, the confraternity officially split in 1681 into two entities to administer to the growing populations of Africans, blacks, and *castas* who had entered in as members.[35] The brotherhood separated into a congregation for the Spanish elite of the town and another under the direction of blacks and mulattos. Unlike its Spanish counterpart, which explicitly specified that members had to be of Spanish descent, the black confraternity maintained a membership requirement open to any individual of all types or *calidad*. Since the confraternity functioned entirely on alms and rental income, the founders suggested that new members who wished to receive the order's benefits should make a humble donation of whatever they could afford, furthering the possibility that membership included individuals of all statuses (free and enslaved) and of various *calidad*. By the early decades of the eighteenth century, documents suggested that leadership included individuals identified as blacks, mulattos, and mestizos with a membership base of all racial classifications that eventually earned the sacred organization a designation as a *casta* confraternity.[36]

34   Ibid. For a more detailed analysis of the legal dispute, see von Germeten, "Black Brotherhoods of Mexico City" and *Black Blood Brothers*.

35   Archivo Histórico del Arzobispado de Michoacán (hereafter, CM), caja 1, exp. 1, Libro de Cofradía de Nuestra Señora de Rosario (1681).

36   Ibid.; CM, caja 1246, exp. 9, Libro de elecciones y constituciones (1733). For an example of a confraternity lead by blacks, mulattos, and mestizos in Mexico City, see AGN, Indiferente Virreinal, caja 2258, exp. 019, Cofradía de la Santa Veracruz (1645).

On occasion, black *cofrades* restricted positions of authority – as *mayordomos*, rectors, deputies, or treasurers – to individuals of African descent. The Confraternity of the Most Precious Blood of Christ in Mexico City stated that their "confraternity should perpetually have a Rector, a Deputy mayor, a *mayordomo*, and thirty-three founders, [all free] blacks and mulattos, who rule and govern." In 1694, the brotherhood received permission from the archbishop to alter their constitutions to include an official known as the *mayoral* "who should be black" like the other officials in the organization.[37] But membership for the confraternity still remained open to "all persons, women as well as men, of whatever state, *calidad*, or condition" as long as they kept their "obligation of giving as their entrance a *real* and a half *real* each week."[38] Similarly, the Confraternity of Saint Nicholas of Tolentino, founded in the *hermita* of Santa Barbara in Amilpas, restricted its leadership to "all blacks and mulattos, men as well as women" who lived in the Valley of Amilpas. They stipulated that "if other persons of whatever *calidad* want to sit as brothers of this Holy Confraternity that, [upon] giving the alms necessary to enjoy the graces and indulgences," they could enter, but only "under the condition [...] that they cannot be elected to any office of this our Confraternity nor can they interfere in any matter of governing."[39]

Restrictions on positions of governance in black confraternities and the general constitutions that maintained policies of open membership at times lead to conflict within the sacred organizations. In most cases, these situations of conflict further underscored the diverse nature of the confraternity despite any specific rules the constitutions contained about the racial designations of its membership or founders. In 1700, Ambrosio Nieto Galindo, a black founder of the Confraternity of Saint Benedict of Palermo petitioned the ecclesiastical authorities for permission to enter a new constitution for the spiritual benefit of the brotherhood. He informed the authorities that "the confraternity, according to its foundation, is for blacks and mulattos by whom it has always been governed." But, in the previous year, "the *mayordomo* and the deputies have admitted Spaniards who have voted," an act that he complained risked the conservation of their order. As such, he requested the permission to add a specific regulation on

37   AGN, Indiferente Virreinal, caja 2235, exp. 23, Cofradía de la Preciosa Sangre de Cristo, f. 3r (1694-1696).
38   AGN, Indiferente Virreinal, caja 3231, exp. 002, Cofradía de la Sangre de Cristo (1686).
39   AGN, Indiferente Virreinal, caja 5109, exp. 007, Cofradía de San Nicólas de Tolentino (1634).

membership, prohibiting any non-Afro-descendant person from entering the confraternity or having a vote in the organization.[40]

Shortly after the ecclesiastical judge extended permission for the new ordinance, the court received another petition from the brotherhood's officials, Nicolás Flores, Tomás de Esquivel, Manuel de la Cruz, and Augustin Francisco de Herrera, who desired to have the new constitution annulled based on the ordinances and customs that had always been observed. To support their claims against Ambrosio's petition, they presented to the court two registers from their confraternity that included the constitutions from their original foundation in 1672. They demonstrated how in the twelfth constitution the founders ordered that they "receive Spaniards in the said Confraternity"[41] and the third constitution further dictated that the brother-hood should "recognize the openness of receiving whatever person."[42] More to their point, they informed the ecclesiastical judge that the confraternity had accepted Spaniards in important positions from the very beginning, and many of these people consisted of "the first and principle persons of this City as well as ecclesiastics such as secular [priests]."[43] They noted that at its formation Fray Cristóbal de San Diego served as the Rector, that multiple "Spaniards were also founders," and that according to the statues the "Treasurer of the Confraternity should be a Spaniard."[44] Speaking on behalf of the brotherhood's entire membership, they pleaded with the ecclesiastical authorities to "recognize the bad intent" of Ambrosio Nieto Galindo, who "wanted to cause disturbance and unease among the brothers." As a countermeasure, they requested permission "to add and put as a new constitution that the said Spaniards can be founders and exercise the charges in which they were elected and vote in all the *cabildos* and gatherings."[45] The ecclesiastical judge, along with the *promotor fiscal*, agreed with the officials, determining that the original statutes permitted Spaniards since "there is no constitution that prohibits [them] as founders and officials of the said confraternity," and therefore upheld the diverse membership of the sacred organization.

For the growing population of black creoles deeply rooted in the complex social formation of the parish, confraternities offered an institutionalized space where they could publicly voice their ideas, beliefs, and practices to

40 AGN, Indiferente Virreinal, caja 0665, exp. 009, Cofradía de San Benito, fol. 1r-2r (1700).
41 Ibid., f. 3v.
42 Ibid.
43 Ibid.
44 Ibid.
45 Ibid.

these diverse congregations without breaking the boundaries of orthodox and unorthodox authority. Creole founders wrote constitutions sanctioned by local authorities that outlined the mutual spiritual commitments required of the brotherhood's diverse members, including alms for their religious devotions, regular attendance at masses and processions, and charitable acts for their members or persons residing in the parish. In these social positions of confraternal leadership supported by church officials, black officers and members exercised a formal, officially recognized form of spiritual authority over a congregation comprised of men and women from disparate social backgrounds. Composing a self-governing body of the faithful, black *mayordomos*, rectors, and deputies possessed the authority to discipline their members for neglecting their spiritual obligations or failing to uphold certain moral or behavioral expectations, all often with limited clerical intervention. Within a colonial Christian society, where participation in Iberian Catholic practices integrated individuals into all aspects of colonial life, such positions of leadership placed black Catholics in a structural role that guided proper religious conduct on the local level. As black Catholics joined or founded confraternities, articulating their personal spiritual choices within the constitutions of the Catholic institution, they produced a mode of sacred organization that inherently affected the cultural landscape of New Spain's confraternal piety.

In the Confraternity of the Most Precious Blood of Christ, for example, the founders Simon de los Santos, Miguel Real, Ignacio de Vera, Antonio Maldonado, and Pedro de la Cruz, among others, delineated the spiritual obligations of the brotherhood and its members.[46] Each *cofrade* upon their entrance received the right to "a doctor and a surgeon to cure them of their attacks and illnesses" and in the event of their passing, received a "good Christian death," a burial with a coffin, two prayed masses, and ten *pesos* to "pay for the parochial rights,"[47] all common benefits in confraternities regardless of racial classification. In return for their care in life and death, the brothers were obligated to participate in a host of communal activities sanctioned by the founders. In addition to their financial contributions "to help with the expenses of the said confraternity," the founders expected all members to participate in the "title feast [of the Ascension of Our Lord], an anniversary, and a procession of disciplines on Holy Thursday"[48] where they would hear a sung mass accompanied by music, a sermon preached by the

46   AGN, Indiferente Virreinal, caja 3231, exp. 002.
47   Ibid., f. 6r.
48   Ibid.

local priest, and prayers at the altar decorated "in all decency, ornamentation, care, and veneration" with wax candles and flowers.[49] The "general anniversary," an offertory mass said in remembrance of "the souls of the officials, brothers, *cofrades* [...] and the souls of Purgatory," required the attendance of all the brothers for vespers, a vigil, an offertory, twenty masses, and a sermon preached by the *sacristan mayor* in the parish church.[50] The black founders of the confraternity selected these spiritual obligations based on their conceptions of communal worship, deeming them essential elements of collective salvation and appropriate religious behavior as they "serve God, Our Lord [and] wait for his infinite mercy."[51]

In the constitutions established for the Confraternity of Our Lady of Tránsito, the black founders Nicólas de Sierra, Pedro Segundo de Luna, Marcos Moreno, Diego Ramirez, and Miguel Sanchez similarly provided the proper communal devotions that guided their sacred organization. They dictated to the notary that each member, upon their acceptance into the brotherhood, contribute to an annual celebration "on the second Sunday of the month of October for the title feast of Our Lady of Tránsito" and the observations for Holy Wednesday, where they would attend the festivities carefully planned in a *cabildo* held six months earlier.[52] They prescribed that the celebration should follow a specific plan of events for the gathering of all the members of their brotherhood. The first item required each member to assist in the adornment of the confraternity's altar before attending a sung mass and a sermon in the same location, indicating that all brothers remained under the strict obligation to join the celebrations unless they "were with a legitimate impediment."[53] Upon completing the mass with prayer for the living and the deceased, the members would "leave in a procession of discipline, light and blood, with the banners of insignias and a bell in memory of the passion and death of Our Lord, Jesus Christ."[54] At the end of the procession, members designated in the previous *cabildo*

---

49 Ibid., f. 6v.

50 Ibid., f. 6v-7r.

51 Ibid, f. 7r.

52 AGN, Bienes Nacionales, caja 1028, exp. 6, Constituciones de la Cofradía del Tránsito, f. 2v (1686).

53 Ibid.

54 Ibid., ff. 2v-3r. In a discipline procession that included "lights and blood," select members would perform acts of contrition, typically a form of flagellation, while other members solemnly carried candles. Often confraternities would be divided the tasks on a gendered basis with male members performing the self-mortification and women carrying the candles. For more see von Germeten, *Black Blood Brothers*, 41-70.

would "carry at last the *paso* of the effigy of Our Lady of Tránsito."[55] Each element of the celebrations – attendance at the masses, the decoration of their communal altar, and a procession "of light and blood" on Holy Wednesday – was carefully selected by the confraternities black officials as important components to Christian veneration that determined the direction of their sacred organization.

Through this articulation of personal religious choices in confraternal piety, black *cofrades* disseminated the cultural practices and customs that shaped communal worship in their local neighborhoods and parishes. Their celebrations of the liturgical calendar, located in the parish streets, the public chapels, or the private altars, publicly displayed their conceptions of a Catholic spirituality that resonated with the spiritual worldview of the diverse members of their congregations. As their devotionals gained notoriety within their social world, individuals of "various status and *calidad*" elected to join their confraternities, considering the sacred organizations founded by individuals of African descent a valuable means to participate in the collective efforts toward divine favor and eternal salvation. They supported the practices by paying entrance fees, donating time, money, and material objects to celebrations, and attending all festivities and devotions. A broader communal acceptance of the devotional practices by fellow parishioners, various *cofrades*, and church officials strengthened the authoritative space afforded to black *cofrades* and their confraternities.

The religious gatherings organized by Isidro de Peralta, for example, reveal the cultural practices and customs determined by its black leadership that gained ground in the religious life of the San Juan de la Penitencia neighborhood. Even though the congregations lacked an official constitution, where elected members of leadership strictly dictated appropriate spiritual behavior for all members in attendance, the daily spiritual activities of religious processions, devotional altars, readings of religious texts, and sermons functioned in much the same manner of an official confraternity. The first congregation, which met in 1699 in a house on the Calle de las Cuadrillas, established the practices surrounding the altar that held their image of their patron saint of Saint Augustine, rituals that would continue into the second congregation described in the testimony from three years later. According to the witness María López, who provided the initial denunciation to the inquisitors, the congregations had occurred for at least a year during which time it gained notoriety among the street's residents. Multiple neighbors had indicated that the "religion [confraternity] left often

55   AGN, Bienes Nacionales, caja 1028, exp. 6, ff. 2v-3r.

with much virtue" for their spiritual processions, giving them the impression that "what they practiced appeared to be very true" to the Catholic faith.[56] Over the course of the year, word about the congregations spread through various social networks, as individuals shared their experiences in the congregations with their friends and family, encouraging them to attend the ceremonies.[57] Isidro de Peralta's congregation, in time, gradually took a lead in the communal devotional practices that defined the religious life of the San Juan de la Penitencia neighborhood.

Functioning within the authoritative space afforded by confraternal piety – in the influential positions as *mayordomos*, rectors, deputies, and treasurers – *cofrades* of African descent governed diverse confraternities with minimal clerical intervention. Despite the church's mandates for ecclesiastical supervision, confraternities generally operated as self-governing institutions with the power to administer to the specific needs of their confraternities. With such independence, they determined the constitutions of their organizations, removing those that negatively affected their community or adding others that would better serve their spiritual endeavors. They controlled the finances that drove their spiritual practices, entered into litigation to defend their organization's rights, and disciplined the moral transgressions of their members.[58] In positions of leadership sanctioned by church authorities, black officers drew from an officially recognized form of spiritual authority to define the boundaries of confraternal piety for their immediate congregations and the neighborhoods and parishes where they enacted their spirituality.

Eight years after their foundation, the officers of the Confraternity of the Most Precious Blood of Christ, located in the parish center of Santa Catalina Mártir, petitioned the ecclesiastical authorities with the request to alter the constitutions and ordinances that governed their brotherhood. They informed the vicar general, Don Antonio de Aunzibay y Anaya, that such changes proved imperative to their effective operation because "without the changes that [they] present [they] cannot comply" with the ordinances that honored God.[59] Upon receiving ecclesiastical approval, the *mayordomo* Nicólas de la Ygera, the deputy mayor Miguel Real, and the rector Luis

---

56   HL, HM 35168, ff. 4v-5r.

57   Ibid., f. 12.

58   For examples of the finances of black confraternities, see the *libros* of finances from the Confraternity of the Most Precious Blood of Christ: AGN, Indiferente Virreinal, caja 4830, exp. 014 (1712-1735); AGN, Indiferente Virreinal, caja 3207, exp. 008 (1734); AGN, Indiferente Virreinal, caja 5128, exp. 012 (1750).

59   AGN, Indiferente Virreinal, caja 2235, exp. 23, f. 2r (1694-1696).

Montaño amended five ordinances from the original constitution, redefining crucial elements of their communal worship. They resolved, for instance, that the organization needed another officer, known as the *mayoral*, who would oversee the devotions practiced by the confraternity's sisters. As *mayoral*, the elected official selected the mother *mayores* who arranged the *pasos* of Our Lady, of the Santo Eccohomo, and of Jesus of Nazareth for the discipline of light and blood on Holy Thursday, placing their devotional practices directly under his control. As a central feature for the procession of discipline on Holy Thursday, a restructuring of the *pasos* lead by the brotherhood's women determined who could participate in the sacred devotions and delineated how those devotions took place.[60] Combined with the other four amendments that addressed the masses held for the major celebration to the Ascension of Christ and financial obligations of the *mayordomo* and the rector, the officers' decision to reform the ordinances centered on their personal choices about the operation of confraternal piety within their brotherhood.

More than merely dictating the spiritual obligations of the confraternity's members, black leaders of local brotherhoods additionally maintained the power to discipline the moral transgressions of their fellow brothers or even expel individuals for their failure to uphold confraternal statutes. Often without major clerical intervention, this moral policing of black confraternal piety remained fully in the hands of the black *mayordomos*, rectors, and deputies who determined appropriate spiritual devotions for communal worship. As leaders of the self-governing body of the faithful with the power to police moral behavior, black *cofrades* shaped the definitions of appropriate communal religious behavior. On May 2, 1696, for example, the *mayordomo*, Diego Real, of the Confraternity of the Spilling of the Blood of Christ, Our Lord and Our Lady of Consolation, petitioned ecclesiastical authorities for permission to hold their *cabildo* the following day, as was the custom. In his request, Diego begged the Cathedral's vicar general to issue a ban against one of their *cofrades*, José de Loaiza, who had proven to the officers to be unworthy of the spiritual graces offered by the brotherhood. During previous *cabildos*, processions, and celebrations, Diego explained, José arrived at the festivities in a drunken state and with a poor temperament, "disrupting and disquieting" the procedures.[61] As a punishment for acting "to the contrary of [the] disposition" of their brotherhood, they wanted José banned from

60 Ibid., f. 3.
61 AGN, Indiferente Virreinal, caja 5173, exp. 050, Cofradía del Derramamiento de Sangre, fol. 1r (1696).

"having a vote or a voice [...] in the said election."[62] For the officials of the confraternity, José could remain a member of the brotherhood, receiving its spiritual benefits. But until he improved his behavior, he would lose the rights to have a say in the brotherhood's religious proceedings. By prohibiting José from participating in the election, which went against the confraternity's constitutions that gave the right to a "vote and a voice" of every member in all cabildos, the *cofrades* acted to curb the moral indecency exhibited by José in the previous gatherings.

Conclusion

Over the course of the seventeenth century, brotherhoods designated as black, pardo, or moreno functioned alongside confraternities and *cofrades* of diverse racial classifications in the spiritual practices that drove the religious life of their neighborhood. Within the specific brotherhoods founded by individuals of African descent, this association with the devotional life of their local parishes rested on their emotional attachment to the personal relationships they forged in the shifting dynamics of the parochial boundaries – in local chapels, the marketplace, or neighborhood streets. As an inherently creole experience, black creoles founded religious brotherhoods closely attached to the colony's parish centers where they enacted their Catholic faith with their friends, family, neighbors, and acquaintances of various status and *calidad*. Even in confraternities where constitutions restricted positions of authority to individuals of African descent, membership remained open to the intergenerational and interracial relationships they had forged in the sacred and secular spaces of the parish.

In time, confraternities founded by persons of African descent served as an integral aspect of the social and cultural landscape of New Spain's parochial centers. They maintained an intimate connection to the fellow parishioners, *cofrades*, and parish priests who formed the social foundation of their communal religious practices. Individuals who composed their parochial social networks, men and women of "various status and *calidad*," entered their sacred organizations, paying entrance fees, donating time, money, and material objects to the spiritual devotions sanctioned by the black founders, and attending all festivities and celebrations. In positions of leadership – as *mayordomos*, rectors, deputy mayors, and treasurers – black *cofrades* delineated the boundaries of conventional communal worship for their friends,

62   Ibid.

family, neighbors, and acquaintances. They wrote constitutions, ordinances, and statutes that outline appropriate religious behavior, maintained financial control over the spiritual obligations of the organization's members, and policed the moral transgressions of any individual associated with their brotherhood. Through the officially recognized authoritative space afforded by confraternities, black *cofrades* fashioned parish-centered devotions that brought together separate social classes around a shared conception of the Catholic Faith. In short, black confraternities situated in the complex, ever-changing social dynamics of the colonial parish functioned as part of the colony's social and cultural milieu, not as a social organization distinct from it.

About the author

Krystle Farman Sweda received her Ph.D. from the Graduate Center, The City University of New York in 2020. Her larger research examines the emergence of Catholicism and its local expressions among Africans and their descendants in seventeenth-century New Spain. She currently works in Research Development under the Office of the Vice President for Research at the University of Kentucky, Lexington.

Archives

Archivo General de la Nación (Mexico City)
Bienes Nacionales
Indiferente Virreinal
Archivo Histórico del Arzobispado de Michoacán (Casa de Morelos)
The Huntington Library (San Marino, CA)
Manuscript Collection

Bibliography

Bennett, Herman. *Colonial Blackness: A History of Afro-Mexico.* Bloomington: Indiana University Press, 2009.
Black, Christopher. "Confraternities and the Parish in the Context of Italian Catholic Reform." In *Confraternities and Catholic Reform in Italy, France, and Spain*, edited by John Patrick Donnelly and Michael W. Maher, 1-26. Kirksville: Thomas Jefferson University Press, 1998.

Bristol, Joan. "Afro-Mexican Saintly Devotion in a Mexico City Alley." In *Africans to Spanish America: Expanding the Diaspora*, edited by Sherwin K. Bryant, Rachel Sarah O'Toole, and Ben Vinson, III, 114-135. Champaign: University of Illinois Press, 2012.

——. *Christians, Blasphemers, and Witches: Afro-Mexican Ritual Practice in the Seventeenth Century*. Albuquerque: University of New Mexico Press, 2007.

Bryant, Sherwin. *Rivers of Gold, Lives of Bondage: Governing through Slavery in Colonial Quito*. Chapel Hill: University of North Carolina Press, 2014.

Flynn, Maureen. *Sacred Charity: Confraternities and Social Welfare in Spain, 1400-1700*. London: Macmillan Press, 1989.

García-Ayluardo, Clara. "Confraternity, Cult, and Crown in Colonial Mexico." Ph.D. diss. University of Cambridge, 1989.

von Germeten, Nicole. "Black Brotherhoods in Mexico City." In *The Black Urban Atlantic in the Age of the Slave Trade*, edited by Jorge Cañizares-Esguerra, Matt D. Childs, and James Sidbury, 248-268. Philadelphia: University of Pennsylvania Press, 2016.

——. *Black Blood Brothers: Confraternities and Social Mobility for Afro-Mexicans*. Gainesville: University of Florida Press, 2006.

Larkin, Brian. "Confraternities and Community: The Decline of the Communal Quest for Salvation in Eighteenth Century Mexico." *Local Religion in Colonial Mexico*, edited by Martin Nesvig, 189-213. Albuquerque: University of New Mexico Press, 2006.

——. *The Very Nature of God: Baroque Catholicism and Religious Reform in Bourbon Mexico City*. Albuquerque: University of New Mexico, 2010.

Mulvey, Patricia A. "Black Brothers and Sisters: Membership in the Black Lay Brotherhoods of Colonial Brazil." *Luso-Brazilian Review*, 17, no. 2 (1980): 253-279.

Patterson, Orlando. *Slavery and Social Death: A Comparative Study*. Cambridge: Harvard University Press, 1982.

Proctor, Frank T., III. *Damned Notions of Liberty: Slavery, Culture, and Power in Colonial Mexico, 1640-1769*. Albuquerque: University of New Mexico Press, 2010.

Restall, Matthew. *The Black Middle: Africans, Mayas, and Spaniards in Colonial Yucatan*. Stanford: Stanford University Press, 2013.

Russell-Wood, A.J.R. "Black and Mulatto Brotherhoods in Colonial Brazil." *Hispanic American Historical Review* 54, no. 4 (1974): 567-602.

——. *Slavery and Freedom in Colonial Brazil*. Oxford: Oneworld, 2002.

Soares, Mariza de Carvalho. *People of Faith: Slavery and African Catholics in Eighteenth Century Rio de Janeiro*. Durham: Duke University Press, 2011.

Sweet, James. *Recreating Africa: Culture, Kinship, and Religion in the African-Portuguese World, 1441-1770*. Chapel Hill: University of North Carolina Press, 2003.

Terpstra, Nicholas. "Ignatius, Confratello: Confraternities as Modes of Spiritual Community in Early Modern Society." In *Early Modern Catholicism: Essays in Honour of John W. O'Malley, S.J.*, edited by Kathleen M. Comerford and Hilmar M. Pabel, 163-182. Toronto: Toronto University Press, 2003.

Vinson, III, Ben. *Bearing Arms for His Majesty: The Free-Colored Militia in Colonial Mexico.* Stanford: Stanford University Press, 2003.

—. *Before Mestizaje: The Frontiers of Race and Caste in Colonial Mexico.* Cambridge: Cambridge University Press, 2017.

Wheat, David. *Atlantic Africa and the Spanish Caribbean, 1570-1640.* Chapel Hill: University of North Carolina Press, 2016.

Part II

Indigenous and Black Confraternities in Peru

4   Confraternal "Collections"

Black and Indigenous *Cofradías* and the Curation of
Religious Life in Colonial Lima

Ximena Gómez
University of Massachusetts Amherst

Abstract
Taking advantage of Lima's rich documentary record, this chapter begins
the process of recovering the images, material culture, and devotional
interactions of black and indigenous confraternities that have been erased
by colonialism. I propose that if we consider each confraternity as a "collection," we can situate their documented sacred images and possession as
"inventory items" that were actively collected and thoughtfully displayed,
rather than objects that were passively owned. I argue that black and
indigenous confraternities curated their religious and social experiences
and, thereby, came to visually define the artistic religious landscape of
Lima in the sixteenth and seventeenth centuries.

Keywords: Peru, Andean Catholicism, black confraternity, colonial art,
material culture

Introduction

A monumental painting depicting a Good Friday procession (c.1660; Figure 4.1),
commissioned by the elite Spanish confraternity of the Virgen de la Soledad,
provides us with one of the only extant pictorial records of the material
grandeur of Holy Week in colonial Lima, the capital of viceregal Peru.[1] At

---

1   Part of a pair, the other painting is equal in size and depicts the front of the procession
in Lima's central plaza and includes earlier scenes from the Passion. Documentation for the
two paintings is no longer extant, but it is presumed that both were commissioned by the elite

Javiera Jaque Hidalgo and Miguel A. Valerio. *Indigenous and Black Confraternities in Colonial
Latin America: Negotiating Status through Religious Practices.* Amsterdam: Amsterdam University
Press, 2022
DOI: 10.5117/ 9789463721547_CH04

the far right of the painting, an ephemeral Calvary tableau is set beneath an awning, against the facade of the Chapel of La Soledad. The central cross is empty with only a loosely draped cloth hanging from the cross bar, indicating that the sculptural image of Christ has already been removed and that the procession depicted is of the *Santo Entierro*, or Holy Burial. With candles in their hands, a continuous line of elite Limeños process along, including regular clergy, members of the military, holy women, and *cofrades* from the Spanish nobility. The stream of wealthy participants is punctuated by sacred images, borne aloft on litters (*andas*). In the painting, at the front of the procession, the image of Christ appears wrapped in a cloth and lying upon an elaborate silver bier adorned with tall candles (*cirios*). The Virgin, wearing a black mantle and kneeling under a canopy (*palio*), follows her son on an elaborate golden platform. A final image tableau represents a scene of the Supper at Emmaus and sits on a simpler, wooden platform, decorated with candles and a dozen flowerpots, overflowing with red and white bunches of flowers (*ramos*). Each of the litters is accompanied by four external bearers, whose faces are concealed, and several more carrying the weight from behind the *andas'* blue skirts (*faldones*). Each element, splendid on its own, combines to create a marvelous religious spectacle in which the Soledad *cofrades* and their images play a starring role.

The procession has drawn a multiracial crowd of Limeños as well, some still exiting the church. In the foreground, people are shown in the act of worship, such as the indigenous men captured in the process of falling to their knees at the sight of the Holy Sepulcher. In front of the Virgin, a black child and his mother approach a *limosnero* (alms collector) in order to make a donation and thereby show their devotion to the image. Much of the crowd in the painting's upper portion sit and dutifully watch the spectacle, including some from the comfort of the carved wooden balconies for which Lima is well-known. Others, meanwhile, engage in commercial activities in the buildings' stalls and social interactions not immediately related to the religious spectacle. These interactions leave the viewer with the impression of a bustling seventeenth-century city, with a fervent piety activated through confraternal visual culture.

With a paucity of extant visual evidence for the colonial period, this painting of a mid-seventeenth century Holy Week procession has come to serve as an exemplary visual document of confraternal devotion in colonial

---

confraternity of the Virgin of la Soledad and were meant to be displayed in the sodality's chapel, adjoining the Church of San Francisco, where they still hang.

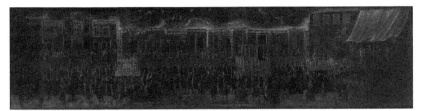

Figure 4.1. Anonymous, *Procesión del Santo Entierro*, c. 1660, Church of Nuestra Señora de la
Soledad, Lima, Peru. Courtesy of the Confraternity of Nuestra Señora de la Soledad, Lima, Peru.

Lima.[2] However, commissioned by an elite *cofradía* and meant for private
display in their confraternal chapel, the painting necessarily and purposefully focuses on its central subjects. While black and indigenous Limeños are
certainly present, they appear primarily as passive onlookers of the religious
festivities being carried out before them. At most, when shown actively
engaging in religious devotion in the painting, subalterns effectively serve
as evidence of the success of the colonial evangelization project. That is to
say, the painting does document confraternal devotion and visual culture
in Lima – but only for the city's small population of elite Spanish people.

But what of all the rest? The black, indigenous, and mixed-race people,
who comprised the vast majority of Lima's population? To date, the sacred
images and *bienes* (movable goods, material possessions) of colonial Lima's
black and indigenous confraternities, have received limited scholarly attention.[3] Lacking extant examples, art historians have largely overlooked these
objects, despite their important role in confraternal devotion, consequently
excluding them and their devotees from art historical accounts. The images
that do remain, such as the miraculous statue of Lima's Virgin of Copacabana
and the copy of the painted Virgin of the Antigua, have predominantly
been examined in a manner that artificially separates them from their
confraternal contexts.[4] Confraternal *bienes*, in turn, have been discussed

2   The painting has been dismissed as being of "sub-par" quality and redeemed by its value
as a glimpse into religious practice in Lima: see, for example: Jorge Bernales Ballesteros, "La
pintura en Lima durante el Virreinato," in *Pintura en el Virreinato del Perú: El libro de arte del
centenario* (Lima: Banco de Crédito del Perú, 2001), 57-58.
3   Guillermo Lohmann Villena discusses some confraternal goods, though only of Spanish
sodalities, in the context of Lima's Holy Week. Guillermo Lohmann Villena and Luis Eduardo
Wuffarden, *La semana santa de Lima* (Lima: Banco del Crédito del Perú, 1996).
4   For a full bibliography and extended discussion on the Virgin of Copacabana and the Virgin
of the Antigua and their respective confraternities, see Chapters 3 and 4 of my dissertation:
"Nuestra Señora: Confraternal Art and Identity in Early Colonial Lima" (University of Michigan,
2019).

by cultural historians interested in Limeño *cofradías*, but very briefly and primarily in terms of their economic value as registered in inventories.[5]

This chapter begins the process of recovering the art and visual culture of Lima's black and indigenous confraternities, as well as the documented ritual practices through which *cofrades* engaged with these objects, in order to incorporate them into the art historical scholarship on early modern Latin America. By focusing on black and indigenous people, we do not just learn about the secondary, "niche" practices of viceregal subjects. Rather, by centering the art and ritual of those who comprised the overwhelming majority of Lima's residents, we get a richer understanding of religious practice in Lima and colonial Spanish America. This is an important distinction to make, as the unrelenting and singular interest in art historical scholarship on colonial Lima on colonial Spanish culture is typically treated as unavoidable or unproblematic, thereby dismissing the artistic and cultural contributions of black and indigenous people.

Given the limitations of the archival record and the epistemological legacies of the colonial world, it is imperative that we approach the *cofrades* as active participants within the colonial visual culture in which they participated.[6] To that end, I propose that, if we use an analogy and consider the material and visual culture related to each confraternity as a kind of "collection," we can situate their documented sacred images and *bienes* as "inventory items" that were collected and displayed through purposeful curation, rather than as objects that were passively owned. The word "collection" evokes images of the early modern *Kunst-und Wunderkammer* or the modern museum designed to educate the public, in both cases an accumulation of objects funded by an elite patron or institution with the intent of display.[7] However,

5   See Teresa Egoavil, *Las cofradías en Lima, siglos XVII y XVIII* (Lima: Universidad Nacional Mayor San Marcos, 1986), 8-12.

6   Many have discussed the limitations and silences of the archive, as well as the ways in which these can be overcome: see, for example: Christina Elizabeth Sharpe, *In the Wake: On Blackness and Being* (Durham: Duke University Press, 2016); Gayatri Chakravorty Spivak, "Can the Subaltern Speak?," in *Can the Subaltern Speak?: Reflections on the History of an Idea*, ed. Rosalind C. Morris (New York: Columbia University Press, 2010), 21-78; Saidiya V. Hartman, *Lose Your Mother: A Journey along the Atlantic Slave Route* (New York: Farrar Straus and Giroux, 2007); Gayatri Chakravorty Spivak, *A Critique of Postcolonial Reason: Toward a History of the Vanishing Present* (Cambridge: Harvard University Press, 2003); John Beverley, *Subalternity and Representation: Arguments in Cultural Theory* (Durham: Duke University Press, 1999).

7   Art historians Lia Markey and Daniela Bleichmar and cultural historian Surekha Davies have looked at the practice of collecting in the early modern world as a means of engaging with the larger historical questions and narratives of the period, though this has been done almost exclusively through the lens of Europeans collecting "exotic" and "foreign" objects: Lia Markey, *Imagining the Americas in Medici Florence* (University Park: Pennsylvania State University Press,

in *Collecting Across Cultures*, Daniela Bleichmar and Peter C. Mancall stated "there was no single individual or group who determined what all [early modern] collections might contain," citing how "African princes [...] captured members of other African groups so they could acquire the newest kinds of cloth produced in Europe" and "Native Americans sought colored glass beads made in Europe, often trading them to other groups."[8] Though these examples are problematic, their contention that the definition of the early modern collection can and should be broadened is useful. Furthermore, Ivan Bargna, whose research addresses modern practices in Bandjoun, Cameroon, begins with the assumption that "collecting is not a Western prerogative or the consequence of colonial domination, but a bundle of different, widespread, transcultural practices of shaping and representing reality." He argues that collections are "forms of concrete thinking operating through things, in ways that are always locally diversified."[9]

In this light, the acts of founding a confraternity, commissioning a primary sacred image, often of the Virgin, as well as other images for devotional use, and acquiring *bienes* that supported religious activities and differentiated individual cults, could be considered as a form of "shaping and representing" their colonial Limeño realities. Thinking about colonial Lima's black and indigenous confraternities in this way, we may understand that subaltern *cofrades* were curating their images and adornments for parochial viewers on a daily basis and for a municipal audience during large celebrations like processions. Reaching a much wider audience than their elite early modern counterparts, required participation in religious processions on principal feast days gave black and indigenous *cofradías* a platform for the public display of their collections. This chapter, then, demonstrates how, through engagements with their sacred images, black and indigenous *cofrades* played active roles in the visual definition of the religious landscape of colonial Lima. In so doing, not only are subaltern participants in confraternal visual culture made visible, but crucially, the vast majority of the city, thereby revealing the constitutive fabric of the religious life of one of early modern Spanish South America's foremost cities.

2016); Daniela Bleichmar, "The Imperial Visual Archive: Images, Evidence, and Knowledge in the Early Modern Hispanic World," *Colonial Latin American Review* 24, no. 2 (2015): 236-266; Surekha Davies, *Collecting Technology in the Age of Empire*, forthcoming.

8   Daniela Bleichmar and Peter C. Mancall, *Collecting across Cultures: Material Exchanges in the Early Modern Atlantic World* (Philadelphia: University of Pennsylvania Press, 2013), 2.

9   Ivan Bargna, "Collecting Practices in Bandjoun, Cameroon: Thinking about Collecting as a Research Paradigm," *African Arts* 49, no. 2 (2016): 20.

Sacred Images

Since Lima was the self-imagined stronghold of Spanish culture in the Andes, subaltern confraternities were limited by the boundaries of colonial normative Catholicism. As such, the documentary record demonstrates that Lima's subaltern sodalities owned and operated with the same kinds of images and goods as their Spanish counterparts. Nevertheless, as with the institution of sodalities, their art and *bienes* were implicated in the process of creating distinctive corporate identities.

Though limited to popular Spanish devotions, Lima's black and indigenous *cofrades* played active roles in the commissioning of their cult statues. At times, such as when a group's central image was a painting, commissioning a sculpture was necessary so that the confraternity could fully engage in many colonial religious practices. The indigenous Candelaria *cofradía*, founded in the Franciscan church, for example, owned both an image for the altar and a separate one for use in processions.[10] Crucially, confraternities were able to commission locally made images, which meant that subaltern *cofrades* had the chance to be involved in the design of their devotional statues.[11] Without extant examples, we cannot know what these images looked like, aside from guessing that those named after specific cult images, such as the Virgen de Aguas Santas or the Virgen de Loreto, might have shared formal similarities with the Spanish originals. However, even that is not necessarily the case, since visual likeness was not strictly necessary for early modern copies.[12] Thus, through the act of generating their own objects of devotion black and indigenous confraternities were effectively visually redefining well-known Spanish images. While this would not necessarily have any implications for the Spanish cults with which these colonial confraternal image advocations were linked, it would have had real implications for the religious visual landscape of Lima, especially in the case of the processional

---

10   AAL, Cof., Leg. 6-A, Exp. 9, fol. 15r (1676).

11   This appears to have been the case with the Virgin of Copacabana: Gómez, *"Nuestra Señora,"* Chapter 3.

12   On the issue of visual likeness, see Jane Garnett and Gervase Rosser, *Spectacular Miracles: Transforming Images in Italy from the Renaissance to the Present* (London: Reaktion Books, 2013), 196. On the reproduction of miraculous images, see: Caroline Walker Bynum, *Christian Materiality: An Essay on Religion in Late Medieval Europe* (New York: Zone Books, 2015), 52-53; Clara Bargellini, "Originality and Invention in the Painting of New Spain," in *Painting a New World: Mexican Art and Life, 1521-1821*, ed. Donna Pierce, Rogelio Ruiz Gomar, and Clara Bargellini (Denver: Denver Art Museum, 2005), 78-91; Thomas B.F. Cummins, "On the Colonial Formation of Comparison: The Virgin of Chiquinquirá, The Virgin of Guadalupe and Cloth," *Anales Del Instituto de Investigaciones Estéticas* 21, no. 75 (1999): 51-77.

sculptures that frequently passed through the capital's streets. In other words, a Virgin that appears to be "Spanish" in text, due to its devotional title, is complicated in its visual form by subaltern patrons in the process of defining their collectivities.

The material qualities and limitations of the polychrome sculptures had an impact on the distinctive visual cultures Lima's black and indigenous *cofrades* fashioned through their devotions. Confraternal images were continually involved in processes of accretion and modification through ritual touch, renovation, and adornment.[13] The process of periodic renewal typically entailed repainting and the replacing missing pieces. In September 1614, the elite indigenous Rosario *cofradía*, in the Church of Santo Domingo, hired the Spanish-born artist, Cristóbal de Ortega (b.1548), to "gild [*dorar*], scratch designs into the gold [*estofar*], paint, apply flesh tones [*encarnar*], and renew [*renovar*] the image of Our Lady of the Rosary again, which they have in the indigenous chapel of the said advocation," so the sodality could place the Virgin on a litter for procession.[14] The wording in the contract seems to purposefully distinguish between processes related to the practical reapplication of missing materials through restoration (*dorar, pintar*) and those related to the renewal and modelling of the Virgin's distinctive features (*estofar, encarnar, renovar*), suggesting that the *cofradía* had hired the painter to do work that was both practical and ritual. Furthermore, Ortega specifies that this was not the first time he had been commissioned by the confraternity for this purpose, which may be an indication that the *cofrades* trusted the painter to carry out the task.[15]

The black confraternity of the Virgen de los Ángeles, founded in the the church of La Merced, appears to have had their image renewed for primarily practical reasons. For example, in 1641, in preparation for the feast of Corpus Christi, the *cofradía* paid three pesos "for the painter who decorated the face and hands of the Virgin, which were mistreated and it

---

13   Megan Holmes, *The Miraculous Image in Renaissance Florence* (New Haven: Yale University Press, 2013), 166.

14   Archivo General de la Nación (hereafter AGN), PNXVII, Prot. 53, fol. 790r (September 15, 1614): "yo el dho xpoval de ortega me obligo de dorar estofar e pintar y encarnar y rrenovar de nuevo la echura de la ymagen denra señora dell rrosario que tienen en la capilla de los naturales de la dha advocación." The confraternity requested that the image be completed in time to be processed in the naval *fiesta* that was to take place in the Dominican monastery that year. Ortega was paid 60 pesos for completing the work.

15   This possibility seems especially likely because Ortega had and maintained many ties to indigenous confraternities in the city, including that of the Virgin of Copacabana, for which Ortega painted and gilded the statue. Furthermore, the confraternity may have sought out Ortega as a direct response to the Virgin of Copacabana's purported sweating miracle in 1591.

was necessary to decorate her."[16] Two years later, the sodality's *mayoralas* (female confraternity officials) spent 35 pesos to restore the Virgin, which included replacing some of her fingers that had "broken."[17] The frequency of repairs is not indicative of the image being cheaply made. To the contrary, the image, commissioned in 1640, cost the confraternity 250 pesos, a substantial sum.[18] To some extent, damage was inevitable, especially, in Lima's extremely humid climate. In 1590, for example, the black confraternity of the Virgin of Aguas Santas had to pay nineteen pesos to restore a sculpted image of the Virgin of Aguas Santas that had been "eaten by moths, degraded, and discolored."[19] More likely, however, the damage sustained by the Virgen de los Ángeles described above came as a result of the confraternity's ongoing interactions with the sculpture at the center of their cult. In these ways, the sculpture's sixteenth- and seventeenth-century *cofrades* left devotional marks on their sacred image, thereby continually redefining the visual qualities of the early colonial image through their active engagement.

Dressing the Virgin

The polychrome wooden statues were rarely displayed unadorned, with their materials of manufacture fully manifest – their carved wooden features and applied pigments and gold. Rather, in the colonial period, as now, Lima's cult images were difficult to discern from beneath continually changing layers of adornments. Even images with fully carved clothing were ritually adorned with mantles, wigs, jewelry, veils, and more.[20] These were among

16   Archivo Arzobispal de Lima (hereafter, AAL), Cof., Leg. 10-B, Exp. 17, fol. 27r (1641): "tres patacones q di a graviel de la vega y a lucas de quiñones para El pintor que adereço El rrostro y manos de la Virgen q estava maltratado y fue nesesario aderesarlo."
17   AAL, Cof., Leg. 10-B, Exp. 17, fols. 34r; 46r (1643). On February 5, 1643 the confraternity paid Diego de Torres, the painter, one peso to paint the fingers. They paid the sculptor, Diego Muñoz y Prado, four pesos for the fingers and another 30 pesos of unspecified work on the image of the Virgin.
18   AAL, Cof., Leg. 10-B, Exp. 17, fol. 46v (1640). The confraternity did not pay for the sculpture in one lump sum. They collected alms specifically for this purpose on at least two occasions in 1640 and paid Doña Catalina in several small installments.
19   AAL, Cof., Leg. 42, Exp. 2, 40r (1590): "mas de aderesar una ymagen de nuestra cofradia de nuestra señora de aguas santa questava comida de polilla y desbrada y descolorida costo dies y nueve pesos." It is unclear if this was the confraternity's primary sculpture of the Virgin or, more likely, just an image in the confraternity's collection, like the canvas painting of the Virgin of Aguas Santas or small sculpture of the Virgin that the *cofrades* used to solicit donations.
20   Dressing sacred images is by no means unique to Peru or the Spanish Americas; the practice had existed for centuries in various parts of Europe well before Lima was founded. See: Richard

the primary items that confraternities acquired for their "collections" and it is through the application of these decorative *bienes* that the curatorial agency of black and indigenous cofradías is most in evidence.

Writing about the early colonial period, the Augustinian chronicler Antonio de la Calancha (1584-1654) described that "it was custom at that time to dress images of the Virgin with clothing, skirts, and head coverings, in the style in which noblewomen dress."[21] The Augustinian church's statue of the Virgen de la Gracia, for example, was dressed with "rich embroideries of gold, silk, and silver, and of brocades and costly fabrics of silver, silk, and gold, adorning her with rich jewelry, pearls, and precious stones."[22] The practice caused concern for the Church, resulting in the Second Lima Council (1576-1581) issuing a decree stating that "the image of Our Lady or of any female saint cannot be adorned with the clothes and garments of women, nor should they put on the cosmetics or colors used by women. [The image] could, instead, wear some rich mantle that the image has with it."[23]

Nevertheless, as early as 1594, the statue of the Virgin of the Repose, which belonged to the multiracial, Spanish-led confraternity in the church of San Lázaro, is recorded to have owned at least three dresses – white, yellow, and green – donated by a widowed devotee on her deathbed.[24] The word used in

C. Trexler, "Dressing and Undressing Images: An Analytic Sketch," in *Religion in Social Context in Europe and America, 1200-1700* (Tempe: Arizona Center for Medieval and Renaissance Studies, 2002), 65; William A. Christian Jr., *Local Religion in Sixteenth-Century Spain* (Princeton: Princeton University Press, 1981), 159; Manuel Trens, *María: iconografía de la Virgen en el arte español* (Madrid: Plus Ultra, 1945), 642.

21   "Usavase entonces vestir a las Imagenes de la Virgen con ropas, sayas i tocas al modo que se visten las mugeres nobles" Antonio de la Calancha, *Coronica moralizada del orden de San Augustin en el Peru: con sucesos egenplares en esta monarquia* [...] (Barcelona: Pedro Lacavalleria, 1639), 569-570.

22   Ibid., 570: "i esmeravase Dona Juana en que los vestidos de la Virgen fuesen de ricos bordados de oro, seda i plata, i brocados i telas costosas de plata, seda i oro, adornandola con ricas joyas de perlas, i piedras preciosas."

23   Rubén Vargas Ugarte, ed., *Concilios Limenses (1551-1772)*, vol. 1 (Lima: Tipogr. Peruana, 1951), 125: "53. que los ovispos vissiten las ymagenes y las que hallaren mal hechas e indecentes o las aderecen o quiten del todo y la imagen de nuestra señora o de qualquiera santa no se adorne con bestidos y trages de mugeres, ni le pongan afeites o colores de que usan mugeres, podrá empero ponerse algún manto rrico que tenga la imagen." Stanfield-Mazzi has argued that dressing practices in the Altiplano followed the Council's decree, suggesting that the clothing placed on the Virgins in this region were limited to gauze gowns with a rich mantle overlay. Maya Stanfield-Mazzi, *Object and Apparition: Envisioning the Christian Divine in the Colonial Andes* (University of Arizona Press, 2013), 81.

24   AAL, Cof., Leg. 40, Exp. 2, fol. 35r (1594): "maria de quiros siendo biuda poco antes que muriesse no se acuerda que tantas dias dio para el dho altar la ymagen de bulto pequeña de nra sra con tres vestidos uno blanco, otro berde y otro leonado."

the inventory, *vestido*, usually means dress, but can also mean clothing, and the confraternity clarified that in the case of the yellow *vestido*, the garment was a skirt (*saya*) paired with a cape (*manto*). However, the subsequent *vestido* was described as a "white taffeta dress *de la china*, adorned with golden fringe, with a cape of lace, [and] a blouse embroidered with a glittery, golden crown." These were immediately followed by the gold and silver head scarf the Virgin was apparently wearing at the time, in addition to a crystalline rosary, all the trappings of elite women at the time.[25] In spite of the recent decree of the Second Lima Council, the confraternity was not dressing their Virgin like this surreptitiously, as *Bachiller* Hernando Martínez, an ecclesiastic *visitador* and beneficiary of the Cathedral, officially approved the confraternal records.[26]

The surviving seventeenth-century inventories of black and indigenous confraternities further attest to the fact that the prohibition was not heeded.[27] Perhaps the most overt evidence of this is the 1676 inventory of the wealthy, indigenous *cofradía* of the Virgin of the Candelaria, in the Church of San Francisco, in which they described their processional Virgin as "a sculpted image of Our Lady that is dressed with a shirt, petticoat, and doublet with an underskirt of red damask."[28] In addition, among a large number of sumptuous *mantos* and opulent pieces of jewelry, the sodality recorded an entire section entitled "dresses and capes," making an explicit differentiation between the two categories of clothing.[29] It included a pink (*carne de doncella*) skirt (*saya*) and doublet of a textile with metallic thread and golden stars, a skirt (*pollera*) of blue lustrous silk with silver flowers, and a black *saya*, *manto*, and doublet that the Virgin wore during lent, veils, and head scarves, all used to adorn the sacred image.[30]

Furthermore, though it does not appear have occurred every time an image's adornments were changed, it was not uncommon for colonial Limeño

25   AAL, Cof., Leg. 40, Exp. 2, fol. 57v (1594): "otro vestido de tafetan de la china blanco guarneçido con una franja de oro ancha con un manto de toca Raxada una camisa de la dicha ymagen bordada con una corona de oro escarchado = un panuelo de cortado de oro y plata q tiene la ymagen en la cabeça – un Rosario de Cristal." The descriptor "de la china" was used in colonial Latin America to denote anything that came vaguely from outside of Europe, but especially from the Spanish Philippines and Japan: "un vestido de tafetan leonado y amarillo que es saya y manto."
26   AAL, Cof., Leg. 40, Exp. 2, fol. 57r (1594).
27   AAL, Cof., Leg. 6, Exp. 14, (1642); AAL, Cof., Leg. 10-B, Exp. 17, fol. 26r (1640-1641); AAL, Cof., Leg. 54, Exp. 10, fol. 5r (1661).
28   AAL, Cof., Leg. 6-A, Exp. 9, fol. 15r (1676): "mas una ymagen de na sa de bulto que se biste con camisa naguas y jubon faldellin de damasco carmesí."
29   AAL, Cof., Leg. 6-A, Exp. 9, fol. 17rv (1676).
30   AAL, Cof., Leg. 6A, Exp. 9, fols. 17v-18v (1676).

confraternities to send their images to a *señora*'s home in preparation for special occasions.[31] *Cuentas* from the indigenous confraternity of the Virgin of Loreto, located in the Church of Santa Ana, give us some insight. On the occasion of the feast of Corpus Christi in 1650, the confraternity sent their Virgin to the home of a woman whom they paid two pesos, two chickens, and a peso worth of fruit to adorn (*aderezar*) their Virgin.[32] Based on the *mayordomo*'s purchases on the day of the *fiesta*, we know that the image was adorned with jasmine, had her hair curled into ringlets, and had a candle affixed to her hands with two large, luxurious ribbons.[33] Once the image was ready, on the morning of the feast, it was transported back to the church of Santa Ana with great pomp, accompanied by a band of musicians, probably all Afro-descendants, playing the *caja* (drum), *clarín* (trumpet), and *chirimías* (shawms).[34]

The above examples make it clear that Lima's black and indigenous confraternities used the *bienes* in their collection to adorn their Virgins "in the style in which noblewomen dress" and did so very deliberately. But why did the *cofrades* dress the Virgin in more than just a *manto* if the clothes beneath were not likely to be visible and it was theoretically prohibited? Writing about the colonial Peruvian Altiplano, Maya Stanfield-Mazzi has argued that dressing images "contributed to an ever-changing image of the statue-as-divinity."[35] This seems apt for the Limeño context as well. Thus, we

---

31   AAL, Cof., Leg. 39-A, Exp. 2, fol. 21v (1654); AAL, Cof., Leg. 10-B, Exp. 17, fol. 26r (1640-1641); AAL, Cof., Leg. 30, Exp. 10, fol. 1r (1654).

32   AAL, Cof., Leg. 30, Exp. 9, fol. 15v (1650). The chickens were worth ten reales each, bringing the total for her payment to three pesos and four reales. Later the same year, the confraternity paid a woman four reales to dress the Christ Child: AAL, Cof., Leg. 30, Exp. 9, fol. 17r (1650). It is possible that the woman was a confraternity member, though affiliation is designated elsewhere in the Loreto confraternity's *cuentas* and *cofrades* were not typically paid for services rendered to their sodality. Moreover, in 1653 the indigenous Rosario *cofradía* (Santo Domingo) similarly contracted a *señora* to adorn their image for the *fiesta* of Nuestra Señora del Naval, specifying that the *cofrades* had paid her twelve pesos "because others were charging 30 pesos": AAL, Cof., Leg. 39-A, Exp. 2, fol. 21v (1653).

33   AAL, Cof., Leg. 30, Exp. 9, fol. 15v (1650). The ribbons (*listones*) cost six pesos and three reales, the jasmine cost two pesos, and the glass and coal or charcoal (*carbón*) used to curl the hair cost four reales.

34   AAL, Cof., Leg. 30, Exp. 9, fol. 15v (1650). They paid two pesos and four reales for the music. According to the research of the musicologist Kydalla Young, when confraternal account books recorded racial categories for musicians, woodwind and brass performers were usually identified as black and sometimes indigenous, while drummers were typically black. Kydalla Etheyo Young, "Colonial Music, Confraternities, and Power in the Archdiocese of Lima" (Ph.D. Diss., University of Illinois, Urbana-Champaign, 2010), 120-121.

35   Stanfield-Mazzi, *Object and Apparition*, 81.

might conclude that cloth's nature as a "transformative medium" provided subaltern *cofradías* the opportunity to use their decorative *bienes* to curate manifestations of the divine that suited their religious experiences.[36]

Beyond Luxury

Black and indigenous Limeño *cofrades* drew from the visual language of luxury as part of the decoration of their sacred images. Indeed, confraternities explicitly detailed the European provenance of their fabric *bienes*, as the indigenous Copacabana confraternity, located in the its eponymous church, did with a chestnut-colored Italian cape worn by their image of Saint Marcellus.[37] At the same time, examples like the Reposo Virgin's white taffeta dress *de la china* show that cosmopolitan splendor was not only derived from Europe. This particular transregional circulation of goods was a feature of colonial Latin America, afforded by a geography positioned between multiple global trade routes.

In the colonial world, as in Golden Age Iberia, sumptuous riches were the visual language of power. Indeed, Susan Webster has argued that the extravagant adornment of sacred images in Seville was popular because it allowed confraternities to "participate in a realm of power, prestige, and glory that once had been exclusively reserved for royalty."[38] If Lima really was the alter-Seville that art historical scholarship characterizes it to be, we might conclude that dressing images with worldly splendor similarly allowed black and indigenous confraternities to engage with the viceregal elite. It would appear, however, that while Lima's subalterns could not afford to ignore the colonial powers in their ritual dressing of sacred images, black and indigenous *cofradías* were also pointedly performing with and for each other.

This may be supported by the many instances in which subaltern confraternities did not rely solely on sumptuousness, foreign or otherwise, to

36 Jane Schneider, "Cloth and Clothing," in *Handbook of Material Culture*, ed. Chris Tilley, Webb Keane, and Susanne Kuechler (London: Sage, 2006), 204.

37 AAL, Cof., Leg. 10A, Exp. 6, fol. 8r (1659). See also AAL, Cof., Leg. 6-A, Exp. 9, fol. 18r (1676), which notes that the indigenous candelaria confraternity had "un capisallo del monto rico con puntas de oro de milan [an undershirt, richly assembled, with golden [puntas] from Milan]" for the Christ Child.

38 Susan V. Webster, "Shameless Beauty and Worldly Splendor on the Spanish Practice of Adorning the Virgin," in *The Miraculous Image in the Late Middle Ages and Renaissance*, ed. Erik Thunø and Gerhard Wolf, Analecta Romana Instituti Danici, Supplementum, 33 (Rome: L'Erma di Bretschneider, 2004), 271.

convey the status of their sacred images. Lima's *cofrades* often incorporated ephemeral elements that augmented and personalized their cult images. The black Rosario Virgin, for instance, was adorned with rosemary and basil on several occasions during Lent in 1668.[39] The aromatic herbs were not commonly used in the *fiestas* of seventeenth-century Lima, suggesting that the value of their addition was particular, and certainly not monetary.[40]

Flowers, meanwhile, were used regularly in the ritual decoration of images, as can be seen in the popular genre of statue paintings. It is not surprising that the indigenous Rosario community would use flowers to decorate their Virgin. What is of interest, however, is the fact that a peso's worth of flowers and other decorations were individually sewn onto the Virgin's *manto*.[41] This is laborious work, but would have added a singular, personalized touch to the Virgin's decoration. Moreover, the effect would have approximated a floral textile, like the *manto* with "flores grandes" worn by the Virgen de los Ángeles, whose confraternity was in La Merced in 1692, a variant of a common colonial type of cloth.[42] These ephemeral additions would have added to the resplendence of the already luxurious textile to which the flowers were affixed.

Returning to the account of Antonio de la Calancha, the Augustinian went on to explain that San Francisco's Virgen de la Gracia had been allowed to continue wearing elite women's clothing after the Second Lima council prohibited it for the rest of the city, because "if richness drew curious eyes, the beauty of the image won over common devotion, which is very important, for as soon as our nature declines in spiritual matters, let the eyes negotiate hearts through delightful images."[43] The Augustinian seems to have drawn a direct correlation between splendor and, specifically, popular devotion. If so, by dressing their images in the elite trappings of noblewomen, black and indigenous confraternities would have called the attention of other faithful like themselves, thereby increasing devotion to their particular images. Put differently, a confraternity's *bienes* had the power to entice

---

39   AAL, Cof., Leg. 31, Exp. 25, fol. 13r (1668).

40   This is the only confraternity that I have seen use these herbs to decorate an image.

41   AAL, Cof., Leg. 39-A, Exp. 2, fol. 21v (1653): "Mas compre tres reales de Alfiler = y otras tres reales de clabito = dos reales de hilo para quajar los floresçitos y otros adornos que le pusieron en el manto de nra señora son un patacon."

42   AAL, Cof., Leg. 10-B, Exp.42, fol. 2r (1692): "un manto de tela blanca con flores grandes guarnesido de puntas grandes y otras pequeñas al buelo aforrado en tafetan nacar."

43   Calancha, *Coronica moralizada*, 570: "Lo rico si se llevava los ojos de la curiosidad, la belleca de la Imagen ganava la comun devocion, que inporta mucho, segun se descaece nuestra naturaleza en las cosas espirituales que sean las Imagenes deleytables, con que los ojos suelen negociar coracones."

Limeños to look at the curated spectacle of their sacred sculptures and, thereby, their reified devotion.

Conclusion

With limited control over the advocation of their cult and a real necessity to adhere to colonial norms of adornment, we might imagine that Lima's black and indigenous *cofrades* were drawn less to a static sculpture and more to the dynamic nature of dressing and presenting it. By putting the image in a continuous state of transformation, the act of dressing allowed subaltern confraternities to define and redefine sacred images at their discretion. Thus, although the sacred image was the primary object in the confraternity's "collection," it was the applied adornment that most empowered black and indigenous *cofrades* in asserting themselves within the religious landscape of Lima.

This calls to mind Richard Trexler's assertion regarding miraculous images: "I wish to stress how mistaken we are when we describe these images as if they were in a museum, stripped to the bone and divested of all the ornaments of clothing and honors with which they were earlier dressed. In fact, they had clearly owed their so-called miraculosity to these features, heaped on them by rustic legends, power-seeking rulers and other devotees."[44] From this perspective, the barrier to the art historical study of Lima's black and indigenous confraternities may not reside in the loss of their sacred images, but in the total lack of extant examples of the clothing, jewelry, wigs, and capes through which they were defined.

To be clear, I am by no means arguing that the confraternal images of Lima were unimportant for their colonial devotees or historians. Indeed, indigenous and black cofrades engaged with their sacred images in numerous ways and mobilized them to their benefit. Rather, I contend that, just as overlooking black and indigenous confraternities problematically limits our view of religious life in colonial Lima, discussing the *cofradías*' devotional sculptures separately from the adornments placed on them and the festive settings in which they were processed prevents us from fully understanding these sacred images.

---

44   Richard C. Trexler, "Being and Non-Being: Paramaters of the Miraculous in the Traditional Religious Image," in *The Miraculous Image in the Late Middle Ages and Renaissance*, ed. Erik Thunø and Gerhard Wolf, *Analecta Romana Instituti Danici*, Supplementum 33 (Rome: L'Erma di Bretschneider, 2004), 18.

In a sense, then, having neither the images nor the clothing of colonial Lima's black and indigenous *cofrades* is a boon. By considering the confraternity as a "collection," we are able to reassign agency to the devotees and see that sacred images were not just linked to numinous visions and miracles, and that the objects used to adorn them were not merely attempts to engage with colonial ideas of wealth. It would appear that the ritual act of dressing images provided black and indigenous people with the ability to activate their statues of painted wood and to "ennoble" them through attentive adornment in valued confraternal possessions. This ritual fashioning (pun intended) of the sculptures was simultaneously a self-defining act of representation for the subaltern sodalities.

Archival evidence thus presents an image of Lima quite distinct from that represented in painting with which this chapter began. While the elite Soledad *cofradía* that commissioned this painting would have us believe that life in the City of Kings and its festival culture were dictated by Spanish customs, Lima was, in reality, defined by its multiracial population. While the colonial Spanish may have held power over the subaltern majority, we have seen how, even within the confines of colonial norms, black and indigenous people defined Lima's religious landscape through their participation in devotion and festivals, and through the display of their confraternal art and *bienes* in their decorated chapels and in public procession.

About the author

Ximena Gómez is Assistant Professor in the Department of the History of Art and Architecture at the University of Massachusetts Amherst. She specializes in the art of colonial Latin America and that of the early modern transatlantic world more broadly. Her work has been published in *Colonial Latin American Review* and the edited volume, *A Companion to Early Modern Lima*. She is currently at work on her first book, which investigates the visual culture of Indigenous and Black lay confraternities in Lima during the sixteenth and seventeenth centuries.

Bibliography

Bargellini, Clara. "Originality and Invention in the Painting of New Spain." In *Painting a New World: Mexican Art and Life, 1521-1821*, edited by Donna Pierce, Rogelio Ruiz Gomar, and Clara Bargellini, 78-91. Denver: Denver Art Museum, 2005.

Bargna, Ivan. "Collecting Practices in Bandjoun, Cameroon: Thinking about Collecting as a Research Paradigm." *African Arts* 49, no. 2 (2016): 20-37.

Bernales Ballesteros, Jorge. "La pintura en Lima durante el Virreinato." In *Pintura en el Virreinato del Perú: El libro de arte del centenario.* Lima: Banco de Crédito del Perú, 2001.

Beverley, John. *Subalternity and Representation: Arguments in Cultural Theory.* Durham: Duke University Press, 1999.

Bleichmar, Daniela. "The Imperial Visual Archive: Images, Evidence, and Knowledge in the Early Modern Hispanic World." *Colonial Latin American Review* 24, no. 2 (2015): 236- 266.

Bleichmar, Daniela, and Peter C. Mancall. *Collecting across Cultures: Material Exchanges in the Early Modern Atlantic World.* Philadelphia: University of Pennsylvania Press, 2013.

Bynum, Caroline Walker. *Christian Materiality: An Essay on Religion in Late Medieval Europe.* New York: Zone Books, 2015.

Calancha, Antonio de la. *Coronica moralizada del orden de San Augustin en el Peru: con sucesos egenplares en esta monarquia* [...] Barcelona: Pedro Lacavalleria, 1639.

Christian Jr., William A. *Local Religion in Sixteenth-Century Spain.* Princeton: Princeton University Press, 1981.

Cummins, Thomas B.F. "On the Colonial Formation of Comparison: The Virgin of Chiquinquirá, The Virgin of Guadalupe and Cloth." *Anales Del Instituto de Investigaciones Estéticas* 21, no. 75 (1999): 51-77.

Egoavil, Teresa. *Las cofradías en Lima, siglos XVII y XVIII.* Lima: Universidad Nacional Mayor San Marcos, 1986.

Garnett, Jane, and Gervase Rosser. *Spectacular Miracles: Transforming Images in Italy from the Renaissance to the Present.* London: Reaktion Books, 2013.

Gómez, Ximena A. "Nuestra Señora: Confraternal Art and Identity in Early Colonial Lima." Ph.D. diss. University of Michigan, 2019.

Hartman, Saidiya V. *Lose Your Mother: A Journey along the Atlantic Slave Route.* New York: Farrar Straus and Giroux, 2007.

Holmes, Megan. *The Miraculous Image in Renaissance Florence.* New Haven: Yale University Press, 2013.

Lohmann Villena, Guillermo, and Luis Eduardo Wuffarden. *La semana santa de Lima.* Lima: Banco del Crédito del Perú, 1996.

Markey, Lia. *Imagining the Americas in Medici Florence.* University Park: Pennsylvania State University Press, 2016.

Schneider, Jane. "Cloth and Clothing." In *Handbook of Material Culture,* edited by Chris Tilley, Webb Keane, and Susanne Kuechler, 203-220. London: Sage, 2006.

Sharpe, Christina Elizabeth. *In the Wake: On Blackness and Being.* Durham: Duke University Press, 2016.

Spivak, Gayatri Chakravorty. *A Critique of Postcolonial Reason: Toward a History of the Vanishing Present*. Cambridge: Harvard University Press, 2003.

——. "Can the Subaltern Speak?" In *Can the Subaltern Speak?: Reflections on the History of an Idea*, edited by Rosalind C. Morris, 21-78. New York: Columbia University Press, 2010.

Stanfield-Mazzi, Maya. *Object and Apparition: Envisioning the Christian Divine in the Colonial Andes*. Tucson: University of Arizona Press, 2013.

Trens, Manuel. *María: iconografía de la Virgen en el arte español*. Madrid: Plus Ultra, 1945.

Trexler, Richard C. "Being and Non-Being: Paramaters of the Miraculous in the Traditional Religious Image." In *The Miraculous Image in the Late Middle Ages and Renaissance*, edited by Erik Thunø and Gerhard Wolf, 15-27. Analecta Romana Instituti Danici, Supplementum, 33. Rome: L'Erma di Bretschneider, 2004.

——. "Dressing and Undressing Images: An Analytic Sketch." In *Religion in Social Context in Europe and America, 1200-1700*, edited by Trexler, 374-408. Tempe: Arizona Center for Medieval and Renaissance Studies, 2002.

Vargas Ugarte, Rubén, ed. *Concilios Limenses (1551-1772)*. Vol. 1. 3 vols. Lima: Tipogr. Peruana, 1951.

Webster, Susan V. "Shameless Beauty and Worldly Splendor on the Spanish Practice of Adorning the Virgin." In *The Miraculous Image in the Late Middle Ages and Renaissance*, edited by Erik Thunø and Gerhard Wolf, 249-271. Rome: L'Erma di Bretschneider, 2004.

Young, Kydalla Etheyo. "Colonial Music, Confraternities, and Power in the Archdiocese of Lima." Ph.D. diss. University of Illinois Urbana-Champaign, 2010.

5 "Of Greater Dignity than the *Negros*"

Language and In-Group Distinctions within Early Afro-Peruvian *Cofradías*[1]

Karen B. Graubart
University of Notre Dame

Abstract

Enslaved and free men and women of African origins or descent in Lima, Peru joined Catholic cofradías in order to form community. The earliest records of Lima's African-descent cofradías reveal some of the ways that members found community, as well as dealt with growing schisms and fissures due to the Atlantic slave trade and local racialized hierarchies. Peruvians of African descent drew upon their contemporary experiences, adapting the European rhetoric of "difference" deployed against them, to identify and police their own divisions during the first century of the institutionalization of African slavery in Spanish America. These documents also provide us with an early history of how African *naciones*, often misdiagnosed as ethnicities, came to be central to diasporic identities.

Keywords: Peru, black confraternity, African diaspora, black Catholicism, race, ethnicity

Introduction

In June 1791, the pseudonymous author Hesperióphylo offered the reading public of the *Mercurio Peruano*, an important journal of Peru's creole

---

1 A previous version of this chapter appeared as "'*So color de una cofradía*': Catholic Confraternities and the Development of Afro-Peruvian Ethnicities in Early Colonial Peru," *Slavery and Abolition* 33, no. 1 (2012): 43-64. I am grateful to Gad Heuman for permission to update and reprint it.

Javiera Jaque Hidalgo and Miguel A. Valerio. *Indigenous and Black Confraternities in Colonial Latin America: Negotiating Status through Religious Practices.* Amsterdam: Amsterdam University Press, 2022

DOI: 10.5117/ 9789463721547_CH05

enlightenment, two short essays titled "Idea de las congregaciones públicas de los Negros Bozales," or a description of the public meetings of African-born Black slaves.[2] Premised on the inhumanity of slavery and the consolation enslaved Africans found in the Catholic Church, the essays contemplated the ways in which these "unhappy men and women" organized themselves into *cofradías* which both deepened their relationship with the Church and provided more secular entertainment and community. Indeed, *cofradías* serving members of African origin or heritage were formed within a decade of the conquest of Peru in 1531-1532, and – like the city's other *cofradías* – flourished in the sixteenth and seventeenth centuries, despite repeated attempts by the Church and the Crown to rein in their enthusiastic increase.[3] Hesperióphylo noted that "the first thing [slaves arriving from Africa] do is join a *cofradía*; these maintain the social networks of their respective communities."

Those "respective communities" were the African ethnicities to which the author claimed the enslaved belonged, the ten major *castas* or *naciones*, which he enumerated as: Terranovos, Lúcumes, Mandingas, Cambundas, Carabalíes, Cangoes, Chalas, Huarochiríes, Congos, and Misangas.[4] These terms, he tells us, did not necessarily refer to birthplaces – some referred to a coastal port of embarkation for the New World, while the enslaved more likely came from interior locations and were transferred to the coast; others he called "arbitrary," including "Huarochiríes," for the highlands just east of Lima, perhaps referring to the slaves sent to work on the agricultural plantations that provisioned the city. The author compared the "savage" behavior of these ethnically distinct *bozales* [African-born, or non-hispanized slaves] with the more "civilized" demeanor of creole slaves, those acclimated to Lima, having shed their originary difference in favor of Peruvianess. Characteristically, the *cofradías* founded by these *castas* would process on holy days in the most obstreperous, noisy and disagreeable fashion, he complained, dressed as devils and animals, bearing weapons, with their faces painted "according to the fashion of their homelands."[5]

2   Hesperióphylo [Joseph Rossi y Rubí], "Idea de Las Congregaciones Públicas de Los Negros Bozales," Pt. 1, *Mercurio Peruano* 48 (June 16, 1791): 112-117; Pt. 2, *Mercurio Peruano* 49 (June 19, 1791): 120-125.

3   For attempts to limit *cofradías*, see *Concilios Limenses (1551-1772)*, ed. Rubén Vargas Ugarte, vol. 1 (1551-1772; reprint: Lima: Tipografia Peruana, 1951), 369; Miguel A. Valerio "'That There be No Black Brotherhood': The Failed Suppression of Afro-Mexican Confraternities, 1568-1612," *Slavery and Abolition* 42, no. 2 (2021): 293-314.

4   Hesperióphylo, "Idea," pt. 1, 115.

5   Ibid., 117.

Hesperióphylo assumed that *casta* – which he already conceived of as an elastic category – was not only the defining factor for the African captives but had always been so. Black *cofradias*, he tells us, were founded by *naciones*: "In past times the Terranovos and Lúcumes were dedicated to the cult of the image of San Salvador in the great church of Nuestra Señora de las Mercedes [...] The Mandingas likewise had an *hermandad* in the Church of the great monastery of San Francisco dedicated to the Virgin under the advocation of Nuestra Señora de los Reyes; nowadays it is in ruins."[6] Most modern scholars of the Atlantic slave trade agree that these names – Mandinga, Congo, Terranova, etc. – privilege the ways that slave merchants and colonial officials imagined the political or cultural organization of the places they had raided rather than consistent geographic, linguistic, religious, or cultural groupings internal to inhabitants of the African continent.[7] But, in the New World, enslaved persons themselves also adopted the framework for their own uses, deploying them to mark communities alongside other means they used to describe their place.

The records of Lima's earliest confraternities provide narratives missing from our understanding of how men and women would come to inhabit the categories that come so readily to modern researchers: Indians, Blacks, and all the mixed-heritage names of great or little traction. These categories began as shorthand for lawmakers, administrators and entrepreneurs, who used them to identify people who owed taxes or received corporate privileges or were legally (or illegally) enslaved.[8] But relatively quickly some of those

6   Hesperióphylo, "Idea," pt. 2, 116.
7   For example, Mariana P. Candido, "Jagas e Sobas No 'Reino de Benguela': Vassalagem e Criação de Novas Categorias Políticas e Sociais No Contexto Da Expansão Portuguesa Na África Durante Os Séculos XVI e XVII," in *África: Histórias Conectadas*, ed. Alexandre Ribeiro, Alexsander Gebera, and Marina Berthet (Niterói: Universidade Federal Fluminense, 2015), 39-76, and "Slave Trade and New Identities in Benguela, 1700-1860," *Portuguese Studies Review* 19, nos. 1-2 (2011): 59-76; Paul E. Lovejoy and David Vincent Trotman, eds., *Trans-Atlantic Dimensions of Ethnicity in the African Diaspora* (London: Bloomsbury, 2004); Joseph Calder Miller, *Way of Death: Merchant Capitalism and the Angolan Slave Trade, 1730-1830* (Madison: University of Wisconsin Press, 1996); Linda M. Heywood, and John K. Thornton, *Central Africans, Atlantic Creoles, and the Foundation of the Americas, 1585-1660* (New York: Cambridge University Press, 2007), Chapter 3; Rachel Sarah O'Toole, "From the Rivers of Guinea to the Valleys of Peru: Becoming a Bran Diaspora within Spanish Slavery," *Social Text* 25, no. 3 (2007): 19-36. The names do provide ways for thoughtful scholars to analyze the experiences of enslaved people: see David Wheat, *Atlantic Africa and the Spanish Caribbean, 1570-1640* (Chapel Hill: University of North Carolina Press, 2016).
8   Critical studies of the use of racial and ethnic categories in the colonial period include David Cahill, "Colour by Numbers: Racial and Ethnic Categories in the Viceroyalty of Peru, 1532-1824," *Journal of Latin American Studies* 26, no. 2 (1994): 325-346; R. Douglas Cope, *The Limits of Racial Domination. Plebeian Society in Colonial Mexico City, 1660-1720* (Madison, Wis.: University of

described by these terms – which ignored existing distinctions of status, local ethnicity and other historically loaded issues – redefined and even embraced them, recognizing the power of appropriating the rhetoric of those in power.

Scholars have long studied the ethnogenesis or creolization of Indigenous, African-descent, and European-descent communities across the Atlantic world.[9] These histories of men and women formulating conjunctural diasporic identities out of variegated experiences have been vital to the development of a truly Atlantic history, one that recognizes connections and transformations in Europe's violent encounters with the Americas and Africa. This scholarship, which had origins in British and Portuguese Atlantic studies, has been critically improved by conversation with the insights of African historians.

Historians of Africans in Spanish America traditionally investigated the worlds of slavery and its resistance, as well as the opportunities free people of color created for themselves; until recently few have asked about the nature of ethnogenesis or the formation of diasporic ethnicities in the mainland Spanish colonies, parallel to that of the British Atlantic and Portuguese Brazil, and rarely in those terms.[10] A new wave of historians has begun to ask how members of the African diaspora, especially in densely populated cities like Lima, where they might live in conditions that allowed for some autonomy and close relationships with Indigenous and Spanish neighbors, transformed and created their own colonial identities.[11] Given the extraordinary archival holdings of Latin America, where African-descent

Wisconsin Press, 1994); O'Toole, "Castas y Representación en Trujillo Colonial," in *Más Allá de La Dominación y La Resistencia: Estudios de Historia Peruana, Siglos XVI-XX*, ed. Leo J. Garofalo and Paulo Drinot (Lima: Institutos de Estudios Peruanos, 2005), 48-76.

9   For the concepts of creolization and ethnogenesis, see Sidney Mintz and Richard Price, *Anthropological Approaches to the Afro-American Past: Caribbean Perspectives* (Philadelphia: Institute for the Study of Human Issues, 1976); Ira Berlin, "From Creole to African: Atlantic Creoles and the Origins of African-American Society in Mainland North America," *William and Mary Quarterly* 53, no. 2 (1996): 251-288; Rachel Corr, and Karen Vieira Powers, "Ethnogenesis, Ethnicity and 'Cultural Refusal': The Case of the Salasacas in Highland Ecuador," *Latin American Research Review* 47 (2012): 5-30.

10   See Herman L. Bennett, "Writing into a Void: Representing Slavery and Freedom in the Narrative of Colonial Spanish America," *Social Text* 93, no. 25:4 (2007): 67-89.

11   For example, Juan Carlos Estenssoro Fuchs, "Los Colores de La Plebe: Razón y Mestizaje En El Perú Colonial," in *Los Cuadros de Mestizaje Del Virrey Amat: La Representación Etnográfica En El Perú Colonial*, ed. Natalia Majluf (Lima: MALI, 1999:, 67-107; José Ramón Jouve Martín, *Esclavos de la ciudad letrada: esclavitud, escritura y coloniliasmo en Lima (1650-1700)* (Lima: IEP, 2005); Christine Hunefeldt, *Paying the Price of Freedom: Family and Labor Among Lima's Slaves, 1800-1854* (Berkeley: University of California Press, 1995); O'Toole, *Bound Lives: Africans, Indians, and the Making of Race in Colonial Peru* (Pittsburgh: University of Pittsburgh Press, 2012); Tamara

peoples appear often, albeit rarely with unmediated voices, it will be possible to tell more stories about the ways that enslaved and free people of African descent imagined their own lives.

This chapter uses the fragmentary *cofradía* records of Lima's Archivo Arzobispal to ask what the rhetoric of African and African-descent *cofrades*, free and enslaved, tells us about the development of racialized hierarchies within early Lima, the capital of the viceroyalty of Peru. It does so by considering their arguments for superiority within the Catholic world in the context of the rhetoric deployed against them by Europeans. These documents demonstrate how the peoples we today group together as Afro-Peruvians recognized distinctions and schisms within that collectivity, and utilized this rhetoric to identify and police their divisions during the period when African slavery was being institutionalized in South America.

African Lima

Lima was founded as a "Spanish" city in 1535, by which its Spanish founders meant that they had removed many of its Indigenous inhabitants, and then imported a Black and Indigenous workforce to provide necessities and comforts for its European elite. The conquistador Francisco Pizarro had received access to the site upon negotiating with the region's *kuraka* or Indigenous local leader, Taulichusco.[12] Taulichusco's town had to be remade in the model of a classical European city: Pizarro maintained the Indigenous ceremonial plaza as the city's centerpiece and deconstructed its adobe *huacas* or ceremonial pyramids, turning them into the adobe houses and gridded streets destined for Spanish notables.[13] Lima's former inhabitants, now tributaries of their new overlords through the labor-tribute mechanism known as *encomienda*, built this new city, likely alongside small numbers of African slaves that arrived with the Spaniards. The city filled with temporary and permanent Indigenous laborers, many migrating from the nearby valleys.

In addition to this fundamental Indigenous presence in the city, Lima was also Black. A few African men accompanied Pizarro's forces into the

---

J. Walker, *Exquisite Slaves: Race, Clothing, and Status in Colonial Lima* (Cambridge: Cambridge University Press, 2017).

12　María Rostworowski de Diez Canseco, *Señoríos indígenas de Lima y Canta* (Lima: IEP, 1978), Chapter 2.

13　Patricia Morgado Maurtua, *Un palimpsesto urbano: del asiento indígena de Lima a la ciudad española de Los Reyes* (Seville: University of Seville, 2007).

Andes, perhaps as *negros de acompañamiento* (or Black conquistadors).[14] The chronicler Pedro de Cieza de León recounted a story from their arrival at coastal Tumbés in 1528: the Spanish author recounted Indigenous residents' supposed surprise when they learned that a conquistador's dark skin did not lighten with washing.[15] The discovery and expropriation of the region's enormous wealth drew settlers with their servants and slaves from the rest of the Americas towards Peru, but the dense Indigenous population made the massive importation of slaves unnecessary for the first few decades, until epidemic disease and the costs of continued warfare changed the balance.

By the 1550s, the importation of African slaves began to take off, particularly along the coast where Indigenous populations declined precipitously and their lands were converted into large agricultural enterprises. Frederick Bowser estimates that Lima contained some 1500 Afro-Peruvians by the mid-1550s, approximately the same number as inhabitants of Spanish origin.[16] The rough parity between Spaniards and Africans continued over the course of the century, according to the sparse (and somewhat incommensurate) documentation we have, including censuses (Table 5.1).

Slavery was crucial for Lima's development as a population center and as the political and ceremonial seat of the viceroyalty. Spanish settlers rapidly purchased lands in surrounding valleys, transforming Indigenous lands into large ranches and haciendas. As coastal Indigenous populations declined, owners of haciendas began to purchase enslaved laborers to replace them. Urban denizens also turned to slave labor. Artisans relied upon enslaved assistants in their workshops, large households – including the massive religious institutions that lined Lima's streets – used them as servants, and elites signaled their status through the ostentatious presentation of enslaved accompaniment, including armed men, in their public life. Slavery underwrote the city's economy and contributed to its sense of spectacle.[17]

Lima's African-descent population included a significant free contingent. Jouve Martín estimates that nearly a quarter of all Black people in the city were free by the turn of the seventeenth century.[18] These men and women mostly achieved manumission because they worked in urban households

---

14 Matthew Restall, "Black Conquistadors: Armed Africans in Early Spanish America," *The Americas* 57, no. 2 (2000): 171-205.

15 The episode appears in Pedro de Cieza de León, *Crónica del Perú*, ed. Francesca Cantù (1553; reprint: Lima: PUCP, 1989), 57. Matthew Restall locates nineteen references to (anonymous, free and enslaved) Africans in Cieza's volume: Restall, "Black Conquistadors," 184.

16 Bowser, *African Slave*, 11.

17 On slavery and status, see Walker, *Exquisite Slaves*.

18 Jouve Martín, *Esclavos de la ciudad letrada*, 41.

Table 5.1: Ethnic breakdown of population of Lima, 1593-1636[19]

	1593		1600		1636	
Blacks		6690		6621	13,620	
Mulatos	(n/a)		(n/a)		861	
Spaniards	6100*		7193		10,758	
Indians		(n/a)		438	1,426	
Mestizos	(n/a)		(n/a)		377	
Total Pop	12,790		14,262		27,394	

* Category of "Spaniards" in 1593 included Indigenous and mixed populations.

or workshops, where they could be rented to others during slow seasons. They could save small amounts of the income they brought in through the institution known as *jornal*, a wage they shared with their masters. Many also earned side incomes by selling food or taking in washing.[20] They might have received manumission as a charitable gift, although this was one to which masters sometimes attached significant strings.[21] Much of Lima's enslaved population was probably in the process of self-purchase, which could take decades of life. The city, then, was full of men and women who were enslaved or slightly removed from enslavement, with profound experience in scrambling for their livelihood.

"So color de una cofradia": Black Brotherhoods in Lima

Africans joined Catholic sodalities from the very first arrivals in Lima. Evidence comes from a complaint heard by Lima's *cabildo* or city council in 1549, stating that slaves were getting together for dances, robbery, and drunken fiestas "*so color de una cofradía,*" or under the guise of a confraternity. In response, the *cabildo* ordered that no groups larger than three Black men

19   Frederick P. Bowser, *The African Slave in Colonial Peru, 1524-1650* (Stanford: Stanford University Press, 1974), 337-341. Lima also had a large transient Indigenous population, housed at its margins and in local valleys, and would have had a large number of enslaved men and women passing through from the port of Callao to endpoints across South America.

20   Emilio, Harth-Terré and Alberto Márquez Abanto, "Perspectiva Social y Económica Del Artesano Virreinal En Lima," *Revista Del Archivo Nacional Del Perú* 26, no. 2 (1962): 46. On the process of *coartación*, or gradual self-purchase see Alejandro de la Fuente, "Slaves and the Creation of Legal Rights in Cuba: Coartación and Papel," *Hispanic American Historical Review* 87, no. 4 (2007): 659-692.

21   Michelle A. McKinley, *Fractional Freedoms: Slavery, Intimacy, and Legal Mobilization in Colonial Lima, 1600-1700* (Cambridge: Cambridge University Press, 2016).

and women could congregate for dances or walking around the city or in a *cofradía*, with the exception of Sundays and holy days, between communion and mass, within the church itself.[22] This concern was reiterated in the reforms of the Catholic Church's Concilio Limense of 1582.[23] The Catholic Church had long mistrusted *cofradías* because of their relative autonomy. Indigenous and Black sodalities raised additional flags because they were new converts and people with languages and cultural practices not readily transparent to Spanish officials.[24]

While many of the *cofradías* established by religious orders for Spanish celebrants may have welcomed Indigenous and African members in the sixteenth century, there are distinct signs that their participation was limited, which likely encouraged them to form their own organizations. Multi-ethnic *cofradías* generally refused the election of non-Spaniards to the positions of *mayordomo* [annually-elected leaders] and *veinticuatro* [voting members who made policy decisions]. For example, the 1603 constitution of the *cofradía* of Nuestra Señora de la Soledad restricted its *veinticuatros* to those who were not "*mulatos* and *mestizos*, and should any of these be accepted as such, the *mayordomos* should eject them without impediment."[25] This demonstrates that non-Spaniards could and likely did participate in some Spanish confraternities, but also that they were not able to do so fully.

We have no direct archival evidence of Black participation in Lima's *cofradías*, however, until the late sixteenth century. Probably the oldest of the African-descent *cofradías* was Nuestra Señora de la Antigua, founded prior to 1574. La Antigua may well have been the subject of the *cabildo*'s

22 *Libros de Cabildos de Lima*, ed. Bertram T. Lee, Juan Bromley, Sophy E. Schofield, and Emilio Harth-Terré, eds., vol. 4 (1534-1821; first printed edition: Lima: San Martín, 1935), 55-56. Valerio shows that a royal decree against Black *cofradías* in New Spain was issued in 1570, and Mexico City's *cabildo* attempted unsuccessfully to enforce it in 1601: "'That There be No Black Brotherhood.'"

23 *Concilios limenses*, 1:360. This suspicion of using confraternities to carry out non-spiritual practices dates back to medieval Iberian kingdoms, where kings often restricted guild-confraternities out of fear of monopolistic practices and scandalous activities: see Susan Verdi Webster, *Art and Ritual in Golden-Age Spain: Sevillian Confraternities and the Processional Sculpture of Holy Week* (Princeton: Princeton University Press, 1998), 20.

24 On the continuation of Indigenous practices within the cofradía, see Rafael Varón Gabai, "Cofradías de indios y poder local en el Perú colonial: Huaraz, siglo XVII," *Allpanchis* 14, no. 20 (2020): 127-146; Olinda Celestino and Albert Meyers, *Las cofradías en el Perú: región central* (Frankfurt: Vervuert, 1981). On analogous local practices in Spain, see William A. Christian, *Local Religion in Sixteenth-Century Spain* (Princeton: Princeton University Press, 1989), 164.

25 As cited in Teresa Egoavil, *Las cofradías en Lima, ss. XVII y XVIII* (Lima: Universidad Nacional de San Marcos, 1986), 80.

complaints in 1549; its membership claimed in 1585 that they had been founded more than 40 years earlier.[26] The Franciscan *cofradía* of Nuestra Señora de los Reyes was, by the turn of the sixteenth century, the city's second oldest long-standing Black confraternity, and was considered the largest and wealthiest by far, according to the church's own census.[27] The few extant wills left by free Blacks in the sixteenth century refer to membership in these two, as well as in Rosario.[28]

Other *cofradías* for Black Limeños survived alongside these. In 1619, the city's archbishop issued a report identifying fifteen *cofradias* devoted to African and African-descent peoples, up from ten in 1585, and there were surely numerous others that briefly came into being and dissolved, due to lack of funds or inconstancy of worshippers.[29]

An active member or *veinticuatro* of a *cofradía* was required to make two kinds of contributions, both of which could be in short supply to an enslaved or newly freed person: an entrance fee, and flexible time for group activities including worship and alms collection.[30] Lima provided some opportunities for both. The *jornal* system and the dependence upon slaves as household or artisan labor meant that both slaves and freedpersons might have the flexibility to attend services or carry out institutional tasks, as well as contribute financially. But their economic and social instability meant that their *cofradías* likewise had precarious existences. The *mayordomos* of the Jesuit *cofradía* of San Salvador complained once that

> the said *cofradia* has not gone out [in procession] for a year [...] it is impossible to gather people together so early, as is ordered, because they are slaves [...] some of them cannot leave their work so early because their

26   Archivo Arzobispal de Lima (hereafter AAL), Cofradías 64:2 (1585).

27   Bowser, *African Slave*, 249.

28   Testamento de José Palomino, Archivo General de la Nación, Perú (hereafter AGN), Protocolos Notariales (hereafter PN) 64, Gutiérrez, ff. 190-191 (July 15, 1553); Testamento de Pedro Hernandes, AGN PN 62, Diego Ruíz, ff. 26-28 (January 8, 1562); Testamento de Magdalena de la Paz, AGN PN 68, Gutiérrez, ff. 662-665v (1566); Testamento de Lorenza de Guinea, AGN PN 136, Esteban Pérez, f. 887 (August 4, 1589); Testamento de Francisco Gamarra, AGN PN 80, Gutiérrez, ff. 1611-1613v (November 26, 1597).

29   Bowser, *African Slave*, 249. According to a 1585 document, there were by then 23 *cofradías* in the city overall, of which seven were for Indians, six for Spaniards, and ten for "*negros* and *mulatos*": Celestino and Meyers, *Las cofradías en el Perú*, 119.

30   Entrance fees varied, from a substantial amount like the 100 pesos required by the Spanish cofradía of Nuestra Señora del Rosario, to the modest four reales asked by the Indigenous and African branches of that brotherhood. In addition, cofrades contributed candles, made irregular donations for masses and other necessities, and often bequeathed property to the institution: Egoavil, *Las cofradías en Lima*, 3-4. AAL Cofradías 31:2 (1608).

masters won't let them, and the others because they support themselves with the work.[31]

The *mayordomo* of Nuestra Señora del Rosario in Lima, in 1608, explained that he could not help indict his predecessor for corruption because

> he is quite busy in taking care of what his master orders, particularly in (going to) make carbon in Pachacamac and other places outside the city where he usually spends one week or two or three and sometimes a whole month, and for this reason he has been absent from membership meetings that are held on Sundays in the chapel.[32]

Cofradías with enslaved membership faced special challenges in maintaining their numbers and their funding over time.

But *cofradías* also could soften the rough edges for enslaved or impoverished city-dwellers, particularly domestic servants and slaves who risked being abandoned by their masters when serious illness or injury struck. The accounts of Nuestra Señora de los Reyes indicate that some of its funds were used to subsidize the funerals of paying members as well as the larger community. One common entry reads, "there are thirty seven pesos and three reales that were spent on the funeral of a *negro biafara*, slave of don Pedro Hoces de Ulloa, because his master only gave twenty pesos and the funeral cost fifty-seven."[33]

This aspect of the *cofradia* – as a kind of mutual aid and burial society for the neediest – also gave Black and *casta cofradias* a reputation for disorder and corruption. Many of the records in the archives accuse officers of mismanagement of funds. In some cases it is clear that there was a lack of oversight, leaving the group open to the predations of con artists or simply incompetent or unskilled leadership.[34] In other cases we can see that, because authorities and elites assumed that Blacks could not manage their own affairs, they exaggerated the brotherhoods' problems, which were quite similar to those of Spanish *cofradías*. This denigration spilled into public acts as well, as crowds taunted the Afro-Peruvian brotherhoods during their

---

31   AAL Cofradías 47:3 (1629-1654).
32   AAL Cofradias 65:1 (1623) and Cofradías 31:2, f.17 (1608).
33   AAL Cofradías 51:2 (1608-1609).
34   Bookkeeping also required literacy and numeracy, skills that few enslaved or freed persons acquired. On the issue of African-descent people (especially slaves) and writing in this period, see Jouve Martín, *Esclavos de la ciudad letrada*.

solemn processions in Holy Week.[35] African and African-descent *cofradías* thus faced prejudicial readings of their everyday activities which drew upon a developing narrative of cultural inferiority.[36]

But segregation also allowed for beneficial limited autonomy. Had Black worshippers been integrated into multi-ethnic cofradías, not only would they have been excluded from positions of authority, but they would likely have been denied access to equal shares of collective funds. The Indigenous *cofradía* of Copacabana in Lima offered a cautionary tale. At the turn of the seventeenth century, it experienced a miraculous apparition that led to an influx of solicitations for membership, from "priests and judges, Inquisitors, and all the great people and the common folk," pouring funds into the organization's coffers. However, all this wealth and attention meant that the Indigenous *mayordomos* lost control over their finances and were left arguing with church officials about their right even to see their account books.[37] Instead, Africans and their New-World-born descendants mostly joined *cofradías* set apart for themselves. Yet within these semi-autonomous institutions, they themselves argued that they were not all the same, and they drew upon the rhetorics of difference and separation often used against them as they navigated their increasingly complicated society.

The Color of Freedom in the Sixteenth Century

In 1574, the mayordomos of Nuestra Señora de la Antigua, the oldest of Lima's longstanding Black *cofradías*, complained to church officials that the Franciscan *cofradía* of Nuestra Señora del Rosario had been given a more prestigious placement for Corpus Christi.[38] In the words of the complainants,

> We, the *moreno* [dark] brothers of the *cofradía* of Nuestra Señora de la Antigua of the Holy Church of this city, state that on the day of the festival of Our Lord last year, in the procession we had a disagreement with the brothers of the *cofradía* of Nuestra Señora of the monastery of San Francisco, because they wished to carry their banner behind ours, and the *alcaldes ordinarios* [...] ordered that the banner of San Francisco

35 See AAL Cofradias 64:1 (1574) and Cofradías 47:2 (1629-1654).

36 On this discourse, see O'Toole, *Bound Lives*.

37 AAL Cofradías 72:4 (1604). See also Alexandre Coello de la Rosa, *Espacios de exclusión, espacios de poder: el cercado de Lima colonial (1568-1606)* (Lima: IEP, 2006), Chapter 4.

38 AAL Cofradías 64:1 (1574).

go behind ours, which upset us, because our *cofradía* ought to receive
preference [...] because it belongs to the Cathedral [*iglesia matriz*], even
though the other's is older.

Apparently, this disagreement turned physical, as the two *cofradías* grabbed
at and tore each other's banner, despite the ruling of the local officials on the
spot that Rosario had the right to the more privileged position. La Antigua
ceded, apparently believing that the officials simply acted in a way to avoid
more conflict, and that this decision would not be binding upon future
processions. When they learned otherwise, they filed suit.

Black participants and witnesses offered testimony in this dispute that
utilized a more subtle tactic of defamation than the simple accusation of
violence. In their brief, the *mayordomos* of La Antigua referred both to
themselves and their foes as *morenos* while the *mayordomos* of Rosario in
their response referred to La Antigua's membership as *negros*, reserving
the term *morenos* only for themselves. This small linguistic point seems to
have been a clear insult, one intended to cast aspersions upon La Antigua's
case. Spanish authorities commonly used the umbrella term *negro* to refer
to all peoples of non-mixed African descent, but it appears that the African-
descent community linked it to slavery. Lima's free Black residents regularly
referred to themselves as *morenos* when they sought out a notary, and so
the Rosario *mayordomos* were attempting to cast aspersions on their rivals
by associating them with debased enslavement.[39]

The linguistic sparring seems to derive from the fact that La Antigua was
founded by enslaved men and women, though its membership, and especially
its officers, included free persons. Yet Rosario confraternities were usually
founded on behalf of the enslaved, and a roster for Rosario from 1608 – the
earliest yet located – names fifty-one members and/or donors; seven of these
are called "esclavos," and only three are labelled "free." The other forty-one
carry no marker of condition, though most of these carry ethnonyms (e.g.,
"Angola," "Anchica," "Biafara," "Sao Tomé") which suggest that they were
bozales, born in Africa, while just four have hispanized surnames, likely

39   While it is difficult, with notarial documents, to know when language comes from the
client or from a lawyer or scribe, in this case the term *moreno* only appears in documents
submitted by the two African-descent *cofradias*, while statements from church officials and
other Spanish-descent people simply call them all *negros*. Further evidence comes from wills
of the period, where free men and women of African heritage likewise referred to themselves
as *moreno* while the authorities only used negro: see Graubart, "The Bonds of Inheritance:
Afro-Peruvian Women's Legacies in a Slave-Holding World," in *Women's Negotiations and Textual
Agency*, ed. Mónica Díaz and Rocío Quispe-Agnoli (New York: Routledge, 2017), 130-150.

second generation or creoles and possibly free.[40] The three specifically marked "free" [*horro*] on the roster were all officers of the sodality, and it is possible that the complaining *mayordomos* were referring to their own condition rather than that of the entire membership. Thirty years earlier there would have been even fewer free Black people in Lima, and the majority of the membership of both *cofradías* would have been enslaved.

The association with freedom mattered to Lima's Black *cofrades*, and they often used this language of *moreno/negro* to underscore their free condition. In 1598, when he was accused of mishandling *cofradía* funds, Antón Aparias called himself *moreno* and referred to his nemesis as "Francisco Gamarra, *negro*." In a follow-up, the latter called himself "Francisco de Gamarra free *moreno*, bricklayer, official of the Holy Inquisition."[41] Gamarra, a Black freedman born in Spain, was demonstrably proud of his accomplishments, and took seriously the aspersions cast upon him by another free man. Because Lima and its *cofradías* were so interwoven with slavery, and because it took hard work plus more than a little luck to manumit oneself, those who were free developed a language that transformed European color distinctions to set themselves off from the less fortunate.

Spanish officials within the Catholic Church used these two terms interchangeably (with a slight preference for *negro* over *moreno*) when referring to African-descent peoples. Since nearly all Black people in the New World shared at least some ancestral link to slavery, Spaniards had little interest in defining how distant that relationship might have been: by the late sixteenth century dark skin was categorically associated with slavery.[42] And when non-Spaniards were naming themselves to themselves, terms like *negro*, *moreno*, *mulato*, *indio* and *mestizo* were often abandoned for more useful associations. In these documents, the so-called *casta* labels of racial hierarchy appear in the mouths of non-Spaniards mostly when casting aspersions on, or correcting, others for an audience. As Lima's population of enslaved people of African descent swelled, its free minority developed its own political language, which drew upon the discourses of those in power, but also reconfigured them. Yet as an attempt to make a winning argument to the Church, it most likely had no resonance.

---

40   AAL Cofradías 31:2 (1608).

41   AAL Cofradías 64:3 (1598-1599). See also his will which states that Gamarra was born in Llerena, Spain, and one of his two homes in Lima sat facing that of a former official of the Inquisition: AGN PN 80 Gutiérrez, ff. 1611-1613 (1597).

42   For this, and a case where Black Christians manipulated language about color in a different way, see Larissa Brewer-García, *Beyond Babel: Translations of Blackness in Colonial Peru and New Granada* (Cambridge: Cambridge University Press, 2020).

"Mulatos, sons of Spanish men": Mixed Parentage and Conflict

As men and women of African descent became a larger share of Lima's population, sexual relationships (both coerced and consensual) with non-Black partners produced children whose status was ambiguous: they might be enslaved or free, depending upon the status of their mother; they might receive privileges or financial benefits, depending upon the relationship with their father.[43] The existence of categories like *mulato* [Black-European], *mestizo* [Indigenous-European], and *zambaigo* [Indigenous-Black] owes in great part to the ambiguity of the place of these children in a legal and fiscal framework predicated upon a simple division between "Indians" and "Spaniards." The crown took contradictory positions depending upon perceived benefits to itself. Free Blacks and *mulatos* owed tribute, like Indians, but they were subject to Spanish authorities rather than their own local legal jurisdictions. Confraternity records reveal that Afro-Peruvians sometimes sought to exploit these ambivalences and, utilizing the discourses of the day, made strong claims for moral and political distinctions between *negros* and *mulatos*.

One early such conflict appears in the records. It was a challenge from the *mayordomos* of La Antigua to the *mayordomos* of Las Vírgenes [Santa Justa y Santa Rufina] over their place in the processions of 1585.[44] The *mayordomos* of Las Vírgenes had asked the ecclesiastic judge "that your Lordship find that we occupy the better place in the Corpus Christi procession than that of the said *negros* because we are sons of Spanish men, and persons, because of this, of greater dignity than the *negros*." This was, of course, met with outrage by the *mayordomos* of La Antigua, who rebutted, "they are *mulatos zanbaigos*, sons of *negra* women and Indian women and *mulata* women, and others of *morena* women and they have no more *calidad* [status] than do the *cofrades* of La Antigua."

La Antigua, as we have seen, was a *cofradía* that called itself *moreno* and free with great pride, an unlikely description undermined by at least one witness in the hearing who spoke of their "many captive" members.[45] Their rival for position, Las Vírgenes, called itself a *cofradía de los mulatos*, though

43   The most important study of the malleability of these categories and what was at stake remains Cope, *The Limits of Racial Domination*. On the gendered heritability of enslavement, see Jennifer L. Morgan, "*Partus sequitur ventrem*: Law, Race, and Reproduction in Colonial Slavery," *Small Axe* 22, no. 1 (2018): 1-17.

44   AAL Cofradías 64:2 (1585).

45   For example, see *mayordomos* mentioned in AAL Cofradías 64:1 (1574), 64:2 (1585), 64:3 (1598-1599). It is unlikely that their membership was even mostly free; in 1630 it had an enslaved *mayordomo*: AAL Cofradías 64:11 (1630).

its own evidence reveals that its membership likewise was more diverse; in the words of a witness there were "three or four *mulatos*, sons of Spaniards, and the rest of them are *zambaigos*, children of *negros* and Indians, and some are *morenos* and free."[46] This conflict is important because it reminds us that "Spanishness" and freedom conferred status, while distinctions between other ethnic groups were not yet entirely fixed, but clearly of interest and import to participants in this debate. As such, the arguments utilized by the *cofradías* were not premised so much on phenotype or descent, but rather on common discourses of civilization and civility, which would eventually become tethered to skin and biology but here were still relatively free signifiers. La Antigua argued their eminence in the city, their antiquity, that they were "free *morenos* and honorable people," and more numerous and wealthier than their counterparts in Las Vírgines. A witness went on to claim that he had seen "the *cofrades* and *mayordomos* [of Las Vírgines] drunk and they are men who have no job nor house." This line of questioning was even assisted by one of Las Vírgenes' own members, who admitted that La Antigua's brothers "have helped and do help [Las Vírgines] with their charity and their wealth." Students of colonial history will recognize this discourse as common both to European descriptions of the barbaric state of many Indigenous and African peoples, as well as the political debates around mestizos and mixing between the groups.

Here we can discern not only the new question of whether *mulatos* fell higher or lower on the social scale than free *morenos* (let alone *negros*) but also what a *mulato* was: was he the son of his Spanish father, or the son of his Black mother? Was he indeed the son of a Spaniard and a Black person or were his parents Black and Indigenous (sometimes called *zambaigo*), with no claim to Spanishness at all? In their own testimony, the Spanish witnesses (including priests and a painter) never invoked ethnic or color language. Instead each spoke of the honor, wealth, marital status, religiousity, and employment history of the aggrieved. It is clear that the inevitable mixtures of the numerically dominant groups were starting to pose interesting problems for some, and provided an opportunity to rethink racial hierarchies, though not yet in normalized ways. It is equally certain that *cofradías* could be mixed and diverse, yet benefitted from ascribing a mythical homogeneity to themselves, propped up with borrowings from colonial discourses of *calidad*.

Black *cofrades* borrowed from at least two contemporary discourses when they formulated these attacks on *mulato* brotherhoods. The first was an ongoing Iberian argument about the best source of slaves. According to Suárez de Figueroa, writing in 1615, Spain had three types of slaves,

> they are either Turks or Berbers or *negros*; the two former kind tend to be treacherous, badly-intentioned, thieves, drunkards, full of a thousand sensualities and commiters of a thousand crimes. They go about continually plotting against the life of their masters; their service is suspicious, dangerous, and thus worthy of avoiding. The *negros* are of a far better nature, easier to deal with, and, once trained, of great utility.[47]

As is well known, this line of thought was picked up and used to differentiate among sub-Saharan Africans as well. Slave traders not only recognized that men and women from certain regions had specific skills (as soldiers, metalworkers, or agriculturalists, for example) but they also priced their wares depending upon assessments of their supposed natures: "docile" *bozales* (non-assimilated or newly arrived Africans) versus lazy, resistant creoles (Spanish speakers or those raised in the colony) or rebellious Wolofs (due to the influence of Islam).[48]

The second discourse that resonates here is the ongoing debate about another group of mixed parentage: *mestizos*. From the early sixteenth century Spanish officials were making concerned pronouncements about *mestizos* "wandering in vagabondage," avoiding employment and causing trouble.[49] The main crime of the first generations of Indigenous-Spanish progeny seems to have been the failure of some parents to fully assimilate their children into one category or the other, leaving them beyond the clutches of any control or tax, and without access to community resources or individual wealth.[50] They were, as a result, collectively characterized as lazy, drunken and unemployed. Such terms were then associated to other liminal peoples, those who fell between the majority groups and thus ran the risk of being perceived as shirking group responsibility or taking unentitled privileges.

47   Cristóbal Suárez de Figueroa, *Plaza universal de todas las ciencias* (Madrid: Luis Sanchez, 1615), f. 307.

48   An important contemporary source is Alonso de Sandoval, *Un tratado sobre la esclavitud*, ed. Enriqueta Vila Vilar (1627; reprint: Madrid: Alianza, 1987).

49   Richard Konetzke, ed., *Coleccion de documentos para la historia de la formación social de Hispanoamérica, 1493-1810*, vol. 1 (Madrid: CSIC, 1953), 147, 168, 320-321, 333-334.

50   Many biological mestizos were likely assimilated into either Spanish or Indigenous societies and thus never counted as mestizos. But since most mulattos had an enslaved mother, there was little likelihood that a free father would recognize them, and thus they were either counted as *negros* or *mulatos*: Elizabeth Kuznesof, "Ethnic and Gender Influences on 'Spanish' Creole Society in Colonial Spanish America," *Colonial Latin American Review* 4, no. 1 (1995): 153-176.

The archives are full of examples of this use of *mulato* as a kind of catch-all for liminality and immorality. In a lawsuit brought by the *cofradía* of Nuestra Señora de Loreto in 1623, Pedro de Paz and Agustín de los Reyes each accused the other of criminal activity. Reyes accused Paz, "*moreno*, who claims to be a *veinticuatro*" of having pawned all the *cofradía*'s possessions (including the Virgin's crown) during his tenure as *mayordomo*. Paz replied, through the hand of his chaplain, that Agustín de los Reyes "*mulato sanbo* [*zambaigo*] who has made himself *mayordomo* and *cofrade* [...] illegitimately [...] has usurped much of the wealth and the charitable contributions of the *cofradía* that were in his power and moreover keeps a false account book."[51] Each time Paz referred to Reyes he repeated the phrase *mulato sanbo*, while calling all the other *cofrades* simply by name, with no epithet. As they did with *negro*, Afro-Peruvians were concocting a denigrating category that reflected internal divisions emerging in their larger community.

By the turn of the seventeenth century, Lima's residents of African descent were becoming even more heterogeneous. The second generation of men and women born to an African parent might have a Spanish or Indigenous parent as well. If the non-African parent was the father, that parentage would have no effect on the child's legal status as slave or free, but it is clear that some *mulatos* wanted to draw upon the privilege that an association with Spaniards could bring them. In response, Black subjects turned the discourse of *mestizaje* as a social problem against *mulatos*. While the membership logs of these *cofradias* show that in most cases they welcomed a broad mixture of members without concern as to parentage, the existence of exclusive *cofradias* – even if only in name – and the contemporaneous discourse demonstrate that African-descent peoples were developing self-images in conversation with the ruling elites. Moving into the seventeenth century, with a rapid increase in the volume of enslaved men and women entering the city, and consequential changes in their African places of origin, Lima's Afro-Peruvian *cofrades* made even more careful parsings as they negotiated their place in a complex colonial society.

Managing Heterogeneity in the Seventeenth Century: Castas and Naciones

Despite Hesperióphylo's insistence, in 1791, that newly arrived Africans in Lima had always sought out members of their own ethnic groups through

---

51   AAL Cofradías 65:1 (1623).

the institution of the *cofradía*, early records indicate that other alignments could be more central to group identity. But over time, *nación* and the elastic concepts the word encapsulated – language groups, cultural heritage, belief systems, histories – did rise to the surface in Lima's Black communities, as the author claimed. This final section examines the process through which some *cofradías* came to narrate their histories and identify their membership through *nación* in the seventeenth century.

The geographic origins of enslaved persons entering Lima's markets changed over the decades, as Portuguese and other European traders moved southward along the western coast of the African continent.[52] But traders also built on, and exacerbated, existing African networks and conflicts, creating what Joseph Miller calls a "violence frontier" on coasts that spread political conflict into internal regions.[53] It is important to note that our knowledge of that geography is, at times, limited. Slave traders gave enslaved men and women surname-like markers, appended to their new baptismal names, that appear to denote ethnic or geographic origins. These names, often referred to as *nación* or *casta* in the records, might more accurately refer to the port where slave merchants loaded them onto ships. Their actual origins might be far from those ports, often inland.[54] For this reason, we cannot assume that the ethnic labels attached to the individuals herein discussed refer necessarily to connections or ethnicities prior to enslavement, nor should we assume that those ethnicities were inevitably static either.[55]

The earliest African slaves in Lima either arrived from Seville or from Upper Guinea into a Caribbean port like Portobelo or Cartagena. From there they would have been taken on an overland route, onto another ship to sail down the Pacific coast to Lima's port of Callao.[56] In the early- to

52 Bowser, *African Slave*, 40-41; Alex Borucki, David Eltis, and David Wheat, "The Size and Direction of the the Slave Trade to the Spanish Americas," in *From the Galleons to the Highlands: Slave Trade Routes in the Spanish Americas*, ed. Borucki, Eltis, and Wheat (Albuquerque: University of New Mexico Press, 2020), 15-46.

53 Miller, *Way of Death*, Chapter 5. See also Toby Green, *The Rise of the Trans-Atlantic Slave Trade in Western Africa, 1300-1589* (Cambridge: Cambridge University Press, 2012).

54 See Candido, "Slave Trade and New Identities."

55 On the ethnogenesis of African cultures, especially those involved in ongoing warfare with resultant captivity and enslavement, see Heywood and Thornton, *Central Africans*, Chapter 3. For examples of cultural affinity in the New World, see also O'Toole, "From the Rivers of Guinea." Clearly a simplistic correlation between "ethnic" names and identities or affinities is not useful.

56 The Spanish Crown initially promoted importation of hispanized (*ladino*) slaves through Spain, but in 1518 called for direct importation from African ports, citing the tendency of ladinos to rebel. The Crown likewise ordered an end to the importation of "Gelofes" and other slaves from Muslim regions in 1526, for the same reasons. Neither policy was completely successful: see Jean-Pierre Tardieu, "Origins of the Slaves in the Lima Region in Peru (Sixteenth and Seventeenth

mid-sixteenth century, captives from West Central Africa predominated, the victims of conflicts that coincided with or were caused by the expansion of demand in the Americas. Lima's African population does not precisely mirror the shifting demographics of the overall Atlantic slave trade, because the city's slave markets were partly fed through a secondary, internal trade that supplemented the infrequent arrival of slave ships at Callao.[57] Bowser argues that the split between Upper Guineans and West Central Africans that characterized the demography of seventeenth-century slavery in Lima also reflected regional buyers' preferences: urban purchasers associated Upper Guineans with skills better suited for domestic service and artisanal labor, while Angolans were marketed for field work, and were thus more commonly sold to work in the valleys that ringed the city.[58] These preferences also explain the greater tendency of Upper Guineans, as domestic servants and artisans, to have the time and financial assets necessary to participate in confraternities. These were the groups most likely to achieve freedom, for the same reasons.

On the other hand, individuals referred to by the *nación* Angola or Congo might have spent time in a region that had frequent contact with Europeans and especially Catholic missionaries. By 1608, the Kingdom of Kongo had already converted to Christianity, and the first Dominican *cofradia* (of Nuestra Señora del Rosario) was founded there in 1610. Kongolese confraternities were the preserve of the upper classes, so few of the men and women who were sold into Atlantic slavery from that region would have had direct experience of participating in one before captivity, but Catholicism was not exotic and its ability to provide social networks for its members would have been common knowledge.[59]

With this growing heterogeneity, and especially the increase in peoples from West Central Africa, some *cofradías* started to take on an "ethnic" association. In some cases, formerly heterogeneous *cofradías* began to group all or part of their membership by *nación*. In other cases new *cofradías* were founded by members of a single group, to the exclusion of others. Creating a group identity became an important way for some to assert affinity and

Centuries)," in *From Chains to Bonds: The Slave Trade Revisited*, ed. Doudou Diène (New York: Berghahn Books, 2001), 51-52.

57 O'Toole, *Bound Lives*, Chapter 2.

58 Bowser, *African Slave*, 40-41 describes his sample of slave sales records in Lima between 1560-1650. For a helpful update to Bowser, see Tardieu, "Origins of the Slaves in the Lima," 40-41.

59 Heywood and Thornton, *Central Africans*, Chapters 2, 4; Cécile Fromont, *Art of Conversion: Christian Visual Culture in the Kingdom of Kongo* (Chapel Hill: University of North Carolina Press, 2014).

community, and to welcome new and dislocated or traumatized arrivals. But it also became ways for individuals to differentiate themselves, based upon perceived alliances, or conflicts in African homelands or in the New World.

The most dramatic case was associated with the bifurcation of Nuestra Señora del Rosario. In Lima, Rosario had been founded by the Franciscans, until the church placed all Rosario confraternities under the auspices of the Dominicans in 1593. The move was contentious, and resulted in the creation of two separate confraternities, the new Rosario de los Morenos, in the monastery of Santo Domingo, and Nuestra Señora de los Reyes, founded in San Francisco for those who chose not to relocate.

In the 1630s and 1640s, both *cofradías* suffered from ongoing crises over the power of different *naciones* within the larger institutional structure, and they utilized Spanish legal theory and customary law to claim their position. For instance, in 1646, Los Reyes, now described as the "*cofradía* of the eight *moreno castas*," suffered through a protracted lawsuit over the seating arrangements for the representatives for each *casta* at *cabildo* meetings, where voting for office holders took place.[60] After debate, the *mayordomos* decided that the primary seat would go to a Bran, and the second to a Terranova, because these were the *castas* of the two *cofrades* who decided to remain in San Francisco after the exodus to Santo Domingo. After these would come a seat for a Jolofo and then a Mandinga, and then the other four *castas*. The list of *veinticuatros* from the founding documents of 1589 shows that these groups were indeed among the best represented in the population, though by no means the only ones.[61] Los Reyes never lost its character as a heterogeneous confraternity, but it did begin to express the contemporary alignments of Lima's Africans rather than claim a creole or non-ethnic identity.

In the Dominican Rosario, we see this process even more clearly. By the 1620s the *morenos* were splitting into eleven subgroups, called *bancos* and headed by a *caporal*, which collected their members' fees, taxes for special occasions, and distributed charity within the group. In 1642 this structure was pressed further when, after the election of *mayordomos* in a poorly attended *cabildo* meeting, the losing parties called for nullification of the vote because "in order to have the election, all the *castas* that exist in the said *cofradia* must be in attendance." Church authorities rejected this claim after examining the constitutional documents, which recorded no such bylaw. The *bancos* were still seen as an innovation, and not a part of institutional culture.

---

60   AAL Cofradías 51:24 (1829)
61   AAL Cofradía 51:24 (1829).

In 1670-1671 internal conflicts came to a head in Rosario over seating arrangements. Domingo Belez, the *caporal* of the Sape *banco*, complained that his Cocolí counterpart was given the privileged first seat "because the [the Cocolíes] claimed *antigüedad*" or preeminence because of their historical position in the *cofradía*. The Cocolíes were *not* founders, he continued, "and if they participated in the *cofradía* that was founded [in Santo Domingo] it was because the Sape brothers brought them in, like orphans, to it, not as founders [...] nor did they give donations even to buy wax or other things."[62] Belez produced the book of the foundation, which listed only one Cocolí member.[63]

Two Cocolí *cofrades*, Miguel and Antón, responded that, "for many years, our Cocolí *nación* has been in possession of the *antigüedad* of the foundation, older than the Sape *nación*."[64] They not only produced their own witnesses, but also the physical title of *antigüedad* issued by the church in a previous litigation, in 1651, which they had won. Indeed they "possessed" the *antigüedad*, in its legal paper form. Church authorities sided again with the Cocolíes in 1671, rather than overturn their previous decision; in Spanish law possession of a title or evidence of customary status nearly always trumped innovation.[65]

The changing demography of Lima in the seventeenth century, affected by changes in the Atlantic slave trade, thus contributed to the formation of new ethnic allegiances and alliances. How this took place is made clearer if we examine just who left Rosario in 1593 to form Los Reyes.[66] As we would expect, the original Rosario was mainly made up of Senegambians and Guineans – Bran, Biafara, Jolofo and Mandinga all refer places or peoples in that region, and these names are used interchangeably in some documents.

---

62 AAL Cofradías 36:28 (1670-1671).

63 However, a document from 1574, prior to the split, shows a mayordomo named Sebastian Cocolí, perhaps part of this memory: AAL Cofradías 64:1.

64 In Africa, the Cocolíes were a subgroup of the Sape kingdoms in the region now known as Sierra Leone. This might reflect a schism that happened in Sierra Leone or later in Lima. Tardieu, "Origins of the Slaves in the Lima," 48.

65 The *bancos* here are using *antigüedad* or seniority in the sense of a property title or of customary law; the legal basis would be as in Spain, *Recopilación de leyes de Indias*, bk. 4, tit. 12, ley xv. On the ways that written words produced *antigüedad* as historical memory, see Alejandra B. Osorio, *Inventing Lima: Baroque Modernity in Peru's South Sea Metropolis* (New York: Palgrave Macmillan, 2008), 41, 154.

66 I do this indirectly by comparing a list of the veintecuatros who founded Los Reyes in 1589 (AAL Cofradías 51:24, 1829) with a list of those who donated to Rosario in 1607 (AAL Cofradías 31:2, 1608). The latter list would include *veintecuatros* as well as those who donated smaller amounts.

But the other large group was Angolans, who did not have much in common with the Guineans prior to arriving in the New World,[67] and these were the majority members of the new Rosario. Nearly all the Guinean brothers and sisters elected to stay in San Francisco in 1593, while many non-Guineans, and especially Angolans, moved on to Santo Domingo. The initial split was not narrowly ethnic so much as between newly establishing and long-established communities in the city.

However, most *cofradias* appealed to long-time residents or to creoles, and thus did not generally split along linguistic or cultural lines; only a few became identified with one or a few *naciones*. La Antigua was undividedly heterogeneous until a conflict erupted, most likely in the 1620s or 30s, which led to its division into at least two *parcialidades*, including one made up of the creoles from Lima, and another called "creoles from Caboverde," referring to (probably Guinean) captives who had spent significant time in the Cape Verde islands before being shipped to Peru.[68] This case is of great interest because the "creoles from Caboverde" and the "creoles from Lima" had each forged a new ethnicity in the land where they were raised, differentiating them from others of their supposed heritage.[69] La Antigua's conflict was serious enough to require elections of a *mayordomo* from each group, which led to a crisis when the Cape Verdean winner refused to serve, leaving a Limeño slave as sole *mayordomo*. The church questioned whether an enslaved man should be trusted with the funds of the largest Afro-Peruvian *cofradía* in the city, eventually ruling that he would have to find a guarantor in order to handle the funds.[70]

At least one sodality had even more serious problems. The *cofradía* of Fray Juan de la Buenaventura was founded in late 1604 by a group of free *morenos* of Guinea-Bissauen descent (*casta Biohoes*, in their words) to honor

67 Heywood and Thornton note that West Central Africans, who formed an increasingly large share of Atlantic slaves after 1600 "shared quite similar linguistic, social, cultural, and political forms, making for a much more uniform set of beliefs and practices than any of the other regions of Atlantic Africa": Heywood and Thornton, *Central Africans*, 49. While we see some Senegambians and Guineans also forming these groupings, it is possible that they were responding to practices begun by Central Africans.
68 Cape Verde acted as a "way-station" for the passage of slaves: A. J. R. Russell-Wood, *The Portuguese Empire, 1415-1808: A World on the Move* (Baltimore: Johns Hopkins University Press, 1998), 40-41. Sandoval believed that the majority of these were of Guinean origin but were "raised from infancy" on the islands: *Un tratado*, 100-101.
69 AAL Cofradías 64:11 (1630).
70 Enslaved men often served as mayordomos, despite the existence of rules against this possibility, leading to uncertain outcomes when they were accused of mishandling funds: AAL Cofradías 64:11 (1630).

a Black Franciscan friar.[71] By 1607 the membership was divided in two, split between the Biohoes born in the New World city of Panama, known in the records as "creoles of Panama," and those Biohoes who were born in Guinea. The Guinean brothers sought to throw the creoles out of their organization, noting that they had been deceived by them:

> [I]t seemed to us that the creole *nación* Biohoes de Panama were virtuous and competent for our brotherhood, [but] over time they have demon-strated themselves to be disruptive people, of poor inclinations, and a lack of respect, raised in vices and libertinage [...] they spoke badly to [the chaplain], and nearly laid their hands on him [...] Since the foundation of the *cofradía* they have been consumed in vices and drunkenness [...] and under the guise of charity they have robbed the community.[72]

Echoes of the earlier discourse about immorality and birth-circumstance resurface here, replete with accusations of violence and drunkenness. But these were a group of men born in Africa using these terms to take down those claiming their own *nación*, corrupted by association with the loose morals of Panamanian slavery. This discourse about immorality had become, by the seventeenth century, a template to place over an internal conflict, to overcome surface similarities. In these final descriptions we have seen that they could also interact with the emerging tendency for many Afro-Peruvians to construct an African ethnicity for themselves. While some of these new ethnic alignments likely drew upon linguistic or cultural similarities that predated enslavement in Africa, it is equally certain that some of them responded to New World conditions and experiences. Afro-Peruvian ethnic-ity must be understood as a construction within the world of colonial slavery which drew from that society's discourses about difference.

Conclusion

African men and women and their descendants were drawn, like many colo-nial subjects, to Catholic *cofradías* in Lima not only for religious fellowship but also for the limited autonomy they could practice there. These sodalities became microcosms of the social world, and this was most evident when they lined up to process on important days in the ritual calendar. *Cofradías*

71   AAL Cofradías 51:1 (1607).
72   AAL Cofradías 51:1 (1607).

were, as the *cabildo* of Lima warned back in 1549, places where people could imagine their own communities, through cultural and social acts under the guise of worship. But rather than the dangerous places *cabildo* members feared – where Africans planned insurrections, had drunken parties, or engaged in religious rites that drew upon non-Catholic practices – the documents reveal sites where Afro-Peruvians deliberated upon colonial group membership and their place in this emerging social hierarchy.

Lima's Afro-Peruvian *cofrades* drew upon their contemporary experiences and needs to formulate community and differentiate themselves from their "others." Their fissures emerge from the fact that some were free and others enslaved; some imagined access to the privileges of Spanishness while others had no such hopes; some arrived to find cultural or linguistic cohorts awaiting them, while others invented their communities from new materials. They did this by adapting a language that was increasingly being deployed against them, one that associated Africans with laziness, violence, drunkenness and crudeness. This language had not yet been inevitably linked with Blackness, it floated as a way of signifying honor, status, and morality for individuals as well as groups. The discourse received numerous iterations, not only describing *negros* and *mulatos*, as discussed here, but also Indians and *mestizos*, and eventually it would be flung against creole Peruvians of Spanish descent by their peninsular relatives. These adjectives represented an attack on public order, and thus were known by Afro-Peruvian complainants to offer the best chance of a favorable hearing from church authorities.

While the documentation offered in this essay only characterizes a small segment of Lima's Afro-Peruvian population – and one deeply engaged with the ecclesiastical authorities, from whom it drew its discourses – it offers a step towards understanding how enslaved and freed people of color saw themselves within the colonial city. This study also presents Afro-Peruvians as not isolated from the rest of Lima but as co-inhabitants with Indigenous, *mestizo* and European men and women. The absence of a larger "African" consciousness, or even a set of more narrowly regional identities, made evident here speaks to the complexities of urban colonial life, and to the parallels and interconnections experienced among and between the groups of peoples we often examine in segregation.

About the author

Karen B. Graubart is Associate Professor of History at the University of Notre Dame. She is the author of two books, *With Our Labor and Sweat: Indigenous*

Women and the Formation of Colonial Society 1550-1700 (Stanford: 2007) and *Republics of Difference: Religious and Racial Self-Governance in the Spanish Atlantic World* (Oxford University Press: forthcoming) as well as numerous articles in *Hispanic American Historical Review, Colonial Latin American Review, Slavery and Abolition, The William and Mary Quarterly*, and other journals. She is a member of the directing collectives of the Tepoztlán Institute for the Transnational History of the Americas and La Patrona Collective for Colonial Latin American Scholarship. Her work has been generously supported by the National Endowment for the Humanities, the American Council of Learned Societies, and the Kellogg Institute for International Studies. An earlier version of this article appeared in *Slavery and Abolition* 33:1 (March 2012).

Bibliography

Bennett, Herman L. "Writing into a Void: Representing Slavery and Freedom in the Narrative of Colonial Spanish America." *Social Text* 93, no. 25:4 (2007): 67-89.

Berlin, Ira. "From Creole to African: Atlantic Creoles and the Origins of African-American Society in Mainland North America." *William and Mary Quarterly* 53, no. 2 (1996): 251-288.

Borucki, Alex, David Eltis, and David Wheat. "The Size and Direction of the Slave Trade to the Spanish Americas." In *From the Galleons to the Highlands: Slave Trade Routes in the Spanish Americas*, edited by Borucki, Eltis, and Wheat, 15-46. Albuquerque: University of New Mexico Press, 2020.

Bowser, Frederick P. *The African Slave in Colonial Peru, 1524-1650.* Stanford: Stanford University Press, 1974.

Brewer-García, Larissa. *Beyond Babel: Translations of Blackness in Colonial Peru and New Granada.* Cambridge: Cambridge University Press, 2020.

Cahill, David. "Colour by Numbers: Racial and Ethnic Categories in the Viceroyalty of Peru, 1532-1824." *Journal of Latin American Studies* 26, no. 2 (1994): 325-346.

Candido, Mariana P. "Jagas e Sobas No 'Reino de Benguela': Vassalagem e Criação de Novas Categorias Políticas e Sociais No Contexto Da Expansão Portuguesa Na África Durante Os Séculos XVI e XVII." In *África: Histórias Conectadas*, edited by Alexandre Ribeiro, Alexsander Gebera, and Marina Berthet, 39-76. Niterói: Universidade Federal Fluminense, 2015.

——. "Slave Trade and New Identities in Benguela, 1700-1860." *Portuguese Studies Review* 19, nos. 1-2 (2011): 59-76.

Celestino, Olinda, and Albert Meyers. *Las cofradías en el Perú: región central.* Frankfurt: Vervuert, 1981.

Christian, William A. *Local Religion in Sixteenth-Century Spain*. Princeton: Princeton University Press, 1989.

Cieza de León, Pedro de. *Crónica del Perú*. Edited by Francesca Cantù. Lima: PUCP, [1553] 1989.

Coello de la Rosa, Alexandre. *Espacios de exclusión, espacios de poder: el cercado de Lima colonial (1568-1606)*. Lima: IEP, 2006.

Consejo de Indias. *Recopilacion de leyes de los reinos de las Indias*. Madrid: Boix, [1680] 1841.

Cope, R. Douglas. *The Limits of Racial Domination: Plebeian Society in Colonial Mexico City, 1660-1720*. Madison: University of Wisconsin Press, 1994.

Corr, Rachel, and Karen Vieira Powers. "Ethnogenesis, Ethnicity and 'Cultural Refusal': The Case of the Salasacas in Highland Ecuador." *Latin American Research Review* 47 (2012): 5-30.

Egoavil, Teresa. *Las cofradias en Lima, ss. XVII y XVIII*. Lima: Universidad Nacional de San Marcos, 1986.

Estenssoro Fuchs, Juan Carlos. "Los Colores de La Plebe: Razón y Mestizaje En El Perú Colonial." In *Los Cuadros de Mestizaje Del Virrey Amat: La Representación Etnográfica En El Perú Colonial*, edited by Natalia Majluf, 67-107. Lima: MALI, 1999.

Fromont, Cécile. *Art of Conversion: Christian Visual Culture in the Kingdom of Kongo*. Chapel Hill: University of North Carolina Press, 2014.

Fuente, Alejandro de la. "Slaves and the Creation of Legal Rights in Cuba: Coartación and Papel." *Hispanic American Historical Review* 87, no. 4 (2007): 659-692.

Graubart, Karen B. "The Bonds of Inheritance: Afro-Peruvian Women's Legacies in a Slave-Holding World." In *Women's Negotiations and Textual Agency*, edited by Mónica Díaz and Rocío Quispe-Agnoli, 130-150. New York: Routledge, 2017.

Green, Toby. *The Rise of the Trans-Atlantic Slave Trade in Western Africa, 1300-1589*. Cambridge: Cambridge University Press, 2012.

Harth-Terré, Emilio, and Alberto Márquez Abanto. "Perspectiva Social y Económica Del Artesano Virreinal En Lima." *Revista Del Archivo Nacional Del Perú* 26, no. 2 (1962): 1-96.

Hesperióphylo [Joseph Rossi y Rubí]. "Idea de Las Congregaciones Públicas de Los Negros Bozales, Pt. 1" *Mercurio Peruano* 48 (June 16, 1791): 112-117.

——. "Idea de Las Congregaciones Públicas de Los Negros Bozales, Pt. 2." *Mercurio Peruano* 49 (June 19, 1791): 120-125.

Heywood, Linda M., and John K. Thornton. *Central Africans, Atlantic Creoles, and the Foundation of the Americas, 1585-1660*. New York: Cambridge University Press, 2007.

Hunefeldt, Christine. *Paying the Price of Freedom: Family and Labor Among Lima's Slaves, 1800-1854*. Berkley: University of California Press, 1995.

Jouve Martín, José Ramón. *Esclavos de la ciudad letrada: esclavitud, escritura y coloniliasmo en Lima (1650-1700)*. Lima: IEP, 2005.

Konetzke, Richard, ed. *Coleccion de documentos para la historia de la formación social de Hispanoamérica, 1493-1810*. Madrid: CSIC, 1953.

Kuznesof, Elizabeth. "Ethnic and Gender Influences on 'Spanish' Creole Society in Colonial Spanish America." *Colonial Latin American Review* 4, no. 1 (1995): 153-176.

Lee, Bertram T., Juan Bromley, Sophy E. Schofield, and Emilio Harth-Terré, eds. *Libros de cabildos de Lima*. Lima: San Martín, [1535-1821] 1935-1948.

Lovejoy, Paul E. "Ethnic Designations of the Slave Trade and the Reconstruction of the History of Trans-Atlantic Slavery." In *Trans-Atlantic Dimensions of Ethnicity in the African Diaspora*, edited by Lovejoy and David Vincent Trotman, 9-42. London: Bloomsbury, 2004.

McKinley, Michelle A. *Fractional Freedoms: Slavery, Intimacy, and Legal Mobilization in Colonial Lima, 1600-1700*. Cambridge: Cambridge University Press, 2016.

Miller, Joseph Calder. *Way of Death: Merchant Capitalism and the Angolan Slave Trade, 1730-1830*. Madison: University of Wisconsin Press, 1996.

Mintz, Sidney, and Richard Price. *Anthropological Approaches to the Afro-American Past: Caribbean Perspectives*. Philadelphia: Institute for the Study of Human Issues, 1976.

Morgado Maurtua, Patricia. *Un palimpsesto urbano: del asiento indígena de Lima a la ciudad española de Los Reyes*. Seville: University of Seville, 2007.

Morgan, Jennifer L. "*Partus sequitur ventrem*: Law, Race, and Reproduction in Colonial Slavery." *Small Axe* 22, no. 1 (2018): 1-17.

Osorio, Alejandra B. *Inventing Lima: Baroque Modernity in Peru's South Sea Metropolis*. New York: Palgrave Macmillan, 2008.

O'Toole, Rachel Sarah. *Bound Lives: Africans, Indians, and the Making of Race in Colonial Peru*. Pittsburgh: University of Pittsburgh Press, 2012.

——. "Castas y Representación en Trujillo Colonial." In *Más Allá de La Dominación y La Resistencia: Estudios de Historia Peruana, Siglos XVI-XX*, edited by Leo J. Garofalo and Paulo Drinot, 48-76. Lima: IEP, 2005.

——. "From the Rivers of Guinea to the Valleys of Peru: Becoming a Bran Diaspora within Spanish Slavery." *Social Text* 25, no. 3 (2007): 19-36.

Restall, Matthew. "Black Conquistadors: Armed Africans in Early Spanish America." *The Americas* 57, no. 2 (2000): 171-205.

Rostworowski de Diez Canseco, María. *Señoríos indígenas de Lima y Canta*. Lima: IEP, 1978.

Russell-Wood, A. J. R, *The Portuguese Empire, 1415-1808: A World on the Move*. Baltimore: Johns Hopkins University Press, 1998.

Sandoval, Alonso de. *Un tratado sobre la esclavitud*. Edited by Enriqueta Vila Vilar. Madrid: Alianza, 1987.

Suárez de Figueroa, Cristóbal. *Plaza universal de todas las ciencias*. Madrid: Luis Sanchez, 1615.

Tardieu, Jean-Pierre. "Origins of the Slaves in the Lima Region in Peru (Sixteenth and Seventeenth Centuries)." In *From Chains to Bonds: The Slave Trade Revisited*, edited by Doudou Diène, 43-54. New York: Berghahn Books, 2001.

Valerio, Miguel. "'That There be No Black Brotherhood': The Failed Suppression of Afro-Mexican Confraternities, 1568-1612." *Slavery and Abolition* 42, no. 2 (2021): 293-314.

Vargas Ugarte, Rubén. *Concilios limenses (1551-1772)*. Lima: Tipografia Peruana, [1551-1772] 1951.

Varón Gabai, Rafael. "Cofradías de indios y poder local en el Perú colonial: Huaraz, siglo XVII." *Allpanchis* 14, no. 20 (2020): 127-146.

Walker, Tamara J. *Exquisite Slaves: Race, Clothing, and Status in Colonial Lima*. Cambridge: Cambridge University Press, 2017.

Webster, Susan Verdi. *Art and Ritual in Golden-Age Spain: Sevillian Confraternities and the Processional Sculpture of Holy Week*. Princeton: Princeton University Press, 1998.

Wheat, David. *Atlantic Africa and the Spanish Caribbean, 1570-1640*. Chapel Hill: University of North Carolina Press, 2016.

6 African-Descent Women and the Limits of Confraternal Devotion in Colonial Lima, Peru

Tamara J. Walker
University of Toronto

Abstract
African-descent women played essential roles in confraternity life in
colonial Latin America. At the same time, however, confraternities often
imposed strictures on African-descent women by tying their place within
organizational hierarchies to their legal condition, marital status, and
ancestral makeup. The unfortunate, uncomfortable truth was that, no
matter how hard they worked or how much they sacrificed for confraternities, there were limits to what African-descent women's confraternal
devotion could yield them. But what alternatives did they have outside of
these institutions? To address this question, this chapter examines a small
collection of eighteenth-century records from Lima's national archive that
feature inventories of material possessions belonging to free women of
African descent. Taken together, within and across each inventory, these
diverse devotional items provide an opportunity to think about African-
descent women's extra-confraternal devotional practices in colonial Lima.

Keywords: Peru, African diaspora, black Catholicism, women, extra-
confraternal devotional practices, material culture

African-descent women played essential roles in confraternity life in colonial
Latin America. From New Spain to Peru, Brazil, and other parts of the
region, in contexts both rural and urban, they collected alms, cared for sick
members, and were front and center in ceremonies, festivals, and public

Javiera Jaque Hidalgo and Miguel A. Valerio. *Indigenous and Black Confraternities in Colonial
Latin America: Negotiating Status through Religious Practices.* Amsterdam: Amsterdam University
Press, 2022
DOI: 10.5117/ 9789463721547_CH06

performances (as well as behind the scenes preparing for and cleaning up after them). These roles provided enslaved and free women alike opportunities to preserve ties to their communities and ancestors, wield autonomy and social influence, and to shape narratives about their histories and cultural identities.[1] At the same time, however, confraternities often imposed strictures on African-descent women by tying their place within organizational hierarchies to their legal condition, marital status, and ancestral makeup. As I have shown elsewhere, in the context of nineteenth century Lima, even when they devoted their time and resources to confraternities, at the expense of pursuing individual freedom and family formation, enslaved women could find their leadership positions usurped by free women who were married to high-ranking men within those same organizations.[2] The

1   For a discussion of women's participation in the daily operations of confraternities in Peru and elsewhere in colonial Latin America, see: Frederick Bowser, *The African Slave in Colonial Peru: 1524-1650* (Stanford: Stanford University Press, 1974), 222-263; Emilio Harth-Terré, *Presencia del negro en el virreinato del Perú* (Lima: Editorial Universitaria, 1971), 13-37; Luis Gómez Acuña, "Las cofradías de negros en Lima (siglos XVII): estado de la cuestión y análisis de caso," *Páginas* 129 (1994): 28-39; Jean-Pierre Tardieu, *Los negros y la Iglesia en el Perú: siglos XVI-XVII* (Quito: Centro Cultural Afroecuatoriano, 1997), 509-563; Diego Lévano Medina, "Organización y funcionalidad de las cofradías urbanas: Lima, siglo XVII," *Revista del Archivo General de la Nación* 24 (May 2002); and Nicole Von Germeten, *Black Blood Brothers: Confraternities and Social Mobility for Afro-Mexicans* (Gainesville: University Press of Florida, 2006), 41-70. On the role of African-descent women on confraternity ceremonies and performances, see: Roberto Rivas Aliaga, "Danzantes negros en el Corpus Christi de Lima, 1756: 'Vos estis Corpus Christi,'" in *Etnicidad y discriminación racial en la historia del Perú*, ed. Ana Cecilia Carrillo S., et al. (Lima: Pontificia Universidad Católica del Perú, 2002), 35-63; José Ramon Jouve Martín, "Public Ceremonies and Mulatto Identity in Viceregal Lima: A Colonial Reenactment of the Fall of Troy (1631)," *Colonial Latin American Review* 16, no. 2 (2007): 179-201; and Miguel Alejandro Valerio, "The Queen Sheba's Manifold Body: Creole Black Women Performing Sexuality, Cultural Identity, and Power in Seventeenth-Century Mexico City," *Afro-Hispanic Review* Vol. 35, no. 2 (2016): 79-98. Finally, Joan Bristol "Afro-Mexican Saintly Devotion in a Mexico City Alley," in *Africans to Spanish America: Expanding the Diaspora*, ed. Sherwin K. Bryant, Rachel Sarah O'Toole, and Ben Vinson (Urbana-Champaign: University of Illinois Press, 2012), 114-135; and Valerio, "'That There Be No Black Brotherhood': The Failed Suppression of Afro-Mexican Confraternities, 1568-1612," *Slavery & Abolition* 42, no. 2 (2021): 293-314, describe how colonial officials and others viewed these organizations and their members with high levels of suspicion. Bristol notes the circulation of rumors in 1611 and 1612 that members of a black confraternity were plotting to overthrow Spanish rule, and Valerio details an instance in which a colonial official characterized the election of queens and kings at a 1609 Christmas party as "the initial act in of a black revolt" (18). Valerio cautions against taking the official at his word, while also noting that the description accurately captured outsiders' angst over the internal workings of black confraternities, which in turn led to a high degree of scrutiny and legal intervention.

2   Tamara J. Walker, "The Queen of *los Congos*: Slavery, Gender, and Confraternity in Colonial Lima, Peru," *The Journal of Family History* 40, no. 3 (2015): 305-322. For further discussion of the kinds of status conflicts that plagued confraternities, see: Ciro Corilla Melchor, "Cofradías en la

unfortunate, uncomfortable truth was that, no matter how hard they worked or how much they sacrificed for confraternities, there were limits to what African-descent women's confraternal devotion could yield them. But what alternatives did they have outside of these institutions?

To address this question, this chapter examines a small collection of eighteenth-century records from Lima's national archive that feature inventories of material possessions belonging to free women of African descent. The inventories stem from a criminal investigation for which the available documentation spanned more than ten years, from 1747 to 1758. My intention here is not to provide a comprehensive view or representative sampling of the broader universe of cases to which my examples belong, but rather to zero in on some key aspects of the records in order to tease out their potential significance (while making occasional references to other archival sources to help contextualize them). Specifically, I am interested in the references these records make to religious paraphernalia, including rosaries, statuary, plaques of the Virgin Mary, and depictions of Marian apparitions. Taken together, within and across each inventory, these diverse devotional items provide an opportunity to think about African-descent women's extra-confraternal devotional practices in colonial Lima.

Race and Religion in Context

Before turning to the inventories and their contents, a brief sketch of the black Catholic tradition in colonial Latin America will be useful. To begin, despite the Catholic Church's profound investment in Africans' religious conversion, people of African descent could not become priests or nuns. There is only one known exception to this rule: in the late-seventeenth century, an African-born woman named Juana Esperanza de San Alberto was veiled as a Carmelite nun as she lay dying in the very convent that had enslaved her and deemed her unworthy of taking monastic orders during her lifetime.[3] In other words, from Africans' earliest arrival in the New World, the Catholic Church expected them and their descendants to convert

ciudad de Lima, siglos XVI y XVII: Racismo y conflictos étnicos," in *Etnicidad y discriminación racial*, 11-34; and Karen Graubart, "'*So color de una cofradía*': Catholic Confraternities and the Development of Afro-Peruvian Ethnicities in Early Colonial Peru," *Slavery & Abolition* 33, no. 1 (2011): 43-64.

3   Joan Cameron Bristol, *Christians, Blasphemers, and Witches: Afro-Mexican Ritual Practice in the Seventeenth Century* (Albuquerque: University of New Mexico Press, 2009), 47-62.

to Catholicism and obey its tenets, all while maintaining a subordinated status within the faith.

Beyond their subordination was the expectation that Africans and their descendants would also bear the weight of suffering without complaint or resistance. As Joan Bristol has shown in the case of Juana Esperanza de San Alberto, it was the enslaved woman's unflagging sense of penitence and commitment to self-mortification that so impressed the priests and nuns in the convent and eventually earned her a deathbed veiling. Similarly, Nancy Van Deusen's close reading of the spiritual diary of Ursula de Jesús, an African-descent woman who was enslaved in a convent in seventeenth-century Peru, shows the links between dignified suffering in bondage and how the Church understood Africans and their descendants' Catholic piety.[4]

This kind of dignified suffering was also embodied by black saints like Martín de Porres, who was born to an enslaved mother in Peru and whose sanctity was linked to pious humility.[5] Yet other black Saints who were venerated around the Iberian world, such as Benedict of Palermo, Anthony of Noto, Iphigenia, and Elesban, who often served as patrons for African-descent confraternities throughout Latin America, represented more varied human conditions and responses.[6] In his analysis of the figure of Iphigenia (or Efigenia) and her cult of worship in Peru, for example, Roberto Sanchez details the emergence of an "alternate history" that both loosely acknowledged her birth, life, and death in Ethiopia during the first century, as per canonical tradition, and linked her arrival in Peru to the transatlantic slave trade. Her presence in Peru took the form not of her corporeal body but as an image hidden among the belongings of the captives on board a slave ship, keeping the passengers safe and allowing them to preserve meaningful and tangible ties to their African heritage. Over time that origin story evolved to take on new details and meanings, with the saint and her

---

4   Nancy Van Deusen, *The Souls of Purgatory: The Spiritual Diary of a Seventeenth-Century Afro-Peruvian Mystic, Ursula de Jesús* (Albuquerque: The University of New Mexico Press, 2011). For more on what one scholar calls the uniquely "Afro-Catholic" features of Ursula de Jesus's writings, see Rachel Spaulding, "Mounting the Poyto: An Image of Afro-Catholic Submission in the Mystical Visions of Colonial Peru's Úrsula de Jesús," *Early American Studies: An Interdisciplinary Journal* 17, no. 4 (2019): 519-544.

5   Erin Kathleen Rowe, "After Death, Her Face Turned White: Blackness, Whiteness, and Sanctity in the Early Modern Hispanic World," *American Historical Review* 121, no. 3 (2016): 727-754.

6   See, for example: Roberto Sanchez, "The Black Virgin: Santa Efigenia, Popular Religion, and the African Diaspora in Peru," *Church History* 81, no. 3 (2012): 631-655; and Valerio, "The Queen Sheba's Manifold Body," 83.

image also representing a spirit of rebellion thanks to the runaway slaves who kept her in their care.[7]

Out of all this emerged two defining traditions of black Catholicism in colonial Latin America, one linking piety to suffering and deference, and the other embracing a legacy of survival and defiance. These were not incompatible notions, and Africans and their descendants excelled at balancing the two. They did so in part because they had to, since the Church imposed limits on their place within the faith, and because of their subjugated status in colonial societies. At the same time, they were also committed to preserving connections to their African heritage, or at least to shaping the contours of faith to suit and affirm their own diverse cultural, social, and individual identities. The existence and practices of black confraternities in the region embodied this balancing act, of course, but additional signs can be found elsewhere as well.

Sumptuous Devotion

When a *parda* named Agustina Balcazar visited a local notary to record her will in March of 1792, she listed the following items among her worldly possessions:

> Two female slaves named Thomasa and Isabel, the latter having a son named
> Carlos, which makes three slaves in total;
> 400 pesos in cash;
> A pair of Pinchbeck bracelets with antique gold finishes;
> A large gold reliquary;
> A rosary with large beads strung on handmade Jerusalem thread with a large gold cross;
> A rosary with large gold beads, a little gold cross, and four charms; and
> A rosary with blue beads and a cross embedded with eleven fine pearls.[8]

---

7   Roberto Sanchez, "The Black Virgin," 651-652. Sanchez also points out that Iphigenia embodied similar attributes in Brazil, where a legendary nineteenth-century slave known as Chico Rei purchased his freedom, helped other enslaved people do the same, and founded a church in Iphigenia's honor.

8   Archivo General de la Nación (AGN), Protocolos Notariales, Teodoro Ayllon Salazar, Protocolo, March 24, 1792. The original Spanish reads, in part: "...declaro que tengo por mis bienes 5 cofradías de a real corrientes, cuyas adoraciones manifestaran las cartas que tengo en mi poder asi lo declaro; que tengo dos esclavas mis propias, nombradas Tomasa e Isabel, y un hijo de esta llamado

In many ways, the will is relatively unremarkable for colonial Lima, where property – and slave – ownership were within reach of women of various colors and classes, including those of African descent. In fact, many such individuals owned personal and immovable property and resources that not only matched but at times even exceeded those of their Spanish and *mestiza* counterparts.[9] Another common feature of the will was the testator's profession of fealty to Christianity. Balcazar's stated recognition of "the Father, Son, and Holy Spirit as three distinct beings," in addition to professing "to have lived and continue to live as a faithful Catholic," was in keeping with standard prefaces to last wills and testaments. No mere catalogues of possessions, wills offered individuals the opportunity to leave written records of their commitment to religiosity – even in consumption. For a testator like Agustina Balcazar, the record represents a balancing act between piety and indulgence. The impressive variety of religious paraphernalia she described, coupled with her apparent penchant for (real and imitation) precious stones and metals, suggests that such a balancing act was resolved through an indulgence in sumptuous rosaries.[10]

Because Balcazar noted in her will that she belonged to five different confraternities, she would have had a busy schedule filled with confraternal

Carlos, que hacen tres esclavos, cuyas boletas que están en mi poder, calificaran el titulo de dominio que sobre ellos tengo; tengo en dinero físico la cantidad de cuatrocientos pesos; tengo por mis bienes: un par de manillas de tumbaga con sus sobrepuestos de oro fabrica antigua; un par de ebillas de oro, de pies; un relicario grande de oro sin cadena; un rosario de cuentas grandes de Jerusalen llano de mano con su cruz de oro grande y masida echava s Alomonica, su santo christo de oro en un lado y al toro envuelto de la Purísima; un par de fandados grandes de oro con sus perlas grandes sin [...] y sus gotas de oro con unas chispas de Diamantes; un rosario de cuentas de oro, grandes, su cruz pequeña de oro, con 4 dijes de oro, en que entra una pajuela grande de lo mismo y a masa lo dicho un cristalito pequeño con su anculo de plata, y un choclito pequeño de perlas finas; un rosario de cuello de cuentas azueles y padres nuestros de oro con cuentecitas chiquitas de oros y en el extremo un choclo grandes de perlas finas y dos cuentas grandes de oro, con su cruz de lo mismo con once perlas finas en ella; un par de cabetes de oro con finas en ella; un par de cabetes de oro con su perla grande cada uno; un rosario de fuentas menudas; una gargantilla con 16 cuentas grandes; una pluma de oro con perlas finas en el extremo en figura de Asahar, y un Pajuelita de oro; una Basánica de plata, de nuda, y un platillo regular de lo mismo [...]" All translations are mine unless otherwise noted.

9   See, for example, my *Exquisite Slaves: Race, Clothing and Status in Colonial Lima, Peru* (Cambridge: Cambridge University Press, 2017); and Danielle Terrazas Williams, "'My Conscience Is Free and Clear': African-Descended Women, Status, and Slave Owning in Mid-Colonial Mexico," *The Americas* 75, no. 3 (2018): 525-554.

10   I also discuss this will in *Exquisite Slaves*, and point out that this kind of indulgence might also have been a way to sidestep legal limitations on sumptuousness in dress, since a trove of religious ornamentation, no matter how costly, could have exemplified piety rather than materialism.

activities that provided her with multiple occasions to make us of – and show off – her rosaries in public settings. But there is no reason to think she would have simply returned home and kept them stored away until her next outing. She likely also prayed with her rosaries in her own time, in her own home. That her inventory also included mention of a reliquary, which was typically used to store items related to saints (such as images, statuary, pieces of hair, clothing, and other relics), provides further indication that for Balcazar, home was also an important center of her devotional life. Other records from the era help to flesh out this notion and push us to consider what those home-based devotional practices may have looked like, whether they were solitary or group pursuits, as well as the possibilities they contained for the women who engaged in them.

After Maria Monserate Santiesteban, a 40-year old *mulata*, was arrested and jailed under suspicion of colluding in a kidnapping and theft case that went before Lima's Inquisition tribunal in 1747, her inventory showed her to be a woman of moderate means.[11] Although she was not a slaveholder like Agustina Balcazar, and rented a room in a home belonging to a woman named Petronila Ortiz (about whom I shall say more below), she had a sizeable number of belongings that included chairs, stools, cushions, and a storage trunk, several items of clothing, and a collection of jewelry. However, the nature of the accusation against Santiesteban set her inventory apart from Balcazar's, since hanging over each entry was the question of whether she was the rightful owner. For the purposes of this chapter, I set that question aside except to note that even though it was not unusual for African-descent women in Peru and elsewhere in colonial Latin America to own valuable property, they rarely escaped scrutiny for it.[12] Among

11   AGN, SO-CO, Caja (C) 199, Documento (DO) 1747, "Maria Monserate Santiesteban." I should note here that, given the fragmentary nature of the record, it is difficult to discern the possible scenarios that opened her and her co-accused up to the suspicion that ultimately ensnared them in the mercurial, and brutally invasive, world of Inquisition tribunals.

12   In addition to falling outside the scope of this chapter, the question of whether Perales and her co-accused were guilty or innocent of kidnapping and theft is difficult to address given the incomplete and fragmentary nature of the records. Typically, records from Inquisition tribunals in Spain, Portugal and their overseas colonies contain detailed accusations of wrongdoing (such as heresy, blasphemy, sorcery, or witchcraft), details of accused suspects' arrest and the confiscation of their belongings, inventories of said belongings, statements from the accused suspects, witness testimonies, resulting judgements, and proposed sentences. The extant records from Lima, however, just include the inventories. Since they only detail goods that were confiscated as part of Inquisitorial proceedings and not the entirety of the proceedings themselves, the documents contain only brief references to the original charges the women faced. They also make no mention of who originally leveled said charges, what evidence the

neighbors, rivals, and other parties, these women often provoked jealousy or suspicion for their access to resources. This was especially true when the women showed no visible signs of patriarchal support, or when they seemed to have what others considered conspicuous access to and leisure, which fueled assumptions that such things were only possible with the help of illegal or nefarious doings.[13]

More relevant to my inquiry are the devotional items that were included in Santiesteban's inventory. In addition to "un rosario de Jerusalén," which most likely referred to a rosary with a centerpiece containing (or that was believed to contain) sand from Jerusalem, there was a statue of Jesus Christ and a glass altar case in which to display it, as well as a dais made of two wooden pallets stacked together.[14] While the rosary was hardly an unusual entry in an individual's inventory, the statue, its altar case, and the dais certainly were. These were the kinds of items that were more often found inside of a church or among a confraternity's possessions. For instance, in a collection of records pertaining to the activities of the African-descent confraternity of Nuestra Senora del Rosario in late-eighteenth and early-nineteenth century Lima, various inventories of belongings include crosses, flags, stools, a statue of Baby Jesus, and a plate bearing the image of the Virgin Mary, among other items.[15] These goods played diverse roles in liturgical events and dinners sponsored by the confraternity, supporting members'

accusers had to substantiate their claims, or whether the accused women had anything to say in their own defense. Nor do they give any indication of the ultimate outcomes of the cases.

13   See, for example: my "'He Outfitted His Family in Notable Decency': Slavery, Honor, and Dress in Eighteenth-Century Lima, Peru," *Slavery & Abolition* 30, no. 3 (2009): 383-402; and Nicole Von Germeten, *Violent Delights, Violent Ends: Sex, Race, and Honor in Colonial Cartagena de Indias* (Albuquerque: University of New Mexico Press, 2013), 152-153, which (among other examples), describes how one African-descent woman's flamboyant appearance that fueled accusations of prostitution that followed her from Cuba to Cartagena de Indias. Paula de Eguiluz, Von Germeten writes, "inspired jealousy in women and obsessive love in men around the Caribbean, even after having several children and into her forties."

14   AGN, SO-CO, C 199, DO 1747, "Maria Monserate Santiesteban," f. 11. The original Spanish reads, in part: "un estrado con dos tarimas [...] un Santo Christo con su dosel de vaso viejo [...]"

15   I sampled records from AGN, Cofradias, "NS del Rosario," including Legajo (L) 3, Cuaderno (C) 227, 1798 "Expediente de cuentas de entradas y salidas perteneciente a la Cofradia de NS del Rosario de los Pardos, administradas por el Mayordomo Ponce Bonifacio, durante el año de 1798;" L 6, C 159, 1822 "Planilla del mes de Febrero de 1822 de los arrendamientos de las fincas que pertenecieron a la Cofradia de los Congos situada en la esquina de Mata Sieta; " L 3, C 37, 1783, "Expediente de cuentas de entradas y salidas perteneciente a la Cofradia de Nuestra Senora del Rosario de Naturales, administrida por el Mayordomo Temoche Ventura desde el 14 de Julio de 1770 hasta otro igual de 1771 y presentadas al juez para su aprobación;" and L 3, C 39, 1783-1819, "Libro de Inventario de bienes y elecciones perteneciente a la Cofradia de NS del Rosario de los Pardos fundada en la Iglesia de Santo Domingo, empieza el ano 1783 y termina en el ano 1819."

conversion and observance of the faith. Statues like those of Jesus Christ and Baby Jesus would have been used as visual aids for daily prayers or liturgical occasions, while the dais would have provided a platform from which a speaker, honored guest, or religious leader might stand to address a congregation. So why were these kinds of items in Santiesteban's room?

Similar questions emerge from a review of the goods confiscated from her landlord and housemate, Petronila Ortiz, and from Maria del Rosario Perales, who also rented a room in Ortiz's home. The two *mulatas* were both arrested under suspicion of their involvement in the same kidnapping and theft case that resulted in Santiesteban's arrest. Like Santiesteban, Ortiz had a (small) dais among her possessions, as well as more than a dozen canvasses depicting various Marian apparitions.[16] For her part, Perales had dozens of rosaries and devotional medals, as well as a series of plaques depicting the life of the Virgin Mary (she also owned a slave who was confiscated following her arrest, along with a much more extensive collection of belongings, including a wardrobe of dresses and shawls, personal jewels, imported dishware such as porcelain teacups, and furniture including stools and storage trunks).[17]

The canvasses depicting Marian apparitions and plaques depicting the life of the Virgin are especially interesting given the place that figure of Mary has occupied in the spiritual lives Africans and their descendants in Latin America. As Russel Lohse has observed, legends of Marian apparitions prevail throughout the region, and both indigenous and African-descent communities hold enduring beliefs that the Virgin has paid them frequent visits over time.[18] In colonial Costa Rica, one such apparition led to the construction of the chapel of Our Lady of the Angels, in the pacific-coastal Puebla de los Pardos in 1639, as a symbol of her "divine favor to former slaves, who were the most degraded members of colonial society."[19] The Virgin has also been the namesake for countless African-descent confraternities throughout Latin America, particularly Our Lady of the Rosary (which existed in colonial Lima, as we saw above). Writing about the Brazilian context, Elizabeth Kiddy cites contemporary oral tradition to help explain

16   AGN, SO-CO, C 199, DO 1748, "Petronila Ortiz, alias Petatalones," f.1. The original Spanish reads, in part: "un estradito...9 lienzos con diferentes advocaciones...13 lienzecitos con sus masquitos de diferentes advocaciones [...]"

17   AGN, SO-CO, C 200, DO 1759, 1758, "Maria del Rosario Perales, alias la musanga." The original Spanish reads, in part: "[...] rosario azul con su cruz de oro, un rosario de Jerusalen con su cruz aforada en oro [...] 5 laminas de la vida de la Virgen [...]"

18   Russel Lohse, "'La Negrita' Queen of the Ticos: The Black Roots of Costa Rica's Patron Saint," *The Americas* 69, no. 3 (2013): 323-355.

19   Ibid., 335.

the centuries-long devotion among Africans and their descendants to Our Lady of the Rosary. It began in Minas Gerais, when two runaway slaves saw her figure bobbing among the waves. "The slaves," Kiddy writes:

> ran back and told their master, and he went down to the shore and tried to convince her to come out of the water, but with no success. Nor were the priest or the bishop able to persuade her to come to the shore. Finally, the white authorities decided to let the blacks have a try at coaxing her out of the water. Various nations of blacks – first the Congo, then the Mozambique – went to the shore with their instruments to dance and sing, trying to lure her from the waves. Only when the 'three oldest blacks' of the candombe (the mythical ancestor of the *congado*), with their three sacred drums went to the shore and played did Our Lady begin to stir. Not until the Congo and the Mozambique joined the candombe and all the African nations played, sang, and danced together, did Our Lady finally come out of the waves and sit on the largest drum.[20]

The devotion to Our Lady of the Rosary has endured over the years, Kiddy argues, thanks to this legend, which casts the Virgin as a figure endowed with heavy symbolism, of cultural resilience in the face of hardship.

When taken together, the assortment of devotional items found in Maria Monserate Santiesteban, Petronila Ortiz, and Maria del Rosario Perales' possessions, coupled with the broader context of Africans and their descendants' particular forms of veneration of the Virgin, raise a compelling possibility about what was going on under the trio's shared roof. What if they had established and been operating their own, informal, all-female confraternity or house of worship? This kind of scenario was not out of the question. All-female confraternities were rare but not unusual in colonial Latin America. Miguel Alejandro Valerio cites an example from the seventeenth century, of the all-female confraternity devoted to St. Iphigenia.[21] And, according to E. Valerie Smith, the all-female *Irmandade de Nossa Senhora da Boa Morte* was founded in nineteenth-century Brazil with the goal of creating space to venerate the Holy Virgin, hold feasts in her honor, and to ensure that the sisterhood's members would all have a "good death."[22] More research is needed

20   Elizabeth Kiddy, "Congados, Calunga, Candombe: Our Lady of the Rosary in Minas Gerais, Brazil," *Luso-Brazilian Review* 37, no. 1 (2000): 47-61; 49.

21   Valerio, "The Queen Sheba's Manifold Body," 83.

22   E. Valerie Smith, "The Sisterhood of Nossa Senhora da Boa Morte and the Brotherhood of Nossa Senhora do Rosário: African-Brazilian Cultural Adaptations to Antebellum Restrictions," *Afro-Hispanic Review* 21, nos. 1-2 (2002): 121-133.

to determine the catalysts for founding these organizations (whether, for example, they emerged out of disputes with mixed-gender confraternities or simply to promote gender-specific forms of religious observance and community), and why there were relatively few of them in comparison to mixed-gender confraternities. For now, though, they provide a context of plausibility for imagining Petronila Ortiz's home as a site of an informal or early-stage attempt at creating another such organization.

It is also worth considering whether the idea of a confraternity – even an all-female one – was even at the front of these women's minds. If we can see within confraternity life the existence of hierarchies on the basis of color, status, and sex, with free men of African descent (and particularly those of mixed-racial ancestry) occupying the highest rungs it is easy to imagine that these women would have found limited space for themselves in these organizations. So why not try to create their own traditions?

As Luiz Mott has shown in his life sketch of Rosa Egípciaca, an African-born woman who had been enslaved and freed in eighteenth-century Rio de Janeiro, it was possible to create all-female spaces for religious observance outside of confraternal contexts that were unbound by those organizations' conventions while also making room for mutual aid and collective worship. In Mother Rosa's case (as Egípciaca came to be known by her devotees), that space provided women who had previously worked in prostitution an opportunity for spiritual retreat. Its existence was made possible thanks to a generous donation from a priest in Minas Gerais, which enabled Mother Rosa to set up operations in a chapel large enough to house at least twenty women. The group consisted of women of African descent as well as those of European ancestry, some of whom had been born and raised in slavery, others who had known juridical freedom but who toiled in sex work at the whims of men's desires. Together, the women spent their days reciting the Office of Our Lady and maintaining their shared home and devotional space.[23]

We also know that African-descent women regularly formed informal communities as ritual practitioners, sorcerers, and witches. In the case of colonial Cartagena de Indias, for example, Nicole Von Germeten describes such women as leaders and members of groups that practiced varying forms

---

23   Luiz Mott, *Rosa Egípciaca: uma santa africana no Brasil* (Rio de Janeiro: Editora Bertrand Brazil, 1993). Mother Rosa was also a controversial figure who eventually devolved into megalomania. For example, in a 250-page spiritual treatise, Mother Rosa claimed that Jesus himself would visit her every day to nurse at her breast, that she herself had died and risen from the dead, and that God had given her the titled Mother of Justice. She also railed against local clergy, which attracted negative attention and ultimately tried before the Inquisition for idolatry, among other offenses.

of divination, incantation, and love magic. Instead of gathering under a cathedral roof, as in the case of Mother Rosa and her devotees in Rio de Janeiro, these enslaved and free women gathered in one another's homes, changing locations as needed to avoid scrutiny or to ensure that an intended recipient of a male target's love and affection would be in the right place at the right time to receive it.[24] Other times, they blended their ritual gatherings with festive ones, where they and others would dance, perform live music, flirt, and have a good time.[25]

If it was possible for African-descent women to gather for the above kinds of purposes, it is not unreasonable to imagine that Maria Monserate Santiesteban, Petronila Ortiz, and Maria del Rosario Perales did the same for the purposes of joint prayer and observance of Catholic traditions in their shared home, with one another as well as, perhaps, members of their wider community. The pair of daises in the women's inventories suggest that the women wanted a physical (and slightly elevated) platform from which to address assembled parties, and the many chairs, stools, and cushions listed in those same inventories indicate that they had the furnishings to comfortably accommodate them. And so, while it might be difficult to imagine the precise forms their collective devotional practices took, there is no doubt that the women were well equipped for it.

Race, Gender, and Spiritual Leadership

Since the women's inventories come from a criminal investigation rather than from wills, they do not indicate whether the women held confraternal memberships. My own research has not, as yet, located the women's names among Lima's testators in the late-eighteenth century, to determine whether they made reference to them in those records. But while that information would be useful to building an understanding of the place of formal confraternities in their lives, it is still possible, without it, to consider the possibility that they may have wanted something more, or something else, out of their spiritual lives than was available through confraternity membership.

Perhaps they wanted to be leaders who people looked up to, without being beholden to societal or organizational rules that would have prohibited them from adopting such positions on the basis of their ancestry, sex, and

24   von Germeten, *Violent Delights,* 38.
25   Ibid., 133.

status. Thinking of them in this way requires us to expand our analytical categories when it comes to African-descent women in Latin America's Catholic tradition, going beyond seeing them as either suffering penitents hopeful for deathbed or posthumous rewards for their piety, unwavering helpmates in convents and confraternities who ultimately answered to European priests, nuns, or to men of African descent, or leaders only when it came to the practice of witchcraft, sorcery, or forms of Love Magic that blended elements of Catholicism with African-derived rites and rituals. Not because these are inaccurate characterizations of their experiences within the faith, but because they are incomplete. They do not make room for women who engaged in self-guided forms of traditional Catholic devotion, in the space of their own homes or as part of informal spiritual networks in which they adhered to biblical convention but also called all the shots they could.

The fragmentary and incomplete nature of these documents necessitates the use of careful, even speculative language. It would be risky to draw concrete or broad conclusions from the few records discussed here. More research will be necessary to draw more meaningful comparisons between these inventories and those of other African descent women, Spaniards, and *mestizas* – regardless of whether they were accused of crimes or the nature of those alleged offenses – and to establish more clearly the context for and conflicts surrounding such accusations. But there is also a risk in refusing to draw any conclusions, particularly given the challenge that defines so much of the work of historians of slavery and slaveholding societies where people of African descent had limited access to writing. The result of this is that their life histories rarely appeared on record and were heavily mediated when they did. My intention here, then, is to simultaneously acknowledge the difficulty of excavating the interior lives of enslaved and free people of African descent as well as to signal the importance of doing as much as possible to glean insights about them anyway. I want to at least elucidate the possibilities raised by the documents I have encountered so far and to explain the importance of taking some time to take them seriously, even in their scant and fragmentary form.

Further, as Mireia Comas-Via notes in her recent examination of widows in Medieval Barcelona, it is possible to rely on evidence of institutional – and therefore extensively documented – forms of support widows relied on to survive, including economic assistance from confraternities (as well as monasteries, convents, and guilds), while also acknowledging less formal forms of support, including companionship from other women and broader "solidarity networks."[26] Comas-Via knows that these solidarity networks left few documentary trails aside from occasional letters between female relatives, friends, and neighbors in which they made promises to provide shelter and care for one another, with the result being that we know little about who formed these networks and why they mattered so much to their members, but does not shy away from highlighting their importance.

Conclusion

There is good reason to engage in speculation, both as a way of better understanding the challenges faced by free, property-holding women of African descent, and of pushing scholarship on African-descent populations in new directions. While there is ongoing work that recognizes the everyday practices and collective acts of worship that took place within the context of cults, confraternities, and convents, what we do not yet have is a complete understanding of the self-guided relationships that enslaved and free people of African descent had to Catholicism outside of those spaces, or of the role that devotional items played as sources of comfort, protection, and divine affinity, of course, but also as tools of self-definition.

With that in mind, it is also worth considering that the presence, ubiquity, and number of the particular species of property that have been at the center of this chapter suggest that women of African descent used the acquisition of devotional items to lay claim to a particular kind of status, one that not only signaled their profound personal fealty to Christianity but that also allowed them to convey it to others. Moreover, perhaps it was precisely the preponderance of Catholic devotional items in their possession that made the African-descent women discussed in this chapter targets of suspicion that ultimately led to their being accused of kidnapping and theft. Such a thing might also have complicated the lives of other women in other times and places as well. As Joan Bristol has shown in her work on colonial New Spain, African descent women often faced accusations of witchcraft for reasons that rarely had anything to do with actual acts of sorcery.[27] Instead, the accusations formed part of attempts to exact punishment when men

---

26   Mireia Comas-Via, "Looking for a Way to Survive: Community and Institutional Assistance to Widows in Medieval Barcelona," in *Women and Gender in the Early Modern World*, ed. Michelle Armstrong-Partida, Alexandra guerson, and Dana Wessell Lightfoot (Lincoln: University of Nebraska Press, 2020), 188.
27   Bristol, *Christians, Blasphemers, and Witches*, 162.

and women of African descent were perceived to be challenging authority figures or stepping outside established norms of behavior. We might add to that the sense that there may have been such a thing as excessive Catholic devotion when it came to women of African descent, at least as it pertained to their material acquisitions of devotional items.

Why might excessive devotion have invited suspicion? By way of an initial attempt at answering, I return to Erin Kathleen Rowe's work. In her analysis of the hagiographies written about Saints Benedict, Iphigenia, and others, Rowe identifies a trend in which hagiographers identified "martyrdom and suffering as integral parts of a larger argument about the role of black Christians in human salvation."[28] Indeed, the very color black signified penance and suffering. Likewise, Juana Esperanza's spiritual biographer detailed his admiration for her capacity to suffer the isolation of being the only person of African descent within the convent, and the treatment at the hands of nuns according to her *calidad*, all without ever having been heard to say a word of sorrow.[29] Perhaps the suspicion Maria Monserate Santiesteban, Petronila Ortiz, and Maria del Rosario Perales attracted – even at their most devotional – owed in part to the fact that they were insufficient in their suffering and penance. This was especially evident in the fact that ten years separated the first arrest in the case, of Maria Monserate Santiesteban in 1747, and the arrest of Maria del Rosario Perales in 1757, during which time it appeared that the home-based devotional practices continued unabated in the house the women shared, even with two of the women being imprisoned (for either the part or all of that time) and the other being heavily scrutinized. Until the end, no matter the cost, the women held on to what they viewed as their place in the faith.

About the author

Tamara J. Walker is an historian of race, gender, and slavery in Latin America. Her research has received support from the Ford Foundation, the Woodrow Wilson Foundation, the American Association of University Women and the John Carter Brown Library, and has appeared in such publications as *Slavery & Abolition: A Journal of Slave and Post-Slave Studies*, *Safundi: The Journal of South African and American Studies*, *Gender & History*, *The Journal of Family History,* and *Souls*. Her first book, *Exquisite*

28   Rowe, "After Death, Her Face Turned White," 741.
29   Bristol, *Christians, Blasphemers, and Witches*, 162.

Slaves: Race, Clothing and Status in Colonial Lima, was published by Cambridge University Press and received the 2018 Harriet Tubman Prize. She is currently at work on two new book projects, one on the history of slavery and piracy in Latin America, and the other on black subjects in Latin American visual culture, which will be published by the University of Texas Press.

Archives

Archivo General de la Nación (Lima, Peru)
    SO-CO, Caja (C) 199, Documento (DO) 1747, "Maria Monserate Santiesteban."
    SO-CO, C 199, DO 1748, "Petronila Ortiz, alias Petatalones."
    SO-CO, C 200, DO 1759, 1758, "Maria del Rosario Perales, alias la musanga."
    Protocolos Notariales, Teodoro Ayllon Salazar, Protocolo, March 24, 1792.
    Cofradias, "NS del Rosario."

Bibliography

Bowser, Frederick. *The African Slave in Colonial Peru: 1524-1650*. Stanford: Stanford University Press, 1974.

Bristol, Joan. *Christians, Blasphemers, and Witches: Afro-Mexican Ritual Practice in the Seventeenth Century*. Albuquerque: University of New Mexico Press, 2009.

—. "Afro-Mexican Saintly Devotion in a Mexico City Alley." In *Africans to Spanish America: Expanding the Diaspora*, edited by Sherwin K. Bryant, Rachel Sarah O'Toole, and Ben Vinson, 114-135. Urbana-Champaign: University of Illinois Press, 2012.

Comas-Via, Mireia. "Looking for a Way to Survive: Community and Institutional Assistance to Widows in Medieval Barcelona." In *Women and Gender in the Early Modern World*, edited by Michelle Armstrong-Partida, Alexandra Guerson, and Dana Wessell Lightfoot, 117-194. Lincoln: University of Nebraska Press, 2020.

Corilla Melchor, Ciro. "Cofradías en la ciudad de Lima, siglos XVI y XVII: Racismo y conflictos étnicos." In *Etnicidad y discriminación racial en la historia del Perú*, edited by Elisa Dasso et al., 11-34. Lima: Pontificia Universidad Católica del Perú, 2002.

van Deusen, Nancy. *The Souls of Purgatory: The Spiritual Diary of a Seventeenth-Century Afro-Peruvian Mystic, Ursula de Jesús*. Albuquerque: The University of New Mexico Press, 2011.

von Germeten, Nicole. *Black Blood Brothers: Confraternities and Social Mobility for Afro- Mexicans*. Gainesville: University Press of Florida, 2006.

——. *Violent Delights, Violent Ends: Sex, Race, and Honor in Colonial Cartagena de Indias*. Albuquerque: University of New Mexico Press, 2013.

Gómez Acuña, Luis. "Las cofradías de negros en Lima (siglos XVII): estado de la cuestión y análisis de caso." *Páginas* 129 (1994): 28-39.

Graubart, Karen. "'*So color de una cofradía*': Catholic Confraternities and the Development of Afro-Peruvian Ethnicities in Early Colonial Peru." *Slavery & Abolition* 33, no. 1 (2012): 43-64.

Harth-Terré, Emilio. *Presencia del negro en el virreinato del Per*. Lima: Editorial Universitaria, 1971.

Jouve Martín, José Ramon. "Public Ceremonies and Mulatto Identity in Viceregal Lima: A Colonial Reenactment of the Fall of Troy (1631)." *Colonial Latin American Review* 16, no. 2 (2007): 179-201.

Kiddy, Elizabeth. "Congados, Calunga, Candombe: Our Lady of the Rosary in Minas Gerais, Brazil." *Luso-Brazilian Review* 37, no. 1 (2000): 47-61.

Lévano Medina, Diego. "Organización y funcionalidad de las cofradías urbanas: Lima, siglo XVII." *Revista del Archivo General de la Nación* 24 (2002).

Lohse, Russell. "'La Negrita' Queen of the Ticos: The Black Roots of Costa Rica's Patron Saint." *The Americas* 69, no. 3 (2013): 323-355.

Mott, Luiz. *Rosa Egípciaca: Uma santa africana no Brazil*. Rio de Janeiro: Editora Bertrand Brazil, 1993.

Rivas Aliaga, Roberto. "Danzantes negros en el Corpus Christi de Lima, 1756: 'Vos estis Corpus Christi.'" In *Etnicidad y discriminación*, 35-63.

Rowe, Erin Kathleen. "After Death, Her Face Turned White: Blackness, Whiteness, and Sanctity in the Early Modern Hispanic World." *American Historical Review* 121, no. 3 (2016): 727-754.

Sanchez, Roberto. "The Black Virgin: Santa Efigenia, Popular Religion, and the African Diaspora in Peru." *Church History* 81, no. 3 (2012): 631-655.

Smith, E. Valerie. "The Sisterhood of Nossa Senhora da Boa Morte and the Brotherhood of Nossa Senhora Do Rosario: African-Brazilian Cultural Adaptations to Antebellum Restrictions." *Afro-Hispanic Review* 21, nos. 1-2 (2002): 121-133.

Spaulding, Rachel. "Mounting the Poyto: An Image of Afro-Catholic Submission in the Mystical Visions of Colonial Peru's Úrsula de Jesús." *Early American Studies* 17, no. 4 (2019): 519-544.

Tardieu, Jean-Pierre. *Los negros y la Iglesia en el Perú: siglos XVI-XVII*. Quito: Centro Cultural Afroecuatoriano, 1997.

Walker, Tamara J. "'He Outfitted His Family in Notable Decency': Slavery, Honor, and Dress in Eighteenth-Century Lima, Peru." *Slavery & Abolition* 30, no. 3 (2009): 383-402.

——. "The Queen of *los Congos*: Slavery, Gender, and Confraternity in Colonial Lima, Peru." *The Journal of Family History* 40, no. 3 (2015): 305-322.

——. *Exquisite Slaves: Race, Clothing and Status in Colonial Lima, Peru.* Cambridge: Cambridge University Press, 2017.

Williams, Danielle Terrazas. "'My Conscience Is Free and Clear': African-Descended Women, Status, and Slave Owning in Mid-Colonial Mexico." *The Americas* 75, no. 3 (2018): 525- 554.

Valerio, Miguel Alejandro. "The Queen Sheba's Manifold Body: Creole Black Women Performing Sexuality, Cultural Identity, and Power in Seventeenth-Century Mexico City." *Afro-Hispanic Review* 35, no. 2 (2016): 79-98.

——. "'That There Be No Black Brotherhood': The Failed Suppression of Afro-Mexican Confraternities, 1568–1612." *Slavery & Abolition* 42, no. 2 (2021): 293-314.

7 Glaciers, the Colonial Archive and the Brotherhood of the Lord of Quyllur Rit'i

Angelica Serna Jeri
University of New Mexico

Abstract
This chapter analyzes the role of dance performances representing Amazonian identities in the annual Andean pilgrimage of Quyllur Rit'i, the most important annual religious pilgrimage in the southern Andes that involves devotional activities including dancing, singing, and dramatized life cycle events centered around both the glaciers and a Catholic shrine to a miraculous image. I argue that these performances allow for the interaction of territorial and ritual practices. My analysis of the history and context of these dances in the pilgrimage will bring into discussion how ethnic identities emerge in relation to places such as glaciers and changes in climate across both time and space.

Keywords: Andean Catholicism, Señor Quyllur Rit'I, Climate, Glaciers, Dancers

Situating the Pilgrimage and the Brotherhood

The Pilgrimage to the Sanctuary of the Lord of Quyllur Rit'i[1] takes place every year in the region of Cuzco in the southern Peruvian Andes between

[1]   The representation of this name and its orthography varies depending on several factors, including how individual scholars decide to approach the issue of vowels in the Southern Peruvian Quechua. The language has three phonemic vowels, two of which have allophonic variants leading to an interpretation along the lines of the five vowels of Spanish. Scholars following

Javiera Jaque Hidalgo and Miguel A. Valerio. *Indigenous and Black Confraternities in Colonial Latin America: Negotiating Status through Religious Practices.* Amsterdam: Amsterdam University Press, 2022
DOI: 10.5117/ 9789463721547_CH07

late May and early June, before the celebration of Corpus Christi. During a week of celebrations, approximately 15,000 people visit the shrine, located at 4,650 meters, at the foot of the glacier Sinaqara in the Vilcanota valley, at the end of an eight km long, narrow canyon. Pilgrims arrive walking individually or in groups of kin and dancing ensembles, or *comparsas,* representing one of many *naciones* that make the pilgrimage to the shrine. Although the site itself is located in the district of Huaro, in the Quispicanchi province, pilgrims arrive from different locations throughout the Cuzco region and elsewhere in Peru. While most of the devotees arrive to the sanctuary on foot, some travel by van, bus, or car to Mahuayani, the nearest town accessible by paved road. Others travel by horse and some even carry family members who are too young, ill, or weak to reach the area where the dancing, singing, and praying takes place. It takes approximately four to five hours to walk to the sanctuary from Mahuayani, and much longer from the surroundings towns and villages.

The pilgrimage is situated in a geographical region where – from before the European invasion through the colonial period and independence – glaciers and humans have maintained a relationship in which their respective identities and personhoods are in constant exchange and association.

In this chapter, I suggest that this relationship with the landscape can help explain why the Brotherhood of the Lord of Quyllur Rit'i – an association devoted to the care and maintenance of the sanctuary at the pilgrimage site as well as to the organization of events – emerged only in the mid-twentieth century, nearly 200 years after the miraculous events that occurred at Sinaqara, and which continue to serve as the origin narrative for contemporary devotees. By contextualizing the contemporary pilgrimage in the colonial history that predates it, I hope to show the ways in which its core devotional practices and ritual performances engage humans with the landscape – especially glaciers – not only in religious terms, but also lead devotees to anchor their economic and political lives in the glacial landscape, and in this *place* in particular. Along parallel lines, I examine some of the oral traditions surrounding Quyllur Rit'i, showing how these, like ritual

this latter model have written the name as Qoyllur Rit'i, using the phonetic system of Spanish. Two other complicating factors are the apostrophe following the /t/, which indicates a glottal ejective. This sound is not present in all Quechua varieties, but it is in the variety spoken in the Cuzco region. Similarly, some scholars have used the colonial orthography which employs /c/ or /cc/ in place of /q/ for the glottal affricate. In this chapter I use the three vowels. However, when I cite other scholars, I do not correct the authors' orthography. For further discussion, see Rodolfo Cerrón-Palomino, *Lingüística Quechua* (Cusco: Centro de Estudios Rurales Andinos Bartolomé de las Casas, 1987), 116.

practices, emphasize the religious, economic, and political importance of human-glacier relationships. These two dimensions of the pilgrimage – ritual and narrative – can be seen as an axis of continuity with past colonial and pre-Hispanic practices. However, the ritual and narrative elements have come to appeal to a much larger public since the second half of the twentieth century because they work together with – and indeed depend crucially on – the Brotherhood of the Lord of Quyllur Rit'i. In conclusion, I suggest that the pilgrimage has persisted as a major force of religious devotion in the region because of the ties to the glacial landscape it fosters among pilgrims, and that it has not only persisted but also grown in large part because the Brotherhood's late emergence grounded it in this crucial territorial axis of Andean religiosity.

In order to show the Brotherhood's embeddedness in the territorial dimensions of Andean religion, I bring into my analysis earlier pre-Hispanic ritual practices and pilgrimages performed by the Incas, such as the *capacocha*, that centered on glaciers and high mountain peaks. I draw these comparisons not simply in order to establish similarity, but more importantly to explore continuities and parallels between earlier, pre-Hispanic pilgrimage practices focused on glaciers and those that characterize the more recent pilgrimage of Quyllur Rit'i. At the same time, the vibrancy of the pilgrimage of Quyllur Rit'i shows that rituals tied to glaciers unite symbolic and material resources, juxtaposing practices that join past and present to generate ritual continuity. In this sense, the Brotherhood of Quyllur Rit'i functions as a disciplined religious group that supervises all elements of the pilgrimage, and moreover does so with the cooperation and support of the Andean Church. This represents a significant contrast with how Christian authorities engaged with indigenous religious groups during the colonial period – by and large through the suppression of Andean ritual.

I begin with the colonial context of the late eighteenth century, reflecting on Quyllur Rit'i's absence from the archive. From there, I turn to a discussion of devotional practices in the pilgrimage, comparing these with the pre-colonial ritual practices like the *capacocha*. I then shift my focus to the oral narratives associated with the pilgrimage. Both analyses of the devotional practices and the narratives emphasize the centrality of the human-landscape relationship not only to religious life, but also to economic and political dimensions of Andean society. Finally, I suggest that these dimensions of the pilgrimage can be read as complementary to a colonial archive that never fails to yield examples of European and Christian impositions on Andean practices, and ultimately that the political, economic, and religious relationships embedded in

ritual practices such as those that constitute the Quyllur Rit'i pilgrimage
constitute a means of securing durability of these relationships through
the end of the colonial period and the formation of the modern Peruvian
nation until today.

The Brotherhood and the Colonial Archive

The Brotherhood of Quyllur Rit'i manages and controls the celebration and
organization of the pilgrimage.[2] It oversees the income of the shrine, the
processions, the donations made by the pilgrims, and it also raises funds
for maintaining the shrine. The present sanctuary, located at the end of
the canyon and close to the foot of the Sinaqara glacier, was erected by the
Brotherhood in 1960. Inside the sanctuary, the Brotherhood has a *celda*
(cell) for its members to sleep in. They also arrange for and fund priests to
conduct masses and hear confessions. Access to and maintenance of the
shrine is also managed by the Brotherhood, and during the pilgrimage they
also supervise the various performative components.[3] The history of the
Brotherhood was only formally recorded in writing in the twentieth century.
As a consequence, this has limited what we know, and has generated the
perception that the pilgrimage, together with Brotherhood – despite its
strong Andean religious components – is a contemporary reinterpretation
of the Andean past. Instead, in this chapter I suggest that the core of the
pilgrimage has been the continuation and maintenance of Andean social,
economic, and political forms through a strategic association of landscape-
oriented ritual with Christian forms of religiosity.

   In the Andes, confraternities and brotherhoods were institutions that
promoted Christian piety in the context of the Church's need for the conversion of indigenous people to Christianity. These associations organized
pilgrimages and led to an increased number of devotees to Christian figures.
However, they did not only result in the Christianization of religious practice
in the region. For example, the religious practices of enslaved Africans
were in some cases incorporated into wider Catholic practice through the

---

2   Guillermo Salas Carreño, "Diferenciación social y discursos publicos sobre la peregrinación
de Quyllurit'i," in *Mirando la Esfera Pública desde la Cultura en el Perú,* ed. Gisela Cánepa and
Maria E. Ulfe (Lima: CONCYTEC, 2006), 243-288; "The Glacier, the Rock, the Image: Emotional
Experience and Semiotic Diversity at the Quyllurit'i Pilgrimage (Cuzco, Peru)," *Signs and Society*
2, no. 1 (2014): 188-214.
3   Michael J. Sallnow, *Pilgrims of the Andes: Regional Cults in Cusco* (Washington, D.C.: Smithsonian Institution Press, 1987).

vehicle of confraternities.[4] Confraternities in the Americas were established by missionaries on the model of those that existed in Europe such as Los Franciscanos de la Vera Cruz and Los Dominicos del Rosario.[5] In the very different context and social world of the Andes, however, confraternities also served, channeled, and defended Andean interests and devotion.[6] Despite their missionary and religious purpose, confraternities were also associations where race and ethnicity played an exclusionary role. In the face of this exclusion, indigenous and black devotees formed their own brotherhoods, showing their capacity for administration and financing while at the same time practicing their own forms of religious devotion. Andean confraternities with indigenous members functioned as associations that united pre-Hispanic and Christian devotional habits, as well as economic and political practices, encompassing the pursuit to fulfill devotees' spiritual needs.

The brotherhood, together with the institution of the *cabildo*, a municipal governing council of Spanish origin that largely represented the land-owning class, formed the basis for what has been called the traditional indigenous community.[7] As the emphasis of brotherhoods was not only on religion and spirituality, but also on mutual aid, these institutions also attended to sociocultural needs that had previously been satisfied by pre-Columbian institutions based on kinship relationships, and which were mostly neglected both by the elite-serving *cabildos* and the limited scope and hold that the Christian church had on indigenous communities.[8] At the same time, these institutions also exercised strict social regulations based on ethnic links and wealth. One example of this is the Brotherhood of the Virgen del Carmen in Jauja during the eighteenth century. This Brotherhood received

4   Hans-Jürgen Prien, *La historia del Cristianismo en América Latina*. (Salamanca: Sígueme, 1985); cited in Fermín Labarga Garcia, "Las cofradías en España e Iberoamérica," in *Corporaciones religiosas y evangelización en Iberoamérica: Siglos XVI-XVIII*, ed. Lévano Medina Diego Edgar and Kelly Montoya Estrada (Lima: Museo de Arqueología y Antropología de San Marcos, 2010), 13.

5   Labarga Garcia, "Las cofradías," 13.

6   Olinda Celestino, "Cofradía: continuidad y transformación de la sociedad andina," *Allpanchis* 20 (1982); Olinda Celestino and Albert Meyers, *Las cofradías en el Perú: región central* (Frankfurt: Vervuert, 1981).

7   Fuenzalida Vollmar, Fernando, "La matriz colonial de las comunidades indígenas del Perú: Una hiótesis de trabajo," *Revista del Museo Nacional Lima* 35 (1970): 92-123.

8   Pedro Carrasco, "The Civil-Religious Hierarchy in Mesoamerican Communities: Pre-Spanish Background and Colonial Development," *American Anthropologist* 65, no. 3 (1967): 483-497; "La posible articulación del ayllu a través de las cofradías," in *Etnohistoria y Antropología Andina: Actas de la Segunda Jornada del Museo Nacional de Historia* (Lima: Museo Nacional de Historia, 1981), 299-310.

monetary, labor, and land donations from important native members but they did not allow indigenous nobles to hold the position of *mayordomo*.[9]

Another example is the confraternity of Santa Ana de los Indios in Lima, comprised of indigenous silversmiths. This confraternity's members, in contrast to their status before the European invasion, had become something like clandestine servants to the Spanish during the colonial period, working for Spanish and clergy, elaborating silver and gold tableware without proper supervision from the viceregal administration.[10] Enslaved and freed black men also formed part of this confraternity as they could work for a silversmith. The brotherhood was devoted to Saint Anne, the mother of the Virgin Mary, in continuation of a Spanish tradition dating from the fourteenth century that associated the cult of Saint Anne with pregnant women and miners by virtue of conventional comparisons of Christ to gold and Mary to silver.[11] Confraternities were corporations that collectively facilitated practices of faith, charity, caring for the sick, and burial of the deceased. For these reasons, they were accepted and promoted by the Catholic Church. At the same time, these groups were criticized because of the nature of the objects of their management – civil and religious domains – and the relative degree of secrecy in their administration.[12] Considering the suspicion with which the Church tolerated confraternities in colonial Andean society, a Brotherhood of Quyllur Rit'i would have faced obstacles in becoming an "official confraternity" in the last decades of the eighteenth century, the time in which oral tradition locates the events of the miracle. The complex colonial power relations that such corporations embodied were constantly unsettled by problems centered around descendance, ethnicity, wealth, and religious purity, all of which would have been stirred up by the focus of Andean ritual organization on *ayllu* (Andean political and kin groups) membership and alliance, and by the geographical focus of devotional practices on the Sinaqara and Qullqipunku glaciers.

9   Olinda Celestino and Albert Meyers, "The Socio-Economic Dynamic of the Confraternal Endowment in Colonial Peru: Jauja in the Eighteenth Century," in *Manipulating the Saints: Religious Brotherhoods and Social Integration in Postconquest Latin America*, ed. Meyers and Diane Elizabeth Hopkins (Hamburg: Wayasbah, 1988), 101-127.

10   Luisa Vetter Parodi, "Plateros indígenas y europeos: de las cofradías de Santa Ana y San Eloy," in *Corporaciones religiosas*, 192.

11   Luisa Vetter Parodi, "Plateros indígenas y europeos: de las cofradías de Santa Ana y San Eloy," in *Corporaciones religiosas*, 189-227.

12   Alberto Díaz A., Paula Martínez S., and Carolina Ponce, "Cofradías de Arica y Tarapacá en los siglos XVIII y XIX: Indígenas andinos, sistema de cargos religiosos y festividades," *Revista de Indias* 74, no. 260 (2014): 103.

In highlighting factors that would have impacted the formation of a Brotherhood of the Lord of Quyllur Rit'i, I want first to emphasize how problematic it would have been to officially formalize an organization that was so deeply couched in Andean political, economic, and religious dynamics, and second to point out that a grasp of the colonial context thus helps to understand the absence of written documents about the early history of devotional practices associated with Quyllur Rit'i. However, as I elaborate further below, the contemporary pilgrimage demonstrates significant continuity with pre-Hispanic practices that continued throughout the Andes during the colonial period. This suggests that the absence of an official confraternity belies the existence of some form of indigenous organization overseeing ritual practices focused on both the site of the miracle and the glacial landscape itself.

In addition to the ways in which the specific context for a brotherhood associated with Quyllur Rit'i challenged colonial religious and political norms, broader contextual factors also shaped its conditions of possibility and, perhaps more importantly, the likelihood that it would appear in the written record. For example, in the late eighteenth century, "indigenous elites of Cusco were simultaneously the most hispanicized sector of indigenous society, and the axiomatic representation of that society."[13] They were engaged in both the "performance of 'Incaness,'" and the Hispanicization of religion and appearance (including dress, residential architecture, etc.).[14] These elite *caciques* also sent their sons to religious schools that inculcated a more rigorous conception of Christianity than commoners'. As such, they would likely have had little incentive to devote their still-limited voices as authors of written documents to something like Quyllur Rit'i that was oriented toward local rather than Spanish political, economic, and religious forms.

At the level of economic context, the southern regions were also impacted by the Bourbon reforms. Other factors in the region were population increase and heightened contestation of caciques' authority. There were over a hundred local riots in the Viceroyalty of Peru from 1700 to 1780, and the Tupac Amaru rebellion can also be understood as part of this trend.[15] These factors help explain why it was that by the late eighteenth and early nineteenth centuries, institutions such as confraternities faced a need for

13   David T. Garrett, *Shadows of Empire: The Indian Nobility of Cusco, 1750-1825* (Cambridge: Cambridge University Press, 2005), 258.

14   Ibid., 52.

15   Ibid.

reconfiguration as a weakening of indigenous authorities loomed with a coming crisis of colonial rule, the rise of the modern state,[16] and ultimately the collapse of the entire colonial order between 1780 to 1825.[17]

The colonial archive *obscures* rather than reveals Andean religious and economic history, and in addition facilitates absences that consequently distort the representation of indigenous religious formation.[18] The relationship with the landscape, and particularly with glaciers, at the heart of the pilgrimage to Quyllur Rit'i may in this sense have prevented its recognition in written documents at that time, and much more so the formation of an official brotherhood. Precedents in pre-colonial rituals can be appreciated when we compare oral tradition with archeological studies of rituals centered on Andean glaciers. As I show in the rest of this chapter, the pilgrimage of Quyllur Rit'i that emerged in the eighteenth century and its contemporary brotherhood are characterized by diverse performative components that are closely connected with pre-Hispanic practices and religious habits as well as colonial practices that juxtapose Andean and Christian elements. Before I turn to examine these continuities through ethnographic, ethnohistorical, and archaeological lenses, however, I first examine the context and the colonial politics that may have led to the absence of official documentation. In doing so, I aim to ask how this absence has been absorbed, how it plays a significant role in our appreciation of the past and present of religious practices in the Andes, and how it can be challenged by looking to continuities of Andean Christian devotion.

In the late-sixteenth- and seventeenth-century Andes, Catholic missionaries' understandings of the relationships that Andean peoples had with places, land or territory, and non-human beings – what de la Cadena calls "earth beings" – that cohabitated with them were filtered by ideas of religious conversion. In that context, native relationships with place and space were very often understood as forms of idolatry and paganism from the Spanish colonial point of view. The knowledge produced by native Andeans about the spaces and places where they had lived since ancestral times was interpreted through Catholic religious dogma. In this sense, the ritual and social relationships between humans and the landscape were not understood as practices or bodies of knowledge that could be translated beyond the sphere of religion. This paradigm of interpretation

16 Díaz et al., "Cofradías de Arica," 105.
17 Garrett, *Shadows of Empire*, 6.
18 My conceptualization of the colonial archive builds on the work of Burns, Verdesio, Trouillot, and Salomon.

is incomplete – indeed, in the Andean world the Earth itself is conceived as a living being, and specifically as a mother, paralleling the figure of the mother of Christ, the Virgin the Spanish brought with them from Europe. But through establishing exchange with the Earth, namely through rituals of giving, "feeding her" by making offering to the most prominent and impressive places, such as glaciers, they also can ask for and hopefully receive what orants need and wish for.[19] In this sense, the relationship can be religious, but it is also grounded in an economy, in a material exchange for the subsistence of humans. The economic component of the relationship with the landscape was obscured or simply not taken into consideration during the colonial period as a pertinent form of knowledge and was instead at best dismissed as only one more example of idolatry and paganism or, perhaps more commonly, ignored altogether.[20]

Confraternities, or *cofradias*, can serve as a useful illustration of the ways in which colonial authorities disarticulated Andean religio-economic formations from Andean understandings of the landscape on the one hand, and from permissible religious practice on the other. For example, in 1636, the archbishop of Lima, F. Arias Ugarte, concerned by the growing formation of *cofradias* without the approval of the Church, expressed the following:

> Because of the work with which they are afflicted, in addition to their tributes and services, and for the excesses to which these Indians go to produce banners in the name of their confraternities, and in making drunken parties and feasts in the same confraternities, this being a widespread vice among the Indians, and the source and root of many other and very grave sins: and the main impediment to their Christianity, and for the fruit of the holy gospel that is preached unto them.[21]

As can be appreciated, for example, in the contemporary vigor of the Quyllur Rit'i pilgrimage, colonial strategies and measures that intended to convert and suppress native religious practices – from the process of conquest to the establishment of the Viceroyalty of Peru – were not entirely successful. Indeed, Arias Ugarte's warning exposes the European suspicion that Andean religious practices continued to even in colonial society. Partly in response

---

19   Salas Carreño develops these ideas at length in *Lugares parientes: comida, cohabitación y mundos andinos* (Lima: Pontifica Universidad Católica del Perú, 2019).

20   I return to this later in the chapter, explaining some of the practical and ideological factors that led to this separation and erasure.

21   *Constituciones Sinodales del Arzobispado de los Reyes en el Perú*, Título de Constitutionibus, IV, ed. J. M Soto (Madrid: Salamanca, 1987), 263.

to such concerns, a series of ecclesiastical councils were held in the city
of Lima, in 1551, 1552, 1567, 1582, 1591, 1601, and 1772, in order to agree on
the use of policies regarding practices and dogma for native conversions
in the Viceroyalty of Peru. Grounded in these councils, the history of the
incorporation of Andeans into the Catholic church has been periodized in
three stages: the "first evangelization," or the period from 1532 to the final
definition of the content of Christian doctrine in 1582; the second period,
approximately from 1610 to 1649, during which the famous campaign of
extirpation of idolatry took place; and the third and shortest, focused on the
persecution of witchcraft and the recognition of indigenous sanctity, from
1650 to 1750.[22] From the first to the last council, the prerogative to control
devotion and create strategies to fight indigenous religious practices with
linguistic, legal, and social tactics persisted.

The rise of brotherhoods during the seventeenth and eighteenth centuries
can offer a point of view from which scholars can explore the significant
negotiations of the intersections between indigenous religious practices
and knowledge production in the colonial world. It is at this intersection
that phenomena such as the pilgrimage of Quyllur Rit'i and its subsequent
brotherhood – in the context of the rise of confraternities – can be seen
as forms of political knowledge production that lay the groundwork both
for later movements of resistance and for emergent indigenous practices
reinterpreting the past and reframing it for future traditions. Indeed, the
number of *cofradías* steadily increased in spite of the dictates of the Second
and Third Councils of Lima. This shows that the latter directives not only
failed in this case but were altogether challenged. By calling out the explosion of *cofradías* in the *pueblos de españoles* and *pueblos de indios*, and by
emphasizing the damage they were causing to the ongoing goal of conversion,
archbishop Arias Ugarte urged attention not only to the *religious* aspect of
cofradías, but moreover to the economic and tributary practices to which
Indians were subjected, or perhaps better, with which they engaged on their
own orthogonal terms when they joined these associations.

How could this be contained or regulated? A partial solution was the
creation of two official administrative bodies: the Real Juzgado de Cofradías,
de ámbito civil, and the Juzgado de Testamentos, cofradías y Obras pías de
ámbito eclesiástico in Lima. Both offices were established to supervise and
regulate economical operations: rent, management of fees, *limosnas* (alms),
accounting, and civil behavior related to religious practices. Although the

22   Juan Carlos Estenssoro and Gabriela Ramos, *Del paganismo a la santidad: la incorporación de los indios del Perú al catolicismo, 1532-1750* (Paris: IFEA, 2003).

increasing number of confraternities that seemed to reframe and reposition Christian and native beliefs in new and unorthodox ways was concerning, it was also predictable. If we follow the definition of confraternities, we see that it emphasizes *accessibility* as a means for the church to draw new devotees into the fold of dogma and practice. In this sense, confraternities were conceived as associations of the faithful, established and guided by the competence of ecclesiastical authority for the promotion of special works of Christian charity or piety.[23] However, as should now be clear, this definition also formalized a paradox: confraternities were seen on the one hand as a means of drawing ever greater segments of the population into the Church, making them into Christians, while on the other hand, the formation of such groups by largely indigenous populations was seen as a threat precisely because these new members were neophytes. It is thus no surprise that practices such as those associated with Quyllur Rit'i, and any formal body dedicated to their organization, would be absent from the written record. While this helps to understand the context in which Quyllur Rit'i emerged as a set of rituals, the following two sections turn to examine the practices and oral narratives at the core of Quyllur Rit'i in order to suggest their continuity through the colonial period despite its absence in the written record. Understanding the resistance and erasure these practices faced in the colonial period helps to demonstrate the difficulty as well as the stakes involved in this continuity.

Devotional Practices and the Andean Landscape

The pilgrimage of the Lord of Quyllur Rit'i encompasses the continuation of various devotional practices that play crucial roles beyond their religious aspects, such as the formation of alliances and social relationship through the performance of dances, prayers, songs, and liturgical Andean Christian practices that manifest in the complex, hybrid emergence of faith during the pilgrimage. Andean religious rituals have been extensively studied from a historical perspective using sixteenth- and seventeenth-century sources written by Spanish missionaries, and have been interpreted through the lens of conversion. Such studies focus on the distinction between true and false religion imposed by Spanish missionaries during the colonial period. Sabine MacCormack's discussion of Christian conversion in the Andes is key here, as she directly addresses the interconnectedness of two sides of

---

23   *New Advent*, http://www.newadvent.org/cathen/04223a.htm

religious change in the colonial Andes – the political and economic on the one hand, and the ritual and theological on the other:

> During the early decades of evangelization in the Andes the model of conversion by persuasion was implemented by some missionaries, in particular by the friend and follower of Las Casas, Domingo de Santo Tomás. Subsequently, however, this model was supplanted by an ever-increasing insistence on the authority, not only of Christianity, but of European concepts of culture, to the exclusion of their Andean equivalents. Conversion to Christianity thus came to entail, not only the acceptance of a set of beliefs and religious observances, but also a broad acceptance of alien customs and values. Indians were therefore faced with a double system of constraints: on the one hand, the economic and political constraints imposed by the secular state, and on the other, the spiritual and cultural constraints of Christian mission.[24]

In the colonial situation, Andeans continued to practice their rituals and devotional practices in a context in which they were also forced to adapt to a different set of beliefs. This new religious paradigm presented both parallels and radical differences, and the identification of elements of each tradition from a scholarly, outsider perspective has become a dominant program of research in the Andes. However, it has also become a tangential distraction from what I argue is the equally – if not more – pressing task of exploring Andean people's ability to adapt without losing sight of the stakes of the force of continuity.

Recognizing the double system of constraints that MacCormack described – both "economic and political [...] and spiritual and cultural" helps not only to sort out tradition from innovation in Andean religion, but also to understand the nature of their historical development. Indeed, the processes of conversion in the Andes were closely tied not only to spiritual practices, but also, crucially, to economic and political ones. Furthermore, as I emphasize here, like the hybrid nature of the religious factors involved, the economic and political factors were grounded not only in colonial society, but also in pre-existing Andean structures of exchange, alliance, tribute, and authority. Indeed, as I suggest below, the rituals and devotional practices centered on glaciers and the eventual formation of the Brotherhood of Lord of Quyllur Rit'i can both be contextualized in their shared relationship to

---

24   Sabine MacCormack, "'The Heart has Its Reasons': Predicaments of Missionary Christianity in Early Colonial Peru," *Hispanic American Historical Review* 65, no. 3 (1985): 447.

dynamics of economic exchange and political alliances with the landscape, and particularly with glaciers.

In order to understand this shared context, consider first how dichotomous Christian concepts of religiosity and economy have steered missionaries, chroniclers, and contemporary scholars alike away from looking at Andean Christian practices of exchange with glaciers as religious practice. This has ultimately led to a lack of comprehension of the ways in which such practices became bound up in the project of conversion. The cultural and religious category of *huaca* – a focal point of colonial missionaries' anti-idolatry fervor – serves as a good starting point for discussing the ways in which colonial authorities thought about and ultimately attempted to intervene in Andean concepts and practices. Frank Salomon defines the term *huaca* as "any material thing that manifested the superhuman: a mountain peak, a spring, a union of streams, a rock outcrop, an ancient ruin, a twinned cob of maize, a tree split by lightning. Even people could be huacas."[25] The Inca Garcilaso defined the term similarly, but from a Christian perspective, writing that "huaca [...] means 'a sacred thing,' such as [...] idols, rocks, great stones or trees which the enemy [Satan] entered to make the people believe he was a god."[26]

In discussions about the historical position that glaciers and mountains have in Andean belief systems, one of the more prominent debates centers on the role of mountains. One side of this debate sees that Andean understandings of mountains as alive or having spirits long pre-dates the European invasion, and that the practices of mountain worship in the Andes resisted colonial proselytization for a number of possible reasons.[27] The other side of the debate, most urgently voiced by Peter Gose,[28] maintains that contemporary Andean mountain worship is in fact the result of the displacement, destruction, and persecution of ancestor worship cults centered on mummies which, Gose argues, constituted the dominant form of religiosity in the Andes prior to colonization. According to his argument, mountains were not truly agents prior to the European invasion, but instead merely the product of ancestors' subterranean burrowing and emergence in a mythic history. Contact with ancestors transformed and sacralized

25   Frank Salomon, *At the Mountains' Altar: Anthropology of Religion in an Andean Community* (Milton Park: Routledge, 2018), 17.
26   Ibid., 52.
27   C.f., Johan Reinhard, "Las Montañas Sagradas: Un Estudio Etho-arqueológico de Ruinas en las Altas Cumbres Andinas," *Cuadernos de Historia* 3 (1983): 27-62.
28   Peter Gose, *Invaders as Ancestors: On the Intercultural Making and Unmaking of Spanish Colonialism in the Andes* (Toronto: University of Toronto Press, 2008).

such places, allowing *ayllus* – Andean socio-political units – ritual access to otherwise distant sources of power.[29] Salomon takes an intermediate position in this debate, arguing that, rather than emerging to replace ancestor worship, the sacred nature of mountains changed its focus during the colonial period from ancestry to territory, leading to an emphasis on the animacy of their natural settings and sometimes absorbing apparitions of Christian divinity.[30]

While I agree with Salomon's intermediate position in this debate, I do not raise the issue here in order to take sides, much less resolve it, but rather mention it because of what is *not* challenged by any of the positions within it: that practices recognized by Christians as idolatrous also played crucial roles in economic and political life. Whether it was mummies or mountains (or both) that stood at the center of Andean religious life, they also articulated networks of exchange of resources, played strategic roles in the negotiation of inter-*ayllu* and inter-ethnic alliances, and were crucial to the way the Inca consolidated such expansive and diverse territories within the Tawantinsuyu. In other words, whatever views one holds on the issue of the worship and sacredness of mountains in the Andes, it is necessary to keep in mind the Spanish fear, ignorance, and, ultimately, inability to recognize the ways in which Andean ritual practices spanned religion, economy, and politics. This failure was due in large part to a simplistic take on the kinds of religious practices that Europeans encountered in the Andes, guided largely by the *idée fixe* that idolatry was at the core of all Andean ritual. As MacCormack explained:

> Among the first things that some of the invaders of the Inca empire noticed was the ubiquitous and "detestable" cult of "dirty" idols. The resulting battle over idols and the beliefs and cultic practices surrounding them is in one sense only an outcrop of debates and conflicts over idols, images, and demons in the ancient Mediterranean and in medieval and Renaissance Europe. Even so, the intricacies of European learned traditions ended up shaping the history and culture of Peru and the other Andean republics until the present. Yet while ancient arguments and beliefs about idols were reiterated in Peru, their effect was not quite what it had been in Europe. Besides, the arguments shifted and changed in the new context. There is also the question, did these arguments ever achieve anything beyond imposing European ideas and cognitive models on the Andean world?

29 Ibid.
30 Ibid., xii.

Or did they succeed in touching upon some aspects at least of Andean religious practice and belief?[31]

While I argue in this chapter that the Quyllur Rit'i pilgrimage exhibits the continuity of core aspects of devotional and ritual practices in the Andes from pre-Hispanic times through the European invasion and colonization until the present, I also want to emphasize that this continuity does not preclude adaptation or change. The imposition and assimilation of Christian practices that ensued from colonial attempts to convert Andeans has certainly shaped the way in which religious practices have continued. The Spanish fixation on idolatry perhaps transformed into a *need* to contemplate practices such as pilgrimages and offerings to mountains as purely religious. This perspective erased important dimensions of mountain or ancestor worship, such as the way in which they helped to maintain social balance among the territories where individual glaciers held authority. Nevertheless, even after the often-violent imposition of Christian religion and anti-idolatry campaigns, most Andean people saw themselves as related to one another by virtue of their connection to these places and held collective memories rooted in these places.

The pilgrimage of Quyllur Rit'i offers an opening for stepping out of this colonially grounded perspective to look at rituals centered on glaciers not only as religious, but also as territorial practices tied to strategies for preserving healthy economic and social relationship both with the glaciers as sentient beings and with other socio-political groups. To look, then, at the processes of change, imposition, assimilation, and adaptation that have shaped Andean ritual practices as they exist today requires taking a moment to contemplate the question of whose position or point of view is taken in defining the category of ritual in the first place. Or, perhaps more to the point, who is making the operation that separates rituals from quotidian habits, categorizing the latter as political, economic, or simply cultural? I address this question by way of two *counter*-examples of the separation which together illustrate how ritual was understood in pre-Hispanic and colonial contexts in the Andes, supporting my position that the separation is indeed an artifact of a colonial Christian ideology that separated religion from the economic and political life.

The first example is the Inca ritual complex known as *capacocha.* I draw here on the writings of Cristóbal de Molina (1529-1585), a priest in the Hospital

---

31   Sabine MacCormack, "Gods, Demons, and Idols in the Andes," *Journal of the History of Ideas* 67, no. 4 (2006): 624.

for the Natives of Our Lady of Succor in Cuzco, a preacher for nearly twenty years in the same city, and an expert in the Quechua language.[32] While Molina's work is not dated, scholars who have worked with the document believe it was written between 1573 and 1575.[33] He described the ritual of the *capacocha* as follows:

> The provinces of Collasuyu, Chinchaysuyu, Antisuyu and Cuntisuyu would bring to this city, from each town and lineage of people, one or two small boys or girls, of ten years old. They would also bring clothes and livestock, as well as sheep [made] of gold, silver, and *mullu*.[34] These were kept in Cuzco [...] there the children and other sacrifices walked around the statues of the creator, sun, Thunders, and Moon, that were already in the plaza for this purpose. They made two turns [around them], and after finishing, the Inca summoned the provincial priest and had the offerings divided into four parts for the four *suyos* [...] And he would tell them "Each of you take your share of these offerings and sacrifices, take it to your principal *huaca*, and sacrifice them [...]"[35]

This description offers a colonial, ethnographic narration of the way the ritual of *capacocha* was enacted before the Spanish invasion and colonization. What I wish to emphasize here is the way in which the ritual enacts a geopolitical strategy, orchestrating the movement of people and sacred objects from far-flung parts of the Tawantinsuyu first to Cuzco, and then to important glacial pilgrimage sites, in order to regulate and govern the extensive territory. Molina later explains that the Inca believed extending human and material offerings to all *huacas* in the four regions would guarantee peace, good health, and food throughout the territory. In Molina's words, "the expert who performs the sacrifices, the *huacamayos* [shrine specialist], which means 'guardian of the *huacas*,' and who were in charge

---

32   Cristóbal de Molina et al., *Account of the Fables and Rites of the Incas* (Austin: University of Texas Press, 2011), xvi.

33   Ibid.; Raúl Porras Barrenechea, ed., *Los Cronistas del Perú (1528-1650)* (Lima: Imprenta DESA, 1986); Carlos A. Romero, *Las crónicas de los Molinas* (Lima: Librería e Imprenta D. Miranda, 1943); Henrique Urbano, "Ediciones de la "Relación," and "Introducción a la vida y obra de Cristóbal de Molina," in *Relación de las fábulas y ritos de los incas,* eds. Urbano and Julio Calvo Pérez (Lima; Universidad de San Martin de Porres Press, 2008).

34   Concha del mar, chaquira, coral, que sacrifican (ofrendaban) los indios, y hoy en día (aún) se hace. Anónimo, *Arte y Vocabulario en la Lengua General del Perú,* (Lima: Publicaciones del Instituto Riva-Agüero, 2014), 133.

35   Molina et al., *Rites of the Incas,* 77.

of them, each received the sacrifice that correspond to their *huaca*."[36] In an essay about Inca state rituals, Gose elaborates further, gathering evidence from other colonial sources that, in addition to offerings, the representatives from each region that gathered in Cuzco also were expected to become possessed by the spirit of the most important *huacas* from their respective territories and offer oracular predictions about the production of resources like corn, potatoes, and camelid fibers, as well as about the outcome of any potential conflicts with neighboring regions not yet incorporated into the Tawantinsuyu.[37] These Inca state rituals underline the fact that *huacas* were not merely of religious import, but were perhaps even principally important for their political and economic value.

The second example is an archeological study of a ceremonial site located on the stratovolcano Llullaillaco, which lies on what is now the border of Argentina and Chile. At an altitude of 6,739 meters, the archeological site at its summit is the highest in the world,[38] and the best preserved, complex ceremonial site at that height in the Andes.[39] Although the Inca presence in this region began approximately after 1470,[40] several ethnic groups inhabited the region at the time of Inca conquest.[41] The ceremonial site corresponds in several ways to the pilgrimage destinations of the *capacocha* described in the first example above, as it is also a pilgrimage destination involving an ascent to a glacial summit and human offerings. Complementing Molina's colonial description, the archaeological studies cited above offer a confirmation of the widespread practice of glacial pilgrimages and offerings in the southern Peruvian Andes before the European invasion.

While ethnographers such as Marisol de la Cadena and Catherine Allen have emphasized the fact that glaciers are salient, sentient authorities in Andean society – earth beings, to use de la Cadena's phrase – colonial and archaeological accounts like those in the two examples above also suggest that glaciers have played a fundamental role in the economic, religious, and cultural life of the Andes for centuries before the European invasion.

36   Ibid., 81.
37   Peter Gose, "Oracles, Divine Kingship, and Political Representation in the Inka State," *Ethnohistory* 43, no. 1 (1996): 1-32.
38   Johan Reinhard, "Heights of Interest," *South American Explorer* 26 (1990), 29.
39   Johan Reinhard and María Constanza Ceruti, *Inca Rituals and Sacred Mountains: A Study of the World's Highest Archaeological Sites* (Los Angeles: Cotsen Institute of Archaeology Press, 2010), 20.
40   Hans Niemeyer, "La ocupación Inkaica de la Cuenca alta del Río Copiapo," *Comechingonia* 4 (1986): 173.
41   Terence N. D'Altroy, *The Incas* (Malden: Blackwell, 2002), 43.

Moreover, as D'Altroy points out, drawing on the work of Kosiba and Bauer, the landscape around Cuzco was not only characterized by sentient land-forms, but the latter were also "active agents in the Incas' relationship to their land's past and present," such that Cuzco was positioned "in the midst of a dynamic social space, which was constantly politically contested."[42] The emergence of Quyllur Rit'i at the end of the eighteenth century as a pilgrimage site that aligned Christian and Andean forms of religiosity while maintaining principally Andean forms of sociality, political alliance, and economic exchange highlights the possibility that here, glaciers had again become key actors in a historical moment of political reconfiguration. I now turn to the oral traditions that narrate the origin of the Quyllur Rit'i pilgrimage – missing from the colonial archive but alive and well among devotees – in order to evince more clearly how the landscape played a key role alongside the Christian church in the site's modern emergence into religious significance.

Glaciers, Narrations, and Apparitions

The oral narratives that scholars and devotees reference in relation to the origin of the Lord of Quyllur Rit'i and the associated pilgrimage centers on a young, indigenous herder and his experience of encountering a white boy of his same age close to the Sinaqara glacier.[43] In my analysis, I emphasize the ways in which the figure of the herder in the context of the Andes evokes the relationship between humans and the living landscape. Through this narrative, both the figure of the herder and the Andean landscape itself are figured as central to the origin of the Lord of Quyllur Rit'i and, I argue, thereby also to that of the Brotherhood of Quyllur Rit'i.

One version of the Quyllur Rit'i miracle was compiled by Sallnow, in this version the priest who served in Ccarca from 1928 to 1946, though its documentary sources are unclear.[44] The *events* of the oral traditions linked to Quyllur Rit'i occurred in the second half of eighteenth century, approximately in 1780. This rough date offers an opportunity to reflect on and interpret the use of temporal paradigms external to this Andean

---

42   Ibid., 202.
43   Juan Andrés Ramírez, "La novena del Señor de Qoyllur Ri"i," *Allpanchis* 1 (1969): 61-88; Salas Carreño, "Diferenciación social"; "The Glacier, the Rock, the Image"; Sallnow, *Pilgrims of the Andes*.
44   Manuel Marzal, *El Mundo Religioso de Urcos* (Cusco: Instituto de Pastoral Andina, 1971); Ramírez, *La novena*; Sallnow, *Pilgrims of the Andes*, 207.

narration. This year, although approximate, generates a point of departure for the analysis of this oral tradition and the cultural conception of time it presupposes. While there are no written records that have been found that relate directly to the history of the Lord of Quyllur Rit'i from that period, the various versions of this narrative converge on this year as an approximate date.[45] Contextual details surrounding the performance of these oral narratives – such as the location, participants, and date – have not been transcribed. Instead, the life of the narrative has persisted in the collective memory of the devotees of the Lord of Quyllur Rit'i as a crucial starting point to participate in or relate to the pilgrimage. As Catherine Allen writes about storytelling in the Andes:

> Like any other cultural production, stories can be treated as having lives of their own, independent of the particular human beings who tell them and listen to them. But this loses the context in which stories actually exist, which is in the telling. Speaking and hearing actualize each other; a narrative exists through its listeners and becomes meaningful in terms of the relationship between speakers and listeners.[46]

The relationship between the oral narrative and the pilgrimage of the Lord of Quyllur Rit'i signals its strength in the gathering of followers and devotees that this narrative has provoked. Scholarship on this pilgrimage has referenced the origin narratives primarily as historical contexts, and as examples of the syncretic nature of Andean-Christian practices since the colonial period. However, by thinking about the narratives' content, structure, and context together with devotees' practices, we can also better understand the way these stories linked together important linguistic, environmental, and religious dynamics that are remarkable for their continuity in the Andean highlands. For example, taking into consideration its physical, social, and historical context – respectively, a high canyon ending at the foot of the Sinaqara glacier, indigenous herders from the nearby town of Ocongate, and the second half of the eighteenth century – I suggest first that this oral narrative circulated not only in Spanish, but also – and perhaps primarily – in Southern Quechua. As the canyon ending at Sinaqara is now

---

45   Guillermo Salas Carreño conducted archival research in the Archivo Regional del Cuzco but did not find relevant documentation in relation to the oral narrative and colonial history of Señor de Quyllur Rit'i: personal communication, March 2021.

46   Catherine J. Allen and Julia Meyerson, *Foxboy: Intimacy and Aesthetics in Andean Stories* (Austin: University of Texas Press, 2011), 1.

both grazing grounds for local herders' alpacas and sheep as well as the site of an annual pilgrimage attended by thousands of devotees to the Lord of Quyllur Rit'i, the narrative also retains a tight connection with its original places and subjects. However, more than simply retaining symbolic ties to the landscape and cultural figures of the Andes, the narrative is the founding story for a regional pilgrimage. As such, it has also given rise to elements independent of the oral tradition, as I will describe in detail in what follows. Finally, in relation to the previous discussion of devotional practices centered on mountains and glaciers, the persistent relationship between the oral narrative and the practices of devotees has helped to maintain ritual ties to the landscape that predate the European invasion.

In the rest of this section, I summarize the narrative, drawing on two similar versions included in the works of previous scholars.[47] I divide the narrative in two parts. In the first part, we witness the encounter between Marianito – the young, indigenous herder – and Manuelito – the white boy of his same age – seeing how the friendship that forms between them helps Marianito to cope with the extreme solitude and physical demands of his work. In the second part, Marianito's father enters, a local priest intervenes, and Manuelito undergoes a transformation.

The story begins as follows:

A family from Ocongate who owns alpacas and sheep sends their two children, one older and the younger approximately ten to twelve years old, to herd in the areas closer to the Sinaqara and Qolqepunco glaciers. The two brothers do not get along well. The older brother mistreats the younger, leaving him alone with no food and in charge of the work, caring for the animals without help, and then lies to their father, blaming his young brother for being lazy and neglecting the herd. Believing the older brother, Marianito's father punishes him, again sending him to herd in the high-altitude areas anyway. Marianito, sad and overwhelmed by his mistreatment, finds himself in a bleak mood, doing the hard work of taking care of the herd with no help and food, despite having an older brother who should be doing the brunt of the work. Marianito suffers and regrets his life. At this moment he decides to leave this situation to avoid more punishment and abuse, and walks toward the glaciers.[48] Along the way, he encounters a young white boy of his own age, also alone. This boy,

---

47   Marzal, *El Mundo Religioso*; Ramírez, *La novena*; Sallnow, *Pilgrims of the Andes*, 207.
48   In another version, Marianito walks toward the glacier seeking a route home that will allow him to avoid running into his older brother.

Manuelito, consoles him and offers him food. They become friends and play together, and Marianito begins to feel content again.

In this first part of the narrative, the difficult condition of the life of a young herder is played out. Herders in the Andes indeed spend long periods of time away from their towns and families. Although they have designated temporal houses in the *punas* (Andean ecological zone above 3,700 meters used primarily for grazing animals) where they live to take care of their camelids and sheep, they also have stable homes where they reside. The houses in the high pasture areas are close to glaciers, lakes, and other places with special topological characteristics, and here herders' relationships with landscape grow stronger. While taking care of their animals, they are physically distant from human interaction. Their experience and knowledge are attuned to the sensorial and physical characteristics of the landscape. Glaciated mountain peaks are particularly important. They are the biggest earth formations in herders' everyday lives, the main source of seasonal increase in river flow, and they figure prominently in stories, rituals, and even dreams – in sum, they play a crucial sociocultural role for herders.[49] Marianito's decision to walk towards the glaciers signals not only his relationship with them, but at the same time presents this closeness with the glaciers as a solution to or exit from the suffering experiences as part of his family in the town of Ocongate. I now continue to the second part:

At first, Marianito lives contentedly in the vicinity of the Sinaqara glacier with Manuelito's help and company while his herd remains healthy and grows. Meanwhile, Marianito's father hears from a neighbor that his son has a white friend who plays with him while watching the herd. His father goes to see Marianito and realizes that he is fine and that the heard is healthy and growing. Marianito tells his father about his friend and how much Manuelito has helped him. His father is happy with the result and gives Marianito new clothes as a reward for his hard work. Marianito returns to the herd, but notices now that his friend's clothes are old and worn. He offers to buy Manuelito new clothes in thanks for his help and friendship, but the white boy responds that he can only use the kind of clothes that he is wearing and no others. Marianito takes a piece of fabric from his friend's clothing and promising to get new clothes for him. When Marianito goes to Cuzco, he finds nothing that

49   Joshua Shapero, "Possessive Places: Spatial Routines and Glacier Oracles in Peru's Cordillera Blanca," *Ethnos* 84, no. 4 (2019): 614-641.

matches the fabric. The vendors tell him that the kind of fabric that he's looking for is only used by the Bishop. The Bishop of Cuzco at the time is Manuel Moscoso Peralta. When Marianito goes to him and insists on receiving the fabric for his friend, the bishop promises to do so. At the same time, Bishop Moscoso feels suspicious about Marianito's story and sends a message to the priest in Ocongate, Pedro de Landa, asking him to investigate Marianito's friend and the fabric. The priest fulfils the bishop's request and, as he approaches Sinaqara, sees not only Marianito and his herd, but also a white boy in a white tunic who emits a bright light that blinds him, making him shield his eyes. The priest suspects a trick, like someone holding a mirror to blind him, and organizes a second expedition, this time accompanied by the local Spanish tribute collector and his successor, neighbors, and the cacique. They see the children from afar and again one child is radiating a blinding light. The group divides in two to try to catch the radiant child, but as they get closer to the child, he moves toward a rock. The priest tries to catch the child, but instead only catches a local tree called *tayanka*.[50] Believing that the child had climbed the tree, the group looks toward it only to see the image of Christ hanging in suffering, looking to the sky. After seeing this, all fall to their knees, but Marianito believes that they have tortured his friend and dies on the spot. After this commotion, the group then sees the sign of the cross on the Tayanka tree. Finally, Marianito is buried beneath the rock where Manuelito disappeared. The miraculous events at Sinaqara are transmitted to the king of Spain, Carlos III, who requests to be sent the *tayanka* cross. This is sent to him, and never returns from Spain. The indigenous people of the area become unsatisfied and, hoping to calm the situation, the priest requests a replica. This image, known now as the Lord of Tayankani, is in a chapel of the same name. To avoid the possibility of idolatry and superstition, the priest lastly orders that the face of Christ be painted on the rock under which Marianito was buried. This is the image now known as "The Lord of Qoyllur Rit'i."

As this narrative reaches its end, the figure of the white boy becomes an apparition. The boy is a human in the eyes of Marianito, and through the time

---

50   Baccharis adorata tree and herbaceous specie from the Andes. Its leaves are used as medicinal treatment for inflammation. De-la-Cruz, Horacio, Graciela Vilcapoma, and Percy A. Zevallos. "Ethnobotanical Study of Medicinal Plants Used by the Andean People of Canta, Lima, Peru," *Journal of Ethnopharmacology* 111 (2007), 292.

they shared, Marianito overcomes his sadness and preoccupation over his intense work. The story thus speaks about an exchange between two ethnic subjects – indigenous and European – in a place that allows them to witness together the manifestation of the Andean landscape. The key elements in the second part continue this pattern, placing church and colonial officials and symbols (the bishop, the priest, the tax collector, the crucified Jesus, and the cross) in counterpoint with the Andean landscape (the tayanka tree, the boulder, and the location itself at Sinaqara). The juxtaposition of the Andean and European boys, and of the Andean landscape with the symbols of Christianity and colonial administration closely parallels the way in which Quyllur Rit'i's emergence in the religious landscape of the late colonial Andes proposed a reconfiguration of Andean and European religious, economic, and political practices. If the colonial archive is silent on this matter, the oral traditions surrounding the pilgrimage are not, and their insistence on the late eighteenth century as the temporal origin, I argue, is no accident. As I wrote above, this was a moment in which Andean society was undergoing significant changes, especially in relation to the respective roles played by indigenous and European forms of religious, economic, and political life. While the written archive offers one point of view, my intervention here is to suggest that the rituals and narrations surrounding Quyllur Rit'i – when seen in the light of their continuation of a long-standing tradition of human-landscape interconnections – offers a different point of view. A full picture can only emerge, then, when the two are juxtaposed, as I have attempted in this chapter.

Conclusion

The physical location where the pilgrimage of the Lord of Quyllur Rit'i occurs is not an inert landscape, but rather contains salient subjects such as glaciers, which have personhood and social relationships with people. The relationship between the landscape and humans in the Andes has a long history before the European invasion and has been adapted and reconfigured by the Spanish Crown and by the Catholic Church. Material efforts to break and prevent these relationships were numerous in the colonial period. These attempts to detach the links that diverse ethnic groups had with ancestors at the time of the European invasion not only entailed the imposition of Spanish colonial laws over indigenous people, but also the implementation of social procedures designed to purify the ecological and human landscape from indigenous relationships with the material world. Among these procedures are the *reducciones*, or resettlements of the Toledan reforms, the spread of Christian institutions throughout the viceroyalty, extirpation campaigns, and the imposition of Spanish political institutions.

In contrast, the rituals and narrations surrounding Quyllur Rit'i tell a different side of the story. Here, Andeans themselves can be seen, not as the sole agents, but rather calling upon the agency of glacial beings like Sinaqara to speak through and with Christian religious and institutional categories in a way that ingeniously cements their continued relevance and centrality as arbiters of spiritual, social, political, and economic order in the region for centuries to come. Ultimately, this continuity did indeed succeed in providing the grounds for the formation of a Brotherhood of the Lord of Quyllur Rit'i – likely impossible in the colonial period – and ultimately in a great increase in the popularity of the pilgrimage throughout the late twentieth and early twenty-first centuries.

About the author

Angelica Serna Jeri is an Assistant Professor of Spanish and Portuguese in the University of New Mexico. She earned her Ph.D. in Romance Languages from the University of Michigan, Ann Arbor. Her teaching and research meet at the intersection of indigenous studies, postcolonial theory, and digital humanities.

Bibliography

Allen, Catherine J. *The Hold Life Has: Coca and Cultural Identity in an Andean Community.* Washington, D.C.: Smithsonian Institution Press, 1988.

Allen, Catherine J, and Julia Meyerson. *Foxboy: Intimacy and Aesthetics in Andean Stories.* Austin: University of Texas Press, 2011.

Anónimo, *Arte y Vocabulario en la Lengua General del Perú.* Lima: Publicaciones del Instituto Riva-Agüero, 2014.

Burns, Kathryn. *Into the Archive: Writing and Power in Colonial Peru.* Durham: Duke University Press, 2010.

Cadena, Marisol de la. *Earth Beings: Ecologies of Practice Across Andean Worlds.* The Lewis Henry Morgan Lectures, 2011. Durham: Duke University Press, 2015.

Carrasco, Pedro. "The Civil-Religious Hierarchy in Mesoamerican Communities: Pre-Spanish Background and Colonial Development." *American Anthropologist* 65, no. 3 (1967): 483-497.

Celestino, Olinda. "Cofradía: continuidad y transformación de la sociedad andina."
     Allpanchis 20 (1982): 147-166.

Celestino, Olinda and Meyers, Albert. *Las cofradías en el Perú: región central.*
     Frankfurt: Vervuert, 1981.

——. "La posible articulación del ayllu a través de las cofradías." In *Etnohistoria
     y Antropología Andina: Actas de la Segunda Jornada del Museo Nacional de
     Historia*, edited by Amalia Castelli, Marcia Koth de Pareces, and Mariana Mould
     de Pease, 299-310. Lima: Museo Nacional de Historia, 1981.

Celestino, Olinda, and Albert Meyers. "The Socio-economic Dynamic of the
     Confraternal Endowment in Colonial Peru: Jauja in the Eighteenth Century."
     In *Manipulating the Saints: Religious Brotherhoods and Social Integration in
     Postconquest Latin America*, edited by Albert Meyers and Diane Elizabeth
     Hopkis, 101-127. Hamburg: Wayasbah, 1988.

Cerrón-Palomino, Rodolfo. *Lingüística Quechua.* Cuzco: Centro de Estudios Rurales
     Andinos "Bartolomé de las casas," 1987.

D'Altroy, Terence N. *The Incas.* Malden: Blackwell, 2002.

De-la-Cruz, Horacio, Graciela Vilcapoma, and Percy A. Zevallos. "Ethnobotanical
     Study of Medicinal Plants Used by the Andean People of Canta, Lima, Peru."
     Journal of Ethnopharmacology 111 (2007): 284-294.

Díaz A., Alberto, Paula Martínez S., and Carolina Ponce. "Cofradías de Arica y
     Tarapacá en los siglos XVIII y XIX: Indígenas andinos, sistema de cargos religiosos
     y festividades." *Revista de Indias* 74, no. 260 (2014): 101-128.

Estenssoro, Juan Carlos, and Gabriela Ramos. *Del paganismo a la lantidad: la
     incorporación de los indios del Perú al catolicismo, 1532-1750.* Lima: IFEA, 2003.

Fuenzalida Vollmar, Fernando. "La matriz colonial de las comunidades indígenas
     del Perú: una hipótesis de trabajo." *Revista del Museo Nacional Lima* 35 (1970):
     92-123.

Garcilaso de la Vega, Inca. *Comentarios reales de los incas.* Lima: Banco de Crédito
     del Perú, 1985.

Garrett, David T. *Shadows of Empire: The Indian Nobility of Cusco, 1750-1825.* Cam-
     bridge: Cambridge University Press, 2005.

Gose, Peter. "Oracles, Divine Kingship, and Political Representation in the Inka
     State." *Ethnohistory* 43, no. 1 (1996): 1-32.

——. *Invaders as Ancestors: On the Intercultural Making and Unmaking of Spanish
     Colonialism in the Andes.* Toronto: University of Toronto Press, 2008.

Kosiba, Steve, and Andrew Bauer. "Mapping the Political Landscape: Toward a GIS
     Analysis of Environmental and Social Difference." *Journal of Archaeological
     Method & Theory* 20, no. 1 (2013): 61-101.

Labarga Garcia, Fermín. "Las cofradías en España e Iberoamérica." *Corporaciones
     religiosas y evangelización en Iberoamérica: Siglos XVI-XVIII*, edited by Lévano

Medina Diego Edgar and Kelly Montoya Estrada, 11-30. Lima: Museo de Arqueología y Antropología de San Marcos, 2010.

MacCormack, Sabine. "'The Heart has Its Reasons': Predicaments of Missionary Christianity in Early Colonial Peru." *Hispanic American Historical Review* 65, no. 3 (1985): 443-466.

——. "Gods, Demons, and Idols in the Andes." *Journal of the History of Ideas* 67, no. 4 (2006): 623-648.

Marzal, Manuel. *El mundo religioso de Urcos*. Cusco: Instituto de Pastoral Andina, 1971.

Molina, Cristóbal de, Brian S. Bauer, Vania Smith-Oka, and Gabriel E. Cantarutti. *Account of the Fables and Rites of the Incas*. Austin: University of Texas Press, 2011.

Niemeyer, Hans. "La ocupación Inkaica de la Cuenca alta del Río Copiapo." *Comechingonia* 4 (1986): 165-294.

Porras Barrenechea, Raúl, ed. *Los Cronistas del Perú (1528-1650)*. Lima: Imprenta DESA, 1986.

Prien, Hans-Jürgen. *La historia del Cristianismo en América Latina*. Salamanca: Sígueme, 1985.

Ramírez, Juan Andrés. "La novena del Señor de Qoyllur Rit'i." *Allpanchis* 1 (1969): 61-88.

Reinhard, Johan. "Las montañas sagradas: un estudio etho-arqueológico de ruinas en las altas cumbres andinas." *Cuadernos de Historia* 3 (1983): 27-62.

——. "Heights of Interest." *South American Explorer* 26 (1990): 24-29.

Reinhard, Johan, and Ceruti María Constanza. *Inca Rituals and Sacred Mountains: A Study of the World's Highest Archaeological Sites*. Los Angeles: Cotsen Institute of Archaeology Press, 2010.

Romero, Carlos A. *Las crónicas de los Molinas*. Lima: Librería e Imprenta D. Miranda, 1943.

Salas Carreño, Guillermo. "Diferenciación social y discursos publicos sobre la peregrinación de Quyllurit'i." In *Mirando la Esfera Pública desde la Cultura en el Perú*, edited by Gisela Cánepa and Maria E. Ulfe, 243-288. Lima: CONCYTEC, 2006.

——. "The Glacier, the Rock, the Image: Emotional Experience and Semiotic Diversity at the Quyllurit'i Pilgrimage (Cuzco, Peru)." *Signs and Society* 2, no. 1 (2014): 188-214.

——. *Lugares parientes: comida, cohabitación y mundos andinos*. Lima: Pontifica Universidad Católica del Perú, 2019.

Salomon, Frank. *At the Mountains' Altar: Anthropology of Religion in an Andean Community*. Milton Park: Routledge, 2018.

Sallnow, Michael J. *Pilgrims of the Andes: Regional Cults in Cusco*. Washington, D.C.: Smithsonian Institution Press, 1987.

Shapero, Joshua. "Possessive Places: Spatial Routines and Glacier Oracles in Peru's Cordillera Blanca." *Ethnos* 84, no. 4 (2019): 614-641.

Trouillot, Michel-Rolph. *Silencing the Past: Power and the Production of History.* Boston: Beacon Press, 1995.

Urbano, Henrique, and Julio Calvo Pérez, eds. *Relación de las fábulas y ritos de los incas.* Lima: Universidad de San Martín de Porres, 2007.

Verdesio, Gustavo. "Para repensar los estudios coloniales: Sobre la relación entre el campo de estudios, las disciplinas, y los pueblos indígenas." *Telar* 11-12 (2013-14): 257-272.

Vetter Parodi, Luisa. "Plateros indígenas y europeos: de las cofradías de Santa Ana y San Eloy." In *Corporaciones religiosas*, 189-227.

Part III

Indigenous Confraternities in the Southern Cone

8 Immigrants' Devotions

The Incorporation of Andean Amerindians in Santiago de Chile's Confraternities in the Seventeenth Century[1]

Jaime Valenzuela Márquez
Pontificia Universidad Católica de Chile

Translated by Javiera Jaque Hidalgo

Abstract

This chapter discusses the main confraternities founded in colonial Santiago de Chile by indigenous immigrants from the Andes. These individuals formed social networks and relations, settled in the periphery of the city and performed artisan labor. This chapter seeks to connect religious practices, social networks and labor spaces through an analysis of the religious corporations that linked these loci of agency to one another.

Keywords: Chile, Andean Catholicism, indigenous confraternities, migration

Following medieval tradition, and under the new doctrinal impulse of the Council of Trent, religious confraternities constituted privileged corporate bodies of Catholic modernity. Confraternities allowed, at least theoretically, monitoring the faithful, channeling devotion institutionally, and applying the ecclesiastical dispositions laid down by the Council of Trent, after its American implementation with the Third Council of Lima (1582-1583).[2]

---

1   This is a translated, revised, and synthesized version of the article: "Devociones de inmigrantes. Indígenas andinos y plurietnicidad urbana en la conformación de cofradías coloniales (Santiago, Chile, siglo XVII)," *Historia* 43, no. 1 (2010): 203-244.
2   Francesco Leonardo Lisi, *El tercer concilio limense y la aculturación de los indígenas sudamericanos* (Salamanca: Universidad de Salamanca, 1990), 195.

Javiera Jaque Hidalgo and Miguel A. Valerio. *Indigenous and Black Confraternities in Colonial Latin America: Negotiating Status through Religious Practices.* Amsterdam: Amsterdam University Press, 2022

DOI: 10.5117/ 9789463721547_CH08

They served to guide the devotion of lay people during religious festivities and to provide spiritual and material support during funeral rites. They also cultivated the remembrance of deceased members through annual masses and supported their members in the face of economic hardship. For the latter, they relied on membership fees, alms collected from the local inhabitants, and – depending on the degree of importance – income from credits or the lease of real estate bequeathed by deceased members.

Confraternities also created a social space for people linked by economic, labor, or ethnic ties. Some were comprised of the local elite and held great prestige, while others corresponded to networks of certain artisanal guilds, or, in the American context, connected people classified by the colonial system into ethnic categories – *morenos* (blacks), *indios* (Indians), and *castas* (castes).[3] There were also, as we will see in this chapter, mixed and pluralistic confraternities where members of different origins and conditions coexisted and practiced their religions.

The system of confraternities implemented in Latin America was thus steeped in the human and cultural diversity of colonial society. With this, indigenous neophytes, enslaved Africans, and mestizo *castas* were fully incorporated into the system of signs and practices deployed by the Church. The confraternity was, then, an organization that provided an identity framework to its members – a corporate identity under which non-Hispanic creoles could present themselves before the colonial system, define their level of commitment to it and, therefore, be allowed to claim a certain degree of symbolic integration and prestige – elements that could be flaunted before the Church, the State, and other groups of society.[4] This was an organization, in short, that contributed to a sense of belonging, a key factor in the context of the displacements associated with the new, colonial forms of labor and administrative organization that were stipulated, such as Viceroy Francisco de Toledo's regime of *reducciones* (labor camps) in Peru.[5]

---

3   See José Luis Martínez, "¿Cómo hablar de indios e identidades en el siglo XVI? Una aproximación a la construcción de los discursos coloniales," *Historia indígena* 8 (2004); 41-55; Alejandra Araya Espinoza and Jaime Valenzuela Márquez, eds., *América colonial. Denominaciones, clasificaciones e identidades* (Santiago: Pontificia Universidad Católica de Chile, 2010).

4   Juan Carlos Estenssoro, *Del paganismo a la santidad. La incorporación de los indios del Perú al catolicismo (1532-1750)* (Lima: IFEA, 2003), 443-444; Albert Meyers and Diane Elizabeth Hopkins, eds., *Manipulating the Saints: Religious Brotherhoods and Social Integration in Postconquest Latin America* (Hamburg: Wayasbah, 1988). On *reducciones*, see Daniel Nemser, *Infrastructures of Race: Concentration and Biopolitics in Colonial Mexico* (Austin: University of Texas Press, 2017).

5   See Akira Saito and Claudia Rosas Lauro, eds., *Reducciones. La concentración forzada de las poblaciones indígenas en el Virreinato del Perú* (Lima: National Museum of Ethnology of Japan, 2017).

In other words, being a member of a religious confraternity, especially for individuals belonging to discriminated, undervalued, or deracinated groups, not only implied a greater closeness to the possibility of post-mortem salvation but also, a certain form of integration, community regeneration, social mobility, and recognition. For those who had already reached these steps, the confraternity could help endorse and enrich one's new social position. This will also be seen in this chapter, since the confraternities where Andean immigrants from Santiago were placed can be viewed not just as instances of corporate identity production, but also, in an inverse sense, as spaces that solidify their settlements, contributed to an integration already achieved, and allowed for a deeper socialization among previous connections.

The visual hierarchy of confraternal ritual participation provided a very clear space for deciphering the nuances of power that circulated among the members. This was crystallized in positions such as the *mayordomo* (leader), who administered income and expenses, organized activities, and served as a link to the religious community that housed the confraternity; the procurator, and the *veinticuatro*, the most influential group, with active and passive votes both in elections and in the confraternity's decision processes. This administrative structure incidentally followed traditional forms of European confraternities, but also, observed at a local level, implied the vindication of symbolic prestige and the allocation of spaces of power between social and ethnic equals.

The Counterreformation world, indeed, highly valued the public experience of devotion that spilled into the streets through processions. In practice, through visual and physical experience, these reinforced the advances of indoctrination and the incorporation of individuals to the parameters of behavior that the colonial system defined for different segments of society.[6]

Processions, in fact, became a useful tool for the process of evangelization and social integration that was deployed, in particular, in indigenous populations. In this strategic context we can observe the different orders of the Chilean capital's regular clergy, striving to support the foundation of confraternities that, at least nominally, were differentiated by social or ethnic origin. These corporate bodies could be seen parading through the streets during Holy Week, on Corpus Christi, and during the respective

6   See Pilar Gonzalbo Aizpuru, "Las fiestas novohispanas: espectáculos y ejemplo," *Mexican Studies/Estudios Mexicanos* 9, no. 1 (1993): 19-45; Berta Ares Queija, "Las danzas de los indios: un camino para la evangelización del virreinato del Perú," *Revista de Indias* 46, no. 174 (1984): 445-463.

annual festivities of their patron saints. Due to its demographic weight and because it was the preferred object of colonial Christianization policies, it was not strange that confraternities of indigenous people, black people, and *castas* were the protagonists of most of the processions that traveled through the streets of Santiago for Holy Week, or for the celebrations organized by convents to celebrate their patron saints and advocations of the Virgin as well as those of their confraternities. These ceremonies were added, as well, to those of the annual liturgical calendar, for which indigenous people also arrived from the city outskirts.[7]

The urban space of Santiago de Chile – peripheral and modest within the viceroyalty of Peru, but representative of the ethnic diversity that characterized the colonial world – reproduced the system of corporate devotion that was deployed in the rest of the continent. It also reproduced the religious practices that were associated with them. Here, too, confraternities were deployed as spaces of shared corporate identity and social positioning for non-Spanish inhabitants. It will be in this context where the specific integration of indigenous people from the Andes, as well as the pluri-ethnic relations that underlaid the processions described above, can be observed.

Andean Immigration in Chile: Displacement and Diversity

The Andean presence in central Chile has antecedents linked to the phase of Tahuantinsuyu expansion toward the south, when colonies of *mitimaes* (Inca emissaries) began to settle on the shores of the Mapocho River – the future enclave of the city of Santiago – in order to protect the southern limit of the Inca empire in the face of hostility from the indigenous people that lived further south. Almost seventy years later, hundreds of *yanaconas* (royal servants) from the Cuzco region and the Aymara plateau of Collao – on the shores of Lake Titicaca – accompanied the expeditions of Diego de Almagro (1535) and Pedro de Valdivia (1540), carrying food and supplies, and providing military support to Spaniards in their invasion of what would later be called Chile.

---

7   For a contemporary description, see Alonso de Ovalle, *Histórica relación del reino de Chile y de las misiones y ministerios que ejercita en él la Compañía de Jesús* (1646; reprint: Santiago: Universidad de Chile, 1969), 184. On Santigo at the time see, Valenzuela Márquez, *Las liturgias del poder. Celebraciones públicas y estrategias persuasivas en Chile colonial (1609-1709)* (Santiago: DIBAM, 2001); Armando de Ramón, *Santiago de Chile (1541-1991). Historia de una sociedad urbana* (Madrid: MAPFRE, 1992); Jean-Paul Zúñiga, *Espagnols d'outre-mer: émigration, métissage et reproduction sociale à Santiago du Chili, au 17e siècle* (Paris: EHESS, 2002).

As servants, "soldiers," translators, and concubines, the indigenous people of the Andes were active assistants to the Europeans. And while forced labor laid the initial foundation for the relationship between the two groups, the fact is that their quick adaptation to the obligations imposed on them by the conquistadors helped both local Indigenous and the Spaniards themselves to see and treat them as true "collaborators" with the Spanish colonization of Chile.

Toward the end of the sixteenth century, the presence of these immigrants in the heart of colonial society had been consolidated.[8] Around 1614, a report prepared by an *oidor* of the Audiencia of Chile highlighted the presence of indigenous peoples from Peru and Tucumán, forming 17% of the city's total indigenous population.[9] On the other hand, in the testaments that several Andean immigrants dictated a few decades later, a more varied geographical origin can be observed. This evidence allows one to believe that, after the first massive wave of immigrants in the mid-sixteenth century, there was a smaller movement that attracted people from places like Huamanga, Huánuco, Jauja, Arequipa, Cochabamba, and even Quito and Guayaquil to Chile.[10]

I recognize that categories such as "Andean indigenous people" are indistinct and clearly generic. The proper aim of an analysis of historical demography, with pretensions of sociocultural study, and that seeks to unravel the complex motivations, circuits, influences, identity crossings, etc., of those migrant actors, would be to explore those actors' ethnogeographical origins; in this case, the ethnic communities of origin, from which it would be possible to give an account of the deeper diversity that feeds the place of their roots. However, we are in the presence of subjects for whom the documentation does not provide more information regarding an "original identity" or a precise community affiliation. Beyond that first wave that accompanied the Spanish invaders, and that we can effectively place among the Aymara inhabitants of the area near Lake Titicaca or among Quechua-speaking people of the Cuzco area, the rest of the references that come from subsequent decades point to general geographic affiliations, noting as origin some main city or its respective jurisdiction.

---

8   Álvaro Jara, "Los asientos de trabajo y la provisión de mano de obra para los no-encomenderos en la ciudad de Santiago, 1586-1600," in *Trabajo y salario indígena, siglo XVI*, ed. Álvaro Jara (Santiago: Universitaria, 1987), 59-63.

9   Antonio Vázquez de Espinosa, *Compendio y descripción de las indias occidentales* (1629, reprint: Madrid: BAE, 1969), 45.

10 Julio Retamal Ávila, *Testamentos de "indios" en Chile colonial: 1564-1801* (Santiago: Universidad Andrés Bello, 2000).

We are therefore faced with references to notions of identity "polluted" by colonial administrative parameters and by the very situation generated by long-distance displacement, in which a generic and easily identifiable geographical origin (a city, a region) acquires greater importance than the reference to an ethnic group or to a more specific place (a community, a locality), a situation that did not occur in contexts of closer intraregional displacement, such as indigenous migrants from the cities of Lima, Potosí, or Quito.[11] On the contrary, in the context of long-distance migratory movements, such as the one we are analyzing in this chapter, ethnic identities experience transformations of different nature, depth, and consequences. Among the most evident is the discursive emergence of the category of "Indian," which even sought to create a specific – and at the same time, homogenizing – "republic" of the wide and diverse universe of indigenous communities. Beyond the failure of this project, the truth is that the category "indio" (Indian) – like that of "negro" (Black), or "español" (Spanish) – quickly acquired a fundamental importance to identify subjects "different" from other categories or denominations, and for whom certain duties and rights were reserved for at the administrative, labor, judicial, and religious levels.[12] The "calidad de indio" (indigenous quality) was then an omnipresent condition stated in every colonial document in which said subjects appeared, after which their nature (geographical origin) and/or their more precise ethnic affiliation (community, partiality, *ayllu*, etc.) could come.

But there is also an opposite effect, under which indigenous subjects began to use, negotiate, or even deny said category from below, in a strategic way, with a view to a better social positioning or escape from their reality. Mestizaje – and the deception of appearances and phenotypes that it

11   Noble David Cook, "Les indiens immigrés à Lima au début du XVIIe siècle," *Cahiers des Amériques Latines* 13/14 (1976): 33-50; Jeffrey Cole, *The Potosí Mita, 1573-1700: Compulsory Indian Labor in the Andes* (Stanford: Stanford University Press, 1985); Paul Charney, "El indio urbano. Un análisis económico y social de la población india de Lima en 1613," *Histórica* 12, no. 1 (1988): 5-33; Jaques Poloni-Simard, *El mosaico indígena. Movilidad, estratificación social y mestizaje en el corregimiento de Cuenca (Ecuador) del siglo XVI al XVIII* (Quito: Abya Yala, 2006); Carlos Ciriza-Mendívil, *Naturales de una ciudad multiétnica. Vidas y dinámicas sociales de los indígenas de Quito en el siglo XVII* (Madrid: Sílex, 2019).

12   See José Luis Martínez Cereceda, "Construyendo mundos: el 'nacimiento' de los indios en los Andes del siglo XVI," in *Del Nuevo al Viejo Mundo: mentalidades y representaciones desde América*, ed. Alejandra Araya, Azún Candina and Celia Cussen (Santiago: Universidad de Chile, 2008), 23-34; Rachel Sarah O'Toole, *Bound Lives: Africans, Indians, and the Making of Race in Colonial Peru* (Pittsburgh: University of Pittsburgh Press, 2012); Eduardo França Paiva, *Nombrar lo nuevo. Una historia léxica de Iberoamérica entre los siglos XVI y XVIII (las dinámicas de mestizajes y el mundo del trabajo)* (Santiago: Universitaria, 2020).

allows – or trades were, then, scenarios that facilitated a certain plasticity of original identities, especially in contexts of diversity such as that which characterizes cities, or those spaces of interaction and coexistence that have been defined as a *middle ground*.[13] If we add to this migration from faraway places, with the uprooting and need for finding a new home that comes with it, that negotiation of "Indian" identity can imply more freedom, to call oneself *Cuzco*, for example. Dynamics that can also contemplate the reconstruction of memory – personal or collective – and the reconstruction of a past adjusted to the demands of the present and the expectations of the future.[14] We could even speak of the emergence of a "ladino" indigenous agenda, understanding by such not only the learning of the Spanish language, but also the awareness of the fissures and interstices of the colonial system that could be used to improve their personal or family situation.[15] This process can be connected, moreover, with the ethnifying dynamics that began to be observed at an early stage, at the midst of the emergence of those mixed and diverse worlds of the post-conquest, and the obsession of colonizers and missionaries to discursively order any ethnic otherness they found in their paths. In a dialectical game that historiography has been unveiling in recent decades, the new "ethnic" denominations or spatialities assigned by colonial agents – such as the invention of "naciones," (nations) "parcialidades" (partialities) or non-existent pre-Hispanic leaderships – were being assimilated and resignified by the indigenous groups concerned, generating in turn colonial processes of ethnogenesis.[16]

13   Berta Ares Queija, "Mestizos en hábito de indios: ¿estrategias transgresoras o identidades difusas?", in *Passar as fronteiras: II coloquio internacional sobre mediadores culturais, séculos XV a XVIII*, ed. Rui Manuel Loureiro and Serge Gruzinski (Lagos: Centro de Estudios Gil Eanes, 1999), 133-146; Marisol de la Cadena, *Indígenas mestizos: Raza y cultura en el Cusco* (Lima: Instituto de Estudios Peruanos, 2004); Ana María Presta, "Significados materiales. Construyendo identidades a través de las profesiones y las cosas que importan. Indias, mulatas y mestizas en La Plata (Charcas), 1575-1635," *2009 Congress of the Latin American Studies Association*, Rio de Janeiro, June 11-14, 2009: http://lasa.international.pitt.edu/members/congress-papers/lasa2009/files/PrestaAnaMaria.pdf, accessed June 11, 2021; Carmen Bernand, "Mestizos, mulatos y ladinos en Hispanoamérica: un enfoque antropológico de un proceso histórico," in *Motivos de la antropología americanista. Indagaciones en la diferencia*, ed. Miguel León-Portilla (Mexico City: FCE, 2001), 105-133.
14   Aude Argouse, "Asignar un pasado al futuro. Los testamentos de indígenas, entre memoria e historia, Cajamarca, Perú, siglo XVII," in *Fronteras y sensibilidades en las Américas*, ed. Frédérique Langue & Salvador Bernabéu (Sevilla: Ediciones Doce Calles, 2011), 45-69.
15   Jaime Valenzuela, "Indios urbanos: inmigraciones, alteridad y ladinización en Santiago de Chile (siglos XVI-XVII)," *Historia rítica* 53 (2014), 13-34.
16   Thérese Bouysse-Cassagne, *La identidad aymara: aproximación histórica (siglo XV, siglo XVI)* (La Paz: IFEA, 1987); Jonathan D. Hill, *History, Power and Identity: Ethnogenesis in the Americas,*

Although they are often fragmentary, the traces left by these immigrants in Chilean archives allow us to generate a series of hypotheses about the process they experienced. These were individuals marked by the experience of being uprooted. This situation is linked, firstly, to the immigrant condition as such, which entails distancing – generally definitively – from the geographic space of origin, as well as the transfer to, and later, settlement and inclusion in the destination. Secondly, at least for those who did not come with the massive displacements of conquering expeditions, is the individuality with which they experienced this process, implicating, in turn, a personal break with the community of origin and the eventual loss of social and cultural ties with its members. Third is the fundamental change entailed by leaving rural and village spaces, and settling in the complexity of a city, regardless of whether or not it was rather modest in its urban ambitions, such as Santiago de Chile. Finally, this uprooting involves the vital need to re-root – to build new social ties and new material networks in the place of settlement. This process is much more evident in the case of their descendants, who carried a foreign family memory and, at the same time, a local personal experience.[17]

Confraternities and Devotions of the "Cuzcos" of Santiago

In the aforementioned context, it is worth asking, then, about the part confraternities played in the traditional role discussed at the beginning of this paper – that is, as an organization of cohesion and social identity, an expression of religiosity, and an example of inclusion and prestige. In other words, it is worth asking to what extent confraternities served as channels to integrate these immigrants into urban life in particular and the colonial system in general; in what way these organizations fed a "pan-Andean" identification under immigrational circumstances; and, finally, under what

1492-1992 (Iowa City: University of Iowa Press, 1996); Stuart Schwartz and Frank Salomon, "New Peoples and New Kinds of People: Adaptation, Readjustment, and Ethnogenesis in South American Indigenous Societies (Colonial Era)," in The Cambridge History of the Native Peoples of the Americas, eds. Frank Salomon and Stuart B. Schwartz, vol. III, part 2 (Cambridge: Cambridge University Press, 1999), 443-501; Guillaume Boccara, "Mundos nuevos en las fronteras del Nuevo Mundo," Nuevo Mundo / Mundos Nuevos: https://journals.openedition.org/nuevomundo/426; Christophe Giudicelli, "Hétéronomie et classifications coloniales. La construction des 'nations' indiennes aux confins de l'Amérique espagnole (XVI-XVIIe siècle)," Nuevo Mundo/Mundos Nuevos: https://journals.openedition.org/nuevomundo/59411

17   Valenzuela, "Indígenas andinos en Chile colonial: inmigración, inserción espacial, integración económica y movilidad social (Santiago, siglos XVI-XVII)," Revista de Indias 250 (2010): 749-778.

conditions they were also a reflection of the interethnic and pluricultural relationships that were woven in that urban space.

This last aspect is fundamental, since the reality of Santiago's confraternities was far from the type of confraternity established by the clergy within indigenous Andean towns. The latter was tied to the community as an ethnic unit and was economically linked to its assets, thereby reinforcing a sense of belonging and social cohesion in the community. The Chilean capital is quite far from this sort of communal confraternity model, as no specific ethnic unity among the immigrants of the Andes can be observed. Moreover, the Andean people about whom we have accurate information are mostly individuals who did not consider any ethnic or geographical link of origin among them, except for the fact of being immigrants and coming from the Peruvian Andes or Quito.

What is clear is that, similar to what happened in other parts of America, various segments of colonial society – and indigenous people in particular – accepted the system of confraternities as a positive fact, incorporating it immediately and energetically into their social and religious practices. In the Chilean case, in fact, they were erected as a basis for inclusion, recognition, and mobility for the actors of that splintered and plural society.[18]

A first empirical line of approach is given by the existence of testaments and work contracts – *asientos* – during the colonial era. Of course, this source is of a fragmentary nature, since it only gives an account of those indigenous people who left their mark by dictating their last wishes or determining their labor obligations in the notarial records of the Chilean capital. In the case of the testaments, their authors are individuals who had achieved certain material autonomy, such as artisans or owners of suburban plots, where they usually grew fruit trees, olive trees, and vineyards. In this same preventative line, it is necessary to relativize the convening capacity and the integrative role of the studied confraternities. This is because they do not appear as massive organizations and we only see them coming together in a few dozen of indigenous peoples, *morenos*, and the *castas* that populated the city of Santiago in the seventeenth century.

Notwithstanding all of the above, the fragments of testaments and contracts examined maintain their validity as interpretive support for

---

18   Dagmar Bechtloff, *Las cofradías en Michoacán durante la época de la colonia. La religión y su relación política y económica en una sociedad intercultural* (Zinacantepec: El Colegio de Michoacán, 1996), 217; Carlos Ruiz Rodríguez, "Cofradías en Chile Central. Un método de evangelización de la población indígena, mestiza y criolla," *Anuario de historia de la Iglesia en Chile* 18 (2000), 30.

broader social and cultural processes by giving us numerous and varied traces that Carlo Ginzburg legitimized through his "indicative paradigm."[9] The individual and isolated experiences that those documents show us, in comparison with other fragments of lives and sociocultural contexts could, then, help us explore more general phenomena. In this way, the testaments dictated by some Andean immigrants allow us to detect their preferences among the variety of confraternities offered by local churches and convents.[20]

A first observation is, as we had already anticipated, the geographical variety of the testators: Cuzco, Lima, Cochabamba, Jauja (Junín), Guayaquil, Quito, Huamanga (Ayacucho), Huánuco, and Pisco. Secondly, by the dates of cofrades' wills (most of the twenty indigenous subjects studied dictated their testaments after 1590) we can infer that most of them were not *yanaconas* who arrived with the first conquerors. They were individuals who migrated later, whose motivations and circuits are currently unknown. This could possibly explain the relative dispersion of their specific origins. Another hypothesis is that these immigrants from the Andes formed part of the original immigration from the conquest of Chile – they would have been very young accompanying their parents – which could be valid for the pre-1600 testators (considering a maximum of sixty years since the arrival of Pedro de Valdivia, in 1540). If true, they could have belonged to groups previously displaced from other regions to Cuzco, and then integrated into the conquering expeditions. This is because practically none of them mentions Collao, the other region that fed *yanaconas* to the armies that conquered Chile in the sixteenth century.

A third tendency that can be observed is the preponderance of the confraternity of Our Lady of Guadalupe, established in the church of La Merced, with the greatest concentration of Andean testators in the second decade of the seventeenth century. Two other confraternities are mentioned along with it: Our Lady of Copacabana – in the church of San Francisco – and Our Lady of Candelaria – in San Agustín. While it is true that the last two appear only once, by observing the choice of confraternities mentioned by

19   Carlo Ginzburg, "Indicios. Raíces de un paradigma de inferencias indiciales," in *Mitos, emblemas, indicios. Morfología e historia* (1979, reprint: Barcelona: Gedisa, 1989).

20   Archivo Nacional Histórico, Escribanos de Santiago (hereafter, ANH.ES), vol. 6, ff. 251-251v; vol. 13, ff. 294-294v; vol. 14, ff. 158-159v; vol. 19, ff. 51v-53; vol. 27, ff. 320-320v; vol. 38, ff. 199-199v; vol. 49, ff. 257-258; vol. 80, ff. 190-191v; vol. 81, ff. 309v-310; vol. 87, ff. 132-133v. See Retamal Ávila, *Testamentos de "indios"*; Álvaro Jara & Rolando Mellafe (comps.), *Protocolos de los escribanos de Santiago. Primeros fragmentos, 1559 y 1564-1566*, vol. 2 (Santiago: DIBAM, 1996), 684.

their *criollo* descendants – many of them mestizos – it is clear that they were highly preferred confraternities.[21]

We now have, then, the main confraternities where most of the indigenous immigrants that came from the Andean space and their descendants settled, socialized, celebrated, were saved, and buried. We anticipate, however, that these three cited confraternities – Guadalupe, Copacabana, and Candelaria, all, in fact, Marian – were spaces where not only Andean immigrants, but also people of very diverse geographical and cultural origins converged; however, all of them were marked under the colonial category of "Indian."

Our Lady of Guadalupe

The preferred confraternity where indigenous people coming from the Andes gathered most likely had its origin in the American journey carried out by the monk Diego de Ocaña, from the Spanish monastery Our Lady of Guadalupe in Extremadura. Ocaña arrived in Lima in 1599 with the intention of spreading the cult to the Virgin of Guadalupe, and its image, to this group. He did the latter through a series of portraits of the Virgin that he painted and distributed in the different places he visited. His work also strategically inserted this devotion among the local patronal devotions, for which he promoted the creation of confraternities devoted to Guadalupe.[22]

Although he would only be in the capital of the viceroyalty a few months, the Guadalupan cult quickly latched on to the image that he left there. In early 1600 Ocaña embarked toward Chile, from whose port in the north, Coquimbo, he would begin his roughly three-month pilgrimage, "until arriving at the end of the land of Chiloé; and in all these years he did not take part in any sitting or resting [...] always walking and I started from the beginning of my governing to set up Our Lady's confreres for all, who were sending their alms."[23]

Ocaña's project reflects the relationship that took place at the time between an image, its devotion, and the organization of corporations of devotees who cared for it. Of course, all these signs lead us to link the rapid

---

21   ANH.ES, vol. 5, ff. 102-103; vol. 6, ff. 9-10v; vol. 30, ff. 7-8v; vol. 51, ff. 210v-211v; vol. 60, f. 9.

22   Kenneth Mills, "Ocaña, Diego de (ca. 1570-1608)," in *Guide to Documentary Sources for Andean Studies, 1530-1900*, ed. Joanne Pillsbury, vol. 3 (Norman: University of Oklahoma Press, 2008), 457-464; Reginaldo de Lizárraga, *Descripción del Perú, Tucumán, Río de la Plata y Chile* (Madrid: Historia 16, 1986), 115-116.

23   Diego de Ocaña, *Viaje a Chile* (Santiago: Universitaria, 1995), 45.

success of this devotion in the space of the Andes with the designation of immigrants to the confraternity that was developed in the city of Santiago de Chile from the beginning of the seventeenth century. This inference speaks to the role that devotional images and their geographic circulation can play, accompanying migrant individuals or groups as support for supernatural protection, as community references, and as bridges to their place of origin and their cultural experiences.[24]

The Andean *cofrades* of the Chilean Guadalupe put all their efforts into fulfilling the commitment signed in 1610 to build their chapel in the church of La Merced in Santiago, perhaps participating with their artisanal skills in the construction or by making monetary donations, resources that could eventually lead to a prominent burial place in the future chapel.[25] Thus, for example, we see the bricklayer Rodrigo, son of an immigrant from Cuzco, who in his 1612 testament left eight pesos "for the work of the chapel of the said confraternity, where I am a member."[26] The following year, the prosperous bricklayer Gaspar, originally from Jauja, declared in Quechua that he was a Guadalupan *cofrade*. In doing so, he also requested to move his future burial from Santo Domingo, where he had previously planned, to the church of La Merced, and leaving fifteen *patacones* (silver ounce coins) for "the said Confraternity of Cuscos."[27] So successful was the activity displayed by the *cofrades* that, as we can see, they could be buried in their chapel beginning in 1613. This is indicated in the testament dictated that year by the "Cuzco" tailor Diego, as well as in that dictated by the "Cuzco" Alonso in 1618.[28]

Indeed, in the same area of the temple where the chapel of the confraternity was located, the order sold a grave to Sebastián de Iturrieta, a mestizo tailor from Lima whose mother was from Cusco, and he openly claimed that origin. Throughout his known life – unfolding since he arrived in Santiago in the 1580s – Iturrieta demonstrated a constant relationship with indigenous people from the Andes, whom he hired as apprentices or tailors, in case he needed quality craftsmen to support his prominent career.[29] This led him to turn his workshop into one of the most sought-after in the Chilean

---

24 See Pierre Ragon, *Les saints et les images du Mexique, XVIe-XVIIIe siècles* (Paris: L'Harmattan, 2003), 344.

25 ANH.ES, vol. 45, ff. 209-210.

26 Retamal Ávila, *Testamentos*, 136.

27 ANH.ES, vol. 81, ff. 309v-310.

28 Retamal Ávila, *Testamentos*, 143, 157; ANH.ES, vol. 7, ff. 305v-306; Emma de Ramón, "La incorporación de las etnias no hispanas a la actividad industrial durante la colonia temprana," *Revista Archivo Nacional* 2 (2004): 42-47.

29 ANH.ES, vol. 6, ff. 251-251v; vol. 35, ff. 267-267v; vol. 36, ff. 34-34v; vol. 39, f. 306v.

capital and even to be counted among the group of select tailors who in 1614 founded another confraternity devoted to the Virgin in the cathedral.[30]

We have seen, then, that the Guadalupan confraternity gathered a significant number of the indigenous immigrants known as *cuzcos*. This denomination responds to a sort of ethnonym, that, used indistinctly by colonial authorities or by those mentioned previously, referred to an identity – an identity that reclaimed a privileged situation the indigenous people of the Andes inherited, as a sort of "meritorious indigenous" – from their forebears. This situation derived from the support provided to the Spanish conquerors by the first immigrants, which allowed for differentiation between local and non-local indigenous people who inhabited the city. It was, of course, a denomination that was not strictly ethnic, but rather historical-geographical, encompassing individuals of different regional origins but who were geographically linked to the Andean space and its legendary Incan capital.[31]

For all these reasons, Guadalupe's internal positions, "named for the devotion of natural Indians and descendants of *cuzcos*," were generally in the hands of these immigrants, at least during its first years of operation.[32] In fact, in 1615 its *mayordomos* (leaders) and *procuradores* (treasurers) authorized the provincial Mercedarian who left for Europe to ask for confirmation of its founding. The document was signed on behalf of all the others by the *cuzco mayordomo* Diego Quispe, as he was the only one who knew how to sign his name. The *cofrades* also asked the friar to request that the privileges supposedly reserved for Andeans and their descendants for the role played in the conquest be granted to them.[33]

Some clues inform us of the changes produced in its composition since the mid-seventeenth century and even of a true crisis in its devotional identity, the latter in relation to an apparent disappearance of immigrants and Andean descendants. On the other hand, regarding the devotional identity of the confraternity, toward the end of this century an important change can be perceived, detectable through the inventories of the church of La Merced. Thus, while in the records from 1676 and 1683 we find in

---

30 ANH.ES, vol. 52, ff. 73v-76; Emma de Ramón, "Juan Chico de Peñalosa, Sebastián de Iturrieta y Martín García, tres sastres en los albores de la industria santiaguina: 1560-1620," in Julio Retamal Ávila (ed.), *Estudios coloniales III* (Santiago: Universidad Andrés Bello, 2004), 100-103.

31 Valenzuela, "Los indios *cuzcos* de Chile colonial: estrategias semánticas, usos de la memoria y gestión de identidades entre inmigrantes andinos (siglos XVI-XVII)," Nuevo Mundo/Mundos Nuevos (2010): http://nuevomundo.revues.org/60271.

32 Ruiz Rodríguez, "Cofradías," 26; ANH.ES, vol. 53, f. 191-191.

33 ANH.ES, vol. 53, ff. 191-191v.

its chapel two busts that represent, respectively, the Virgin of Guadalupe and the risen Christ, the *guadalupana* (image of the Virgin of Guadalupe) disappears abruptly, replaced by Our Lady of Nieves, four years later, in an inventory from 1687.[34] It is worth noting that there was already a confraternity in La Merced, mentioned for the first time in 1645, and whose relationship with Andean immigrants had been confirmed in the testament dictated in 1657 by the cobbler Andrés Machado (originally from Quito), who at that date was concurrently the *mayordomo* of this confraternity as well as that of Our Lady of Copacabana, in the Church of San Francisco.[35]

Following the 1687 inventory – and in the absence of other documents – we can infer that either the two corporate bodies merged – with Guadalupe being subsumed into that of Las Nieves – or the *guadalupana* had simply lost its devotional strength, replaced by this other, more active devotion. In any case, for these or other reasons, the Virgin of Nieves appeared in a central place, presiding over the chapel that had been dedicated to Guadalupe, accompanied by other previously unknown Marian images.[36]

Toward the end of the seventeenth century, as we can see, both the votive orientation and the ethnic composition of the confraternity had changed, diluting its Andean component. It can also be argued that such an evolution could be directly related to the change in the demographic backdrop of the city itself. Indeed, a substantive part of the Andean immigration that had fueled this confraternity and others in the city had already experienced its migratory boom during the second half of the sixteenth century and the first decades of the next. By the end of the seventeenth century, then, one can infer that most of these foreigners had died and that, perhaps, their descendants, especially those of the second generation, could have had other votive or associative inclinations. This tendency is reflected in the Mercedarian inventory of 1701, in which the confraternity is not only officially called Our Lady of Nieves – definitively displacing the original devotion – but the name "of the *cuzcos*," with which it traditionally appeared linked, also disappears, and is not mentioned again in subsequent inventories.[37]

---

34 Archivo de la Provincia Mercedaria de Chile (APMCh), "Libro de visitas (1676-1702)," ff. 5, 51v-52, 65v.

35 Retamal Ávila, *Testamentos*, 194-197; Ruiz Rodríguez, "Cofradías," 39n72.

36 APMCh, Libro de visitas (1676-1702), f. 65v (inventory of 1687).

37 APMCh, Libro de visitas (1676-1702), f. 142v. I looked at several documents from the years 1714 until 1766: APMCh, Libro de visitas, Convento Grande: 1714-1843.

Our Lady of Copacabana

With less demand than that of Guadalupe in terms of the number of Andean immigrants registered, is the confraternity of Copacabana, established in the church of San Francisco prior to 1608. In its Andean origin, this corporation corresponded to a variant of the Virgin of the Candelaria, appearing around 1582 on the shores of Lake Titicaca (in the Collao region).[38]

This was a favorite confraternity for Chilean indigenous people in particular, as it appears in a document from 1613.[39] A few years later, in 1616, this feature is again highlighted by the indigenous *mayordomos*, Gaspar and Sancho, who refer to it as a "confraternity of the natural Indians of this city."[40] It is interesting to highlight that the apparent ethnic-geographical unity that prevailed among the confraternity's members was crossed by other identitary references that diversified it, such as the members' working conditions; apparently many of these indigenous people were artisans and worked in different specialties. To mention an example, there is the case of "brother" Juan, the "*ladino* Indian tailor" who in 1611 received one hundred pesos lent by the confraternity thanks to the support of another indigenous man, Miguel, a "cobbler's deputy" of the same confraternity.[41]

The above case also reflects the economic solvency of the corporation, which we have not found in other indigenous confraternities studied from the time period and which probably derived from the preeminence of artisans committed to its financing. This solvency and availability of surpluses would explain the fact that for those same years in which 100 pesos were lent to brother Juan, a similar sum was given to the Spanish cobbler Pedro Mancera and his wife who, apparently, were not members.[42]

On the other hand, the "ethnic unity" of the members of Copacabana only implied a nominal mask that concealed the great geographic and cultural diversity that was hidden behind the urban indigenous world.[43] This is considering that a good part – if not the majority – of the indigenous people

38   See Gabriela Ramos, "Nuestra Señora de Copacabana ¿Devoción india o intermediaria cultural?," in *Passeurs, mediadores culturales y agentes de la primera globalización en el Mundo Ibérico, siglos XVI-XIX*, ed. Scarlett O'Phelan Godoy and Carmen Salazar-Soler (Lima: PUCP, 2005), 163-65, 170.

39   ANH.ES, vol. 51, ff. 19-20v.

40   Archivo del Arzobispado de Santiago (AAS), Secretaría, vol. 61, ff. 272-275.

41   ANH.ES, vol. 41, f. 60v. *Ladino* was used for acculturated Amerindians (and blacks) who spoke Spanish.

42   ANH.ES, vol. 51, ff. 19-20v.

43   Valenzuela, "Indios urbanos: inmigraciones, alteridad y ladinización en Santiago de Chile (siglos XVI-XVII)," *Historia crítica* 53 (2014), 13-34.

in the city were also immigrants. In fact, among the confreres of Copacabana who gave testaments throughout this century, not only were there people from the capital, but also from the central valley of Chile (Rapel), Araucanía (Villarrica), and even the distant island of Chiloé. The first information found appears in the testament of an indigenous native of Tucumán, in 1608.[44] Half a century later its *mayordomo* was the cobbler Andrés Machado, originally from Quito – the same one who, as seen before, exercised that function at the same time in the Mercedarian confraternity of the Virgin of Nieves.[45]

But Copacabana not only thoroughly fulfilled the role we have assigned to the confraternities as channels of socio-ethnic integration, but it also constituted a space of baroque expression and Tridentine monitoring of religious practices of its members. Indeed, the document from 1616, cited above, underscored its penitential character by calling it, at the same time, a "confraternity of the blood of the *naturales*" (Amerindians). In fact, the text is a request raised by the *mayordomos* to the *protector de indios* (Indian defender) so that he would authorize the money needed to pay for the candles that would illuminate the corporation's participation in the procession on the night of Holy Thursday.[46] For his part, the Jesuit Alonso de Ovalle also took this position in his chronicle, adding that "it has the most penitents of them all."[47] And, at the end of the same century we continue to find the denomination of "Indian confraternities," as well as the subsidy for Holy Week – coming from the *Caja de censos de indios* (Indian welfare fund) – and the penitential nature of their participation in it.[48]

However, in a similar way to what happened with the Guadalupan confraternity, the indigenous exclusivity of its original composition was progressively extended to the mestizo and even Spanish realms, even attracting renowned members of the local elite. In 1681, in fact, its eldest confrere was Pablo de Villela, a merchant born in the Basque Country.[49] In those same years, Catalina de Irarrázaval y Andía, granddaughter of Francisco Bravo de Saravia, one of the richest *encomenderos* of Chile, also participated as a confrere.[50]

We must add to the above the great change that took place at the end of the 1680s after the crisis of the confraternities dependent on the Jesuits of

44 Testamento de Alonso Rodríguez, ANH.ES, vol. 45, f. 494.
45 Retamal Ávila, *Testamentos*, 194-197; Ruiz Rodríguez, "Cofradías," 39.
46 AAS, Secretaría, vol. 61, ff. 272-275.
47 Ovalle, *Histórica relación*, 187.
48 AAS, Provisor, sección "Asuntos diversos," expediente 480, f. 2.
49 Ruiz Rodríguez, "Cofradías," 30-31.
50 Hernán Rodríguez Villegas, "Historia de un solar de la ciudad de Santiago, 1554-1909," *Historia* 11 (1972-1973), 119.

Santiago. This crisis coincides, symptomatically, with the transformation seen in the Guadalupana de la Merced. In fact, throughout that decade, the Society of Jesus came into conflict with indigenous confraternities (of the Christ Child) and black confraternities (of Bethlehem), founded in their *Colegio* (school) of Santiago. This conflict derived, apparently, from the new Jesuit attitude that sought to strengthen the orthodoxy of these cofrades by extirpating their more "pagan" devotional and festive forms.[51] Faced with confreres' rejection, the Order decided to expel them from their church, along with their images, decorations, and belongings. This decision was canonically stipulated in the diocesan synod celebrated in Santiago in 1688, where several Jesuits participated prominently. There it was indicated that the dissolved confraternity of the Niño Jesús had to be "added" to that of Copacabana (San Francisco) or definitively dissolved.[52]

There is no further information regarding the outcome of this situation, but it can be assumed that the arrival of this new contingent and its devotional objects prompted an important transformation in the Copacabana confraternity. On the one hand, this reinforced its "indigenous" content and the ethnic complexity implied by the diversity that hid behind the colonial category of "Indian." On the other hand, this merger could imply a reinforcement of the internal organization and of the relative weight of the confraternity within the corporative-devotional system of the city of Santiago, which would be reflected in the survival of its religious participation in public spaces in the mid-eighteenth century.[53]

Our Lady of Candelaria

Andean indigenous people also formed part of the confraternity of Candelaria, established in the convent of San Agustín around 1600.[54] It was

51 Francisco Enrich, *Historia de la Compañía de Jesús en Chile*, vol. 2 (Barcelona: Imprenta de Francisco Rosal, 1891), 8-9. This situation is described in detail in Víctor Rondón, *Jesuitas, música y cultura en el Chile colonial* (Ph.D. diss., Pontificia Universidad Católica de Chile, 2009), 378, 382-384.
52 *Sínodos diocesanos del Arzobispado de Santiago de Chile celebrados por los ilustrísimos señores doctor don fray Bernardo Carrasco Saavedra [1688] y doctor don Manuel de Alday y Aspee* (1763; reprint: New York: Eduardo Dunigan y Hermano, 1858), 55.
53 See, for example, the confraternity expense records of the year 1752: AAS, Provisor, section Asuntos diversos, file 503.
54 Jorge Falch, "Cofradía de Nuestra Señora de la Candelaria de los mulatos en el Convento de San Agustín de Santiago de Chile," *Anuario de historia de la Iglesia en Chile*, vol. 13, 16 (1995, 98): 17-30, 167-199. For Perú, the initial development of this cult in the Arequipa region is described in Alejandro Málaga Núñez-Zeballos, "La Virgen Candelaria en el obispado de Arequipa: origen

founded by – and conceived for – free blacks, but it quickly acquired a plural makeup by incorporating the city's indigenous population. It appears as such in its constitutions since 1610, when it was defined as an entity composed of "freed mulatos" and "native officials." This highlighted the preeminence granted to the entry of indigenous people who worked as artisans.[55] The same document even makes clear that the internal positions of the confraternity had to be divided into equal conditions and responsibilities between both "nations," with the *veinticuatro* members appearing equally divided between "morenos" and "naturales," and each group with its respective *mayordomo* and *procurador*.[56] This "ethnic" differentiation also occurred in records regarding gender because, at least since the approval of the constitutions, there were female "mayordomas" elected annually, and concurrently, for "mulatas" and female "naturales."[57]

Certainly, this diversity of the Candelaria also must have projected onto the universe of its religious expressions, helping to make richer the practices that poured out into public spaces. Among these, the annual feast – the day of the Purification – where every member had to participate with burning candles in their hands, stands out. There was also the "blood procession" that took place on Easter Tuesday. In the latter, as pointed out by the Jesuit Ovalle, the brothers paraded "with their black robes and took many and very devoted steps of passion, accompanied by much wax, and the music is among the best there."[58] In fact, the inventory of goods registered by the confraternity for 1614 takes into account a series of images, crosses, banners, black cloths, and more than 100 *hacheros* (torches) used to illuminate the Stations of the Cross that were carried on the shoulders of the confreres in the streets of Santiago.[59]

With regard to the participation of indigenous peoples of the Andes, the book that kept the confraternity's accounts and records for the first half of the seventeenth century allows us to see how, in the twenty years that followed its official organization – from when the constitutions went into effect in 1615 – these immigrants played an important role in its internal functioning. In this sense, the regular appearance of some of them among

y milagros," in *Incas e indios cristianos. Elites indígenas e identidades cristianas en los Andes coloniales*, ed. Jean-Jacques Decoster (Lima: Centro Bartolomé de Las Casas, 2002), 347-358.

55   Falch, "Cofradía," pt. 1, 26; Ruiz Rodríguez, "Cofradías," 30.

56   Falch, "Cofradía," pt. 1, 26 (const. n. 2).

57   Archivo Provincial de San Agustín, Santiago (APSA), Libro de la Cofradía de Nª Sra. de la Candelaria, en el Convento de San Agustín (1606-1651).

58   Ovalle, *Histórica relación*, 187.

59   APSA, Libro de la Cofradía, ff. 187-188v.

those chosen to administer the institution is striking. In fact, in September of that year the master tailor Juan de Luna, "Indian of Cuzco," who two years before leased a plot in *la Chimba*, at the margins of the city, took on the role of *mayordomo de naturales* (leader of Indians).[60] In 1615, Andrés Bañado Pongo, the silkweaver and hatter originally from Huánuco, was also elected as *alférez* (lieutenant).[61] Furthermore, in 1616, another Andean, Agustín Quispe, appears as *procurador* of the confraternity. 1617 was the year in which Bañado was positioned as *mayordomo de naturales*, a position for which he would be reelected successively until the beginning of 1619. Moreover, in this last year, Francisco Cuzco, of whom no more information is known, but whose Andean origin is evident through his "patronymic," becomes an *alférez*. In the following election, carried out at the beginning of 1622, the position of *alférez* would fall on another Andean, Diego Quispe, probably a relative of the procurator from 1616. As a matter of fact, we have already come across Diego in relation to the confraternity of Guadalupe, where in 1615 he served as one of its *mayordomos*.[62]

At the start of 1623, Andrés Bañado returned as *mayordomo*, to be replaced the following year by the aforementioned Diego Quispe, whose rapid rise showed, thus, his "political" skills, undoubtedly supported by his "literate" talents; in the document of Guadalupe cited, Quispe had been the only one who knew how to sign it.[63] Bañado remained within the leading group of Copacabana throughout the year of 1624, taking on the role as its oldest member, despite the health problems that, we think, could have led him to dictate his testament.[64] In fact, his active presence within the corporation is confirmed when, in 1626, he is again elected as *mayordomo*. An Andean, Juan Cuzco, appears next to him as *alférez*. The following year, meanwhile, we see the return of Juan de Luna to the *mayordomía* of the *naturales*, taking turns at the position with Bañado in the elections of 1628 (Bañado) and 1629 (Luna). Both *cuzcos* repeat this rotation again in 1632 (Bañado) and 1633 (Luna).

Within this dynamic, I would like to highlight the apparent decline in influence of the "morenos" in leadership positions at the same time. From the start of the decade of 1630, *cofrades* eligible to occupy the positions reserved for their "nation" were scarce. This situation led to a crisis in the 1633 *mayordomos* election, a moment in which it was determined that,

60 ANH.ES, vol. 46, f. 56.
61 ANH.ES, vol. 51, f. 262.
62 ANH.ES, vol. 53, ff. 191.
63 Cf. ANH.ES, vol. 85, f. 249v.
64 ANH.ES, vol. 87, f. 132.

in the future, there would only be one acting *mayordomo*. Next to him, a deputy "of a nation different from that of the *mayordomo*," who would have to assume the position in the following period based on a system of taking turns, would be elected. As we have seen, after all the confreres voted in that year's election, the Andean tailor Juan de Luna was elected. This occurred despite the fact that the previous year an immigrant from the Andes had been elected – not a black man, as stipulated by the internal regulations – with Andrés Bañado holding the position in the turn reserved for the "pardos."[65] This shows the predominant influence of these immigrants within the Candelaria, even beyond the institution's own indigenous sector, as Bañado also voted for the "morenos."

The year 1637 would be the last one in which we see Luna appear as *mayordomo* and Bañado as "*alférez* of *naturales*" – the latter again occupying the space that corresponded to a "moreno," in light of the continuing shortage of these candidates.[66] From that moment Andeans stopped appearing in those positions, nor were they registered among the other confreres settled in those years.

Considering the above, it seems pertinent, then, to return to the question surrounding the "decline" in the presence of Andeans that we have seen with other confraternities beginning in the mid-seventeenth century – an absence that seems more evident in light of their active participation during the previous decades. This situation is combined with what we have also seen in the other corporations studied, in the sense that in La Candelaria there was a "Hispanicization" of its membership – a process that derived from the arrival of mestizos and Hispano-Creoles who, from the 1620s, began to change the initial "bi-ethnic" orientation. In fact, the testament dictated in 1619 by the mestizo blacksmith Diego Mejía (originally from Quito) stipulated that he be buried in the church of San Agustín, "in the place where the brothers of the Candelaria confraternity are buried, where I command to be settled as a confrere."[67] That same year the confrere Francisca Cardoso testified that, being a mestizo, she had entered the Candelaria as "Spanish." Among the Hispano-Creoles we find that one of the most prominent members of the elite, Juan Rodulfo Lisperguer, settled in 1633 with his wife and children.[68] Even some Portuguese appear in the second half of the century.[69]

---

65   APSA, Libro de la Cofradía, ff. 58-59, 181.
66   Ibid., f. 184.
67   ANH.ES, vol. 59, f. 95.
68   APSA, Libro de la Cofradía, f. 9. The consulted book is made up of about 30 Spanish settlements until 1642, last year that we have its records.
69   Ruiz Rodríguez, "Cofradías," 31n33.

The growing presence of Spaniards even led them to attempt to position themselves as a nucleus in similar political conditions as the other "nations" – an intention finalized in 1634, when the confreres managed to elect their "elder sister of the female Spaniards." The following year, however, the traditional strata – "morenos" and "naturales" – would react, deciding that Spaniards could have an active vote, but could not be elected to positions of the corporation.[70]

In Search of Common Threads

As we have seen in each of the confraternities studied here, these were built as spaces that brought together people with very different social, ethnic, and geographical origins. The indigenous immigrants from the Andes, who experienced the same diversity among themselves, but who were seen by Chilean society – and presented themselves – with a common "identity" based precisely on identification with Andean space, came to form part of these corporate channels of devotion, often in their foundational and leadership ranks.

Confraternities were established, thus, amid the ethnic complexity and the multiplicity of identitarian references of the urban population, and they did so by creating a new sense of institutional belonging – in this case, religious – to its various components. From this perspective, we can see them as an inclusive space, but in a "depersonalized" context characterized by fragmented, uprooted, or threatened ethnic identities typical of a colonial urban context.[71]

In addition, in the case of Santiago, the fact that there were practically no confraternities linked to specific artisan guilds, unlike what happened in other places, helped. This situation was probably due to how, beyond their nominal existence, the Chilean "guilds" ultimately did not exist as organic corporations. Rather, the artisans of Santiago participated in this or that trade and defined themselves – or were defined by the municipal authorities – as members of a hypothetical guild within the corporate socio-political imaginary of the time.[72] In this way, Santiago's confraternities were also erected as channels for a devotion that was transverse in terms of labor, incorporating craftsmen from different trades and latitudes into its center.[73]

---

70   APSA, Libro de la Cofradía, f. 181-184.

71   Valenzuela Márquez, *Las liturgias*.

72   See Sergio Villalobos, *Historia del pueblo chileno*, vol. 2 (Santiago: Zig-Zag, 1983), 129.

73   ANH.ES, vol. 52, f. 73v, Carta de constitución de la cofradía de los sastres en la catedral de Santiago (Santiago, June 3, 1614).

If we view the studied confraternities as socio-ethnic kaleidoscopes – that is, as a diverse and changing group, which fragments as well as integrates – we can then confirm their role in the successful deployment of a system such as the Spanish one – a system that, after its breakdowns – resulting from the demographic, social, labor, cultural, and political processes implied by the colonial organization itself – now "offered" channels of symbolic integration and social belonging that ended up being useful to their collective legitimation.[74]

However, from a point of view that privileges the construction of networks and common referents, much like the institutions offered by the system, there are some indications that allow us to decipher certain tendencies in relation to some relational patterns between, at least, a part of their members. Let's direct our attention, for example, to a fourth confraternity in which Andean immigrants participated: Jesús Nazareno, established in the beginning of the seventeenth century in the convent of La Merced. Among its founders, alongside the Andean cobbler, Hernando Muñoz, was the mestizo tailor Juan Chico de Peñalosa. Also, during those first years its members were the blacksmith Mateo Naranjo, the Portuguese cutler Manuel González Guimaraes, the mulato swordsman of Portuguese origin Pedro González, and the carpenters Juan Bernal and Juan de Lepe, among other artisans.[75] We have, then, a first common thread between all of them – they are all artisans – beneath which lie inter-ethnic relations defined by the different origins of at least Muñoz (probable mestizo, Huánuco) and González (mulato, from Lisbon). The latter, for his part, became a prosperous artisan, with a shop for making and repairing swords. This store also received, as was customary for a cash-deficit economy like Chile's, numerous objects traded or pawned by other people. And in this list of debtors – which González included in his testament – we find again his co-confreres Muñoz, González Guimaraes, and Chico, as well as several other local artisans of various specializations.[76]

If we continue to explore the individual lives of these confreres-artisans, taking an interest in their most personal relationships or the spaces where they lived, we observe certain coincidences that open new and interesting perspectives within the framework of the hypotheses presented in this paper. If we focus on the case of Juan Chico, for example, we see that, although

74 See Valenzuela Márquez, *Las liturgias*.

75 Emma de Ramón, "Juan Chico de Peñalosa," 100; ANH.ES, vol. 51, fs. 116-116v.

76 Emma de Ramón, "Artífices negros, mulatos y pardos en Santiago de Chile: siglos XVI y XVII," *Cuadernos de historia* 25 (2006): 74-79.

this tailor was originally from Concepción, he was married for some time to Isabel de Gálvez, a mestizo daughter of an indigenous woman from Quito. His connection to the world of the Andes was such that he knew the Quechua language perfectly – so much so that, on one occasion, he went as a translator to the house of his neighbor, the indigenous "Cuzco" Gaspar Guanca, a bricklayer who apparently did not speak Spanish – or did not speak it easily – who wanted to dictate a new testament. Previously he had dictated at least two other testaments and a codicil. Furthermore, the other witness to Guanca's testament was a son of Chico, who also understood Quechua.[77]

Thus, there were two artisans (a tailor and a bricklayer), who shared a cultural proximity to the Andes (language, family, etc.) but who also lived in the same sector of the city: la Chimba, a word of Quechua origin that alluded to the neighborhood that can be translated as "on the other side of the river;" in this case, of the Mapocho river, which crosses the city of Santiago. In fact, the farm that Isabel had contributed as a dowry to her marriage with Juan Chico in 1587, and where her mother-in-law, an indigenous immigrant from Quito, also lived, was in la Chimba.[78]

The city's residential space was, then, an additional axis that must be included in the analysis of the social and ethnic complexity observed here. This axis not only relates to the participation of indigenous Andeans in the confraternities, but also, in a broader sense, to their integration into the urban life of Santiago.

In this same vein we can identify nuclei of people whose place of residence – la Chimba – and shared confraternity – la Candelaria – converge in the trio formed by Lorenzo Ramírez Yañez (son of a "cuzca" Indian) and the indigenous Andeans Pedro Lima and Andrés Bañado Pongo, with only five years separating their testaments. Their trades, as it were, were connected: the first two worked as tailors, while Bañado was a silkweaver and hatter. Moreover, one of the executors of Lima's testament was, in fact, Bañado, who was called "my *compadre.*"[79] Regarding Bañado, who arrived in Chile around 1600, it is interesting to note that when he made his testament in 1624, he declared that he was married to an indigenous woman named Inés, and that "when we married we had nothing." However, by that date he

---

77 ANH.ES, vol. 80, fs. 190-191v. Juan Chico had also participated as witness in Gaspar's last will in 1613: ANH.ES, vol. 81, fs. 309v-310v.

78 Diego González Holguín, *Vocabulario de la lengua general de todo el Perú llamada lengua quichua o del inca* (1608, reprint: Lima: Universidad Nacional Mayor de San Marcos, 1989), 109-110; ANH.ES, vol. 6, fs. 9-10v.

79 Retamal Ávila, *Testamentos*, 166-167.

had managed to accumulate not only certain material assets equivalent to those of a moderately well-to-do urban craftsman – which included a black slave – but he had also woven a network of clients and connections with other artisans who undoubtedly endorsed the positioning he had achieved within the Candelaria confraternity, as we have seen.[80]

The so-called Chimba area began to consolidate in the early 1560s, precisely with the settlement of some of the Andean *yanaconas* that had come to the service of the conquistadors. In fact, the majority of indigenous married couples registered in the last decades of the sixteenth century who claimed to live in said neighborhood, are from the Andes.[81] However, as previously said, la Chimba was not an exclusive space for immigrants of the conquest; it was also a place for those who arrived later, coming from other regions and through individual routes, like the aforementioned Bañado Pongo. It was also the place that harbored the city's ethnic diversity, as *naturales* from a variety of origins – Mapuches from southern Chile, Huarpes from Cuyo, Juríes from Tucumán, black freemen, *ladinos*, poor Hispanic creoles, and the wide range of mestizos that were born from their unions, settled there.[82] To cite an example linked to this complexity and with the superposition of religious and spatial settings, consider Pascual de Jesús, an indigenous tailor. In 1682 he was a confrere of Copacabana, but at the same time he acted as procurator of the Confraternity of Our Lady of Renca, established in the parish of the same name, in a semi-agricultural suburb north of Santiago, next to la Chimba.[83]

It was in the daily life and work in this marginal urban sector, then – many of those who lived there were craftsmen – where the inter-ethnic relations that were later seen reflected in the practices deployed within the city, particularly in the composition and organization of the religious confraternities, crystallized.

80   ANH.ES, vol. 87, fs. 132-133v.
81   Armando de Ramón, "Bautizos de indígenas según los libros del Sagrario de Santiago correspondientes a los años 1581-1596," *Historia* 4 (1965), 232; Tomás Thayer Ojeda, *Santiago durante el siglo XVI. Constitución de la propiedad urbana i noticias biográficas de sus primeros pobladores* (Santiago: Imprenta Cervantes, 1905), 102.
82   Carlos Ruiz Rodríguez, *La zona norte de Santiago: población, economía y urbanización, 1540-1833* (BA thesis, Pontificia Universidad Católica de Chile, 1986); Hugo Contreras Cruces, "'Siendo mozetón o *güeñi* salió de su tierra a vivir entre los españole': Migración y asentamiento mapuche en Chile central durante el siglo XVIII, 1700-1750," *Historia indígena* 9, 2005-2006, pp. 7-32; Carlos Ruiz Rodríguez, "Presencia de los mapuche-huilliche en Chile central en los siglos XVI-XVIII. Desarraigo y mestizaje," *Boletín del Museo y Archivo Histórico Municipal de Osorno* 4, 1998, pp. 1-71; Valenzuela Márquez, "Indios urbanos...".
83   Ruiz Rodríguez, "Cofradías," 45.

Indeed, from early on, interaction and contact between different individuals gathered in that space gave way to the construction of networks of interests, families, or friendships – networks that helped to configure those processes of sociocultural "interdigitation" that are central to the configuration of inter-ethnic dynamics.[84] Along with this, strategies and spaces of formal integration to the colonial system were developed, both in the labor sphere – artisan activity, work seats, trade – as well as in the associative sphere – confraternities, "guilds" – and legal and judicial spheres – the use of Western inheritance and transaction mechanisms (testaments and notarial contracts) and the use of colonial justice to settle conflicts, to mention a few of these scenarios.[85]

Thus, the experiences of immigration, of the insertion into an urban context defined by rules of the Spanish colonial system, of economic integration, and of the deep and daily interaction with the "others" that inhabited the city, allowed the Andean indigenous people of Santiago an "anchor" based on new community and corporate weavings, such as confraternities. This also allowed them to build new social and cultural identities and, eventually, new ethnic references, as revealed by the use of the term "cuzco" by the various Andean immigrants studied.

About the author

Jaime Valenzuela Márquez is professor of history at the Pontificia Universidad Católica de Chile. He has been a fellow at the Centro Diego Barros Arana of the Biblioteca Nacional de Chile (1991-1993) and the John Carter Brown Library. He has been a visiting professor at many French and Latin American universities. Some of his books include: *Las liturgias del poder. Celebraciones públicas y estrategias persuasivas en Chile colonial (1609-1709); Fiesta, rito y política. Del Chile borbónico al republicano; América en diásporas. Esclavitudes y migraciones forzadas en Chile y otras regiones americanas (siglos XVI-XIX).*

84 Jacques Poloni Simard, "Redes y mestizajes: propuestas para el análisis de la sociedad colonial," in *Lógica mestiza*, 113-138; José Luis Martínez, "Ayllus e identidades interdigitadas. Las sociedades de la puna salada," ibid., 85-112.

85 See Valenzuela Márquez, "Indias esclavas ante la Real Audiencia de Chile (1650-1680): los caminos del amparo judicial para mujeres capturadas en la guerra de Arauco," in *América en diásporas. Esclavitudes y migraciones forzadas en Chile y otras regiones americanas (siglos XVI-XIX),* ed, Valenzuela Márquez (Santiago: Pontificia Universidad Católica de Chile, 2017), 319-380.

Bibliography

Araya Espinoza, Alejandra, and Jaime Valenzuela Márquez, eds. *América colonial. Denominaciones, clasificaciones e identidades*. Santiago: PUCC, 2010.

Ares Queija, Berta. "Las danzas de los indios: un camino para la evangelización del virreinato del Perú," *Revista de Indias* 174 (1984): 445-463.

—. "Mestizos en hábito de indios: ¿estrategias transgresoras o identidades difusas?" In *Passar as fronteiras. II coloquio internacional sobre mediadores culturais, séculos XV a XVIII*, edited by Rui Manuel Loureiro and Serge Gruzinski, 133-146. Lagos: Centro de Estudios Gil Eanes, 1999.

Argouse, Aude. "Asignar un pasado al futuro. Los testamentos de indígenas, entre memoria e historia, Cajamarca, Perú, siglo XVII." In *Fronteras y sensibilidades en las Américas*, edited by Frédérique Langue and Salvador Bernabéu, 45-69. Sevilla: Ediciones Doce Calles, 2011.

Bechtloff, Dagmar. *Las cofradías en Michoacán durante la época de la colonia. La religión y su relación política y económica en una sociedad intercultural*. Zinacantepec: Colegio de Michoacán, 1996.

Bernand, Carmen. "Mestizos, mulatos y ladinos en Hispanoamérica: un enfoque antropológico de un proceso histórico." In *Motivos de la antropología americanista. Indagaciones en la diferencia*, edited by Miguel León-Portilla, 105-133. Mexico City: FCE, 2001.

Boccara, Guillaume. "Mundos nuevos en las fronteras del Nuevo Mundo." *Nuevo Mundo/Mundos Nuevos* (2001). https://journals.openedition.org/nuevomundo/426

Bouysse-Cassagne, Thérèse. *La identidad aymara: aproximación histórica (siglo XV, siglo XVI)*. La Paz: IFEA, 1987.

Cadena, Marisol de la. *Indígenas mestizos: Raza y cultura en el Cusco*. Lima: IEP, 2004.

Carrasco Saavedra, Bernardo, y Manuel de Alday y Aspee. *Sínodos diocesanos del Arzobispado de Santiago de Chile celebrados por los ilustrísimos señores doctor don fray Bernardo Carrasco Saavedra [1688] y doctor don Manuel de Alday y Aspee*. New York: Eduardo Dunigan y Hermano, [1763] 1858.

Charney, Paul. "El indio urbano. Un análisis económico y social de la población india de Lima en 1613." *Histórica* 12, no. 1 (1988): 5-33.

Ciriza-Mendívil Carlos. *Naturales de una ciudad multiétnica. Vidas y dinámicas sociales de los indígenas de Quito en el siglo XVII*. Madrid: Sílex, 2019.

Cole, Jeffrey. *The Potosí Mita, 1573-1700: Compulsory Indian Labor in the Andes*. Stanford: Stanford University Press, 1985.

Contreras Cruces, Hugo. "'Siendo mozetón o güeñi salió de su tierra a vivir entre los españoles': migración y asentamiento mapuche en Chile central durante el siglo XVIII, 1700-1750." *Historia indígena* 9 (2005-2006): 7-32.

Cook, Noble David. "Les indiens immigrés à Lima au début du XVIIe siècle." *Cahiers des Amériques Latines* 13-14 (1976): 33-50.

Enrich, Francisco. *Historia de la Compañía de Jesús en Chile*. Barcelona: Imprenta de Francisco Rosal, 1891, 2 vols.

Estenssoro, Juan Carlos. *Del paganismo a la santidad. La incorporación de los indios del Perú al catolicismo (1532-1750)*. Lima: IFEA, 2003.

Falch, Jorge. "Cofradía de Nuestra Señora de la Candelaria de los mulatos en el Convento de San Agustín de Santiago de Chile." *Anuario de historia de la Iglesia en Chile* 13 (1995): 17-30.

França Paiva, Eduardo. *Nombrar lo nuevo: una historia léxica de Iberoamérica entre los siglos XVI y XVIII (las dinámicas de mestizajes y el mundo del trabajo)*. Santiago: Universitaria, 2020.

Ginzburg, Carlo. *Mitos, emblemas, indicios: morfología e historia*. Barcelona: Gedisa, 1989.

Giudicelli, Christophe. "Hétéronomie et classifications coloniales. La construction des 'nations' indiennes aux confins de l'Amérique espagnole (XVI-XVIIe siècle)." *Nuevo Mundo/Mundos Nuevos* (2021). https://journals.openedition.org/nuevomundo/59411

Gonzalbo Aizpuru, Pilar. "Las fiestas novohispanas: espectáculos y ejemplo." *Mexican Studies/Estudios Mexicanos* 9, no. 1 (1993): 19-45.

González Holguín, Diego. *Vocabulario de la lengua general de todo el Perú llamada lengua quichua o del inca*. Lima: Universidad Nacional Mayor de San Marcos, [1608] 1989.

Hill, Jonathan D. *History, Power and Identity: Ethnogenesis in the Americas, 1492-1992*. Iowa City: University of Iowa Press, 1996.

Jara, Álvaro, and Rolando Mellafe, eds. *Protocolos de los escribanos de Santiago. Primeros fragmentos, 1559 y 1564-1566*. Santiago: DIBAM, 1996. 2 vols.

Lisi, Francesco Leonardo. *El tercer concilio limense y la aculturación de los indígenas sudamericanos*, Salamanca: Universidad de Salamanca, 1990.

Lizárraga, Reginaldo de. *Descripción del Perú, Tucumán, Río de la Plata y Chile*. Madrid: Historia 16, 1986.

Málaga Núñez-Zeballos, Alejandro. "La Virgen Candelaria en el obispado de Arequipa: origen y milagros." In *Incas e indios cristianos. Elites indígenas e identidades cristianas en los Andes coloniales*, edited by Jean-Jacques Decoster, 347-358. Lima: Centro Bartolomé de Las Casas, 2002.

Martínez, José Luis. "¿Cómo hablar de indios e identidades en el siglo XVI? Una aproximación a la construcción de los discursos coloniales." *Historia Indígena* 8 (2004): 41-55.

——. "Ayllus e identidades interdigitadas. Las sociedades de la puna salada." In *Lógica mestiza en América*, edited by Guillaume Boccara and Sylvia Galindo, 85-112. Temuco: Universidad de la Frontera, 2000.

Martínez Cereceda, José Luis. "Construyendo mundos: el 'nacimiento' de los indios en los Andes del siglo XVI." In *Del Nuevo al Viejo Mundo: mentalidades y representaciones desde América*, edited by Alejandra Araya, Azún Candina and Celia Cussen, 23-34. Santiago: Universidad de Chile, 2008.

Meyers, Albert, and Diane Elizabeth Hopkins, eds. *Manipulating the Saints. Religious Brotherhoods and Social Integration in Postconquest Latin America*. Hamburg: Wayasbah, 1988.

Mills, Kenneth. "Ocaña, Diego de (ca. 1570-1608)." In *Guide to Documentary Sources for Andean Studies, 1530-190*, edited by Joanne Pillsbury, 3:457-464. Norman: University of Oklahoma Press, 2008.

Nemser, Daniel. *Infrastructures of Race: Concentration and Biopolitics in Colonial Mexico*. Austin: University of Texas Press, 2017.

Ocaña, Diego de. *Viaje a Chile*. Santiago: Universitaria, 1995.

O'Toole, Rachel Sarah. *Bound Lives: Africans, Indians, and the Making of Race in Colonial Peru*. Pittsburgh: University of Pittsburgh Press, 2012.

Ovalle, Alonso de. *Histórica relación del reino de Chile y de las misiones y ministerios que ejercita en él la Compañía de Jesús*. Santiago: Universidad de Chile, [1646] 1969.

Poloni-Simard, Jacques. "Redes y mestizajes: propuestas para el análisis de la sociedad colonial." In *Lógica mestiza en América*, edited by Guillaume Boccara and Sylvia Galindo, 113-138. Temuco: Universidad de la Frontera, 2000.

Ragon, Pierre. *Les saints et les images du Mexique, XVIe-XVIIIe siècles*. Paris: L'Harmattan, 2003.

Ramón, Armando de. *Santiago de Chile (1541-1991). Historia de una sociedad urbana*. Madrid: MAPFRE, 1992.

——. "Bautizos de indígenas según los libros del Sagrario de Santiago correspondientes a los años 1581-1596." *Historia* 4 (1965): 229-235.

Ramón, Emma de. "Artífices negros, mulatos y pardos en Santiago de Chile: siglos XVI y XVII." *Cuadernos de historia* 25 (2006): 59-82.

——. "La incorporación de las etnias no hispanas a la actividad industrial durante la colonia temprana." *Revista Archivo Nacional* 2 (2004): 42-47.

——. "Juan Chico de Peñalosa, Sebastián de Iturrieta y Martín García, tres sastres en los albores de la industria santiaguina: 1560-1620." In *Estudios coloniales III*, 95-112. Edited by Julio Retamal Ávila. Santiago: Universidad Andrés Bello, 2004.

Ramos, Gabriela. "Nuestra Señora de Copacabana ¿Devoción india o intermediaria cultural?" In *Passeurs, mediadores culturales y agentes de la primera globalización en el Mundo Ibérico, siglos XVI-XIX*, edited by Scarlett O'Phelan Godoy and Carmen Salazar-Soler, 163-179. Lima: PUCP, 2005.

Retamal Ávila, Julio. *Testamentos de "indios" en Chile colonial: 1564-1801*. Santiago: Universidad Andrés Bello, 2000.

Rodríguez Villegas, Hernán. "Historia de un solar de la ciudad de Santiago, 1554-1909." *Historia* 11 (1972-1973): 103-162.

Rondón, Víctor. *Jesuitas, música y cultura en el Chile colonial.* Ph.D. diss., Pontificia Universidad Católica de Chile, 2009.

Ruiz Rodríguez, Carlos. "Cofradías en Chile Central. Un método de evangelización de la población indígena, mestiza y criolla." *Anuario de historia de la Iglesia en Chile* 18 (2000): 23-58.

—. "Presencia de los mapuche-huilliche en Chile central en los siglos XVI-XVIII. Desarraigo y mestizaje." *Boletín del Museo y Archivo Histórico Municipal de Osorno* 4 (1998): 1-71.

—. *La zona norte de Santiago: población, economía y urbanización, 1540-1833.* BA thesis. Pontificia Universidad Católica de Chile, 1986.

Saito, Akira, and Claudia Rosas Lauro, eds. *Reducciones. La concentración forzada de las poblaciones indígenas en el Virreinato del Perú.* Lima: National Museum of Ethnology of Japan, 2017.

Salomon, Frank, and Stuart Schwartz. "New Peoples and New Kinds of People: Adaptation, Readjustment, and Ethnogenesis in South American Indigenous Societies (Colonial Era)." In *The Cambridge History of the Native Peoples of the Americas*, eds. Frank Salomon and Stuart B. Schwartz, 3. 2:443-501. Cambridge: Cambridge University Press, 1999.

Thayer Ojeda, Tomás. *Santiago durante el siglo XVI: constitución de la propiedad urbana i noticias biográficas de sus primeros pobladores.* Santiago: Cervantes, 1905.

Valenzuela, Jaime. "Indias esclavas ante la Real Audiencia de Chile (1650-1680): los caminos del amparo judicial para mujeres capturadas en la guerra de Arauco." In *América en diásporas: esclavitudes y migraciones forzadas en Chile y otras regiones americanas (siglos XVI-XIX)*, edited by Valenzuela, 319-380. Santiago: PUCP, 2017.

—. "Indios urbanos: inmigraciones, alteridad y ladinización en Santiago de Chile (siglos XVI-XVII)." *Historia Crítica* 53 (2014): 13-34.

—. "Indígenas andinos en Chile colonial: inmigración, inserción espacial, integración económica y movilidad social (Santiago, siglos XVI-XVII)." *Revista de Indias* 250 (2010): 749-778.

—. "Los indios *cuzcos* de Chile colonial: estrategias semánticas, usos de la memoria y gestión de identidades entre inmigrantes andinos (siglos XVI-XVII)." Nuevo Mundo/Mundos Nuevos (2010). http://nuevomundo.revues.org/60271

—. *Las liturgias del poder. Celebraciones públicas y estrategias persuasivas en Chile colonial (1609-1709).* Santiago: DIBAM, 2001.

Vázquez de Espinosa, Antonio. *Compendio y descripción de las indias occidentales.* 1629; reprint: Madrid: BAE, 1969.

Villalobos, Sergio. *Historia del pueblo chileno*. Santiago: Zig-Zag, 1983.

Zúñiga, Jean-Paul. *Espagnols d'outre-mer: émigration, métissage et reproduction sociale à Santiago du Chili, au 17e siècle*. Paris: EHESS, 2002.

9 The Marian Cult as a Resistance Strategy

The Territorialized Construction of Devotions in the Province of Potosí, Charcas, in the Eighteenth Century[1]

Candela De Luca
IDIHCS/UNLP

Translated by Javiera Jaque Hidalgo

Abstract
This chapter studies indigenous confraternities' Marian devotion in eighteenth-century Potosi. This period saw an explosion in Marian devotion, manifested through a proliferation of images, particularly paintings and statues, around which developed local devotions, articulated through numerous confraternities. This chapter proposes to draw a devotional map, highlighting the mechanism of devotion around these images and their relation to the Church and indigenous confraternities. This analysis will underscore the tensions among the different social groups in this space and their competition for sacred space, as well as point out how these transformations were projected unto the political and religious imaginary.

Keywords: Charcas, Marian devotion, indigenous confraternities

1   A first version of this work was presented in Third Symposium on Gender and Resistance at the Pontificia Universidad Católica de Chile, Santiago de Chile, in May 2019. This work is included within the framework of the RESISTANCE Project – Rebellion and Resistance in the Iberian Empire, 16th-19th centuries, Horizon 2020 program of the European Commission, through the grant Marie Skłodowska-Curie RISE (Research and Innovation Staff Exchange), under grant agreement no. 778076.

Javiera Jaque Hidalgo and Miguel A. Valerio. *Indigenous and Black Confraternities in Colonial Latin America: Negotiating Status through Religious Practices.* Amsterdam: Amsterdam University Press, 2022
DOI: 10.5117/ 9789463721547_CH09

A Brief Tour: Mary in the Andes

Mary has been a controversial icon of American culture and politics since the beginning of the conquest until today, representing both European militarism and universal motherhood, as well as a "difficult" model of femininity.[2] This figure and her importance in the configuration of Christianity in the New World has been approached through very different perspectives, from different disciplines that range from theology, sociology, and anthropology to history and art history. As a symbol, Mary is as precarious as she is versatile – virgin, woman, mother, queen, teacher, mediator, conqueror, liberator – as well as variable in relation to the particular historical context in which popular fervor formed around her.[3]

Regarding these variations, the Argentine historian Patricia Fogelman uses the concept of "refraction," understood as an explanatory instrument that allows one to unravel the transformations of the Marian cult in its transfer from Europe to America.[4] Refraction is the change of direction of light rays that occurs after passing from one medium to another, in which the light propagates at different speeds. By equating the Marian cult with the path of light that is transformed generating different optical phenomena, this metaphor is now used as a theoretical tool. Using this concept, Fogelman analyzes the actions that various agents in different media implemented in the processes of construction, transformation, and incorporation of the religious practices that developed around Marian fervor. Referring specifically to this cult, which spread widely following the Counter-Reformation, the author analyzes a certain "matrix" of visible practices from the Spanish Reconquest process, which are reproduced during the Conquest of America and the colonial period. In this trajectory, the persistence of certain practices

2   Patricia Fogelman, "El culto mariano y las representaciones de lo femenino: Recorrido historiográfico y nuevas perspectivas de análisis," *La Aljaba* 10 (2006): 175-188. Theologians such as Silvia Moreira da Silva denounce the macho bias of the Marian cult, which is represented as a model of "ideal femininity," since it carries women's own values such as passivity, resignation, and modesty. These are understood as "virtues" to which the global dimension of the feminine being is reduced: "La mujer en la teología: reflexión biblicoteológica," in *Mujer latinoamericana: Iglesia y teología* (México: MPD, 1981), 155-156.

3   In line with Julia Costilla's approach, we understand the figure of Mary as a symbol while resulting in a fencing tool used by different sectors and by different social actors to generate mechanisms of social cohesion, access certain spaces and/or benefits, or to legitimize positions: "El milagro en la construcción del culto a Nuestra Señora de Copacabana (virreinato del Perú, 1582-1651)," *Estudios Atacameños. Arqueología y Antropología Surandinas* 39 (2010): 35-56.

4   Patricia Fogelman, "Simulacros de la virgen y refracciones del culto mariano en el Río de la Plata Colonial," *Eadem Utraque Europa* 2, no. 3 (2006): 11-34.

"are the result of a capitalizable cultural experience that gives recourse to an understandable and at the same time legitimizing explanatory scheme."[5] While the transformations – understood as "detours" in this journey – "come from the conjunctural adaptations of new agents in new media."[6] The concept of "refraction" is particularly interesting since it takes into account the dynamism of the models of development of Marian devotions, as well as the common denominators present in both the Old World and the New: the development of local devotions to an image (especially in the form of busts), the importance of geographical and political positions in the construction of each sanctuary built for its contemplation, and the presence of miracles attributed to it. However, one of the differences observed in American lands is that local actors modified and adapted the resources and practices woven around devotional figures, since on this side of the Atlantic there were different geographical, ethnic, and social borders which, added to the particular weight that pre-Hispanic traditions had in each place, acquired different characteristics in each case. In this sense, it is interesting to analyze these different processes of refraction, understanding their impact on the configuration of local religiosity.[7]

These issues are present from the beginning of the evangelization process, and are able to be reconstructed based on the information that the documents carry, as well as on other material sources. It is interesting, then, to address the characteristics and the path of various depictions – either paintings and/or engravings – in which Mary is portrayed at different stages, such as childhood, joy, pain, glorification – or sculptures corresponding to different devotions.[8] These types of images were especially convincing, and they became the structuring vectors of the religious brotherhoods. These associations, made up mostly of lay brothers, had a well-defined group of directors and an absolutely regulated annual calendar of activities.

---

5   Ibid., 29.

6   Ibid.

7   We agree with Julia Costilla and incorporate as a theoretical instrument the concept coined by William Christian of "local religiosity," while enabling us to analyze the configuration of Catholic religiosity in a specific historical and geographical context, avoiding that of "popular religiosity": "El milagro en la construcción."

8   Undoubtedly, the most iconic case of Hispanic America is that of the Virgin of Guadalupe, who in 1531 appeared to Juan Diego, a native of Cuauhtitlan, to request that he go to see the bishop with the goal of erecting a chapel in her name. According to tradition, it would be an image "not made by human hands," and therefore a bearer of divine design. In her representation, both the darkness of her face, as well as of her hands and facial features, made her especially suggestive to indigenous people. In this case, the link to Juan Diego clearly defines Mary's role as articulator and, fundamentally, as mediator, from early on.

Membership in these types of institutions meant being part of a network in which one could obtain benefits and privileges. These associations were considered useful vehicles for the consolidation of Christianity, which took root strongly on American soil over the sixteenth and seventeenth centuries. With the arrival of the Bourbons to the Iberian Peninsula in the eighteenth century, a period of restructuring began, during which confraternities were attacked by the imperial administration.[9] Rather than weakening the confraternities, they proliferated and the different Marian devotions around which the confreres gathered became local social symbols, either generating or re-signifying collective identities that, through practices such as processions and pilgrimages, defined particular geographies.[10] The metaphor of refraction is still useful in this chaotic context of transformation and deconstruction of the old doctrinal and parochial jurisdictions. On a general level, something of a noteworthy occurrence is the "Marian emergence" in the area, manifested in the pro-liferation of diverse depictions – particularly paintings and busts – around which local devotions developed, articulated through numerous religious confraternities.[11] The refraction of the Virgen de la Candelaria, developed in Copacabana, diversified in the area of Charcas into other devotions, such as the Virgen de Cocharcas, in Nuestra Señora de Sabaya, in the Virgen de Urkupiña, and the Virgen del Socavón de Oruro, to name but a few. As a result of the modifications in the iconography, the faithful ceased to recognize a single Mary, fueling these localisms.[12] Thus, the mestizo face

9   The Synod of Charcas specifies that the Confraternities foundations should have authoriza-tion from both the Archbishop and the Crown. See Argandoña Pastén and Salazar, *Constituciones sinodales*, 86-87.

10   Dolores Estruch agrees to mention that the same phenomenon is repeated in Jujeño space; see *El ejercicio del poder en el Jujuy colonial: enlaces y tensiones entre la jurisdicción civil y eclesiástica, siglos XVI-XVIII.* (Buenos Aires: La Bicicleta Ediciones, 2017).

11   An abundant corpus of images of Marian devotion appears in the material record of *potosino* churches. Among them appear in large numbers, in addition to several Candelarias – there is no parish that does not present one or more images advocated to the Virgin of Copacabana, – la Virgen de la Guadalupe, la Inmaculada Concepción, and Nuestra Señora de los Dolores. As a particular topic there are three images where the Virgin Hill of Potosi is represented. A first approach to the analysis of this survey appears in Candela De Luca, "'…De la importante devoción a la celestial Reina María Señora Nuestra…' Religiosidad mariana en las cofradías de indígenas de Potosí (Alto Perú) en el siglo XVIII," in *Cofradías en el Perú y en otros ámbitos del mundo hispánico (siglos XVI al XIX)*, edited by David Fernández Villanova, Diego Egar Lévano Medina, and Kelly Montoya Estrada (Lima: Conferencia Episcopal Peruana, 2015), 405-422.

12   Teresa Gisbert and José De Mesa, "La virgen María en Bolivia: la dialéctica barroca en la representación de María," in *Barroco Andino, Memoria del I Encuentro Internacional* (La Paz: Unión Latina, 2003).

of Mary in her many devotions continued to be configured as the emblem of Christianity in the Andes.

In the Central Andes, the image of Mary has been present practically since the beginning of the Conquest. However – and unlike in New Spain, where the process was less problematic and violent than in the Andes – some of the earliest sources do not associate the Virgin with lavish favors toward subalterns. Writings by Guamán Poma and the Inca Garcilaso describe how the Virgin descended on the Spaniards to defend them from the siege of indigenous peoples who, under the command of Manco Inca II, surrounded the city of Cuzco in 1535-1536 in an attempt to retake it. The role of the Virgin does not appear in the first-hand documents that relate this event – like Pedro Pizarro's sources – but in later accounts. Guamán Poma narrates:

> When the said heathen Indians revolted and surrounded a great number of Christian Indians to kill them, the Virgin Mary appeared in the sky as a very young, beautiful, and resplendent maiden. And the Indians say that she emitted sun rays and that her dress was whiter than snow, and that she defended the Christian Indians by throwing dirt in the eyes the heathen Indians.[13]

In this case, Mary appears as a protector of the Spaniards who found themselves in a rudimentary chapel, located in what would have previously been a place of vital importance to the indigenous people, identified as the house of Viracocha, or the Sunturhuasi ("Casa Privilegiada"). This event is represented on different seventeenth- and eighteenth-century canvases known as *La Virgen del Sunturhuasi* and *Aparición y milagro de la Virgen en el sitio de Cusco*.[14] In these paintings, the Virgin is seen descending from the sky and spreading her mantle over the Spaniards to extinguish the flames, to the surprised and terrified gaze of the indigenous.[15]

---

13   Felipe Guaman Poma de Ayala, *El primer nueva crónica y buen gobierno* (México: Siglo XXI, 1980), 402.

14   The former is in a private collection in Lima and the latter is in the Enrique Udaondo Museum complex in Luján, Argentina.

15   Although the statue has been traditionally considered to have been made in the mid-eighteenth century, an analysis by Gabriela Siracusano and her team suggest that it was probably made in the seventeenth century. This means that the narrative was more advanced in the eighteenth century: see Gabriela Siracusano, Rosanna Kuon, and Marta Maier, "Colores para el milagro: una aproximación interdisciplinaria al estudio de pigmentos en un caso singular de la iconografía colonial andina," in *Investigación en conservación y restauración: II Congreso del Grupo Español del IIC* (Barcelona: Museu Nacional d'Art de Catalunya, 2005), https://ge-iic.com/files/2congresoGE/Colores_para_el_milagro.pdf

The reference to this previously described event is important for several reasons. First, the figure of Mary appears here linked directly to the Spaniards, and her role as protector is not associated with the natives; instead, she is shown as a conqueror.[16] This very early representation differs from what is usually found throughout Hispanic America, in which the Virgin traditionally manifests herself as a mediating figure in times of chaos and cultural disintegration, and is linked to subaltern, humble, or directly marginal agents: children, slaves, indigenous people, and women.[17] But although we initially observe a radical difference regarding the role of the Virgin, certain elements form a common matrix of practices of diffusion and incorporation of the cult mentioned previously: a) the miraculous appearance of Mary, who intervened in a critical situation in defense of the righteous – in this case she presents herself as an intermediary for the Spanish troops under indigenous siege – b) the place where the Virgin acts is significant in that it has a sacred character to the indigenous people – *Sunturhuasi* – c) that space is "re-sacralized," by subsequently establishing a church there – the Church of Triumph – which initially functioned as the Cathedral of Cuzco. This implied the "re-symbolization" of religious practices, now oriented around the figure of Mary.

These types of actions can be identified on numerous occasions, especially in the Andean area. Surely the most emblematic case is that of the Virgin of Copacabana, whose image was enthroned on the shores of Lake Titicaca in 1583. The writings of Alonso Ramos Gavilán describe how the bust was sculpted in *maguey* by the indigenous Tito Yupanqui in Potosí, similar to Nuestra Señora de la Candelaria.[18] This devotion, spread by the Augustinians, was presented with the goal of founding a confraternity that brought

---

16   It is another reason why we agree with Siracusano, Kuon and Maier in thinking that these canvases – or perhaps the canvases that inspired them – are of much earlier production, which both in representation and in narrative can be compared to the figure of Santiago Mataindios (who in turn was represented during the Reconquest as Santiago Matamoros): Siracusano, Kuon, and Maier, "Colores para el milagro," 37.

17   See Elina Vuola, "María, mujer en la política. Nuevos desafíos para la teología latinoamericana." *Albertus Magnus* 4, no. 2 (2012): 59-71; Patricia Fogelman, "La omnipotencia suplicante: el culto mariano en la ciudad de Buenos Aires y la campaña en los siglos XVII y XVIII" (Ph.D. diss., Universidad de Buenos Aires, 2003); Antonio González Dorado, *De María conquistadora a María liberadora: mariología popular latinoamericana* (Madrid: Sal Terrae, 1988).

18   Alonso Ramos Gavilán, *Historia del santuario de Nuestra Señora de Copacabana* (1621; reprint: La Paz: MUSEF, 1988). This advocation originated in the evangelical episode of the Purification of Mary, and her feast day was set on February 2, 45 days after the Birth of Christ. From the fifth century, the use of candles was introduced to this holiday, which refers both to the radiance that the encounter with Christ implies, as well as humility, malleability, and docility in the work of Mary, represented in the wax of which they composed the candles. See also Hector Schenone, *Santa María: iconografía del arte colonial* (Buenos Aires: Educa, 2008), 326-327.

together indigenous peoples, divided into Anansaya and Urinsaya factions. Although at first rejected by the latter faction, which proposed to dedicate the confraternity to San Sebastián, the realization of the Virgin's miracles in favor of primarily indigenous people (although also of blacks, mestizos, mulattos, Spaniards, and creoles of different social conditions) culminated with the establishment of the cult of Mary in the Andean world's most sacred pre- and Hispanic space. In this case, we observe that, unlike in the previous example, the figure of the Virgin appears as a mediator in favor of the humble, bringing together social subjects from different cultural, political, and ethnic backgrounds.[19] This "refraction" demonstrates the plasticity of Mary as mediator, since her figure is re-signified when she passes from conqueror to protector. However, fundamentally, she presents herself to the dispossessed as a healer, teacher, and above all, mother.

One of the miracles recounted by Ramos Gavilán describes how an Uro Indian, noting the existence of the miraculous Sanctuary of the Virgin in Copacabana, went there to request that his disability be cured and

> Quiso la buena suerte de este indio tullido que llegase a su noticia, que en Copacabana estaba una saludable piscina o fuente de salud, contra todo género de enfermedades, que era la Santísima Virgen.[20]

> The good fortune of this crippled Indian wanted that he reached its news, that in Copacabana was a healthy pool or source of health, against all kinds of diseases, which was the Blessed Virgin.

This fragment makes evident the complete identification between the sacred lake and the Virgin, as what appears as a "source of health" cannot be distinguished. The description continues, fundamentally appealing to the pedagogical character of Mary by saying that:

> Apareciósele llena de luz, y acompañda de Ángeles, hablole amorosamente, y examinole si sabía rezar para tomar ocasión de enseñarle, no le dio el indio buena cuenta, porque ni aun persignarse sabia; reprendiole blandamente la

---

19   See Gabriela Ramos, "Nuestra Señora de Copacabana ¿devoción india o intermediaria cultural?" in *Passeurs, mediadores culturales y agentes de la primera evangelización en el mundo ibérico, s. XVI-XIX,* ed. Scarlett O'Phelan and Carmen Salazar Soler (Lima: Pontificia Universidad Católica del Perú, 2005), 163-179.

20   *Documentos históricos relativos al orijen y milagros con que se estableció el culto de la imajen de María Santísima que se venera en el santuario de Copacabana, publicados por un devoto* (Lima: Imprenta del Pueblo, 1849), 6.

Virgen, y tomo a su cargo el enseñarle por su misma persona, sin encargarlo, como pudiera a uno de los muchos Ángeles que la venían sirviendo. [...] Empezó desde aquella noche a enseñarle a persignarse, y por espacio de aquellos nueve días que duró el novenario, todas las noches venía la santísima Virgen a enseñarle las demás oraciones, y explicarle todos los misterios de nuestra Santa Fe, hasta que los supo muy bien todos, y para esto compuso la misma Virgen un humo elegantísimo en lengua aimara.[21]

She appeared to him full of light, and accompanied by Angels, she spoke to him lovingly, and examined him if he knew how to pray to take the opportunity to teach him, the Indian did not give her a good account, because he did not even know how to cross himself; the Virgin rebuked him softly, and took charge of teaching him by herself, without command-ing him, as she could to one of the many angels who had been serving her. [...] She began teaching him to cross himself from that night, and for the space of those nine days that the novena lasted, every night the Blessed Virgin came to teach him the other prayers, and explain all the mysteries of our Holy Faith, until he knew each one very well, and for this the Virgin herself composed a very elegant smoke in Aymara language.

However, and as noted, the main reference and role with which the figure of Mary is identified is first that of the Mother of Christ, and by exten-sion, Mother of all Christianity, upon which collective identities configure and bind together. The persistence of that role is evidenced in the cult of Copacabana from very early on, and in a very curious way, to the point that the maguey sculpture was literally modified with that objective; her wrist was broken, since the position of the child initially prevented devotees from contemplating the face of the Divine Mother. When the priest of Tiquina, a town through which the image passed before being enthroned, noticed this situation, he told Tito Yupanqui to correct it. The next day,

queriéndola bajar del altar, hallaron al niño reclinado, y como desviado de la suerte que está el día de oy, sobre el braço yzquierdo de la Madre, y tan bien puesto, que en ninguna manera estorva la vista del Virginal, y Materno rostro, aunque le pongan corona por grande que sea, quedó juntamente tan alegre [...] dando muestras del regozijo grande que siente de ver que miren los fieles a su Madre con tanta devoción.[22]

21   Ibid.
22   Ramos Gavilán, *Historia del santuario,* 243-244.

wanting to bring her down from the altar, they found the reclined child, and as diverted from the fortune that to this day he is, on the left arm of the Mother, and so well put, that in no way hinders the view of the virginal and maternal face, even if they put a crown on him, no matter how great, it was so cheerful together [...] showing signs of the great joy he feels to see the faithful look at his Mother with such devotion.

As Mother of Christ, the assimilation of Mary to archaic deities associated with Mother Earth and fertility has been quite frequent since the beginning of the evangelization process, both in the New World and in the Old. In the Andes especially, traditional cults to the land and the hills, which were articulated with the Christian rites, persist strongly (albeit with modifications). This is particularly visible in the resignification of the sacredness of Titicaca in the Virgin of Copacabana.[23] The association of the landscape with the maternal breast has been present, according to Mircea Eliade, since the first human religious experiences. The Earth, as the foundation of the cosmos, is a source of *existence* since it is what sustains, contains, and, therefore, constitutes a great *unity* and, we might add, by extension, identity:

> Men were related to each other through their mothers only, and that relationship was precarious enough. But they were related to their natural surroundings far more closely than any modern, profane mind can conceive. They were literally, and in no mere allegorical sense, "the people of the land."[24]

The sanctuary of Copacabana was built in relation to the lake and therefore with the rock of Isla del Sol, the great *pacarina,* articulating an Andean worldview. This concept refers to "place of origin" as *waka*. In general, *wakas* are social, political, and religious complexes that can be defined as "the materiality of the sacred," which are composed of both the natural and supernatural, and are linked to collective identity, in line with the worship of ancestors.[25] Thus,

---

23   Costilla, "El milagro en la construcción," 48.

24   Mircea Eliade, *Patterns in Comparative Religion*, trans. Rosemary Sheed (Lincoln: University of Nebraska Press, 1958), 243.

25   In the Andean worldview there are different types of *wakas* – sacred polymorphic objects intervened or not by human hands, or spaces such as hills, water courses, rocks, – which simultaneously have different categories: there are smaller *wakas*, linked to family worship – as the mummies of the ancestors – and older *wakas* – like the *apus* – in which much larger collective identities come together: see María Alba Bovisio, *Las huacas del NOA: objetos y conceptos* (Buenos

they also articulate different social subjects' rights over territory and access to resources. In this sense, the ritual practices developed in this context permanently renew the social and political centrality of these complexes. This is especially interesting as we consider that fundamentally, these practices unite the social subjects who take part in them, consolidating the conformation, resignification, and legitimization of collective identities around a concrete devotional figure. We choose the concept of identity as this term implies a relational, procedural, and dynamic character that is developed in power relations, and which implies "a self-understanding, the recognition of shared attributes and the creation of communal bonds and a feeling of belonging."[26]

The radiation of the cult of the Virgin of Copacabana and the reconfiguration of religious geography in Andean space has already been studied extensively, especially in the Titicaca area.[27] However, and as we mentioned previously, these types of practices can be observed in different places during the evangelizing process. Therefore, it is not surprising that to observe a continuum of these kinds of strategies in the *potosino* space in the early colonial period. The writings of Bartolomé de Arzáns y Orsua reference on numerous occasions how "among the most miraculous images of the Blessed Mary that are venerated in the temples of Potosí," it is the Virgin of the Candelaria who miraculously intercedes for the life of the natives in different moments of danger, especially those associated with mines and hills, which, as we know,

Aires: Mimeo, 2006). The *wakas* also function as territorial demarcators and transition sites between the "ecumenum" and "anecumen" space. The sacredness of the *wakas* and the interactions of men with them show the eminent relationship that exists between religious conception and the organization of society in that geography; see Pablo Cruz, "Mundos permeables y espacios peligrosos: consideraciones acerca de punkus y qaqas en el paisaje altoandino de Potosí, Bolivia," *Boletín del Museo Chileno de Arte Precolombino* 11, no. 2 (2006): 35-50; Liliana Regalado de Hurtado, "Espacio andino, espacio sagrado: visión ceremonial del territorio en el período incaico," *Revista Complutense de Historia de América* 22 (1996): 85-96.

26   See Julia Costilla, "Itinerarios religiosos y espacios sacralizados: santuarios, devotos y peregrinos en el culto al Señor del Milagro de Salta y la peregrinación a la Virgen de Copacabana en Jujuy," in *Espacialidades altoandinas. Nuevos aportes desde la Argentina,* eds. Alejandro Benedetti and Jorge Tomassi. vol. 2 (Buenos Aires: Universidad de Buenos Aires, 2014), 145.

27   Thérèse Bouysse-Cassagne, "El sol de adentro: wakas y santos en las minas de Charcas y en el lago Titicaca siglos XV a XVI," *Boletín de Arqueología PUCP,* no. 8 (2004): 59-97; "Las minas de centro-sur andino, los cultos prehispánicos y los cultos cristianos," *Boletín del Instituto Francés de Estudios Andino*s 34, np. 3 (2005): 443-462; Teresa Gisbert, *Iconografía y mitos indígenas en el arte* (1980, reprint: La Paz: Editorial Gisbert, 2008); Gabriela Siracusano, "Polvos y colores en la pintura colonial andina: prácticas y representaciones del hacer, el saber y el poder" (Ph.D. diss., Universidad de Buenos Aires, 2002); Verónica Salles Reese, *De Viracocha a la Virgen de Copacabana*, (La Paz: Plural editores, 2008). Among the vast existing bibliography, we cite only some works that are in more direct dialogue with this article.

have a sacred character.[28] I am interested in contextualizing such actions as resistance strategies; the reconfiguration of sacred spaces around figures of Christian devotion – that is, the conformation of a colonial infrastructure over the pre-Hispanic structure – does not imply only violent ploys of imposition, but also rejection, appropriation, re-signification, in which the decisions and creativity of individuals can be recognized. In fact, and in line with Christian's statement, which proposes that sharing the same devotions becomes a cohesive instrument in disaggregated societies, such as in the Andes, we consider the Marian cult as a resistance strategy in this space, since Mary, as mother, brings together social groups that are identified in certain *wakas* of greater or lesser scope, such as the Titicaca *pacarina* or that of Porco Hill, for example.[29] The cult is projected in religious topography with territorial implications and, therefore, refers both to senses of belonging and to the rights wielded in that space.[30]

The (Many?) Faces of Mary in the Eighteenth Century

The eighteenth century presented special characteristics in accordance with the transformations carried out by the Bourbon administration.[31]

28   Bartolomé Arzáns de Orsúa y Vela, *Relatos de la Villa Imperial de Potosí* (eighteenth century; reprint: La Paz: Plural, 2009). See Tristan Platt, Thérèse Bouysse-Cassagne, and Olivia Harris, *Qaraqara, Charka, Mallku, Inka y Rey en la Provincia de Charcas (siglos XVI – XVII): historia antropológica de una confederación Aymara* (La Paz: Institut Français D'études Andines, 2006); Platt and Pablo Quisbert, "Sobre las huellas del silencio: Potosí, los incas y el virrey Francisco de Toledo (siglo XVI)," in *Minas y metalurgias en los Andes del Sur, entre la época prehispánica y el siglo XVII*, eds. Pablo Cruz and Jean-Joinville Vacher, (Sucre: Instituto Francés de Estudios Andinos, 2008), 231-377; Pablo Cruz, "Huacas olvidadas y cerros santos. Apuntes metodológicos sobre la cartografía sagrada en los Andes del sur de Bolivia," *Estudios Atacameños* 38 (2009): 55-74; Carmen Salazar Soler, "La Villa Imperial de Potosí" cuna del mestizaje (siglos XVI – XVII)," in *Colonización, resistencia y mestizaje en las Américas, siglos XVI-XX*, ed. Guillaume Boccara (Lima: IFEA, 2002), 139-160.
29   William A. Christian Jr., *Local Religion in Sixteenth-Century Spain* (Princeton: Princeton University Press, 1981). William Christian, *Religiosidad local en la España de Felipe II* (Madrid: Editorial Nerea 1991), 81.
30   The concept of *waka* can be associated with that of hierophany, coined by Mircea Eliade. In that sense, the sacred space also implies time, while the sacredness of that space is constantly renewed through an intricate network of ritual practices that return and perpetrate its strength; see Eliade, *Patterns in Comparative Religion*.
31   Beyond the regulations promulgated by the Crown, the dynamics of structuring and exercising power over that territory must be analyzed in a long-term perspective that contemplates the logic and disputes between the different sectors that traditionally settled in that space. This type of analysis must also question the traditional vision that regards the process of "Bourbon secularization" as an attack by the "centralized State" on the prerogatives of the "colonial

Among the reforms brought about, we will focus on those aimed at limiting
the foundation of confraternities, as well as others referring to indigenous
people in particular and the treatment they should receive. Also included
among the provisions issued by the Crown were those that reduced the
jurisdiction of the parish priests through the subdivision of doctrines that
had a large number of followers and which limited the number of celebrations
carried out during the year. Although the climate of reforms prompted
by the Bourbon monarchs limited the number of religious festivals, those
devoted to Marian worship continued to take place. In the Synod of Charcas
(celebrated between 1771 and 1773) they appear as feasts:

> La dominica de Resurrección sin los dos días siguientes – La Asención
> del Señor – La dominica Pentecostal sin los dos días siguientes- La fiesta
> del Corpus Cristi – Todas las dominicas del año – La circunsición del
> Señor – La epifanía del Señor – La Purificación de Nuestra Señora – El
> día de los Santos Apóstoles San Pedro y San Pablo – La Anunciación de
> Nuestra Señora – El día de la Natividad del Señor.[32]

> The Dominican Resurrection without the next two days – The Assump-
> tion of the Lord – The Dominican Pentecostal without the next two
> days – The feast of Corpus Christi – All the Dominicans of the year – The
> circumcision of the Lord – The Epiphany of the Lord – The Purification of
> Our Lady – The day of the Holy Apostles Saint Peter and Saint Paul – The
> Annunciation of Our Lady – The day of the Nativity of the Lord.

Importantly, two of them are Marian in character: La Purificación de Nuestra
Señora (celebrated on February 2) and the Anunciación de Nuestra Señora
(celebrated on March 25).

Such innovations generated opposition on the part of priests, as they
implied a decrease in their income, since the money they received for
sponsoring these activities grew smaller. These changes were likewise
opposed by indigenous communities, since alterations in the festive calendar
did not align with the logic that sustained a large part of the community
structure.[33] For indigenous peoples, rituals were the counterpart to their

Church," observing that these processes affect and resolve differently, by different sectors and
in different spaces; see Dolores Estruch, *El ejercicio del poder*.

32   Pedro Miguel de Argandoña Pastén y Salazar, *Constituciones sinodales del Arzobispado de
La Plata* (Cochabamba: Imprenta de los Amigos, 1854), 261.

33   Mónica Adrián, "Estrategias políticas de los curas de Charcas en un contexto de reformas y
de conflictividad creciente," *Andes* 11 (2000): 135-160; "El espacio Sagrado y el ejercicio del poder.

economic activities, such as land purchase. For this reason, they carried out different resistance strategies against these innovations.

Within the general framework of these transformations, the Synod of Charcas strongly promoted Marian religiosity. As Chapter 6 indicates, "De la importante devoción a la celestial Reina María Señora Nuestra que deben encargar los curas a sus feligreses" [Of the important devotion to the heavenly Queen Mary Our Lady that the priests must entrust to their parishioners]:

> a efecto de que en los indios no se escuse medio para desterrar de sus engañados ánimos, la inclinación a la superstición e idolatría, y aficionarlos al culto del verdadero dios y a los oficios sagrados, siendo uno de los más oportunos el de la devoción a María Santísima, virjen y madre de Dios: encargamos a nuestros Curas, promuevan este asunto de tanta importancia con el más dilijente estudio, procurando persuadir a estos miserables, a que con afecto fervoroso se acojan con el soberano patrocinio de esta celestial Reina.[34]

> to the effect that there is no method not used to banish from the Indians their deceived tempers, the inclination to superstition and idolatry, and to bring them of the cult of the true God and sacred offices, one of the most appropriate being that of devotion to Holy Mary, virgin and mother of God: we entrust our priests, promote this matter of such importance with the most diligent study, trying to persuade these wretches, to fervently embrace the sovereign patronage of this celestial Queen.

Teaching the prayer of the Rosary and of the Salve, and celebrating Mass sung to Mary on Saturdays was emphasized, "aunque no hubiese cofradía que le mande decir" [although there was no confraternity who requested to be said].[35] When cross-checking this regulation with the logbooks from indigenous parishes in the Municipality of Potosí, we observed that indigenous confraternities consistently requested that Mass be said.[36] Although

---

Las doctrinas de Chayanta durante la segunda mitad del siglo XVIII," in *Actas del IV Congreso internacional de Etnohistoria*, ed. José Luis Martínez, vol. 1 (Lima: PUCP, 1998), 17-37.

34 Argandoña Pastén y Salazar, *Constituciones sinodales*, 139-140.

35 Argandoña Pastén y Salazar, *Constituciones sinodales*, 141.

36 Founded in 1782, Potosi included the Imperial town and its rural annexes, as well as the provinces of Chayanta, Tarija, Porco, Lípez, Atacama, and Chichas. The intendance differs from the rest of those who made up the recently formed Viceroyalty of the Río de la Plata, whose territory was delimited with its corresponding Bishopric following the illustrated logic that sought to match the civil and ecclesiastical administration.

the available information is incomplete and fragmented, through a survey carried out in the Archives of the Bishopric of Potosí,[37] two types of valuable information can be obtained: first, the inventories of material goods that these parishes had and the income received by priests for baptisms, marriages, and burials; and second, the confraternities that operated there, who their authorities were – sometimes all of their members – and which activities they carried out, with their corresponding costs. Likewise, these documents enable us to reconstruct how the parish and doctrinal jurisdiction of the municipality was configured, since in its creation the original fourteen parishes of the Imperial Village were grouped into seven (each with its corresponding sub-parish); at the same time, the doctrines had many followers, as mentioned above.[38]

To analyze urban areas, there is information about the parishes of San Cristóbal, Nuestra Señora de la Concepción, San Pablo, San Sebastián, and Nuestra Señora de Copacabana. The parishes of San Pedro, Santiago, and San Francisco el Chico are not included, since we only have inventories of their assets, in which the existence or activity of confraternities is not specified. Thus, we identified the presence of twenty-five confraternities made up of indigenous people that existed in the parishes located within the city limits of Potosí (Table 9.1). Among the devotions around which the faithful congregated, Blessed Sacrament (three brotherhoods distributed in the parishes of San Cristobal, Nuestra Señora de la Concepción, and San Sebastián) and Nuestra Señora de la Purificación, either in the form of Nuestra Señora of Copacabana or Nuestra Señora de la Candelaria, appointments in the parishes of San Cristóbal, Nuestra Señora de la Concepción and San Pablo predominate. There are also confraternities devoted to the Ángel de la Guarda, the Benditas Ánimas del Purgatorio, San Miguel Arcángel, Santa María Magdalena, San Sebastián, Santa Ana, Santa Lucía, San Cristóbal, San Salvador, and San Gerónimo. Likewise, a large number of confraternities of Marian devotion can be accounted for, including:

- N. S. de la Inmaculada Concepción
- N. S. de la Asunción

37   Archivo del Obispado de Potosí (hereafter, AOP). In the year of 1980, the parish archives of the Diocese of Potosí were centralized in the AOP. The archives of many parishes were mislaid in the move, thus losing a large amount of information that had not previously been recorded by scholars.
38   We previously addressed the doctrinal and parochial organization of Potosí in Candela de Luca, "'…y que olviden los errores de sus antiguos ritos y ceremonias supersticiosas, vivan en concierto y policía…': transformaciones y continuidades en la organización parroquial indígena potosina durante el siglo XVIII," *Revista de Historia Americana y Argentina* 51, no. 1 (2016): 11-37.

- N. S. del Rosario
- N. S. de los Dolores
- N. S. de la Soledad
- N. S. de la Misericordia
- N. S. de la Gracia[39]

On the other hand, among the institutions surveyed in rural areas are the parish of Nuestra Señora de la Concepción, the vice parish of San Cristóbal, the parish of San Bartolomé, the parish of San Pedro de Uru and Carasi, the parish of San Francisco de Micani, the vice parish of Santa Lucía, the parish of Nuestra Señora de Surumi, the vice parish of San Salvador de Salinas de Yocalla. Also, this information can be complemented with the logbook from the parish of San Marcos de Miraflores, currently lost, but which Tristan Platt reproduces entirely in his article on the feast of Corpus Christi published in 1987.[40] Based on such documents, at least 65 confraternities in rural churches can be accounted for. Thanks to the information provided by these documents, an overview of the religious festivities actually celebrated in the Indigenous churches of Potosí can also be traced, since each of the confraternities could celebrate their patron's day, a celebration that was added to the holy days authorized by the Synod of Charcas.[41]

Listed below are the confraternities that were located in those parishes, based on information obtained from the contributions of these institutions that appear in logbooks (Table 9.2). It was previously clarified that the vice parish of San Salvador de Salinas de Yocalla was not included because only inventories of goods were recorded in its logbook, which is why its confraternities and the festivities that were carried out within its framework cannot be accounted for. I would like to emphasize, however, the importance of the sanctuary that housed the image of Nuestra Señora de Turqui, to which we will return later.

It is notable that the devotions around which *cofrades* congregated are often repeated, predominantly the confraternities devoted to the worship of saints such as Santa Barbara and San Miguel,[42] and of the Virgen del

39   The latter also known in the territory of Charcas as the Virgin of Pucarani.
40   Tristan Platt, "The Andean Soldiers of Christ: Confraternity Organization, the Mass of the Sun and Regenerative Warfare in Rural Potosi (18th-20th centuries)," *Journal de la Société des Americanistes* 83 (1987): 139-192.
41   Carnival, Holy Week, and Easter holidays should be added, as well as the celebration of the Transfiguration of the Lord held in the parish of San Francisco de Micani. However, in its logbook, which confraternities or in what order they paid for such festivities is not specified.
42   Five confraternities devoted to Santa Barbara and four devoted to San Miguel were identified.

Table 9.1. Confraternities in Urban Parishes of Potosí, Eighteenth Century[43]

Brotherhood / Parish	San Cristóbal	Nuestra Señora de la Concepción	San Pablo	San Sebastián	Nuestra Señora de Copacabana
Santísimo Sacramento	X	X		X	
Ángel de la Guarda				X	
Ánimas del Purgatorio				X	
N. S. de la Purificación/ N. S. de Copacabana/ N. S. de la Candelaria	X	X	X		
N. S. de la Inmaculada Concepción		X			
N. S. de la Asunción		X			
N. S. del Rosario				X	
N. S. de los Dolores			X		
N. S. de la Soledad					X
N. S. de la Misericordia		X			
N. S. de la Gracia				X	
San Miguel Arcángel	X			X	
Santa María Magdalena				X	
San Sebastián				X	
Santa Ana	X				
Santa Lucía	X				
San Cristóbal	X	X			
San Salvador		X			
San Gerónimo		X			

Rosario and of the Immaculate Conception. It should be noted that in all parishes there were confraternities devoted to the Santísimo Sacramento – we identified seven – and to Nuestra Señora de la Candelaria (either as Nuestra Señora de la Purificación or the Virgen de Copacabana),[44] which appeared as the most popularly venerated figure, even in the sanctuary of Nuestra Señora de Surumi, where the primary venerated figure was the

43 Author's table based on the data extracted from AOP, Libro de Fábrica de La Concepción (1756-1780); Libro de Fábrica de La Concepción y San Cristóbal (1797-1801); Libro de Fábrica de San Cristóbal, 1756-1803; Libro de Fábrica de San Sebastián (1682-1808); ACMP, I, C. 51, Inventario de la Iglesia de San Pedro, entregado por su cura interino Pedro Méndez de la Parra D. Fr. Manuel Rodríguez, que quedó en su lugar (1791); C. 52, Inventario de las iglesias de Santiago y de Copacabana, entregado a su nuevo párroco (1779).

44 In particular cases, devotions are identified, in others, broken down. This particularity must be analyzed according to the time and place where they are mentioned in the documents. We hope to resolve that question in future work.

Table 9.2.   Confraternities in Rural Parishes of Potosí, Eighteenth Century[45]

Brotherhood \ Parish	San Bartolomé de Porco	San Francisco de Micani	Santa Lucía	San Pedro de Uru y Carasi	San Marcos de Miraflores	Nuestra Señora de Surumi	San Juan de Talina
Santísimo Sacramento	X	X	X	X	X	X	X
Santa Cruz	X						X-X
Espíritu Santo	X						
Benditas Ánimas del Purgatorio							X
N. S. de la Purificación/ N. S. de Copacabana/ N. S. de la Candelaria	X	X	X	X	X	X	X-X-X
N. S. del Rosario		X		X			
N. S. de la Inmaculada Concepción	X			X			X- X
Natividad de Nuestra Señora						X	
N. S. de Loreto		X					
N. S. de la Encarnación			X(*)				
N. S. de las Nieves		X					
N. S. de Surumi						X	
San Pedro	X			X	X		
San Rafael							X
San Bartolomé	X						
San Antonio	X						
Santiago	X		X(*)				
San Miguel	X	X	X(*)	X	X		
San Benito	X						
Santa Rosa		X					X
San Salvador		X	X				
San Gerónimo							
San Juan		X	X	X			
San Blas		X					
Santa Bárbara		X		X	X		X-X
San Roque			X(*)	X		X	X- X-X
San Bernabé						X	

45   Author's table based on the data extracted from AOP, Libro de Fábrica de Porco (1771-1835); Libro de Fábrica de Micani (1779-1835); Libro de Fábrica de Nuestra Señora de Surumi (1779-1810); Libro de Fábrica de Uru y Carasi (1797-1804); Libro de Fábrica de Santa Lucía (1724-1815); Libro de Fábrica de Talina (1703-1808); Libro de Fábrica de la Parroquia de San Marcos de Miraflores, Anexo Documental; Platt, "The Andean Soldiers," 181-191.

Virgin of the same name. Likewise, three confraternities were devoted to San Pedro, three to Santa Cruz, three to San Juan, five to San Roque, two to San Salvador, one to the Benditas Ánimas del Purgatorio, one to San Rafael, one to San Bartolomé, one to San Antonio, one to the apostle Santiago, one to San Benito, one to Santa Rosa, one to San Gerónimo, one to San Blas, and, finally, one to San Bernabé.

Thus, we observe that the confraternities devoted to the Virgin had, throughout the eighteenth century, a by no means negligible role. The following appear:

- Nine brotherhoods devoted to Nuestra Señora de la Purificación, (N. S. de la Candelaria/N. S. de Copacabana)[46]
- Four brotherhoods devoted to Nuestra Señora de la Inmaculada Concepción
- Two brotherhoods advocate Nuestra Señora del Rosario
- One devoted to Nuestra Señora de la Misericordia
- One devoted to Nuestra Señora de Loreto
- One devoted to Nuestra Señora de la Encarnación de Tarapaya
- One devoted to Nuestra Señora de la Asunción
- One devoted to Nuestra Señora de Surumi
- Another devoted to the Natividad de Nuestra Señora

The proliferation of Candelarias "refracted" into images that allude to the Virgin of Copacabana suggests that the territory, and therefore, the configuration of social identities acknowledged within it, continues to be concretely referenced. The allusion to Copacabana as a reference to a sacred space alters the original hierophany. Copacabana, as Mother and/or Andean *pacarina*, welcomes all her children under her mantle as a large collective.

On the other hand, when cross-checking the documents with material records, we observe that in Potosí, Candelaria's process of refraction into Copacabana materializes in two distinct cases. In this space we observe that two completely local devotions emerged from the period in which the

---

46 Particularly in Potosí, the reference in the sources made to the Virgen de la Candelaria, not necessarily in Copacabana, is still a question for us. In the written record there are intermixed mentions of the festivities of Copacabana, Purification, Candelaria, where it is not clear what feast is being mentioned. That is to say: we find cases, as in the parish of San Juan de Talina, in which the advocations appear differentiated from each other, while in most cases they appear superimposed. It is important to recognize this in order to be able to reconstruct the different itineraries that articulate the holiday calendar, an issue that we try to address in other works.

doctrinal and parochial jurisdictions were restructured. These are two Candelarias, known as Nuestra Señora de Turqui and the Virgen de Surumi.

Regarding the Virgen de Turqui, it is a bust image of a Candelaria that was venerated in the church of Salinas de Yocalla. This church was founded by the Augustinians in 1743, at the time of the jurisdictional transformation. It was directly dependent on the Imperial Villa, along with its annex, called Ormini. This temple, a jewel of the Andean baroque, presents a series of peculiarities. Its facade is completely full of reliefs that emulate those of the parish of San Lorenzo. As it appears in their inventories, their greatest wealth – not only in terms of money, but fundamentally because of its affective and cultural implications – came from housing the image of Nuestra Señora de Turqui.[47] It is an image of the Virgen de la Candelaria of which a photographic assessment could not be performed.[48] However, it is described in detail in the logbook, with the image's trousseau, which were traded as indicated by the liturgical calendar, standing out in the inventory:

La señora de Turqui, vestida de Brocato azul de plata encaje assi mesmo, forrado en tafetán Carmessi doblete, boleado con encaje de dedo, y medio ordinario, alva de Clarin, con encaje a la delantera, y otras puntas gruesas, sengulo de plata afondada azul, con sus serafines al extremo, Corona de plata, con varias piedras falzas: Una Gargantilla, con quatro sartas de Perlas chicas y unos sarcillos de oro con Diamantes chispas, que al uno le falta la mitad el pendienta de avajo: En el pecho dos sartas de perlas finas con una Cruz de esmeraldas engarzada en Oro, Contiene diez y nueve esmeraldas: Yten otra Zarta que Comprhende Catorce cuentas de oro chicas, y sus botoncitos igualmente de perlas: Um tembleque de oro filigrana con cinco perlas pequeñas. Su cena en la mano de plata a pedazos

47 Among its many assets was a magnificent altarpiece and a large number of paintings on canvas, which were subsequently transferred to the church of San Martín.

48 We refer to this image as a Candelaria, relying on Hector Schenone's text which describes it as "una de las tantas surgidas en el amplio ámbito de dispersión del fervor despertado por la Virgen del Lago. En el Museo Charcas (Sucre, Bolivia) hay un lienzo que la reproduce con sus vestidos y adornos, teniendo a sus pies los santos franciscanos Buenaventura y posiblemente Juan de Capistrano" [one of the many [advocations] emerging in the wide range of dispersion of the fervor awakened by the Virgin of the Lake. In the Charcas Museum (Sucre, Bolivia) there is a canvas that reproduces it with its dresses and ornaments, having at its feet the Franciscan Sts. Bonaventure and possibly Juan de Capistrano] (Schenone, *Santa María*, 535). Querejazu Leyton states that this image derives from another Candelaria, the work of Luis Niño, which is located in the Recoleta de Sucre museum. Querejazu Leyton, "Iconografías Marianas locales y la pintura de imágenes durante el siglo XVIII en la Audiencia de Charcas," in *Barroco iberoamericano: territorio, arte, espacio y sociedad* (Sevilla: Universidad Pablo de Olavide, 2001), 366.

dorada, assi mesmo la Candileja; Baston de Cristal con puño y extremo de plata, – canastilla ssi mesmo de plata dorada, Una sortija con cinco esmeraldas que parecen Cristal. Otra dha con tres esmeraldas, la una grande, Otra dha de metal con cristal morado, Otra de plata sin piedra: El Niño vestido de Brocato con sombrero de plata.[49]

The Lady of Turqui, dressed in blue brocade silver lace likewise, lined in crimson doublet taffeta, bowling with finger lace, and half ordinary, [...] with lace at the front, and other thick tips, silver seam embossed blue, with its seraphim at the end, silver crown, with several false stones: A choker, with four strings of small pearls and some gold twigs with diamond sparks, which one is missing half the slope below: On the chest two strings of fine pearls with a cross of emeralds set in gold. It contains nineteen emeralds: And it has another string that includes fourteen small gold beads, and its equally pearl buttons: A filigree gold tremble with five small pearls. His dinner in the hand of golden silver pieces, likewise the Candileja; crystal cane with a silver fist and end, – layette of golden silver likewise, a ring with five emeralds that look like crystal. Another with three emeralds, the large one, another metal with purple crystal, another silver without stone: The Christ Child dressed as brocade with a silver hat.

The contrast between the baroque paraphernalia of the now-abandoned temple and the large number of luxury objects present in it is also curious, as is the total absence of documents that mention it, except for the aforementioned inventory and the images that today lie in the Charcas Museum. On the other hand, we might also wonder what the conditions that enabled us to identify the image of this Candelaria as a different devotion, the Virgen de Turqui, were. In this case, there are no references to miracles or any other particular sign, nor have we been able to observe any ethnohistoric or ethnographic sources regarding the groups that occupied this space and were part of the religious community that belonged to the parish and devoted to the Virgin. Although the reorganization that was carried out in the Bolivian ecclesiastical archives in the 1980s correlated with the loss of a large part of the repositories, the dearth of records is striking. This perhaps shows a lack of receptivity "from below" towards this devotion, which, unlike the others mentioned, is not widely recognized even today. I propose as a hypothesis with which I will continue to work, that this was an imposition "from above" that did not have enough support to be taken

49   AOP, Libro de Fábrica de Salinas de Yocalla, f. 3.

up, in that it did not respect the cultural logic of the community, that is, the territorial references associated with the *wakas*.

This particular case, in which the Virgen de la Candelaria/Copacabana "refracts" in a local devotion, differs from the case of Nuestra Señora de Surumi. From the beginning of the Spanish conquest, the symbolism of these figures was used many times as a binding element around which collective identities were woven. This allowed for a better spatial organization of the population suppressed for the benefit of the crown and/or members of the clergy. In his work on the doctrines of Chayanta, Adrián analyzes how a similar strategy was used by the priests of this region to counteract the adverse effects caused by the division of the doctrine of San Marcos de Miraflores from that of Surumi in 1779.[50] As a matter of fact, the conformation of this doctrine was carried out due to the fact that it supposedly had enough resources to be a leading parish, since it housed the miraculous image of Nuestra Señora de Surumi.[51]

This image had been introduced in August 1769 in the city of La Plata, headquarters of the Archbishopric and the Royal Audience of Charcas. The figure of the Virgin was taken there in a procession from Potosí by clergy who requested donations in order to build a sanctuary to house it, ending their route at the Iglesia de Nuestra Señora de los Remedios. By not obtaining a license to beg for alms, the prelates were immediately asked to suspend their demands. Such requests were unsuccessful, as this prohibition, far from achieving the expected result, caused a multitude of people to congregate around the city. This crowd

> salió acompañando a la dicha Ymagen manifestando sentimientos inducidos por dichos demandantes a que era echada y expelida de la Ciudad por las Justicias Reales contra quienes se vertieron en el vulgo con ese motivo sediciosas tumultantes especies relativas a desautorizar y desacreditar su religión y christiandad.[52]

> came out accompanying the said image expressing feelings induced by said claimants that were thrown out and expelled from the city by the Royal Justices against those who poured into the populace with that

50 Adrián, "El espacio sagrado."
51 While the miraculous character of the image is mentioned by Platt, "The Andean Soldiers" and Adrián, "El espacio Sagrado," I have been unable to find documentation that describes it.
52 Archivo y Biblioteca Nacional de Bolivia, Expediente formado acerca de la introducción a esta ciudad de la imagen titulada Nuestra Señora de Surumi y el modo que tuvieron para ella los cuatro que la condujeron, f. 53 (1769).

seditious motive tumultuous species related to disavow and discredit their religion and Christianity.

The document continues, stating that:

y el haver depocitado dicha Ymagen en una caseria inmediata a la Ciudad, donde concurre el pueblo en qadrillas de cuia ocacion se aprovechan dichos questores para continuar la exacción de limosnas que están recogiendo en el campo fomentando para este efecto la mal entendida compacion de la plebe y poniendo la Ciudad en un inminente riesgo de un alboroto.[53]

and having deposited said image in a farmhouse adjacent to the city, where the town attends in groups of which occasion such cheaters take advantage to continue the exaction of alms they are collecting in the field, promoting for this purpose the misunderstood compassion of the plebs and putting the city at an imminent risk of a riot.

In 1779, far from enforcing the prohibition on the request for alms, Nuestra Señora de Surumi became the leading chapel of the doctrine. Years later, this sanctuary was almost exclusively maintained by the donations from pilgrims who frequented it, seeking the Virgin's grace:

Por ser santuario se mantiene y subsiste esta Iglecia. De lo contrario ya hubiera estado arruinada y destruida. Porque los estraños que vienen de Romería la socorren con Limosnas, Dones, O Dadivas a esta Portentosa imagen. El mes de Septiembre por la Natividad de Nuestra Señora y su novenaria se hacen las Fiestas principales y en tonces concurre mucha gente y se [...] en el Platillo con el Niño Limosna de los medios que dan los fieles en todo el Novenario se juntan ya cien pesos ya ciento y mas según el maior o menor concurso de cada año. Esta es la Renta de esta Iglecia y de lo que se forma ella. A esto se agregan las dadivas o dondes de algunas alajitas y piedritas de plata labrada y otras cositas su adoro que todo se pondrá en su lugar, año por año.[54]

Because it is a sanctuary, this church is maintained and subsists. Otherwise it would have been ruined and destroyed. Because strangers who

53 Ibid.
54 AOP, Libro de Fábrica de la Parroquia de Nuestra Señora de Surumi, ff. 26v-27r (1797).

come from Romería help her with alms, or gifts to this portentous image. The month of September for the Nativity of Our Lady and her *novenaria* the main festivities take place and then many people attend and [...] in the plate with the Christ Child. From the alms of half pesos the faithful give in the whole *novenario* [novena] they collect already one hundred pesos and one hundred and more according to the major or minor contest of each year. This is the rent of this church and of what it is formed. To this are added the gifts or gifts of some small boxes and pebbles of carved silver and other little things his adoration that everything will be put in place, year by year.

Through these fragments it can be observed how, as Adrián expresses, the image of the Virgin was used by the *doctrineros* priests as an element of social bonding that summoned thousands of followers grouped in the area. For these prelates, this advocation was an effective tool that brought indigenous people into its orbit when restructuring the doctrines. However, this was not only a tool for priests. The collective identities grouped around the image that the restructuring generated also enabled the logics of resource exploitation to continue, maintaining their rights in the highlands and also in the valleys. The register of the San Marcos parish states that:

que hace el territorio de la Parroquia ser los adultos mil ochocientos y siete, y lo que hace al territorio de santuario aparece ser los adultos seicientos quarenta y sinco y los Parbulos ciento diez y ocho absteniéndose, como se nota en los mesmos padrones, que esta sola es la Feligrecia Vecina estante, y perpetua en uno y otro territorio sin contar los que entran y salen en tiempo de siembra y cosecha y que tienen su residencia en la Puna y pertenecen a otros curatos, den donde se suponen en Padronados por sus propios párrocos.[55]

and what makes the territory of the parish to be the adults one thousand eight hundred and seven, and what makes the territory of the sanctuary appears to be the adults six hundred and forty-five and the *párvulos* one hundred and eighteen abstaining, as noted in the same census, that this alone is the neighboring parish that is, and perpetual in one or another territory without counting those that enter and leave in time of sowing and harvesting and that have their residence in la Puna and belong to other curates, where they are supposed to be registered by their own pastors.

55   ANB, Expediente 23, Testimonio de la división del curato de San Marcos, f. 7 (1797).

The space occupied by these parishes was divided by the Rio Grande (Mayu Grande) and was composed of:

> su feligresía de perpetua residencia, llega a mil quatrocientas almas: setecientas a la una vanda y otras setecientas a la otra pero en tiempo de cosechas, y también de siembras pasaran de siete mil almas, las que vienen al territorio donde esta la Parroquia, a cultivas, y recojo de sus grano.[56]

> its parishioner of perpetual residence, reaches one thousand four hundred souls: seven hundred to one band and another seven hundred to the other but in time of harvests, and also of plantings will pass from seven thousand souls, those who come to the territory where the parish is, to grow, and I pick up its grain.

As observed in this source, the agricultural calendar demarcated the movements of the Puna and Valle regions' populations. For the inhabitants of each side, the River was the meeting place par excellence, where *ch'allas* and libations were also held, often in the presence of the area priest, which is why we consider it to be a *waka*.[57] In this sense we agree with Costilla, who states that:

> los usos y apropiaciones del espacio en términos consagratorios, desde erigir una iglesia hasta conformar una apacheta o disponer de un altar, nos remiten a procesos identitarios: a la construcción de referentes de carácter religioso y/o a la expresión de sentimientos de pertenencia e identificaciones sociopolíticas, culturales, ideológicas, etc.[58]

> the uses and appropriations of space in consecrational terms, from erecting a church to forming an *apacheta* or having an altar, refer us to identity processes: to the construction of religious references and/or to the expression of feelings of belonging and socio-political identifications, cultural, ideological, etc.

56 Ibid.
57 See Platt, "The Andean Soldiers," 181-191.
58 Julia Costilla, "Itinerarios religiosos y espacios sacralizados: santuarios, devotos y peregrinos en el culto al Señor del Milagro de Salta y la peregrinación a la Virgen de Copacabana en Jujuy," in *Espacialidades altoandinas: nuevos aportes desde la Argentina*, eds. Alejandro Benedetti and Jorge Tomassi (Buenos Aires: Universidad de Buenos Aires, 2014), 119-163.

It is clear to us that building devotions around the image of the Virgin was so effective that it wove around it a religious practice that involved the formation of a new collective identity strong enough to support the new territorial organization. This type of practice was interpreted and used by both priests and indigenous people during the parish transformation carried out by the new administration. While the prelates found mechanisms through which they were able to reduce the decline in their income by spreading this new devotion, for the natives, the congregation around the image of Nuestra Señora de Surumi meant the possibility of maintaining their communal ties both in the highlands and the lowlands, corresponding with the "double domicile system," as well as to preserve the festive environment that sealed the sacralization of this space through ritual practices – such as processions and pilgrimages – developed around the image/*waka* of the Virgin.

The Cultural (Re-?) Structuring of *Potosino* Space

At present, the paradigm maintaining that the Bourbons' arrival to the throne of Castile came hand in hand with the implementation of an articulated and coherent reform package, primarily regarding aspects related to ecclesiastical organization, has been called into question. On the contrary, we agree with Estruch, who expresses that the indigenous institutional apparatus had various means of not complying with these regulations and, conversely, of strengthening certain traditional political behaviors.[59]

The resistance strategies mentioned here are oriented in that direction. The new administrative division is justified or resisted, depending on the case, through "re-symbolized" practices that involve aspects susceptible to both the formation of collective identities and the defense of territorial communal rights. In this context, the Marian cult operates as an identitary social matrix that legitimizes and re-signifies social practices that are associated with the expression of the cult. We agree with Barelli and Nicoletti, who understand these representations "como imaginarios sociales dominantes en un conjunto social, que se manifiestan a través de símbolos, ideas, imágenes, valores, etc. y reproducen un poder establecido, construyendo su propia identidad colectiva representándose a sí mismas, marcando territorio, alteridades y memorias" [as dominant social imaginary in a social group, manifested through symbols, ideas, images, values, etc. and reproduces

---

59   Estruch, *El ejercicio del poder*, 200.

an established power, building their own collective identity representing themselves, marking territory, alterities, and memories].[60]

In Potosí, Marian refraction is permanent. Marian devotions in Potosí constitute "refractions" of the Virgen de Copacabana – which in turn is a refraction of the Candelaria – that refer to their Andean "origin," the Titicaca *pacarina*. This refraction is also understood as the matrix of practices present in the evangelizing process developed in a different context – the eighteenth century. Like in the case of Surumi, the matrix that we had mentioned for Copacabana is renewed, encompassing: 1) the miracles associated with the image, 2) enthronement in a "hierophanic" space, and 3) the resignification of that space and the renewal of its practices. In that sense, the sacred space is (re)constructed as a hierotopy.[61] Furthermore, and beyond the sacred nature of the space, practices of spatialization, such as the pilgrimage – devotees' journey toward an encounter with the image – and the procession – the path the image takes in the context of public ritual – in large part build, define, and territorialize it. It is precisely those practices that articulate and enable the existence of the community, while defining its identity.

The "refracted" Marian devotions of Copacabana and, moreover, local devotions, shaped territoriality and reconfigured identities in this context of de-structuring. Beyond being a new process, references to Mary/Mother evoke a connection to the particular territory, and therefore, to collective identities. Nevertheless, this is not an ancestral question, considering the more than 200 years of "Christian rule" in the area, and especially considering that this process culminates with the Panamanian uprising that shook the region at the end of the eighteenth century. When observing that one of the common denominators in the three epicenters (Cuzco, La Paz, Chayanta) is a re-appropriation and vindication of Iberian institutions, we agree with Abercrombie's statement, which proposes that:

En los Andes, la hegemonía española se nutrió y reprodujo a través de la imposición de nuevas formaciones políticas – asentamientos y

---

60 Inés Barelli y María Andrea Nicoletti, "Devociones marianas en la ciudad de San Carlos de Bariloche (Argentina): construcciones identitarias sociales y marcas territoriales," *Revista Brasileira de História das Religiões* 7, no. 19 (2014): 3.

61 Hierotopies allude to the dynamics of sacred spaces, capturing both its symbolic and material dimensions, as well as its performative ones. Hierotopies represent human creations that articulate the memory of hierophany: see Astrid Windus y Andrés Eichmann Oehrli, "La (re)construcción de espacios sagrados: los proyectos hierotópicos de la Isla del Sol/Copacabana, Carabuco y La Plata," in *Barroco: mestizajes en diálogo*, ed. Norma Campos Vera (La Paz: Fundación Visión Cultural, 2017), 383-389.

puestos de autoridad civil modelados sobre, pero mantenidos aparte de un molde de pueblo español – y a través de muchas formas de teatro público y rituales mediante los cuales los andinos habrían de expresar públicamente sumisión al dominio colonial (y de esta manera, civilizarse a sí mismos). Es mi argumento que los grupos andinos modernos, tal como los conocemos en el presente, emergieron en los procesos en que los andinos tomaron en sus manos estrategias administrativas impuestas, tales como la reducción y las instituciones de doctrina, para reconstruir un sistema de articulación que servía tanto para sus propios fines como los de sus dominadores. En este proceso, los mismos vehículos con que la hegemonía debía producirse se tornaron en canales para expresar algo muy poco parecido a los que los arquitectos de la colonia habían previsto. Un tipo de resistencia "táctica" que en oportunidades deviene en terreno fértil para la rebelión.[62]

In the Andes, Spanish hegemony was nurtured and reproduced through the imposition of new political formations – settlements and civil authority positions modeled on, but kept apart from, a mold of Spanish people – and through many forms of public theater and rituals whereby the Andean people would publicly express submission to colonial rule (and thus, civilize themselves). It is my argument that modern Andean groups, as we know them today, emerged in the processes in which Andeans took into their hands imposed administrative strategies, such as the *reducciones* and doctrine institutions, to reconstruct an articulation system that served both for its own purposes and those of its dominators. In this process, the same vehicles with which hegemony had to occur became channels to express something very little similar to those that the architects of the colony had foreseen. A type of "tactical" resistance that sometimes becomes fertile ground for rebellion.

On the contrary, in the de-structuring process brought about by the reorganization of the Bourbon administration, new identities are configured in which the so-called "indigenous" or "neo-Inca" does not involve the continuation of a prevailing imaginary, but instead, the configuration of a new one that includes certain traditional elements. Within this framework exists a re-appropriation of European discourses, practices,

---

62   Thomas Abercrombie, "Articulación doble y etnogénesis," in *Reproducción y transformación de las sociedades andinas Siglos XVI-XX,* eds. Segundo Moreno and Frank Salomon (Quito: Abya Yala, 1991), 202-203.

values, symbols, and institutions, as the case of religious confraternities makes clear.

About the author

Candela De Luca is a professor of history at the Universidad Nacional de La Plata. Her research focuses on indigenous Catholic practices in the colonial Andes. De Luca has been part of CONICET. She currently is a member of the project "RESISTANCE: *Rebellion and Resistance in the Iberian Empire, 16th-19th centuries*," sponsored by the *Research and Innovation Staff Exchange* (RISE) of the European Union.

Archives

Archivo del Obispado de Potosí
  Libro de Fábrica de La Concepción 1756-1780
  Libro de Fábrica de La Concepción y San Cristóbal 1797-1801
  Libro de Fábrica de Micani 1779-1835
  Libro de Fábrica de Nuestra Señora de Surumi 1779-1810
  Libro de Fábrica de Porco 1771-1835
  Libro de Fábrica de Salinas de Yocalla 1789-1931
  Libro de Fábrica de San Cristóbal 1756-1803
  Libro de Fábrica de San Sebastián 1682-1808
  Libro de Fábrica de Santa Lucía 1724-1815
  Libro de Fábrica de Talina 1703-1808
  Libro de Fábrica de Uru y Carasi 1797-1804

Archivo de la Casa de la Moneda de Potosí
  I. y C. 51. *Inventario de la Iglesia de San Pedro, entregado por su cura interino Pedro Méndez de la Parra D. Fr. Manuel Rodríguez, que quedó en su lugar.* 1791.
  I. y C. 52. *Inventario de las iglesias de Santiago y de Copacabana, entregado a su nuevo párroco.* 1779.

Archivo y Biblioteca Nacional de Bolivia
  E.C. 53. *"Expediente formado acerca de la introducción a esta ciudad de la imagen titulada Nuestra Señora de Surumi y el modo que tuvieron para ella los cuatro que la condujeron."* 1769.
  E. C. 1779. Expediente 23. Testimonio de la división del curato de San Marcos. May 22, 1797.

Bibliography

Abercrombie, Thomas. "Articulación doble y etnogénesis." In *Reproducción y transformación de las sociedades andinas Siglos XVI-XX*, edited by Segundo Moreno and Frank Salomon, 197-212. Quito: Abya Yala, 1991.

Adrián, Mónica. "El espacio Sagrado y el ejercicio del poder. Las doctrinas de Chayanta durante la segunda mitad del siglo XVIII." In *Actas del IV Congreso Internacional de Etnohistoria*, edited by José Luis Martínez, 17-37. Lima: PUCP, 1998.

——. "Estrategias políticas de los curas de Charkas en un contexto de reformas y de conflictividad creciente." *Andes* 11 (2000): 135-160.

Anonymous. *Documentos históricos Relativos al orijen y milagros con que se estableció el culto de la imajen de María Santísima que se venera en el santuario de Copacabana, publicados por un devoto*. Potosi: Imprenta del Pueblo, 1849.

Argandoña Pastén y Salazar, Pedro Miguel. *Constituciones Sinodales del Arzobispado de La Plata*. Cochabamba: Imprenta de los Amigos, 1854.

Arzáns de Orsúa y Vela, Bartolomé. *Relatos de la Villa Imperial de Potosí*. La Paz: Plural editores, 2009.

Barelli, Inés, and Maria Nicoletti. "Devociones marianas en la ciudad de San Carlos de Bariloche (Argentina): construcciones identitarias sociales y marcas territoriales." *Revista Brasileira de História das Religiões* 7, no. 19 (May 2014): 5-30.

Bouysse-Cassagne, Thérèse. "El sol de adentro: wakas y santos en las minas de Charcas y en el lago Titicaca siglos XV a XVI." *Boletín de Arqueología* 8 (2004): 59-97.

——. "Las minas de centro-sur andino, los cultos prehispánicos y los cultos cristianos." *Boletín del Instituto Francés de Estudios Andinos* 34, no. 3 (2005): 443-462.

Bovisio, María Alba. *Las huacas del NOA: objetos y conceptos*. Buenos Aires: Mimeo, 2006.

Costilla, Julia. "El milagro en la construcción del culto a Nuestra Señora de Copacabana (virreinato del Perú, 1582-1651)." *Estudios Atacameños. Arqueología y Antropología Surandinas* 39 (2010): 35-56.

——. "Itinerarios religiosos y espacios sacralizados: santuarios, devotos y peregrinos en el culto al Señor del Milagro de Salta y la peregrinación a la Virgen de Copacabana en Jujuy." In *Espacialidades altoandinas. Nuevos aportes desde la Argentina*, edited by Alejandro Benedetti and Jorge Tomassi, 2:119-163. Buenos Aires: Universidad de Buenos Aires, 2014.

Cruz, Pablo. "Mundos permeables y espacios peligrosos. Consideraciones acerca de punkus y qaqas en el paisaje altoandino de Potosí, Bolivia." *Boletín del Museo Chileno de Arte Precolombino* 11, no. 2 (2006): 35-50.

——. "Huacas olvidadas y cerros santos. Apuntes metodológicos sobre la cartografía sagrada en los Andes del sur de Bolivia." *Estudios Atacameños* 38 (2009): 55-74.

De Luca, Candela. "'…De la importante devoción a la celestial Reina María Señora Nuestra…' Religiosidad mariana en las cofradías de indígenas de Potosí (Alto Perú) en el siglo XVIII." In *Cofradías en el Perú y en otros ámbitos del mundo hispánico (siglos XVI al XIX)*, edited by David Fernández Villanova, Diego Egar Lévano Medina, and Kelly Montoya Estrada, 405-422. Lima: Conferencia Episcopal Peruana, 2015.

—. "'…y que olviden los errores de sus antiguos ritos y ceremonias supersticiosas, vivan en concierto y policía…' Transformaciones y continuidades en la organización parroquial indígena potosina durante el siglo XVIII." *Revista de Historia Americana y Argentina*, 51, no. 1 (2016): 11-37.

Eliade, Mircea. *Tratado de Historia de las Religiones*, vol. 2. Madrid: Ediciones Cristiandad, 1974.

Estruch, Dolores. *El ejercicio del poder en el Jujuy colonial. Enlaces y tensiones entre la jurisdicción civil y eclesiástica. Siglos XVI-XVIII.* Buenos Aires: La Bicicleta, 2017.

Fogelman, Patricia. "El culto mariano y las representaciones de lo femenino: Recorrido historiográfico y nuevas perspectivas de análisis." *Aljaba* 10 (2006): 175-188.

—. "Simulacros de la virgen y refracciones del culto mariano en el Río de la Plata Colonial." *Eadem Utraque Europa* 2, no. 3 (2006): 11-34.

—. *La omnipotencia suplicante. El culto mariano en la ciudad de Buenos Aires y la campaña en los siglos XVII y XVIII.* Ph.D. diss. Universidad de Buenos Aires, 2003.

Gisbert, Teresa. *Iconografía y mitos indígenas en el arte.* La Paz: Gisbert, 2008.

Gisbert, Teresa and José de Mesa. "La virgen María en Bolivia. La dialéctica Barroca en la representación de María." In *Barroco Andino, Memoria del I Encuentro Internacional*, 21-36. La Paz: Unión Latina, 2003.

González Dorado, Antonio. *De María conquistadora a María liberadora. Mariología popular latinoamericana.* Madrid: Sal Terrae, 1988.

Guaman Poma de Ayala, Felipe. *El primer nueva crónica y buen gobierno.* México City: Siglo XXI, [c. 1615] 1980.

Moreira, Vilma da Silva. "La mujer en la teología: reflexión biblicoteológica." In *Mujer latinoamericana: Iglesia y teología*, edited by Mujeres para el Diálogo, 140-166. México: MPD, 1981.

Platt, Tristan. "The Andean Soldiers of Christ: Confraternity Organization, the Mass of the Sun and Regenerative Warfare in Rural Potosi (18th-20th centuries)." *Journal de la Société des Américanistes* LXXXIII (1987): 139-192.

Platt, Tristan, and Pablo Quisbert. "Sobre las huellas del silencio: Potosí, los incas y el virrey Francisco de Toledo (siglo XVI)." In *Minas y metalurgias en los Andes del Sur, entre la época prehispánica y el siglo XVII,* edited by Pablo Cruz and Jean-Joinville Vacher, 231-277. Sucre: Instituto Francés de Estudios Andinos, 2008.

Platt, Tristan, Thérese Bouysse-Cassagne, and Olivia Harris. *Qaraqara, Charka, Mallku, Inka y Rey en la Provincia de Charkas (siglos XVI – XVII): historia antropológica de una confederación Aymara.* La Paz: Institut Français D'études Andines, 2006.

Ramos Gavilán, Alonso. *Historia del santuario de Nuestra Señora de Copacabana.* 1621, reprint: La Paz: MUSEF, 1988.

Ramos, Gabriela. "Nuestra Señora de Copacabana ¿devoción india o intermediaria cultural?" In *Passeurs, mediadores culturales y agentes de la primera evangelización en el mundo ibérico, s. XVI-XIX*, edited by Scarlett O'Phelan and Carmen Salazar Soler, 163-179. Lima: Pontificia Universidad Católica del Perú, 2005.

Regalado de Hurtado, Liliana. "Espacio andino, espacio sagrado: visión ceremonial del territorio en el período incaico." *Revista Complutense de Historia de América* 22 (1996): 85-96.

Salazar Soler, Carmen. "La Villa Imperial de Potosí" cuna del mestizaje (siglos XVI XVII)." In *Colonización, resistencia y mestizaje en las Américas, siglos XVI-XX*, edited by Guillaume Boccara, 139-160. Lima: IFEA, 2002.

Salles Reese, Verónica. *De Viracocha a la Virgen de Copacabana.* La Paz: Plural, 2008.

Schenone, Hector. *Santa María. Iconografía del arte colonial.* Buenos Aires: Educa, 2008.

Siracusano, Gabriela. "Copacabana, lugar donde se ve la piedra preciosa: imagen y materialidad en la región andina." In *Actas del seminario internacional de estudios de arte en América Latina: temas y problemas*, 2003. http://www.esteticas.unam. mx/edartedal/PDF/Bahia/complets/siracusano_bahia.pdf

Siracusano, Gabriela, Rosanna Kuon, and Marta Maier. "Colores para el milagrona aproximación interdisciplinaria al estudio de pigmentos en un caso singular de la iconografía colonial andina." In *Investigación en conservación y restauración: II Congreso del Grupo Español del IIC*. Barcelona: Museu Nacional d'Art de Catalunya, 2005. https://ge-iic.com/files/2congresoGE/Colores_para_el_milagro.pdf

Vuola, Elina. "María, mujer en la política. Nuevos desafíos para la teología latinoamericana." *Albertus Magnus* 4, no. 2, (2012): 59-71.

Windus, Astrid, and Andrés Eichmann Oehrli. "La (re) construcción de espacios sagrados. Los proyectos hierotópicos de la Isla del Sol/Copacabana, Carabuco y La Plata." In *Barroco: mestizajes en diálogo: VIII Encuentro Internacional sobre Barroco*, edited by Norma Campos Vera, 383-390. La Paz: Fundación Visión Cultural, 2017.

10   Between Excess and Pleasure

The Religious Festivals of the Indigenous People of Jujuy,
Seventeenth-Nineteenth Centuries[1]

Enrique Normando Cruz
UE CISOR- CONICET and Universidad Nacional de Jujuy

Grit Kirstin Koeltzsch
UE CISOR- CONICET and Universidad Nacional de Jujuy

Translated by Javiera Jaque Hidalgo

Abstract
This chapter studies the religious festivals staged by the indigenous
confraternities of colonial Jujuy, in the viceroyalty of Peru. It argues
that these festivals help consolidate Spanish rule over these individuals,
sustaining that this festival culture helped legitimize the indigenous
governors' authority and popularized a penchant for the excess of food
and drink.

Keywords: Jujuy, indigenous confraternities, Feasting, food, alcohol

Introduction

This work analyzes Indigenous religious festivals in the Viceroyalty of Peru.
Our hypothesis is that indigenous parishioners engaged in festive spending
that enabled colonial legal domination by the State, the Church, and its agents
of exploitation because the festivities reinforced the authority of *curacas*

1   This chapter is part of the project "Construcciones de soberanía en las fronteras de la Colonia
y la Independencia (Jujuy en Salta del Tucuman, 1780-1821)" (PIP-CONICET 112-201301-00074-CO).

Javiera Jaque Hidalgo and Miguel A. Valerio. *Indigenous and Black Confraternities in Colonial*
Latin America: Negotiating Status through Religious Practices. Amsterdam: Amsterdam University
Press, 2022
DOI: 10.5117/ 9789463721547_CH10

and Indian governors and popularized an overindulgence in drinking and feasting. The case study is Jujuy, a district located in the Peruvian regional space with a dominant indigenous population, like Charcas, Potosí, and La Paz. This geographical context allows us to establish historical comparisons to determine the different types of festivals, the legality and legitimacy of economic exploitation, as well as how these festive performances fell within the framework of colonial rule.

Regarding the historiographical perspective, we consider that festivities favor processes of group revitalization. With respect to the documents that we will use, it is necessary to critique sources before analyzing the religious festivals of the Indigenous people of Jujuy, because, as Jacques Heers puts it, as for identity, resistant, and rebellious behaviors in the festivities of the seventeenth and eighteenth centuries are actually reputed as such in sources by the State and the Church to combat paganism and to continue evangelization with more sober religious practices and devotions.[2] For this reason, the sample was prepared with documents that could be contrasted among themselves. Thus, documents generated by the Crown, the governors and councils, and also, by the ecclesiastical jurisdictions of the bishoprics, the church councils, the local parishes, and the native parishioners were selected, which allowed us to confront the dominant agency with the subaltern agency.[3] For example, when identifying that the *cédulas reales* (royal decrees) prohibited the festivals, the ecclesiastical tariffs that funded them were enumerated. The denunciations made against doctrinal priests for imposing festivals were compared with inventories of the churches that recognized them, and the complaints by ethnic authorities that the festivals were an excessive economic burden for the community were refuted with records of elections by indigenous authorities for the exercise of stewardships and festivals. It is estimated that this is how a sample was created that accounts for the totality, diversity of the different "voices" documented in the religious festivals in Jujuy in the Peruvian space at the end of the colonial period.[4]

---

2   Jacques Heers, *Carnavales y fiestas de locos* (Barcelona: Península, 1988), 253.

3   Sahid Amin, "Testimonio de cargo y discurso judicial: el caso de Chauri Chaura," in *Debates post coloniales: una introducción a los estudios de la sulbalternidad*, ed. Silvia Rivera Cusicanqui and Rossana Barragán (La Paz: Historia, 1997), 119-156.

4   Research was conducted in local archives in Jujuy (Archivo del Obispado, Archivo de Tribunales, Archivo Histórico de la Provincia, Archivo del Convento de San Francisco), regional archives (Archivo Histórico de Salta), and national archives with documents about colonial Jujuy (Archivo General de la Nación Argentina, Archivo Arquidiócesis de Sucre, Archivo y Biblioteca Nacional de Bolivia).

Period and Space Studied

The historical period chosen to study the religious festivals of Indians in Jujuy goes from the end of the seventeenth century to the first two decades of the nineteenth. It is possible to identify this portion of time as an autonomous unit, because Spain's American territories had the common characteristics of government prevalence with respect to the State, constitution of social spaces in which the group predominates before the individual (which enables a participatory agency of the individual in the public), dominion of credit regarding production, and cultural crystallization of global miscegenation.[5] With reference to the historical space, it is the Peruvian region, with a focus on Potosí mining. A spatial context "open" to the Andean world that includes Tucumán, and from which the case of Jujuy will be specifically analyzed. Tucumán was conquered from Peru with the foundation of a series of cities in the sixteenth century and colonial dominance was consolidated through a commercial communication route known as the *camino real*, which linked Lima with Buenos Aires, passing by Potosí and the cities of Córdoba, Tucumán, Salta, and Jujuy.[6]

The importance of Tucumán as a route of commercial circulation was consolidated in the eighteenth century, especially after the port of Buenos Aires became the viceregal capital of Río de la Plata, supplying Potosí mining with livestock and various products *de la tierra* (agricultural goods).[7] In 1692, a century after the foundation of Jujuy in 1593, the *aduana seca* ["Dry" Customs] was installed to try to control smuggling between the mining region of Alto Peru and the port of Buenos Aires and from that year on the city began an accelerated economic development boosted by the trade of

5   Jacques Le Goff, *¿Realmente es necesario cortar la historia en rebanadas?* (Mexico City: FCE, 2016), 96-97; Francois-Xavier Guerra, Annick Lempérière, et al., *Los espacios públicos en Iberoamérica. Ambigüedades y problemas. Siglos XVIII- XIX* (Mexico City: Fondo de Cultura Económica, 1998); Annick Lempérière, "La 'cuestión colonial'," Nuevo Mundo/Mundos Nuevos (2014), http://nuevomundo.revues.org/437; David A. Brading, *Mineros y comerciantes en el México borbónico (1763-1810)* (Mexico City: FCE, 1997) and *Orbe Indiano: de la monarquía católica a la república criolla, 1492-1867* (Mexico City: FCE, 1991); Jürgen Habermas, Thomas Burger, and Frederick Lawrence, *The Structural Transformation of the Public Sphere: An Inquiry into a Category of Bourgeois Society* (Cambridge: Polity, 2020); Serge Gruzinski, *Las cuatro partes del mundo. Historia de una mundialización* (Mexico City: FCE, 2010).
6   Carlos S. Assadourian, *El sistema de la economía regional. El mercado interior. Regiones y espacio económico* (Mexico City: Nueva Imagen, 1983), 160-161; Víctor Tau Anzoátegui, "Introducción," in *Nueva Historia de la Nación Argentina,* edited by Tau Anzoátegui, vol. 2 (Buenos Aires: Planeta, 1999), 11-12.
7   Assadourian, *El sistema de la economía,* 161.

cattle and various products to the mining markets of Potosí, as well as the legal and illegal circulation of silver.[8]

As for the jurisdictions of Spanish government in the region, in 1563 the Tucumán governorate was created, encompassing Jujuy, Salta, Tucumán, Santiago del Estero, Catamarca and Córdoba, which subsisted until 1783, the year in which it was divided into the administration of Córdoba del Tucumán (Córdoba, La Rioja, and the Province of Cuyo) and the Municipality of Salta del Tucumán (Salta, Jujuy, San Miguel de Tucuman, Santiago del Estero, and Catamarca). In ecclesiastical terms, in 1570 the diocese of Tucumán was erected under the jurisdiction of Lima until 1609 when it became dependent on the archbishopric of Charcas-La Plata.[9] These Hispanic jurisdictions administered a plethora of Spanish parishioners, Creoles, Indians, mulattos, zambos, free Blacks, and slaves, which, according to the census prepared by the *cantor* in charge of the bishopric in 1779, was 126,004 souls in 46 ecclesiastical *beneficios* (privileges).[10] Among these *beneficios*, Jujuy is distinguished because from 70% to 82% of its population was indigenous; at the end of the eighteenth century these indigenous parishioners were organized into the parishes of Jujuy, Perico, Río Negro, Tumbaya, Humahuaca, Juan Bautista de Cerrillo, Santa Catalina, San José de la Rinconada, and Nuestra Señora de la Candelaria de Cochinoca, most of them entrusted and tributary to the King.[11]

Summarizing, this case is optimal to carry out a study of the religious festivals of Indians, because it is linked to the Tucumán space and, in the

---

8   Zacarías Moutoukias, "Gobierno y sociedad en el Tucuman y el Río de la Plata, 1550- 1800," in *Nueva Historia Argentina*, 2:381.

9   Moutoukias, "Gobierno y sociedad en el Tucumán"; Nelson C. Dellaferrera, "La iglesia diocesana: las instituciones," in *Nueva Historia de la Nación Argentina*, 2:94.

10   "Padrón del Tucumán, 1778/1779, elaborado por Don José Antonio de Ascasubi chantre de la iglesia del Tucumán provisor y gobernador de la diócesis por orden del obispado de 1777 en 1778 y publicado en 1779," in *Documentos del Archivo de Indias para la historia del Tucumán*, ed. Antonio Larrouy, vol. 1 (1591-1700, first print edition: Buenos Aires: L. J. Rosso, 1923), 380-381.

11   Extracto general de los siete curatos de indios tributarios a Su Majestad que abraza la jurisdicción de esta ciudad según los Repartimientos y totales que contiene, Archivo General de la Nación (hereafter AGN), Buenos Aires, Argentina, Sala IX, Interior, 30.4.7 (December 23, 1791); Beatriz Rasini, "Estructura demográfica de Jujuy. siglo XVIII," *Anuario del Instituto de investigaciones Históricas* 8 (1965): 119-150; Ernesto J. Maeder, *La formación de la sociedad argentina desde el siglo XVI hasta mediados del XVIII* (Resistencia: IIGHI, 1984); Raquel Gil Montero, "La población de Jujuy entre 1779 y 1869" (bachelor's thesis, Universidad Nacional de Córdoba, 1993); Raquel Gil Montero, "Familia campesina andina. Entre la colonia y el nuevo estado independiente en formación" (Ph.D. diss., Universidad Nacional de Córdoba, 1999); Jorge Comadrán Ruíz, *Evolución demográfica argentina durante el período hispano (1535-1810)* (Buenos Aires: EUDEBA, 1969), 89.

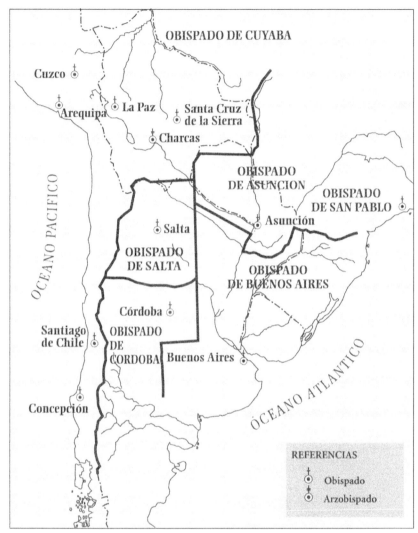

Map 10.1. Bishoprics (1620-1806). Source: Dellaferrera, "La iglesia diocesana," 393. With author's permission.

middle of the commercial circuits of the Peruvian regional system, it depends jurisdictionally and ecclesiastically on the bishopric of Charcas and there was a predominance of indigenous among the parishioners. The latter aspect enables a local and synchronous historical comparison with the regions of Charcas, Potosí, La Paz, and Peru in general.[12]

12   Magnus Mörner, "En torno al uso de la comparación en el análisis histórico de América Latina," *Jahrbuch fur Gerschichte Von Staat, Wirtschaft Lateinamerikas* 31 (1994): 388-389.

Types of Indigenous Religious Festivals

Throughout Spanish America, indigenous people carried out different religious festivities with similar economic structures, institutional hierarchies,
agents, and institutions in interaction and festive performance. These festivities can be grouped into the brotherhoods' festivities, civic festivals, and the
festivities of the *mayordomías* (stewardship) and *alferazgos* (lieutenantship).
For example, the festivals that were held in religious brotherhoods of the
Peruvian highlands were long-term, so the elements that constitute them,
that we named above, had less coercive pull, thus, being more open to the
entire community.[13] These festivities were of a complex nature, with different
levels of authority and jurisdictional and institutional competencies, as well
as a temporality bounded to the time recorded in the brotherhoods' books.

Another aspect of the religious brotherhoods is that the economic resources of the association were only partially generated in the festivals and
they were not always under the exclusive orbit of the ethnic authorities, but
were disputed and sometimes monopolized by the priests. This is the case of
the festivals of the religious brotherhoods of the Purificación, Copacabana,
and San Lorenzo del Molino of the vice-parish of the rectory parish of
Jujuy (1670). These brotherhoods were founded by don Pedro Chavúcar
(chief *curaca* of the Yalas indigenous people) and don Juan Ochoa de Zárate
(*encomendero* and owner of the Yala hacienda) and from 1637 onward they
held parties to raise money to pay the priest's salary. These brotherhoods also
had resources of goods and work that the community provided, in addition
to the alms collected in the area.[14] In the year 1726, the ecclesiastical visitor
of the Bishopric of Tucumán, Antonio Suárez, denounced the rector priest
for appropriating the goods collected by the community and declared that
the priest did not hold the festivals for which goods and alms were collected,
as inferred from the lack of records in the chapel's account books.[15]

The second type of festivals were those that took place outside the
brotherhoods' communities. These were the festivals that, for example,
the doctrinal priest José Alejo de Alberro informed to his superiors in 1795
that were held in the parish of Tumbaya, an ecclesiastical jurisdiction of
Jujuy that, according to the record of Carlos III of 1778 and early 1779, was

13   Olinda Celestino y Albert Meyers, *Las cofradías en el Perú: región central* (Frankfurt: Verlag
Klaus Dieter Vervuert, 1981), 129.
14   Autorización para formar la cofradía de la Purificación y Copacabana en San Lorenzo del
Molino y títulos de las viceparroquias e Iglesias de la Parroquial de esta ciudad de San Salvador
de Jujuy, Archivo del Obispado de Jujuy (hereafter AOJ), 6.9, 2:73 (1637-1723).
15   AOJ, 6.9, 2:73, sf.

the one with the largest native population.[16] Thus, in the vice-parish of Purmamarca de Santa Rosa, the festivities of the Niño Jesús (Child Jesus) and the Ánimas (Souls of Purgatory) took place, in the chapel of the parish of Tumbaya of the Virgen María (Virgin Mary), del Señor Crucificado (Our Lord Crucified) y de las Ánimas (Souls of Purgatory); in the Tilcara chapel of Francisco Solano, Nuestra Señora de los Dolores (Our Lady of Sorrows), Santo Domingo de Guzmán, Nuestra Señora del Rosario (Our Lady of the Rosary), Saint Francis of Assisi, el Señor Crucificado (Our Lord Crucified), Rosario (Rosary), and Ánimas (Souls of Purgatory); and in the Huacalera chapel of Nuestra Señora de la Limpia Concepción (Our Lady of the Immaculate Conception), and Ánimas (Souls of Purgatory).[17]

The group of Christian devotions had a system of governing positions similar to that of the festivals of the religious brotherhoods, but, apparently, there was less community pressure to participate or to be chosen as an authority of the festivities.[18] Another aspect is that income in *metálico* (coins) to carry out the festivities predominates: in the elections of 1794 for 1795 festivities, 403 *pesos* of eight *reales* were collected, in addition to sung masses and processions, dresses for the image of the Virgin, wax, and rockets. Finally, these indigenous religious festivals were held every year for as long as the festive eagerness of the parish' *ayllus* lasted.[19]

The third type of festivals were those held by the *mayordomías* and *alferazgos* of Christian religious devotions. As the Hispanic *mayordomías* and *alferazgos* established for the devotion of the Ánimas of the Villa de Oropeza, the Ánimas [Souls], and Nuestra Señora de la Limpia Concepción of the cities of Potosí and Cochabamba in the eighteenth century. In these festive celebrations, the party *mayordomos* were the trustees, captains, priests, and "aldermen twenty-four," who exercised the trades in property because it allowed them to control valuable advocations' real estate.[20]

---

16 "Relevamiento del ministro Gálvez y llevado adelante por el alcalde provincial de Jujuy Diego de la Corte el 10 setiembre 1779," in *Censo de la Provincia de Jujuy, 1778- 1779*, vol. 2, ed. Ricardo Rojas (Buenos Aires: Imprenta de Coni Hermanos, 1913).

17 Libro de fiestas que se hacen en el curato de Tumbaia para los años 1795-1796 y elección de autoridades, AOJ, 28-18, 11:1 (1795).

18 Alejandro Diez Hurtado, *Fiestas y cofradías: asociaciones religiosas e integración en la historia de la comunidad de Sechura (siglos XVII al XX)* (Piura: CIPCA, 1994).

19 AOJ, 28-18, 11:1, sf.

20 Diligencias por la posesión de la administración de la cofradía de las Animas de Joaquín de Tejerina y Hurtado actual síndico procurador y las fianzas de 12000 pesos, Archivo Arquidiócesis de Sucre (hereafter AAS), Cofradías 1 (1804); Presentación del presbítero Pablo de Orozco para que se le restituya la mayordomía de la cofradía de las animas de su padre, por mala administración de su titular, AAS, Cofradías 1, (1781); Autos seguidos por la parte de la cofradía de Nuestra Señora

This is similar to the system used by the confraternal *mayodormos* of the mining city of Guanajuato: wealthy gentlemen who administered their funds, organized the functions, and covered the deficits of the festivals of the religious associations themselves.[21]

In the *mayordomías* and *alferazgos* of indigenous festivals, in addition to the economic, status, and of *calidad* (quality) motivations, the indigenous authorities were subordinated and state-exploited by local ecclesiastical agents.[22] We learn about this situation through, for example, an *auto* made by the *corregidor* of Potosí dated in 1662, which maintains that the priests introduced brotherhoods and festivals at the expense of the "indios principales" (indigenous leaders), native authorities that in some cases, as in the Humahuaca parish of Jujuy, turned the position of festivity authority into a strategy of colonial integration.[23] This is what seems to have been done by the chief cacique of Uquía, Don Andrés Toronconti who in his will, in addition to arranging to be buried in the church of San Antonio de Humahuaca (parish headquarters), acknowledges that 62% of his assets were debts he had with the brotherhoods of Nuestra Señora de la Candelaria, Benditas Ánimas, Señor San Antonio, and Santa Bárbara.[24] This is also the case of the *alférez* Bernardo Madrigal, founder and authority of the feast of Nuestra Señora del Rosario de Iruya [Our Lady of the Rosary of Iruya], who at the beginning of the eighteenth century handled at his discretion the money collected in the vicinity of the parish and the products of the "sementeras" of the virgin (crops of wheat, potatoes, and straw for fodder and to make earth bricks). Goods and resources that he did not return in an equivalent way but rather with ornaments for worship: for thirteen loads of potatoes, he "paid" the brotherhood five pounds of wax, a "lana de ruan" (cotton fabric printed in colors manufactured in Rouen,

de la Limpia Concepción fundada en la Iglesia Matriz de esta Villa de Potosí contra el regidor del Ilustre Cabildo Don Manuel Jauregui, AAS, Cofradías 1, (1801).

21   David A. Brading, *Una iglesia asediada: el obispado de Michoacán, 1749-1810* (Mexico City: FCE, 1994), 158.

22   Norbert Elias, *La sociedad cortesana* (Mexico City: FCE, 1982); Eugenia Bridikhina, *Theatrum mundi. Entramados del poder en Charcas colonial* (La Paz: Plural, 2007). *Calidad* is a circumstantial label for the context and moment under scrutiny: see, Joanne Rappaport, *The Disappearing Mestizo: Configuring Difference in the Colonial New Kingdom of Granada* (Durham/London: Duke University Press, 2014).

23   Auto de averiguación sobre los excesos en las fiestas de cofradías y designación de alféreces, Archivo y Biblioteca Nacional de Bolivia (hereafter ABNB), Real Cédula 456 (August 3, 1662).

24   Memoria de Don Andrés de Toronconti difunto y Autos obrados en su razón en 2 días del mes de Agosto de 1710 años, Juez el Capitán Camacho, Archivo de Tribunales de Jujuy (hereafter ATJ), 27:834 (August 2, 1710).

France) with its tassels, twelve ribbon wands, and one *sarda* (rustic wicker fabric).[25]

Legalization and Festive Legitimacy

In documents prepared by the Archbishopric of La Plata in the seventeenth century (1619, 1654, and 1692) and which were still in force in the Jujuy parishes in the eighteenth century, it was established with respect to the festivals, brotherhoods and *alferazgos* that:

- The people designated as festivities' *alféreces* were in charge of contributing goods, resources, and work in a private or familiar way to carry out the festivities.
- The doctrinal priest exercised some violence in the imposition of festivals and in the appointment of the Indians who carried the banner of the position of *alférez*, on whom fell the economic responsibility of the festival as well as the transfer of resources to the priest.
- Doctrinal priests, ethnic authorities, and Indian parishioners agree that the festivities of brotherhoods and saints enable excess food and drink, acts of disorder in general, lack of respect for the authorities, and violence and sexual relations. That is to say, "*muchas malas obras y pecados*" [many evil deeds and sins].[26]

The documentary series informs us of the existence, at southern Charcas in the seventeenth and eighteenth centuries, a combination between the legality and legitimacy of colonial festive. Legal festivals received the "imprimatur" of the Church and the State, as the festivals appear in all the ecclesiastical tariffs published in the region between 1619 and 1797.[27] These festivities were also characterized by the presence of ecclesiastical authorities, elections, and ordered social and economic life of the parishes. This is what is reported in detail by the inventories carried out by the doctrinal priests of the parishes of Jujuy de Casabindo and Cochinoca between 1798 and 1826, which record that the religious in "consorcio" (consortium) with

25   Imposición de la fiesta de la virgen del Rosario de Iruya con elección de autoridades, libro de cofradía, AOJ, 8.7, 12:633, 640 and 689 (February 20, 1708).

26   Archivo Histórico de la Provincia de Jujuy (herafter AHR), Archivo Marquesado del Valle de Tojo, 61, 72.

27   Edward P. Thompson, *Tradición, revuelta y conciencia de clase: estudios sobre la crisis de la sociedad preindustrial* (Barcelona: Crítica, 1984), 129-130.

caciques, governors, and *segundas indígenas* (female native leaders) build temples, hold festivals, and attend regularly to the chapels of the brother-hoods and the fiestas to make inventories and the "yerra" (registration with marks) of the cattle.[28]

The presence of Spanish authorities at festivals and in brotherhoods has been evaluated in the historiography as an instance of competition between the ecclesiastical and the royal jurisdiction, a dispute over jurisdictions that increased in the Bourbon context since the mid-eighteenth century, when it provided, for example, by means of the Royal Decree of 1791, that the meetings or assemblies of the religious brotherhoods should always be held under the presence of a royal minister.[29] It mandated that, in Jujuy, officials of the Crown must always be present at the festive "juntas" (meetings).[30]

In order for colonial rule in the Old Regime to be possible, in addition to festive legality, a legitimate "moralidad multitudinaria" [multitudinous morality] was required.[31] That is why the tariffs that regulate religious festivals were used by doctrinal priests to legalize the festive overexploitation of their parishioner communities;[32] and also, by indigenous ethnic leaders to argue the limits of exploitation. It is what the governor of Cochinoca, Fernando Bilti did, who had a tariff on his property to establish clearly in various articles, what the Indians must give as alms for the festivals of local devotions and of the brotherhoods – legal instrument in which the validity of the coercive introduction of "fiestas añadidas" (added festivals)

28 Inventarios realizados por los curas excusadores del curato de Casabindo y Cochinoca, de los bienes capellánicos de Nuestra Señora de la Asunción (patrona del pueblo de Casabindo), y de las cofradías de Nuestra Señora de la Asunción, Candelaria y Purificación, Archivo Ricardo Rojas (hereafter ARR), Papeles eclesiásticos, box 1 (1775-1826). Previoulsy at the Archivo Histórico de Jujuy (herafter AHJ).

29 Se prohíbe reunirse en Asamblea de cofradías sin la presencia del ministro real, AGN, Sala IX, Justicia, 8.10.5, Asamblea de cofrades, ff. 241-245 (October 12, 1791); Ana de Zaballa y Ianire Lanchas, "Los conflictos entre la jurisdicción real y episcopal a fines del siglo XVIII: el caso del obispo José Gregorio Ortigoza," in *Cultura legal y espacios de justicia en América, siglos XVI-XIX*, ed. Macarena Cordero, Rafael Gaune, and Rodrigo Moreno (Santiago de Chile: Universidad Adolfo Ibañez, 2017), 93-117; Clara García Ayluardo, *Desencuentros con la tradición: los fieles y la desaparición de las cofradías de la ciudad de México en el siglo XVIII* (Mexico City: FCE, 2015), 201-232.

30 Oficio y copia de real cédula sobre las reuniones de las cofradías y hermandades y la presencia de las autoridades civiles, AOJ, 8.23, 700-701 (November 26,1791); El cabildo de Jujuy dictamina en particular quienes deben asistir a las "juntas" de las cofradías el 28 de noviembre del mismo año, AHJ, ARR, 45, 79 (November 28, 1791).

31 Thompson, *Tradición, revuelta y conciencia*, 65-66.

32 Causa criminal contra el cura de Cochinoca Maestro Don Valentín Albornoz Ladrón de Guevara, AOJ, 8-15, 653, 656 (1735).

was recognized, but limiting the economic contribution to the "propia voluntad" (own will) of each indigenous parishioner.[33]

Thus, a paradox appears in the class relations between the Indians who recognize and promote the legality of the dominance and exploitation of the Hispanic patriciate and in which the state dominator (represented locally by the doctrinal priests) tries to limit, and that consequently sometimes they are harmed by the use of festive legality by the dominated indigenous people.[34] It is about the acceptance of economic and noneconomic contributions that the indigenous governor of Cochinoca Fernando Bilti and the edict of 1783 issued by the Bishop of San Alberto de Tucumán recognized, which commands the priests and lieutenants to "abstenerse" (refrain themselves) from "concurrir y promover" (attend and promote) the religious festivals of Indians, by the "juntas" [meetings] of men and women, drunkenness and games that took place among the people who participated in the festivities.[35] It is also what can be seen in the 1619 tariff – which is later replicated in the following century – formed by the Archbishop of La Plata, Fray Gerónimo Méndez de Liedra, in a Diocesan Synod that brought together the dean, cathedral chapter, priests, and vicars of the entire archbishopric; in which he orders that when the religious festivals were held, the banner should not be removed from the church because the indigenous people wear it as a badge of their "vicios" (vices).[36] In 1662, the *corregidor* (mayor) of Potosí, Francisco de Sarmiento de Mendoza, made an inquiry about the inconveniences that the suspension of the festivities of brotherhoods would cause, because the priests imposed them in almost all the Indigenous parishes of the Villa Imperial, damaging the convocation and the service of the mining *mita* of Indians to Potosí.[37] Various regional cases of the Peruvian space demonstrate, in the festive environment, the legal and legitimate contradictions of colonial domination.

Festive Economy

The festive economy oriented to the control of goods and resources is historically related to the State. Whether the pre-Hispanic structures of

---

33   Ibid.

34   Thompson, *Tradición, revuelta y conciencia*, 45.

35   Edicto del obispo San Alberto a los curas y tenientes del Tucuman, AOJ, box 16, 3 (1783-1788).

36   Arancel del arzobispo de La Plata, fray Gerónimo Méndez de Liedra, AHPJ, Archivo Marquesado del Valle de Tojo, 61 and 72 (December 11, 1619).

37   Auto de averiguación sobre los excesos en las fiestas de cofradías y designación de alféreces, ABNB, Real Cédula, 456 (August 3, 1662).

the Tawantinsuyu or Spanish rule, they enable private and state ownership of the lands, determine the actors (priests, parish priests, and *doctrineros*, *corregidores*, *encomenderos*, poor indigenous people, and their *caciques*), establish the public festive event (in temples, streets, and especially the plaza), and sacralize compulsory labor.[38]

For this reason, colonial corporations organized brotherhoods and religious festivals to institutionalize the benefits of the colonial economy. As did the expelled Jesuits from the Colegio of the city of La Paz and from the congregation of San Salvador and the annex chapel of Loreto, which they administered through brotherhoods, buildings, and rural and urban establishments valued at 120,678 *pesos* of eight *reales*.[39] This economic profitability also explains the development of festivals and brotherhoods among the Indians of the region. Some imposed in a constant and coercive way by doctrinal priests, as denounced by *curacas* and ecclesiastical authorities in the central area of the *audiencia* (royal tribunal) de Charcas de Chayanta and Laimes, and others generated in part by the parishioners themselves and the indigenous ethnic authorities, as in Tucumán, where the brotherhoods and festivals of the Humahuaca and Casabindo and Cochinoca parishes allowed the recompositing of identity, the practice of some aspects of traditional religion, the reinforcement of ethnic authority and the administration of labor, livestock, salt, and fabrics.[40]

38   Divinity associated with St. James: Jan Szeminski, *Vocabulario y textos andinos de don Felipe Guaman Poma de Ayala* (Lima: FCE, 1993), 149; Felipe Guaman Poma de Ayala, *Nueva corónica y buen gobierno*, ed. Franklin Pease (sixteenth century; first printed edition: Lima: FCE, 1993), 805-819.

39   Plan de las tres fincas pertenecientes a la cofradía del Señor de las Piedades del colegio de La Paz y de las doce que tocan a la congregación de San Salvador y capilla anexa de Nuestra Señor a de Loreto que fue de los regulares extinguidos de la compañía del nombre de Jesús, AGN, Sala IX, 5-1-6 (1772-1777).

40   Solicitud de los curas de Chayantacas y Laimes para producir información sobre los sobrantes de las fiestas los daban voluntariamente los indios a sus párrocos, AGN, Sala IX, Justicia, 31.7.1 (1797); Sobre la formación de planes de fiestas de Chayantacas y Laymes, AGN, Sala IX, Justicia, 31.7.3 (1797); Antonio Acosta, "Los clérigos doctrineros y la economía colonial (Lima, 1600-1630)," *Allpanchis* 19 (1982): 117-149; Nicholas A. Robins, *Comunidad, clero y conflicto: las relaciones entre la curia y los indios en el Alto Perú, 1750-1780* (La Paz: Plural, 2009); David Cahill, "Curas and Social Conflict in the Doctrinas of Cuzco, 1780-1814," *Journal of Latin American Studies* 16, no. 2 (1984): 241-276; Christine Hünefeldt, "Comunidad, curas y comuneros hacia fines del período colonial: ovejas y pastores indomados en el Perú," *HISLA* 2 (1983): 3-31; Bernard Lavallè, "Las doctrinas de indios como núcleos de explotación colonial (siglos XVI y XVII)," *Allpanchis* 19 (1982): 151-171; Guillermo Pons Pons, "Abancay en la época colonial: una doctrina peruana," *Hispania Sacra* 42, no. 86 (1990): 593-633; Ariel J. Morrone, "Curas doctrineros y caciques andinos en la construcción de legitimidades: las iglesias rurales de La Paz, Audiencia de Charcas, 1570-1630," *Jahrbuch für Geschichte Lateinamerikas* 50 (2013): 29-54; Mónica Adrián,

In some cases, coercion is more extra-economic at festivities than in brotherhoods. According to Fernando Vilti, governor of the town of Cochinoca
(Jujuy), the voluntary nature of the economic contribution was subrogated
by the violence of the catechizing priest, who appropriated the work of
the Indians (especially the freight of cattle), made indigenous woman spin
and weave, and did not pay them for this work, instead keeping the goods
handed over as alms and violently punishing the ethnic authorities. As a
consequence of these actions, the young indigenous neophytes fled from
the doctrine, they were "alzados" [hiding in the woods] and "no asisten a
las confesiones" [they did not attend confessions].[41]

Thus, in the Audiencia de Charcas, the indigenous parishioners supported the Church and its agents financially. The multitude of festivals that
the Indians carried out paid for masses, festive supplies (wax, rockets, etc.),
feeding and keeping the priest in the rural chapel while the ceremonies
lasted, and food and drink for those attending the event.[42] Ecclesiastical
rights that were charged for the festivals that were added to those that
the Church received for the first fruits, gifts, and alms of various kinds,
giving rise to a kind of "repartimiento forzoso," [forced distribution], to
the extent that this overexploitation is considered to be one of the causes

"Estrategias políticas de los curas de Charcas en un contexto de reformas y conflictividad
creciente," *Andes* 11 (2000): 135-160; Thierry Saignes, "Lobos y ovejas: formación y desarrollo de
los pueblos y comunidades en el sur andino siglos XVI-XX," in *Reproducción y transformación
de las sociedades andinas siglos XVI-XX*, ed. Segundo Moreno y Frank Salomón (Quito: Abya
Yala, 1991), 91-136; Daniel J. Santamaría, "Iglesia y economía campesina en el alto Perú, siglo
XVIII," *Occasional papers series* 5 (1983): 1-21; María Candela De Luca, "Las cofradías de indios en
el territorio de Charcas (siglo XVIII): balance historiográfico y nuevas propuestas de análisis,"
Segundas Jornadas Nacionales de Historia Social, La Falda, Córdoba, 2009; Gabriela Caretta
e Isabel Zacca, "'Benditos ancestros'": comunidad, poder y cofradía en Humahuaca en el siglo
XVIII," *Boletín Americanista* 62 (2011): 51-72; Carlos Zanolli, "Entre la coerción, la oportunidad
y la salvación. Las cofradías de indios de San Antonio de Humahuaca. Siglos XVII y XVIII,"
Andes 19 (2008): 345-369; Enrique N. Cruz, "Poder y adaptación al Sur de Charcas en el siglo
XVIII. Curas doctrineros y curacas en San Antonio de Humahuaca," *Boletín Americanista* 67
(2013): 71-83; "Poder y relaciones sociales en curatos de indios. El curato de Cochinoca en el
siglo XVIII (Puna de Jujuy- Argentina)," *Hispania Sacra* 58, no. 117 (2006): 355-381; Enrique N.
Cruz y Adolfo Rodrigo Ramos, "El proceso de construcción y mantenimiento de iglesias en
curatos indígenas del altiplano argentino, siglos XVIII y XIX," *Colonial Latin American Historical
Review* 19, no. 2 (2014): 159-189.
41   Causa criminal contra el cura de Cochinoca Maestro Don Valentín Albornoz Ladrón de
Guevara, AOJ, 8-15, 653, 656 (1735).
42   Jorge Hidalgo Leuedé, "Tierras, exacciones fiscales y mercado en las sociedades andinas de
Arica, Tarapacá y Atacama, 1750-1790," in *La participación indígena en los mercados surandinos.
Estrategias y reproducción social. Siglos XVI a XX*, ed. Olivia Harris, Brooke Larson, and Enrique
Tandeter (La Paz: CERES, 1987), 193-231.

of the Andean rebellions of the late eighteenth century.[43] In this context of religious festivals that enable rural indigenous overexploitation, the *ayllus* of the Audiencia de Charcas will permit and even develop them because they also allow them to recreate cultural traditions and reinforce the power of ethnic authorities. In a report from the Audiencia of 1768, the distribution of useless things to the Indians, the appointment of *mayordomos* and *alféreces*, and that the "curas cargan a los indios con muchas fiestas" [priests burden the Indians with many festivals] are denounced, but also that in the festivities everyone is invited, it is celebrated with food and drink for two or three days "quedando todos embriagados" [all being drunk] and that although the priests and *corregidores* tried for this reason "desarraigar esta perniciosa corruptela nunca han podido conseguirlo por reusarlo los indios con pretexto de que no quieren ser menos que sus antecesores que hacían lo mesmo" [to uproot this pernicious corruption they have never been able to achieve because the Indians refuse on the pretext that they do not want to be less than their ancestors who did the same].[44]

Also, in 1790, and in the context of the Bourbon reforms, in the Peruvian Andean region the possibility of suppressing religious festivals is discussed, the archbishop saying that priests depend entirely on tax collectors, and that suppressing festivals and gifts as a source of complementary income of the synod, priests and *doctrineros* would be "subordinados, dependientes de unos hombres ignorantes, ebrios sin educación, sin cristiandad" [subordinate, dependent on ignorant men, drunk without education, without Christianity].[45]

To summarize, in the archbishopric of Charcas and in the parishes of Jujuy, the economic income of the festivities involved a diversity of actors and contradictory relationships between the colonial state, its religious agents, indigenous parishioners, and ethnic authorities. All this due to the economic importance of festivities in the operation of the system of colonial domination, as evidenced by the fact that 75% of the income of the doctrinal priest for the benefit of Rinconada came from religious festivals, as reported in 1791 by Gregorio Funes, "Canónigo de la catedral de Córdoba

43   Eduardo Saguier, "Charcas y su articulación comercial al espacio colonial rioplatense. Las presiones mercantiles y el reparto forzoso en el siglo XVIII," *DATA* 6 (1996): 75; Scarlett O'Phelan Godoy, *Un siglo de rebeliones anticoloniales, Perú y Bolivia 1700-1783* (Cuzco: CERA, 1988); Juan Marchena Fernández, "Al otro lado del mundo. Josef Reseguín y su 'generación ilustrada' en la tempestad de los Andes, 1781-1788," *Tiempos de América* 12 (2005): 43-111.

44   Real Cédula y Real provisión sobre fiestas y excesos de indios, AGN, IX-Interior, 30.1.3 (1770).

45   Mónica Adrián, "Los curatos rurales en la provincia de Chayanta," *DATA* 6 (1996): 102.

y visitador de los curatos de la Puna por el obispo Ángel Mariano Moscoso"
[Canon of the Cathedral of Córdoba and *visitador* of the Puna parishes for
Bishop Ángel Mariano Moscoso].[46]

Festive Performance

The Bourbon historical conjuncture of state control over the religious sphere,
will lead to the interference of authorities in festivals and brotherhoods
and even provisions that tried to prohibit them, such as that of the Concilio
Provincial de La Plata (Diocesan Council of La Plata) from 1774 to 1778,
concerned with containing abuses in "relaciones entre distintos sexos en los
campos," [relations between different sexes in the fields], excessive intake
of food and drinks, and "bailes y cantares poco honestos y con malicia"
[dances and songs that are not honest and malicious].[47] The festive excesses
have to do, among other things, with the historical conjuncture of a colonial
baroque culture with high doses of theatricality in public festivals, in which
individuals act in a relaxed way as if nobody saw them and, at the same
time, in theatrical performances for a group of observers.[48]

   Although it is considered that the content of the feast cannot be reduced
in a certain way and cannot be limited, the festive act can be delimited
in space and in the sacred order.[49] Like the spatial and devotional limits
established in 1798 by the doctrinal priest of Cochinoca, Manuel Benito
Arias, for festive ceremonies with a procession through the town square of
the body of the *cacique* Pedro Quipildor, the main person in charge of the
construction of the new temple. A performance that had to be carried out
with "solemnidad fúnebre," [funereal solemnity], celebrating "dos misas

---

46   The other 25% came from burial, extreme unction, and land leased: AOJ, 1-4, Inventario de
bienes del curato a cargo de José Torino (May 28, 1791).

47   Roberto Di Stefano, "De la cristiandad colonial a la iglesia nacional. Perspectivas de investigación en historia religiosa de los siglos XVIII y XIX," *Andes* 11 (2000), 94-95.

48   Carmen Espinosa Valdivia y Bruno Mestries Bazarte, "Monjas a escena. Teatro y vida
conventual de las jerónimas novohispanas," in *Obra novohispana de teatro: la conquista de
México por Carlos V*, ed. Alicia Bazarte Martínez and José G. Herrera Alcalá (México: Instituto
Politécnico Nacional, 2016), xxxviii; Eva Valero, "Las relaciones de fiestas: copiar la historia "fuera
de costumbre," in *Historia de las literaturas en el Perú*, vol. 2, ed. Raquel Chang-Rodríguez and
Carlos García-Bedoya M. (Lima: Pontificia Universidad Católica del Perú, 2017), 252-253; Erving
Goffman, *The Presentation of Self in Everyday Life* (Edinburgh: University of Edinburgh Press,
1956).

49   Mikhail Bakhtin, *Rabelais and His World*, trans. Helene Iswolsky (Bloomington: Indiana
University Press, 1984), 248-249.

rezadas y una cantada, vigiliada de cuerpo presente, y se soterró el cadáver puesto en un cajón en medio del crucero de la propia Iglesia nueva, por el mérito contraído por dicho don Pedro en haber a su costa emprendido la referida obra, llevado de su celo y religión, y que sirva de recuerdo a los fieles la piedad de este bienhechor" [two prayed masses and one sung, watched over the present body, and the corpse placed in a coffin in the middle of the crossing of the new Church itself was buried, due to the merit contracted by said Don Pedro in having undertaken the aforementioned work at his expense, carried away by his zeal and religion, and that serves as a reminder to the faithful the piety of this benefactor].[50] The festivals also vary in time and determine the festive movements. The main event of the festival takes place on the day the dedication is celebrated and, also, an annual chronological conjuncture is generated that is repeated cyclically without limitations. As it happens with the celebrations of the parish of Tumbaya de Jujuy: on the day of the celebrations the ethnic authorities were chosen who had to take charge of paying for the next festivities, so that they had a whole year to recover the goods and resources to be able to carry them out.[51]

Regarding the scope of the festive act, it is recognized that, through the practice of "pedir limosnas" [begging for alms], the distinction between urban and rural was diluted. That is why in 1790 the stewards of the churches of Cochabamba requested and obtained authorization to collect alms in the city and in the "campaña" (countryside) and in the "San Pedro de Naturales" brotherhood of Jujuy, between 1752 and 1776 specific authorities were elected to raise money and donations: the "diputados de la ciudad" [deputies of the city] and the "diputados del campo," [deputies of the field].[52]

As an Old Regime performance that is usually practiced for a public, a legal guideline and state control are needed so that social obligation is not "[se] descuide" [neglected]. This is what the interim priest and vicar Romualdo Jijena pointed out in 1791 when he took over the *beneficio* of

50   Informe del cura excusador y vicario pedáneo Manuel Benito Arias de la doctrina de Cochinoca, acerca de la fábrica de la nueva iglesia de Casabindo, Pueblo de Casabindo, Colección Archivo Ricardo Rojas, Papeles eclesiásticos, box 1 (December 17, 1798).

51   Fiestas que se hacen en el curato de Tumbaya para los años 1795-1796 y elección de autoridades, AOJ, 28-18, 11:1 (1795).

52   Cofradía de Jesús Nazareno. Pedido del mayordomo de la Iglesia de San Juan de licencia para pedir limosna por la campaña, AGN, Sala IX, Justicia, 31.5.7 (1790); Cochabamba. Los mayordomos de la villa de Cochabamba sobre que se les conceda licencia para pedir limosna para la refacción del templo de Nuestra Señora del Rosario, AGN, Sala IX, Justicia, 31.3.5 (1790); Libro de Colecturia de la cofradía de San Pedro, AOJ, Libro de Matrimonios, Catedral (1693-1836), n. 4, Naturales (1752-1776).

Rinconada in Jujuy, that there were no books that recorded the income of the annex of the chapel of the Río de San Juan, and by no means books of festivals: "de lo que resulto que no habiendo de donde constasen los alférez, priostes y mayordomos que se habían asentado y no teniendo yo por otra parte conocimiento alguno de los indios, muchos se ocultaron, la fiestas fueron en decadencia y no quedo derecho alguno de fiestas a favor de esta viceparroquia" [from which it turned out that for not having record of the *alférez*, *priostes*, and *mayordomos* who had settled and, on the other hand, having no knowledge of the Indians, many hid, the festivities were in decline and there was no right for any festivities in favor of this vice-parish].[53]

Finally, in this festive performance the protagonism belongs to the celebrants. According to the *Nueva Corónica y Buen Gobierno* by Felipe Guamán Poma de Ayala, the election of ethnic authorities as festive authorities and brotherhoods should be controlled, "porque siendo principal o mandón o indio borracho, coquero o jugador, se lo bebe con los alcaldes ordinarios y regidores, y los demás mandoncillos lo gastan y lo consume los bienes de la Iglesia y de cofrades" [because being the leader or *mandón* or drunk Indian, *coquero* or player, he drinks it with the mayors and aldermen, and the other *mandoncillos* spend and consume the goods of the Church and of confreres].[54] Drunkenness and excesses of food seemed to be generalized in the eighteenth century, going from the *caciques* to the poor Indians, structuring a more "popular" and ethnically communal legitimacy.[55]

Conclusion

The Indigenous religious festivals of the Peruvian space of Jujuy allowed colonial domination because they were legalized by a corpus of state and ecclesiastical guidelines and contradictory practices of the State, the Church, and doctrinal priests. At the same time, they were legitimized by the *ayllus*, the *curacas*, and governors of Indians and the native parishioners, because they reinforced the authority of the ethnic leaders and popularized the excesses in drink and food.

53 Cuenta de los derechos por servicios eclesiásticos cobrados en la iglesia de Rinconada por Romualdo Jijena, AOJ, 24-6, 7:1 (1791).
54 Poma de Ayala, *Nueva corónica y buen gobierno*, 807-821.
55 Thierry Saignes, "De la borrachera al retrato: Los caciques andinos entre dos legitimidades (Charcas)," *Revista Andina* 5, no. 1 (1987): 152-170.

What is not clear is whether the Indigenous religious festivals contributed to the reinforcement of ethnic identity, as if it seems to have happened in the festivals of Blacks, *mulatos*, and *pardos* of the Archconfraternity of San Benito de Palermo de Jujuy, who chose a "hermana reina" (sister queen) a local American reference to the African and tropical cults.[56]

And also, in the Hispanic festivals, such as the ones carried out in 1808 by the authorities of the neighboring city of Salta to ask for the end of the drought to the "todo poderoso" (almighty) and to the "intercesores, y medianeros, que son los Santos, entre los cuales deben ser preferentes nuestros patronos," [intercessors and mediators, who are the Saints, among whom should be preferred by our patron saints], natural disasters that the dominators also faced with festivals, vows, brotherhoods, and oratories in Guadalajara, Madrid, Toledo, Ciudad Real, and Cuenca.[57] As for the goods and resources generated by the festive economy, when the festivals were held in the religious confraternities, various actors dispute their control (priests, *doctrineros*, parish priests, landowners, *curacas*, Indian governors, *mayordomos*, and *alféreces*). When they are held for an annual devotion, the dispute is between the doctrinal priest and the festive authorities (usually the ethnic authorities) and when it comes to the feast of *mayordomías* and *alferazgos*, the authorities had the economic monopoly.

Finally, according to the *Nueva corónica y buen gobierno* from 1615, festive devotions, resources, and religious practices are matters of "policía" [order] and "servicio a Dios" [service to God].[58] That is why the expense to give "esplendor" [splendor] to the festival is related to the State, which uses the festival to regulate excesses (eating and drinking), organize work, and regulate the celebrants sexually and socially. On the other hand, the Indigenous parishioners consented with "gusto" [pleasure] to the exploitation of doctrinal priests, *curacas*, and their indigenous governors, because the party allowed them to act in a relaxed way, as if unobserved, reinforcing the authority of their ethnic leaders, overindulging in food and drink, working

---

56 Constituciones de la Archicofradía de San Benito de Palermo de esta ciudad de Jujuy, formadas por los Religiosos de este convento del Salvador, Archivo del Convento de San Francisco de Jujuy (1809); José María Nunes Pereira, "Cultura afro-brasileira," in *Introdução a historia da África e da cultura afro-brasileira*, ed. Beluce Belluci (Rio de Janeiro: UCAM, 2003), 119-126.

57 Acta capitular y resolución del Gobernador sobre rogativas y ceremonias religiosas a favor del patrono San Felipe y Santiago con motivo de la sequía del año, Archivo Histórico de Salta, Libros Copiadores, Legislativas, 161 (1808); William Christian, Jr., *Religiosidad local en la España de Felipe II* (Madrid: Editorial Nerea, 1991), 45.

58 Poma de Ayala, *Nueva corónica y buen gobierno*, 879-893.

at their discretion for the splendor of the festival and freeing themselves sexually and socially.[59]

About the authors

Enrique Normando Cruz is professor of history at the Universidad Nacional de Jujuy. He has been a researcher at the Escuela de Estudios Hispanoamericanos in Seville, Spain, and the University of Bonn, and guest lecturer at several Latin American and European universities. His work has appeared in *GLADIUS*, *TEMPUS*, *América Latina en la Historia Económica* y *LATINOAMERICA*.

Grit Kirstin Koeltzsch is a Ph.D. candidate at the National Scientific and Technical Research Council of Argentina (CONICET). She was a Research Scholar in the George A. Smathers Libraries at the University of Florida and was awarded a Graduate Student Paper Award from the Latin American Studies Association in 2017. Her work has appeared in the *Oxford Research Encyclopedia of Latin American History*, *Canadian Journal of Latin American and Caribbean Studies*, *Intercontinental Journal on Physical Education*, *Revista Interdisciplinar de Literatura e Ecocrítica*, *América Latina en la Historia Económica* and *TEMPUS: Revista en Historia General*.

Bibliography

Acosta, Antonio. "Los clérigos doctrineros y la economía colonial (Lima, 1600-1630)." *Allpanchis* 19 (1982): 117-149.

Adrián, Mónica. "Los curatos rurales en la provincia de Chayanta." *DATA* 6 (1996): 97-117.

——. "Estrategias políticas de los curas de Charcas en un contexto de reformas y conflictividad creciente." *ANDES* 11 (2000): 135-160.

Amin, Sahid. "Testimonio de cargo y discurso judicial: el caso de Chauri Chaura." In *Debates post coloniales. Una introducción a los estudios de la sulbalternidad*, edited by Silvia Rivera Cusicanqui and Rossana Barragán, 119-156. La Paz: Historia, 1997.

59   We concluded, therefore, that the political life of other farmers in Sedaka must have been similar, in other words, that they availed themselves of disguise in their political behavior: see Jim Scott, *Los dominados y el arte de la Resistencia: discursos ocultos* (Mexico City: Era, 2000), 41.

Assadourian, Carlos S. *El sistema de la economía regional. El mercado interior. Regiones y espacio económico*. Mexico City: Nueva Imagen, 1983.

Bajtín, Mijaíl. *La cultura popular en la Edad Media y en el Renacimiento. El contexto de Francois Rabelais*. Madrid: Alianza, 1988.

Bourdieu, Pierre. *El sentido social del gusto: Elementos para una sociología de la cultura*. Buenos Aires: Siglo Veintiuno Editores, 2013.

Brading, David, A. *Orbe Indiano. De la monarquía católica a la república criolla, 1492-1867*. Mexico City: Fondo de Cultura Económica, 1991.

——. *Una iglesia asediada: el obispado de Michoacán, 1749-1810*. Mexico City: Fondo de Cultura Económica, 1994.

——. *Mineros y comerciantes en el México borbónico (1763-1810)*. Mexico City: FCE, 1997.

Bridikhina, Eugenia. *Theatrum mundi. Entramados del poder en Charcas colonial*. La Paz: Plural, 2007.

Cahill, David. "Curas and Social Conflict in the Doctrinas of Cuzco, 1780-1814." *Journal of Latin American Studies* 16, no. 2 (1984): 241-276.

Caretta, Gabriela, and Isabel Zacca. "'Benditos ancestros': comunidad, poder y cofradía en Humahuaca en el siglo XVIII." *Boletín Americanista* 62 (2011): 51-72.

Celestino, Olinda and Albert Meyers. *Las cofradías en el Perú: región central*. Frankfurt: Vervuert, 1981.

Christian Jr., William A. *Local Religion in Sixteenth-Century Spain*. Princeton: Princeton University Press, 1981.

Comadrán Ruíz, Jorge. *Evolución demográfica argentina durante el período hispano (1535-1810)*. Buenos Aires: EUDEBA, 1969.

Cruz, Enrique N. "Poder y relaciones sociales en curatos de indios. El curato de Cochinoca en el siglo XVIII (Puna de Jujuy-Argentina)." *Hispania Sacra* 57, no. 117 (2006): 355-381.

——. "Poder y adaptación al Sur de Charcas en el siglo XVIII. Curas doctrineros y curacas en San Antonio de Humahuaca." *Boletín Americanista* 67 (2013): 71-83.

Cruz, Enrique N., and Adolfo Rodrigo Ramos. "El proceso de construcción y mantenimiento de iglesias en curatos indígenas del altiplano argentino, siglos XVIII y XIX." *Colonial Latin American Historical Review* 19, no. 2 (2014): 159-189.

Dellaferrera, Nelson C. "La iglesia diocesana: las instituciones." In *Nueva Historia de la Nación Argentina*, edited by Tau Anzoátegui, 2:385-415. Buenos Aires: Planeta, 1999.

Di Stefano, Roberto. "De la cristiandad colonial a la iglesia nacional. Perspectivas de investigación en historia religiosa de los siglos XVIII y XIX." *ANDES* 11 (2000): 83-113.

Diez Hurtado, Alejandro. *Fiestas y cofradías. Asociaciones religiosas e integración en la historia de la comunidad de Sechura (siglos XVII al XX)*. Piura: CIPCA, 1994.

Elias, Norbert. *La sociedad cortesana*. Mexico City: FCE, 1982.

Engels, Friedrich. *Der Ursprung der Familie, des Privateigenthums und des Staats.* Stuttgart: Dietz Verlag, 1892.

Espinosa Valdivia, Carmen, and Bruno Mestries Bazarte. "Monjas a escena. Teatro y vida conventual de las jerónimas novohispanas." In *Obra Novohispana de Teatro. La Conquista de México por Carlos V*, edited by Alicia Bazarte Martínez and José G. Herrera Alcalá, xxxviii-xlv. Mexico City: Instituto Politécnico Nacional, 2016.

García Ayluardo, Clara. *Desencuentros con la tradición. Los fieles y la desaparición de las cofradías de la ciudad de México en el siglo XVIII*. Mexico City: FCE, 2015.

Gil Montero, Raquel. "Familia campesina andina. Entre la colonia y el nuevo estado independiente en formación." Ph.D. diss. Universidad Nacional de Córdoba, 1999.

Goffman, Erving. *The Presentation of Self in Everyday Life*. Edinburgh: University of Edinburgh Press, 1956.

Gruzinski, Serge. *Las cuatro partes del mundo. Historia de una mundialización*. Mexico City: FCE, 2010.

Guaman Poma de Ayala, Felipe Guaman. *Nueva corónica y buen gobierno*. Edited by Franklin Pease. Lima: FCE, 1993. 2 vols.

Guerra, Francois-Xavier, and Annick Lempérière, et al. *Los espacios públicos en Iberoamérica. Ambigüedades y problemas. Siglos XVIII-XIX*. Mexico City: FCE, 1998.

Habermas, Jürgen, Thomas Burger, and Frederick Lawrence. *The Structural Transformation of the Public Sphere: An Inquiry into a Category of Bourgeois Society*. Cambridge: Polity, 2020.

Heers, Jacques. *Carnavales y fiestas de locos*. Barcelona: Península, 1988.

Hidalgo Leuedé, Jorge. "Tierras, exacciones fiscales y mercado en las sociedades andinas de Arica, Tarapacá y Atacama, 1750-1790." In *La participación indígena en los mercados surandinos. Estrategias y reproducción social. Siglos XVI a XX*, edited by Olivia Harris, Brooke Larson, and Enrique Tandeter, 193-231. La Paz: CERES, 1987.

Hünefeldt, Christine. "Comunidad, curas y comuneros hacia fines del período colonial: ovejas y pastores indomados en el Perú." *HISLA* 2 (1983): 3-31.

Larrouy, Antonio. *Documentos del Archivo de Indias para la historia del Tucumán, vol. I (1591-1700)*. Buenos Aires: L. J. Rosso, 1923.

Lavallè, Bernard. "Las doctrinas de indios como núcleos de explotación colonial (siglos XVI y XVII)." *Allpanchis* 19 (1982): 151-171.

Le Goff, Jacques. *¿Realmente es necesario cortar la historia en rebanadas?* Mexico City: FCE, 2016.

Lempérière, Annick. "La 'cuestión colonial'." Nuevo Mundo/Mundos Nuevos (2016). http://nuevomundo.revues.org/437

Maeder, Ernesto J. *La formación de la sociedad Argentina desde el siglo XVI hasta mediados del XVIII*. Resistencia: IIGHI, 1984.

Marchena Fernández, Juan. "Al otro lado del mundo. Josef Reseguín y su 'generación ilustrada' en la tempestad de los Andes. 1781-1788." *Tiempos de América* 12 (2005): 43-111.

Mörner, Magnus. "En torno al uso de la comparación en el análisis histórico de América Latina." *Jahrbuch fur Gerschichte Von Staat, Wirtschaft Lateinamerikas* 31 (1994): 373-390.

Morrone, Ariel J. "Curas doctrineros y caciques andinos en la construcción de legitimidades: las iglesias rurales de La Paz, Audiencia de Charcas, 1570-1630." *Jahrbuch für Geschichte Lateinamerikas* 50 (2013): 29-54.

Moutoukias, Zacarías. "Gobierno y sociedad en el Tucumán y el Río de la Plata, 1550-1800." In *Nueva Historia Argentina*, 2:355-411.

Nunes Pereira, José Maria. "Cultura afro-brasileira." In *Introdução a historia da Africa e da cultura afro-brasileira*, edited by Beluce Belluci, 119-126. Rio de Janeiro: UCAM, CEEA, 2003.

O'Phelan Godoy, Scarlett. *Un siglo de rebeliones anticoloniales, Perú y Bolivia 1700-1783*. Cuzco: CERA Bartolomé de Las Casas, 1988.

Pons Pons, Guillermo. "Abancay en la época colonial: una doctrina peruana." *Hispania Sacra* 62, no. 86 (1990): 593-633.

Rappaport, Joanne. *The Disappearing Mestizo: Configuring Difference in the Colonial New Kingdom of Granada*. Durham: Duke University Press, 2014.

Rasini, Beatriz. "Estructura demográfica de Jujuy. Siglo XVIII." *Anuario del Instituto de investigaciones Históricas* 8 (1965): 119-150.

Robins, Nicholas A. *Comunidad, clero y conflicto. Las relaciones entre la curia y los indios en el Alto Perú, 1750- 1780*. La Paz: Plural, 2009.

Rojas, Ricardo. *Censo de la Provincia de Jujuy, 1778- 1779*. Buenos Aires: Coni Hermanos, 1913.

Saguier, Eduardo. "Charcas y su articulación comercial al espacio colonial rioplatense. Las presiones mercantiles y el reparto forzoso en el siglo XVIII." *DATA* 6 (1996): 73-95.

Saignes, Thierry. "De la borrachera al retrato: Los caciques andinos entre dos legitimidades (Charcas)." *Revista Andina* 5, no. 1 (1987): 152-170.

——. "Lobos y ovejas: formación y desarrollo de los pueblos y comunidades en el sur andino siglos XVI-XX." In *Reproducción y transformación de las sociedades andinas siglos XVI-XX*, edited by Segundo Moreno and Frank Salomón, 91-136 Quito: Abya Yala, 1991.

Santamaría, Daniel J. "Iglesia y economía campesina en el alto Perú, siglo XVIII." *Occasional Papers Series* 5 (1983): 1-21.

Scott, Jim. *Los dominados y el arte de la resistencia. Discursos ocultos*. Mexico City: Era, 2000.

Szeminski, Jan. *Vocabulario y textos andinos de don Felipe Guaman Poma de Ayala*. Edited by Franklin Pease. Lima: Fondo de Cultura Económica, 1993.

Tau Anzoátegui, Víctor. "Introducción." In *Nueva Historia de la Nación Argentina*, 2:9-18.

Thompson, Edward P. *Tradición, revuelta y conciencia de clase. Estudios sobre la crisis de la sociedad preindustrial*. Barcelona: Crítica, 1984.

Valero, Eva. "Las relaciones de fiestas: copiar la historia 'fuera de costumbre.'" In *Historia de las literaturas en el Perú. Volumen II. Literatura y Cultura en el Virreinato del Perú: apropiación y diferencia*, edited by Raquel Chang-Rodríguez and Carlos García-Bedoya M., 252-289. Lima: PUCP, 2017.

Zaballa, Ana de, and Ianire Lanchas. "Los conflictos entre la jurisdicción real y episcopal a fines del siglo XVIII: el caso del obispo José Gregorio Ortigoza." In *Cultura legal y espacios de justicia en América, siglos XVI-XIX*, edited by Macarena Cordero, Rafael Gaune, and Rodrigo Moreno, 93-117. Santiago de Chile: Universidad Adolfo Ibañez, 2017.

Zanolli, Carlos. "Entre la coerción, la oportunidad y la salvación. Las cofradías de indios de San Antonio de Humahuaca. Siglos XVII y XVIII." *Andes* 19 (2008): 345-369.

Part IV

Black Brotherhoods in Brazil

11   Black Brotherhoods in Colonial Brazil

Devotion and Solidarity

Célia Maia Borges
Federal University of Juiz de Fora

Translated by Bruna Dantas Lobato
and Miguel A. Valerio

Abstract
There were innumerable black brotherhoods in colonial Brazil. With the objective of promoting devotional practices and Catholic practices, brotherhoods had a central role in fostering solidarity among the members. Afro-Brazilians and enslaved Africans made up the black Rosary brotherhoods of colonial Brazil. Endorsed by the Church and Crown, these institutions constituted Afro-Brazilians' sole means of social association. This chapter studies the meaning of membership in Afro-Brazilian brotherhoods and emphasizes the centrality of rituals in the formation of new social identities.

Keywords: Brazil, Afro-Brazilian Brotherhoods, Afro-Catholicism, solidarity

Introduction

Numerous black religious brotherhoods or lay Catholic confraternities – made up of enslaved and manumitted as well as free-born Afro-descendants – were formed in Brazil during the colonial (1500-1822) and imperial (1822-1889) periods.[1] With the goal of promoting Catholic devotional practices, these

---

[1]   This chapter draws on my previous research, which resulted in the book *Escravos e libertos nas irmandades do Rosário* (Juiz de Fora: Editora da UFJF, 2005).

Javiera Jaque Hidalgo and Miguel A. Valerio. *Indigenous and Black Confraternities in Colonial Latin America: Negotiating Status through Religious Practices.* Amsterdam: Amsterdam University Press, 2022
DOI: 10.5117/ 9789463721547_CH11

brotherhoods took on an important role in developing solidarity among their members. People coming from different ethnic groups in Africa, along with free and enslaved blacks born in Brazil, made up these confraternities, mainly under the advocation of Nossa Senhora do Rosário (Our Lady of the Rosary).[2] Officially legalized through their own bylaws and with the approval of the Portuguese Crown and the Church, these brotherhoods were the only possible way for black men and women to congregate within a slave society, of which Brazil was the largest in the eighteenth and nineteenth centuries.[3]

In Latin America, confraternities of the Rosary spread across Venezuela, Argentina, Peru, and Uruguay.[4] In Brazil, high numbers of lay confraternities began to appear under this denomination. The Jesuit priests in Portugal's overseas colonies were largely responsible for the creation of Rosary confraternities in plantations and sugar mills, as well as the dissemination of Marian devotion.[5] In São Paulo, Father José de Anchieta erected the first confraternity of the Rosary in the sixteenth century. Likewise, the Franciscans played a prominent role in spreading this devotion in other parts of the country. Eduardo Hoornaert writes about two Capuchin friars who founded Rosary confraternities in Rio de Janeiro thanks to the catechetical work developed within African communities.[6]

These brotherhoods followed the model of white Portuguese organizations in Brazil. They were stratified according to the colonial social structure with white brotherhoods for the colonial elites holding greater status than black confraternities of enslaved and free/d blacks or indigenous groups. These brotherhoods, moreover, were mostly composed of lay people. With a distinct capacity for organization and mobilization, the brotherhoods and Third Orders renewed members' social lives and promoted public rituals and religious festivals by hiring priests and musicians, in addition

2   The creation and spread of Rosary brotherhoods is attributed to the Dominican Order in Europe. The oldest known record of such a brotherhood is from 1475, in the Dominican monastery of Cologne. Portugal had various Rosary brotherhoods in Lagos, Évora, Leiria, Alcácer-do-Sal, Elvas, Setúbal, and Moura. Rosary brotherhoods also spread to Africa, the Americas, and Asia, especially Portuguese Goa and Macau. There is record of Rosary brotherhoods in Luanda (Angola) in religious festivities in the late seventeenth century.

3   The *Tribunal da Mesa de Consciência e Ordens* (Court of Conscience and Orders) was responsible for controlling the brotherhoods based on the regulations presented in the *Ordenações do Reino* (Orders from the King).

4   Roger Bastide, *As religiões africanas no Brasil* (Sao Paulo: Pioneira, 1971), 79. Patricia Mulvey offers a list of black brotherhoods in the Americas, Africa, and the Iberia Peninsula: "The Black Lay Brotherhoods of Colonial Brazil: A History," (Ph.D. diss., City University of New York, 1976).

5   Arlindo Rubert, *Historia de la Iglesia en Brasil* (Madrid: MAPFRE, 1992), 20.

6   Eduardo Hoornaert, *História da Igreja no Brasil*, vol. 2 (Petrópolis: Vozes, 1977), 67-68.

to investing financial resources in the construction of churches.[7] Each one of these groups had their own patron saints and hosted festivities to honor their heavenly protectors.

The major goals of these associations included promoting the rituals in the Catholic calendar; celebrating saints; assisting the sick, old, and poor; taking care of the deceased; arranging coffins and burials in their churches or cemeteries; and promoting individual and collective masses for deceased members' souls. With different organizational and mobilization capacities, these brotherhoods played an active role in the lives of many enslaved, manumitted, and free-born Afro-descendants.

Each confraternity had its own bylaws, which listed the objectives of the organization, the brothers' duties, and the services they would perform. Such handbooks had to be approved by the Crown and the bishop. Brotherhoods also had a book recording the names and origins of all of the members; an income and expense log that included the institution's cash flow; and, in some cases, a Book of Goods, where they recorded the brotherhood's material possessions. The brotherhoods also commonly had a board (*mesa*) usually composed of twelve members (called *juizes*) responsible for supervising the brotherhood's activities and promoting their festivals and rituals.

Within the confraternity, each member had distinct functions and power. The *juizes* were responsible for compliance with the organization's rules, holding accountable those who did not pay their annual fees. In the case of disagreements or conflict, it was up to the *juizes* to resolve disputes.

Black Rosary confraternities stipulated in their bylaws that *juizes* should be black men in good standing as they would oversee and reprimand those who neglected their duties, such as those who did not follow the established social norms. *Irmãos* (members) were required not to overconsume alcohol or practice concubinage, and those who were suspected of taking part in witchcraft were expelled. In this way, the brotherhoods came to be controlling, disciplinary bodies. In addition to the *juizes*, the clerk, the treasurer, and the board (which usually had twelve members), black brotherhoods differed from white ones in that each year they elected a king and a queen for the feast of their patron, Our Lady of the Rosary, which usually fell on the first Sunday of October.

The brotherhood's king and queen carried out important roles within the confraternal community and were largely responsible for promoting the

---

7   Third Orders were lay associations connected to the regular orders (Franciscans, Carmelites, etc.), which approved their statutes and guided them spiritually. They were normally reserved for colonial elites.

annual celebration where their replacements would be crowned. Taking on any role in the brotherhood meant bearing higher financial costs, in addition to requiring more of a time commitment. For this reason, many members could not take on this responsibility, since as slaves they could not make such a commitment without their masters' consent.

This model was used broadly throughout the colony, though confraternal groups often varied in their capacity for mobilization and organization, depending on their financial reach and relationship with local authorities. Black brotherhoods, composed of enslaved and free blacks, had resources from begging and charity, the entrance fee paid by members, or donations inherited from people outside the brotherhood who bequeathed goods to them in their wills out of devotion to the Virgin of the Rosary. With such resources, they built churches, procured liturgical vestments, funded religious celebrations, and paid their (white) chaplains' salaries.

Black Rosary Confraternities: Devotion and Solidarity

Mostly composed of slaves, Rosary brotherhoods played an important role in organizing the social and religious lives of Afro-descendants in Lusophone America. Originally from a variety of communities in Africa, along with the members born in Brazil, the Rosary *irmãos* integrated themselves into Catholicism, the only religion allowed on colonial soil. As such, they had to reorganize their traditions within the religious matrix of the colonizer. In the great ethnic mosaic that was colonial Brazil, they produced a variety of ways of reorganizing these experiences. In Bahia, for example, Catholic saints veiled Yoruba *orixás*, and soon their adaptations and recreations appeared in the Catholic calendar as well, mixed with African traditions.[8]

In Minas Gerais, a region of high Portuguese influx from the end of the seventeenth century to the end of the eighteenth century, because of the discovery of large deposits of precious metals and stones in the 1690s, ethnic groups of different origins often participated in the same black brotherhoods.[9] During the colonial period, in the captaincy of Minas Gerais alone, 63 Rosary brotherhoods (*irmandades*) were founded, amounting to a total of approximately 340 confraternal associations. However, contrary

8   See Miguel A. Valerio, "Architects of Their Own Humanity: Race, Devotion, and Artistic Agency in Afro-Brazilian Confraternal Churches in Salvador and Ouro Preto," *Colonial Latin American Review* 30, no. 2 (2021): 238-271.
9   Célia Maia Borges, *Escravos e libertos*, 119-126.

to what might be expected, life in the brotherhood did not always prove peaceful among its members; besides solidarity, conflicts were also present, especially with black members opposing the admission of members of other ethnic backgrounds. Additionally, there were squabbles between black confraternities over precedence in public processions. Despite this, brotherhoods established contracts with chaplains and invested in the preparation of services and their celebrations.

For the enslaved, it was difficult to obtain financial resources to pay the membership dues required to join the brotherhood, amass the expected annual contribution, or take on roles in the governing board. They often counted on the support of their respective masters who, being Catholic themselves, helped them with the belief that they would achieve salvation in the hereafter by joining, and also for the purpose of promoting the Catholic faith among their captives.

However, another requirement weighed heavily on the spirit of slave owners: the duty imposed by the Crown for masters to be responsible for the annual confession and funeral arrangements of their captives. There is documentation showing that the registration of some captives was also given as a favor to the brotherhood's kings and queens. We have no way of knowing whether the dues were paid by the kings and queens themselves or whether they had the power to exempt some candidates from paying these membership fees.

The chaplains hired by *irmandades* also offered important support. For example, when the Crown insisted that confraternal organizations send their bylaws (called *compromisso* (sing) in Portuguese) to be considered by the Chancellery in Lisbon, there is evidence that many *compromissos* had to be amended and updated with clauses that benefited black members. I thus contend that some chaplains took the side of black *irmãos* and did not only assume a more strict attitude toward confraternities because of the vigilance exercised by the Crown. A very illustrative case is perhaps Father Bernardo Madeira, who led the Rosary brotherhood of Alto da Cruz for about 25 years in Vila Rica (today Ouro Preto), in Minas Gerais.[10] It is no coincidence that this brotherhood was one of the richest and best organized in Minas Gerais. Madeira helped the *irmãos* accumulate a large estate that allowed them to borrow money and invest in the construction and ornamentation of their church, in addition to hiring musicians for their celebrations.[11]

---

10 Ouro Preto was the economic center of Brazil's eighteenth century "golden age."
11 On the churches Afro-Brazilian brotherhoods built, see Valerio, "Architects of Their Own Humanity."

Colonial documents show conflicts between the diocesan vicar and black *irmandades* and their chaplains.[12] This was common in several parishes, showing signs of a much greater tension in this region. Competition for control of the sacred occurred both in Europe and the overseas colonies. The vicars' interference in brotherhoods' internal affairs points to a fierce dispute to monopolize how the *irmãos* exercised devotion. If the chaplain did not submit to the vicar's orders, the vicar sought to impose himself by force.

The brotherhoods experienced, throughout the eighteenth century, similar ecclesiastical interference in the autonomy of the brotherhoods.[13] One such example were the conflicts experienced by the Alto da Cruz Rosary brotherhood mentioned above. Against the vicar's attacks, this *irmandade* met several times, showing a remarkably resilient spirit, which was characteristic of this community. Eighty-five members' signatures were recorded in a book (almost all signed with an X, indicating a high level of illiteracy among the *irmãos*). The chaplain, Leonel de Abreu Lima's signature is recorded among these, and it seems as though he led the movement and instructed the *irmãos*, recording the meeting minutes himself. The relationship between the chaplain and the *irmandade* lasted for fourteen years, and upon analysis of his acts, while a member of the brotherhood, it is clear he did not accept external interferences. The vicars claimed parochial rights. The most important one was to celebrate chanted masses because they would provide them with financial means.

The confraternal community was well-organized and often held meetings to address internal affairs. In response to the local vicar's arrogance, members considered recording their *compromisso* in the notary's office and hiring a lawyer to represent them. The *irmandade*'s executor, the slave João Moreira Crespo, was appointed to record the new statutes, find a lawyer, and attend the confraternity's official meetings, where he proposed reducing festival expenses to save funds for other matters.[14] In the year 1799, the vicar managed to ruin part of the *irmandade*'s festivities. The following year, the brotherhood spent a considerable amount of money on their legal defense. Paying such a high amount was not easy on the brotherhood. What is notable about this, however, is how the members mobilized to defend the

12   Arquivo Histórico Ultramarino (hereafter AHU), Minas Gerais, cx. 139, doc. n. 10 (1794); AHU, Minas Gerais, cx, 119, doc.13; AHU, Minas Gerais, cx. 152, doc. n. 30., AHU, Minas Gerais, cx. 11, doc. n. 67.
13   See Célia Maia Borges, *Escravos e libertos*, 71-77.
14   AHU, Minas Gerais, cx. 152, doc. n. 5.

confraternity, which gave them a common goal through which they could overcome internal disagreements.

At the celebration for Santa Luzia (St. Lucy), the vicar fired the chaplain and hired another in his place, against the *irmandade*'s will. This gave them reason to request an intervention from the district's magistrate, helping the *irmandade* select a new chaplain. The crux of the matter was who had jurisdiction over the confraternal organization. The *irmãos* claimed to be the founders of the chapel themselves.[15]

The members were aware of the disagreements opposing the temporal and spiritual powers in the colony. The dispute became part of the public sphere and the community became privy to the insults being exchanged. One example is the case that took place in the village of São João del Rei in Minas Gerais. Records show conflicts in which physical violence was equally present; the *irmãos* witnessed this and took sides, seeking support from secular officials in a strategy of political survival. The vicars, in most cases, were seen as great enemies of the *irmandades*.

Vicars, as authorities, demanded respect proportionate with their dignity as well as exclusive rights to conduct religious services. In addition, vicars also demanded their lawful financial gains. However, the spiritual power of the parish priest, as shown, was questioned every step of the way by lay organizations. Bourdieu highlights that the dispute for the legitimate monopoly of religious power for the Church also meant preserving control, as well as the reproduction and the distribution of salvific goods.[16]

Along these lines, the management of the sacred, which is symbolic, allowed the vicars to control the representation of religious practices, granting them "the principle that generates all thoughts, perceptions, and actions."[17] The Church, using a language unknown to laypeople made access to the tools of service more difficult and consequently reaffirmed its supremacy and the vicars' power, duly recognized by the ecclesiastical hierarchy. In this symbolic power structure, the Church concentrated its strength and the dependency of its members in an "economy of salvation."[18] In colonial Brazil, this control of the religious explains the actions of parish priests who sought in every moment, through religious monopoly, to guarantee the recognition of their authority in the Church hierarchy and in the ideological

15 Arquivo Nacional, MCO, cx. 249, doc. 49. The vicar would still have jurisdiction as a diocesan official.
16 Pierre Bourdieu, *A economia das trocas simbólicas* (Sao Paulo: Perspectiva, 1992), 58.
17 Ibid.
18 Ibid., 63.

control over their members. Brotherhood members, facing restrictions, sought alliances with other brotherhoods mainly to organize the annual feast in honor of their patron saint.

The Great Festival in Honor of Our Lady of the Rosary

The highlight of confraternal life was the annual celebration in honor of Our Lady of the Rosary and black saints, whose images, usually in statue form, were placed on the lateral altars of confraternal churches or parishes' churches when brotherhoods did not have their own church. Organizing the festivities for the Virgin and black saints had been part of confraternal life since the Medieval period.[19] At the end of the sixteenth century, Pope Gregory XIII (r. 1572-1585) instituted the solemnity (feast) of the Rosary on the first Sunday of October, with attending indulgences for Rosary brotherhoods who observed it.[20] Later, in 1681, Innocent XI reaffirmed the decision to celebrate the feast of the Virgin of the Rosary "with the rite of the office of the hours" in order to celebrate the victory over the Ottoman Empire at the Battle of Lepanto (1571).[21]

The Jesuits had celebrated this feast in Brazil since the seventeenth century. The confraternities recreated rituals that were common in Portugal, filled with the same choreographic complexity of the Iberian Peninsula, and added elements of their distinct cultures to the Catholic service. Among the rituals at the celebration was the practice of crowning *reis congos* (Congo kings and queens).[22] Even though the origins of the crowning of Congo monarchs could have been a political strategy from the kings of Portugal, as a symbol of recognizing the authority of African kings, the *irmãos* still elected the royal figureheads. This circumstance added more symbolic meanings to these cults.

This chapter seeks to highlight the meaning behind the election of kings and queens among Rosary *irmaos* in Minas Gerais. This is particularly

19   See Maria Helena da Cruz Coelho, *"As confrarias medievais portuguesas*: cofradias, grêmios, solidariedades en la Europa medieval," *Semana de Estudios Medievales* 9 (1992): 166.

20   Arquivo Nacional da Torre do Tombo (hereafter ANTT), Convento de São Domingos de Lisboa, livro 30, Breve Recompilação [...] das graças e indulgencias por diversos Summo Pontífices são concedidas aos confrades de Nossa Senhora do Rosário.

21   Bull of Innocent XI, *Sollicitudo Pastoralis Officii*, June 11, 1681, in Santo Abranches, *Suma do Bulário Português*, 183, n. 1331.

22   See Marina de Mello e Souza, *Reis negros no brasil escravista. história da festa de coroação de rei congo* (Belo Horizonte: UFMG, 2002) and her chapter in this volume.

relevant as meanings are constantly recreated and "negotiated" in each situation and moment. The figures of the king and queen in brotherhoods were, as previously stated, essential and above all seen as figures of authority. The brotherhoods in Minas Gerais were composed of men and women of various "ethnicities." Choosing a royal couple and acknowledging their authority was a process of symbolic exchange within distinct cultural systems. When wearing the mantle and wielding the scepter and sitting on a throne, the monarchs were recognized as powerful and capable of reigning over their "subjects," in this case the other brotherhood members.

Rosary brotherhood kings and queens belonged to different groups formed by Africans and their descendants. Being a monarch meant prestige, even to a slave, for being recognized with such a high honor among their peers. If the monarchs' authority was particularly strong during the celebration, it was thanks to the anointing they received. They were sworn in as rulers of Congo, even if they were actually Benguelas, Angolas, Minas (Costa da Mina – Golfo da Guiné), all ethnonyms used to designate different African groups, or even *crioulos*, or American-born.[23] Social groups of diverse origins and ethnicities attended various rituals. As such, it is not entirely accurate to say that these rituals symbolized direct representation of the kingdom of Congo. It represented a new, panethnic group altogether, re/constructed in the colonial context. After all, different groups projected different forms and meanings onto Catholic rituals celebrated in the Luso-American world, according to the history of each place.

On the Brazilian coast, the groups were divided as each one demanded the right to elect their own royalty. In Minas Gerais, the mining region, the process was unique: Rosary brotherhoods brought together several groups, which meant they had to accept the monarchs elected by the majority. When they did not accept the results of the election of monarchs, conflicts ensued. For this reason, the election was grounded in an arduous negotiation process which was updated regularly to prevent factions from clashing with one another. When being sworn in as sovereigns, the elected king and queen adopted a position of symbolic authority at the climax of the celebration.

23 The Rosary brotherhood of Casa Branca had a "Mina" royal couple in 1748 and a "Benguela" couple in 1751. At the end of the *compromisso* of the Rosary brotherhood of Guarapiranga, one can read "rei Angola." This brotherhood's scribe, treasurer, and almoner were "Mina": Arquivo Eclesiástico da Arquidiocese de Mariana (hereafter AEAM), Irmandade do Rosário, Livro de Miscelânia de Casa Branca; AEAM, Compromisso da Irmandade do Rosário de Guarapiranga.

Congadas

The annual feast of Rosary brotherhoods was preceded by a great organizational action that unfolded in various phases: hiring of musicians, making the attire for the ritual participants, rehearsals for *congadas* or dramatic dances that were performed at the celebration, and the preparations for a great banquet.[24] *Congadas* in Minas Gerias, and even in Goiás and São Paulo, had a scenographic structures of representation wherein black groups played the role of whites, and black dressed as "Indians" staged a mock battle with the kings' guard, which the latter always won, receiving the protection of the Virgin of the Rosary. Without realizing it, irmãos built a symbolic language in which, contrary to what was their lived experience, affirmed the superiority of blacks over other groups.

The celebration during the colonial period was intervened by all social sectors, which resulted in the modification of the ritual structure. For this reason, pressure from political, social, and religious forces affected the ceremony, which eventually led to modifications in its structure or in some cases even prevented the staging of the ritual altogether.[25] As previously shown, the most authoritarian repression came from diocesan vicars and other church officials, since they were the guardians of Catholic ideologies originating from the Council of Trent, and because it was in their interest to control popular culture, in addition to them feeling their parish rights were being attacked as they were pushed away from liturgical practices in these ceremonies.

The reforming clergy's investment, alongside a few brotherhoods, however, was not enough to implement a unique new model of ritual organization. A few brotherhoods resisted. Ouro Preto's brotherhoods, for example, fought and received permission from the Crown to have their chaplain officiate sung mass. Upon winning the dispute with the vicar, they immediately headed outside and threw a great party, with "candles, bells, and fireworks," to celebrate it.[26]

---

24   In Brazil, *congadas* are still performed today, some of which revive the ritual fight from the colonial period. These ritual fights gained permanence in Minas Gerais, surviving to the present day. Another Brazilian tradition only entails the monarchs processing with their regalia. Another iteration includes ambassadors who announce the monarchs.

25   In some places, the feast was removed from the liturgical calendar, taking place in July and August, and in others, it is still celebrated in October. The election of black monarchs for the feasts alarmed colonial authorities. For example, in 1719, the Count of Assumar, Pedro Miguel de Almeida Portugal e Vasconcelos, who was Captain General of São Paulo and Minas Gerais, connected black rebellion to the coronations of festive kings and queens. Arquivo Público Mineiro (Belo Horizonte, Minas Gerais/Brazil) códice 4, f. 648.

26   AHU, Minas Gerais, cx. 139, doc. n. 10.

As the liturgical component of the ceremony suffered strong repression, members fought back with even greater strength. Regardless of censorship, there were brotherhoods that managed to preserve, to some extent, their original model with support from the chaplains as well as political and economic groups from the interested elites who wanted to safeguard the autonomy of the brotherhoods. This was partly due to the fact that Portuguese colonizers appreciated the festivities and celebrations and felt equally oppressed by vicars. Interventions by ecclesiastical authorities in confraternal ceremonies happened everywhere. In numerous instances, ecclesiastical visitors questioned the excessive spending on fireworks, such as in 1731, when Manoel de Andrade scolded the Rosary brotherhood of Alto da Cruz for their spending on fireworks.[27] The brotherhoods appreciated pyrotechnics, and as such did not spare any expenses on them. Following in the footsteps of Rosary brotherhoods, other brotherhoods in the eighteenth century also received warnings regarding excessive spending on fireworks. Rosary *irmãos*, even though admonished, continued to enjoy their festivities without giving up on fireworks. What the authorities saw as superfluous, brotherhood members saw as important to paying tribute to the Virgin of the Rosary.

White *irmãos* from other brotherhoods showed solidarity with the black members for defending a cause that affected everyone in the community in different ways. In other words, they supported the defense of religious autonomy of black brotherhoods. In this way, the dominant class put together a complex and dialectic strategy of rule, going back and forth between concession and repression, as it suited their interests. Exactly because the ceremony was targeted by the counter-reformist sector of the Catholic Church throughout the eighteenth century, brotherhoods' *compromissos* had to be updated and adapted as a political strategy of survival that reflected the new conflicts they experienced.

These brotherhoods and their ceremonies relied for the most part on how much funds and influence they had in the local sociopolitical fabric. To survive, as such, they depended on the strengthening of a network of generosity across several internal groups within the brotherhood, which in turn needed to overcome their differences to prioritize the confraternal organization.

In addition to the election of a board of directors and new officials, several activities filled the week of the ceremony: a procession in honor

---

27   Arquivo Eclesiástico da Paróquia de Antônio (hereafter AEPAD), Livro de receita e despesa da Irmandade de Nossa Senhora do Rosário dos Pretos do arraial do Padre Faria, f. 53 (1726-1798).

of the Virgin of the Rosary, a novena, high mass, and a banquet. All these parts of the festivity demanded several meetings to be organized well, ranging from deciding on the food and preparing it to making the costumes for participants, and preparing the procession route and the royal throne.

It was (and still is) a custom in rural towns of Minas Gerais for participants to ask for and collect money from house to house to help with the celebration. The flag of Our Lady of the Rosary opens the parade; men dressed in ornamental and colorful attire followed it, dancing and singing songs that have pleas for donation in their lyrics. When a donation is made, *irmãos* thank the contributor, always through singing, accompanied by instrumentalists. Some of these rituals still survive to this day in São João del Rei, in Ouro Preto, and northern Minas Gerais. Almoners do not stop collecting donations the whole week of the feast of the Rosary. Women elected as stewardesses are equally in charge of collecting. As such, the ceremony demands months of preparation in which the *irmãos'* participation is essential.

Missionary Pedagogy and the Reorganization of Religious Myths

The Virgin and the mostly black saints played an essential role in the conversion of the black population to Catholicism. The Virgin and the saints' hagiographies/life stories were part of a missionary pedagogy for that population. The hagiographic narratives told by preachers filled with miracle scenes that prominently emphasized their seemingly magical and protective powers against adversity, which ended up creating myths that granted power to their images. These myths were responsible for creating a religious imaginary.[28]

Since around the sixteenth century, there has been a literary arsenal dedicated to the lives of black saints. Along with catechism and Christian compendiums, booklets on the saints' lives had a central place in the set of works the press produced for missionary work.[29] The Virgin and the saints could aid supporters both in adversity and in countless dilemmas of daily life. The various images inside churches were available to the brothers as intercessors with God. These images of saints, who were often black, were used by black brotherhoods, who had the task of ornamenting the altars and watching over the services of their patrons.

28   See Erin K. Rowe, *Black Saints in Early Modern Global Catholicism* (Cambridge: Cambridge University Press, 2019).
29   C.R. Boxer, *A Igreja e a expansão ibérica* (Lisbon: Edições 70, 1989), 57.

Roger Bastide suggested that Bantu people would have been more receptive to accepting Catholic brotherhoods, precisely because black saints expressed an idea of ancestry, being therefore integrated into those groups' symbolic cosmologies.[30] In the colonial context, saints fulfilled the role of a stabilizing element, organizing symbolic goods as they helped integrate blacks into the new religion. In short, they took on not only a religious but also a political function of adapting Africans to a new reality. Regarding this position, it can be said that saints acquired an ideological function. By adding a new meaning to the *irmãos*' actions, (black?) saints nourished them with hope. Hence the religious reconstruction carried out in the brotherhoods also became a cultural reconstruction, shaped by new meanings, through a permanent process of reorganizing collective representations.

All social groups that inherited European traditions maintained emotional relationships with the Virgin and the saints, resorting to them in times of distress. Offerings were infallible remedies. Pleasing the saints was part of the worldview in which the notion of sacrifice was implicit. Maintaining a reciprocal relationship with the saints was essential as a way of gaining control over the sacred. The saint fulfilled their part of the contract if the orant did the same. Obtaining divine protection was part of the European religious imaginary. Black saints were adopted as protectors of the big family (the *irmandade*), thus entering the process of cultural negotiation. Saints, at the same time that they were far away in the hereafter, were also close in the images in churches.

Offers to Catholic saints as well as to *orixás* were subject to differentiated services and were part of an exchange relationship that made it possible for black *irmãos* to reorganize their sacred symbols. This is the case of groups that, faced with the dangers of everyday life and the need to safeguard transcendental security, sought support within a larger set of social relationships that were familiar to them. The heirs of Portuguese religious traditions, when expressing their religiosity, did so by decorating the Virgin and the saints, as they adorned the churches and images. According to the beliefs at the time, it was necessary to be on good terms with the Virgin and the saints and to have an intimate relationship with them.

Given this model, Our Lady of the Rosary played an essential role for the *irmãos*, despite the light color of her skin. First of all, she had the role of a mediator, given her role as a protector, which made her fully integrated

30   Roger Bastide, *As religiões africanas no Brasil: contribuição a uma sociologia das interpretações de civilizações* (Sao Paulo: Livraria Pioneira, 1971), 88.

into the black Catholic universe. Along with black saints, she was part of
a large family where each of its members had different powers used on
diverse ways and occasions.

Masses and Processions

Festivities that had the participation of all the brotherhoods were held
periodically and each one of them, depending on their status, assumed
the structure of the great event, in the collective rituals or in the private
rituals that took place in churches. During religious feasts (Lent, Holy
Week, and Corpus Christi), all brotherhoods were involved, dressing the
Virgin and saints, collecting money, hosting and attending masses, and
preparing for Good Friday services.[31] In some Rosary brotherhoods, it was
common practice to promote Lenten rituals on Saturdays, during which the
brothers went out in a procession praying the Rosary, while the chaplain
read meditations on the Mysteries of the Passion.[32]

Great scenes were prepared in the villages on the days of the festivities.
Torches and lit candles provided light effects, in addition to the sounds of
rattles, and the ringing of church bells; the whole scenic apparatus was
profusely framed with choral music in a spectacle that attracted the attention
of those present and brought them over to religion. Despite the measures
in the First Constitutions of the Archbishopric of Bahia (1717) to prohibit
processions at night, brotherhoods did not give up on them – they celebrated
them in the light of torches and candles, which enchanted everyone for
their beautiful scenic effects. In these manifestations of Baroque culture,
the conjunction of colors and lights, plus the various religious symbols
(canopy, crosses, script, incense), helped to produce in the churchgoers a
state of ecstasy that numbed the senses.

The participation of confraternal organizations in these processions
followed certain rules, as each *irmandade* had its designated place in
the procession. The order of confraternities in the ceremonies followed a
hierarchy that had to do with the seniority of each brotherhood. Certain
places in the procession conferred prestige, and many brotherhoods fought

31   AEPAD, código 132. In the books of expenses of the Alto da Cruz Rosary brotherhood, one
finds entries for amounts "spent preparing the chapel for Holy Week" and "Holy Week donations":
AEPAD, Livro de receita e despesa da Irmandade do Rosário do Alto da Cruz.
32   AHU, Minas Gerais, código 1286, Irmandade do Rosário dos Homens Pretos da Freguesia
de Lagoa Dourada, cap. 16 (1793).

to obtain better placements.[33] The distinction in processions thus reflected a system based on a hierarchy of power, a fact that, in a way, reflected peculiar phenomena from society itself. By the integration of the rituals, in spite of their intentions, they legitimized their own order, reinforcing their place in the system they belonged. The religious processions formed the set of ceremonials characteristic of the Ancien Régime, performing, in scenic apparatus, the same symbolic function of consecration of the social hierarchy.

Funeral Practices

An important part of confraternal life was devoted to caring for the dead. With the death of any member, sacristans were responsible for announcing it with a knell, walking around the village with a bell and a cross in hand, a sign that the deceased was one of the members. Not participating in the funeral procession would result in a rebuke from the entire confraternal community, since the fate of the dead depended on the solidarity of the living. The death of a member mobilized the entire community, and some Rosary brotherhoods had their own houses for funerals.[34]

Funeral processions generally took place at night when the brothers were free from their professional duties. Wearing white capes, they took their predefined places in the ritual and took charge of fetching the corpse to be shrouded. At the head of the procession was the chaplain, followed by the sacristan with the cross and, immediately behind him, four *irmãos* carrying the coffin, after which came the head *juiz* carrying his staff in his right hand.[35] Upon arriving at the door of the deceased member's house, the chaplain entered the house in order to proceed with the service.[36]

After completing this ritual, the head *juiz* deposited the body in the coffin and then the procession continued towards the church, accompanied

33   Caio César Boschi, *Os leigos e o poder: irmandades leigas e política colonizadora em Minas Gerais* (Sao Paulo: Atica, 1986), 1.

34   AHU, Minas Gerais, códice 1534, Compromisso da Irmandade de N.ª Sr.ª do Rosário dos Homens Pretos incorporada na sua igreja cita na vila da Campanha da Princesa. Chapter 12 reads: "because so many *irmãos* of this brotherhood are kept a league and half away from this city by their masters, the governing board [*mesa*] should build a house to wake *irmaos*, from where the corpse will be taken to the church, as stated above, the which will be done as the brotherhood sees useful, lest it should fall into poverty."

35   ANTT, Chancelaria Antiga da Ordem de Cristo, livro 296, cap. 24, Irmandade do Rosário da freguesia N.ª Sr.ª do Pilar de Vila Rica, ff. 49v-59v.

36   Ibid.

by the *irmãos* with lit candles and torches.[37] The spatial distribution of
graves followed distinctions from the confraternal hierarchy; the higher
the position of the member on the board, the closer his body would be to
the altar or the images of the saints along the church walls. The interior
of the temple was thus marked by distinct levels of sacredness. On the
other hand, being buried in the church gave the brother a feeling of being
constantly remembered, since they were granted physical proximity to the
world of the living. Still, placement was not the only sign of distinction for
board members. The number of votes to be received was also a marker of
uniqueness. The higher their positions, the greater the number of masses
ordered for the salvation of their souls. All confraternal *compromissos*
showed a greater number of masses for voting officials who held positions
of greater power in the brotherhood's hierarchy.

In the Christian imaginary, the postmortem moment is considered
crucial for the fate of the soul, requiring the help of the living to influence
the deceased person's salvation. Thus members strictly followed a series
of pious precepts, ranging from ordering masses to praying the Rosary
on behalf of the dead.[38] The passage to the hereafter, being so important,
required absolute generosity from the living. Interceding for the dead had a
caveat: reciprocity. On several occasions the dead could assist the living in a
communicational relationship, the advantages of which were not exclusive
to the Catholic religion. Consider the case of some African peoples, where
the living and the dead belonged to a single family structured around
networks of solidarity.[39]

Among the Bantu people, the dead, like the living, had their own existence, which contributed to greater attention paid to the deceased through
a sequence of funeral rites. Among the various ethno-cultural formations
in Angola, rituals were guided by dances, weeping, games, drinks, and
food. Funeral dances varied according to the circumstances in which death
occurred or according to the social status of the deceased. For the death of
a Congo king, the dance prescribed at that time was called *lemba*; among
the Mbundu ethnic group,[40] a *maringa* involving a ritual cleansing was

37   AEAM, Livro n. 15, cap. 4, Compromisso da Irmandade de Nossa Senhora do Rosário de
Itaverava, f. 9; Livro H-30, cap. 18, "Compromisso da Irmandade de Nossa Senhora do Rosário
de Congonhas do Campo," (1807).
38   AEAM, Livro W-15, Compromisso da Irmandade do Rosário de São Brás do Sauçuí, cap. 13,
f. 15 (1757).
39   On confraternal mortuary practices, see Leonara Lacerda Delfino, *O Rosário das almas
ancestrais* (Belo Horizonte: Clio, 2017).
40   *Mbundus* settled along the coast of Congo, south of the rivers N'Dande and Kwanza.

performed when death was caused by witchcraft.[41] Other types of dances with their own meanings were added to these manifestations of ancestral traditions: obituary dances, ceremonial dances, propitiatory dances, magic-healing dances, and even dances to evoke the dead.

Caring for the dead was also part of the life of the Sudanese people, who buried them inside their homes. In Benin, more precisely close to Uidá, the basements of houses belonged to the dead. The house was seen as a place of conviviality between those in the hereafter and the living. Dying was seen as a form of encounter with ancestors. From their perspective, the dead did not interfere as much in the lives of the living as they did for the Bantu peoples; there, deities became the source of misfortune, disease, or abundance. For Bantu people, ancestral spirits coexisted with the living, interacted and influenced their behaviors, and were responsible for events such as illnesses, misfortunes, hexes, and so on. Through a sequence of rituals, the groups sought to guarantee the place of the dead, as a symbolic representation of how the event was framed in the religious imagination. In other words, Bantus believed they could establish paths for the non-living.

Despite the particularities of each group, everyone in general devoted their energies to rituals as a way of guaranteeing the dead a good passage to the afterlife. In all African cultures, as in Portuguese culture, the deceased was the object of care: a haircut, shaving, nail trimming, baths, farewell ceremonies, and so on.[42] This was an essential practice designed to prepare one for the afterlife.[43] In the imaginary of these African cultures, death presupposed first and foremost the opening of doors to allow the encounter with one's ancestors. African eschatology was complex and diverse. In Yoruba culture, the idealization of a hereafter included paths to be followed by the deceased, who, according to merit, would go to the good *Orum* or the bad *Orum*, meaning they either would turn into an animal or reincarnate as a person. In the *Nagô* system (a Yoruba group), the understanding of the world was explained through two planes of existence: the *Aiye* (concrete universe) and the *Orum* (supernatural space), inhabited by the *orixás* (spirits) and the *eguns* (ancestors), connected to men's stories, to the life of the ancestors. In their origin story, at first there was only one plane. Death would be, therefore,

---

41   José Redinha, *Etnias e culturas de Angola* (Luanda: Instituto de Investigação Científica de Angola, 1974), 330.

42   João José Reis, *A morte é uma festa: ritos fúnebres e revolta popular no Brasil do século XIX* (Sao Paulo: Letras, 1991), 90.

43   Arthur Ramos, *As culturas negras no Novo Mundo* (Sao Paulo: Editora Nacional), 1979.

a reunion, the passage from one world to another, which is why the Ewes of Dahomey (present-day Benin) danced and ate on their way there.

In this coexistence between ancestors and the living, the religious practices of Bantu peoples included veneration of the dead, given their ability to interfere with the world of the living.[44] Therefore, the passage to the afterlife was important for these different traditions. Upon joining brotherhoods, Africans assumed the funeral rituals of Christian traditions, bringing new meaning from their original cultural backgrounds. In view of this, it is understood why Maria da Costa, an African of Sudanese origin, from the Ardrá nation, living in of Minas Gerais, left in her will a request for 100 masses on behalf of her soul.[45] The dead in the Sudanese tradition went through a predestined cycle that led them to meet their ancestors. In the Christian tradition, the living interceding for the deceased could guarantee their safe passage to heaven, without getting stuck in purgatory.

Conclusion

Funeral rites not only contributed to the reconstruction of the original structures that supported different African cultures, but also gave them new meanings by integrating these rituals. For this new process of cultural symbiosis, the baroque rituals of the Christian tradition, which the brotherhoods celebrated, had much to contribute. For them, the vision of death was very present in the daily lives of *irmãos*. As they had more contact with Catholic rites, black *irmãos* began to adapt their beliefs to the dominant cultural matrix. Fully integrated in the dynamics of other confraternities, they gradually began to add new ideas to their original notion of eschatology. In this way, the devotional experience of black *irmãos* carries signs of intercultural exchange. In the different situations they experienced, forms of negotiation, cultural and religious, occurred through a dynamic process, having generated a common layer of understanding. As Marshall Sahlins shows us, culture is renewed through the acts of its subjects.[46] In this process, cultural interpretation may change and inevitably end up affecting other meanings. History is culturally ordered, just as cultural schemes are historically ordered.[47]

44   Ibid., 101, 118.
45   Luiz Mott, *Rosa Egipcíaca: uma santa africana no Brasil* (Rio de Janeiro: Bertrand, 1993), 140-141.
46   Marsahll Sahlins, *Ilhas de história* (Rio de Janeiro: Jorge Zahar, 1990), 7.
47   Ibid.

Although they came from different places and cultures, black *irmãos* in their respective religious communities were able to reinvent themselves in their new spaces. In a constant dialogic process and influenced mainly by new experiences of ritual, they recreated their religious matrices. Belonging to an *irmandade* and taking part in its rituals gave brothers the opportunity to interact with members of different groups and form new identities, even while facing the most extreme oppression. The brotherhoods made it possible to reorganize the captives' cultural and religious matrices by enabling African brothers to meet. Together, *irmãos* had the ability to redefine their religious space and time of worship and shape a new awareness of themselves before other social categories.

About the author

Célia Maia Borges is professor of history at the Universidade Federal de Juiz de Fora. Her research focuses on religious orders, popular saints, and black brotherhoods in Portugal and Brazil. She is the author of *Escravos e Libertos nas Irmandades do Rosário* and numerous articles.

Bibliography

Bastide, Roger. *As religiões africanas no Brasil: contribuição a uma sociologia das interpretações de civilizações*. Sao Paulo: Livraria Pioneira, 1971.

Borges, Célia Maia. *Escravos e libertos nas Irmandades do Rosário*. Juiz de Fora: Editora da UFJF, 2005.

Bourdieu, Pierre. *A economia das trocas simbólicas*. Sao Paulo: Perspectiva, 1992.

Boxer, C.R. *A Igreja e a expansão ibérica*. Lisbon: Edições 70, 1989.

Coelho, Maria Helena da Cruz. "As confrarias medievais portuguesas: espaços de solidariedades na vida e na morte." In *Cofradias, grêmios, solidariedades en la Europa medieval: XIX Semana de Estudios Medievales*. Pamplona: Government of Navarre, 1993, 149-184.

Delfino, Leonara Lacerda. *O Rosário das almas ancestrais*. Belo Horizonte: Clio, 2017.

Fromont, Cécile. "Dancing for the King of Congo from Early Modern Central Africa to Slavery-Era Brazil." *Colonial Latin American Review* 22, no. 2 (2013): 184-208.

Hoornaert, Eduardo. *História da Igreja no Brasil*. Petrópolis: Vozes, 1977.

Mott, Luiz. *Rosa Egipcíaca: uma santa africana no Brasil*. Rio de Janeiro: Bertrand, 1993.

Mulvey, Patrícia. "The Black Lay Brotherhoods of Colonial Brazil: A History." Ph.D. diss. City University of New York, 1976.

Ramos, Arthur. *As culturas negras no Novo Mundo*. Sao Paulo: Ed. Nacional, 1979.

Redinha, José, *Etnias e culturas de Angola*. Luanda: Instituto de Investigação Científica de Angola, 1974.

Reis, João José. *A morte é uma festa: ritos fúnebres e revolta popular no Brasil do século XIX*. Sao Paulo: Letras, 1991.

Rowe, Erin K. *Black Saints in Early Modern Global Catholicism*. Cambridge: Cambridge University Press, 2019.

Rubert, Arlindo. *Historia de la Iglesia en Brasil*. Madrid: MAPFRE, 1992.

Sahlins, Marshall. *Ilhas de história*. Rio de Janeiro: Zahar, 1990.

Souza, Marina de Mello e. *Reis negros no brasil escravista. história da festa de coroação de rei congo*. Belo Horizonte: UFMG, 2002.

Valerio, Miguel A. "Architects of Their Own Humanity: Race, Devotion, and Artistic Agency in Afro-Brazilian Confraternal Churches in Eighteenth-Century Salvador and Ouro Preto." *Colonial Latin American Review* 30, no. 2 (2021): 238-271.

12   Cultural Resistance and Afro-Catholicism in Colonial Brazil

Marina de Mello e Souza
University of Sao Paulo

Translated by Bruna Dantas Lobato
and Miguel A. Valerio

Abstract
Lay brotherhoods were a major form of social organization in colonial Brazil. These brotherhoods were dedicated to mutual aid and devotion to the Virgin Mary and certain saints. There were white, mestizo, black, rich, mid-income and poor brotherhoods. Black brotherhoods elected a king among its charges. His authority was recognized by the community he represented, and he was a respected mediator with slave-owners, priests, and colonial authorities. Brotherhoods offered Afro-Brazilian possibilities of affirming their identity and a social space. Afro-Brazilian brotherhoods show that Afro-Brazilians did not only achieved their own space through revolt and resistance, but also through negotiation and the adoption of European institutions.

Keywords: Brazil, Afro-Brazilian Brotherhoods, Afro-Catholicism, Royal Pageantry, resistance

Irmandades de homens pretos

It was common in the vast area around the Atlantic Ocean, where slavery and colonial relations prevailed, for Africans and their descendants to organize into lay brotherhoods devoted to Catholic saints and the Virgin. These brotherhoods had existed in Portugal, Spain, and their American

Javiera Jaque Hidalgo and Miguel A. Valerio. *Indigenous and Black Confraternities in Colonial Latin America: Negotiating Status through Religious Practices.* Amsterdam: Amsterdam University Press, 2022
DOI: 10.5117/ 9789463721547_CH12

colonies since the arrival of the first enslaved Africans, who were obliged to convert to Christianity and find new ways of organizing themselves in their new world. In some places in Africa, such as Cape Verde, São Tomé, Luanda, and Mozambique, brotherhoods dedicated to the Virgin or certain saints were introduced by the Catholic Church in conjunction with the Portuguese Crown and adopted by the mixed-race communities taking shape at the time.

Irmandades de homens pretos (black brotherhoods, literally "brotherhoods of the blacks"), as they were called in Brazil, were lay associations made up of black men and women – enslaved, manumitted, and free-born Afro-descendants – devoted to the Virgin or certain saints, whose "image" – in statue or painted form – was deposited on an altar or which had their own confraternal church. They were governed by a set of rules recorded in a *compromisso* (statutes), a written document signed by the *juizes* (board members) who held management positions and were recognized by royal, ecclesiastical, and colonial authorities alike. The *compromisso* defined the profile of the *irmãos* (literally brothers, or members) to be admitted, the terms for their admittance, the ways they should contribute to the *irmandade* or brotherhood's common funds, the composition and selection of the administrative board (the *juizes*, literally "judges"), the *irmaos* and *juizes*' duties, and how they would celebrate their patron's annual feast.

These associations fulfilled several functions: religious worship, mutual aid, socialization, and entertainment. Through them, groups of Africans and Afro-descendants established relationships of solidarity in an environment that oppressed them, especially in the face of death and illness. Brotherhoods could also collaborate to obtain the freedom of enslaved members. Joining a brotherhood allowed Africans and their descendants to further integrate into the society that subjugated them. These associations were primarily spaces for religious practice and functioned as mutual aid societies but could also be a path to some social mobility, even operating as channels through which slaveowners negotiated and exercised their authority.

A board of directors (*juizes*), elected annually on the patron's feast day, was responsible for the good administration of the common funds and the fulfillment of the *compromisso*. The brotherhoods accumulated wealth through testamentary bequests, gifts for the saints, contributions made when joining the brotherhood, and the annual fees paid by members. Some brotherhoods owned houses that they rented, lent money at interest, and charged for funeral services and burials. Those in management positions made greater contributions. The expenses for festivities were covered by donations from the ceremonial monarchs elected each year and the *juizes* were responsible for carrying out the festivities and their roles were laid out in the *compromisso*. The *irmãos*, in turn, were responsible for maintaining the altars for their patron saints when they were housed in churches belonging to other brotherhoods and building their own churches when resources allowed. For this, extra donations were requested from members.

In the *compromisso*, the main items referred to aid for the sick and needy; burial of the deceased, at which all brothers were to appear in a solemn procession dressed in their confraternal habit; recitation of masses for their souls; and the annual celebration in honor of the patron saint. A justification commonly invoked for the creation of *irmandades de homens pretos* was the need to give Christian burial to black men who were often abandoned by their masters at the time of death. Thus, the small contributions paid throughout their lives, in the form of the annual fee, guaranteed a dignified burial for those whose earthly remains would have been discarded without the support of the brotherhood to which they belonged.

If we think about the importance that funerals have in African societies, representing the moment when the dead pass from the world of the living to the world of the ancestors and spirits, with the help of special rituals, songs, and dances, it becomes easier to understand the speed with which Africans and their descendants adapted these Catholic associations of an eminently Iberian nature. Governed by the norms of the metropolitan administration, these organizations at first glance had as their objectives the dissemination of the Christian faith and the maintenance of greater control over the black community in the colony.

In addition to these cultural links to their places of origin, joining a brotherhood was an acceptable way for Africans and their descendants to enter the colonial social fabric. It was also important for them to belong to Catholic religious brotherhoods, institutions that were an integral part of Iberian colonial societies based on existing social categories. For Africans and their descendants, belonging to a brotherhood represented one of the few opportunities to organize, meet, celebrate, and commiserate together, with the approval of their masters and the colonial administration.

Although not a general norm, it was common for brotherhoods to consist of members from the same regions of Africa, whether of the same ethnicity or from the same *nação* or nation, that is, having incorporated such distinctions from colonial relations.[1] This adoption of the same labels used by the colonizers becomes clear in the brotherhoods that called themselves *angolas* (Angolan), as was the case of the first groups created, since the

---

[1]   The term *nação* was used to identify the different places of origin of enslaved Africans.

term was coined by the Portuguese for an area that encompassed multiple distinct ethnicities. Organizing brotherhoods by members' national origins was part of the processes of constitution of new identities, and of new institutions and social relations in a slave society. Africans took on the labels attributed to them in the composition of new identities, after the radical rupture of enslavement. Therefore, the groups based on nations created in the Atlantic trade circuits was operational not only among traffickers and masters, but also among the enslaved. The same can be said for brotherhoods, which, according to João José Reis, though they were an instrument aimed at domesticating the African spirit, also functioned as a means of cultural affirmation and of building identities and alterity formed in the diasporic process on the way to America.[2]

Ethnic labels, when they could be used, were important for building ties for enslaved Africans in the colonial world, but these identities were not the same as those that prevailed in their homelands. The smallest identifications were valued by people removed from their original social structures, in a context where everyone was a foreigner and sought to reconstruct social ties based on what they brought from Africa and what slave society allowed. Ethnic origin could have greater or lesser weight in the formation of *irmandades de homens pretos*. Julita Scarano, the author of one of the first research projects about Afro-Brazilian *irmandades*, did not find any organized by ethnic differences in Diamantina, Minas Gerais and, though she noted rivalries between ethnic groups, she pointed to the unity brought by the same social conditions, with brotherhoods playing an important role in creating cohesive groups despite being culturally diverse. In coastal cities, with a greater presence of newly arrived Africans, organizations founded on cultural affinities were more predominant.[3]

Upon arriving in the Americas, Africans who had been captured and launched into the colonial slave system from the Atlantic trade found in

---

2   João José Reis, *A morte é uma festa: ritos fúnebres e revolta popular no brasil do século XIX* (Sao Paulo: Companhia das Letras, 1991), 55. The same author notes that Afro-Brazilian brotherhoods "were formed along the widest African identities created in the diaspora": "Identidade e diversidade étnicas nas irmandades negras no tempo da escravidão," *Tempo* 2, no. 3 (1997): 29. The author describes "ethnic engineering" as the alliances and rivalries among slave-era Afro-Brazilian groups.

3   Julita Scarano, *Devoção e escravidão: a Irmandade de Nossa Senhora do Rosário dos Pretos no Distrito Diamantino no século XVIII* (Sao Paulo: Editora Nacional, 1978). On brotherhoods where group of origin was influential, see Mariza de Carvalho Soares, *Devotos da cor: identidade étnica, religiosidade e escravidão no Rio de Janeiro, século XVIII* (Rio de Janeiro: Civilização Brasileira, 2000); Lucilene Reginaldo, *Os Rosários dos Angolas: irmandades de africanos e crioulos na Bahia setecentista* (São Paulo: Alameda, 2011).

brotherhoods a sanctioned way of building bonds of solidarity and cultural affirmation. Their enormous popularity among Afro-Brazilians was fundamentally since confraternities fulfilled functions that were as much in the interest of the master class as of freed, manumitted, and free-born Afro-descendants. In colonial Brazil brotherhoods were exclusive to certain ethnic and social categories, grouping people according to the color of their skin and their place in the social hierarchy. *Irmandades de homens pretos* were, according to Caio Boschi, the only institutions in which black men and women could manifest themselves with relative autonomy and freedom. However, they were, contradictorily, effective agents of colonization. As Boschi puts it, "as well as being a privileged place for the affirmation of the cultural, ethnic, or social identities of members," confraternities were also aligned with the colonizing European rule.[4]

Adaptation Strategies

Catholicism was an essential element of the Portuguese empire, especially in colonization areas. Missionary action was a major argument for the recognition of Portuguese rights over the regions in which Portugal had established its presence. At the same time, the Portuguese Crown had to find ways to make itself present in distant places despite the small population. In the case of Portuguese America (i.e. colonial Brazil), due to the modest investment by the Portuguese Crown in the construction of temples and the insufficient number of priests to meet the religious needs of the colonizers spread over such a large territory, Catholicism developed mostly around the lay brotherhoods. Brotherhoods invested in the construction of churches and took on several religious responsibilities, especially those related to the worship of their patron saints. Boschi analyzed the confraternities with regard to their relations with the government and showed how brotherhoods were an "auxiliary, complementary and substitute force for the Church," being responsible for hiring religious representatives and building temples, especially during Brazil's eighteenth-century "golden age."[5] His analysis shows how the brotherhoods took on various tasks that should have been the responsibility of the public sector in an agreement between the absolute monarchy, the Church, and the brotherhoods.

---

4   Caio César Boschi, *Os leigos e o poder: irmandades leigas e política colonizadora em Minas Gerais* (Sao Paulo: Ática, 1986), 68.
5   Ibid., 3. Our translation.

In addition to their political role, brotherhoods were instrumental in cultivating colonial and baroque religiosity, characterized by the cult of saints, personal devotions, and processions and festivities, marked by the grandeur of the outward manifestations of faith, in which sacred and profane elements coexisted. To this display of colonial Catholicism was added a practical and immediate character, which sought solace and solution to daily issues, mainly through the intercession of saints, to whom promises were addressed that would be fulfilled after the realization of the requested grace. This pragmatism of colonial religiosity directed at the saints was also present in the brotherhoods, as they had as fundamental objectives a series of acts aimed at the welfare of destitute members and served as associations of mutual aid. For Africans, the brotherhoods might occupy the place of lineages and relationships of kinship, which defined social places and one's position within the group, which also guaranteed protection. Perhaps they were spaces to articulate the visible and invisible sphere of existence, guaranteeing the well-being of their members.

Irmandades de homens pretos were the subjects of multiple interpretations, as they had different functions for those who experienced them and could be perceived in different ways by the different social groups. They were seen as corporate bodies intended to Christianize Africans and provide mutual aid, being also a place to vent tensions, to maintain members' ancestral heritage, in addition to contributing to the improvement of the lives of enslaved members.[6] They were also seen as a physical and political space that gave their members a sense of identity and pride,[7] or conversely, as a space for the acculturation of Afro-descendants.[8] On the other hand, they were also viewed as a bastion of resistance and defense of Afro-Brazilians against slavery and as a form of counter-culture insofar as "native idols" would be worshiped under the guise of the saints,[9] and as centers of cultural resistance, a space for the concentration of racial demands and the formation of leaders.[10] Additionally, they were seen as a means of integrating black men and women into local society and humanizing the

6   André João Antonil [João Antonio Andreoni], *Cultura e opulência do Brasil* (1711; reprint: Sao Paulo: Editora Nacional, 1966).
7   Arthur Ramos, *A aculturação negra no Brasil* (Sao Paulo: Editora Nacional, 1942).
8   Carlos Ott, "A Irmandade de Nossa Senhora do Rosário dos Pretos do Pelourinho," *Afro-Ásia* no. 6-7 (1968): 119-126.
9   Veríssimo de Mello, "As confrarias de N. S. do Rosário como reação contra aculturativa dos negros do Brasil," *Afro-Ásia* 6-7 (1968): 107-118.
10   Roger Bastide, *As Américas negras: as civilizações africanas no Novo Mundo*, trans. Eduardo de Oliveira e Oliveira (Sao Paulo: Difel, 1974).

slaves who could gather and entertain there, however without challenging the slavocratic system.[11] And finally confraternities were understood as having an important role in the formation of a "black consciousness," even if divided by ethnic differences, and as an instrument of resistance and the construction of identities.[12]

As a subject studied for a long time, recent work done in Brazil on *irmandades de homens pretos* has proliferated significantly thanks to the expansion of postgraduate courses and recognition of the contribution of black communities to the formation of Brazilian society, a perception that was largely aroused by the actions of black activists. Despite the variety of approaches brought by research aimed mainly at particular cases, a prevalent perspective considers brotherhoods spaces for the autonomous construction of identities and social ties.

For some scholars, African religious practices took place within the brotherhoods, away from the watchful eyes of masters and their representatives. But there is little evidence documenting these practices, which would have been carried out under the protective cloak of the brotherhoods. The documents about the activities of *irmandades de homens pretos*, consisting mainly of *compromissos*, elections, board meeting minutes, membership logs, and financial expenses, are an expression of the rules dictated by colonial society and show their legal aspects. Thus, even though these are documents produced by the brothers themselves, they do not provide clues about the possible African traditions maintained under the law. The only indication that they might have existed is the reference to the ban on "witchcraft" that appears in some *compromissos*. What can be seen both in the documents produced by the brotherhoods and in the reports from outside observers is the adoption of the colonizing white religion by Africans and their descendants in their own different ways. In the case of Africans coming from the region of Angola, there was already contact with Christianity since the work of Catholic priests in the region dates to the sixteenth century. In the areas of more intense catechesis, such as Luanda, Massangano, and São Salvador do Congo, there were lay brotherhoods that brought together native Catholics, whose practices coexisted with local religious traditions.

With the shattering of family and community relations when they were trafficked, enslaved Africans sought to rebuild the fundamental bonds that united them on a new basis. Meeting through organizations that brought together people of the same ethnicity, from nearby regions, or belonging to

11 Scarano, *Devoção e escravidão*; Boschi, *Os leigos e o poder*.
12 Reis, *A morte é uma festa*.

the same cultural complex was a way they found to recreate the affinities previously founded on kinship relations, in organizations that grouped members by age group, activity, or specific spiritual ties. Roger Bastide writes regarding confraternities that congregating around a saint, more than mystical affinity expressed a kind of ethnic kinship.[13] Kátia Mattoso, emphasizing the importance of ethnicity in the religious, social, and political life of Africans brought to Bahia in the eighteenth and nineteenth centuries, writes that people of the same ethnic group called themselves "relatives," with essential links between them in the process of redefining solidarities, previously founded on familial relations.[14] João José Reis also points out that Africans "redefined the semantic scope of the word relative to include everyone of the same ethnicity," inventing the concept of "relative of nation." These symbolic kinships were the result of the impact of trafficking and enslavement on people from "societies based on complex kinship structures, of which ancestor worship was a very important part."[15]

Just as nations can be considered a substitute for kinship among African communities in the New World, so brotherhoods can be seen as spaces for the reconstruction of social ties informed by the pattern of familial structures, which aimed to integrate people into groups that would guarantee some protection and solidarity, such as support during illness or extreme need and presence in funeral rites, when the boundaries between the world of the living and that of the dead were crossed. But in addition to lineage, African power structures informed other practices experienced within *irmandades de homens pretos*, such as the election of festive monarchs, who played a central role in organizing festivities to honor the *irmandades*' patron, be it Nossa Senhora do Rosário (Our Lady of the Rosary), São Benedito (St. Benedict the Moor), Santo Elesbão (St. Kaleb of Axum) or Santa Efigênia (St. Iphigenia of Ethiopia), the most common patrons. The annual feast in honor of the patron saint was the most important moment for the brotherhood, in which there was a greater circulation of money, and on which the attention of most brothers converged.

Mintz and Price argued that the monopoly of power exercised by Europeans strongly influenced the ways in which cultural continuities remained, as well as the ways in which innovation occurred in the African

---

13   Roger Bastide, *Le religion africaine au Brésil* (Paris: Presses Universitaires de France, 1960), 161.

14   Kátia de Queirós Mattoso, *Bahia do Século XIX: uma província do império* (Rio de Janeiro: Nova Fronteira, 1992), 163-175.

15   Reis, *A morte é uma festa*, 55. Our translation.

diaspora.[16] In this sense, the permission given by representatives of colonial society to Africans and their descendants to elect kings, as well as the use of confraternal institutions to control black communities, was fundamental for the dissemination of this custom, founded on African political traditions. The election of black monarchs in this space forged from the Atlantic slave trade is the result of relations between Africans and Europeans. In the case of Brazil, the inequality of relations and power did not prevent the culture brought by enslaved Africans from contributing to the establishment of these institutions that guided their social life, consistent with their particular cultures, and allowed them some autonomy. It was the symbolic strength that a political leader, or a ruler, had for Africans that made them seek to organize themselves around leaders chosen according to the characteristics of their personalities and the positions they occupied in the social structure.

Black Kings and Queens

The society the Portuguese encountered at the end of the fifteenth century at the mouth of the Congo River was identified by them as a *reino* or kingdom, composed of several provinces, subordinated to a capital and a king. The history of ancient Congo, the Kingdom of Congo in Portuguese sources, is well known, and continues to be the subject of investigation in several areas of knowledge. What is relevant for this analysis is that it was a hierarchical society, with territorial scope and prominence over its neighbors, which made it a kingdom for the Portuguese. Many of the enslaved people who were brought to Brazil came from the central African coast, where Congo and the societies that were integrated into the Portuguese conquest of Angola in the seventeenth century were located. In Brazil, the memory of Congo and its contact with the Europeans, the Portuguese in particular, was evoked in a demonstration called a "dramatic dance" by one of the greatest scholars of Brazilian culture, Mário de Andrade.[17] Since the seventeenth century, there had been reports of festive parades in Brazil, in which the *rei congo* or "king of Congo" performed with his court, parading to the sound of African music and rhythms but dressed in European style.[18]

---

16   Sidney Mintz and Richard Price, *The Birth of African-American Culture: An Anthropological Perspective* (Boston: Beacon Press, 1992).

17   Mário de Andrade, *Os congos: danças dramáticas do Brasil*, vol. 2 (Belo Horizonte: Itatiaia; Brasília: Instituto Nacional do Livro, 1982), 9-105.

18   See, for example, Andreoni, *Cultura e opulência*. Urbain Souchu Rennefort states, "Their captivity does not bar them from having some fun. On Sunday, September 10, they have their

In Portugal, where there have been *irmandades de homens pretos* since the sixteenth century, on feast days kings, queens, and their courts went out in public procession with dance, music, special attire, and rituals that referred both to their societies of origin and to European courts. Such processions were often incorporated into official public ceremonies, in which they introduced a hint of exoticism and represented the power of the Portuguese empire over distant territories, incorporated into Portugal's sphere of influence through commercial and diplomatic relations, as well as evangelization and military conquest.[19]

Therefore, in Portugal and in Portuguese America, *irmandades de homens pretos* elected festive kings and queens as representatives of their groups on feast days, and they were recognized as such by the instituted powers. The king was responsible for collecting donations throughout the year for the feast of the patron saint, when he then paraded in various public ceremonies. Often masters paid for their slaves' contributions to the festivities partially or in full. The celebration of black kings is directly related to the history of contact between the Portuguese and the Congolese, which began in the late fifteenth century and which decisively interfered in the history of Congo. Considered an African Catholic kingdom, which at the beginning of the seventeenth century developed diplomatic relations with Portugal and the Vatican, Congo adopted a series of elements of Catholicism introduced by the Portuguese and coming directly from Rome via the missionaries sent by

feast in Pernambuco. There were 400 men and 100 women at mass. They elect a king and queen and parade through the streets singing, dancing, and reciting their own verses, written for the occasion, led by oboes, trumpets, and tambourines. They were dressed in their masters' clothes, with gold necklaces and earrings, some wearing masks. The king and his officers did nothing else that week but walk the streets solemnly with their swords and daggers": *A estada em Pernambuco, em 1666, de François de Lopis, Marquês de Mondevergue, segundo o relato de Souchou de Rennefort (1688)* (São Paulo: IEB-USP, 2016), 31. For the eighteenth century, see, among others, Francisco Calmon, *Relação das faustíssimas festas* (Rio de Janeiro: FUNARTE, 1982). Nineteenth-century accounts include Hermann Burmeister, *Viagem ao Brasil através das províncias do Rio de Janeiro e Minas Gerais* (Belo Horizonte: Itatiaia, 1980); Luiz Edmundo, *O Rio de Janerio no tempo dos cice-reis, 1763-1808* (Rio de Janeiro: Imprensa Nacional, 1932); Henry Koster, *Viagens ao nordeste do Brasil*, trans. Luiz da Camara Cascudo (São Paulo: Companhia Editora Nacional, 1942); Mello Moraes Filho, *Festas de tradições populares do Brasil* (Rio de Janeiro: F. Briguiet & Cia, 1946); J. B. von Spix and C. F. P. von Martius, *Viagem pelo Brasil*, trans. Lúcia Furquim Lahmeyer (Rio de Janeiro: Imprensa Nacional, 1938).

19   On black kings and queens in Lisbon, see Marina de Mello e Souza, *Reis negros no Brasil escravista: história da festa de coroação de rei congo* (Belo Horizonte: Editora UFMG, 2001), 165. On the role of Catholicism in the Portuguese colonization of Congo and Angola, see Mello e Souza, *Além do visível: poder, catolicismo e comércio no Congo e Angola, séculos XVII e XVIII* (Sao Paulo: USP, 2018).

Propaganda Fide, the Vatican's overseas evangelization branch. The incorporation of elements of Catholicism, integrated especially in rites of power, was directly related to the exercise of authority by the chiefs and was central to the maintenance of a certain political and territorial unity in the Congo until the beginning of the twentieth century, when Portuguese colonialism deepened its roots in the region that today forms part of northern Angola.[20]

In Brazil the election of kings, always associated with the feasts of the patron saints, especially of Our Lady of the Rosary on the first Sunday of October, appears only briefly in confraternal statutes, and was an aspect of the feast that was not welcomed by the Church. Along with the administrative positions of the brotherhoods, kings, queens, and a festive court were chosen annually, with titles referring to the European courts but also to the Congolese hierarchical powers, where European titles, such as king, queen, count, duke, ensign, butler, had been common since the sixteenth century. Therefore, European elements of the performance of festive kings and queens in Brazil were also present in Congo and Angola, where some social segments had contact with European state ceremonies and Catholic processions since the arrival of the Portuguese. The same can be said for other insignias of power, such as luxurious clothes and ornaments with precious stones and metals, which referred to the Portuguese court and were also linked to the African elites of the regions that had greater contact with the Portuguese, such as Congo, and the Ndembo and Ndongo, where chiefs began to show their power through clothing acquired in relations with Europeans, generally received as gifts of distinction. Also in Brazil, robes, elaborate clothes, crowns, scepters, and thrones appear in the descriptions of the dances and representations that were part of the festive processions known as *congadas* from the beginning of the nineteenth century. The coexistence of European clothing such as long dresses, coats, and robes, with turbans and *tangas* (a kind of sarong), in the same way that jewels and sabers were used together with ostrich feathers and masks, materialized a synthesis of diverse elements, rearticulated in the construction of new identities in a colonial slave society.

The playful and popular character of the parade of black kings and queens, with dances and songs performed in the streets, the ingestion of large amounts of food and alcohol, the temporary inversion of hierarchies, and the

---

20   On the presence of Congo elites in European visual culture in the seventeenth and eighteenth centuries, as well as the repercussions of the embassy sent by D. Álvaro II to Rome in 1607, see Cécile Fromont, *The Art of Conversion: Christian Visual Culture in the Kingdom of Kongo* (Chapel Hill: University of North Carolina Press, 2014). There are many studies on Catholicism in the Congo, and besides those mentioned, I would like to note the work of John K. Thornton, who has written several important volumes on the topic.

liberation of normally prohibited behaviors, provoked the fear of a definitive rupture of social order, and caused the administrative and ecclesiastical authorities to set limits proportionate to the threat of destabilization that the party suggested. But often, these feasts also made sense to slaveowners and colonial administrators, who argued that allowing enslaved men to celebrate in their own fashion for a few days would appease them and make them work better. In the eighteenth century, André João Antonil, an Italian Jesuit who lived in Brazil from 1681 until his death in 1716, wrote in his book *Cultura e opulência do Brasil* (Culture and Opulence of Brazil) that masters let the slaves stage their celebrations, in addition to crown and celebrate their kings and queens, because to keep them from these activities, "the only relief from their captivity, would be to make them inconsolable and melancholy, with little life and health."[21] Whether they were convinced for reasons of faith, which even went as far as to justify captivity, or whether it was for the pursuit of rationality in production, as Antonil advised, masters should allow their slaves to be absent when involved in religious celebrations. In this context, it is not surprising that enslaved as well as free men and women joined black brotherhoods in such large numbers, as attested by the number of them scattered throughout Brazil.

Conclusion

The evocation of Central African history at the time of the slave trade and the role that the Portuguese had there is essential in understanding the reasons internal to African cultures that led to the election of black kings and queens in Lisbon at ancient times and in Brazil, where the tradition continues today. The celebration of a Christian Congo king, who defeats his pagan enemy in a ritual battle and dramatic dance, is interpreted here as an element of strengthening a black Catholic identity based on the African past, and renewed annually in the festive celebration.[22] Previously understood as an expression of the subordination of Africans and their descendants to the Catholic slaveholding social order, I argue that the festive celebrations of black kings and queens, and kings of Congo in particular, were an affirmation of identity linked to the African Catholic experience. Reminding that elements of Catholicism and some of its symbols were incorporated by the ruling elite of Congo and by part of its population, I point to processes that

---

21   Andreoni, *Cultura e opulência*, 64.
22   I develop this argument in *Reis negros*.

led to forms of organization of black communities where multiple meanings converged. While for the slave owners, black brotherhoods were a means of pacifying slaves and instilling the values of a European Catholic society, for their members brotherhoods were forms of organization and exercise of solidarity that referred to their societies of origin. The elections of black kings in these brotherhoods were ways of celebrating an authority that *irmãos* recognized as representative and protective of the group, which recreated bonds that could be associated with those of kinship, such as respect for elders, bonds that supported networks of solidarity.

I approach the elections of black kings and queens within the scope of the Catholic lay brotherhoods from the perspective of the encounter between different cultures in certain historical contexts. To this end, I consider, on the one hand, that the Congolese elite incorporated elements of European culture, and on the other that brotherhoods and their celebrations were forms permitted by colonial slave society for the integration of enslaved Africans. Colonial domination and Catholic missionary action always happened in tandem, and the compulsory baptism of every slave embarking in Luanda, by the hundreds and frequently without any introduction to Christian doctrine, was only the first step in a long process of Christianization, the greatest expression of which was proliferation of black brotherhoods, organized around saints preferred by Africans and their descendants. Considering the multiple meanings of Catholic lay brotherhoods, my intention is to understand the reinterpretations of models sanctioned by the mainstream made by oppressed people originally from another sociocultural universe. To this end, it is essential to consider their environments of origin and the historical processes in which they were inserted. When speaking of the dances performed in the parades of kings of Congo, the ritual embassies and wars then staged, with the history of the Congo and some of its traditions, it becomes clear that these performances evoked an African past. The election of black kings, even forged in the context of colonial domination, served as a link between the black community and an idealized past, connected to an abstract idea of the homeland.

The fundamentally African characteristics of such customs were not only present in their most obvious aspects and highlighted by observers, generally Europeans shocked by the dances and masks seen as symbols of the inferiority of blacks, they were also present in the act of electing ceremonial monarchs to which the community reported to resolve its internal issues and whose authority was accepted by wider society. Combining elements of the cultures in contact with one another, that is, African and Portuguese, the elections of black kings and queens and the festive rituals that accompanied them were part of the general framework of colonization of the Americas and the constitution of identities specific to the groups forming these societies. Spaces permitted by slave owners, such as lay brotherhoods devoted to Catholic saints, were adopted by groups of Africans and their descendants, including enslaved, manumitted, and free-born Afro-descendans. On the other hand, many of those who came from Angola, the main embarkation point for slaves in Central Africa, could associate Catholicism with their cultures of origin, since Catholic missionaries had worked in the region from the beginning of the sixteenth century.

The king of Congo, which in the nineteenth century became the only title adopted by festive black monarchs, was a symbol of a mythical Africa, built out of the slave trade, of the history of evangelization, and the insertion of Africans and their descendants into a colonial social order in which ethnic differences were set aside in favor of building a common black identity with Catholic traditions rooted in their homelands. The rituals surrounding the Congo king, such as the festive annual parade and the staging of dances and war battles in which the Catholic *rei Congo* (Congo king) subdue the pagan enemy, ritualized a memory that constituted a community identity founded on a mythical Africa, in which Catholicism was somehow integrated. The Congo kings were the living ancestor, the representation of the founding hero, and he provided to the communities that elected him an identity that linked them to their native Africa, while opening up spaces of possibility within colonial slave society.

The product of the meeting of different cultures under the conditions of the colonial slave system, the festive king and queen celebration, and the dramatic dances performed brought together symbols decoded differently by black *irmãos* and white masters. For black *irmãos*, they were an affirmation of African characteristics, in addition to ways of exercising religiosity and recognizing leaders chosen internally. For white masters and colonial administrators, they were an example of submission and adaptation to slave society, a way to reinforce patriarchal relations and build intermediaries in dealing with black communities. The nature of these festivals was polysemic; the black kings took on a variety of meanings and attributions, attesting to the continuity of institutions that are distinguished by their malleability.

In Brazil, even today *irmandades* have festive kings and queens that parade on their patron's feast accompanied by musicians and dancers. *Congadas*, *mozambiques*, and *maracatus* – as the performance is variously called today – take place in different Brazilian regions, organized by groups that maintain the traditions of their ancestors, including these festive parades with dances done to the beat of specific rhythms, conducted by leaders who are knowledgeable in such traditions. Contemporary Brazilian society, post-slavery and post-colonial, still celebrates not only these customs from the past but also lives with violent forms of segregation of the first inhabitants of the land, generically called Indians, and of former enslaved Africans whose blood and cultures fertilized Brazilian soil and society. The white elite, no longer Portuguese, but the result of arrivals since the end of the nineteenth century of a large number of migrants of diverse origins, keeps the reins of politics and the economy firmly in its hands, sometimes relaxing its hold, sometimes grasping it more strongly, without ever losing control or any of its privileges. Continuously a target of economic and political violence, the black population creates and recreates ways of existing, of resisting, of facing the social exclusion to which it is subjected explicitly. As post-colonial studies teach us, the colonial experience must be incorporated into current, contemporary society, itself the result of colonial experience and not merely what followed it. Recent attitudes that have sought to erase the past have not resulted in positive outcomes.

About the author

Marina de Mello e Souza is professor of history at the University of Sao Paulo. She is the author of *Paraty, a Cidade e as Festas*; *Reis Negros no Brasil Escravista*: *História da Festa de Coroação de Rei Congo*; *África e Brasil africano*; *Além do Visível: Poder, Catolicismo e Comércio no Congo e em Angola* (*Séculos XVI e XVII*). She currently is conducting research on the Congo in the eighteenth and nineteenth centuries.

Bibliography

Andrade, Mário de. *Os congos: danças dramáticas do Brasil*. Belo Horizonte: Itatiaia: Instituto Nacional do Livro, 1982.

Andreoni, João Antonio [André João Antonil]. *Cultura e opulência do Brasil*. Sao Paulo: Companhia Editora Nacional, [1711] 1966.

Bastide, Roger. *Le religion africaine au Brésil*. Paris: Presses Universitaires de France, 1960.

——. *As Américas Negras*: *as civilizações africanas no Novo Mundo*. Translated by Eduardo de Oliveira e Oliveira. Sao Paulo: Difel, 1974.

Boschi, Caio César. *Os leigos e o poder: irmandades leigas e política colonizadora em Minas Gerais*. Sao Paulo: Ática, 1986.

Burmeister, Hermann. *Viagem ao Brasil através das províncias do Rio de Janeiro e Minas Gerais*. Belo Horizonte: USP, 1980.

Calmon, Francisco. *Relação das faustíssimas festas*. Rio de Janeiro: FUNARTE, [1762] 1982.

Edmundo, Luiz. *O Rio de Janerio no tempo dos cice-reis, 1763-1808*. Rio de Janeiro: Imprensa Nacional, 1932.

Fromont, Cécile. *The Art of Conversion*: *Christian Visual Culture in the Kingdom of Kongo*. Chapel Hill: University of North Carolina Press, 2014.

Koster, Henry. *Viagens ao Nordeste do Brasil*. Translated by Luiz da Camara Cascudo. Sao Paulo: Editora Nacional, 1942.

Mattoso, Kátia de Queirós. *Bahia do século XIX: uma província do império*. Rio de Janeiro: Nova Fronteira, 1992.

Mello, Veríssimo de. "As Confrarias de N. S. do Rosário como reação contra aculturativa dos negros do Brasil." *Afro-Ásia* 6-7 (1968): 107-118.

Mintz, Sidney, and Richard Price. *The Birth of African-American Culture*: *An Anthropological Perspective*. Boston: Beacon Press, 1992.

Moraes Filho, Mello. *Festas de tradições populares do Brasil*. 3rd ed. Rio de Janeiro: F. Briguiet, 1946.

Ott, Carlos. "A Irmandade de Nossa Senhora do Rosário dos Pretos do Pelourinho." *Afro-Ásia*, 6-7 (1968): 119-126.

Ramos, Arthur. *A aculturação negra no Brasil*. Sao Paulo: Companhia Editora Nacional, 1942.

Reginaldo, Lucilene. *Os Rosários dos Angolas: Irmandades de Africanos e Crioulos na Bahia Setecentista*. Sao Paulo: Alameda, 2011.

Reis, João José. *A Morte é uma Festa: Ritos Fúnebres e Revolta Popular no Brasil do Século XIX*. Sao Paulo: Companhia das Letras, 1991.

—. "Identidade e Diversidade Étnicas nas Irmandades Negras no Tempo da Escravidão." *Tempo* 2, no. 3 (1997): 7-33.

Rennefort, Urbain Souchu. *A estada em Pernambuco, em 1666, de François de Lopis, Marquês de Mondevergue, segundo o relato de Souchou de Rennefort (1688)*. Sao Paulo: IEB, [1668] 2016.

Scarano, Julita, *Devoção e Escravidão: A Irmandade de Nossa Senhora do Rosário dos Pretos no Distrito Diamantino no século XVIII*. Sao Paulo: Editora Nacional, 1978.

Soares, Mariza de Carvalho. *Devotos da cor: nidentidade étnica, religiosidade e escravidão no Rio de Janeiro, século XVIII*. Rio de Janeiro: Civilização Brasileira, 2000.

Souza, Marina de Mello e. *Reis negros no Brasil escravista: História da festa de coroação de Rei Congo*. Belo Horizonte: UFMG, 2002.

—. *Além do Visível. Poder, Catolicismo e Comércio no Congo e Angola, séculos XVII e XVIII*. Sao Paulo: EDUSP, 2018.

Spix, J. B. von, and C. F. P. von Martius. *Viagem pelo Brasil*. Translated by Lúcia Furquim Lahmeyer. Rio de Janeiro: Imprensa Nacional, [1823] 1938.

13   "Much to See and Admire"

Festivals, Parades, and Royal Pageantry among Afro-Bahian
Brotherhoods in the Eighteenth Century

Lucilene Reginaldo
University of Campinas

Translated by Bruna Dantas Lobato
and Miguel A. Valerio

Abstract
Brotherhoods' patron feasts were their main devotional and social activity.
Celebrated annually, it was the most notable as well as the moment of
the greatest public visibility for members. The celebration could bring a
great deal of prestige to the governing board and the whole brotherhood,
attracting new members. Beyond this, the feast was an opportunity for
the brotherhood to show its capacity to organize funerals, along with
burial at a holy place, which constituted a key source of income and a
major attractive to potential members. This was also another aspect of
the celebrations: they functioned as a space for dancing, music, and the
consumption of food and alcoholic beverages. The election and coronation
of kings and queens was a unique part of this aspect of the celebration.
This chapter analyzes the festivities organized by black brotherhoods
in eighteenth-century Salvador, Brazil, underscoring various aspects of
their confraternal life and the economic and political activity (within and
without the brotherhood) undertaken to stage these festivities.

Keywords: Bahia, Afro-Brazilian Brotherhoods, Festivals, Parades, Royal
Pageantry

For Afro-Brazilian brotherhoods, called *irmandades*, the feast of their patron
is the main annual event. It is the most conspicuous moment of confraternal

Javiera Jaque Hidalgo and Miguel A. Valerio. *Indigenous and Black Confraternities in Colonial
Latin America: Negotiating Status through Religious Practices.* Amsterdam: Amsterdam University
Press, 2022
DOI: 10.5117/ 9789463721547_CH13

life, marked with the greatest mobilization and public visibility for the brotherhood. During the colonial period, black brotherhoods rivaled each other as well as their white counterparts, taking this competition to the streets in the form of colorful displays, music, and dances. According to a contemporary account, they often surpassed "the whites in everything, going to great lengths to outdo everyone."[1] Behind these rivalries lay the desire for distinction in colonial society. The patron's feast was also a unique opportunity to entice new members and even secure the benevolence of colonial elites and civil and ecclesiastical authorities, which could guarantee "strong supporters in the defense of their interests."[2] However, confraternal celebrations had other aspects, as they constituted the spaces for dance, music, and feasting least likely to attract the interference of colonial authorities. The coronation of the king and queen were the central component of the festivities, giving visibility to the most complex political dimensions of Afro-Brazilians' relations with the slavocratic establishment. In this chapter, I argue that the festivities organized by eighteenth-century Afro-Bahian brotherhoods reveal, and at the same time, constitute privileged spaces of confraternal life, economic relations, and conflict and governance within the brotherhoods.

Father Manuel Cerqueira Torres, a local priest in Salvador, wrote an account of the feast for Our Lady of the Rosary where he states the black Rosary brotherhood in the Portas do Carmo neighborhood was principally responsible for the grandeur of celebration, one of the most lauded in the city's history:

> The feast of the ever victorious Most Blessed Virgin of the Rosary was observed with majestic pomp. The church was richly adorned. In the afternoon, its procession went out with just as much order and pomp, and this being one of the most praiseworthy processions in the city because of the great effort this confraternity puts into it, and on this occasion they outshone themselves.[3]

1   Frei Agostinho de Santa Maria, *Santuário mariano e história das imagens milagrosas de Nossa Senhora milagrosamente manifestadas e aparecidas em o Arcebispado da Bahia*, vol. 9 (1707-1723; reprint: Salvador: Instituto Histórico e Geográfico da Bahia, 1949), 86.
2   Marcos Magalhães Aguiar, "Vila Rica dos confrades. A sociabilidade confrarial entre negros e mulatos no século XVIII" (master's thesis, University of São Paulo, 1993), 220.
3   Torres, *Narração panerírico-histórica das festividades con que a Cidade da Bahia solenizou os felicíssimos desposórios da Princesa Nossa Senhora com o Sereníssimo Senhor Infante Dom Pedro*, in *O movimento academicista no Brasil, 1641-1820/22*, ed. José Aderaldo Castello, vol. 3, part 3 (1760; reprint: São Paulo: Conselho Estadual de Cultura), 205.

Table 13.1.   Black brotherhoods in eighteenth-century Salvador

PARISH	BROTHERHOOD
São Salvador da Sé	Bom Jesus da Ressurreição; São Benedito; Santa Ifigênia
Nossa Senhora da Vitória	Nossa Senhora do Rosário dos Pretos
Nossa Senhora da Conceição da Praia	Nossa Senhora do Rosário dos Pretos; São Benedito; Senhor Bom Jesus da Redenção
Santo Antônio Além do Carmo	Nossa Senhora do Rosário dos Pretos
São Pedro	Nossa Senhora do Rosário dos Pretos; Santo Antônio de Categeró; Santo Rei Baltazar
Senhora Santana	Nossa Senhora do Rosário dos Pretos
Santíssimo Sacramento da Rua do Passo	Nossa Senhora do Rosário dos Pretos; Senhor Bom Jesus dos Martírios
Nossa Senhora da Penha de França de Itapagipe	Nossa Senhora do Rosário dos Pretos; São Benedito

SOURCES: ANTT, Chancelarias Antigas, Ordem de Cristo; Santa Maria, *Santuário mariano*; Luís Monteiro Costa, "A devoção de N.S. do Rosário na cidade do Salvador," *Revista do Instituto Genealógico* 10 (1959): 95-117; Silva Campos, "Procissões tradicionais da Bahia," *Anais do Arquivo Público da Bahia* 27 (1941); Manoel da Silveira Cardozo, "As irmandades da antiga Bahia," *Revista de História* 47 (1973): 235-261.

The date, organization, and procedures of the ceremony were prescribed in brotherhoods' constitutions, called *compromissos*. In the second half of the eighteenth century, almost all parishes in the city of Salvador had one or more black brotherhoods (Table 13.1).[4]

The city's calendar of religious festivities included celebrations from several confraternities. At the beginning of the year, preferably on January 6 (the feast of the Epiphany), the feast of the black Confraternity of St. Baltazar the Magus would take place, since the three magi have included a black magus since the late thirteenth century.[5] On the first octave of Easter, it was the turn of the brotherhoods of St. Benedict the Moor (sixteenth c. CE) in the city's Franciscan monastery and the parish of Itapagipe to hold their annual celebrations. The brotherhood of St. Iphigenia of Ethiopia (first c.

---

4   Looking at various sources, especially the *compromissos* approved by the Portuguese Crown in the 1760s, I counted sixteen black *irmandades* in Salvador: Reginaldo, *Os Rosários dos Angolas. Irmandade de africanos e crioulos na Bahia Setecentista* (São Paulo: Alameda, 2011), 123.

5   Paul H. D. Kaplan, *The Rise of the Black Magus in Western Art* (Ann Arbor: UMI Research Press, 1985).

CE), also in the city's Franciscan monastery, held its feast in September, on the day dedicated to St. Matthew. In the month of October, there were ceremonies for the Rosary brotherhoods in the parishes of Conceição da Praia and Rosário de João Pereira, as well as in the confraternal church of the Rosary in the Portas do Carmo (today's Pelourinho) neighborhood. On the fourth Sunday of November, the feast in honor of St. Anthony of Carthage (sixteenth c. CE) took place. In the second octave of Christmas it was the turn of the Rosário da Vitória brotherhood to host their own annual feast. These represent but a few examples.

In the Recôncavo neighborhood, the brotherhoods' ceremonies conformed to a more rigid calendar (see Map 13.1). Most festivities were concentrated on Christmas octaves, that is, the sixteen days that followed the celebration of Christ's birth. This time of the year was safe from the great rains that made paths in the area hard to use for priests who traveled long and painful distances to tend to the needs of their parishioners.[6]

The organization of the annual festivities was the responsibility of the brotherhood. They usually celebrated their patron saint with a sung mass, music, and preaching specifically prepared for this date. Some even made a point of choosing an especially "suitable preacher," like the brotherhood of Rosário de João Pereira.[7] The sermon was an act of great importance within the feast. As such, whenever possible, the brotherhoods hired well-known preachers, with the payment proportionate to the prestige of the speaker.[8]

Sacred vespers, adoration of the Blessed Sacrament, organ music, and processions were also employed by black *irmãos* (brotherhood members). The procession was another highlight of the celebrations, but it was not always possible for a confraternity to bear its high costs. The Rosary brotherhood of João Pereira had in its *compromisso* all the appropriate steps for the organization of the procession: the position of the officers and *irmãos* in the procession, the insignia each carried according to hierarchy, ornaments with the image of the Virgin of the Rosary, duration, posture required by the act, etc. However, it was declared in the same statutes that, if there were not enough stewards to sponsor the full array of celebrations in a

6   Santa Maria, *Santuário mariano*, 88; D. Sebastião Monteiro da Vide, "Notícias do Arcebispado da Bahia para suplicar a Sua Majestade. Em favor do culto divino e das almas, 1712" (1712), reprinted in *Revista do Instituto Histórico e Geográfico Brasileiro* 54 (1891): 323-364.

7   Arquivo Nacional da Torre Tombo (hereafter ANTT), Lisbon, Portugal, Chancelarias Régias, Ordem de Cristo, Livro 297, Compromisso da Irmandade de N. S. do Rosário dos Pretos de João Pereira, Freguesia de São Pedro, f. 169v (1768).

8   Julita Scarano, *Devoção e scravidão: irmandade de N.S. do Rosário dos Pretos do Distrito Diamantino no Século XVIII* (São Paulo: Editora Nacional, 1978), 76-77.

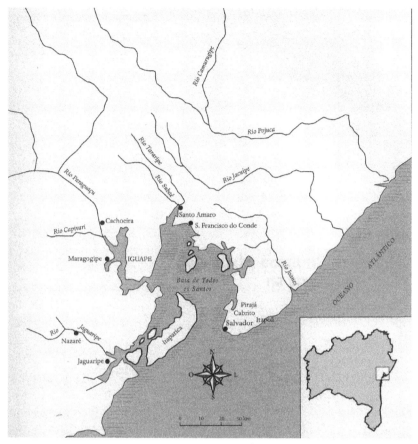

Map 13.1. The Bahian Recôncavo. Source: João José Reis, *A rebelião escrava na Bahia*, 10. Reproduced with the author's permission.

given year, this would be reduced to "a sung mass and communion without a procession."[9]

Despite the difficulties, whenever possible and at great sacrifice, Afro-Bahian brotherhoods made a point of taking to the streets around the parishes or villages in high style. In the parish of São José das Itapororocas in the countryside, the feast for the Virgin of the Rosary sponsored by the black brotherhood was held annually on Pentecost, preceded by a novena on nine consecutive afternoons. On the day of the ceremony,

> The procession came out with the leader in ornate vestments and the most upright brotherhoods in the same chapel. One of the *juizes* guided the

9   Compromisso da Irmandade do Rosário na Igreja Paroquial de João Pereira, f. 169v.

procession of the past and present year or any other year in its absence with a new white cape, and the clerk before the leader, and behind the canopy, the *juizes* of that year.[10]

The processions were separate events, since they required specific ceremonial etiquette. Participants had to play well this game of veiled messages, full of symbolism. For "the slightest change in the place assigned to a person in a ceremony was tantamount to a change in their social position."[11] For this reason, the Portuguese Royal Bureau of Lay Orders demanded changes to the *compromisso* of the brotherhood of Rosário de São José das Itapororocas, located in Recôncavo, especially in the chapter that regulated the feast of its patron, the Virgin of the Rosary. The authorities rejected the *juizes'* position in front of the canopy, claiming that it was only up to the main *juiz* to open the procession of his own brotherhood, and not those of any other brotherhood in the same chapel.[12] The baldachin, which was carried in processions; beneath it was the celebrated saint or the priest who carried it. It was the center of the procession, the most prominent place. Thus, the individual's position in relation to the canopy translated into the broader social hierarchy.

It is important to distinguish the different processions that took place in colonial Bahia. There were solemn processions, also called precepts, as well as general ones. These public processions did not need a license to be performed, as they were "ordered by Canon Law, Royal Laws and Ordinances, and customs" established in the archbishopric.[13] Processions organized by the brotherhoods were called devotional, requiring prior authorization from the bishop. The entourage was led by the sponsoring brotherhood and, when sharing the temple space with others, they also participated in the procession. The *irmãos* at the Portas do Carmo, in the

10 Arquivo da Freguesia de São José das Itapororocas, Bahia, Compromisso da Irmandade de Nossa Senhora do Rosário dos homens pretos na Capela de Paramirim, f. 79v (1786). Brotherhoods were governed by a board (*mesa*) made up of *juizes* (literally, judges).

11 José Pedro Paiva, "Etiqueta e cerimonias públicas na esfera da Igreja (séculos XVII-XVIII)," in *Festa: cultura e sociabilidade na América Portuguesa*, ed. Istaván Jancsó and Iris Kantor, vol. 1 (São Paulo: Imprensa Oficial, 2001), 85.

12 ANTT, Chancelarias Antigas da Ordem de Cristo, D. Maria I, Livro 16, Provisão de aprovação do Compromisso da Irmandade de Nossa Senhora do Rosário dos homens pretos na Capela de Paramirim, Freguesia de São José das Itapororocas, f. 82.

13 Processions approved by the bishop varied, among which were the Onze mil Virgens (eleven thousand virgins) staged by the Jesuits; Holy Friday, organized by the Carmelites; Sts. Francis Xavier and Sebastian, staged by the City Council; and Corpus Christi: Arcebispado de São Salvador, *Constituições Primeiras do Arcebispado da Bahia*, Livro III, Títulos XIII, XIV, XV.

early decades of the nineteenth century, had the participation of "the most upright brotherhoods in the same chapel with their decently decorated leaders, following the order of seniority for the places" in the procession for the Virgin.[14] Other significant expenses in the budget for festivals were the decorations and improvements for the temples and chapels, "with all the necessary cleanliness."[15] The dress and insignia displayed by *juizes* and *irmãos* also had to be appropriate to the grandeur of the event. Dressed in white capes and holding torches or candles in their hands, the *irmãos* and *juizes* accompanied all scheduled events. All of these fineries were costly.

Irmandades generally had resources dedicated to covering feast day expenses. In addition to donations (from people on the streets), in many confraternities board members, especially the *juizes* and stewards, contributed in a special way to these events. In the St. Iphigenia brotherhood in the Franciscan monastery in Salvador, the contributions offered by the *juizes* helped with the preparations for the ceremony.[16] In the nearby Magus Baltazar brotherhood, the entire feast was "paid for by the *juizes* and stewards."[17] The difficulties were certainly greater among black *irmandades* in rural regions. In order to guarantee more funds for the patron's feast, the black *irmãos* of the Rosary brotherhood of Vila Nova Real in Rio São Francisco, in the district Sergipe de El Rei, instituted specific *juizes* for this purpose, in addition to a large number of stewards. Faced with the poverty of the *irmãos*, whose donations were not enough to fund the ceremony, they instituted "a male *juiz* and a female *juiza* as well as 15 stewards in honor of the 15 mysteries of the Rosary, so that all together their donations could do more for the feast of the Blessed Virgin."[18]

Extravagance was common at these events. In the year 1742, for example, the ecclesiastical visitor Fr. João da Cruz, at the behest of the Bishop of Rio de Janeiro, was in the parish of Santo Antonio de Itatiaia, in Ouro Preto,

14 "Compromisso da Irmandade de Nossa Senhora do Rosário das Portas do Carmo, 1820" as reproduced in Sara Oliveira Farias, "'Irmãos de cor, de caridade e de crença': a Irmandade do Rosário do Pelourinho na Bahia do século XIX" (master's thesis, Universidade Federal da Bahia, 1997).
15 Compromisso da Irmandade do Rosário na Igreja Paroquial de João Pereira, f. 169v.
16 ANNT, Chancelarias Antigas, Ordem de Cristo, Livro 301, Compromisso da Irmandade de Santa Ifigênia no Convento de São Francisco, f. 108 (1770).
17 ANNT, Chancelarias Antigas, Ordem de Cristo, Livro 297, Compromisso da Irmandade do Santo Rei Baltazar na Freguesia de São Pedro Velho, f. 252v (1768).
18 Arquivo Histórico Ultramarino (hereafter AHU), Lisbon, Portugal, Bahia, Códice 1958, Compromisso da Irmandade de Nossa Senhora do Rosário ereta em Igreja própria que as suas custas fundaram os Homens Pretos na Vila Nova Real Del Rey do Rio São Francisco, chap. III (1800). These *juizes* had crowns but were not addressed by royal titles.

Minas Gerais. The visitor was scandalized by the prodigality of the *irmaos* of the Rosary and St. Benedict, who used "the funds of the brotherhoods for human ostentation."[19] The excessive spending on the festivities has been interpreted by several scholars as a kind of escape valve, a release permitted in the difficult daily life of slavery and continuous labor. It was also imbued with exaggeratedly pompous behavior and Baroque culture, itself "marked by the pleasure of contemplating the exuberance of images, incense, music, sermons and processions with the chimes of bells and the lighting of fireworks."[20] For the men and women of the eighteenth century, known as Brazil's "golden age," which carried many residues of the Baroque, this spectacular homage to the Virgin or a saint, which aimed towards more than simple pleasures of contemplation, also had an influence on the relationships established with saints venerated.[21]

It is also important to relativize the notion of the escape valve and baroque inspiration, and this pompousness as an essential element for the economic health of black confraternities. To this end, I suggest paying attention to the material aspect of the ceremonies funded by black confraternities, in view of the interests of conservation and maintenance of their physical and symbolic heritage.

Elections of new brotherhood officers used to take place during the patron's feast. Members of the Rosary brotherhood of Santo Amaro da Purificação, about 50 miles from Salvador, recorded their concern for this moment of much turmoil and of several "disputes and disagreements" in their *compromisso*.[22] The concern with the regulation of the electoral processes makes us believe that, in these associations, the management positions were very coveted. It is important to remember that the old board ended its mandate with the most important event in the annual life of the brotherhood, its patron's feast. Possibly the grandeur or modesty of the festivities represented the crowning jewel or proof of the failure of the outgoing administration.

The gains offered by the celebrations could go beyond a political game. In this sense, the historian Marcos Magalhães Aguiar points out the importance of festivals not only as a wasteful moment, but also as a catalyst for income:

19   Alisson Eugênio, "Tensões entre os visitadores eclesiásticos e as irmandades negras no século XVIII mineiro," *Revista Brasileira de História*, 22, no. 14, (2002): 34, 36, 37.
20   Ibid., 38.
21   João José Reis, *A morte é uma festa: ritos fúnebres e revolta popular no Brasil do século XIX* (São Paulo: Companhia das Letras, 1991), 61.
22   AHU, Bahia, Códice 1931, Compromisso da Irmandade de N. S. do Rosário dos Pretos da Vila de Santo Amaro da Purificação, f. 19 (1803).

Typically, elections and parties took place on subsequent days or weeks, when they did not take place on the same day. These occasions coincided with the giving of alms and the payment of annual fees and entrance fees for the brothers [...] These were, therefore, the strongest moments of economic contribution by the brotherhoods, and the brothers knew very well the risks of the absence of the celebrations for the survival of devotion.[23]

The ceremony provided prestige to board members as well as the association itself, contributing very effectively to attract new members and maintain old ones. Furthermore, the beauty, pomp, and solemnity of the patron's feast celebration could also be an indication of their ability to celebrate funeral rituals, which, together with the guarantee of a grave in a sacred place, was another unquestionable point of attraction for new members to join.

Reading the *compromissos* of both black and white brotherhoods reveals a continuous desire for decent burial of its members – in other words, guaranteed burial in a sacred place. The certainty of proper liturgy presided over by one or more priests, and accompaniment to the grave by the *irmãos*, if not ostentatious at least worthy and honorable. According to the historian José João Reis, "funeral pomp was part of the ceremonial tradition of the confraternities, forming, alongside the patron saint festivals, an important source of prestige."[24] The brotherhood of St. Benedict in Salvador's Franciscan convent accompanied the deceased brothers to the grave with candles and wore their capes.[25] This attitude was common in the daily life of the brotherhoods. In fact, the black and white brotherhoods were primarily responsible for the grandeur of colonial funerals. These truly public spectacles stood out for the profusion of signs, gestures, and symbolic objects, and, above all, for the size and impact of the procession.

"They use so many of their own instruments": Festivities and Royalty

Aside from Catholic rites and political and economic interests, there were other dimensions to the Afro-confraternal festivities. A few records allow

23   Marcos Magalhães Aguiar, "Festas e rituais de inversão hierárquica nas irmandades negras de Minas Gerais," in *Festa*, 1: 370.
24   Reis, *A morte é uma festa*, 144.
25   ANTT, Chancelarias Antigas, Ordem de Cristo, Livro 293, Compromisso da Irmandade de São Benedito do Convento de São Francisco da Bahia, f. 121 (1770).

us to glimpse less "orthodox" aspects of the celebrations sponsored by the black sodalities in the parishes of old Bahia. In his ten-volume history of Marian devotion in the Portuguese Empire, *Santuário mariano* (Lisbon, 1707-1723), the Augustinian friar Agostinho de Santa Maria (1642-1728), for example, observed that black *irmãos*

> make the feast of the Our Lady [of the Rosary] on one of the Christmas octaves for the reasons mentioned [i.e. their devotion] and with so much joy and so many instruments from their country, which with their great celebrations is much to see and admire, to the point that it seems this is all they do; and in this great joy the wonders of God, and the favors, and favors of the Most Holy Virgin Mary, are recognized, for her devotion makes her black children so happy they look out of their minds.[26]

But the celebrations organized by the black brotherhoods were not limited to the liturgical acts prescribed by the Church. They were also occasions for less restrained and solemn manifestations of joy. These celebrations, which took place outside the scope of the church, with music, dance, and food, all sprinkled with a lot of *geribita* (cachaça or sugarcane alcohol), are hardly mentioned in brotherhoods' official records, for obvious reasons, since they were not wanted by the colonial church, the crown, or colonial elites. Certainly, because they were devoid of devotional purposes, the expenses destined to these secular ends rarely appear in the *irmandades*' financial records.[27] During the festivities for the patron saint, black devotees played their instruments, could sing and dance "in their own way" as "happy people," as Friar Santa Maria put it. There is no doubt that the festivities of black confraternities were unique occasions for cultural manifestations for Africans and their descendants in Bahia. In 1786, for example, black devotees of the Virgin of the Rosary in Salvador asked Queen D. Maria I "to be allowed for greater and general applause for the festivity masks, dances in the local language of Angola, with instruments, songs and praises."[28] According to the petitioners, such practices, previously permitted by the authorities, were common in many Christian countries. The appeal from the

26 Frei Agostinho de Santa Maria, *Santuário mariano*, 86. All Portuguese books before 1810 were printed in Lisbon.
27 See, for example, Scarano, *Devoção e escravidão*; Aguiar, "Festas e rituais"; Farias, "*Irmãos de cor*'."
28 AHU, Bahia, cx. 71, doc. 12235 (cota antiga), Requerimento dos Pretos Devotos da Senhora do Rosário da Bahia, 1786. The author is grateful to Maria Inês Cortes de Oliveira for sharing a copy of this document with her.

Virgin of the Rosary devotees presented an interesting justification, although African cultural manifestations took on very different roles, depending on the context in which they became public, as will be explained below.

African customs had a prominent place in public celebrations promoted by the Crown.[29] Africans, with all the peculiarities of their dances, songs, and "exotic" instruments, were present at the triumphal entries, weddings, birthdays, acclamations, and other events of the Portuguese royal family.[30] According to the historian A. Saunders, in Portugal, since the Middle Ages, "events of an official character were frequently marked by the participation of subjugated minority peoples."[31] On these occasions, Moors and Jews were called upon to show their "exotic" songs and dances.[32] The participation of "conquered or converted peoples" was not restricted to civilian processions; they were also present at public religious ceremonies such as bishops' entries, processions, and ecclesiastical visits.

In Lisbon in the fifteenth and sixteenth centuries, in the great processions of Corpus Christi, there was no lack of representation of dances from Jews, Gypsies, and Moors; all this in the midst of clowns, snakes, devils, raised crosses, holy hymns, priests, and nuns.[33] The demonstrations of perceived "exotic" customs were for more than pure entertainment; it was an important opportunity to reaffirm the power of the Portuguese empire over the territories incorporated through commercial, diplomatic, and religious relations.[34]

Since their incorporation into the Portuguese Empire, Africans have also been part of public civil and ecclesiastical processions. In 1451, for instance, black and Canarian dancers participated in the celebrations in honor of the wedding of Leonor of Portugal to Emperor Frederick III.[35] In 1521, moreover,

29 On spectacles by blacks in the Hispanic context, see Miguel A. Valerio, "A Mexican Sangamento? The First Afro-Christian Performance in the Americas," in *Afro-Catholic Festivals in the Americas: Performance, Representation, and the Making of Black Atlantic Tradition*, ed. Cécile Fromont (State College: Pennsylvania State University Press, 2019), 59-72.

30 Marina de Melo e Souza, *Reis negros no Brasil escravista: história da coroação do rei Congo* (Belo Horizontes: Editora da UFMG, 2002), 160.

31 A. C. de C. M. Saunders, *História social dos escravos e libertos negros em Portugal (1441-1555)* (Lisbon: Imprensa Nacional, 1994), 105.

32 On the exotic genre, see Peter Mason, *Infelicities: Representations of the Exotic* (Baltimore: Johns Hopkins University Press, 1998).

33 Pierre Verger, "Procissões e carnaval no Brasil" *Ensaios/Pesquisas* 5 (1980): 3.

34 Ver Silvia Lara, "Significados cruzados: um reinado de congos na Bahia setecentista," in *Carnavais e outras frestas. Ensaios de História Social da Cultura*, ed. Clementina Pereira Cunha (Campinas: UNICAMP, 2002), 71-100.

35 Spain colonized the Canary Islands in the fourteenth century, and Canarians were considered brown and enslaved accordingly.

during the festivities of the entry into Lisbon of King Manuel I with his new queen, the *irmãos* of Lisbon's black Rosary brotherhood, based in the city's Dominican monastery, represented an interlocution, a kind of playful small farce of one act of a popular or palatial character, generally closing with a sung musical number and whose origins date back to the twelfth century.[36] The meanings attributed by Africans and their descendants to these spectacles could differ from the objectives of the Empire. In addition, the performances alluded to African culture, shared and recreated in the diaspora.[37]

The manifestation of African customs was not seen with the same tolerance when they took place on slaves' days off and without the control or sponsorship of imperial and colonial authorities. In 1461, for example, the municipal council of the city of Santarém, in Portugal, banned black people from holding celebrations on Sundays and holy days, a custom sanctioned since the early fifteenth century. They argued when justifying the prohibition that to sustain their celebrations, the slaves stole ducks and chickens, in addition to embezzling money from their masters to buy bread and wine.[38]

Wine in Portugal, *geribita* in Brazil, the consumption of alcoholic beverages was a hallmark of these black celebrations.[39] In his poem about the festivities of Our Lady of the Rosary in Salvador, seventeenth-century Bahian satirist Gregório de Matos (1636-1696) highlights the excessive alcoholic consumption of brandy by the "brazen" devotees.[40] According to the literary

---

36   Saunders, *História social*, 142-143. The Dominicans were the first to institute Rosary brotherhoods, for Europeans, starting in the thirteenth century, and the fifteenth for Afro-descendants: Elizabeth W. Kiddy, "*Congados, Calunga, Candombe*: Our Lady of the Rosary in Minas Gerais, Brazil," *Luso-Brazilian Review* 37, no. 1 (2000): 47-61.

37   Valerio, "A Mexican Sangamento?," 61.

38   Saunders, *História social*, 143-144. Similar complaints were made elsewhere in the Iberian world: see Karen B. Graubart, "'*So color de una cofradía*': Catholic Confraternities and the Development of Afro-Peruvian Ethnicities in Early Colonial Peru," *Slavery and Abolition* 33, no. 1 (2012): 43-64.

39   On alcohol consumption in Afro-Brazilian merrymaking, see Julita Scarano, "Bebida alcoólica na sociedade colonial," in *Festa*, 2: 467-486.

40   "Senhor, os negros juízes/Da Senhora do Rosário / Fazem por uso ordinário / Alarde nestes países: / Como são tão infelizes, / Que por seus negros pecados / Andam sempre mascarados / Contra as leis da polícia, / Ante vossa Senhoria / Pedem licença prostrados. // A um General capitão / Suplica a Irmandade preta, / Que não irão de careta, / Mas descarados irão. / Todo o negregado irmão / Desta Irmandade bendita, / Pendem que se lhe permita / Ir ao alarde enfascados / Não de pólvora atacados / Calçados de geribita" [Your Lordship, in this land, the blacks of the Rosary ordinarily have their festivities. They are so unhappy that, for their black sins, they always go masked against the order of law. They ask for permission kneeling before Your Lordship. The blacks of the brotherhood tell a Captain-General that they will not wear masks, but rather go

scholar Fernando Peres, the poem by Matos was inspired by a prohibition by colonial authorities at the time on African manifestations during the festivities.[41]

Idleness in a slave's life was seen as an opportunity for transgression and therefore a threat to the colonial order. Theft, flight, contempt, and drunkenness could also cover up plans for escapes and rebellions. In view of the evangelizing project, the festivals for patron saints were a fundamental part of devotional life, even though their "excesses" were harshly punished by colonial officials.[42]

The warm reception of black processions in church or state-sponsored celebrations, in contrast to the reluctance to accept communal, intragroup black festivities, draws attention to the danger of the "progressive continuities" trap. As suggested by the historian Silvia Lara, it is necessary to pay attention to the "differences between the theatrical crowning of religious festivals and the processions of black kings of public dynastic festivities." Failure to recognize these differences "implies disregarding which subjects maintain control over the festival."[43] In addition to religious festivals and processions at public events, there is yet another form of manifestation by the black performances.

The Brazilian ethnomusicologist José Ramos Tinhorão, although he did not find documented evidence of the event, suggested the possibility of coronations of festive black kings and queens in Portugal as early as the sixteenth century. For the author, these coronations would be contemporary and, at the same time, "a reflection on the new policy put in practice since D. João II in relation to African business."[44] In addition to the symbolic "recognition" of African royalty, the institution of festive black kings and queens seems to have occupied, in different historical contexts, a function of "mediation" between the constituted powers and the black, enslaved, and free population.

The tradition of crowning kings and queens among slaves and free men in the African diaspora goes beyond the Portuguese slave experience. Since the

unmasked. All the blacks of this blessed confraternity ask to be allowed to drink cachaça on their feast and not be chased by the police]: Gregório de Matos, *Obras completas de Gregório de Matos*, vol. 1 (Salvador: Editora Janaina, 1970), 186.

41   Peres, "Negros e mulatos em Gregório de Matos," *Afro-Ásia* 4 (1967): 73.

42   See particularly, Vera Lucia Amaral Ferlini, "Folguedos, feiras e feriados: aspectos socioeconômicos das festas no mundo dos engenhos," in *Festa*, 2: 449-463.

43   Lara, "Significados cruzados," 90.

44   José Ramos Tinhorão, *Os negros em Portugal: uma presença silenciosa* (Lisbon: Editorial Caminho, 1988), 148.

fifteenth century, cities such as Lisbon and Seville began to face the problem
of controlling the slave population of African origin, resident or in transit, as
these centers had become large slaveholding buildings. The solution found
by the local authorities "was to transfer part of the police responsibility
to the captives themselves, which was done through the appointment of
chiefs chosen from among the members of the slave community deemed
more responsible and reliable."[45] If no Portuguese document on the subject
has reached the hands of contemporary researchers,

> in relation to Spain, it is known that even in the fifteenth century the
> Catholic monarchs Fernand II of Aragon and Isabella of Castile, in an
> order of 11 November 1478, already granted the title of *mayoral* (steward)
> to a black man named Juan de Valladolid, which gave him responsibility
> for black captives and manumitted slaves in Seville, subject by the same
> documents to his judgements in their disputes.[46]

The institution of these stewards crossed the Atlantic and took root in the
Hispanic colonies. The French sociologist Roger Bastide listed a series of
black kings and queens spread across Spanish-American colonies in the
eighteenth and nineteenth centuries. In Hispaniola, there were reports
of black kings or governors, chosen by their respective nations, since the
1540s. Black kings and governors were also elected in Martinique, Cuba,
Colombia, Saint Lucia, Jamaica, Venezuela, Peru, Mexico, Uruguay, and
Argentina. This role almost always carried a mark of ethnic distinction.[47] It
is possible that the national or ethnolinguistic group *cabildos*, or communal
associations, organizations of paramount importance to the history of the
black population in Cuba, originated from this tradition of the election of
black kings and queens.[48]

In the New World, black kings and queens chosen by ethnic groups
maintained in some regions more effective links with colonial power, that

---

45 Ibid., 155.

46 Ibid., 155-156. See Isidoro Moreno, "Plurietnicidad, fiestas y poder: cofradías y fiestas andaluzas
de negros como modelo para la América colonial," in *El mundo festivo en España y América*, ed.
Antonio Garrido Aranda (Cordoba: Universidad de Córdoba, 2005), 169-188; Graubart, "*So color
de una cofradía*"; Carmen Fracchia, "*Black but Human*": *Slavery and the Visual Arts in Hapsburg
Spain, 1480-1700* (Oxford: Oxford University Press, 2019), 48-55.

47 Roger Bastide, *As Américas negras* (São Paulo: DIFEL, 1974), 91-94.

48 Martha Escalona Sánchez, "Matanzas colonial e los cabildos congos," in *Actas del VII Taller
Internacional de África en el Caribe (Ortiz a Lachatañeré)*, ed. Zaylen Clavería Centurión and
Yadine M. Yara González (Santiago de Cuba: Centro Cultural Africano Fernando Ortiz, 2003),
143-148.

is, exercising the function of "control" of the slave community, sometimes acting as an intermediate authority and, at the same time, colonial or provincial authorities.[49] On the other hand, these royal roles did not fail to have a subversive character within the colonial order, supporting revolts and contempt or even petty disputes. It is possible that the spectacular dimension, as well as the political authority of black royalty came to life in the brotherhoods.

The coronations of kings and queens, although not exclusively limited to black brotherhoods, had privileged visibility within these associations, partly because of the preservation of varied written records where they are described. A broadside published in 1729 prohibited black kings in the festivities for the Virgin of the Rosary in Bahia, claiming that "the black people, in order to do that act with grandeur steal even off the altars." The same document states that, at the time of the black kings, "unexplained disorders" such as violent invasions "occurred in the homes of many residents, taking from them slaves on the stocks or prisoners in punishment." For this reason, the Governor and Captain General Vasco Fernandes de Menezes, decreed that from the proclamation of the gang "there is no function of black kings, and only the *juizes* of Nossa Senhora do Rosário can host their parties in the Churches."[50]

Marina de Melo e Souza has suggested that the intense repression of the black kingdoms, associated with the strong and growing influence of Yoruba culture in Bahia, made the nature of festive black kings and queens disappear, and the author found no reference to these kingdoms in the black brotherhood *compromissos* at the beginning of nineteenth century.[51] It is important to note, first, that the omission of the event in confraternal *compromissos* does not necessarily mean its absence or suppression. Marcelo Mac Cord found that in Recife's Rosary brotherhood, in the second half of the nineteenth century, festive kings and queens were not mentioned in *compromissos*, but were elected and continued to be important. The "hierarchies of the king of Congo" ended up constituting an institution separate from the brotherhood, even though it maintained close corporate bonds to it. This independence removed "the hierarchies of the king of Congo" from the control and persecution of the Church in the nineteenth-century process

49   On festive black king and queens' involvement in political movements in Pernambuco, see Marcelo Mac Cord, "O Rosário dos homens pretos de Santo Antônio: Alianças e conflitos na história social do Recife, 1848-1873" (master's thesis, UNICAMP, 2001).

50   AHU, Bahia, Avulso, Caixa 33, doc. 2978, Consulta do CU ao Rei D. João V sobre os abusos do reinado dos negros e seus folguedos, Cópia do Bando que se publicou sobre não haver Reinados nas Festas de Nossa Senhora do Rosário, f. 1 (1729).

51   Melo e Souza, *Reis negros*, 236. See also her chapter in this volume.

of secularization.[52] This institution, in turn, gave rise to the *maracatus* (as black kings were known in the Northeast), which gradually purified from its most political aspects, ended up becoming one of the most beautiful popular *folguedos* (diversion) in Pernambuco.[53] Bastide observed a similar process in the Brazilian Southeast, where the *congadas* (festive king and queen performances), were expelled from churches by secularization, "little by little lost the domain of religion to enter the camp of folklore."[54]

The disturbances caused by black kingdoms and their consequent repression by colonial authorities were not restricted to Bahia. Célia Borges found that in Minas Gerais "local authorities repeatedly asked Portuguese officials in Lisbon for clear provisions that would prevent the exercise of royalty in the brotherhoods."[55] However, despite complaints from local authorities, the Crown never established a definitive policy towards black royalty. What actually happened were localized measures like the one that banned, in 1720, the election of black kings in Serro Frio.

Despite this, black kings continued to be crowned in the Minas brotherhoods throughout the eighteenth and nineteenth centuries. In the year 1771, a Mariana parish priest denounced a series of disturbances in the city involving black kings and queens. In one of the complaints, he said that the king and queen of the city's Rosary brotherhood came to the disrepute of going to the public jail and demanding the release of a few prisoners. What really worried the cleric, then, was not the "harmless" ritual role played by kings at the brotherhood patron's feast, but the actual authority of these characters in the daily life of black community.[56]

It is likely that the kings elected in Bahia in the early eighteenth century also had authority recognized by their subjects. And, precisely based on this delegated power, they invaded houses, removing slaves from the stocks and from punishment. The prohibition of black kings, proclaimed in 1729, was not respected by Afro-Bahian brotherhoods. At least that is what some of

---

52   On the secularization of this practice, see Mac Cord, *O Rosário de D. Antonio: irmandades negras, alianças e conflitos na historia social do Recife, 1848-1872* (Recife: Ufpe, 2005).

53   On *maracatus* in Pernambuco, see Leonardo Dantas da Silva, "A instituição do Rei do Congo e sua presença nos maracatus," in *Estudos sobre a escravidão negra*, ed. Silva, vol. 2 (Recife: FUNDAJ, 1988), 13-53; Peter Fryer, *Rhythms of Resistance: African Musical Heritage in Brazil* (London: Pluto Press, 2000).

54   Roger Bastide, *As religiões africanas no Brasil: contribuição a uma sociologia das interpretações de civilizações*, vol. 1 (São Paulo: Pioneira, 1971), 178.

55   Célia Borges, "Devoção branca de homens negros: As irmandades do Rosário em Minas Gerais no século XVIII" (Ph.D. diss., Universidade Federal Fluminense, 1998), 96. See also her chapter in this volume.

56   Ibid., 97.

the approved *compromissos* attest, without restriction by royal authority, in the second half of the eighteenth century. The black Rosary brotherhood in the parish of Matriz da Vitória, for example, determined in their *compromisso*, approved in Lisbon in 1767, that the elected officials should define "the king and queen for the year on the following Sunday, on the day of the feast, who will then notify their masters, and determine the day to crown themselves so that everyone will know."[57] Almost forty years after the proclamation of the broadside that prohibited black reigns, this brotherhood chose its king and queen on the Sunday following the annual celebration. The chosen black monarchs reigned for a year and culminated their term in a brotherhood ceremony. At first, all the efforts during this period would be concentrated in collecting donations for the ceremony's organization, mainly through begging.

The black royalty chosen by the *irmãos* of the Rosary *irmandade* in the parish of Matriz da Vitória were to be presented to their masters before their coronation. It is possible that their masters, mentioned in the text of the *compromisso*, were the constituted authorities. In this sense, the presentation ritual could be both a gesture of submission by the black *irmãos*, and an acknowledgment by colonial authorities of the practice. Another hypothesis would be the possibility of the masters being the owners of the elected slaves. In that case, before taking on this outstanding position, they would need the approval of their masters. The Brotherhood of the Rosary of Vila de Santo Antônio in Recife, for example, established that "every brother or sister, whether black, white, or brown who by their devotion wants to serve as king or queen could not participate in the election if those who are captive did not have permission from their master" to prevent future problems with those elected to the positions of king and queen.[58]

The Rosary brotherhood at parish of São Pedro Velho also elected its kings and queens, despite prohibitions. At least that was how it was established in its *compromisso*, approved in 1767. It is worth noting that the wording of the chapter that regulates the election of the king and queen said that filling these positions was not mandatory.[59] Borges suggests that pressure from church members and Crown officials against coronations in the brotherhoods led many of them to abolish these positions, passing their duties to

---

57 ANTT, Chancelarias Antigas, Ordem de Cristo, Livro 297, Compromisso de Nossa Senhora do Rosário da Matriz de Nossa Senhora da Vitória da cidade da Bahia, ff. 58-63 (1767).

58 ANTT, Chancelarias Antigas, Ordem de Cristo, Livro 283, Compromisso da Irmandade do Rosário dos homens pretos da Vila de S. Antonio do Recife, f. 117 (1767).

59 Compromisso da Irmandade do Rosário dos Pretos na Matriz de São Pedro Velho, f. 170v.

the *juizes*. In other brotherhoods, *compromissos* were simply silent on this point, which could mean that there was a strategy by the *irmãos* to escape pressure from the authorities and, in the same way, facilitate the approval of their statutes at higher levels.[60]

In addition to the omission, the change in terms was also used by black members to circumvent the vigilance of ecclesiastical and crown officials. The Rosary brotherhood of Vila de Nova Real de El Rei, for example, concerned with holding the annual patron's feast, instituted in the year 1800 a special board. In addition to the presiding *juiz* and the ordinary *juizes*, the brotherhood also elected a male *juiz* and a female *juiza*.[61] The black *irmãos* of Itabira, Minas Gerais, moreover, also opted to create male and female *juizes*.[62] Thus, the monarchs became a *reis-juizes*, losing their title but not their majesty.

The statutes of the brotherhoods of Vitória and São Pedro Velho were particularly succinct when dealing with the positions of king and queen. There is a marked contrast between the concision with regard to black royalty and the careful detailing of the duties, rights, and obligations of the other board officials. I believe that the brief mention as well as the omission and the new title were part of an effort to avoid dangerous polemics that would affect the good relationship with authorities. The *irmãos* of the parish of Freguesia de N. S. do Rosário da Várzea, in Recife, abused their decision when dealing with black royalty. The text is short and to the point: "In this brotherhood due to ancient traditions pledges to make an officer in the mantle of the king and queen of Congo who pay 40 *réis* [the basic monetary unit] worth of contributions each to help with the expenses of the annual patron feast and more expenses for our church."[63] In this sense, discretion could be a strategy to minimize the importance of the event in the eyes of the authorities responsible for approving *compromissos*. For this reason, I believe that further details about the coronations and feasts of the black kings and queens were not described in *compromissos*, since they were tolerated events, but not fully accepted by ecclesiastical authorities.[64]

The tradition of festive black kings and queens in eighteenth-century Bahia points to connections with Central African culture and people

---

60 Borges, "Devoção branca," 95-96.
61 Compromisso da Irmandade do Rosário dos homens pretos na Vila Nova Real de El Rei, cap. III (1800).
62 Borges, "Devoção branca de homens negros," 96.
63 ANTT, Chancelarias Antigas, Ordem de Cristo, Livro 297, Compromisso da Irmandade do Rosário dos homens pretos da Freguesia e matriz de N. S. do Rosário da Várzea de Pernambuco, f. 179 (1767).
64 Souza, *Reis negros*, 193.

in the region. With the exception of Benedict of Cairu, all Afro-Bahian brotherhoods who left record of royal coronations had the Virgin of the Rosary as their patroness and mentioned their "Angolan" members in their *compromissos*.

Nina Rodrigues linked the coronations to the large presence of Central Africans in the black population of certain regions of Brazil. This explains, according to the author, the persistence of the practice in late-nineteenth-century Pernambuco, while it disappeared in Bahia in the eighteenth century. Notwithstanding her error in thinking the practice had disappeared in Bahia in the eighteenth century, Rodrigues established a link, later confirmed by several scholars, between Afro-Brazilian festive kings and queens and the Afro-descendants from Angola present in Rosary brotherhoods.[65] According to Luís Viana Filho, another scholar of the black presence in Bahia, "the idea of king, of a royal court, in religious solemnities is a fact that points to a Bantu presence. It is peculiar to that culture."[66] Julita Scarano, a researcher of black brotherhoods in eighteenth-century Diamantina, also links the performance to Angolan and Congolese culture.[67] Souza in a more recent study, arrived at the same conclusion.[68]

The coronation of kings and queens among brotherhoods with other patrons or even of other ethnic groups was exceptional both in Portugal and Portuguese America.[69] In Lisbon, in the 1730s, at least two black brotherhoods elected king and queen: the Rosary brotherhood of the convent of Salvador elected an Angolan royal couple; and that of St. Benedict, a Mina one.[70] In Portugal as well the coronations were more frequent in Angolan and Congolese Rosary brotherhoods.[71]

The Central African origins of the tradition, observed by scholars from different epochs, was until recently interpreted through prejudice and

65 Raimundo Nina Rodrigues, *Os africanos no Brasil* (São Paulo: Editora Nacional, 1988), 32

66 Luís Viana Filho, *O negro na Bahia* (Rio de Janeiro: Nova Fronteira, 1988).

67 Scarano, *Devoção e escravidão*, 113.

68 Souza, *Reis negros*, 192.

69 On the coronation of "Minas" kings and queens in Rio de Janeiro, see Mariza de Carvalho Soares, *Devotos da cor: identidade étnica, religiosidade e escravidão no Rio de Janeiro, século XVIII* (Rio de Janeiro: Civilização Brasileira, 2000), 154-161. As other chapters in this volume show, in Spanish America the case was different.

70 Didier Lahon, *Os negros no coração do Império: uma memória a resgatar, séculos XV-XIX* (Lisbon: Secretariado Coordenador dos Programas Multiculturais, 1999), 71; Maria do Rosário Pimentel, "El Rei do Congo em Portugal e no Brasil: da realidade à ficção," in *Portugal e Brasil no advento do mundo moderno*, ed. Pimentel (Lisbom: Colibri, 2001), 387.

71 Pimentel, "El Rei do Congo," 358; Lahon, *Os negros em Portugal, séculos XV a XIX* (Lisbon: Comissão Nacional para as Comemorações dos Descobrimentos Portugueses, 1999), 146-147.

ignorance of the experience of African slaves and freepersons in the Lusophone world.[72] Recent studies, attentive to the importance of African
references in the diaspora, suggest that the tradition should be interpreted
by attending to its Central African political and religious aspects. In this
manner, the African influence on the ritual and formal aspects of the
performance (dance, music, rhythms), understood as reminiscences frozen
in time, became a fundamental interpretive key for a deeper reading of the
phenomenon. In this sense, Souza calls attention to the political and social
representations of initial contacts between African and Europeans, most of
all what it says about the conversion of the Congo ruler and the formation of
Central African Catholicism.[73] According to the late Elizabeth Kiddy, the
tradition among brotherhoods and other contexts expressed "the legendary
political and ritual power of the King of Kongo, well known both among
Central African slaves and among Europeans," representing "the triumph
of a continuing strategy to preserve a link to Africa."[74] Cécile Fromont has
convincingly traced the practice to a Congolese martial dance, known as
sangamento, that was well recorded in the region. *Sangamento* constituted
a ritual performance that accompanied the paying of tributes and the
making of vows of fealty to the Christian ruler of Congo, recognizing the
kingdom's political hierarchy. It "consisted of ritual battles that reenacted
the two successive foundations of the kingdom, first, in the distant past,
by Lukeni, the original civilizing hero of Kongo oral history, and then by
Afonso, the realm's first great Christian ruler."[75]

Conclusion

The patron's feast was the main activity for Afro-Bahian brotherhoods. Held
annually, it was the most notable and most publicly visible moment for the
irmãos. The ceremony could bring great prestige to the board in particular,

72 Luís Viana Filho, for example, emphasized the existence of a Bantu "temperament" which,
more open to integration and syncretism, had a fundamental tendency toward "cultivating
public exteriorities, dances, and festivals on the streets": *O negro*, 92-96.
73 Souza, *Reis negros*, 181. See also Cécile Fromont, *The Art of Conversion: Christian Visual
Culture in the Kingdom of Kongo* (Chapel Hill: University of North Carolina Press, 2014).
74 Kiddy, "Who is the King of Congo?: A New Look at African and Afro-Brazilian Kings in Brazil,"
in *Central Africans and Cultural Transformations in American Diaspora*, ed. Linda Heywood
(Cambridge: Cambridge University Press, 2002), 182.
75 Fromont, "Dancing for the King of Congo from Early Modern Central Africa to Slavery-Era
Brazil," *Colonial Latin American Review* 22, no. 2 (2013), 188.

but also to the entire brotherhood, thereby attracting new members. In addition, the patron's feast was an example of the brotherhood's ability to organize funeral processions, which, together with the guarantee of burials in a sacred place, was a source of income and an important selling point for new members. There was still another side to this festivity, including spaces for dancing, music, food, and alcohol. On this side of the festivities, the elections and coronations of kings and queens were particularly relevant. Confraternal coronations attest to the presence of Central African culture in eighteenth-century Bahia, yet that culture acquired its own life in the Bahian context. In sum, I consider that the festivities promoted by Afro-Bahian brotherhoods are privileged spaces for the study of brotherhoods' internal dynamics as well as their relations to their broader slavocratic world.

About the author

Lucilene Reginaldo is professor of history at the Universidade Estadual de Campinas. Her researches focuses on the Church and black brotherhoods in colonial Bahia, Brazil. She is the author of *Os Rosários dos Angolas: irmandades de africanos e crioulos na Bahia Setecentista,* for which she was awarded the Prêmio Katia Mattoso for best book on Bahian history in 2011.

Bibliography

Aguiar, Marcos Magalhães. "Vila Rica dos confrades. A sociabilidade confrarial entre negros e mulatos no século XVIII." Master's thesis, University of São Paulo, 1993.
Bastide, Roger. *As Américas negras.* São Paulo: DIFEL, 1974.
—. *As religiões africanas no Brasil: contribuição a uma sociologia das interpretações de civilizações.* São Paulo: Pioneira, 1971.
Borges, Célia. "Devoção branca de homens negros: As irmandades do Rosário em Minas Gerais no século XVIII." Ph.D. diss. Universidade Federal Fluminense, 1998.
Eugênio, Alisson. "Tensões entre os visitadores eclesiásticos e as irmandades negras no século XVIII mineiro." *Revista Brasileira de História* 22, no. 14 (2002): 33-46.
Farias, Sara Oliveira. "'Irmãos de cor, de caridade e de crença': a Irmandade do Rosário do Pelourinho na Bahia do século XIX." Master's thesis. Universidade Federal da Bahia, 1997.
Ferlini, Vera Lucia Amaral. "Folguedos, feiras e feriados: aspectos socioeconômicos das festas no mundo dos engenhos." In *Festa: cultura e sociabilidade na América*

portuguesa, edited by Istaván Jancsó and Iris Kantor, 2:449-463. Sao Paulo: Imprensa Oficial, 2001.

Fromont, Cécile. "Dancing for the King of Congo from Early Modern Central Africa to Slavery Era Brazil." *Colonial Latin American Review* 22, no. 2 (2013): 184-208.

——. *The Art of Conversion: Christian Visual Culture in the Kingdom of Kongo.* Chapel Hill: University of North Carolina Press, 2014.

Fryer, Peter. *Rhythms of Resistance: African Musical Heritage in Brazil.* London: Pluto Press, 2000.

Graubart, Karen B. "*So color de una cofradía*': Catholic Confraternities and the Development of Afro-Peruvian Ethnicities in Early Colonial Peru." *Slavery and Abolition* 33, no. 1 (2012): 43-64.

Kaplan, Paul H. D. *The Rise of the Black Magus in Western Art.* Ann Arbor: UMI Research Press, 1985.

Kiddy, Elizabeth W. "Congados, Calunga, Candombe: Our Lady of the Rosary in Minas Gerais, Brazil." *Luso-Brazilian Review* 37, no. 1 (2000): 47-61.

——. "Who is the King of Congo?: A New Look at African and Afro-Brazilian Kings in Brazil." in *Central Africans and Cultural Transformations in American Diaspora,* edited by Linda Heywood, 153-182. Cambridge: Cambridge University Press, 2002.

Lahon, Didier. *Os negros no coração do Império: uma memória a resgatar, séculos XV-XIX.* Lisbon: Secretariado Coordenador dos Programas Multiculturais, 1999.

Lara, Silvia. "Significados cruzados: um reinado de congos na Bahia setecentista." In *Carnavais e outras frestas: ensaios de História Social da Cultura,* edited by Clementina Pereira Cunha, 71-100. Campinas: UNICAMP, 2002.

Mac Cord, Marcelo. "O Rosário dos homens pretos de Santo Antônio: Alianças e conflitos na história social do Recife, 1848-1873." Master's thesis, UNICAMP, 2001.

Mason, Peter. *Infelicities: Representations of the Exotic.* Baltimore: Johns Hopkins University Press, 1998.

Matos, Gregório de. *Obras completas de Gregório de Matos.* Salvador: Editora Janaina, 1970. 7 vols.

Moreno, Isidoro. "Plurietnicidad, fiestas y poder: cofradías y fiestas andaluzas de negros como modelo para la América colonial." In *El mundo festivo en España y América,* edited by Antonio Garrido Aranda, 169-188. Cordoba: University of Córdoba, 2005.

Paiva, José Pedro. "Etiqueta e cerimonias públicas na esfera da Igreja (séculos XVII-XVIII)." In *Festa,* 1:75-94.

Peres, Fernando. "Negros e mulatos em Gregório de Matos." *Afro-Ásia* 4 (1967): 59-75.

Pimentel, Maria do Rosário. "El Rei do Congo em Portugal e no Brasil: da realidade à ficção." In *Portugal e Brasil no advento do mundo moderno,* edited by Pimentel, 371-392. Lisbon: Colibri, 2001.

Reis, João José. *A morte é uma festa: ritos fúnebres e revolta popular no Brasil do século XIX*. São Paulo: Companhia das Letras, 1991.

Reginaldo, Lucilene. *Os Rosários dos Angolas. Irmandade de africanos e crioulos na Bahia Setecentista*. Sao Paulo: Alameda, 2011.

Rodrigues, Raimundo Nina. *Os africanos no Brasil*. Sao Paulo: Editora Nacional, 1988.

Sánchez, Martha Escalona. "Matanzas colonial e los cabildos congos." In *Actas del VII Taller Internacional de África en el Caribe (Ortiz a Lachatañeré)*," edited by Zaylen Clavería Centurión and Yadine M. Yara González, 143-148. Santiago de Cuba: Centro Cultural Africano Fernando Ortiz, 2003.

Santa Maria, Frei Agostinho de. *Santuário Mariano e História das imagens milagrosas de Nossa Senhora milagrosamente manifestadas e aparecidas em o Arcebispado da Bahia*. Salvador: Instituto Histórico e Geográfico da Bahia, [1707-1723], 1949. 9 vols.

Saunders, A. C. de C. M. *História social dos escravos e libertos negros em Portugal (1441-1555)*, Lisbon: Imprensa Nacional, 1994.

Scarano, Julita. *Devoção e escravidão: irmandade de N.S. do Rosário dos Pretos do Distrito Diamantino no Século XVIII*. São Paulo: Editora Nacional, 1978.

——. "Bebida alcoólica na sociedade colonial." In *Festa*, 2:467-486.

Silva, Leonardo Dantas da. "A instituição do Rei do Congo e sua presença nos maracatus." In *Estudos sobre a escravidão negra*, edited by Silva, 2:13-53. Recife: FUNDAJ, 1988.

Soares, Mariza de Carvalho. *Devotos da cor: identidade étnica, religiosidade e escravidão no Rio de Janeiro, século XVIII*. Rio de Janeiro: Civilização Brasileira, 2000.

Souza, Marina de Melo. *Reis negros no Brasil escravista: história da coroação do rei Congo*. Belo Horizonte: Editora da UFMG, 2002.

Tinhorão, José Ramos. *Os negros em Portugal: uma presença silenciosa*. Lisbon: Caminho, 1988.

Torres, Manuel Cerqueira. *Narração panerírico-histórica das festividades con que a Cidade da Bahia solenizou os felicíssimos desposórios da Princesa Nossa Senhora com o Sereníssimo Senhor Infante Dom Pedro*. In *O movimento academicista no Brasil, 1641-1820/22*, edited by José Aderaldo Castello, 3.3:191-227. São Paulo: Conselho Estadual de Cultura, [1760] 1970-1978.

Verger, Pierre. *Procissões e carnaval no Brasil*. Salvador: UFB, 1980.

Viana Filho, Luís. *O negro na Bahia*. Rio de Janeiro: Nova Fronteira, 1988.

Vide, D. Sebastião Monteiro da. "Notícias do Arcebispado da Bahia para suplicar a Sua Majestade: em favor do culto divino e das almas, 1712." *Revista do Instituto Histórico e Geográfico Brasileiro* 54 ([1712] 1981): 323-364.

Afterword

Indigenous and Black Confraternities in Colonial Latin
America

Nicole von Germeten
Oregon State University

Brotherhood, sisterhood, community formation, even allyship... the history of
indigenous and African-descent Catholic organizations in the Iberian Empires
illuminates twenty-first century readers on all of the above. On the less positive
side, archival documentation generated by these groups, known as *cofradías*
and *hermandades*, also exposes stories of racialized embodiment, imperial
religious proselytization, and the divide and conquer strategy so effective for
maintaining a massive transoceanic empire in an era of slow communication.
This collection of essays has brought together scholars of Portuguese and
Spanish America with amazing breadth, all discussing this fundamental
institution, in locations as far-flung as Santiago de Chile, Lima, Mexico City, and
Salvador de Bahia. Many of the excellent essays in this volume help complicate
traditional interpretations of religious organizations and push us to go further.
For example, Ximena Gómez evoked visual and material aspects of *cofradía*
life to stress the *cofrades* and *cofradas* as active participants in their own pious
display, which most likely sought to impress their peers. The common conflicts
caused by jockeying for prominent positions in processions backs up this
competitiveness among urban *castas*. In this Afterword, while acknowledging
the contributors' deep and incisive scholarship, I take advantage of their
ideas as a springboard to jump in a less examined area: multiethnic African,
African-descent, and indigenous brother/sisterhoods as political organizations.

For decades, scholars have noticed the political aspects of both indigenous
cofradías and Afro-Brazilian brotherhoods.[1] As noted throughout this volume,

---

[1]   See John Chance and William B. Taylor, "Cofradías and Cargos: An Historical Perspective
on the Mesoamerican Civil-Religious Hierarchy," *American Ethnologist* 12, no. 1 (1985): 1-26; and

---

Javiera Jaque Hidalgo and Miguel A. Valerio. *Indigenous and Black Confraternities in Colonial
Latin America: Negotiating Status through Religious Practices.* Amsterdam: Amsterdam University
Press, 2022
DOI: 10.5117/ 9789463721547_CONC

sodalities and confraternities of various kinds represented a reaction to the conditions of imperialism and enslavement, often based on colonial identities relating to race and place of origin. While they helped their members survive, these organizations also provided opportunities for celebrations, socializing, and the promise of a "good death," which was interpreted as a communal remembrance of one's life and a coming together of friends and acquaintances to honor one's path to the afterlife and pray for the eternal fate of members' souls. It is somewhat less common to discuss these groups as a kind of training for citizenship within nineteenth-century nation states, although for centuries, *cofrades* and *cofradas* organized elections, enjoyed a variable degree of autonomy, and both raised and managed their own funds.[2]

Hints of politicalization can be seen even in medieval cofradías. In the final essay in this volume, Lucilene Reginaldo reminded readers that the institution of crowning kings and queens as part of yearly festivities combines with the Iberian strategy of allowing a governor or steward to represent groups of enslaved Africans, a policy that began in places like Seville (see Karen Graubert's discussion of the *alcalde* there), and Lisbon, but extended to the Caribbean. Reginaldo notes that the elected kings and queens of Rosario brotherhoods faced suspicion for their recognized authority over other African-descent residents of Rio de Janeiro. In Mexico City, as presented in Cristina Verónica Masferrer León's essay, an Angolan king and queen led a movement of group mourning over an enslaved woman's death by abuse, led to fears of riots and an, albeit ineffective, suppression of cofradías. In the case of indigenous festivities, the essay by Enrique Normando Cruz and Grit Kirstin Koeltzsch moved away from colonial exploitation to highlight how these events instead reinforced the authority of ethnic leaders. The observations of scholars such as Graubert, who researched deeply into the archival documents generated by diocesan courts, can attest to many cases relating to cofradía leaders' assertions of autonomy from local Spaniards, even if this required proclaiming a stronger tie to race labels such as *pardo, mulato,* or *moreno.*[3]

A.J.R. Russell-Wood, "Black and Mulatto Brotherhoods in Colonial Brazil: A Study in Collective Behavior," *Hispanic American Historical Review* 54, no. 4 (1974): 567-602.

2   The best examples of scholarship crossing the bridge from imperial subjects to political citizens of modern nation states include Philip A. Howard, *Changing History: Afro-Cuban Cabildos and Societies of Color in the Nineteenth Century* (Lafayette: Louisiana State University Press, 1998); and Elizabeth Kiddy, *Blacks of the Rosary: Memory and History in Minas Gerais, Brazil* (University Park: Penn State University Press, 2007).

3   See Nicole von Germeten, *Black Blood Brotherhoods: Confraternities and Social Mobility for Afro-Mexicans* (Gainesville: University Press of Florida, 2006), 188-220, for several examples of conflicts relating to control of resources and access to leadership.

Indigenous cofradías helped shape the long transition from pre-colonial local identities through to participation in rebellions and insurgencies in the eighteenth and nineteenth centuries, and even to the pilgrimages that persist to the twenty-first century. While resistance to Spanish rule often manifested itself in violence, religious organizations more steadily affirmed community ties across the centuries. Laura Dierksmeier's contribution offers numerous examples of the Nahua Christianity that can be found in cofradías in New Spain, as well as noting the many other organizations that maintained indigenous rituals and ways of thinking about the divine and worship in the Viceroyalty of Peru. Confraternity documents used Nahuatl in their accounts, and processions included native costumes for decades after the Spanish invasion. Angelica Serna Jeri focuses on the "embeddedness" of landscape which strengthened indigenous rituals for centuries – and continues to do so to the present day. This is a key distinction to keep in mind when looking at African-descent versus indigenous organizations – the urban and rural differences, and the ways that place and geography inform their history in diverse and distinctive ways.

We can find a burgeoning political consciousness among urban sodality participants who defined themselves as upwardly mobile tradesmen and skilled artisans. As Krystle Farman Sweda aptly stated in her essay, multi-generational and interracial connections within parishes hosting cofradías need further study. Jaime Valenzuela Márquez also urged us to contextualize ethnically diverse brotherhoods within their urban settings. In response these contributors' calls to action, a brief discussion of the regional center of Valladolid, Michoacán (now Morelia, Mexico) can provide a useful test case. Morelia's notarial, parish, and diocesan archives offer plentiful data attesting to how multiethnic working men in the eighteenth century moved from pious participants' Baroque religiosity towards citizenry through their involvement in confraternities. It cannot be a coincidence that a group of men, all of them members and leaders of local *cofradías de castas* who labeled themselves *plebe*, organized for a political goal in the precise time and place that shaped the education, and perhaps also the revolutionary outlook, of the future insurgent priests Miguel de Hidalgo y Costilla and José María de Morelos.

African-descent men and women living in Valladolid organized, led, and joined *cofradías* from the late sixteenth century until the early nineteenth-century insurgency era and even beyond. For my 2006 book *Black Blood Brothers: Confraternities and Social Mobility for Afro-Mexicans*, I analyzed over four thousand baptism, marriage, and funeral records to trace general trends over time in terms of the very basic life contours of this group of

Valladolid residents. From the mid-seventeenth century until the end of the eighteenth century, an increasing number of infants, inscribed with the labels of *negra/o, morena/o, parda/o,* and *mulata/o* at the baptism font, were born into legal freedom. From 1597 to 1798, the number of babies baptized with "unknown fathers," (the presiding priest's term for a father not present at the baptismal font), decreased from over 76% to under 30%. Over the course of two centuries, dynasties of prominent men carrying the labels of *pardo, mulato,* and *mestizo* began to lead the two enduring *cofradías de castas* in the town. The first of these organizations was dedicated to the Incarnation of Christ and Saint Blaise. The more famous and long-lasting local *cofradía* was known as the *Rosario de los mulatos,* although members used the term *pardo* to describe themselves.[4]

Starting by reading all of the existing confraternity record books, I attempted to do a prosopography of certain families who passed on leadership roles over the generations. Using a list of around 200 confraternity members and leaders, I tried to uncover their biographies through the traces they left in their interactions with parish priests. Unfortunately, I could not find out too much about African-descent women who led these organizations, because of the anonymity of their names (such as the very common Ana, Juana or María *negra*), but the men who played active roles in *cofradías* tended to have Spanish last names which stand out in the documents. In very general terms, the founding members and early leaders of these *cofradías* changed their status from enslaved to free in the course of their lives. Some may have ended up in Valladolid at the end of journeys from Europe or Africa, and others moved into this regional urban center from the surrounding countryside. The men who held leadership positions in Rosario and Incarnation and Saint Blaise tended to come from families of urban craftsmen with a wide range of race labels applied in their encounters with bureaucrats and clerics. They never received the honorific *don,* but they did refer to themselves as *maestros* of their crafts and trades. Evidence suggests that these men lived into their fifties and beyond, and married multiple times in succession, as their wives most likely suffered ailments relating to frequent pregnancies and childbirth. Their wives and children, like them, experienced or crafted fluid identities encompassing a variety of

4   See Germeten, *Black Blood Brothers,* 104-158 for the history of these *cofradías* and their members. The classic book on the rise of racially mixed plebeians in New Spain is R. Douglas Cope, *The Limits of Racial Domination: Plebeian Society in Colonial Mexico City, 1660-1720* (Madison: University of Wisconsin Press, 1994). More recently, for another superb urban study, see Pablo Miguel Sierra Silva, *Urban Slavery in Colonial Mexico: Puebla de los Ángeles, 1531-1706* (Cambridge: Cambridge University Press, 2018).

race labels, although usually they did not form family ties with an *español* or *española*. This group of men began to lead the Rosary confraternity in the late seventeenth century, and handed down their positions for the next century or more.

One of the most fascinating men of African descent who led both the cofradía del Rosario and a small 1766 political movement was a *maestro arquitecto* named Diego Durán. Born in 1721 to a woman labeled both *mulata* and *india* and a father described as *mulato*, Durán descended on the maternal side from a family of renowned local builders, credited for the beautiful Valladolid/Morelia cathedral and other superb structures that draw tourists to the city into the twenty-first century. Durán married four times over the course of his life, with seven known children, all but one from his final wife. He appears multiple times in the notarial records of the city, inspecting properties, making loans, and serving as an executor of last wills and testaments. He began his leadership of the Rosary confraternity in 1776, and worked for the group up until his final days in 1795.

In his mid-40s, Durán organized 150 Valladolid self-described plebeian men to petition the viceroy in Mexico City for their favorite candidate to continue as *alcalde mayor* (an honorary judicial appointment) of the province of Michoacán. Many of the petitioners came from the local families who had led *casta* cofradías over the course of decades. They argued for the incumbent *alcalde mayor* on the grounds of his care for the poor, orphans, and indigenous people. According to the petition, not only had this *alcalde* helped increase the prosperity of the region, he also reduced the government fees that residents had to pay, and he seemed immune to the temptations of wealth and power. Although his *cofrades* did not have the education to sign this document, Durán used his literacy and well-established good reputation to give a voice to his peers so they could communicate their will on issues beyond the sacred, social, self-help, and celebratory foci typical of their cofradías.

My comments in this Afterword aim to inspire future paths for scholarship. Although all scholars of the Iberian world recognize the strong ideological and practical cooperation between church and state in the Spanish and Portuguese empires, politicizing cofradías highlights their importance outside of what non-specialists might perceive as "just" the religious and pious realm. Now more than ever, it is vitally important to acknowledge the long tradition of activism and political organization which energizes the global African Diaspora. Along with enduring rebel communities and violent revolt, cofradías provide a complicated and detailed paper trail documenting the centuries of resistance to European colonialism in the Americas. The essays in this volume offer important contributions to this critical chapter in African Diaspora history, one which we cannot ignore any longer. I invite the contributors and other cofradía scholars to continue to collaborate and communicate the history of organizing among Africans and their descendants in the Americas.

About the author

Nicole von Germeten, a professor of Latin American History at Oregon State University, has worked as the Director of the School of History, Philosophy, and Religious studies since 2017. She received her PhD from the University of California Berkeley in 2003 with research funded by the Fulbright Garcia Robles Scholarship and the Muriel McKevitt Sonne Endowment. She was a Fellow at the Princeton Center for the Study of Religion in 2004 and was affiliated with the Stanford University Center for Latin American Studies in 2008 and 2009. She has contributed essays, reviews, and articles in close to sixty edited volumes and academic journals. She has published three single-authored books and one edited book-length translation since 2006, most recently *Profit and Passion: Transactional Sex in Colonial Mexico* (California, 2018). Her fifth book, coming out in 2022 with the University of Nebraska Press, *The Enlightened Patrolman: The Early History of Law Enforcement in Mexico City*, examines how the Spanish viceroys attempted to modernize policing to suppress popular revolt and to curb what they viewed as an out-of-control drinking culture. This book focuses on the perspective of the men walking the beat. Her previous publications range in topics from sexuality, religion, legal history, and gender in Spain and the Iberian empires, to Afro-descended populations in Spanish America, Catholic brotherhoods and Jesuit proselytization. Her scholarship has also explored transactional sex, honor, violence, witchcraft, sodomy, and suicide. She is currently writing a manuscript entitled *Death in Old Mexico: The 1789 Dongo Murders* and a translation from Spanish to English of an 1869 novel which focuses on the same case.

Bibliography

Chance, John, and William B. Taylor. "Cofradías and Cargos: An Historical Perspective on the Mesoamerican Civil-Religious Hierarchy." *American Ethnologist* 12, no. 1 (1985), 1-26.

Cope, R. Douglas. *The Limits of Racial Domination: Plebeian Society in Colonial Mexico City, 1660-1720.* Madison: University of Wisconsin Press, 1994.

Germeten, Nicole von. *Black Blood Brotherhoods: Confraternities and Social Mobility for Afro- Mexicans*. Gainesville: University Press of Florida, 2006.

Howard, Philip A. *Changing History: Afro-Cuban Cabildos and Societies of Color in the Nineteenth Century*. Lafayette: Louisiana State University Press, 1998.

Kiddy, Elizabeth. *Blacks of the Rosary: Memory and History in Minas Gerais, Brazil*. University Park: Penn State University Press, 2007.

Russell-Wood, A.J.R. "Black and Mulatto Brotherhoods in Colonial Brazil: A Study in Collective Behavior." *Hispanic American Historical Review* 54, no. 4 (1974): 567-602.

Sierra Silva, Pablo Miguel. *Urban Slavery in Colonial Mexico: Puebla de los Ángeles, 1531- 1706*. Cambridge: Cambridge University Press, 2018.

Bibliography

Abercrombie, Thomas. "Articulación doble y etnogénesis." In *Reproducción y transformación de las sociedades andinas Siglos XVI-XX*, edited by Segundo Moreno and Frank Salomon, 197-212. Quito: Abya Yala, 1991.

Acosta, Antonio. "Los clérigos doctrineros y la economía colonial (Lima, 1600-1630)." *Allpanchis* 19 (1982): 117-149.

Adams, Richard. *Etnias en evolución social: estudios de Guatemala y Centroamérica.* Mexico City: UAM, 1995.

Andrade, Mário de. *Os congos: danças dramáticas do Brasil.* Belo Horizonte: Instituto Nacional do Livro, 1982.

Andreoni, João Antonio [André João Antonil]. *Cultura e opulência do Brasil.* Sao Paulo: Companhia Editora Nacional, [1711] 1966.

Adrián, Mónica. "El espacio Sagrado y el ejercicio del poder. Las doctrinas de Chayanta durante la segunda mitad del siglo XVIII." In *Actas del IV Congreso internacional de Etnohistoria*, edited by José Luis Martínez, 17-37. Lima: PUCP, 1998.

—. "Estrategias políticas de los curas de Charkas en un contexto de reformas y de conflictividad creciente." *Andes* 11 (2000): 135-160.

—. "Los curatos rurales en la provincia de Chayanta." *DATA* 6 (1996): 97-117.

Aguirre Beltrán, Gonzalo. *La población negra de México.* Mexico City: FCE, 1972.

Alberro, Solange. *Inquisición y Sociedad en México, 1571-1700.* Mexico City: FCE, 2004.

—. "Las representaciones y realidades familiares de los negros bozales en la predicación de Alonso de Sandoval (Cartagena de Indias, 1627) y Nicolás Duque de Estrada (La Habana, 1796)." In *La familia en el mundo iberoamericano*, edited by Pilar Gonzalbo and Cecilia Rabell, 73-89. Mexico City: IIS-UNAM, 1994.

Allen, Catherine J. *The Hold Life Has: Coca and Cultural Identity in an Andean Community.* Washington, D.C.: Smithsonian Institution Press, 1988.

—, and Julia Meyerson. *Foxboy: Intimacy and Aesthetics in Andean Stories.* Austin: University of Texas Press, 2011.

Amin, Sahid. "Testimonio de cargo y discurso judicial: el caso de Chauri Chaura." In *Debates post coloniales. Una introducción a los estudios de la sulbalternidad*, comp. Silvia Rivera Cusicanqui y Rossana Barragán, 119-156. La Paz: Historia-Aruwiyiri- SEPHIS, 1997.

Araya Espinoza, Alejandra, and Jaime Valenzuela Márquez, eds. *América colonial. Denominaciones, clasificaciones e identidades.* Santiago: PUCC, 2010.

Ares Queija, Berta. "Las danzas de los indios: un camino para la evangelización del virreinato del Perú." *Revista de Indias* 44, no. 174 (1984): 446-462.

—. "Mestizos en hábito de indios: ¿estrategias transgresoras o identidades difusas?" In *Passar as fronteiras. II coloquio internacional sobre mediadores culturais, séculos XV a XVIII*, ed. Rui Manuel Loureiro and Serge Gruzinski, 133-146. Lagos: Centro de Estudios Gil Eanes, 1999.

Argandoña Pastén y Salazar, Pedro Miguel. *Constituciones Sinodales del Arzobispado de La Plata*. Cochabamba: Amigos, 1854.

Argouse, Aude. "Asignar un pasado al futuro. Los testamentos de indígenas, entre memoria e historia, Cajamarca, Perú, siglo XVII." In *Fronteras y sensibilidades en las Américas*, edited by Frédérique Langue and Salvador Bernabéu, 45-69. Sevilla: Ediciones Doce Calles, 2011.

Armenteros Martínez, Iván. "De hermandades y procesiones: la cofradía de esclavos y libertos negros de *Sant Jaume* de Barcelona y la asimilación de la negritud en la Europa premoderna (siglos XV-XVI)," *Clio: Revista de Pesquisa Histórica* 29, no. 2 (2011): http://www.revista.ufpe.br/revistaclio/index.php/revista/article/viewFile/234/130

Arzáns de Orsúa y Vela, Bartolomé. *Relatos de la Villa Imperial de Potosí*. La Paz: Plural editores, 2009.

Badde, Paul. *María of Guadalupe: Shaper of History, Shaper of Hearts*. San Francisco: Ignatius Press, 2008.

Bakhtine, Mikhail M. *Rabelais and His World*. Bloomington: Indiana University Press, 1984.

Barelli, Inés, and Maria Nicoletti. "Devociones marianas en la ciudad de San Carlos de Bariloche (Argentina): construcciones identitarias sociales y marcas territoriales." *Revista Brasileira de História das Religiões* 7, no. 19 (2014): 5-30.

Bargellini, Clara. "Originality and Invention in the Painting of New Spain." In *Painting a New World: Mexican Art and Life, 1521-1821*, edited by Donna Pierce, Rogelio Ruiz Gomar, and Clara Bargellini, 78-91. Denver: Denver Art Museum, 2005.

Bargna, Ivan. "Collecting Practices in Bandjoun, Cameroon: Thinking about Collecting as a Research Paradigm." *African Arts* 49, no. 2 (2016): 20-37.

Barth, Frederik. Introduction to *Ethnic Groups and Boundaries: The Social Organization of Culture Difference*, edited by Barth, 9-38. Long Grove: Waveland Press, 1998.

Bartolomé, Miguel. "Conciencia étnica y autogestión indígena." In *Indignidad y descolonización en América Latina*, 309-324. Mexico City: Nueva Imagen, 1979.

Bastide, Roger. *The African Religions of Brazil: Toward a Sociology of the Interpenetration of Civilizations*. Baltimore: John Hopkins University Press, 2007.

—. *African Civilisations in the New World*. New York: Harper & Row, 1971.

Bazarte, Alicia. *Las cofradías de españoles en la Ciudad de México (1526-1869)*. Mexico City: UAM, 1989.

Bennett, Herman. *Colonial Blackness: A History of Afro-Mexico*. Bloomington: Indiana University Press, 2009.

Bechtloff, Dagmar. *Las cofradías en Michoacán durante la época de la colonia. La religión y su relación política y económica en una sociedad intercultural.* Zinacantepec: Colegio de Michoacán, 1996.

Bejarano, Ignacio, ed. *Actas del cabildo de la Ciudad de México,* 52 vols. Mexico City: Aguilar e Hijos, 1889-1911.

Bernales Ballesteros, Jorge. "La pintura en Lima durante el Virreinato." In *Pintura en el Virreinato del Perú: el libro de arte del centenario,* edited by Luis Nieri Galindo, 211- 238. Lima: Banco de Crédito del Perú, 2001.

Bernand, Carmen. "Mestizos, mulatos y ladinos en Hispanoamérica: un enfoque antropológico de un proceso histórico." In *Motivos de la antropología americanista. Indagaciones en la diferencia,* ed. Miguel León-Portilla, 105-133. Mexico City: FCE, 2001.

Berlin, Ira. "From Creole to African: Atlantic Creoles and the Origins of African-American Society in Mainland North America." *William and Mary Quarterly* 53, no. 2 (1996): 251- 288.

Beverley, John. *Subalternity and Representation: Arguments in Cultural Theory.* Durham: Duke University Press, 1999.

Black, Christopher. "Confraternities and the Parish in the Context of Italian Catholic Reform." In *Confraternities and Catholic Reform in Italy, France, and Spain,* edited by John Patrick Donnelly and Michael W. Maher, 1-26. Kirksville: Thomas Jefferson University Press, 1998.

Bleichmar, Daniela. "The Imperial Visual Archive: Images, Evidence, and Knowledge in the Early Modern Hispanic World." *Colonial Latin American Review* 24, no. 2 (2015): 236- 266.

—, and Peter C. Mancall. eds. *Collecting across Cultures: Material Exchanges in the Early Modern Atlantic World.* Philadelphia: University of Pennsylvania Press, 2013.

Blumenthal, Debra. "'La Casa dels Negres': Black African Solidarity in Late Medieval Valencia." In *Black Africans in Renaissance Europe,* edited by Thomas F. Earle and Kate J. P. Lowe, 225-246. Cambridge: Cambridge University Press, 2010.

Boccara, Guillaume. "Mundos nuevos en las fronteras del Nuevo Mundo." *Nuevo Mundo/Mundos Nuevos,* 2001. https://journals.openedition.org/nuevomundo/426, accessed June 11, 2021

Borges, Célia. *Escravos e libertos nas irmandades do Rosário.* Juiz de Fora: Editora da UFJF, 2005.

Borucki, Alex, David Eltis, and David Wheat. "The Size and Direction of the Slave Trade to the Spanish Americas." In *From the Galleons to the Highlands. Slave Trade Routes in the Spanish Americas,* edited by Borucki, Eltis, and Wheat, 15-46. Albuquerque: University of New Mexico Press, 2020.

Boschi, Caio César. *Os leigos e o poder: irmandades leigas e política colonizadora em Minas Gerais.* Sao Paulo: Atica, 1986.

—. *Distinction: A Social Critique of the Judgement of Taste*. New York: Routledge, 2015.

Bouysse-Cassagne, Thérese. "El sol de adentro: wakas y santos en las minas de Charcas y en el lago Titicaca siglos XV a XVI." *Boletín de Arqueología* 8 (2004): 59-97.

—. "Las minas de centro-sur andino, los cultos prehispánicos y los cultos cristianos." *Boletín del Instituto Francés de Estudios Andinos* 34, no. 3 (2005): 443-462.

—. *La identidad aymara: aproximación histórica (siglo XV, siglo XVI)*. La Paz: IFEA, 1987.

Bovisio, María Alba. *Las huacas del NOA: objetos y conceptos*. Buenos Aires: Mimeo, 2006.

Bowser, Frederick P. *The African Slave in Colonial Peru, 1524-1650*. Stanford: Stanford University Press, 1974.

Boxer, Charles R. *The Church Militant and Iberian Expansions, 1440-1770*. Baltimore: Johns Hopkins University Press, 1978.

Boxt, Matthew A., and Brian D. Dillon, eds. *Fanning the Sacred Flame: Mesoamerican Studies in Honor of H. B. Nicholson*. Boulder: University Press of Colorado, 2012.

Brading, David A. *Mexican Phoenix: Our Lady of Guadalupe, Image and Tradition across Five Centuries*. Cambridge: Cambridge University Press, 2001.

—. *The First America: The Spanish Monarchy, Creole Patriots, and the Liberal State 1492-1867*. Cambridge: Cambridge University Press, 2004.

Brewer-García, Larissa. *Beyond Babel. Translations of Blackness in Colonial Peru and New Granada*. Cambridge: Cambridge University Press, 2020.

Bridikhina, Eugenia. *Theatrum mundi: entramados del poder en Charcas colonial*. La Paz: Plural Editores e IFEA, 2007.

Bristol, Joan Cameron. "Afro-Mexican Saintly Devotion in a Mexico City Alley." In *Africans to Spanish America: Expanding the Diaspora*, edited by Sherwin K. Bryant, Rachel S. O'Toole, and Ben Vinson III, 114-135. Urbana: University of Illinois Press, 2014.

—. *Christians, Blasphemers, and Witches: Afro-Mexican Ritual Practice in the Seventeenth Century*. Albuquerque: University of New Mexico Press, 2007.

Bryant, Sherwin. *Rivers of Gold, Lives of Bondage: Governing through Slavery in Colonial Quito*. Chapel Hill: University of North Carolina Press, 2014.

Burkhart, Louise M. *The Slippery Earth: Nahua-Christian Moral Dialogue in Sixteenth-Century Mexico*. Tucson: University of Arizona Press, 1989.

—. *Holy Wednesday: A Nahua Drama from Early Colonial Mexico*. Philadelphia: University of Pennsylvania Press, 1996.

—, Barry D. Sell, and Gregory Spira. *Nahua Christianity in Performance*. Norman: University of Oklahoma Press, 2009.

Burmeister, Hermann. *Viagem ao Brasil Através das Províncias do Rio de Janeiro e Minas Gerais*. Belo Horizonte: EDUSP, 1980.

Burns, Kathryn. *Into the Archive: Writing and Power in Colonial Peru*. Durham: Duke University Press, 2010.

Bynum, Caroline Walker. *Christian Materiality: An Essay on Religion in Late Medieval Europe*. New York: Zone Books, 2015.

Cadena, Marisol de la. *Earth Beings: Ecologies of Practice Across Andean Worlds*. Durham: Duke University Press, 2015.

—. *Indigenous Mestizos: The Politics of Race and Culture in Cuzco, Peru, 1919-1991*. Durham: Duke University Press, 2012.

Cahill, David. "The Long Conquest: Collaboration by Native Andean Elites in the Colonial System, 1532-1825." In *Technology, Disease, and Colonial Conquests, Sixteenth to Eighteenth Centuries: Essays Reappraising the Guns and Germs Theories*, edited by George Raudzens, 85-126. Boston: Brill, 2003.

—. "Colour by Numbers: Racial and Ethnic Categories in the Viceroyalty of Peru, 1532-1824." *Journal of Latin American Studies* 26, no. 2 (1994): 325-346.

—. "Curas and Social Conflict in the Doctrinas of Cuzco, 1780-1814." *Journal of Latin American Studies* 16, no. 2 (1984): 241-276.

Calancha, Antonio de la. *Coronica moralizada del orden de San Augustin en el Peru: con sucesos egenplares en esta monarquia [...]*. Barcelona: Pedro Lacavalleria, 1639.

Calmon, Francisco. *Relação das faustíssimas festas*. Rio de Janeiro: FUNARTE-INF, [1762] 1982.

Campos y Fernández de Sevilla, F. Javier. *Catálogo de cofradías del Archivo del Arzobispado de Lima*. Lima: IEIH, 2014.

Candido, Mariana P. "Tracing Benguela Identity to the Homeland." In *Crossing Memories: Slavery and African Diaspora,* edited by Ana Lucia Araujo, Mariana P. Candido, and Paul Lovejoy, 183-208. Trenton: World Press, 2011.

—. "Jagas e Sobas No 'Reino de Benguela': Vassalagem e Criação de Novas Categorias Políticas e Sociais No Contexto Da Expansão Portuguesa Na África Durante Os Séculos XVI e XVII." In *África: Histórias Conectadas*, edited by Alexandre Ribeiro, Alexander Gebera, and Marina Berthet, 39-76. Niterói: Universidade Federal Fluminense, 2015.

—. "Slave Trade and New Identities in Benguela, 1700-1860." *Portuguese Studies Review* 19, nos. 1-2 (2011): 59-76.

Carrasco Pizana, Pedro. *The Tenochca Empire of Ancient Mexico: The Triple Alliance of Tenochtitlan, Tetzcoco, and Tlacopan*. Norman: University of Oklahoma Press, 1999.

—. "The Civil-Religious Hierarchy in Mesoamerican Communities: Pre-Spanish Background and Colonial Development." *American Anthropologist* 65, no. 3 (1967): 483-497.

Carrasco Saavedra, Bernardo, and Manuel de Alday y Aspee. *Sínodos diocesanos del Arzobispado de Santiago de Chile celebrados por los ilustrísimos señores doctor*

INDIGENOUS AND BLACK CONFRATERNITIES IN COLONIAL LATIN AMERICA

don fray Bernardo Carrasco Saavedra [*1688*] *y doctor don Manuel de Alday y Aspee*. New York: Eduardo Dunigan y Hermano, [1763] 1858.

Carrera Stampa, Manuel. *Los gremios mexicanos: la organización gremial en Nueva España, 1521-1861*. Mexico City: Iberoamericana, 1954.

Caretta, Gabriela y Zacca, Isabel. "'Benditos ancestros': comunidad, poder y cofradía en Humahuaca en el siglo XVIII." *Boletín Americanista* 62 (2011): 51-72.

Carvalho Soares, Mariza de. *People of Faith: Slavery and African Catholics in Eighteenth- Century Rio de Janeiro*. Durham: Duke University Press, 2011.

—. "La posible articulación del ayllu a través de las cofradías." In *Etnohistoria y Antropología Andina: Actas de la Segunda Jornada del Museo Nacional de Historia*, edited by Amalia Castelli, Marcia Koth de Pareces, and Mariana Mould de Pease, 299-310. Lima: Museo Nacional de Historia, 1981.

—, and Meyers, Albert. *Las cofradías en el Perú: región central*. Frankfurt: Vervuert, 1981.

Celestino, Olinda, and Albert Meyers. "The Socio-economic Dynamic of the Confraternal Endowment in Colonial Peru: Jauja in the Eighteenth Century." In *Manipulating the Saints: Religious Brotherhoods and Social Integration in Postconquest Latin America*, edited by Albert Meyers and Diane Elizabeth Hopkis, 101-127. Hamburg: Wayasbah, 1988.

Chance, John, and William B. Taylor. "Cofradías and Cargos: An Historical Perspective on the Mesoamerican Civil-Religious Hierarchy." *American Ethnologist* 12, no. 1 (1985), 1-26.

Charney, Paul. "'Much Too Worthy...': Indians in Seventeenth-Century Lima." In *City Indians in Spain's American Empire: Urban Indigenous Society in Colonial Mesoamerica and Andean South America, 1530-1810*, edited by Dana Velasco Murillo, Mark Lentz, and Margarita R. Ochoa, 87-103. Eastbourne: Sussex Academic Press, 2012.

—, "El indio urbano: un análisis económico y social de la población india de Lima en 1613." *Histórica* 12, no. 1 (1988): 5-33.

Chasteen, John Charles. *National Rhythms, African Roots: The Deep History of Latin American Popular Dance*. Albuquerque: University of New Mexico Press, 2004.

Chávez Carbajal, María Guadalupe. "La negritud en Michoacán, época colonial." In *Presencia Africana en México*, edited by Lax Maria Matinez Montiel, 119-124. Mexico City: Conaculta, 1994.

Chimalpahin, Domingo. *Annals of His Time: Don Domingo de San Antón Muñón Chimalpahin Quauhtlehuanitzin*. Edited by James Lockhart, Susan Schroeder, and Doris Namala. Stanford: Stanford University Press, 2006.

Christian Jr., William A. *Local Religion in Sixteenth-Century Spain*. Princeton: Princeton University Press, 1981.

Christensen, Mark Z. *Nahua and Maya Catholicisms: Texts and Religion in Colonial Central Mexico and Yucata*n. Stanford: Stanford University Press, 2013.

Cieza de León, Pedro de. *Crónica del Perú*. Edited by Francesca Cantù. Lima: PUCP, [1553] 1989.

Ciriza-Mendívil Carlos. *Naturales de una ciudad multiétnica: vidas y dinámicas sociales de los indígenas de Quito en el siglo XVII*. Madrid: Sílex, 2019.

Coelho, Maria Helena da Cruz. "As confrarias medievais portuguesas: espaços de solidariedades na vida e na morte." In *Cofradias, gremios, solidariedades en la Europa medieval: XIX Semana de Estudios Medievales*, 149-184. Pamplona: Government of Navarre, 1993.

Coello de la Rosa, Alexandre. *Espacios de exclusión, espacios de poder: el cercado de Lima colonial (1568-1606)*. Lima: IEP, 2006.

Cole, Jeffrey. *The Potosí Mita, 1573-1700: Compulsory Indian Labor in the Andes*. Stanford: Stanford University Press, 1985.

Comadrán Ruíz, Jorge. *Evolución demográfica argentina durante el período hispano (1535-1810)*. Buenos Aires: EUDEBA, 1969.

Comas-Via, Mireia. "Looking for a Way to Survive: Community and Institutional Assistance to Widows in Medieval Barcelona." In *Women and Gender in the Early Modern World*, edited by Michelle Armstrong-Partida, Alexandra Guerson, and Dana Wessell Lightfoot, 117-194. Lincoln: University of Nebraska Press, 2020.

Consejo de Indias. *Recopilacion de leyes de los reinos de las Indias*. Madrid: Boix, [1680] 1841.

Contreras, Hugo. "'Siendo mozetón o *güeñi* salió de su tierra a vivir entre los españoles': migración y asentamiento mapuche en Chile central durante el siglo XVIII, 1700-1750." *Historia indígena* 9 (2005-2006): 7-32.

——. "Indios de Tierra adentro en Chile central. Las modalidades de la migración forzosa y el desarraigo (fines del siglo XVI y comienzo del siglo XVII)." In *América en Diásporas: esclavitudes y migraciones forzadas en Chile y otras regiones americanas (siglos XVI-XIX)*, edited by Jaime Valenzuela, 161-196. Santiago: RIL Editores, 2017.

Cook, Noble David. "Les indiens immigrés à Lima au début du XVIIe siècle." *Cahiers des Amériques Latines* 13-14 (1976): 33-50.

Cope, R. Douglas. *The Limits of Racial Domination. Plebeian Society in Colonial Mexico City, 1660-1720*. Madison: University of Wisconsin Press, 1994.

Cordero Fernández, Macarena. "La cofradía de Nuestra Señora de Guadalupe. Querellas y defensas indígenas ante la justicia eclesiástica. Colina, Chile, siglo XVII-XVIII. Un estudio de caso." *Revista de Humanidades*, no. 33 (2016): 79-104.

Corilla Melchor, Ciro. "Cofradías en la ciudad de Lima, siglos XVI y XVII: Racismo y conflictos étnicos." In *Etnicidad y discriminación racial en la historia del*

Perú, edited by Ana Cecilia Carrillo, et al., 11-34 Lima: Pontificia Universidad Católica del Perú, 2002.

Corr, Rachel, and Karen Vieira Powers. "Ethnogenesis, Ethnicity and 'Cultural Refusal': The Case of the Salasacas in Highland Ecuador." *Latin American Research Review* 47 (2012): 5-30.

Costilla, Julia. "El milagro en la construcción del culto a Nuestra Señora de Co-pacabana (virreinato del Perú, 1582-1651)." *Estudios Atacameños* 39 (2010): 35-56.

—. "Itinerarios religiosos y espacios sacralizados: santuarios, devotos y peregri-nos en el culto al Señor del Milagro de Salta y la peregrinación a la Virgen de Copacabana en Jujuy." In *Espacialidades altoandinas: nuevos aportes desde la Argentina*, edited by Alejandro Benedetti and Jorge Tomassi, 2:119-63. Buenos Aires: Universidad de Buenos Aires, 2014.

Cruz, Enrique. "'Esclavos españoles, indios y negros': notas para el estudio de las relaciones interétnicas en las cofradías religiosas del norte del Virreinato del Río de la Plata," *Boletim do Museu Paraense Emílio Goeldi* 8, no. 2 (2013): 449-458.

—. "Poder y relaciones sociales en curatos de indios. El curato de Cochinoca en el siglo XVIII (Puna de Jujuy-Argentina)." *Hispania Sacra* LVIII-117 (2006): 355-381.

—. "Poder y adaptación al Sur de Charcas en el siglo XVIII. Curas doctrineros y curacas en San Antonio de Humahuaca." *Boletín Americanista* 67 (2013): 71-83.

— and Adolfo Rodrigo Ramos. "El proceso de construcción y mantenimiento de iglesias en curatos indígenas del altiplano argentino, siglos XVIII y XIX." *Colonial Latin American Historical Review* 19, no. 2 (2014): 159-189.

Cruz, Pablo. "Mundos permeables y espacios peligrosos. Consideraciones acerca de punkus y qaqas en el paisaje altoandino de Potosí, Bolivia." *Boletín del Museo Chileno de Arte Precolombino* 11, no. 2 (2006): 35-50.

—. "Huacas olvidadas y cerros santos. Apuntes metodológicos sobre la cartografía sagrada en los Andes del sur de Bolivia." *Estudios Atacameños* 38 (2009): 55-74.

Cummins, Thomas B.F. "On the Colonial Formation of Comparison: The Virgin of Chiquinquirá, the Virgin of Guadalupe and Cloth." *Anales Del Instituto de Investigaciones Estéticas* 21, no. 75 (1999): 51-77.

D'Altroy, Terence N. *The Incas*. Malden: Blackwell, 2002.

Dávila y Padilla, Agustín. *Historia de la fundación y discurso de la provincia de Santiago de México de los Predicadores*. Brussels: Ivan de Meerbeque, 1625.

De Luca, Candela. "'...de la importante devoción a la celestial Reina María Señora Nuestra...' Religiosidad mariana en las cofradías de indígenas de Potosí (Alto Perú) en el siglo XVIII." In *Cofradías en el Perú y en otros ámbitos del mundo hispánico (siglos XVI al XIX)*, edited by David Fernández Villanova, Diego Egar Lévano Medina, and Kelly Montoya Estrada, 405-422. Lima: Conferencia Episcopal Peruana, 2015.

—. "'…y que olviden los errores de sus antiguos ritos y ceremonias supersticiosas, vivan en concierto y policía…': Transformaciones y continuidades en la organización parroquial indígena potosina durante el siglo XVIII." *Revista de Historia Americana y Argentina*, 51, no. 1 (2016): 11-37.

Delfino, Leonara Lacerda. *O Rosário das almas ancestrais*. Belo Horizonte: Clio, 2017.

Dellaferrera, Nelson C. "La iglesia diocesana: las instituciones." In *Nueva Historia de la Nación Argentina*, 2:385-415. Buenos Aires: Planeta, 1999.

Deusen, Nancy E. van. "The 'Alienated' Body: Slaves and Castas in the Hospital de San Bartolomé in Lima, 1680 to 1700." *The Americas* 56, no. 1 (1999): 1-30.

Dewulf, Jeroen. *From the Kingdom of Kongo to Congo Square: Kongo Dances and the Origins of the Mardi Gras Indians*. Lafayette: University of Louisiana at Lafayette Press, 2017.

Díaz A., Alberto, Paula Martínez S., and Carolina Ponce. "Cofradías de Arica y Tarapacá en los siglos XVIII y XIX: indígenas andinos, sistema de cargos religiosos y festividades." *Revista de Indias* 74, no. 260 (2014):101-28.

Díaz, Mónica. *Indigenous Writings from the Convent: Negotiating Ethnic Autonomy in Colonial Mexico*. Tucson: University of Arizona Press, 2010.

Dibble, Charles. "The Nahuatilization of Christianity." In *Sixteenth-Century Mexico: The Work of Sahagún*, edited by Munro Emerson, 225-233. Albuquerque: University of New Mexico Press, 1974.

DiCesare, Catherine R. *Sweeping the Way: Divine Transformation in the Aztec Festival of Ochpaniztli*. Boulder: University Press of Colorado, 2009.

Dierksmeier, Laura. *Charity for and by the Poor: Franciscan-Indigenous Confraternities in Mexico, 1527-1700*. Norman: University of Oklahoma Press, 2020.

Diez Hurtado, Alejandro. *Fiestas y cofradías. Asociaciones religiosas e integración en la historia de la comunidad de Sechura (siglos XVII al XX)*. Piura: CIPCA, 1994.

Edmundo, Luiz. *O Rio de Janerio no tempo dos vice-reis, 1763-1808*. Rio de Janeiro: Imprensa Nacional, 1932.

Egoavil, Teresa. *Las cofradías en Lima, siglos XVII y XVIII*. Lima: Universidad Nacional Mayor San Marcos, 1986.

Eliade, Mircea. *Tratado de Historia de las Religiones*. Madrid: Cristiandad, 1974.

Elias, Norbert. *La sociedad cortesana*. Mexico City: FCE, 1982.

Engels, Friedrich. *The Origin of the Family, Private Property, and the State*. Edited by Alick West. Brooklyn: Verso [1892] 2021.

Enrich, Francisco. *Historia de la Compañía de Jesús en Chile*. Barcelona: Francisco Rosal, 1891. 2 vols.

Espinosa Valdivia, Carmen y Mestries Bazarte, Bruno. "Monjas a escena: teatro y vida conventual de las jerónimas novohispanas." En *Obra novohispana de teatro: la conquista de México por Carlos V*, edited by Alicia Bazarte Martínez and José G. Herrera Alcalá, xxxvii-xlv. Mexico City: Instituto Politécnico Nacional, 2016.

Estenssoro Fuchs, Juan Carlos. "Los Colores de La Plebe: Razón y Mestizaje En El Perú Colonial." In *Los Cuadros de Mestizaje Del Virrey Amat: La Representación Etnográfica En El Perú Colonial*, edited by Natalia Majluf, 67-107. Lima: Museo de Arte de Lima, 1999.

——, and Gabriela Ramos. *Del paganismo a la lantidad: la incorporación de los indios del Perú al catolicismo, 1532-1750.* Lima: IFEA, 2003.

Estruch, Dolores. *El ejercicio del poder en el Jujuy colonial. Enlaces y tensiones entre la jurisdicción civil y eclesiástica. Siglos XVI-XVIII.* Buenos Aires: La Bicicleta, 2017.

Eugênio, Alisson. "Tensões entre os visitadores eclesiásticos e as irmandades negras no século XVIII mineiro." *Revista Brasileira de História* 22, no. 14, (2002): 33-46.

Evans, Susan Toby. *Ancient Mexico and Central America: Archaeology and Culture History.* New York: Thames & Hudson, 2013.

Falch, Jorge. "Cofradía de Nuestra Señora de la Candelaria de los mulatos en el Convento de San Agustín de Santiago de Chile." *Anuario de historia de la Iglesia en Chile* 13 (1995): 17- 30.

Farman Sweda, Krystle. "Black Catholicism: The Formation of Local Religion in Colonial Mexico." Ph.D. diss., City University of New York, 2020.

Ferlini, Vera Lucia Amaral. "Folguedos, feiras e feriados: aspectos socioeconômicos das festas no mundo dos engenhos." In *Festa: cultura e sociabilidade na América portuguesa,* edited by Istaván Jancsó and Iris Kantor, 2: 449-463. Sao Paulo: Imprensa Oficial, 2001.

Flynn, Maureen. *Sacred Charity: Confraternities and Social Welfare in Spain, 1400-1700.* Ithaca: Cornell University Press, 1989.

Fogelman, Patricia, and Marta Goldberg. "*El rey de los congos*: The Clandestine Coronation of Pedro Duarte in Buenos Aires, 1787." In *Afro-Latino Voices: Narratives from the Early Modern Ibero-Atlantic World, 1550-1812*, edited by Kathryn Joy McKnight and Leo J. Garofolo, 155-173. Indianapolis: Hacket, 2009.

——. "El culto mariano y las representaciones de lo femenino: Recorrido historiográfico y nuevas perspectivas de análisis." *Aljaba* 10 (2006): 175-188.

——. "Simulacros de la virgen y refracciones del culto mariano en el Río de la Plata Colonial." *Eadem Utraque Europa* 2, no. 3 (2006): 11-34.

——. "*La omnipotencia suplicante: el culto mariano en la ciudad de Buenos Aires y la campaña en los siglos XVII y XVIII.*" Ph.D. diss. Universidad de Buenos Aires, 2003.

Fonseca, Jorge. *Religião e liberdade: os negros nas irmandades e confrarias portuguesas (séculos XV à XIX).* Lisbon: Humus, 2016.

Fracchia, Carmen. *"Black but Human": Slavery and the Visual Arts in Hapsburg Spain, 1480- 1700.* Oxford: Oxford University Press, 2019.

França Paiva, Eduardo. *Nombrar lo nuevo: una historia léxica de Iberoamérica entre los siglos XVI y XVIII (las dinámicas de mestizajes y el mundo del trabajo)*. Santiago: Editorial Universitaria, 2020.

Fromont, Cécile. "Dancing for the King of Congo from Early Modern Central Africa to Slavery- Era Brazil," *Colonial Latin American Review* 22, no. 2 (2013); 184-208.

——. *The Art of Conversion: Christian Visual Culture in the Kingdom of Kongo*. Chapel Hill: University of North Carolina Press, 2014.

Fryer, Peter. *Rhythms of Resistance*: African Musical Heritage in Brazil. London: Pluto Press, 2000.

Fuente, Alejandro de la. "Slaves and the Creation of Legal Rights in Cuba: Coartación and Papel." *Hispanic American Historical Review* 87, no. 4 (2007): 659-92.

Fuenzalida Vollmar, Fernando. "La matriz colonial de las comunidades indígenas del Perú: una hipótesis de trabajo." *Revista del Museo Nacional Lima* 35 (1970): 92-123.

Gage, Thomas. *The English-American, His Travail by Sea and Land, or a Survey of the West India's*. London: R. Cotes, 1648.

Galindo, David R. *To Sin No More: Franciscans and Conversions in the Hispanic World, 1683- 1830*. Stanford: Stanford University Press, 2018.

Galván Rivera, Mariano, ed. *Concilio III Provincial Mexicano, celebrado en México el año 1585, confirmado en Roma por el Papa Sixto V, mandado observar por el gobierno español, en diversas órdenes*. Barcelona: Miro y Barsa, [1585] 1870.

García-Ayluardo, Clara. "Confraternity, Cult, and Crown in Colonial Mexico." Ph.D. diss., University of Cambridge, 1989.

——. García Ayluardo, Clara. *Desencuentros con la tradición: los fieles y la desaparición de las cofradías de la ciudad de México en el siglo XVIII*. Mexico City: FCE/ CONACULTA, 2015.

Garnett, Jane, and Gervase Rosser. *Spectacular Miracles: Transforming Images in Italy from the Renaissance to the Present*. London: Reaktion Books, 2013.

Garrett, David T. *Shadows of Empire: The Indian Nobility of Cusco, 1750-1825*. Cambridge: Cambridge University Press, 2005.

Gemelli Careri, Giovanni F. *Viaje a Nueva* España. Mexico City: UNAM, [1700] 1976.

Germeten, Nicole von. *Black Blood Brothers: Confraternities and Social Mobility for Afro- Mexicans*. Gainesville: University Press of Florida, 2006.

——. "Juan Roque's Donation of a House to the *Zape* Confraternity, Mexico City, 1623." In *Afro-Latino Voices*, 83-103.

——. *Violent Delights, Violent Ends: Sex, Race, and Honor in Colonial Cartagena de Indias*. Albuquerque: University of New Mexico Press, 2013.

——. "Colonial Middle Men: Mulatto Identity in New Spain's Confraternities." In *Black Mexico: Race and Society from Colonial to Modern Times*, edited by Ben

Vinson III and Matthew Restall, 136-154. Albuquerque: University of New Mexico Press, 2009.

——. "Black Brotherhoods in Mexico City." In *The Black Urban Atlantic in the Age of the Slave Trade*, edited by Jorge Cañizares-Esguerra, Matt D. Childs, and James Sidbury, 248-268. Philadelphia: University of Pennsylvania Press, 2013.

Gibson, Charles. *The Aztecs Under Spanish Rule: A History of the Indians of the Valley of Mexico, 1519-1810*. Stanford: Stanford University Press, 1964.

Gil Montero, Raquel. "Familia campesina andina. Entre la colonia y el nuevo estado independiente en formación." Ph.D. diss. Universidad Nacional de Córdoba, 1999.

Gisbert, Teresa. *Iconografía y mitos indígenas en el arte*. La Paz: Gisbert, 2008.

——, and José de Mesa. "La virgen María en Bolivia. La dialéctica Barroca en la representación de María." In *Barroco Andino: memoria del I Encuentro Internacional*, 21-36. La Paz: Unión Latina, 2003.

Ginzburg, Carlo. *Myths, Emblems, Clues*. London: Hutchinson Radius, 1990.

——. *The Cheese and the Worms: The Cosmos of a Sixteenth-Century Miller*. Baltimore: Johns Hopkins University Press, 2013.

Giudicelli, Christophe. "Hétéronomie et classifications coloniales: la construction des 'nations' indiennes aux confins de l'Amérique espagnole (XVI-XVIIe siècle)." *Nuevo Mundo/Mundos Nuevos* (2010). https://journals.openedition.org/nuevomundo/59411

Goffman, Erving. *The Presentation of Self in Everday Life*. Edinburgh: University of Edinburgh Press, 1956.

Gómez Acuña, Luis. "Las cofradías de negros en Lima (siglos XVII): estado de la cuestión y análisis de caso." *Páginas* 129 (1994): 28-39.

Gómez, Ximena A. "Nuestra Señora: Confraternal Art and Identity in Early Colonial Lima." Ph.D. diss., University of Michigan, 2019.

Gonzalbo Aizpuru, Pilar. *Historia de la familia*. Mexico City: UAM, 1993.

——. "Reflexiones sobre el miedo en la historia." In *Una historia de los usos del miedo*, edited by Pilar Gonzalbo, Anne Staples, Valentina Torres Septién, 21-36. Mexico City: Colmex, 2009.

——. "Las fiestas novohispanas: espectáculos y ejemplo." *Mexican Studies/Estudios Mexicanos* 9, no. 1 (1993); 19-45.

González Dorado, Antonio. 1988. *De María conquistadora a María liberadora. Mariología popular latinoamericana*. Madrid: Sal Terrae, 1988.

González Holguín, Diego. *Vocabulario de la lengua general de todo el Perú llamada lengua quichua o del inca*. 1608; reprint: Lima: Universidad Nacional Mayor de San Marcos, 1989.

Gose, Peter. "Oracles, Divine Kingship, and Political Representation in the Inka State." *Ethnohistory* 43, no. 1 (1996): 1-32.

——. *Invaders as Ancestors: On the Intercultural Making and Unmaking of Spanish Colonialism in the Andes*. Toronto: University of Toronto Press, 2008.

Gran Diccionario Náhuatl de la Universidad Nacional Autónoma de México. http://www.gdn.unam.mx/

Graubart, Karen B. "'*So color de una cofradía*': Catholic Confraternities and the Development of Afro-Peruvian Ethnicities in Early Colonial Peru." *Slavery and Abolition* 33, no. 1 (2012): 43-64.

Green, Toby. *The Rise of the Trans-Atlantic Slave Trade in Western Africa, 1300-1589*. Cambridge : Cambridge University Press, 2012.

Greenleaf, Richard E. "The Inquisition Brotherhood: Cofradía de San Pedro Martir of Colonial Mexico." *The Americas* 40, no. 2 (1983): 171-207.

Greer, Allan, and Jodi Bilinkoff. *Colonial Saints: Discovering the Holy in the Americas, 1500- 1800*. New York: Routledge, 2003.

Goffman, Erving. *The Presentation of Self in Everday Life*. Edinburgh: University of Edinburgh Press, 1956.

Guaman Poma de Ayala, Felipe. *El primer nueva crónica y buen gobierno*. Mexico City: Siglo XXI, 1980.

Guerra, Francois-Xavier y Lempérière, Annick, et al. *Los espacios públicos en Iberoamérica. Ambigüedades y problemas. Siglos XVIII- XIX*. Mexico City: FCE, 1998.

Guevara Sanginés, María. "El proceso de liberación de los esclavos en la América Virreinal." In *Pautas de convivencia étnica en la América latina colonial: indios, negros, mulatos, pardos y esclavos,* edited by Juan Manuel de la Serna, 111-162. Guanajuato: Government of Guanajuato, 2005.

Gutiérrez Azopardo, Ildefonso. "Las cofradías de negros en la América Hispana. Siglos XVI XVIII." https://www.africafundacion.org/IMG/pdf/LOS_NEGROS_Y_LA_IGLESIA_EN_LA_SPANA_DE_LOS_SIGLOS_XV_y_XVI.pdf

——. "Los negros y la iglesia en la España de los siglos XV y XVI." https://www.africafundacion.org/IMG/pdf/LOS_NEGROS_Y_LA_IGLESIA_EN_LA_ES-PANA_DE_LOS_SIGLOS_XV_y_XVI.pdf

Habermas, Jürgen. *The Structural Transformation of the Public Sphere: An Inquiry into a Category of Bourgeois Society*, edited by Thomas Burger and Frederick Lawrence. Cambridge: Polity, 2020.

Hanke, Lewis. *Aristotle and the American Indians: A Study in Race Prejudice in the Modern World*. Chicago: Regnery, 1959.

Harth-Terré, Emilio. *Presencia del negro en el virreinato del Per*. Lima: Universitaria, 1971.

——, and Alberto Márquez Abanto. "Perspectiva social y económica del artesano virreinal en Lima." *Revista del Archivo Nacional del Perú* 26, no. 2 (1962): 1-96.

Hartman, Saidiya V. *Lose Your Mother: A Journey along the Atlantic Slave Route*. New York: Farrar, Straus and Giroux, 2007.

Heers, Jacques. *Fêtes des fous et carnavals*. Paris: Hachette, 2007.

Henderson, John. *Piety and Charity in Late Medieval Florence*. Oxford: Clarendon, 1994.

Herrera, Robinson A. "Surviving the Colonial City: Native Peoples in Early Santiago de Guatemala." In *City Indians in Spain's American Empire: Urban Indigenous Society in Colonial Mesoamerica and Andean South America, 1530-1810*, edited by Dana Velasco Murillo, Mark Lentz, and Margarita R. Ochoa, 48-62. Eastbourne: Sussex Academic Press, 2012.

Hesperióphylo [Joseph Rossi y Rubí]. "Idea de Las Congregaciones Públicas de Los Negros Bozales, Pt. I." *Mercurio Peruano* 48 (June 16, 1791): 112-117.

——. "Idea de Las Congregaciones Públicas de Los Negros Bozales, Pt. II." *Mercurio Peruano* 49 (June 19, 1791): 120-125.

Heywood, Linda M., and John K. Thornton, eds. *Central Africans, Atlantic Creoles, and the Foundation of the Americas, 1585-1660*. New York: Cambridge University Press, 2007.

Hidalgo Leuedé, Jorge. "Tierras, exacciones fiscales y mercado en las sociedades andinas de Arica, Tarapacá y Atacama, 1750-1790." In *La participación indígena en los mercados surandinos. Estrategias y reproducción social. Siglos XVI a XX*, edited by Olivia Harris, Brooke Larson and Enrique Tandeter, 193-231. La Paz: CERES, 1987.

Hill, Jonathan D. *History, Power and Identity. Ethnogenesis in the Americas, 1492-1992*. Iowa City: University of Iowa Press, 1996.

Holmes, Megan. *The Miraculous Image in Renaissance Florence*. New Haven: Yale University Press, 2013.

Hoornaert, Eduardo. *História da Igreja no Brasil*. Petrópolis: Vozes, 1977.

Howard, Philip A. *Changing History: Afro-Cuban Cabildos and Societies of Color in the Nineteenth Century*. Lafayette: Louisiana State University Press, 1998.

Hunefeldt, Christine. *Paying the Price of Freedom: Family and Labor Among Lima's Slaves, 1800-1854*. Berkley: University of California Press, 1995.

——. "Comunidad, curas y comuneros hacia fines del período colonial: ovejas y pastores indomados en el Perú." *HISLA* 2 (1983): 3-31.

Israel, Jonathan I. *Race, Class and Politics in Colonial Mexico, 1610-1670*. London: Oxford University Press, 1975.

Jara, Álvaro, and Rolando Mellafe, eds. *Protocolos de los escribanos de Santiago. Primeros fragmentos, 1559 y 1564-1566*. Santiago: DIBAM, 1996. 2 vols.

Jesús, Úrsula de. *The Souls of Purgatory: The Spiritual Diary of a Seventeenth-Century Afro-Peruvian Mystic, Ursula de Jesús*, edited b Nancy van Deusen. Albuquerque: The University of New Mexico Press, 2011.

Jouve Martín, José Ramón. *The Black Doctors of Colonial Lima: Science, Race, and Writing in Colonial and Early Republican Peru*. Montreal: McGill-Queen's University Press, 2014.

——. "Death, Gender, and Writing: Testaments of Women of African Origin in Seventeenth-Century Lima, 1651-1666." In *Afro-Latino Voices*, 105-125.

——. *Esclavos de la ciudad letrada: Esclavitud, escritura y colonialismo en Lima (1650-1700)*. Lima: IEP, 2005.

——. "Public Ceremonies and Mulatto Identity in Viceregal Lima: A Colonial Reenactment of the Fall of Troy (1631)." *Colonial Latin American Review* 16, no. 2 (2007): 179-201.

Kaplan, Paul H. D. *The Rise of the Black Magus in Western Art*. Ann Arbor: UMI Research Press, 1985.

Katzew, Ilona. *Casta Painting: Images of Race in Eighteenth-Century Mexico*. New Haven: Yale University Press, 2004.

Kellogg, Susan, and Matthew Restall, eds. *Dead Giveaways. Indigenous Testaments of Colonial Mesoamerica and the Andes*. Salt Lake City: The University of Utah Press, 1998.

Kiddy, Elizabeth W. "*Congados, Calunga, Cadombe*: Our Lady of the Rosary in Minas Gerais, Brazil." *Luso-Brazilian Review* 37, no. 1 (2000): 47-61.

——. *Blacks of the Rosary: Memory and History in Minas Gerais, Brazil*. University Park: Pennsylvania State University Press, 2007.

———. "Who is the King of Congo?: A New Look at African and Afro-Brazilian Kings in Brazil." in *Central Africans and Cultural Transformations in American Diaspora*, edited by Linda Heywood, 153-182. Cambridge: Cambridge University Press, 2002.

Konetzke, Richard, ed. *Coleccion de documentos para la historia de la formación social de Hispanoamérica, 1493-1810*. Madrid: CSIC, 1953.

Kosiba, Steve, and Andrew Bauer. "Mapping the Political Landscape: Toward a GIS Analysis of Environmental and Social Difference." *Journal of Archaeological Method and Theory* 20, no. 1 (2013): 61-101.

Koster, Henry. *Travels in Brazil by Henry Koster in the Years from 1809 to 1815*. Philadelphia: M. Carey & Son, 1817.

Kuznesof, Elizabeth. "Ethnic and Gender Influences on 'Spanish' Creole Society in Colonial Spanish America." *Colonial Latin American Review* 4 (1995): 153-176.

Labarga Garcia, Fermín. "Las cofradías en España e Iberoamérica." In *Corporaciones religiosas y evangelización en Iberoamérica: Siglos XVI-XVIII*, edited by Lévano Medina Diego Edgar and Kelly Montoya Estrada, 11-30. Lima: Museo de Arqueología y Antropología de San Marcos, 2010.

Lahon, Didier. *Os negros no coração do Império: uma memória a resgatar, séculos XV-XIX*. Lisbon: Secretariado Coordenador dos Programas Multiculturais, 1999.

Lara, Silvia Hunold. "Significados cruzados: um reinado de congos na Bahia setecen-
    tista." In *Carnavais e outras frestas: ensaios de história social da cultura*, edited
    by Clementina Pereira Cunha, 71-100. Campinas: Editora da UNICAMP, 2002.

Larkin, Brian. "Confraternities and Community: The Decline of the Communal
    Quest for Salvation in Eighteenth Century Mexico." In *Local Religion in Colonial
    Mexico*, edited by Martin Nesvig, 189-213. Albuquerque: University of New
    Mexico Press, 2006.

——. *The Very Nature of God: Baroque Catholicism and Religious Reform in Bourbon
    Mexico City*. Albuquerque: University of New Mexico, 2010.

Larrouy, Antonio. *Documentos del Archivo de Indias para la historia del Tucumán*.
    Vol. 1. Buenos Aires: L.J. Rosso, 1923.

Lasso de la Vega, Luis. *The Story of Guadalupe: Luis Laso de la Vega's Huei Tlama-
    huiçoltica of 1649*. Edited by Lisa Sousa, Stafford Poole, James Lockhart, and
    Miguel Sánchez López. Stanford: Stanford University Press, 1998.

Lavallè, Bernard. "Las doctrinas de indios como núcleos de explotación colonial
    (siglos XVI y XVII)." *Allpanchis* 19 (1982): 151-171.

León-Portilla, Ascensión H. de. *Tepuztlahcuilolli, impresos en náhuatl: historia y
    bibliografía*. Mexico City: UNAM, 1988.

Lee, Bertram T., and Juan Bromley, eds. *Libros de cabildos de Lima*. Lima: San
    Martín, [1534- 1821] 1935-1948.

Le Goff, Jacques. *¿Realmente es necesario cortar la historia en rebanadas?* Mexico
    City: FCE, 2016.

Lempérière, Annick. "La 'cuestión colonial'." Nuevo Mundo/Mundos Nuevos (2016).
    http://nuevomundo.revues.org/437;DOI:10.4000/nuevomundo.437

Lévano Medina, Diego. "Organización y funcionalidad de las cofradías urbanas:
    Lima, siglo XVII." *Revista del Archivo General de la Nación* 24 (2002): 77-114.

Lisi, Francesco Leonardo. *El tercer concilio limense y la aculturación de los indígenas
    sudamericanos*. Salamanca: University of Salamanca, 1990.

Lizárraga, Reginaldo de. *Descripción del Perú, Tucumán, Río de la Plata y Chile*.
    Madrid: Historia 16, 1986.

Lockhart, James, and Enrique Otte, eds. *Letters and People of the Spanish Indies,
    Sixteenth Century*. Cambridge: Cambridge University Press, 1976.

Lohmann Villena, Guillermo, and Luis Eduardo Wuffarden. *La semana santa de
    Lima*. Lima: Banco del Crédito del Perú, 1996.

Lohse, Russell. "'La Negrita' Queen of the Ticos: The Black Roots of Costa Rica's
    Patron Saint." *The Americas* 69, no. 3 (2013): 323-355.

Lorenzana, Francisco Antonio, ed. *Concilios Provinciales, Primero y Segundo,
    celebrados en la muy noble, y muy leal Ciudad de México, Presidiendo el ILLmo y
    Rmo. Señor D.F Alonso de Montúfar, en los años 1555, y 1565*. Mexico City: Impenta
    de el Superior Gobierno, [1555 and 1565] 1769.

Lovejoy, Paul E. "Ethnic Designations of the Slave Trade and the Reconstruction of the History of Trans-Atlantic Slavery." In *Trans-Atlantic Dimensions of Ethnicity in the African Diaspora*, edited by Lovejoy and David Vincent Trotman, 9-42. London: Bloomsbury, 2004.

Luna García, Sandra Nancy. "Espacios de convivencia y conflicto. Las cofradías de la población de origen africano en Ciudad de México, siglo XVII." *Trashumante* 10 (2017): 32-52.

MacCormack, Sabine. "'The Heart has Its Reasons': Predicaments of Missionary Christianity in Early Colonial Peru." *Hispanic American Historical Review* 65, no. 3 (1985): 443-466.

——. "Gods, Demons, and Idols in the Andes." *Journal of the History of Ideas* 67, no. 4 (2006): 623-648.

Maeder, Ernesto J. *La formación de la sociedad Argentina desde el siglo XVI hasta mediados del XVIII*. Resistencia: IIGHI, 1984.

Maffie, James. *Aztec Philosophy: Understanding a World in Motion*. Boulder: University Press of Colorado, 2014.

Málaga Núñez-Zeballos, Alejandro. "La Virgen Candelaria en el obispado de Arequipa: origen y milagros." In *Incas e indios cristianos. Elites indígenas e identidades cristianas en los Andes coloniales*, edited by Jean-Jacques Decoster, 347-358. Lima: Centro Bartolomé de Las Casas, 2002.

Marchena Fernández, Juan. "Al otro lado del mundo. Josef Reseguín y su 'generación ilustrada' en la tempestad de los Andes. 1781-1788." *Tiempos de América* 12 (2005): 43-111.

Markey, Lia. *Imagining the Americas in Medici Florence*. University Park: Pennsylvania State University Press, 2016.

Martínez, José Luis. "¿Cómo hablar de indios e identidades en el siglo XVI? Una aproximación a la construcción de los discursos coloniales." *Historia Indígena* 8 (2004): 41-55.

——. "Ayllus e identidades interdigitadas. Las sociedades de la puna salada." In *Lógica mestiza en América*, edited by Guillaume Boccara and Sylvia Galindo. 85-112. Temuco: Universidad de la Frontera, 2000.

——. "Construyendo mundos: el 'nacimiento' de los indios en los Andes del siglo XVI." In *Del Nuevo al Viejo Mundo: mentalidades y representaciones desde América*, edited by Alejandra Araya, Azún Candina and Celia Cussen, 23-34. Santiago: Universidad de Chile, 2008.

Martínez Ferrer, Luis. "Pedro López y los negros y mulatos de la ciudad de México (1582- 1597." In *Socialización y religiosidad del médico Pedro López (1527-1597): de Dueñas (Castilla) a la ciudad de México*, edited by Ferrer and María Luisa Rodríguez-Sala, 179- 216. Mexico City: UNAM, 2013.

Martínez Montiel, Luz María. *Negros en América*. Mexico City: Colecciones Mapfre, 1992.

Marzal, Manuel. *El mundo religioso de Urcos*. Cusco: Instituto de Pastoral Andina, 1971.

Masferrer León, Cristina. *Muleke, negritas y mulatillos. Niñez, familia y redes sociales de los esclavos de origen africano de la Ciudad de México*. Mexico City: INAH, 2013.

——. "*Por las ánimas de los negros bozales*: Las cofradías de personas de origen africano en la ciudad de México (siglo XVII)." *Cuicuilco*, 18, no. 51 (2011): 83-104.

Mason, Peter. *Infelicities: Representations of the Exotic*. Baltimore: Johns Hopkins University Press, 1998.

Mattoso, Kátia de Queirós. *Bahia do século XIX: uma província do império*. Rio de Janeiro: Nova Fronteira, 1992.

McKinley, Michelle A. *Fractional Freedoms: Slavery, Intimacy, and Legal Mobilization in Colonial Lima, 1600-1700*. Cambridge: Cambridge University Press, 2016.

McLeod, Alexus. *Astronomy in the Ancient World: Early and Modern Views on Celestial Events*. Cham: Springer, 2016.

Megged, Amos. "The Religious Context of an 'Unholy Marriage': Elite Alienation and Popular Unrest in the Indigenous Communities of Chiapa, 1570-1680." *Ethnohistory* 46, no. 1 (1999): 149-172.

Mello, Veríssimo de. "As Confrarias de N. S. do Rosário como reação contra aculturativa dos negros do Brasil." *Afro-Ásia* 6-7 (1968): 107-118.

Meyers, Albert, and Diane Elizabeth Hopkins, eds. *Manipulating the Saints: Religious Brotherhoods and Social Integration in Postconquest Latin America*. Hamburg: Wayasbah, 1988.

Miller, Joseph Calder. *Way of Death: Merchant Capitalism and the Angolan Slave Trade, 1730- 1830*. Madison: University of Wisconsin Press, 1996.

Mills, Kenneth. "Ocaña, Diego de (ca. 1570-1608)." In *Guide to Documentary Sources for Andean Studies, 1530-190*, edited by Joanne Pillsbury, 3:457-464. Norman: University of Oklahoma Press, 2008.

Mintz, Sidney and Richard Price. *The Birth of Africa-American Culture: An Anthropological Perspective*. Boston: Beacon Press, 1992.

——, and Richard Price. *Anthropological Approaches to the Afro-American Past: Caribbean Perspectives*. Philadelphia: Institute for the Study of Human Issues, 1976.

Molina, Cristóbal de, Brian S. Bauer, Vania Smith-Oka, and Gabriel E, eds. Cantarutti. *Account of the Fables and Rites of the Incas*. Austin: University of Texas Press, 2011.

Mondragón Barrios, Lourdes. *Esclavos africanos en la Ciudad de México: el servicio doméstico durante el siglo XVI*. Mexico City: Euram, 1999.

Moraes Filho, Mello. *Festas de Tradições Populares do Brasil*. Rio de Janeiro: F. Briguiet, 1946.

Moreira, Vilma da Silva. "La mujer en la teología: reflexión biblicoteológica." In *Mujer latinoamericana: Iglesia y teología*, edited by Mujeres para el Diálogo, 140-166. México: MPD, 1981.

Moreno, Isidro. *La antigua hermandad de los negros de Sevilla: etnicidad, poder y sociedad en 600 años de historia*. Seville: University of Seville, 1997.

——. *Cofradías y hermandades andaluzas: estructura, simbolismo e identidad*. Seville: Governemt of Andalucía, 1985.

——. "Plurietnicidad, fiestas y poder: cofradías y fiestas andaluzas de negros como modelo para la América colonial." In *El mundo festivo en España y América*, edited byAntonio Garrido Aranda, 169-188. Cordoba: University of Córdoba, 2005.

——, Teresa Eleazar, and Ricardo Jarillo, eds. *Cofradías de indios y negros: Origen, evolución y continuidades*. Mexico City: INAH, 2018.

Morgado Maurtua, Patricia. "Un palimpsesto urbano: del asiento indígena de Lima a la ciudad española de Los Reyes." Ph.D. diss., University of Sevilla, 2007.

Morgan, Jennifer L. "Partus Sequitur Ventrem: Law, Race, and Reproduction in Colonial Slavery." *Small Axe* 22, no. 1 (2018): 1-17.

Morgan, Ronald J. *Spanish American Saints and the Rhetoric of Identity, 1600-1810*. Tucson: University of Arizona Press, 2002.

Mörner, Magnus. "En torno al uso de la comparación en el análisis histórico de América Latina." *Jahrbuch fur Gerschichte Von Staat, Wirtschaft Lateinamerikas* 31 (1994): 373-390.

Morrone, Ariel J. "Curas doctrineros y caciques andinos en la construcción de legitimidades: las iglesias rurales de La Paz, Audiencia de Charcas, 1570-1630." *Jahrbuch für Geschichte Lateinamerikas* 50 (2013): 29-54.

Moutoukias, Zacarías. "Gobierno y sociedad en el Tucumán y el Río de la Plata, 1550-1800." In *Nueva Historia Argentina*, edited by Tau Anzoátegui, 2:355-411. Buenos Aires: Sudamericana, 2000.

Mott, Luiz. *Rosa Egípciaca: uma santa africana no Brazil*. Rio de Janeiro: Editora Bertrand Brazil, 1993.

Mulvey, Patricia Ann. "The Black Lay Brotherhoods of Colonial Brazil: A History." Ph.D. diss., City University of New York, 1976.

——. "Slave Confraternities in Brazil: Their Role in Colonial Society." *The Americas* 39, no. 1 (1982): 39-68.

——. "Black Brothers and Sisters: Membership in the Black Lay Brotherhoods of Colonial Brazil." *Luso-Brazilian Review*, 17, no. 2 (1980): 253-279.

Naveda, Adriana. "De San Lorenzo de los negros a los morenos de Amapa: cimarrones veracruzanos, 1609-1735." In *Rutas de la esclavitud en África y América Latina*, edited by Rina Cáceres, 157-174. San José: Universidad de Costa Rica, 2001.

Negro, Sandra and Manuel Marzal, eds. *Esclavitud, economía y evangelización. Las haciendas jesuitas en la América Virreinal*. Lima: PUCP, 2005.

Nemser, Daniel. *Infrastructures of Race: Concentration and Biopolitics in Colonial Mexico*. Austin: University of Texas Press, 2017.

Ngou-Mvé, Nicolás. "Mesianismo, cofradías y resistencia en el África Bantú y América Colonial." http://bibliotecavirtual.clacso.org.ar/ar/libros/aladaa/nico.rtf

Niemeyer, Hans. "La ocupación Inkaica de la Cuenca alta del Río Copiapo." *Comechingonia* 4 (1986): 165-294.

Nunes Pereira, José Maria. "Cultura afro-brasileira." In *Introdução a historia da Africa e da cultura afro-brasileira*, edited by Beluce Belluci, 119-126. Rio de Janeiro: UCAM, 2003.

O'Brien, Terry J. *Fair Gods and Feathered Serpents: A Search for Ancient America's Bearded White God*. Bountiful: Horizon Publishers, 1997.

Ocaña, Diego de. *Viaje a Chile*. Santiago: Universitaria, [1600] 1995.

O'Phelan Godoy, Scarlett. *Un siglo de rebeliones anticoloniales, Perú y Bolivia 1700-1783*. Cusco: CERA Bartolomé de Las Casas, 1988.

Osorio, Alejandra B. *Inventing Lima: Baroque Modernity in Peru's South Sea Metropolis*. New York, NY: Palgrave Macmillan, 2008.

O'Toole, Rachel Sarah. *Bound Lives: Africans, Indians, and the Making of Race in Colonial Peru*. Pittsburgh: University of Pittsburgh Press, 2012.

——. "Castas y representación en Trujillo colonial." In *Más Allá de La Dominación y La Resistencia: Estudios de Historia Peruana, Siglos XVI-XX*, edited by Leo J. Garofalo and Paulo Drinot. 48-76. Lima: IEP, 2005.

——. "From the Rivers of Guinea to the Valleys of Peru: Becoming a Bran Diaspora within Spanish Slavery." *Social Text* 25, no. 3 (2007): 1936.

Ott, Carlos. "A Irmandade de Nossa Senhora do Rosário dos Pretos do Pelourinho." *Afro-Ásia*, 6-7 (1968): 119-126.

Ovalle, Alonso de. *Histórica relación del reino de Chile y de las misiones y ministerios que Ejercita en él la Compañía de Jesús*. Santiago: Universidad de Chile, [1646] 1969.

Pagden, Anthony. *The Fall of Natural Man: The American Indian and the Origins of Comparative Ethnology*. Cambridge: Cambridge University Press, 1982.

Paiva, José Pedro. "Etiqueta e cerimonias públicas na esfera da Igreja (séculos XVII-XVIII)." In *Festa*, 1: 75-94.

Palmer, Colin. *Slaves of the White God: Blacks in Mexico, 1570-1650*. Cambridge: Harvard University Press, 1976.

Patterson, Orlando. *Slavery and Social Death: A Comparative Study*. Cambridge: Harvard University Press, 1982.

Penry, Elizabeth. "Canons of the Council of Trent in Arguments of Priests and Indians over Images, Chapels and Cofradías." In *The Council of Trent: Reform and Controversy in Europe and Beyond (1545-1700)*, edited by Wim François and Violeta Soen, 3:277-299. Göttingen: Vandenhoeck and Ruprecht, 2018.

Peres, Fernando. "Negros e mulatos em Gregório de Matos," *Afro-Ásia* 4 (1967): 59-75.

Pérez Puente, Leticia. "La sangre afrentada y el círculo letrado. El obispo Nicolás del Puerto, 1619-1681." In *Promoción universitaria en el mundo hispánico. Siglos XVI al XX*, edited by Armando Pavón Romero, 271-293. Mexico City: UNAM, 2012.

Perry, Jonathan S. *The Roman Collegia: The Modern Evolution of an Ancient Concept*. Leiden: Brill, 2006.

Peterson, Jeanette Favrot. *Visualizing Guadalupe: From Black Madonna to Queen of the Americas*. Austin: University of Texas Press, 2014.

Pimentel, Maria do Rosário. "El Rei do Congo em Portugal e no Brasil: da realidade à ficção." In *Portugal e Brasil no advento do mundo moderno*, edited by Pimentel, 371-392. Lisbon: Colibri, 2001.

Plate, S. Brent. *Key Terms in Material Religion*. New York: Bloomsbury Academic, 2015.

Platt, Tristan. "The Andean Soldiers of Christ. Confraternity Organization, the Mass of the Sun and Regenerative Warfare in Rural Potosi (18th-20th centuries)." *Journal de la Société des Américanistes* 83 (1987): 139-192.

—, and Pablo Quisbert. "Sobre las huellas del silencio: Potosí, los incas y el virrey Francisco de Toledo (siglo XVI)." In *Minas y metalurgias en los Andes del Sur, entre la época prehispánica y el siglo XVII,* edited by Pablo Cruz and Jean-Joinville Vacher, 231-277. Sucre: Instituto Francés de Estudios Andinos, 2008.

—, Thérèse Bouysse-Cassagne, and Olivia Harris. *Qaraqara, Charka, Mallku, Inka y Rey en la Provincia de Charkas (siglos XVI-XVII): historia antropológica de una confederación Aymara*. La Paz: Institut Français D'études Andines, 2006.

Poloni-Simard, Jacques. "Redes y mestizajes: propuestas para el análisis de la sociedad colonial." In *Lógica mestiza en América*, edited by Guillaume Boccara and Sylvia Galindo, 113-138. Temuco: Universidad de la Frontera, 2000.

Pons Pons, Guillermo. "Abancay en la época colonial: una doctrina peruana." *Hispania Sacra* 62, no. 86 (1990): 593-633.

Poole, Stafford. *Our Lady of Guadalupe: The Origins and Sources of a Mexican National Symbol, 1531-1797*. Arizona: University of Arizona Press, 1995.

Porras Barrenechea, Raúl, ed. *Los cronistas del Perú (1528-1650)*. Lima: Imprenta DESA, 1986.

Prien, Hans-Jürgen. *La historia del cristianismo en América Latina*. Salamanca: Sígueme, 1985.

Proctor, Frank T., III. *Damned Notions of Liberty: Slavery, Culture, and Power in Colonial Mexico, 1640-1769*. Albuquerque: University of New Mexico Press, 2010.

Ragon, Pierre. *Les saints et les images du Mexique, XVIe-XVIIIe siècles*. Paris: L'Harmattan, 2003.

Ramírez, Juan Andrés. "La novena del Señor de Qoyllur Rit'i." *Allpanchis* 1 (1969): 61-88.

Ramón, Armando de. *Santiago de Chile (1541-1991). Historia de una sociedad urbana*. Madrid: MAPFRE, 1992.

——. "Bautizos de indígenas según los libros del Sagrario de Santiago correspondientes a los años 1581-1596." *Historia* 4 (1965): 229-235.

Ramón, Emma de. "Artífices negros, mulatos y pardos en Santiago de Chile: siglos XVI y XVII." *Cuadernos de Historia* 25 (2006): 59-82.

——. "La incorporación de las etnias no hispanas a la actividad industrial durante la colonia temprana." *Revista Archivo Nacional* 2 (2004): 42-47.

——. "Juan Chico de Peñalosa, Sebastián de Iturrieta y Martín García, tres sastres en los albores de la industria santiaguina: 1560-1620." In *Estudios coloniales III*, edited by Julio Retamal Ávila, 95-112. Santiago: Universidad Andrés Bello, 2004.

Ramos, Arthur. *As culturas negras no Novo Mundo.* São Paulo: Editora Nacional, 1979.

Ramos, Gabriela. "'Mi Tierra': Indigenous Migrants and their Hometowns in the Colonial Andes." In *City Indians in Spain's American Empire: Urban Indigenous Society in Colonial Mesoamerica and Andean South America, 1530-1810*, edited by Dana Velasco Murillo, Mark Lentz, and Margarita R. Ochoa, 128-147. Eastbourne: Sussex Academic Press, 2012.

——. "Nuestra Señora de Copacabana ¿Devoción india o intermediaria cultural?" In *Passeurs, mediadores culturales y agentes de la primera globalización en el Mundo Ibérico, siglos XVI-XIX*, edited by Scarlett O'Phelan Godoy and Carmen Salazar-Soler, 163-179. Lima: PUCP, 2005.

Ramos Gavilán, Alonso. *Historia del santuario de Nuestra Señora de Copacabana.* La Paz: MUSEF, [1621] 1988.

Rappaport, Joanne. *The Disappearing Mestizo. Configuring Difference in the Colonial New Kingdom of Granada.* Durham: Duke University Press, 2014.

——, and Tom Cummins. *Beyond the Lettered City: Indigenous Literacies in the Andes.* Durham: Duke University Press, 2012.

Rasini, Beatriz. "Estructura demográfica de Jujuy. Siglo XVIII." *Anuario del Instituto de Investigaciones Históricas* 8 (1965): 119-150.

Real Academia Española. *Diccionario de Autoridades*, vol. 1. Barcelona: Editorial Herder, [1732] 1987.

Redinha, José, *Etnias e culturas de Angola.* Luanda: IICA, 1974.

Regalado de Hurtado, Liliana. "Espacio andino, espacio sagrado: visión ceremonial del territorio en el período incaico." *Revista Complutense de Historia de América* 22 (1996): 85-96.

Reginaldo, Lucilene. *Os Rosários dos Angolas: Irmandades de africanos e crioulos na Bahia setecentista.* São Paulo: Alameda, 2011.

Reinhard, Johan. "Las montañas sagradas: un estudio etho-arqueológico de ruinas en las altas cumbres andinas." *Cuadernos de Historia* 3 (1983): 27-62.

——. "Heights of Interest." *South American Explorer* 26 (1990): 24-29.

——, and Ceruti María Constanza. *Inca Rituals and Sacred Mountains: A Study of the World's Highest Archaeological Sites.* Los Angeles: Cotsen Institute of Archaeology Press, 2010.

Reis, José João. *Death is a Festival: Funeral Rites and Rebellion in Nineteenth-Century Brazil.* Translated by H. Sabrina Glehill. Chapel Hill: University of North Carolina Press, 2003.

——. "Identidade e diversidade étnicas nas irmandades negras no tempo da escravidão." *Tempo* 2, no. 3 (1997): 7-33.

Remensnyder, Amy G. *La Conquistadora: The Virgin Mary at War and Peace in the Old and the New Worlds.* New York: Oxford University Press, 2014.

Rennefort, Urbain Souchu. *A Estada em Pernambuco, em 1666, de François de Lopis, Marquês de Mondevergue, Segundo o relato de Souchou de Rennefort (1688).* São Paulo: IEB, 2016.

Restall, Matthew. "Black Conquistadors: Armed Africans in Early Spanish America." *The Americas* 57, no. 2 (2000): 171-205.

——. *The Black Middle: Africans, Mayas, and Spaniards in Colonial Yucatan.* Stanford: Stanford University Press, 2013.

Retamal, Julio. *Testamentos de "Indios" en Chile colonial: 1564-1801.* Santiago: RIL, 2000.

Richie, Annette D. "Confraternity and Community: Negotiating Ethnicity, Gender, and Place in Colonial Tecamachalco, Mexico." Ph.D. diss., New York State University, Albany, 2011.

Rivas Aliaga, Roberto. "Danzantes negros en el Corpus Christi de Lima, 1756: 'Vos estis Corpus Christi.'" In *Etnicidad y discriminación*, 35-63

Robins, Nicholas A. *Comunidad, clero y conflicto. Las relaciones entre la curia y los indios en el Alto Perú, 1750-1780.* La Paz: Plural, 2009.

Rodríguez, Jaime E. *"We Are Now the True Spaniards": Sovereignty, Revolution, Independence, and the Emergence of the Federal Republic of Mexico, 1808-1824.* Stanford: Stanford University Press, 2012.

Rodriguez, Junius P. *Encyclopedia of Slave Resistance and Rebellion.* Westport: Greenwood Press, 2007.

Rodríguez León, Mario. "Invasion and Evangelization in the Sixteenth Century." In *The Church in Latin America, 1492-1992*, edited by Enrique Dussel, 43-54. Tunbridge Wells: Burns & Oates, 1992.

Rodríguez Villegas, Hernán. "Historia de un solar de la ciudad de Santiago, 1554-1909." *Historia* 11 (1972-1973): 103-162.

Rojas, Ricardo. *Censo de la Provincia de Jujuy, 1778-1779.* Buenos Aires: Coni Hermanos, 1913.

Romero, Carlos A. *Las crónicas de los Molinas.* Lima: D. Miranda, 1943.

Rondón, Víctor. *Jesuitas, música y cultura en el Chile colonial.* Ph.D. diss. Pontificia Universidad Católica de Chile, 2009.

Roselló Soberón, Estela. "La Cofradía de San Benito de Palermo y la integración de los negros y los mulatos en la ciudad de la Nueva Veracruz en el siglo XVII." In *Formaciones religiosas en la América colonial*, cedited by María Alba Pastor and Alicia Mayer, 229- 242. Mexico City: UNAM, 2000.

Rostworowski de Diez Canseco, María. *Señoríos indígenas de Lima y Canta*. Lima: IEP, 1978.

Rowe, Erin Kathleen. "After Death, Her Face Turned White: Blackness, Whiteness, and Sanctity in the Early Modern Hispanic World." *American Historical Review* 121, no. 3 (2016): 727-754.

——. *Black Saints in Early Modern Global Catholicism*. Cambridge: Cambridge University Press, 2019.

Rubert, Arlindo. *Historia de la Iglesia en Brasil*. Madrid: MAPFRE, 1992.

Ruiz Rodríguez, Carlos. "Cofradías en Chile Central. Un método de evangelización de la población indígena, mestiza y criolla." *Anuario de Historia de la Iglesia en Chile* 18 (2000): 23-58.

——. "Presencia de los mapuche-huilliche en Chile central en los siglos XVI-XVIII: desarraigo y mestizaje." *Boletín del Museo y Archivo Histórico Municipal de Osorno* 4 (1998): 1-71.

——. *La zona norte de Santiago: población, economía y urbanización, 1540-1833*. BA thesis, Pontificia Universidad Católica de Chile, 1986.

Russell-Wood, A.J.R. "Black and Mulatto Brotherhoods in Colonial Brazil." *Hispanic American Historical Review* 54, no. 4 (1974): 567-602.

——. *Slavery and Freedom in Colonial Brazil*. Oxford: Oneworld, 2002.

——. *The Portuguese Empire, 1415-1808: A World on the Move*. Baltimore: Johns Hopkins University Press, 1998.

Saguier, Eduardo. "Charcas y su articulación comercial al espacio colonial rioplatense. Las presiones mercantiles y el reparto forzoso en el siglo XVIII." *DATA* 6 (1996): 73-95.

Sahlins, Marshall. *Islands of History*. Chicago: University of Chicago Press, 1985.

Saignes, Thierry. "De la borrachera al retrato: Los caciques andinos entre dos legitimidades (Charcas)." *Revista Andina* 5, no. 1 (1987): 152-170.

——. "Lobos y ovejas: formación y desarrollo de los pueblos y comunidades en el sur andino siglos XVI-XX." En *Reproducción y transformación de las sociedades andinas siglos XVI-XX*, edited by Segundo Moreno y Frank Salomón, 91-136. Quito: Abya Yala, 1991.

Saito, Akira, and Claudia Rosas Lauro, eds. *Reducciones. La concentración forzada de las poblaciones indígenas en el Virreinato del Perú*. Lima: National Museum of Ethnology of Japan, 2017.

Salas Carreño, Guillermo. "Diferenciación social y discursos publicos sobre la peregrinación de Quyllurit'i." In *Mirando la Esfera Pública desde la Cultura en el Perú,* edited by Gisela Cánepa and Maria E. Ulfe, 243-288. Lima: CONCYTEC, 2006.

—. "The Glacier, the Rock, the Image: Emotional Experience and Semiotic Diversity at the Quyllurit'i Pilgrimage (Cuzco, Peru)." *Signs and Society* 2, no. 1 (2014): 188-214.

—. *Lugares parientes: comida, cohabitación y mundos andinos.* Lima: PUCP, 2019.

Salazar Soler, Carmen. "La Villa Imperial de Potosí" cuna del mestizaje (siglos XVI-XVII)." In *Colonización, resistencia y mestizaje en las Américas, siglos XVI-XX,* edited by Guillaume Boccara, 139-160. Lima: IFEA, 2002.

Salles Reese, Verónica. *De Viracocha a la Virgen de Copacabana.* La Paz: Plural, 2008.

Sallnow, Michael J. *Pilgrims of the Andes: Regional Cults in Cusco.* Washington, D.C.: Smithsonian Institution Press, 1987.

Salomon, Frank. *At the Mountains' Altar: Anthropology of Religion in an Andean Community.* Milton Park: Routledge, 2018.

—, and Stuart Schwartz. "New Peoples and New Kinds of People: Adaptation, Readjustment, and Ethnogenesis in South American Indigenous Societies (Colonial Era)." In *The Cambridge History of the Native Peoples of the Americas,* edited by Frank Salomon and Stuart B. Schwartz, 3.2:443-501. Cambridge: Cambridge University Press, 1999.

Sánchez, Martha Escalona. "Matanzas colonial e los cabildos congos." In *Actas del VII Taller Internacional de África en el Caribe (Ortiz a Lachatañeré),*" edited by Zaylen Clavería Centurión and Yadine M. Yara González, 143-148. Santiago de Cuba: Centro Fernando Ortiz, 2003.

Sanchez, Roberto. "The Black Virgin: Santa Efigenia, Popular Religion, and the African Diaspora in Peru." *Church History* 81, no. 3 (2012): 631-655.

Sánchez Gaete, Marcial. "Desde el Mundo Hispano al Cono Sur americano: una mirada a las Cofradías desde la historiografía en los últimos 50 años." *Revista de Historia y Geografía* no. 28 (2013): 59-80.

Sandoval, Alonso de. *Treatise on Slavery.* Translated by Nicole von Germeten. Indianapolis: Hacket, [1627] 2008.

Santamaría, Daniel J. "Iglesia y economía campesina en el alto Perú, siglo XVIII." *Occasional Papers Series* 5 (1983): 1-21.

Saunders, A.C C. M. *A Social History of Black Slaves and Freedmen in Portugal, 1441-1555.* Cambridge: Cambridge University Press, 2010.

Scarano, Julita, *Devoção e escravidão: a irmandade de Nossa Senhora do Rosário dos Pretos no Distrito Diamantino no século XVIII.* São Paulo: Editora Nacional, 1978.

—. "Bebida alcoólica na sociedade colonial." In *Festa,* 2:467-486.

Scott, James C. *Arts of Resistance: Hidden Transcript of Subordinate Groups.* New Haven: Yale University Press, 1990.

Schenone, Hector. *Santa María. Iconografía del arte colonial.* Buenos Aires: Educa, 2008.

Schneider, Jane. "Cloth and Clothing." In *Handbook of Material Culture*, edited by Chris Tilley, Webb Keane, and Susanne Kuechler, 203-220. London: Sage, 2006.

Schroeder, Susan. *Chimalpahin and the Kingdoms of Chalco*. Tucson: University of Arizona Press, 1991.

Serna, Juan Manuel de la. "Integración e identidad, pardos morenos en las milicias y cuerpo de lanceros de Veracruz en el siglo XVIII." In *Fuerzas militares en Iberoamérica siglos XVIII y XIX*, edited by Juan Ortiz Escamilla, 61-74. Mexico City: Colmex, 2005.

Serrano, Lilia. "Población de color en la ciudad de México. Siglos XVI y XVII." In *Memoria del III Encuentro de Afromexicanistas*, edited by Luz María Martínez Montiel and Juan Carlos Reyes, 72-88. Mexico City: CNCA, 1993.

Shapero, Joshua. Possessive Places: Spatial Routines and Glacier Oracles in Peru's Cordillera Blanca. *Ethnos* 84, no. 4 (2019): 614-641.

Sharpe, Christina Elizabeth. *In the Wake: On Blackness and Being*. Durham: Duke University Press, 2016.

Sierra Silva, Pablo Miguel. *Urban Slavery in Colonial Mexico: Puebla de los Ángeles, 1531-1706*. Cambridge: Cambridge University Press, 2018.

Silva, Leonardo Dantas da. "A instituição do Rei do Congo e sua presença nos maracatus." In *Estudos sobre a escravidão negra*, edited by Silva, 2:13-53. Recife: FUNDAJ, 1988.

Silva Prada, Natalia. "El año de los seises (1666) y los rumores conspirativos de los mulatos en la ciudad de México: coronaciones, pasquines, sermones y profecías, 1608-1665," *Nuevo Mundo/Mundos Nuevos* (2012). http://journals.openedition.org/nuevomundo/64277

Siracusano, Gabriela. "Copacabana, lugar donde se ve la piedra preciosa: imagen y materialidad en la región andina." In *Actas del seminario internacional de estudios de arte en América Latina: temas y problemas*, 2003. http://www.esteticas.unam.mx/edartedal/PDF/Bahia/complets/siracusano_bahia.pdf

Siracusano, Gabriela, Rosanna Kuon, and Marta Maier. "Colores para el milagro. Una aproximación interdisciplinaria al estudio de pigmentos en un caso singular de la iconografía colonial andina." In *Investigación en conservación y restauración: II Congreso del Grupo Español del IIC*. Barcelona: Museu Nacional d'Art de Catalunya, 2005. https://ge-iic.com/files/2congresoGE/Colores_para_el_milagro.pdf

Smith, E. Valerie. "The Sisterhood of Nossa Senhora da Boa Morte and the Brotherhood of Nossa Senhora Do Rosario: African-Brazilian Cultural Adaptations to Antebellum Restrictions." *Afro-Hispanic Review* 21, nos. 1-2 (2002): 121-133.

Soares, Mariza de Carvalho. *People of Faith: Slavery and African Catholics in Eighteenth Century Rio De Janeiro*. Durham: Duke University Press, 2011.

Socolow, Susan Migden. *The Women of Colonial Latin America*. Cambridge: Cambridge University Press, 2000.

Sordo, Emma. "Our Lady of Copacabana and her Legacy in Colonial Potosí." In *Early Modern Confraternities in Europe and the Americas: International and Interdisciplinary Perspectives*, edited by Christopher F. Black and Pamela Gravestock, 187-203. Aldershot: Ashgate Publishing, 2006.

Souza, Marina de Mello e. *Reis negros no Brasil escravista: História da festa de coroação de Rei Congo*. Belo Horizont: UFMG, 2002.

—. *Além do Visível. Poder, Catolicismo e Comércio no Congo e Angola, séculos XVII e XVIII*. São Paulo: EDUSP, 2018.

Spaulding, Rachel. "Mounting the Poyto: An Image of Afro-Catholic Submission in the Mystical Visions of Colonial Peru's Úrsula de Jesús," *Early American Studies* 17, no. 4 (2019): 519-544.

Spivak, Gayatri Chakravorty. *A Critique of Postcolonial Reason: Toward a History of the Vanishing Present*. Cambridge: Harvard University Press, 2003.

—. "Can the Subaltern Speak?" In *Can the Subaltern Speak?: Reflections on the History of an Idea*, edited by Rosalind C. Morris, 21-78. New York: Columbia University Press, 2010.

Spix, Johann B, and Carl F. P. Martius. *Travels in Brazil in the Years 1817-1820: Undertaken by Command of His Majesty the King of Bavaria*. Translated by Hannibal E. Lloyd. New York: Cambridge University Press, 2013. 2 vols.

Stanfield-Mazzi, Maya. *Object and Apparition: Envisioning the Christian Divine in the Colonial Andes*. Tucson: University of Arizona Press, 2013.

Stefano, Roberto di. "De la cristiandad colonial a la iglesia nacional. Perspectivas de investigación en historia religiosa de los siglos XVIII y XIX." *ANDES* 11 (2000): 83-113.

Suárez de Figueroa, Cristóbal. *Plaza Universal de Todas las Ciencias*. Madrid: Luis Sanchez, 1615.

Sweet, James H. *Recreating Africa: Culture, Kinship, and Religion in the African-Portuguese World, 1441-1770*. Chapel Hill: University of North Carolina Press, 2003.

Szeminski, Jan. *Vocabulario y textos andinos de don Felipe Guaman Poma de Ayala: Tomo III Nueva corónica y buen gobierno*. Edited by Franklin Pease. Lima: Fondo de Cultura Económica, 1993.

Tardieu, Jean-Pierre. "Origins of the Slaves in the Lima Region in Peru (Sixteenth and Seventeenth Centuries)." In *From Chains to Bonds: The Slave Trade Revisited*, edited by Doudou Diène, 43-54. New York: Berghahn Books, 2001.

—. *Los negros y la Iglesia en el Perú: siglos XVI-XVII*. Quito: Centro Cultural Afroecuatoriano, 1997.

Tau Anzoátegui, Víctor. Introduction to *Nueva Historia de la Nación Argentina*, 2:9-18.

Teixeira Leite, José Roberto "Negros, pardos e mulatos na pintura e na escultura brasileira do século XVIII." In *A mão afro-brasileira: significado da contribuição artística e histórica*, edited by Emanoel Araújo, 13-54. Sao Paulo: Técnica Nacional de Engenharia, 1988.

Terpstra, Nicholas. "De-institutionalizing Confraternity Studies: Fraternalism and Social Capital in Cross-Cultural Contexts." In In *Early Modern Confraternities in Europe and the Americas: International and Interdisciplinary Perspectives*, edited by Christopher F. Black and Pamela Gravestock, 264-284. Aldershot: Ashgate Publishing, 2006.

——. "Ignatius, Confratello: Confraternities as Modes of Spiritual Community in Early Modern Society." In *Early Modern Catholicism: Essays in Honour of John W. O'Malley, S.J.*, edited by Kathleen M. Comerford and Hilmar M. Pabel, 163-182. Toronto: Toronto University Press, 2003.

Thayer Ojeda, Tomás. *Santiago durante el siglo XVI. Constitución de la propiedad urbana noticias biográficas de sus primeros pobladores*. Santiago: Cervantes, 1905.

Thompson, Edward P. *Making of the English Working Class*. London: Open Road, 2016.

Tinhorão, José Ramos. *Os negros em Portugal: uma presença silenciosa*. Lisboa: Caminho, 1988.

Torre Villar, Ernesto de la, and Ramiro Navarro de Anda. *Testimonios históricos guadalupanos*. Mexico City: FCE, 1982.

——. *Nuevos testimonios históricos guadalupanos*. Mexico City: FCE, 2007.

Trens, Manuel. *María: iconografía de la Virgen en el arte español*. Madrid: Plus Ultra, 1945.

Trexler, Richard C. "Being and Non-Being: Paramaters of the Miraculous in the Traditional Religious Image." In *The Miraculous Image in the Late Middle Ages and Renaissance*, edited by Erik Thunø and Gerhard Wolf, 15-27. Rome: L'Erma di Bretschneider, 2004.

——. "Dressing and Undressing Images: An Analytic Sketch." In *Religion in Social Context in Europe and America, 1200-1700*, edited by Trexler, 374-408. Tempe: Arizona Center for Medieval and Renaissance Studies, 2002.

Trouillot, Michel-Rolph. *Silencing the Past: Power and the Production of History*. Boston: Beacon Press, 1995.

Truitt, Jonathan. *Sustaining the Divine in Mexico Tenochtitlan: Nahuas and Catholicism, 1523- 1700*. Norman: University of Oklahoma Press, 2018.

Urbano, Henrique, and Julio Calvo Pérez, eds. *Relación de las fábulas y ritos de los incas*. Lima: Universidad de San Martín de Porres, 2007.

Valenzuela Márquez, Jaime. "Devociones de inmigrantes. Indígenas andinos y plurietnicidad urbana en la conformación de cofradías coloniales (Santiago de Chile, siglo XVII)." *Historia* 1, no. 43 (2010): 203-244.

——. "Indias esclavas ante la Real Audiencia de Chile (1650-1680): los caminos del amparo judicial para mujeres capturadas en la guerra de Arauco." In *América en diásporas: esclavitudes y migraciones forzadas en Chile y otras regiones americanas (siglos XVI-XIX)*, edited by Valenzuela, 319-380. Santiago: PUCC, 2017.

——. "Indios urbanos: inmigraciones, alteridad y ladinización en Santiago de Chile (siglos XVI-XVII)." *Historia Crítica* 53 (2014): 13-34.

——. "Indígenas andinos en Chile colonial: inmigración, inserción espacial, integración económica y movilidad social (Santiago, siglos XVI-XVII)." *Revista de Indias* 250 (2010): 749-778.

——. "Los indios *cuzcos* de Chile colonial: estrategias semánticas, usos de la memoria y gestión de identidades entre inmigrantes andinos (siglos XVI-XVII)." Nuevo Mundo/Mundos Nuevos (2010). http://nuevomundo.revues.org/60271

——. *Las liturgias del poder: celebraciones públicas y estrategias persuasivas en Chile colonial (1609-1709)*. Santiago: DIBAM, 2001.

Valerio, Miguel A. "'That There Be No Black Brotherhood': The Failed Suppression of Afro Mexican Confraternities, 1568-1612." *Slavery and Abolition* 42, no. 2 (2021): 293-314.

——. "Black Confraternity Members Performing Afro-Christian Identity in a Renaissance Festival in Mexico City in 1539." *Confraternitas* 29, no. 1 (2018): 31-54.

——. "A Mexican *Sangamento*?: The First Afro-Christian Performance in the Americas." In *Afro-Catholic Festivals in the Americas: Performance, Representation, and the Making of Black Atlantic Tradition*, edited by Cécile Fromont, 59-74. University Park: Pennsylvania State University Press, 2019.

——. "The Queen of Sheba's Manifold Body: Creole Black Women Performing Sexuality, Cultural Identity, and Power in Seventeenth-Century Mexico City." *Afro-Hispanic Review* 35, no. 2 (2016): 79-98.

——. "Architects of Their Own Humanity: Race, Devotion, and Artistic Agency in Afro-Brazilian Confraternal Churches in Eighteenth-Century Salvador and Ouro Preto." *Colonial Latin American Review* 30, no. 2 (2021): 238-271.

Valero, Eva. "Las relaciones de fiestas: copiar la historia 'fuera de costumbre'." In *Historia de las literaturas en el Perú*, edited by Raquel Chang-Rodríguez y Carlos García-Bedoya M., 2:252-289. Lima: PUCP, 2017.

Vargas Ugarte, Rubén, ed. *Concilios limenses (1551-1772)*. 3 vols. Lima: Tipografía Peruana, [1551-1772] 1951.

Varón Gabai, Rafael. "Cofradías de indios y poder local en el Perú colonial: Huaraz, siglo XVII." *Allpanchis* 14, no. 20 (2020): 127-146.

Vázquez de Espinosa, Antonio. *Compendio y descripción de las indias occidentales.* Madrid: BAE, [1623] 1969.

Vega, Garcilaso de la Inca. *Comentarios reales de los incas.* Lima: Biblioteca Clásicos del Perú, Banco de Crédito, [1609] 1985.

Velázquez, María Elisa. *Mujeres de origen africano en la capital novohispana, siglos XVII y XVIII*. Mexico City: INAH, 2006.

Verdesio, Gustavo. "Para repensar los estudios coloniales: Sobre la relación entre el campo de estudios, las disciplinas, y los pueblos indígenas." *Telar* 11-12 (2013-14): 257-272.

Verger, Pierre. *Procissões e carnaval no Brasil*. Salvador: UFB, 1980.

Vetancourt, Agustín de. *Chronica de la Provincia del Santo Evangelio de México.* Mexico City: Porrúa, [1697] 1982.

Vetter Parodi, Luisa. "Plateros indígenas y europeos: de las cofradías de Santa Ana y San Eloy." In *Corporaciones religiosas,* 189-227.

Viana Filho, Luís. *O negro na Bahia.* Rio de Janeiro: Nova Fronteira, 1988.

Vieira-Powers, Karen. *Andean Journeys: Migration, Ethnogenesis, and the State in Colonial Quito.* Albuquerque: University of New Mexico Press, 1995.

Villalobos, Sergio. *Historia del pueblo chileno.* Santiago: Zig-Zag, 1983. 2 vols.

Vincent, Catherine. *Les confréries médiévales dans le royaume de France: XIIIe-XVe siècle.* Paris: Albin Michel, 1994.

Vinson III, Ben. "Los milicianos pardos y la relación estatal durante el siglo XVIII en México." In *Fuerzas militares en Iberoamérica siglos XVIII y XIX,* edited by Juan Ortiz Escamilla, 47-59. Mexico City: Colmex, 2005.

———. *Bearing Arms for His Majesty: The Free-Colored Militia in Colonial Mexico.* Stanford: Stanford University Press, 2003.

Vuola, Elina. "María, mujer en la política. Nuevos desafíos para la teología latinoamericana." *Albertus Magnus* 4, no. 2 (2012): 59-71.

Walker, Tamara J. "The Queen of *los Congos*: Slavery, Gender, and Confraternity Life in Late Colonial Lima, Peru." *Journal of Family History* 40, no. 3 (2015): 305-322.

———. *Exquisite Slaves: Race, Clothing, and Status in Colonial Lima.* Cambridge: Cambridge University Press, 2017.

———. "'He Outfitted His Family in Notable Decency': Slavery, Honor, and Dress in Eighteenth-Century Lima, Peru." *Slavery and Abolition* 30, no. 3 (2009): 383-402.

Webster, Susan V. "Shameless Beauty and Worldly Splendor on the Spanish Practice of Adorning the Virgin." In *The Miraculous Image in the Late Middle Ages and Renaissance,* edited by Erik Thunø and Gerhard Wolf, 249-271. Rome: L'Erma di Bretschneider, 2004.

———. *Art and Ritual in Golden-Age Spain: Sevillian Confraternities and the Processional Sculpture of Holy Week.* Princeton: Princeton University Press, 1998.

Wells, E.C., and Karla L. Davis-Salazar. *Mesoamerican Ritual Economy: Archaeological and Ethnological Perspectives.* Boulder: University Press of Colorado, 2007.

Wheat, David. *Atlantic Africa and the Spanish Caribbean, 1570-1640.* Chapel Hill: University of North Carolina Press, 2016.

Williams, Danielle Terrazas. "'My Conscience Is Free and Clear': African-Descended Women, Status, and Slave Owning in Mid-Colonial Mexico." *The Americas* 75, no. 3 (2018): 525- 554.

Windus, Astrid, and Andrés Eichmann Oehrli. "La (re) construcción de espacios sagrados. Los proyectos hierotópicos de la Isla del Sol/Copacabana, Carabuco y La Plata." In *Barroco: mestizajes en diálogo,* edited by Norma Campos Vera, 383-390. La Paz: Fundación Visión Cultural, 2017.

Wood, Stephanie. "Adopted Saints: Christian Images in Nahua Testaments of Late Colonial Toluca." *The Americas* 47, no. 3 (1991): 259-293.

Yacher, Leon. *Marriage, Migration and Racial Mixing in Colonial Tlazazalca, (Michoacán, Mexico), 1750-1800*. Syracuse: Syracuse University, 1977.

Yannakakis, Yanna. *The Art of Being In-between: Native Intermediaries, Indian Identity, and Local Rule in Colonial Oaxaca*. Durham: Duke University Press, 2008.

Young, Kydalla Etheyo. "Colonial Music, Confraternities, and Power in the Archdiocese of Lima." Ph.D. diss. University of Illinois Urbana-Champaign, 2010.

Zaballa, Ana de y Lanchas, Ianire. "Los conflictos entre la jurisdicción real y episcopal a fines del siglo XVIII: el caso del obispo José Gregorio Ortigoza." In *Cultura legal y espacios de justicia en América, siglos XVI-XIX*, edited by Macarena Cordero, Rafael Gaune y Rodrigo Moreno, 93-117. Santiago: Universidad Adolfo Ibañez, 2017.

Zafra Oropeza, Aurea. *Las cofradías de Cocula, Guadalajara, Jalisco*. Guadalajara: Governement of Guadalajara, 1996.

Zanolli, Carlos. "Entre la coerción, la oportunidad y la salvación. Las cofradías de indios de San Antonio de Humahuaca. Siglos XVII y XVIII." *Andes* 19 (2008): 345-369.

Zedillo, Antonio. "Presencia de África en América Latina. El caso de México." In *Memoria del III Encuentro de Afromexicanistas*, edited by Luz María Martínez Montiel y Juan Reyes, 208-210. Mexico City: Conaculta, 1993.

Zúñiga, Jean-Paul. *Espagnols d'outre-mer. Émigration, métissage et reproduction sociale à Santiago du Chili, au 17e siècle*. Paris: EHESS, 2002.

Contributors

Célia Maia Borges
Célia Maia Borges is professor of history at the Universidade Federal de Juiz de Fora. Her research focuses on religious orders, popular saints, and black brotherhoods in Portugal and Brazil. She is the author of *Escravos e Libertos nas Irmandades do Rosário* and numerous articles.

Enrique Normando Cruz
Enrique Normando Cruz is professor of history at the Universidad Nacional de Jujuy. He has been a researcher at the Escuela de Estudios Hispanoamericanos in Seville, Spain, and the University of Bonn, and guest lecturer at several Latin American and European universities. His work has appeared in *GLADIUS*, *TEMPUS*, *América Latina en la Historia Económica* y *LATINOAMERICA*.

Laura Dierksmeier
Laura Dierksmeier is a postdoctoral researcher in the German Research Foundation (DFG) research group "Resource Cultures" at the University of Tübingen in Germany. Previously, she worked as a researcher in the research group "Religious Knowledge in Pre-Modern Europe, 800 – 1800." Her dissertation, completed in 2016 at the University of Tübingen, focused on indigenous confraternities in colonial Mexico. Dierksmeier received the Bartolomé de las Casas Dissertation Award from the University of Fribourg in Switzerland in 2017. She recently finished an edited book together with Fabian Fechner and Kazuhisa Takeda entitled: *Indigenous Knowledge as a Resource: Transmission, Reception, and Interaction of Knowledge between the Americas and Europe, 1492-1800.*

Krystle Farman Sweda
Krystle Farman Sweda received her Ph.D. from the Graduate Center, The City University of New York in 2020. Her larger research examines the emergence of Catholicism and its local expressions among Africans and their descendants in seventeenth-century New Spain. She currently works in Research Development under the Office of the Vice President for Research at the University of Kentucky, Lexington.

Nicole von Germeten
Nicole von Germeten, a professor of Latin American History at Oregon State University, has worked as the Director of the School of History, Philosophy,

and Religious studies since 2017. She received her PhD from the University of California Berkeley in 2003 with research funded by the Fulbright Garcia Robles Scholarship and the Muriel McKevitt Sonne Endowment. She was a Fellow at the Princeton Center for the Study of Religion in 2004 and was affiliated with the Stanford University Center for Latin American Studies in 2008 and 2009. She has contributed essays, reviews, and articles in close to sixty edited volumes and academic journals. She has published three single-authored books and one edited book-length translation since 2006, most recently *Profit and Passion: Transactional Sex in Colonial Mexico* (California, 2018). Her fifth book, coming out in 2022 with the University of Nebraska Press, *The Enlightened Patrolman: The Early History of Law Enforcement in Mexico City*, examines how the Spanish viceroys attempted to modernize policing to suppress popular revolt and to curb what they viewed as an out-of-control drinking culture. This book focuses on the perspective of the men walking the beat. Her previous publications range in topics from sexuality, religion, legal history, and gender in Spain and the Iberian empires, to Afro-descended populations in Spanish America, Catholic brotherhoods and Jesuit proselytization. Her scholarship has also explored transactional sex, honor, violence, witchcraft, sodomy, and suicide. She is currently writing a manuscript entitled *Death in Old Mexico: the 1789 Dongo Murders* and a translation from Spanish to English of an 1869 novel which focuses on the same case.

Ximena Gómez

Ximena Gómez is Assistant Professor in the Department of the History of Art and Architecture at the University of Massachusetts Amherst. She specializes in the art of colonial Latin America and that of the early modern transatlantic world more broadly. Her work has been published in *Colonial Latin American Review* and the edited volume, *A Companion to Early Modern Lima*. She is currently at work on her first book, which investigates the visual culture of Indigenous and Black lay confraternities in Lima during the sixteenth and seventeenth centuries.

Karen B. Graubart

Karen B. Graubart is Associate Professor of History at the University of Notre Dame. She is the author of two books, *With Our Labor and Sweat: Indigenous Women and the Formation of Colonial Society 1550-1700* (Stanford: 2007) and *Republics of Difference: Religious and Racial Self-Governance in the Spanish Atlantic World* (Oxford University Press: forthcoming) as well as numerous articles in *Hispanic American Historical Review, Colonial Latin American Review, Slavery and Abolition, The William and Mary Quarterly*, and other journals. She is a member of the directing collectives of the Tepoztlán Institute for the Transnational History of the Americas and La Patrona Collective for Colonial Latin American Scholarship. Her work has been generously supported by the National Endowment for the Humanities, the American Council of Learned Societies, and the Kellogg Institute for International Studies. An earlier version of this article appeared in *Slavery and Abolition* 33:1 (March 2012).

Javiera Jaque Hidalgo

Javiera Jaque Hidalgo is an assistant professor of Spanish in the Department of Modern and Classical Languages and Literatures in Virginia Tech. Her topic of research is the literature and culture of Colonial Latin America with a focus on Jesuit missions in Chile. More recently her research focus is on indigenous migration to urban spaces. She has published her research in *A Contracorriente, Una revista de estudios latinoamericanos, Rocky Mountain Review, Revista Chilena de Literatura, and Revista Provinciana. Revista de literatura y pensamiento.* She is currently working in her first monograph entitled *Misiones Jesuitas en la Frontera de Arauco: Resistencia Mapuche, Negociación y Movilidad Cultural en la Periferia Colonial (1593-1641)*, in which she analyzes the frontier dynamics among Mapuche people and Jesuit missionaries in the seventeenth century.

Grit Kirstin Koeltzsch

Grit Kirstin Koeltzsch is a Ph.D. candidate at the National Scientific and Technical Research Council of Argentina (CONICET). She was a Research Scholar in the George A. Smathers Libraries at the University of Florida and was awarded a Graduate Student Paper Award from the Latin American Studies Association in 2017. Her work has appeared in the *Oxford Research Encyclopedia of Latin American History, Canadian Journal of Latin American and Caribbean Studies, Intercontinental Journal on Physical Education, Revista Interdisciplinar de Literatura e Ecocrítica, América Latina en la Historia Económica* and *TEMPUS: Revista en Historia General.*

Candela De Luca

Candela De Luca is a professor of history at the Universidad Nacional de La Plata. Her research focuses on indigenous Catholic practices in the colonial Andes. De Luca has been part of CONICET. She currently is a member of the project "RESISTANCE: *Rebellion and Resistance in the Iberian Empire, 16th-19th centuries*," sponsored by the *Research and Innovation Staff Exchange* (RISE) of the European Union.

Cristina V. Masferrer León

Cristina Masferrer is professor and researcher at the Ethnology and Social Anthropology Direction of the National Institute of Anthropology and History of Mexico (DEAS-INAH). Author of *Muleke, negritas y mulatillos. Niñez, familia y redes sociales de los esclavos de origen africano de la Ciudad de México* (INAH, 2013), as well as several publications on Afromexican population, childhood, education and racism. She studied Ethnohistory and Psychology, with a master's degree in Social Anthropology and a Ph.D. in History and Ethnohistory. She was awarded the National Prize "Francisco Javier Clavijero 2010." She coordinates the Seminar on Anthropology and History of the Racisms, Discriminations and Inequalities (DEAS-INAH/ SURXE-UNAM) with Olivia Gall.

Lucilene Reginaldo

Lucilene Reginaldo is professor of history at the Universidade Estadual de Campinas. Her researches focuses on the Church and black brotherhoods in colonial Bahia, Brazil. She is the author of *Os Rosários dos Angolas: irmandades de africanos e crioulos na Bahia Setecentista,* for which she was awarded the Prêmio Katia Mattoso for best book on Bahian history in 2011.

Angelica Serna Jeri

Angelica Serna Jeri is an Assistant Professor of Spanish and Portuguese in the University of New Mexico. She earned her Ph.D. in Romance Languages from the University of Michigan, Ann Arbor. Her teaching and research meet at the intersection of indigenous studies, postcolonial theory, and digital humanities.

Marina de Mello e Souza

Marina de Mello e Souza is professor of history at the University of Sao Paulo. She is the author of *Paraty, a Cidade e as Festas*; *Reis Negros no Brasil Escravista: História da Festa de Coroação de Rei Congo*; *África e Brasil africano*; *Além do Visível: Poder, Catolicismo e Comércio no Congo e em Angola (Séculos XVI e XVII)*. He currently conducting research on the Congo in the eighteenth and nineteenth centuries.

Jaime Valenzuela Márquez

Jaime Valenzuela Márquez is professor of history at the Pontificia Universidad Católica de Chile. He has been a fellow at the Centro Diego Barros Arana of the Biblioteca Nacional de Chile (1991-1993) and the John Carter Brown Library. He has been a visiting professor at many French and Latin

American universities. Some of his books include: *Las liturgias del poder. Celebraciones públicas y estrategias persuasivas en Chile colonial (1609-1709)*; *Fiesta, rito y política. Del Chile borbónico al republicano*; *América en diásporas. Esclavitudes y migraciones forzadas en Chile y otras regiones americanas (siglos XVI-XIX)*.

Miguel A. Valerio

Miguel A. Valerio is assistant professor of Spanish at Washington University in St. Louis. His research focuses on the African diaspora in the literatures and cultures of the early modern Iberian world, particularly Afro-confraternities' festive practices. His work has appeared in *Afro-Hispanic Review, Confraternitas, Slavery and Abolotion, Colonial Latin American Review* and the *Journal of Festive Studies*. His book, *Sovereign Joy: Afro-Mexican Kings and Queens, 1539-1640*, which studies Afro-Mexican confraternities' festive practices, will be published with Cambridge University Press in 2022.

Tamara J. Walker

Tamara J. Walker is an historian of race, gender, and slavery in Latin America. Her research has received support from the Ford Foundation, the Woodrow Wilson Foundation, the American Association of University Women and the John Carter Brown Library, and has appeared in such publications as *Slavery & Abolition: A Journal of Slave and Post-Slave Studies, Safundi: The Journal of South African and American Studies, Gender & History, The Journal of Family History,* and *Souls*. Her first book, *Exquisite Slaves: Race, Clothing and Status in Colonial Lima*, was published by Cambridge University Press and received the 2018 Harriet Tubman Prize. She is currently at work on two new book projects, one on the history of slavery and piracy in Latin America, and the other on black subjects in Latin American visual culture, which will be published by the University of Texas Press.

Acknowledgements

We would like to thank Stephanie Kirk who urged us into this project; the contributors for their hard work, collegiality, and patience; Erika Gaffney and the Amsterdam University Press team for making the process smooth; Gaby Martin and Bruna Dantas Lobato for their help with translating some of the essays; Kathryn Santner for her assistance copy-editing some of the chapters; the anonymous readers for their comments and suggestions; the editors of this series for their reception of the project and comments and suggestions throughout; our respective departments and the Center for the Study of Race, Ethnicity, and Equity at Washington University in St. Louis for their financial support; the journals that gave permission to build on previous versions of essays that appeared in them; and our spouses and families for their love and support.

Index

(References to illustrations are in *italics*. References to tables are in **bold**).